D1796412

The Dyeing of Cellulosic Fibres

Yorkshire Chemicals Limited

LEEDS

TECHNICAL INFORMATION BUREAU

Accession No.: 11010

Date: 8th July, 1986

Location: T.S. LABORATORY

K220

The Dyeing of Cellulosic Fibres

Edited by Clifford Preston PhD BSc

YORKSHIRE CHEMICALS LIMITED
LEEDS

TECHNICAL INFORMATION BUREAU

| Worshipful Company of Dyers | Society of Dyers and Colourists |

1986

Dyers' Company Publications Trust

Published by the Dyers' Company Publications Trust, and distributed by the Society of Dyers and Colourists, P O Box 244, Perkin House, 82 Grattan Road, Bradford, West Yorkshire BD1 2JB, England.

Printed by The Eastern Press Ltd, London and Reading.

ISBN 0 901956 43 0

Contents

Dyers' Company Publications Trust

The Dyers' Company Publications Trust was instituted by the Worshipful Company of Dyers of the City of London in 1971 to encourage the publication of textbooks and other aids to learning in the science and technology of colour and coloration and related fields. The Society of Dyers and Colourists acts as trustee for the fund.

Contributors

Ulrich Baumgarte Dr rer nat
Marketing Textilchemie Department, BASF AG, Ludwigshafen

David A Clarke PhD CChem MRSC
Technical director, James Robinson and Co. Ltd, Huddersfield

Kenneth Dickinson BSc
Technical manager, Interox Chemicals Ltd, Warrington

(The late) **Maurice R Fox** CGIA CChem FRSC CText FTI CCol FSDC
Formerly manager, Cellulosics Dyeing Section, ICI plc, Organics Division, Manchester

Hans Herzog Dr phil II
Assistant vice president, Rohner AG, Pratteln

Ian Holme PhD Bsc CChem FRSC CText FTI CCol FSDC
Senior lecturer, Department of Textile Industries, University of Leeds

Bernard Kramrisch CChem FRSC CText FTI CCol FSDC
Formerly assistant technical service manager, CIBA Clayton Ltd, Manchester

William J Marshall BSc CChem FRSC
Consultant in dyeing and finishing, Shirley Institute, Manchester

Thomas P Nevell DSc PhD CChem FRSC
Formerly senior lecturer in polymer and fibre science, University of Manchester Institute of Science and Technology

Colin Senior CCol ASDC
Chief colourist, James Robinson and Co. Ltd, Huddersfield

John Shore BScTech AMCST CChem MRSC CCol ASDC
Senior scientist, Research Department, ICI plc, Organics Division, Manchester

Harry H Sumner BSc CChem FRSC CCol FSDC
Formerly manager, Technological Services and Dyeing Research Section, ICI plc, Organics Division, Manchester

Preface

Prefaces to previous books in the series have drawn attention to the Dyers' Company Publications Trust and to the trust fund generously established by the Worshipful Company of Dyers for the publication of new textbooks.

The need for new books on colour and coloration technology has been evident in many ways, partly because substrates, dyes, auxiliaries and application techniques have been changing rapidly. But the main reason for producing the books has been to provide authoritative information on the principles and practice of coloration for students preparing for the Associateship examinations of the Society of Dyers and Colourists. It is hoped that the books in the series will prove equally valuable to those already engaged in industry, research and education.

In this present book the first three chapters discuss various aspects of the substrate and the remainder cover the principles and application technology of the relevant classes of dyes. One of the latter chapters deals specifically with the dyeing of polyester/cotton blends that receives relatively brief treatment in the chapter on blends in the second book published by the Trust, *The Dyeing of Synthetic-polymer and Acetate Fibres*. Also one of the original manuscripts included material on the application of ingrain dyes and oxidation bases, but this has been omitted as these colorants are no longer of significant commercial importance.

Grateful thanks is expressed to authors, referees, members of the Trust's Technical Subcommittee and the Society's staff; in particular to Paul Dinsdale, the Society's editor, and to John Shore, who has given valuable assistance in technical editing.

In Chapter 1 some photomicrographs have been taken from the 4th Edition of *Identification of Textile Materials* (published by the Textile Institute) but the publisher has pointed out that the 7th Edition is now available. The author of Chapter 2 acknowledges the permission granted by Interox Chemicals Ltd to prepare the manuscript and to use information from the company's publications. The author of Chapter 5 gratefully acknowledges the assistance given to him by many individuals in the preparation of his chapter.

CLIFFORD PRESTON

CHAPTER 1

Cellulose – Its Structure and Properties

THOMAS P NEVELL

1.1 INTRODUCTION

Cellulose is the most abundant of all naturally occurring organic polymers, thousands of millions of tonnes being produced by photosynthesis throughout the world every year [1]. Recent reports based on spectroscopic evidence even suggest its existence in interstellar space [2]. In addition, the possibility that industrial cellulose may be produced by bacteria instead of by plants is now real, although still somewhat remote [3]. The production of cellulose on a small scale by *Acetobacter xylinum* and other micro-organisms has been known for over a century, but recent work on its mechanism [4] opens the way for the application of genetic engineering to the development of a micro-organism that would combine the photosynthesis of glucose with its polymerisation to form cellulose. For the time being, however, industry will have to rely on the traditional vegetable sources for its supply of cellulose.

Cellulose constitutes the main structural material of land plants. The fact that the cell walls of all such plants are constructed from the same substance was first recognised by Payen [5], who invented the name cellulose. Besides being an essential constituent of plants, it has great industrial importance, being the raw material of a large part of the textile industry, the paper industry and several others. Cellulose for paper is derived almost entirely from wood and a good deal of that required for textiles comes from the same source. Wood fibres themselves are too short for spinning into textile yarns, and the cellulose they contain has to be dissolved in a suitable solvent and then regenerated in order to render it usable. Longer cellulosic fibres can be extracted from certain plants by relatively simple purification treatments. Cotton is pre-eminent amongst these, but flax, hemp, jute, and China grass provide other fibre types. Linen is obtained from flax; hemp and jute are used mainly for industrial textiles. Ramie (from China grass), with a supramolecular structure of particular scientific interest, has few industrial applications.

1.2 CELLULOSE TEXTILE FIBRES

1.2.1 Cotton

Cotton is the seed hair of plants of the genus *Gossypium* [6]. Many species are grown for commercial use, but they may be conveniently divided into three types.

Type 1 comprises fibres having staple lengths (i.e. average fibre lengths) varying from 25 to 60 mm; it includes the highest quality fine cottons such as the Egyptian, Sudanese and Sea Island varieties. Type 2 comprises coarser species with shorter staple lengths (about 13 to 33 mm) such as American upland cottons, and type 3 species of still shorter staple length (about 9 to 25 mm) commonly produced in India and other parts of Asia. The mature cotton fibre forms a flat ribbon varying between 12 and 20 μm in width. It is highly convoluted, probably on account of the twisting that takes place when the tubular shape that it possesses during growth collapses as the fibre dries out. The number of convolutions varies between four and six per millimetre, and they reverse their direction every millimetre or so along the fibre. These unique characteristics of cotton are easily recognised under the microscope.

Cotton fibres are illustrated both lengthwise and in cross-section in Figure 1.1. Each fibre consists of three main parts: primary wall, secondary wall and lumen, as shown in Figure 1.2. The primary wall consists of a network of cellulose fibrils covered with an outer layer, or cuticle, of pectin, protein, mineral matter and wax. It is the wax that renders the fibre impermeable to water and aqueous solutions unless a wetting agent is present. The secondary wall constitutes the bulk of a mature fibre and consists almost entirely of fibrils of cellulose arranged spirally around the fibre axis, the direction of the spiral reversing (i.e. changing from S- to Z-twist and vice versa) many times along a single fibril. Reversal points frequently correspond with reversals of the exterior convolutions. Although fibrils may be seen under a high-power microscope, there is considerable uncertainty about their dimensions. The resolution limit of the optical microscope is around 0.2 μm and it is probable that the objects seen are really bundles of smaller microfibrils, which appear in the electron microscope to be from 0.02 to 0.03 μm thick and at least 10 μm long. The microfibrils are themselves believed to consist of still smaller 'elementary' fibrils that are approximately 0.004×0.006 μm in cross-section. The secondary wall consists of several layers and the spiral angle of the fibrils varies from one layer to the next, from about 20 to 35°. Thus the cotton fibre consists of an assembly of fibrils in which the cellulose is accessible to most (but not all) chemical reagents only at fibrillar surfaces by way of a system of voids and channels [7, 8]. The lumen is what remains of the central canal from which the layers of cellulose were laid down in the secondary wall while the fibre was growing; it contains some residual protein.

It is instructive to compare the composition of the primary wall of a cotton fibre with that of the fibre as a whole, since it is the primary wall which has to be broken down in some way in preparing cotton for dyeing and printing. Although it accounts for only 5% of the weight of the fibre, it contains a greater proportion of the non-cellulosic constituents. Table 1.1 gives comparative data for a typical cotton [9]. The 'other substances' are mostly water-soluble organic acids and sugars.

1.2.2. Bast Fibres

The bast fibres [6] are obtained from the stalks of a group of dicotyledonous plants the most important of which is *Linum usitatissimum*, generally known as flax. They

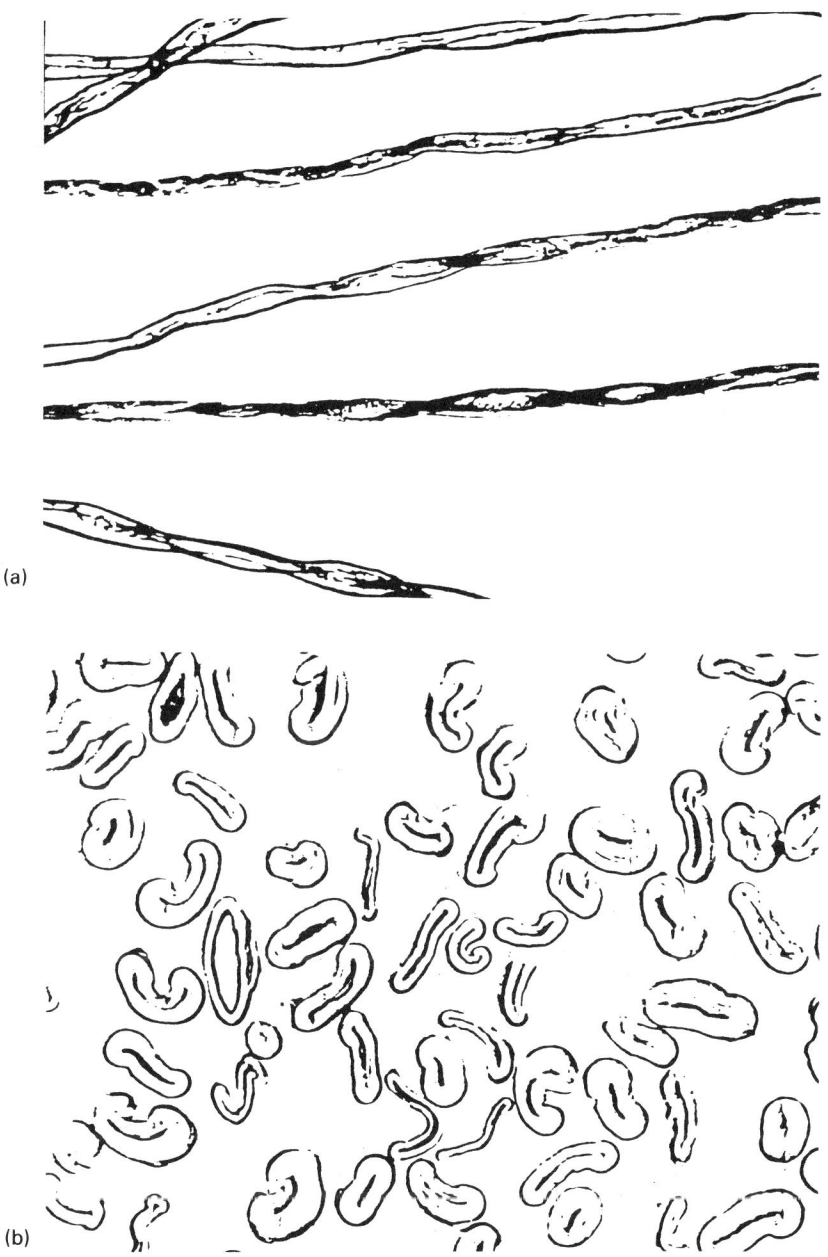

(a)

(b)

Figure 1.1 – Raw cotton fibres (a) × 180, (b) × 500 (reproduced from 'Identification of Textile Materials' by permission of the Textile Institute, Manchester)

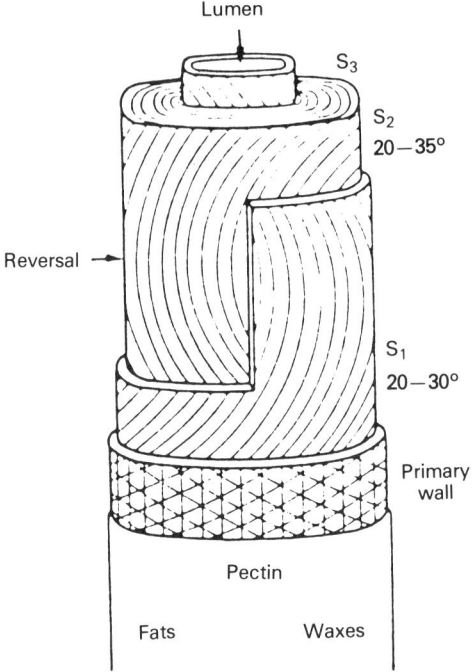

Figure 1.2 – Idealised morphology of cotton fibre (reproduced from 'Liquid Ammonia Treatment of Cellulosic Textiles' by permission of Shirley Institute, Manchester)

TABLE 1.1

Composition of a Typical Cotton

	Proportion of dry weight (%)	
Constituent	Whole fibre	Primary wall
Cellulose	94.0	54.0
Protein (%N × 6.25)	1.3	14.0
Pectin	1.2	9.0
Wax	0.6	8.0
Ash	1.2	3.0
Other substances	1.7	12.0

occur on the outsides of the stalks, forming a strength-giving protective layer around the woody central portion, and are themselves protected by an outermost cuticle which contains waxes and other substances. The fibres consist of bundles of thick-walled cells held together by gummy substances. The ultimate fibres vary in dimensions from one species to another. For example, in flax the length varies from 25 to 30 mm and the diameter from 15 to 35 μm. On the other hand the individual cells of ramie are unusually long (about 150 mm), whilst their width (30 to 50 μm) is of the same order as that of flax. In the bast bundles the ends of the individual fibres overlap so as to produce continuous filaments extending along the length of the stalk. Most bast fibres are used as full-length bundles, but flax is separated into its ultimate fibres for the production of fine linen yarns, and ramie is always similarly separated before spinning. The microscopic features of these fibres are characteristic, as illustrated in Figures 1.3–1.5.

The separation of the fibre bundles from the harvested stalks is a complicated and time-consuming process. In most cases the first stage is 'retting', i.e. soaking the stalks for periods of several weeks in water, traditionally in slow-moving rivers or bogs, until the effect of bacterial action in the intercellular matter loosens the fibres sufficiently to enable them to be separated mechanically. The treatment time can be reduced to a few days by retting in tanks controlled at temperatures within the range 27–32°C. This applies particularly to the production of linen from flax. The subsequent stages of separation involve a variety of mechanical procedures. They differ in detail from one fibre to another and go under such names as stripping (jute), scutching (flax) and hackling (flax). The decortication of ramie is carried out without preliminary retting.

The crude fibres contain far less cellulose than cotton, as may be seen from Table 1.2.

TABLE 1.2

Composition of Typical Bast Fibres

	Proportion of dry weight (%)		
Constituent	Jute	Raw flax	Decorticated ramie
Cellulose	71.3	80.1	83.3
Polymeric intercellular matter	27.1	10.5	7.5
Wax	0.4	2.6	0.2
Ash	0.8	1.5	2.1
Other substances	0.4	5.3	6.9

The polymeric intercellular matter consists of pectins and hemicelluloses (both rather ill-defined types of polysaccharide) and lignin (a highly complex cross-linked aromatic polymer based on substituted phenylpropane units and found in large quantities in wood). Jute is frequently used without further purification, but flax

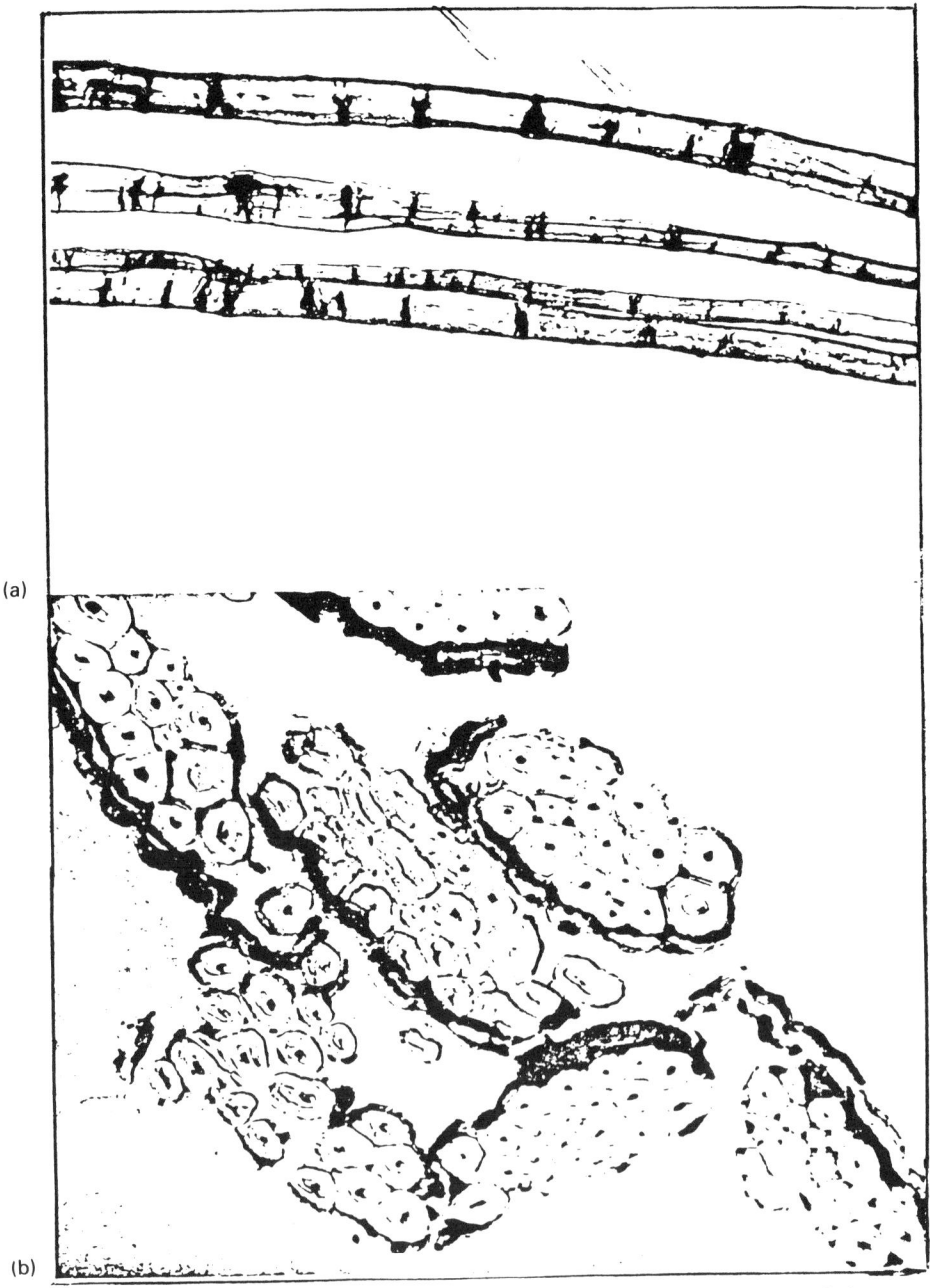

(a)

(b)

Figure 1.3 – Flax (a) fibre ultimates ×180, (b) cross-section of bundles ×340 (reproduced from 'Identification of Textile Materials' by permission of the Textile Institute, Manchester)

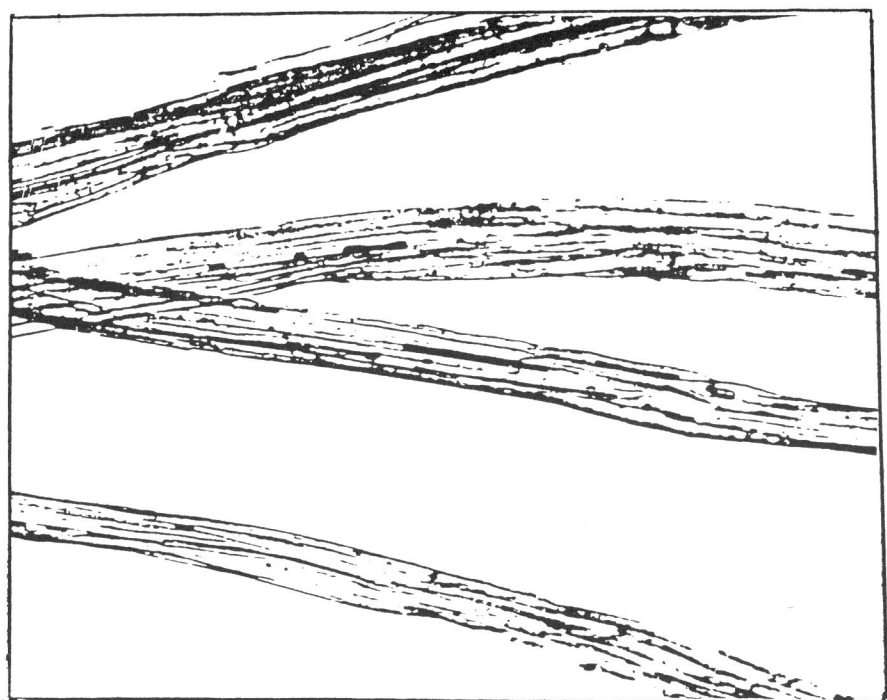

Figure 1.4 – Jute bundles × 180 (reproduced from 'Identification of Textile Materials' by permission of the Textile Institute, Manchester)

and ramie are usually scoured and sometimes bleached. Much of the non-cellulosic material is removed, to an extent depending on the quality required in the product. Flax containing 'sprit' (remnants of the woody core of the stem of the plant) may be difficult to dye satisfactorily because of the different substantivities of many dyes for the fibre proper and the sprit. The problem is similar to that of motes (remnants of seed coat) in raw cotton. If jute is to be dyed, it too must be prepared by scouring, but considerable quantities of lignin usually remain, which leads to poor light fastness in the final product.

1.2.3 Regenerated Fibres

The conversion of short cellulosic fibres into useful textile filaments was first achieved by Chardonnet [10] around 1885. The cellulose was nitrated and dissolved in a mixture of diethyl ether and ethanol. The solution was extruded through a fine orifice either into water (wet spinning) or into a hot-air chamber (dry spinning) to produce continuous filaments of cellulose nitrate. Since these were highly inflammable they were denitrated with ammonium hydrosulphide. The final product was the first regenerated cellulose to enjoy any commercial success, but it is now completely obsolete. It has been superseded almost entirely by various types of viscose,

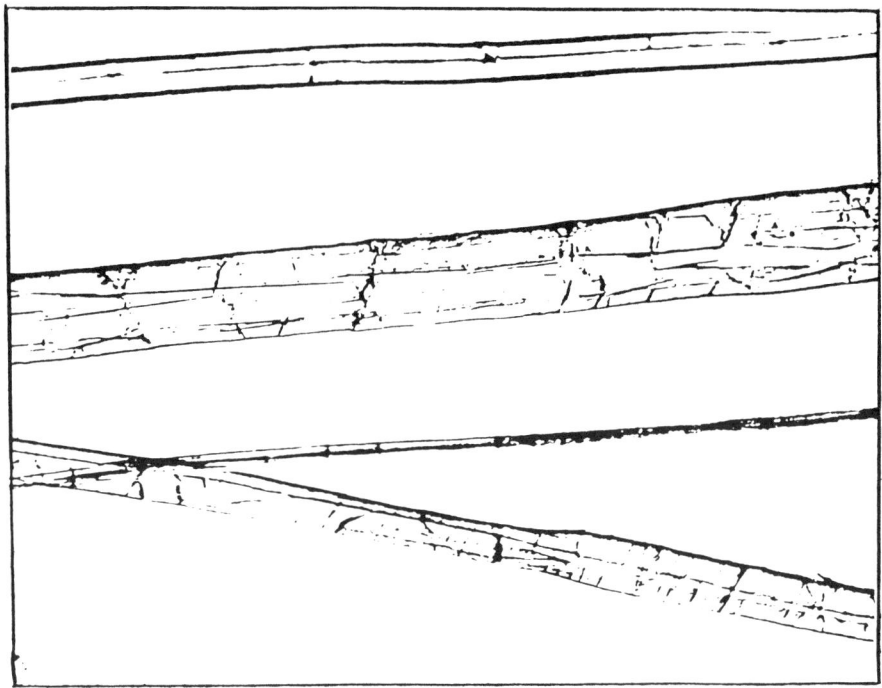

Figure 1.5 – Ramie fibre ultimates × 180 (reproduced from 'Identification of Textile Materials' by permission of the Textile Institute, Manchester)

although very small quantities of its other rival cupro (cuprammonium rayon) are still produced.

The main raw material from which viscose is manufactured is specially purified wood pulp, usually known as dissolving pulp. In the past, particularly for cupro, cotton linters have been used. These are very short cotton seed hairs left after those suitable for spinning directly into yarns have been separated. Although they were easier to purify than wood pulp, they were more expensive and are now unobtainable in the quantities required for modern industry.

Cupro was first produced commercially in 1901 although it had been made experimentally some years earlier [10]. Linters or wood pulp are dissolved in cuprammonium hydroxide and the solution extruded into water. The filaments so formed are stretched and passed through dilute sulphuric acid to complete the regeneration of the cellulose.

The viscose process was discovered by C F Cross and E J Bevan at the end of the 19th century [10], but it was not until 1910 that appreciable quantities of what is now called regular viscose were produced. Even then it was a comparative rarity. The viscose solution consists of sodium cellulose xanthate dissolved in aqueous sodium hydroxide. Cellulose filaments are obtained by extruding the solution through a spinneret into an aqueous solution whose main constituents are sodium sulphate and sulphuric acid. The chemistry of the process will be described later (see p. 47). The filaments are stretched mechanically [10] during regeneration and their properties are determined by the concentration of the viscose solution, the rate at which it is allowed to coagulate, the rate of stretching and the point at which stretching occurs during coagulation. The rate of coagulation is controlled by the temperature at which it occurs and by the addition of small quantities of substances such as zinc sulphate and glucose to the coagulation baths.

Regular, or ordinary, viscose differs from cotton in being non-fibrillar, having no lumen and having a much lower degree of polymerisation (see p. 12). Although viscose filaments consist wholly of cellulose, their skin and core differ somewhat in supramolecular structure. Under the microscope they appear striated longitudinally and in cross-section their circumference is irregularly serrated due to the contraction of an originally cylindrical shape during the later stages of the regeneration process (see Figure 1.6). Compared with cotton, regular viscose suffers from the disadvantage of much lower breaking strength, particularly in the wet state. Whilst this does not preclude its use in apparel, it does render viscose unsuitable as a reinforcing cord for rubber tyres. High-tenacity viscose fibres for this purpose have now been in production for half a century. Their formation depends mainly on retarding the regeneration process in order to increase the degree of orientation of the cellulose molecules in the filaments. More extensive variations in the conditions of manufacture have led to the production of the so-called polynosic fibres. These viscose fibres are far more like cotton than the regular and high-tenacity varieties. They possess a fibrillar structure, exhibit stress/strain curves similar to those for cotton, and are similarly insoluble in aqueous sodium hydroxide solutions up to a concentration of about 8%. Regular viscose is partially soluble in this reagent.

Cellulose acetate is also regenerated from solution on a large scale for textile purposes. Two distinct types are now produced, the main difference between them being their degree of substitution. Filaments of cellulose triacetate were first 'dry-spun' from chloroform solution in 1914, but because of the high toxicity of the solvent the process was never practised on a large scale and was discontinued after about ten years [10]. It was reintroduced during the 1950s after the cheaper and safer solvent dichloromethane had become available, and the value of hydrophobic polyester fibre as a textile raw material had been demonstrated. Cellulose triacetate is marketed under various trade names, Tricel being the commonest in the UK.

The term cellulose acetate is usually reserved for the material with a degree of substitution of about 2.3 and derived from the triacetate by partial hydrolysis [10]. Because of its method of preparation it is also called secondary cellulose acetate to distinguish it from the 'primary' triacetate. It is sold in the UK under the name of Dicel. Unlike the triacetate it is soluble in acetone, from which it is obtained in continuous-filament form by dry spinning. It is much less hydrophilic than cellulose itself but more so than the triacetate. Both fibres are thermoplastic at moderate temperatures and Tricel fabrics can be permanently pleated.

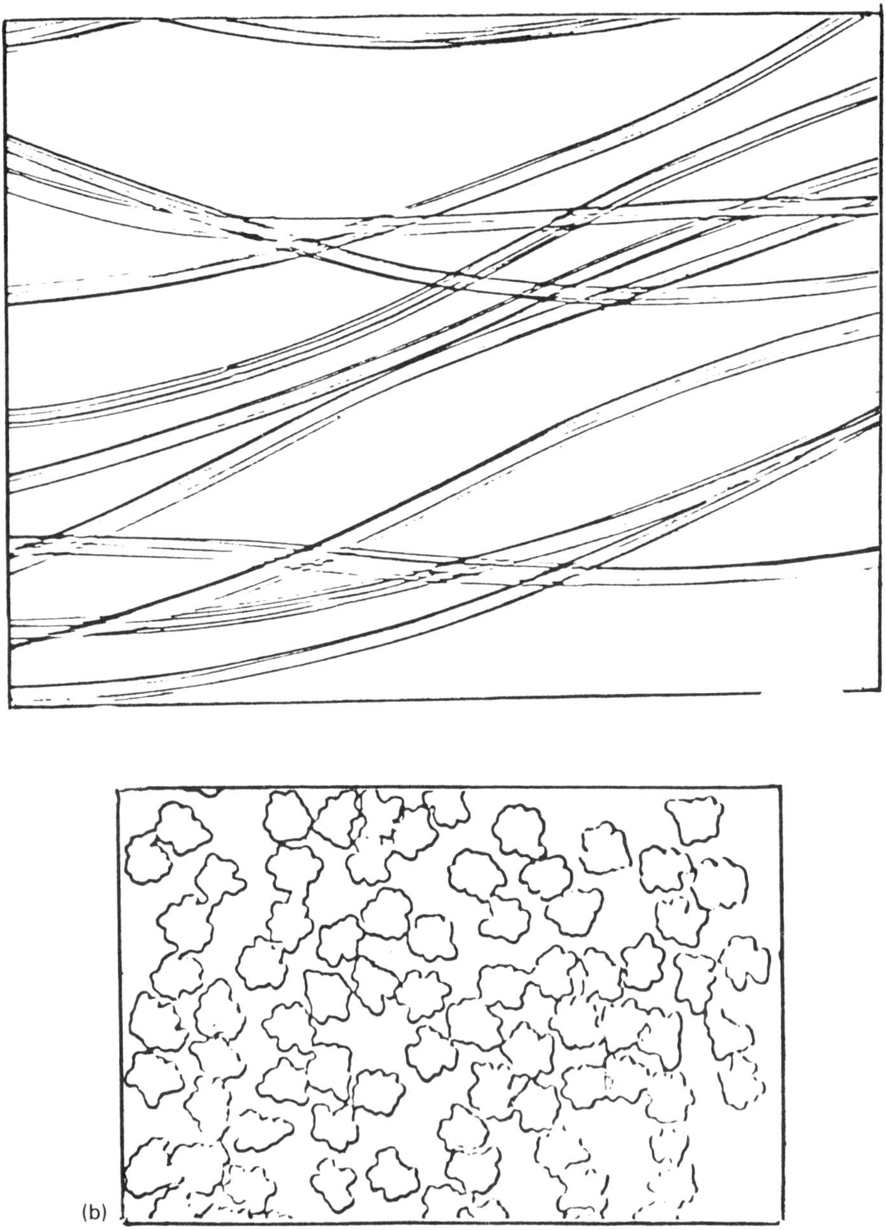

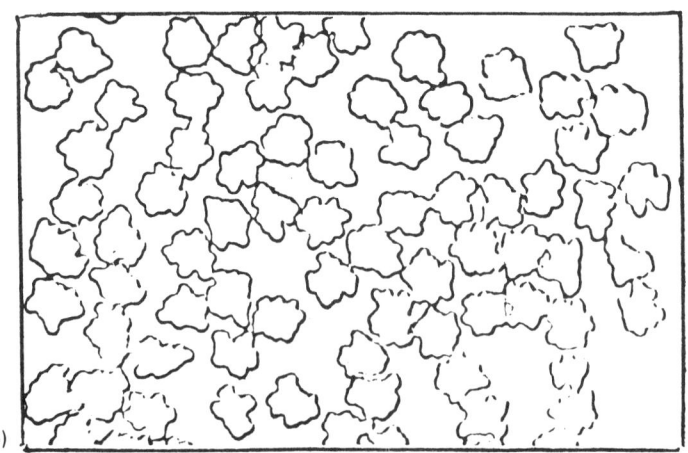

Figure 1.6 – Viscose fibres (a) × 180, (b) × 500 (reproduced from 'Identification of Textile Materials' by permission of the Textile Institute, Manchester)

1.3 MOLECULAR STRUCTURE

The main features of the chemical structure of cellulose are well known and have been summarised many times (e.g. [1,11]). It may most conveniently be described as a 1,4-β-D-glucan, i.e. a condensation polymer of β-D-glucopyranose with 1,4-glycosidic bonds.

The pyranose rings are in the 4C$_1$ conformation (see Figure 1.7 (a)). In this formula it should be noted that, for the sake of clarity and in accordance with convention, all secondary carbon atoms and hydrogen atoms linked directly to a carbon atom other than a primary carbon atom are omitted. The Haworth projection formula is shown in Figure 1.7 (b). Being easier to write, it is frequently used and is usually entirely adequate. It does, however, obscure some important stereochemical aspects of the cellulose molecule [12]. The conventional numbering of the six carbon atoms of each chain unit is shown in Figure 1.7 (b), but it is, of course,

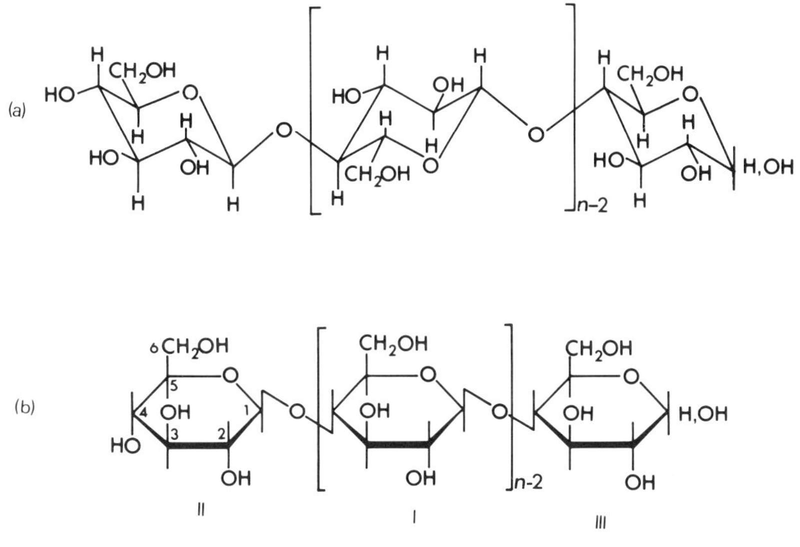

Figure 1.7 – Representation of cellulose (n = degree of polymerisation)

not normally included. The essential features of the polymer chain are the main sequence of intermediate units (I), the non-reducing end group (II), the reducing end group (III) and the glycosidic linkages. The intermediate chain units possess one primary and two secondary alcohol groups each. The reducing end group (capable of reducing Fehling's solution or ammoniacal silver nitrate) is a cyclic hemiacetal which exhibits the characteristics of both an alcohol and an aldehyde under appropriate conditions (Scheme 1.1).

The degree of polymerisation of cellulose (DP) varies with its source, and is usually expressed as an average, since a wide distribution is always found in any

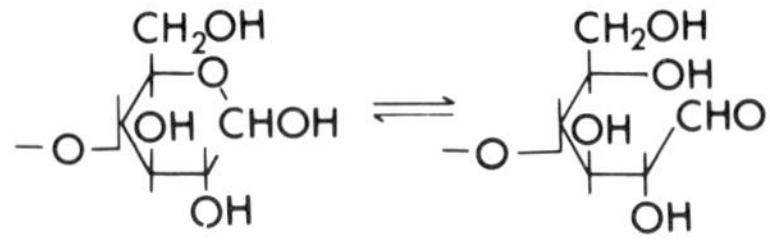

$$\begin{array}{ccc}
CH_2OH & & CH_2OH \\
\end{array}$$

Scheme 1.1

particular sample. In unpurified native cellulose it may well exceed 10 000 [13], but purification involving treatment with alkali usually reduces this to about 1 000–2 000. Furthermore the hemiacetal end groups are converted to acid groups (see p. 34); thus, purified native cellulose is usually devoid of reducing power. Regenerated celluloses have DPs of about 250–300 and may contain small numbers of aldehyde, ketone and carboxylic acid groups, introduced during manufacture. Chemically they are nearly identical with native cellulose, and differences between the two types arise mainly in their supramolecular structure. Polynosic fibres have higher DPs (about 500–700) than other forms of regenerated cellulose.

1.4 SUPRAMOLECULAR STRUCTURE

Cellulose is a highly crystalline material, but it does not form discrete crystals like those of glucose, from which it is derived. In its native form it consists of crystalline fibrils of varying degrees of complexity and of indeterminate length. These fibrils combine together to form fibres and may be interspersed with material in which the chain molecules are less well ordered than in a crystal. The same chain molecule may occur in crystalline and non-crystalline parts of a fibre, along different portions of its length. As already stated, the polynosic fibres are fibrillar, unlike the traditional forms of regenerated cellulose. The supramolecular structure of cellulose, i.e. the overall arrangement of chain molecules in a fibre, may be considered under two headings: crystalline structure and fine structure. The former will now be considered in some detail, and the latter will be considered in Chapter 3.

Cellulose exists in at least five polymorphic forms [14], but only cellulose I and cellulose II are important from the textile point of view. Cellulose I is the form found in nature and cellulose II (formerly, and misleadingly, called 'hydrate cellulose') is the thermodynamically stable form produced when cellulose is regenerated from solution or is subjected in the solid state to the process of mercerisation. The main features of the crystal structures of the two forms were established about 50 years ago by X-ray analysis [15, 16], but uncertainties in the precise details of these structures remain to this day, in spite of the prodigious amount of work that has been done [14, 17].

X-ray analysis alone has proved insufficient to define the unit cells of cellulose I and II. However, more detailed information on structure has been provided with the aid of infra-red spectroscopy [18] and electron diffraction. The most useful work relied on the model proposed by Liang and Marchessault [19] for cellulose I, concerning the hydrogen bonding system. Apparently the cellulose chains exist, at least to a close approximation, in the so-called 'bent-chain' conformation originally proposed by Hermans [20]. In this form contiguous anhydroglucose units (as, for example, units II and I, or I and III, in Figure 1.7) are oriented with their mean planes at an angle of 180° to each other. The glycosidic bonds, instead of being in a plane perpendicular to the mean planes of the adjacent rings, as in the Meyer and Misch model [15], are inclined at a small angle alternately positive and negative to these planes. The chain molecules are thus fully extended in the form of flat ribbons having the minimum possible thickness in the direction perpendicular to the mean plane of the rings. These flat ribbons pack together into a monoclinic unit cell of dimensions approximately $a = 0.82$, $b = 0.79$ and $c = 1.035$ nm (fibre axis), and $\gamma = 97°$, in the case of cellulose I. A cross-section of the cell in the ab plane, looking along the fibre axis, is shown in Figure 1.8. Originally Meyer and Misch believed that the 'centre' and 'corner' chains were antiparallel to one another, but the latest evidence [17] strongly favours the parallel arrangement with the centre chains staggered by approximately $0.25c$ (0.26 nm) with respect to the corner chains (see Figure 1.9 (a)). Adjacent chains are held together in a system of hydrogen-bonded sheets in the ac planes as shown in Figure 1.10, alternate sheets being staggered with respect to each other in accordance with the arrangement indicated in Figure 1.9 (a). Thus there are two interpenetrating sets of sheets, one comprising the corner chains and the other the centre chains. There is no hydrogen bonding between corner and centre chains. Since the surfaces of the chain molecules at right angles to the mean planes of the rings are hydrophobic, the sheets of chains are held together in that direction by van der Waals forces.

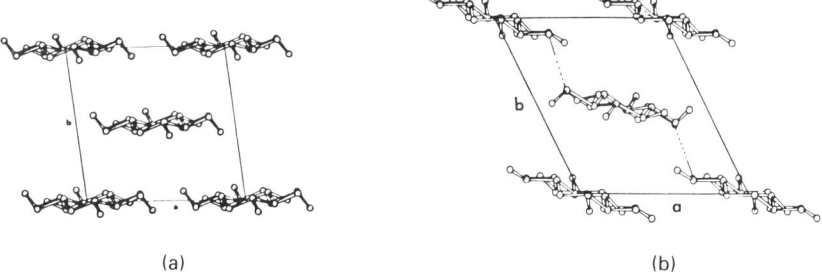

(a)   (b)

Figure 1.8 – Unit cell of (a) cellulose I and (b) cellulose II, looking along the fibre axis (reproduced from ref. 17 by permission of the American Chemical Society, Washington DC)

Three features of the structure of cellulose I should be emphasised. Firstly the cellulose chains are fully extended. Thus the repeat distance in the chain direction is equal to the length of the two anhydroglucose units, i.e. one anhydrocellobiose unit. The degree of polymerisation is the average number of anhydroglucose units per chain molecule. Secondly the unit cell parameters have been stated in terms of the modern crystallographic convention [21]. Unfortunately in most of the literature of cellulose structure the fibre axis has been identified with the b direction; according to this older usage the unit cell would be $a = 0.82$, $b = 1.035$ (fibre axis) and $c = 0.79$ nm, and $\beta = 83°$. Care must be taken to avoid confusion between the

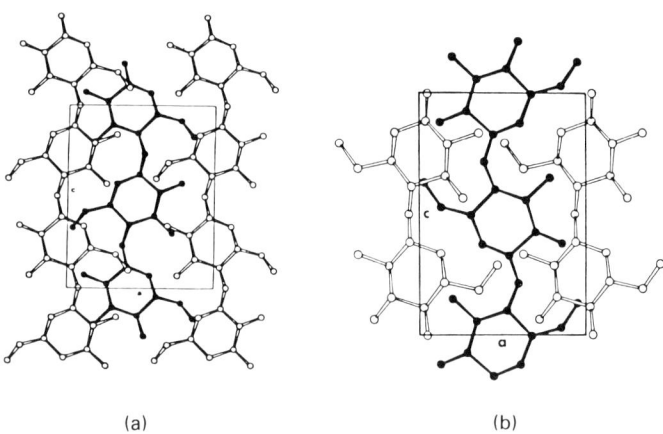

(a)   (b)

Figure 1.9 – (a) Parallel-chain model of cellulose I perpendicular to the ac *plane,
(b) antiparallel-chain model of cellulose II perpendicular to the* ac *plane (reproduced
from ref. 17 by permission of the American Chemical Society, Washington DC)*

two conventions. Lastly it may be wondered why the unit cell dimensions have not
been quoted with a higher degree of precision, since X-ray analysis is certainly
capable of achieving it. The reason is that the precise values of the parameters
differ by up to about 1% according to the source of the cellulose. The values given
here are averages; more precise figures are readily obtainable for a particular
sample of cellulose.

The unit cell of cellulose II is also monoclinic; it has average dimensions $a = 0.81$,
$b = 0.91$ and $c = 1.035$ nm, and $\gamma = 117°$. The cross-section in the ab plane is shown
in Figure 1.8 (b). The chain arrangement differs from that in cellulose I in two respects. Firstly, the planes of the glucose rings are inclined at a small angle to the ac
plane. Secondly the centre chains are oriented antiparallel to the corner chains.
They are still staggered with respect to the corner chains in the c direction, in the
same way as in cellulose I (see Figure 1.9 (b)). However, the hydrogen bonding
system is rather more complicated than in cellulose I. Not only are there hydrogen
bonds in the ac planes between parallel corner chains and between parallel centre
chains, but there are also hydrogen bonds between antiparallel corner and centre
chains. Detailed illustrations of the system have been published [17], along with X-
ray evidence for the antiparallel orientation of alternate chains. Such an arrangement would be expected in regenerated cellulose since there is no reason to
suppose that the molecules would be other than randomly oriented in solution. It is
more difficult to reconcile with the fact that cellulose I is converted into cellulose II
by mercerisation – a process that does not involve dissolution of the material. A
possible explanation has been given [17], but further work on the subject is
desirable.

Chain folding in cellulose has been postulated [14], but the existence of a
parallel-chain structure effectively disposes of the suggestion for cellulose I, since it

is incompatible with any reasonable picture of the synthesis of cellulose in nature. It would also be difficult to reconcile with the low extensibility of native cellulose fibres. The antiparallel arrangement in cellulose II is compatible with chain folding. However, it seems unlikely that the two forms would differ, especially since, by carefully choosing the conditions of regeneration, filaments that are much more like native cotton than ordinary viscose can be readily produced. Rejection of the folded-chain hypothesis for cellulose in fibrous form does not mean that chain-folded structures may not be formed under special conditions. For example, single crystals of cellulose triacetate containing folded chains can be obtained from solution in a mixture of nitromethane and butan-1-ol, and it is possible that some chain folding survives subsequent saponification [22]. Similarly, under suitable conditions, cellulose of moderate degree of polymerisation may be crystallised from solution in aqueous sodium hydroxide in folded-chain form [23].

Cellulose III is not itself important in textile applications, but it may be mentioned here because it is sometimes formed as a result of treating cellulose I with liquid ammonia or aliphatic amines (see p. 24). It has a monoclinic unit cell with the following dimensions: $a = 0.77$, $b = 1.00$ and $c = 1.03$ nm, and $\gamma = 122°$ [14].

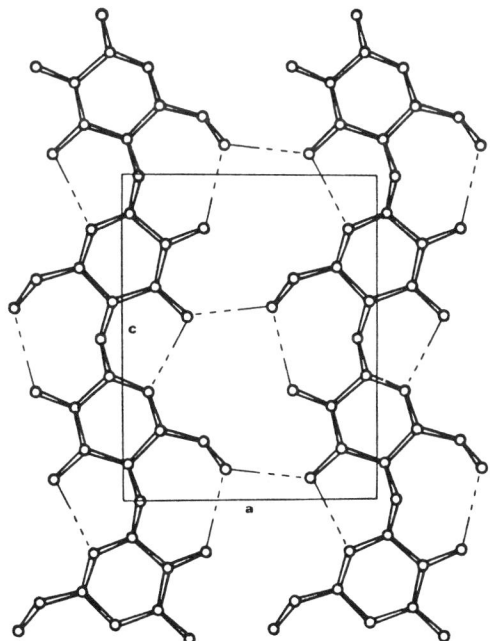

Figure 1.10 – Hydrogen bonding network in cellulose I (reproduced from ref. 17 by permission of the American Chemical Society, Washington DC)

1.5 AFFINITY FOR WATER AND ORGANIC LIQUIDS

1.5.1 Water

The affinity of cellulose for water is of great industrial importance for several reasons:

(a) Water is essential for many processes (e.g. dyeing and finishing)
(b) Cellulose cannot normally be freed from water completely (the moisture regain depends on the ambient humidity and has commercial implications)
(c) The mechanical properties of cellulosic materials vary with moisture content; thus cotton is stronger wet than dry, but viscose is weaker when wet
(d) The comfort of clothing made from cotton or viscose is associated to a large extent with moisture sorption.

This affinity is not difficult to understand. Indeed, a cursory look at the formula (Figure 1.7) might lead one to expect that cellulose would be soluble in water. It possesses an abundance of hydroxyl groups to be solvated, but the majority of these are combined with one another in such a way that dissolution cannot occur. The reason why the hydrogen bonding system cannot be completely disrupted by water is not that its intramolecular hydrogen bonds are stronger than those between cellulose and water. The cellulose molecules are too inflexible for the inter-chain bonds to break successively, allowing the material to dissolve, and it is highly improbable that all these bonds would break simultaneously [24]. Thus the insolubility of cellulose in water is a direct consequence of the equatorial orientation of all the hexose substituents, including the glycosidic bonds, a feature distinguishing cellulose from all other polysaccharides. It is noteworthy that some methyl-celluloses with low degrees of substitution are soluble in water. This is because, although methyl groups are hydrophobic, their size distorts the conformation of the cellulose chains so that crystallisation is inhibited and the remaining hydroxyl groups are capable of being solvated [24].

Although cellulose is insoluble in water, it readily absorbs water vapour. This is because not all the hydroxyl groups are bound together in crystalline regions. A proportion of them exists in a sufficiently accessible state in micellar surfaces and in imperfectly crystalline regions in the fibres to attract water molecules. The moisture relations of cellulose have been extensively studied over many years [1, 25, 26]. The early work of Urquhart and Williams [27] on scoured cotton, illustrated in Figure 1.11, demonstrates the essential features of the sorption isotherms. Sorption is expressed as moisture regain (weight of water per 100 g of bone-dry cotton) rather than moisture content (weight of water per 100 g of moist cotton). The former is more valuable for comparing the hygroscopicity of different materials, although the latter may be more useful in practical applications. Under average conditions in the UK (say 65% relative humidity (r.h.) and 20°C) scoured cotton has a moisture regain around 7.5%, which corresponds to a moisture content of 7%. Fully mercerised cotton and regular viscose have regains of about 11% and 13% respectively under similar conditions.

The sigmoidal curves in Figure 1.11 may conveniently be divided into three sections:
(a) Low humidity (0–10% r.h.) – probably a monomolecular layer of water is adsorbed by direct association of one water molecule with each accessible hydroxyl group
(b) Medium humidity (10–50% r.h.) – a multilayer of increasing thickness is formed progressively
(c) High humidity (50–100% r.h.) – water is sorbed virtually in liquid form, gradually swelling the fibres so that more hydroxyl groups become accessible.

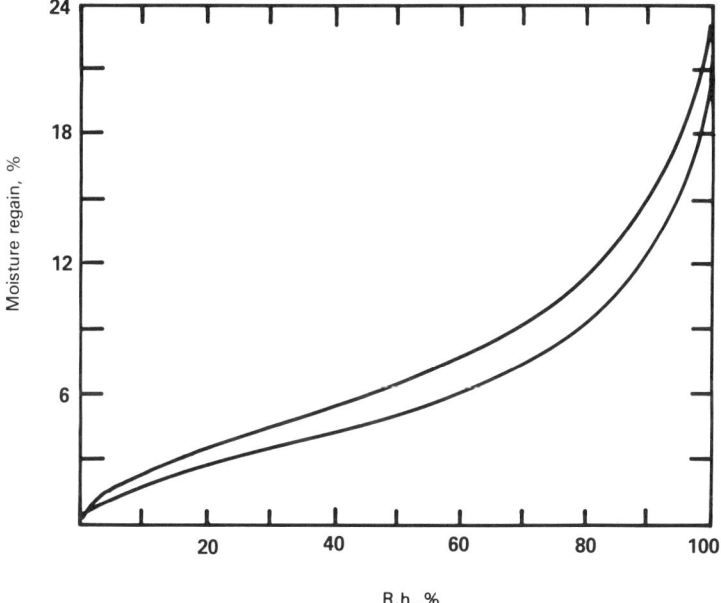

Figure 1.11 – Moisture adsorption (lower) and desorption (upper) isotherms of scoured cotton at 25°C (reproduced from ref. 1 by permission of Wiley Interscience, New York)

At all humidities below 50°C, and below 85% r.h. at higher temperatures, moisture regain decreases as temperature increases. When both humidity and temperature are above these limits, however, the breaking of inter-chain hydrogen bonds becomes so extensive that the moisture regain begins to increase again with further rise in temperature [25].

A notable feature of the sorption of water vapour by cellulose is the phenomenon known as hysteresis, i.e. the greater regain found at a given relative humidity when equilibrium is approached from the wet than from the dry state. In Figure 1.11 the upper curve represents the moisture regain when a sample first exposed to an atmosphere saturated with water vapour is brought to equilibrium with atmospheres of successively decreasing relative humidity. The lower curve represents a bone-dry sample in equilibrium with successively increasing humidities. If a sample of cellulose that has been conditioned to constant weight at some intermediate relative humidity is examined it will give desorption and adsorption curves somewhere between the two limiting curves shown in Figure 1.11. Thus the precise moisture regain of any sample of cellulose at a particular relative humidity and temperature is determined by its previous patterns of hydrogen bond interchange. When cellulose is first formed in plants most of the hydroxyl groups are bonded to water. As it begins to lose water, strong inter-chain hydrogen bonds are formed while the cellulose remains swollen and the chain molecules can move relatively freely. Only relatively weak inter-chain bonds can form when the fibre is approaching dryness. On exposing the dry cellulose to a moist atmosphere, water is first adsorbed on whatever free hydroxyl groups remain, and then on those groups held together by weak hydrogen bonds which are momentarily broken by thermal vibration. The chain molecules are pushed apart, exposing more free hydroxyl groups. But the increase in the number of available hydroxyl groups during adsorption from one relative humidity to another is less than the corresponding decrease during desorption, because the amplitude of vibration of one molecule held to another molecule by hydrogen bonding is less than that of the same molecule when its hydroxyl groups are free to bear water molecules and it is less restricted in its movement [25].

Cellulose fibres imbibe considerably more water when immersed in the liquid than they sorb at a relative humidity of 100% [28]. The extra water is doubtless held by capillary condensation [1]. Precise estimates of the amount of imbibed water cannot be made because of the difficulty of devising a procedure that removes mechanically entrained water from the test samples without removing any truly imbibed water at the same time. In the so-called centrifuge method the saturated sample is centrifuged for 5–10 min, weighed, dried and reweighed. Cotton yarn gives a water imbibition of about 45–50% by this method [28], but somewhat greater retention is likely in the processing of cloth when excess liquor from a padding bath is expressed by means of a mangle.

1.5.2 Organic Liquids

Organic liquids, other than the aliphatic amines (see p. 24), are less strongly attracted to cellulose than is water [1]. The vapours of small molecules with a hydrogen bonding capacity, such as methanol and ethanol, are sorbed, but to a smaller extent than water. As the size of the molecule increases, the degree of sorption decreases, and butan-1-ol is not sorbed at all. Non-polar vapours, such as benzene and carbon tetrachloride, are sorbed to a very slight extent.

Although only very small quantities of non-polar liquids are imbibed by cellulose under normal conditions, it has proved possible to introduce them into the structure by first swelling the material in water and then treating it successively with a series of solvents of decreasing polarity, finishing with the particular non-polar solvent. Removal of the excess liquid by pumping leaves a material containing an appreciable amount of non-polar solvent that cannot be removed further, however high a vacuum is used. Such products have been called 'inclusion celluloses' because their solvent content is not held by ordinary valency forces but is trapped in the cellulose structure in the manner of a clathrate (i.e. cage) compound. It appears that the originally swollen structure gradually collapses during the removal of the solvent by pumping. The chief interest in these compounds [14, 29] lies in their higher reactivity towards processes such as acetylation. They are stable only in the absence of water, which rapidly displaces the non-polar liquid. For example, if cyclohexane inclusion cellulose is viewed under a microscope whilst being wetted, beads of liquid cyclohexane can be seen forming on individual fibres [29].

1.6 SWELLING

1.6.1 General
When bone-dry cotton fibres are immersed in water their average diameter increases by about 20% [30]. However, many aqueous solutions cause much greater swelling than this and it is usual to define the degree of swelling as the percentage increase in either the average diameter or cross-sectional area of a fibre initially in the water-swollen state. This is more useful than basing measurements on bone-dry fibres, which are seldom encountered in practice.

Swelling always entails the breaking of hydrogen bonds between adjacent chain molecules, and a number of substances other than the aqueous solutions referred to above can cause it. Since Mercer's pioneering work [31, 32] the subject has been widely studied [8, 14, 33]. The degree of swelling depends both on the reagent used and on the morphology of the fibre. Thus the same swelling agent has different effects on cotton and on viscose. Nevertheless, the fundamental process involved is the same in all cases.

The swelling of cotton and other native cellulose fibres takes place in two ways; it may be interfibrillar or intrafibrillar. The first can occur without the second, but the second is always accompanied by the first. The most extensive changes arise from intrafibrillar swelling, which sometimes involves the formation of a different molecular arrangement with a definite X-ray diagram. When the swelling agent is removed by washing or other means the cellulose contracts again and usually forms cellulose II. Sometimes, however, it forms cellulose III or reverts to cellulose I. In all cases a more accessible fine structure is produced. The properties of the product depend markedly on the method of removal of the swelling agent.

It has been suggested [34] that when cellulose undergoes intrafibrillar swelling the solid structure is only partially disrupted. Sheets of cellulose in which the chain molecules are held together in the 110 planes mainly by van der Waals forces are pushed apart in the 110 direction by the breaking of hydrogen bonds and the intrusion of molecules of the swelling agent. This is illustrated in Figure 1.12, which shows the cross-section of part of a fibre, looking along the fibre axis. The sheets maintain their identity during swelling although, probably because a certain amount of interchain hydrogen bonding within them is possible, some rearrangement of the chains may occur.

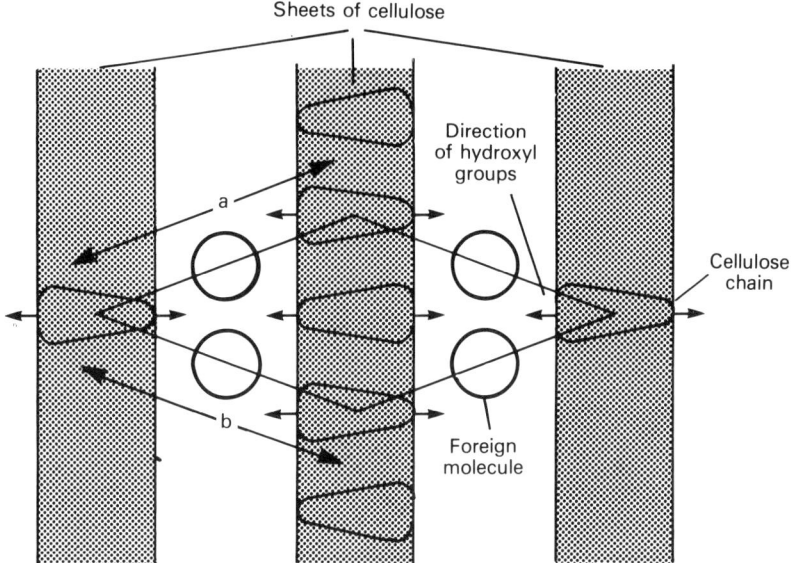

Figure 1.12 – Swelling of cellulose by penetration of reagent between sheets, looking along fibre axis (reproduced from 'Liquid Ammonia Treatment of Cellulosic Textiles' by permission of Shirley Institute, Manchester)

1.6.2 Aqueous Alkalis

The literature on the swelling of cellulose by aqueous alkalis is a jungle, but it is possible to pick one's way through it with the help of a suitable review [14, 33]. The hydroxides of the alkali metals cause extensive swelling over a limited range of concentrations. The range and the concentration at which maximum swelling occurs differ from one metal to another and from one type of cellulose to another. By far the greatest amount of work has been done with sodium hydroxide because of its importance in mercerising.

The basic facts are now well established; they are generally interpreted in terms of sorption of alkali by the cellulose and the consequent imbibition of water. There have always been those who have preferred to postulate stoichiometric compound formation, and the existence of complexes with the general formula: $C_6H_{10}O_5 . NaOH . nH_2O$ (where $n = 1$, 2, 3 or 5) as well as $2C_6H_{10}O_5 . NaOH$ have been inferred from the X-ray diagrams of cellulose at various stages of swelling in sodium hydroxide [35]. These inferences, however, ignore the fact that X-ray diagrams may be reasonably well defined when only part of a cellulose–alkali system is geometrically ordered. Furthermore, because differences in fibre morphology at various stages of swelling produce differences in accessibility of the cellulose to alkali, no air-dry solid sample with an overall composition corresponding to any of the proposed formulae has ever been reported.

One of the reasons for the early belief in compound formation was that, when the apparent amount of sodium hydroxide sorbed by cellulose (as measured by titration of the solution) was plotted against the equilibrium concentration of the solution, a curve with distinct plateaux was obtained. This is illustrated in Figure 1.13 [36]. It was subsequently shown, however, that the change in titre of the sodium hydroxide represented the net effect of two separate processes, namely the sorption of sodium hydroxide and a preferential imbibition of water [37]. The water uptake passed through a maximum at a concentration of sodium hydroxide of about 100 to 200 g/l (2.5 to 5 mol/l), whereas the uptake of sodium hydroxide rose steadily in a manner characteristic of sorption. This conclusion has been fully justified in many later investigations, although the stoichiometric-compound theory continued to attract supporters for a long time [38].

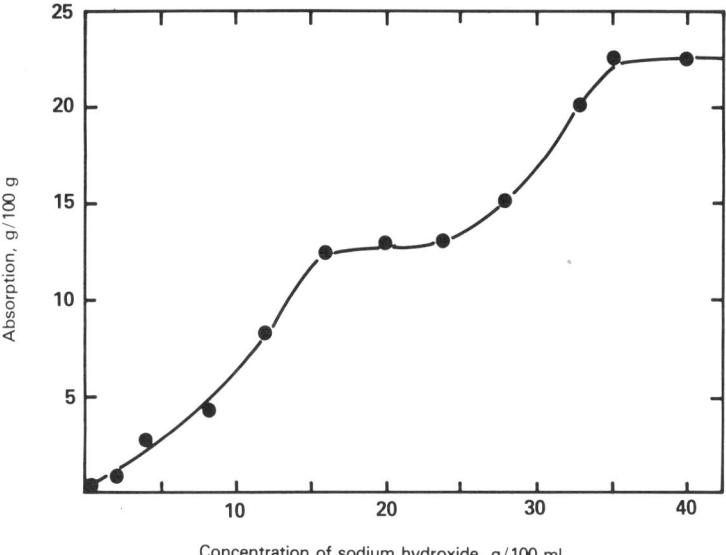

Figure 1.13 – Apparent uptake of sodium hydroxide by cotton (reproduced from ref. 14, by permission of Wiley Interscience, New York)

The degree of swelling of cotton in sodium hydroxide depends on the amount of water imbibed, which in turn depends on the concentration of alkali in the liquor. Maximum swelling occurs at concentrations between 2.5 and 5 mol/l, according to the temperature. This is illustrated in Figure 1.14, which also shows that swelling increases as the temperature decreases, as would be expected, since the sorption of alkali is exothermic [33, 39, 40]. The particularly high maximum at 0°C has been attributed to bursting of the primary wall of the cotton fibres [14]. Other fibres such as ramie and viscose, which have much weaker outer walls, swell more extensively than cotton at 25°C [41].

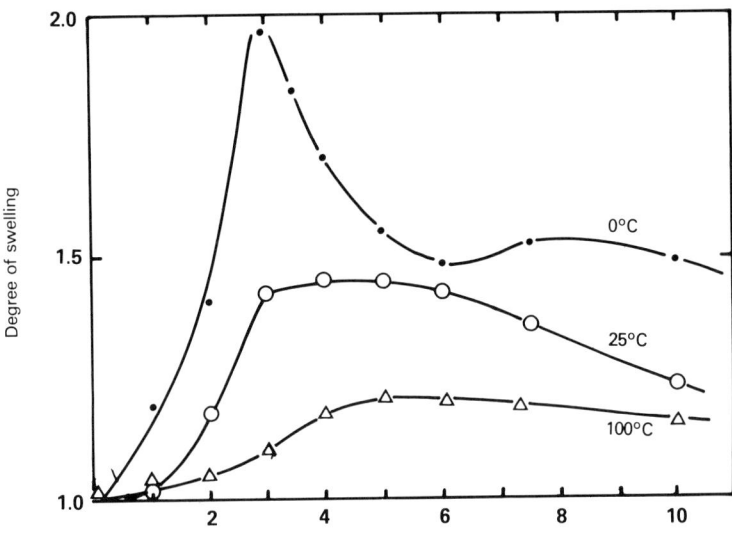

Concentration of sodium hydroxide, mol/l

Figure 1.14 – Swelling of cotton in sodium hydroxide solutions (reproduced from ref. 14 by permission of Wiley Interscience, New York)

The first quantitative theory of the swelling of cellulose in alkali was due to Neale [42]. He applied Donnan's equation for the distribution of diffusable ions between two phases separated by a membrane, through which another ion in one of the phases is unable to diffuse. He treated cellulose as a very weak monobasic acid ($pK_a \sim 13.7$), and assumed that when immersed in sodium hydroxide it may be considered as the two-phase system shown in Table 1.3, the 'membrane' between the phases being the outer surface of the fibres. Because of the high alkalinity of the external (liquid) phase the concentration of hydrogen ions in it was regarded as negligible.

TABLE 1.3

Distribution of Ions in a Two-phase (Cellulose and Liquid) System

Cellulose phase (1)		Membrane ↓	Liquid phase (2)
Undissociated acid	$R_{cell}OH$		
Hydrogen ions	H^+		
Cellulose ions	$R_{cell}O^-$		
Sodium ions	Na^+		Na^+
Hydroxyl ions	OH^-		OH^-
Water	H_2O		H_2O

Since the ion $R_{cell}O^-$ cannot diffuse:

$$[Na^+]_1[OH^-]_1 = [Na^+]_2[OH^-]_2 \qquad (1.1)$$

The osmotic pressure P tending to drive water from phase 2 into phase 1 may be calculated roughly from the difference between the total concentration of diffusable ions in each phase:

$$P = RT([Na^+]_1 + [OH^-]_1 - [Na^+]_2 - [OH^-]_2) \qquad (1.2)$$

Remembering that each phase is electrically neutral and neglecting concentration changes resulting solely from the increase in volume that accompanies swelling, Eqns 1.1 and 1.2 may be used to calculate values of P and $[NaOH]_2$ for arbitrarily chosen values of $[NaOH]_1$. In Figure 1.15 the results so obtained are compared with measured values of the amount of water taken up by a regenerated cellulose film (used instead of cotton fibres because it is easier to handle experimentally). The similarity between the two curves lends support to Neale's theory. However, the theory has several defects, not least of which is that it cannot distinguish one alkali metal hydroxide from another, although considerable differences do exist [14].

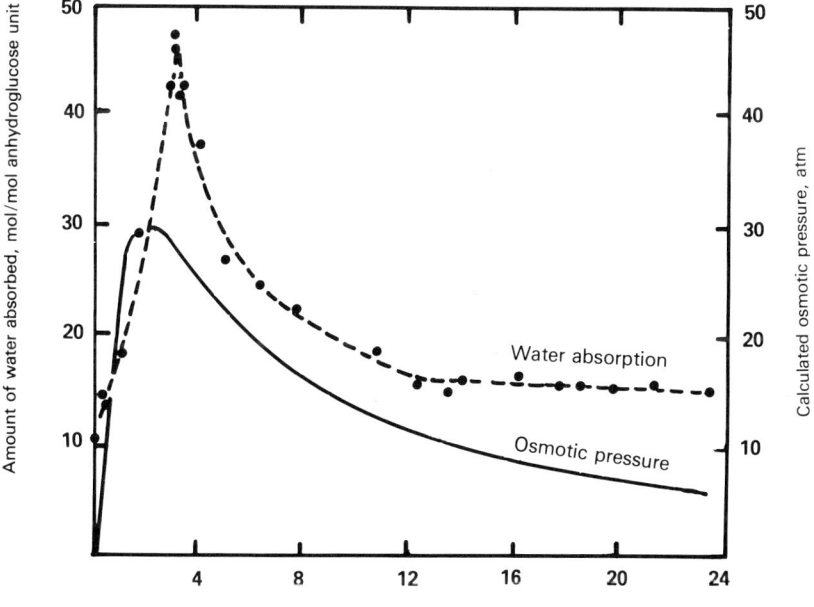

Figure 1.15 – Osmotic pressure (calculated) and water absorption (measured) of cellulose film immersed in sodium hydroxide solution (reproduced from ref. 33 by permission of Wiley Interscience, New York)

Furthermore, approximations such as equating activities with concentrations and neglecting changes in volume in the swollen fibres are hard to justify. In spite of these defects the theory has provided valuable insight into the mechanism of swelling.

One aspect of the subject not yet considered is the extent to which swelling is controlled by the degree of hydration of the cations in alkaline solutions. The importance of ionic hydration has been recognised for a long time [14, 41], and Chédin and Marsaudon [43] have visualised the swelling process as arising from the substitution of some of the water of hydration of the dissolved metal hydroxide by cellulosic hydroxyl groups, as represented by Scheme 1.2. When the hydrated ion

$$Na^+OH^-.nH_2O + R_{cell}(OH)_3 \rightleftharpoons R_{cell}(OH)_3.Na^+OH^-.(n-3)H_2O + 3H_2O$$

Scheme 1.2

pairs are sorbed by the cellulose, three molecules of water are released and are replaced by three cellulosic hydroxyl groups, which are not necessarily all from the same anhydroglucose unit. The liberated water molecules occupy a greater volume than when they were associated with sodium ions, and so cause swelling [44]. This theory of swelling is more general than Neale's. Not only can it account for the different behaviour of different alkali metal hydroxides (in terms of different hydrate equilibria in aqueous solution), but it can also be applied to other aqueous systems where ionic hydration is extensive. It is not, of course, applicable to non-aqueous swelling agents.

1.6.3 Liquid Ammonia and Amines

When cellulose is treated with liquid ammonia at temperatures near its boiling point (33.4°C) a 1:1 complex, with a monoclinic cell having $a = 1.27$, $b = 1.075$ and $c = 1.03$, and $\gamma = 133.5°$, is formed [45–48]. This complex is fairly stable; it loses ammonia by evaporation, quite slowly at room temperature [48] but more rapidly on heating, to give cellulose III. These changes are illustrated schematically in Figure 1.16, which shows that the distance between the 110 planes remains nearly constant, the distention of the lattice by the ammonia being almost entirely within these planes (cf. Figure 1.9). If the ammonia is removed by washing with water instead of by evaporation, the material reverts to cellulose I. The morphology, and therefore some of the technically important properties, of native cellulose fibres are also differently affected by the method of removal of the ammonia.

When cellulose is treated at 0°C with ethylamine (b.p. 16.6°C) a 1:1 complex similar to that formed with ammonia results, but the lattice is further distended in the 110 direction to accommodate the larger molecule (see Figure 1.16). Once again the spacing between 110 planes remains practically unchanged [49, 50]. Propylamine cellulose, with a still greater 1̄10 spacing, is formed in the same way, but higher amines are too large to penetrate the cellulose I lattice directly. However, if the cellulose is first 'primed' with ethylamine or liquid ammonia, complexes of the higher primary aliphatic monoamines, various diamines (including some

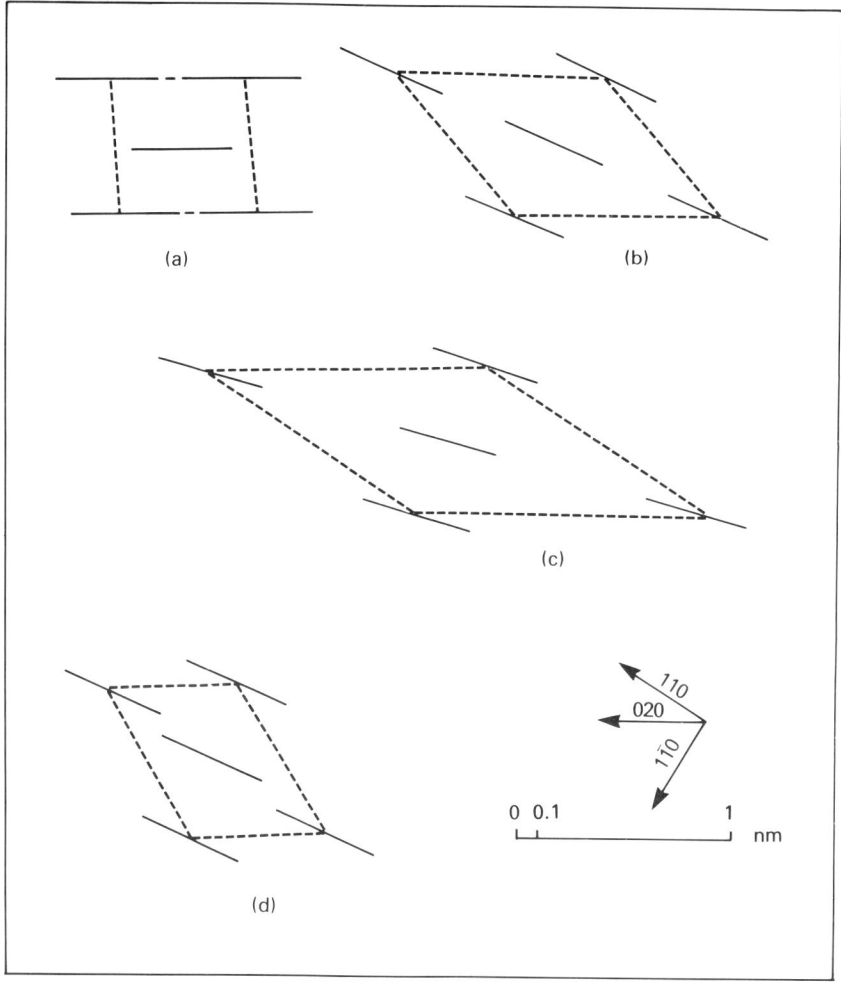

Figure 1.16 – Schematic representation of conversion of (a) cellulose I to (b) ammonia–cellulose, (c) ethylamine–cellulose, and (d) cellulose III

secondary and tertiary amines) and certain cyclic amines are readily formed [51, 52]. With the diamines the increase in the 1Ī0 spacing depends not on the distance between amino groups, but on the total size of the molecule [52]. Thus, cellulose–nitrogen bonding involving a single hydrogen bond is the basis of intrafibrillar swelling by ammonia and amines. It may be noted that water does not inhibit the process, provided that the amount is less than that required to form the mono-hydrate of the amine (28.6% wt/wt in the case of ethylamine). If more water than this is present no complex is formed [53].

When ethylamine is removed from its complex with native cellulose the structure reverts either to cellulose I or to cellulose III, according to the method of removal of the amine. However, the product has a much lower degree of crystallinity than the original cellulose, and for this reason has been called 'decrystallised cellulose' [54]. Besides being less crystalline it is chemically more reactive. This is illustrated in Figure 1.17, which shows the effect of ethylamine treatment on the rate of acetylation of cotton by acetic anhydride in pyridine at 25°C (see p. 47). Figure 1.17 also shows the effect on reactivity of the method of ethylamine removal. Extraction with pyridine leaves far more hydroxyl groups accessible to acetic anhydride than washing with water, which has the effect of drawing together the chain molecules of the highly swollen material. The relevant difference between pyridine and water is that pyridine can form only one hydrogen bond per molecule, but water can form two. It should be noted that the pyridine-washed material had been further washed with water and dried in the air before being introduced into the acetylating mixture in order to standardise the final treatment of the three samples before acetylation. It is apparent that once the ethylamine has been removed with pyridine, the extent to which water can draw the chain molecules together is much less than when it is used directly.

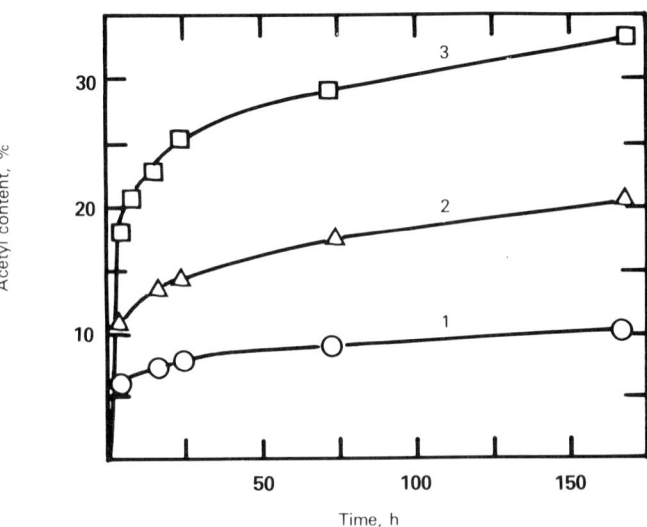

1 — No pretreatment
2 — Ethylamine treated, water washed
3 — Ethylamine treated, pyridine washed

Figure 1.17 – Rate of acetylation of cotton (reproduced from ref. 54 by permission of Merrow Publishing Co., Shildon, Durham)

The treatment of cellulose with liquid ammonia is practised on a considerable scale industrially, sometimes as an alternative to mercerisation. Whilst hopes were at one time entertained that ethylamine treatment might be similarly exploited, they have not so far been realised.

1.6.4 Other Swelling Agents

Many other substances have been recognised as swelling agents for cellulose [14]. In his patent [32] on the effect of sodium hydroxide, Mercer also described the swelling of cellulose using 62% sulphuric acid at room temperature and 59% zinc chloride at about 70°C. The parchmentisation of paper with 70% sulphuric acid is still a commercial process, and in the past special finishes were obtained on cotton cloth in a similar way, but with somewhat lower concentrations of acid [55]. Other mineral acids also swell cellulose at appropriate concentrations. Care must be taken, generally by keeping the time of treatment to a minimum and the temperature low, to avoid simultaneous degradation or esterification of the material. Phosphoric acid has been claimed to have little degradative effect, but the claim has been disputed.

Zinc chloride is typical of a group of metal halides that, in suitable concentrations, swell (and sometimes even dissolve) cellulose at elevated temperatures; calcium thiocyanate behaves similarly. Lastly it must be mentioned that polar organic solvents, both protic and aprotic, swell cellulose to a small extent. The swelling power of a solvent appears to depend on the strength of the hydrogen bonds that it can form with the cellulose [56, 57]. The swelling of cellulose in N,N-dimethylformamide takes place more rapidly than in water, but the final degree of swelling is less [58].

1.7 SOLVENTS FOR CELLULOSE

Although many reagents swell cellulose very few are capable of dissolving it. Much effort has been put into the search for cellulose solvents [14, 59, 60], for two reasons:

(a) To determine molecular weight and other properties
(b) To manufacture regenerated cellulosic fibres.

For many years the only known solvents for cellulose at ordinary temperatures were moderately concentrated mineral acids (such as 70% sulphuric acid or 78% phosphoric acid) and cuprammonium hydroxide. Dissolution in the former is due to protonation of the cellulosic hydroxyl groups to give species of the type $R_{cell}OH_2^+$. A saturated solution of calcium thiocyanate at its boiling point (133°C) also dissolves cellulose, almost certainly due to its hydrolysis to thiocyanic acid. The cellulose in these solutions is always seriously degraded after a short time, so they are of little practical importance. Cuprammonium hydroxide, on the other hand, dissolves cellulose without degradation provided that atmospheric oxygen and light are excluded. Originally discovered by Schweizer [61], the dissolution of cellulose in cuprammonium hydroxide forms the basis of the now obsolescent process for manufacturing cupro and of the well-known fluidity test for chemical degradation in cellulosic textiles [62, 63]. In this test a standard solvent containing 15 g/l of copper and 200 g/l of ammonia is used. This solvent is frequently referred to as cuprammonium or cuam. Solutions containing 0.5 g (cotton) or 2 g (viscose) per 100 ml are prepared in a special viscometer and their flow times between two marks are measured at 20°C. Results are expressed as 'fluidities', i.e. as reciprocals of the dynamic viscosities; the unit of fluidity is the reciprocal poise or rhe (1 rhe $= 10$ m^2 N^{-1} s^{-1} in SI units). The conditions of the test ensure an approximately linear relation between fluidity and loss of tensile strength for cotton tendered to an extent of up to 50%. The fluidity of undegraded scoured cotton is about 3 rhes and rises to about 30 rhes at 50% loss of strength. Therefore expressing results as fluidities is more meaningful than expressing them as viscosities, which fall roughly hyperbolically with loss of strength and so constitute an insensitive measure of tendering except in its very early stages [64]. Another important feature of the fluidity measurement is that cuprammonium hydroxide is strongly alkaline. It will be shown later (p. 41) that certain forms of chemical tendering do not become apparent until after the material has received some alkaline treatment, as in ordinary laundering. The 'latent' tendering, which is only detectable by measuring tensile strength after the material has been treated with alkali, is automatically taken into account in the fluidity measurement because of the alkalinity of the solvent.

It is interesting to speculate on the reason why cellulose dissolves in cuprammonium hydroxide. It seems that a 1:1 complex is formed between the cuprammonium ion and the 2,3-diol group of the anhydroglucose chain units [65]. A plausible reaction would be the formation of the uncharged square-planar copper(II) complex shown in Scheme 1.3 [66]. The formation of this complex

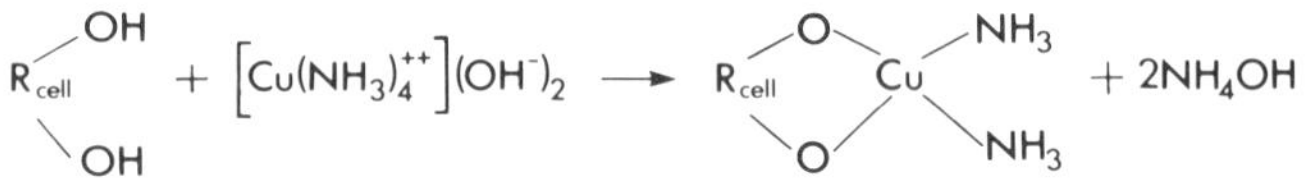

$$R_{cell}\overset{\displaystyle OH}{\underset{\displaystyle OH}{\Big\langle}} + \left[Cu(NH_3)_4^{++}\right](OH^-)_2 \longrightarrow R_{cell}\overset{\displaystyle O}{\underset{\displaystyle O}{\Big\langle}}Cu\overset{\displaystyle NH_3}{\underset{\displaystyle NH_3}{\Big\rangle}} + 2NH_4OH$$

Scheme 1.3

involves distortion of the pyranose ring, and this is strongly indicated by the large difference between the optical rotation of cellulose with a low degree of polymerisation in cuprammonium hydroxide and in 2 mol/l sodium hyroxide. Furthermore, the electrical conductivity of cuprammonium falls sharply when cellulose dissolves in it because some of the strongly basic cuprammonium hydroxide is converted into the weakly basic ammonium hydroxide.

It has been known for a long time that cellulose dissolves in solutions of copper(II) hydroxide in aqueous, 1,2-diaminoethane (ethylenediamine) [67]. Such solutions, which are usually called cupriethylenediamine or cuen, are now preferred by many workers to cuprammonium for testing purposes, because ethylenediamine is much less volatile than ammonia, and it is widely believed that the dissolved cellulose is less susceptible to photochemical oxidation. The standard TAPPI [68] and ASTM [69] methods both use a reagent concentration of 0.5 mol/l with respect to copper and 1.0 mol/l with respect to the amine. The TAPPI method recommends using 0.5% solutions of cellulose and expressing the results as viscosities; objections to this have already been noted. The ASTM method specifies that the results be expressed in terms of intrinsic viscosity ($[\eta]$) and that the cellulose concentration (c) used should be such that $[\eta]c = 3.0 \pm 0.5$. This makes the procedure more tedious than the other methods because preliminary rough experiments have to be made to find out what concentration to use for the test proper. Also, since the relation between tendering and intrinsic viscosity is an empirical one, it seems to offer little advantage. If molecular weight (M) is to be determined, the measurement of intrinsic viscosity is essential. So too is a knowledge of the constants in the Mark–Houwink equation: $[\eta] = KM^a$. Typical values of these constants are $K = 0.101$ ml/g and $a = 0.66$ for cuprammonium, and $K = 0.00395$ ml/g and $a = 1.0$ for cupriethylenediamine, both at 25°C [70]; there are considerable discrepancies between the K and a values reported by different workers for supposedly the same system.

Several other metals (e.g. cadmium, cobalt, nickel and zinc) have been found to form complexes with ethylenediamine capable of dissolving cellulose [14]. Jayme has developed the use of an alkaline solution of iron(III) hydroxide in sodium tartrate, which probably contains the complex Na_6^+ [Fe(III)$(C_4H_3O_6)_3^{6-}$], as a solvent for cellulose. Neither this reagent nor the newer amine complexes has yet achieved the same importance as cuoxam and cuen, but the complex of cadmuim with ethylenediamine (cadoxen) is rapidly showing signs of doing so. The preparation and properties of cadoxen have been fully described by Henley [71]. Solutions containing 5% cadmium and 28% ethylenediamine in 0.35 mol/l sodium hydroxide are suitable, although small variations in composition are permissible. As a solvent for measuring viscosities, cadoxen has the great advantage of being colourless and giving solutions of cellulose that are remarkably stable in the presence of oxygen and light. It should be noted that it degrades alkali-sensitive materials slowly and may not, therefore, be as satisfactory as cuprammonium for detecting latent tendering [72].

A quite different type of solvent for cellulose has been developed during the last 15 years. It comprises binary (and occasionally ternary) mixtures of a variety of non-aqueous polar liquids with certain other substances that are capable of reacting with cellulose in some way to give a product soluble in the polar medium [17, 60]. The first inklings that non-aqueous solvents might be found for cellulose itself, as opposed to cellulose derivatives, were obtained by Fowler et al. [73] in the late 1940s. They published a list of 40 different cellulose solvents, consisting of dinitrogen tetroxide mixed with a range of substances as diverse as nitrobenzene and cellobiose octa-acetate. The proportion by weight of dinitrogen tetroxide was usually between 80 and 90% and was never less than 50%. Little further work was done on these lines until 1969 when Schweiger [74] showed that cellulose could be dissolved in solutions of dinitrogen tetroxide or nitrosyl chloride in N,N-dimethylformamide (DMF) or N,N-dimethylacetamide. It is now generally believed [60] that dissolution is due to the formation of cellulose nitrite, which is soluble in DMF (Scheme 1.4).

$$R_{cell}OH + N_2O_4 \xrightarrow{DMF} R_{cell}ONO + HNO_3 \xrightarrow{DMF} \text{Solution}$$

Scheme 1.4

The latest addition to the list of non-aqueous solvents for cellulose is a mixture of paraformaldehyde and dimethylsulphoxide (DMSO) [60, 75]; the solution can also be prepared by bubbling formaldehyde into a suspension of cellulose in boiling DMSO [76]. In all probability it is the methylol derivative of cellulose that is soluble (Scheme 1.5). The current interest in this and other non-aqueous solutions

$$R_{cell}OH + HCHO \xrightarrow{DMSO} R_{cell} O CH_2OH \xrightarrow{DMSO} \text{Solution}$$

Scheme 1.5

of cellulose lies in the possibility of their use for the production of fibres by regeneration in water. The pressure to find an alternative to the viscose process that would be less harmful to the environment is very strong. It has already proved possible to regenerate fibres from some of the solutions studied, but as yet the products are not of an acceptable commercial quality [60].

1.8 DEGRADATION OF CELLULOSE

1.8.1 General

In many applications textile fibres require high tensile strength and resistance to chemical attack. Even slight degradation of cellulose is invariably accompanied by loss of strength. The study of degradation mechanisms therefore has important practical implications for the production of satisfactory finished fabrics.

From a chemical point of view the complete degradation of cellulose is its conversion into carbon dioxide and water. Any intermediate stage in this process may be described as partial degradation, and it is the very early stages of degradation that are important in the textile field. Quite small changes in chemical composition may affect the physical properties of cellulose profoundly, sometimes so much so that a fibrous material falls to powder. The types of degradation to be considered in this section are those produced by acids, alkalis, oxidising agents, heat, radiation and enzymes. The water-insoluble products of the action of acids and oxidising agents will be referred to by the long-established [77–79] trivial names of hydrocellulose and oxycellulose respectively, in spite of certain objections to them by purists [80].

Before the introduction of modern physico-chemical analytical techniques, the only method of determining unequivocally the structure of a particular sample of degraded cellulose was to hydrolyse it, or a derivative of it, completely and to isolate in quantitative yield the fragments of each and every chain unit in the original material. This was a monumental task by the methods of classical organic chemistry and was seldom achieved. However, a great deal of useful information was, and still can be, obtained by means of the less rigorous approach to the problem perfected by Clibbens and his collaborators at the Shirley Institute [81]. Series of materials are prepared with particular degrading agents. These are characterised by measuring properties related to chain length (such as tensile strength and cuprammonium fluidity) and those related to the content of carbonyl and carboxyl groups. A variety of methods exist for the determination of carbonyl groups (e.g. aldehyde and ketone groups, and hemiacetal end groups), but they are not of universal applicability and are sometimes insufficiently sensitive for materials containing only small proportions of carbonyl [25].

The long-established empirical measure of reducing power known as the copper number [82] has proved of great value in cellulose research. It is defined as the weight in grams of Cu(II) in alkaline solution reduced to Cu(I) by 100 g of dry material under specified conditions, which include conducting the reaction at 100°C. The amount of copper reduced per carbonyl group varies greatly with the precise nature of the group and its position in the chain molecule. For example, the two aldehyde groups in periodate oxycelluloses reduce 1.6 and 8.9 atoms of copper respectively [83], and the end groups in hydrocelluloses reduce 22 atoms [84]. Thus the copper number is a very sensitive measure of hemiacetal end groups, and the fact that the copper number of scoured cotton is practically zero is good evidence of the absence of such groups in this material.

A large number of methods, with known stoichiometry, are available for the determination of carboxyl groups in cellulose [25]. They nearly all depend on the simple cation exchange shown in Scheme 1.6. The methods differ from one another

$$R_{cell} \, COOH + M^+ \rightleftharpoons R_{cell} \, COOM + H^+$$

Scheme 1.6

in the way in which it is ensured that equilibrium in Scheme 1.6 is pushed to the right, and in the way in which either the decrease in concentration of the cation M^+ or the increase in concentration of the hydrogen ion H^+ is measured in the supernatant liquid. Among the most popular methods are the methylene blue absorption method [82], the alkalimetric method [82] and the iodometric method [85]. Uronic acid groups (i.e. carboxyl groups at C6 in the pyranose ring), but not other carboxyl groups, are driven off as carbon dioxide by boiling the material containing them with 12% hydrochloric acid, and can thus be quantitatively determined [82].

1.8.2 Degradation by Acids

The degradation of cellulose by aqueous acids consists in the hydrogen-ion catalysed hydrolysis of the glycosidic linkages according to Scheme 1.7 [86].

The properties of the hydrocelluloses so formed depend solely on the number and distribution of glycosidic linkages broken, which vary with pH, temperature and time of treatment. The nature of the anion is immaterial. It thus happens that tensile strength, copper number and fluidity of a hydrocellulose are uniquely related to one another, irrespective of the conditions under which the hydrocellulose has been made [1, 87]. The products of the early stages of hydrolysis are fibrous, but those having a fluidity greater than about 44 rhes are usually powders. The rate of increase of fluidity depends on the supramolecular structure of the cellulose, as may be seen from Figure 1.18. After a time the fluidity reaches a plateau, the height of which also depends on the nature of the starting material

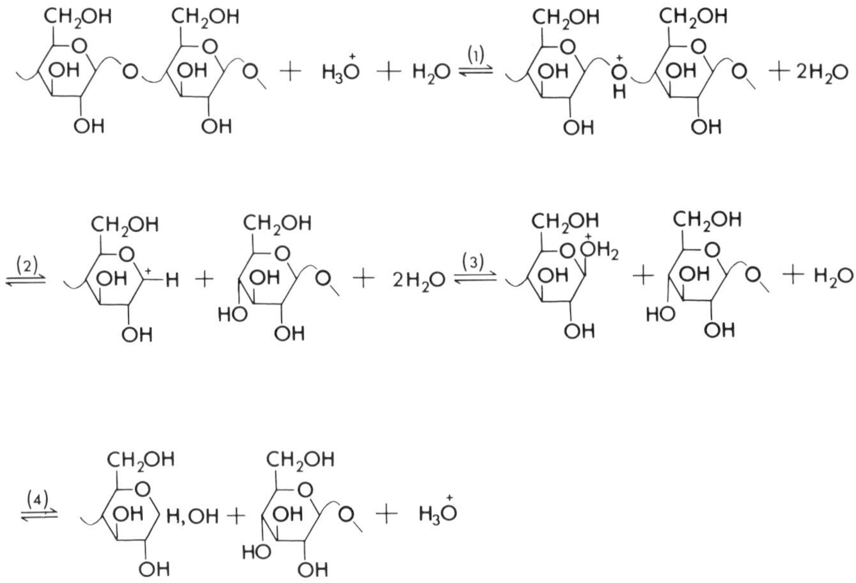

Scheme 1.7

[88]. The degree of polymerisation calculated from one of these plateaux is often called the levelling-off degree of polymerisation (LODP).

It must not be inferred that because a constant degree of polymerisation has been reached the reaction has ceased. Far from it; the material continues to lose weight. This is because, once the completely accessible glycosidic bonds have been randomly hyrolysed, further reaction occurs at chain ends in the previously inaccessible regions of the fibres (sometimes referred to as 'crystallites'). Hence the slow final reaction consists in the removal of small soluble fragments from chain ends and produces no noticeable effect on the average degree of polymerisation. It has been shown that, if the accessible regions involved in the first stage of the reaction are randomly distributed along the microfibrils of the original cellulose, an exponential distribution of crystallite lengths will result from hydrolysis and a constant particle-size distribution will be maintained as end-wise degradation continues [89, 90a].

For many years there was considerable controversy as to whether cellulose contained 'weak bonds', i.e. glycoside linkages capable of being hydrolysed more rapidly than normal completely accessible 1,4-β-glucosidic linkages [91,92]. Three possible causes of such acid sensitivity have been identified [90a]. The first is the presence of electron-attracting groups at certain points in the chain molecules. Certain types of wood cellulose seem to be more susceptible than cotton to acid degradation, probably because they contain a small proportion of aldehyde groups resulting from the oxidation of a few of the primary alcohol groups. Secondly a few

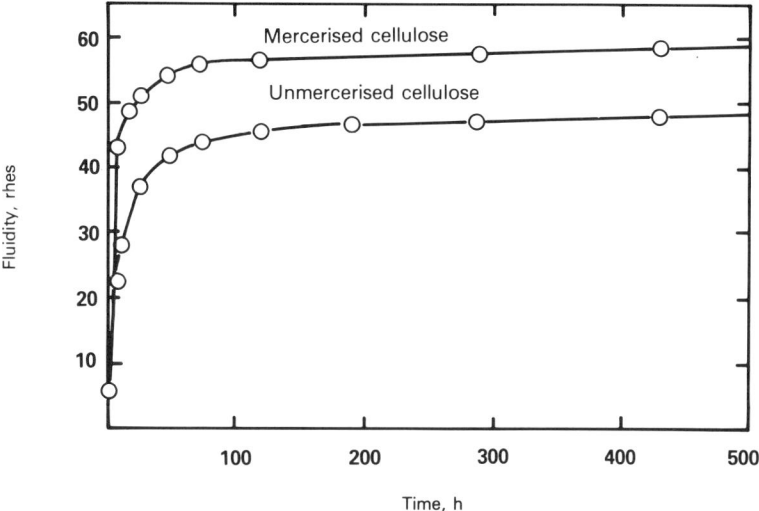

Figure 1.18 – Hydrolysis of cellulose in 6 mol/l hydrochloric acid at 20°C (reproduced from ref. 1 by permission of Wiley Interscience, New York)

of the monosaccharide units may not be anhydroglucose. A glycosidic linkage involving xylose would be expected to hydrolyse more rapidly than one between two glucose units. Various workers have reported the presence of xylose in the soluble hydrolysis products of cellulose, but it does not follow that it was originally present in the cellulose itself. It might have come from associated hemicelluloses not completely removed during purification. Although it is to some extent a matter of faith, it is generally believed that genuine cellulose from cotton and wood is a 1,4-β-D-glucan containing no 'rogue' units of any kind. The third possible cause of acid sensitivity is physical. Rate constants 10000 times greater than normal have been found in the very early stages of the hydrolysis of native cellulose. This enhanced susceptibility has been attributed to the development of abnormal physical stresses at a small number of localised points while the fibres are being formed.

1.8.3 Degradation by Alkalis

The glycosidic linkages in cellulose are not attacked by alkali at temperatures lower than about 170°C. Nevertheless, the industrial purification of cellulose, as in the scouring of cotton with dilute sodium hydroxide or in the soda and kraft processes of wood pulping, is always accompanied by losses of weight greater than can be accounted for by the removal of the non-cellulosic constituents of the raw material. The losses are large enough to be commercially significant. They may be of the order of 3–4% with cotton boiled in a kier at about 140°C [93] and considerably more with wood pulp, which is often cooked at temperatures above 170°C. Davidson [94] first recognised that the losses were caused by stepwise removal of anhydroglucose units from the reducing ends of the cellulose chains, but it was not until the 1950s that Kenner et al. [90b, 95] elucidated the mechanism. The fact that the alkaline degradation of cellulose is dependent upon the reducing end groups is evident from the enhanced susceptibility to degradation of hydrocelluloses. Indeed, the loss of weight on alkaline boiling under standard conditions is proportional to the copper number. For purposes of investigation, therefore, hydrocelluloses are to be preferred to cellulose itself, because they differ from it only in that they contain more end groups. When these end groups are converted into carboxyl or alcohol groups [96] the materials become stable towards alkali. Kenner's contribution was to institute a systematic study of the alkaline decomposition of O-substituted glucose derivatives in which it was conclusively shown that Isbell's mechanism [97] for the formation of saccharinic acids by the action of alkali on glucose could be applied both to the alkyl ethers of sugars and to polysaccharides.

Taking glucose as an example, the first effect of cold dilute alkali is to convert some glucose to mannose and fructose (see Scheme 1.8); this is usually known as

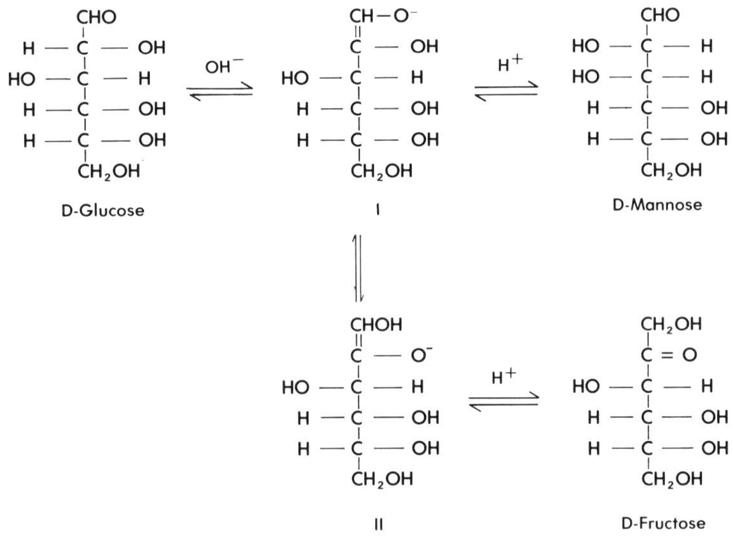

Scheme 1.8

the Lobry de Bruyn/Alberda van Ekenstein transformation, after its discoverers [98, 99]. If the action of the alkali is prolonged more profound changes occur that lead to the production of three isomeric saccharinic acids (see IV, V and VI in Scheme 1.9) by the elimination of the hydroxyl group attached to the carbon atom

```
      CH–O⁻              CHO                CHO                 COOH
      ‖                  |                  |                         BAR
      C — OH             C — OH             C = O              CH (OH)
      |                  ‖                  |          ────►   H — C — H
HO — C — H   ⇌          CH        ⇌        CH₂                 |
      |                  |                  |                   H — C — OH
H — C — OH          H — C — OH         H — C — OH               |
      |                  |                  |                   H — C — OH
H — C — OH          H — C — OH         H — C — OH               |
      |                  |                  |                   CH₂OH
      CH₂OH              CH₂OH              CH₂OH
        I                                                         IV

      ⇵

      CHOH               CH₂OH              CH₂OH
      ‖                  |                  |              BAR
      C — O⁻             C = O              C = O                 COOH
      |                  |                  |          ────►      |
HO — C — H   ⇌          C — OH  ⇌          C = O                  C (OH) (CH₂OH)
      |                  |                  |                      |
H — C — OH          H — C — H          H — C — H              H — C — H
      |                  |                  |                      |
H — C — OH          H — C — OH         H — C — OH             H — C — OH
      |                  |                  |                      |
      CH₂OH              CH₂OH              CH₂OH                  CH₂OH
        II                                                         V

      ⇵

      CH₂OH              CH₂                CH₃
      |                  ‖                  |              BAR
      C — OH             C — OH             C = O                  COOH
      ‖                  |                  |          ────►       |
      C — O⁻   ⇌        C = O    ⇌         C = O                   C (OH) (CH₃)
      |                  |                  |                       |
H — C — OH          H — C — OH         H — C — OH              H — C — OH
      |                  |                  |                       |
H — C — OH          H — C — OH         H — C — OH              H — C — OH
      |                  |                  |                       |
      CH₂OH              CH₂OH              CH₂OH                   CH₂OH
       III                                                          VI
```

Scheme 1.9

next but one to that carrying the negatively charged oxygen in the intermediate ion. This process has therefore been called β-hydroxycarbonyl elimination. It is immediately followed by a 'benzilic acid rearrangement' (designated BAR) of the resulting dicarbonyl compound. When the hydroxyl group that can be eliminated in one of these ways has been previously alkylated, the elimination of the resulting alkoxyl group occurs more rapidly, but otherwise the reaction is the same.

The reason for the end-wise alkaline degradation of cellulose and hydrocelluloses is now apparent. The reducing end group is first converted into a fructose residue which, having a carbonyl group in the β-position with respect to the glycosidic bond, becomes detached from the end of the chain and appears in solution as D-glucoisosaccharinic acid (V). At the same time a new reducing end group is revealed, and the process of erosion would continue indefinitely if it were not stopped at some point by a competing stabilising reaction. This reaction consists in the elimination of the hydroxyl group at C3 from the reducing end group with formation a D-glucometasaccharinic acid residue (cf. IV) still attached at C4 to the rest of the chain by the original glycosidic bond (VII). This bond is not susceptible to scission by alkali. The two processes are formulated in Scheme 1.10.

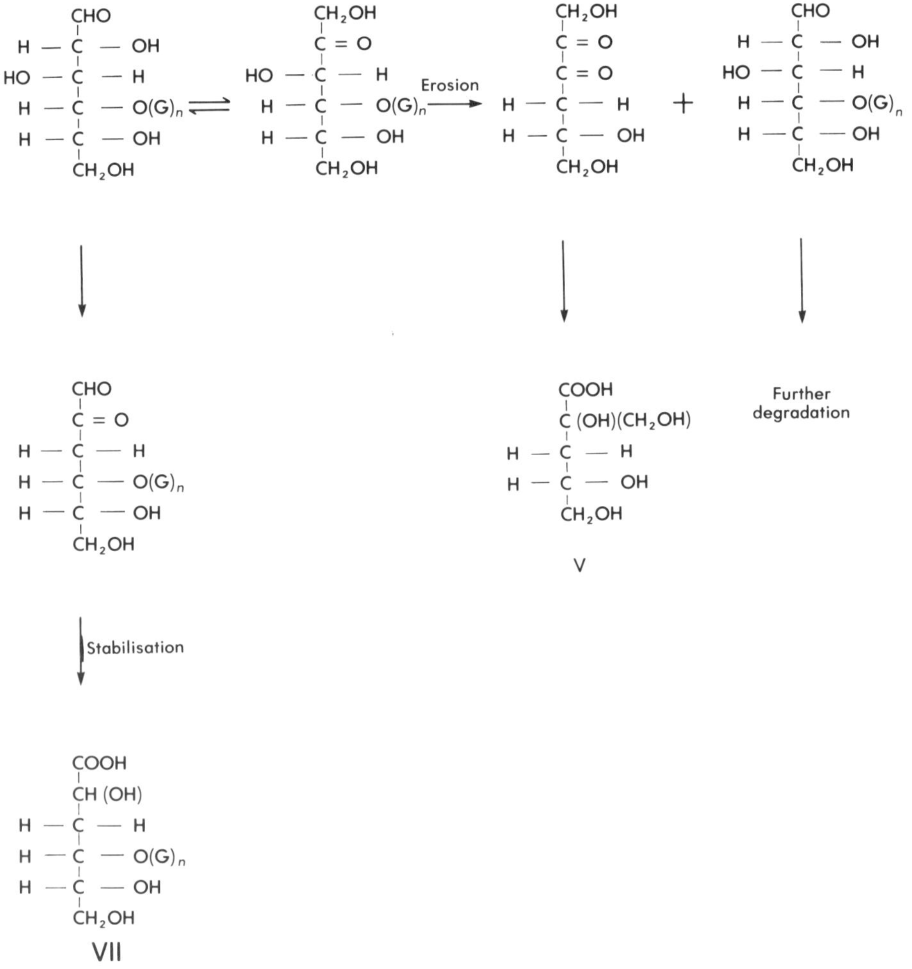

$$\begin{array}{c} CHO \\ | \\ H - C - OH \\ | \\ HO - C - H \\ | \\ H - C - O(G)_n \\ | \\ H - C - OH \\ | \\ CH_2OH \end{array} \rightleftharpoons \begin{array}{c} CH_2OH \\ | \\ C = O \\ | \\ HO - C - H \\ | \\ H - C - O(G)_n \\ | \\ H - C - OH \\ | \\ CH_2OH \end{array} \xrightarrow{Erosion} \begin{array}{c} CH_2OH \\ | \\ C = O \\ | \\ C = O \\ | \\ H - C - H \\ | \\ H - C - OH \\ | \\ CH_2OH \end{array} + \begin{array}{c} CHO \\ | \\ H - C - OH \\ | \\ HO - C - H \\ | \\ H - C - O(G)_n \\ | \\ H - C - OH \\ | \\ CH_2OH \end{array}$$

$$\begin{array}{c} CHO \\ | \\ C = O \\ | \\ H - C - H \\ | \\ H - C - O(G)_n \\ | \\ H - C - OH \\ | \\ CH_2OH \end{array} \qquad \begin{array}{c} COOH \\ | \\ C (OH)(CH_2OH) \\ | \\ H - C - H \\ | \\ H - C - OH \\ | \\ CH_2OH \\ \\ V \end{array} \qquad \begin{array}{c} Further \\ degradation \end{array}$$

Stabilisation

$$\begin{array}{c} COOH \\ | \\ CH (OH) \\ | \\ H - C - H \\ | \\ H - C - O(G)_n \\ | \\ H - C - OH \\ | \\ CH_2OH \\ \\ VII \end{array}$$

Scheme 1.10

Scheme 1.10 represents only the main reactions of cellulose with dilute alkali; other processes undoubtedly occur even at temperatures below 170°C, but they are not well understood. Above 170°C dilute sodium hydroxide causes scission of glycosidic bonds randomly along the chain [100, 101] and the newly formed shorter chains are then degraded further by erosion in the way that has just been described.

1.8.4 Degradation by Oxidation

Since each intermediate unit in a cellulose molecule contains three alcohol groups, the number of possible oxidation products is considerable. End groups can also be oxidised and this may be important if primary oxidation is accompanied by chain scission, as often happens when the reaction is carried out under alkaline conditions. Moreover, only a small proportion of a cellulose fibre is readily accessible to most oxidising agents, which therefore react rapidly at first and then very much more slowly. The action of most oxidising agents, including those that are industrially important, is non-specific and complex, and it has seldom proved possible to elucidate either the mechanism of the reaction or the precise constitution of its products. Nevertheless considerable insight into these questions has resulted from the Shirley Institute's approach [81], extended to the study of oxidation by sodium metaperiodate. This oxidant is both specific in its mode of action and capable of penetrating the whole solid structure of cellulose. Its use permits the preparation of oxycelluloses whose constitution is known with a fair degree of certainty. Relationships between properties and constitution can be recognised and the knowledge so obtained can be used to explain, by analogy, the behaviour of other oxycelluloses. The literature of cellulose oxidation is extensive; four useful reviews may be mentioned here [1, 25, 82, 90c].

The oxidation of cellulose by sodium hypochlorite (NaClO) has been studied chiefly because of the importance of preventing tendering during cotton bleaching. Hypochlorite is still used for this purpose in some parts of the world. Clibbens and his co-workers [102, 103] established that both the rate of oxidation and the nature of the products depend on the pH of the solution used. Under alkaline conditions, where the oxidant is mainly the hypochlorite ion, the reaction is slow and leads to acidic oxycelluloses with low reducing powers. In mildly acid solutions (pH 3–5), where most of the oxidant is in the form of undissociated hypochlorous acid, the reaction is also rather slow, but the products possess high reducing power and contain few acid groups. Oxidation is most rapid at pH 7 and oxycelluloses of hybrid type (containing both acid and reducing groups in appreciable amounts) are formed. Later work [104] has shown that the reducing groups produced in acid solutions comprise both aldehyde and ketone groups. The ratio COOH:CHO:CO is 2:7:9 at pH 5, while at pH 10 it is 5:1:0. The total number of acidic and reducing groups in the oxycelluloses accounts for only about 40% of the hypochlorite consumed; the rest has been used in oxidising the small proportion of short-chain primary reaction products that have been passed into solution.

Following Clibbens's work the pH of hypochlorite bleach liquor was adjusted with sodium carbonate in order to maintain a high pH, to minimise degradation of the cellulose and to ensure that any oxidation occurring did not lead to the formation of reducing groups. The presence of such groups impairs both the stability of the bleached cotton on storage and its resistance to damage during laundering.

Hypochlorite has now been largely replaced by alkaline hydrogen peroxide (H_2O_2) and to a lesser extent by acidified sodium chlorite ($NaClO_2$) in the bleaching of cellulosic textiles. Hydrogen peroxide is a 'safe' bleaching agent in the sense that it seldom damages the cloth, although under unfavourable conditions it can cause serious degradation. The nature of the degradation is not well understood; workers attempting to study the problem have found great difficulty in obtaining reproducible results. This is almost certainly due to the strong catalytic influence of metal ions, such as those of iron and copper, which may be found both in the cellulose and in the sodium hydroxide used for the oxidising liquor. The amounts having an appreciable effect on the reaction rate are so small that precisely reproducible oxidation systems are not easily prepared. Oxidation by alkaline peroxide almost certainly involves peroxy radicals and leads to materials containing carboxyl groups and a small proportion of reducing groups. Chain scission also occurs. Acidified chlorite is a particularly safe bleaching agent, although if used in excessively high concentrations it results in the slow formation of carboxyl and reducing groups together with a certain amount of depolymerisation [105]. The effect is probably due not to the chlorite itself, but to the chlorine dioxide formed by its spontaneous decomposition in the presence of acid (Scheme 1.11). It must not be thought,

$$4NaClO_2 + 4H^+ \longrightarrow 4Na^+ + 4HClO_2 \longrightarrow 2ClO_2 + HClO_3 + HCl + H_2O$$

Scheme 1.11

however, that chlorine dioxide degrades cellulose at all easily. In moderate concentrations it has little effect and is, in fact, widely used for bleaching in the wood pulp industry.

Cellulosic textiles may be subjected to unwelcome oxidative degradation during other alkaline processes, e.g. scouring that usually precedes bleaching. Thus in the traditional kier boil complete exclusion of air was essential if the goods were not to be damaged; even with the milder scouring conditions now employed it is desirable to exclude as much air as possible. The oxidation of cellulose by molecular oxygen in the presence of alkali is not always to be avoided, however. It constitutes the process of 'ageing', which is an essential step in the production of viscose fibres (see p. 47). The main functional groups formed are carboxyl groups, but some of the initially produced carbonyl groups remain intact, which explains why commercial viscose has an appreciable content of carboxyl groups and a low copper number. The oxidation of alkali cellulose by oxygen has been shown to proceed by a radical mechanism involving peroxides [106]. It is catalysed by transition-metal ions, e.g. those of iron, manganese and cobalt.

A curious phenomenon (the 'brown line' effect) involving the formation of both acidic and reducing groups in cellulose may be mentioned here, although it is not certain whether or not oxidation is responsible. A coloured line develops at the boundary between wet and dry cellulose in a piece of fabric hung vertically with its lower end dipping into water [107–109]. When oxygen is rigidly excluded from the system no brown colour appears, but a line containing acidic and reducing groups is still detectable using methylene blue or alkaline silver thiosulphate. The brown contaminant (soluble in water or ethanol) may be a low molecular weight secondary product resulting from the action of oxygen on the primary products. These, it is suggested, are reducing end groups, formed by hydrolysis arising from increased acidity at the wet–dry boundary, and carboxyl groups formed from them in a

Cannizzaro-type rearrangement [110]. These explanations are speculative. The effect itself, however, is of considerable practical importance. For example, brown lines have been found in window curtains that have been wetted by rain from time to time over a period of years [109].

Sodium metaperiodate ($NaIO_4$) is a reagent that is widely used in carbohydrate chemistry. It was first applied to cellulose by Jackson and Hudson [111] and by Davidson [112]. The reaction is best conducted at a pH between 2 and 5, when a yield of dialdehyde chain units (VIII) in excess of 90% of that indicated by Scheme 1.12 is obtained [112].

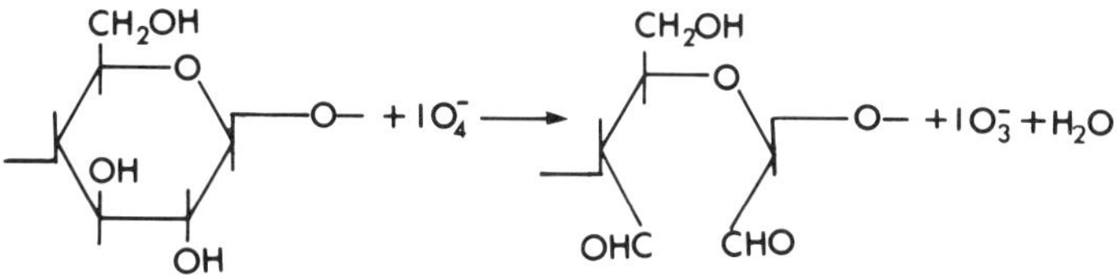

VIII

Scheme 1.12

One of the most notable properties of periodate oxycelluloses is their extreme sensitivity to degradation by dilute alkalis. This arises from the aldehyde groups they contain, which allow the β-alkoxycarbonyl elimination mechanism (see p. 35) to operate [113]. When the aldehyde groups are oxidised with chlorous acid to carboxyl groups [83, 114] or reduced with sodium borohydride to primary alcohol groups [115], as shown in Scheme 1.13, stability to alkali is restored. Thus the periodate oxycelluloses provide an extreme example of latent tendering. They have high fluidities in cuprammonium becuase of the alkalinity of the solvent, but when their aldehyde groups are either oxidised or reduced their fluidities fall. They

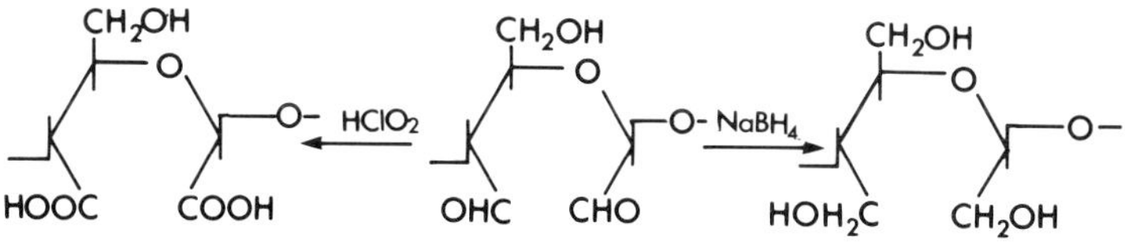

Scheme 1.13

never revert to the fluidity of the original cellulose, however, most probably because of degradative side reactions during the periodate oxidation.

1.8.5 Degradation by Heat
Cellulose can be heated for many hours at temperatures up to about 120°C without any serious deleterious effect. In dry air at higher temperatures, however, considerable depolymerisation takes place, accompanied by the formation of both carbonyl and carboxyl groups [116, 117]; simultaneously water, carbon monoxide and

carbon dioxide are evolved. Degradation involves oxidation and chain scission, with a consequent loss of tensile strength, and is accelerated by the presence of water [116].

The presence of aldehyde groups in cellulose renders it inherently unstable [118]. Cotton that has been overbleached with hypochlorite under acid or neutral conditions goes yellow on storage even at room temperature. Raising the pH or temperature accelerates the rate of yellowing. Oxycelluloses containing large numbers of aldehyde groups, such as those made with periodate, go yellow or brown rapidly on heating to 100°C, but if the aldehyde groups are first reduced with sodium borohydride most of their susceptibility to yellowing disappears. The yellowing of cellulose containing aldehyde groups is enhanced in the presence of alkali. The constitution of the yellow product is unknown, but it can be extracted by boiling with 5% sodium bicarbonate, and the absorbance of the solution can be correlated with the aldehyde content of the material [119]. Viscose fibres always contain a small number of reducing groups formed by ageing of the alkali cellulose during manufacture. They are considerably more susceptible to yellowing in hot alkali than properly bleached cotton, and this can cause difficulties in the dyeing of pastel colours by the continuous thermofixation process.

At around 250°C pyrolysis becomes significant, and this has been extensively studied over a number of years because of the fire hazard associated with cellulosic textiles [118, 120]. The number of pyrolysis products is very large indeed; at least 50 have been identified with varying degrees of certainty but many more exist. The most important of the solid products is levoglucosan (IX) (Figure 1.19) and among the volatile products are water, hydrogen, methane and other hydrocarbons, carbon monoxide and dioxide, and glyoxal. In a much simplified picture of

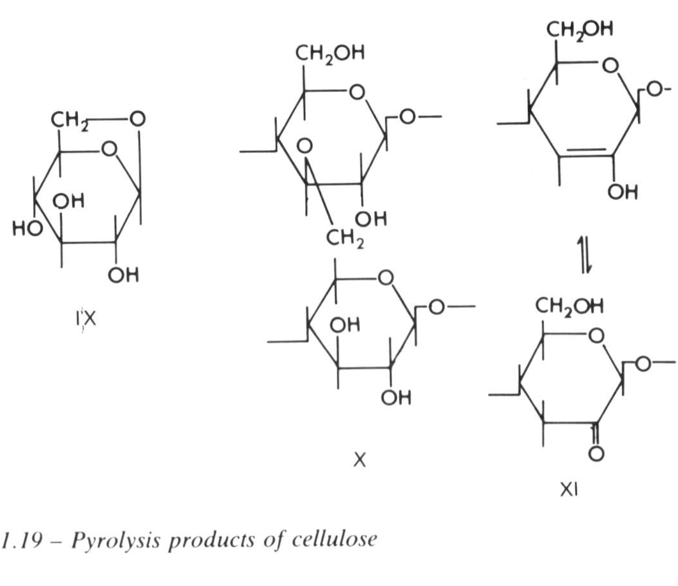

Figure 1.19 – Pyrolysis products of cellulose

pyrolysis, decomposition is represented as occurring by two paths, namely dehydration and levoglucosan formation. Dehydration, which is slightly endothermic, probably leads to the formation of intra- and inter-molecular ether linkages, the latter constituting a form of cross-linking (X) (Figure 1.19). The formation of unsaturated rings tautomeric with 2-keto-3-deoxyanhydroglucose units (XI) (Figure 1.19) may also occur. The complex mixture may be loosely referred to as 'dehydrocellulose'; it decomposes further exothermically, with the evolution of gaseous products and leaves a mass of carbon, which is often known as 'char'. Many of the gaseous products are inflammable and the char glows in the presence of air, being slowly converted into carbon dioxide. The other pyrolysis pathway results in the formation of a tar, the main constituent of which is levoglucosan. This reaction is strongly endothermic and occurs to a greater extent than dehydration at higher temperatures. The two pathways are summarised in Scheme 1.14. It is evident that the flameproofing of cellulose is likely to be most easily achieved by treatments that increase the amount of levoglucosan formed at the expense of dehydration.

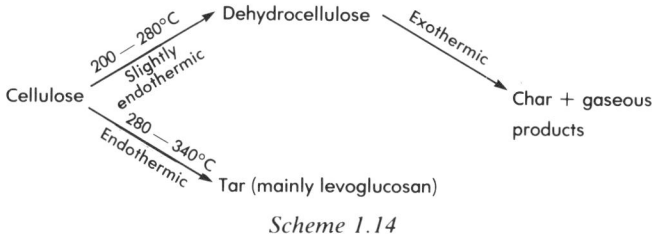

Scheme 1.14

1.8.6 Degradation by Radiation

From a practical point of view the most important type of photochemical degradation that can affect cellulose is that caused by radiation in the visible and near-ultra-violet regions of the spectrum. This must, of necessity, be a photosensitised reaction since the radiation itself is not sufficiently energetic to disrupt the molecule. The energy needed to cleave carbon–carbon or carbon–oxygen bonds in cellulose is about 330 to 380 kJ/mol, from which it can be calculated that, to be effective, radiation must have a wavelength less than about 340 nm [90d]. Since the visible region of the spectrum runs roughly from 800 to 400 nm, it is not surprising that pure cellulose is hardly at all affected by exposure to daylight. However, in the presence of oxygen and of a photosensitiser considerable degradation occurs and is enhanced by the presence of moisture. The oxycellulose formed is of the alkali-sensitive type and can be particularly objectionable in domestic fabrics such as curtain materials, because the full effect of its presence may not become apparent until after they have been laundered. The most important group of photosensitisers comprises the yellow, orange and red vat dyes, but sulphur and basic dyes in the same colour range and certain metallic oxides, such as those of zinc and titanium, are also active.

The photosensitised degradation of cellulose is complex [1, 90d] and its precise mechanism has not been determined with certainty. It was shown by Egerton [121] that not only are suitably dyed cotton threads degraded by exposure to sunlight in a moist atmosphere, but undyed threads placed up to 8 mm away from a dyed thread are also affected (see Figure 1.20). Egerton concluded that a volatile agent must have been the immediate cause of oxidation, and suggested that light energy absorbed by the dye was transferred to molecular oxygen which, in its 'activated' form, reacted with water to give hydrogen peroxide. Later he identified the activated oxygen with the radical ion O_2^- [121]. This may oxidise cellulose directly, or it may react with water to form peroxide ions and hydroxyl radicals, as shown in Scheme 1.15. The hydroxyl radical itself would be expected to oxidise cellulose. The formation of free radicals during the irradiation of vat-dyed cellulose has been demonstrated by e.s.r. spectroscopy [122].

$$O_2^- + H_2O \longrightarrow HO_2^- + \cdot OH$$

Scheme 1.15

The direct photolysis of cellulose is a simpler reaction than photosensitised degradation. It can be brought about by sufficiently energetic u.v. radiation, but,

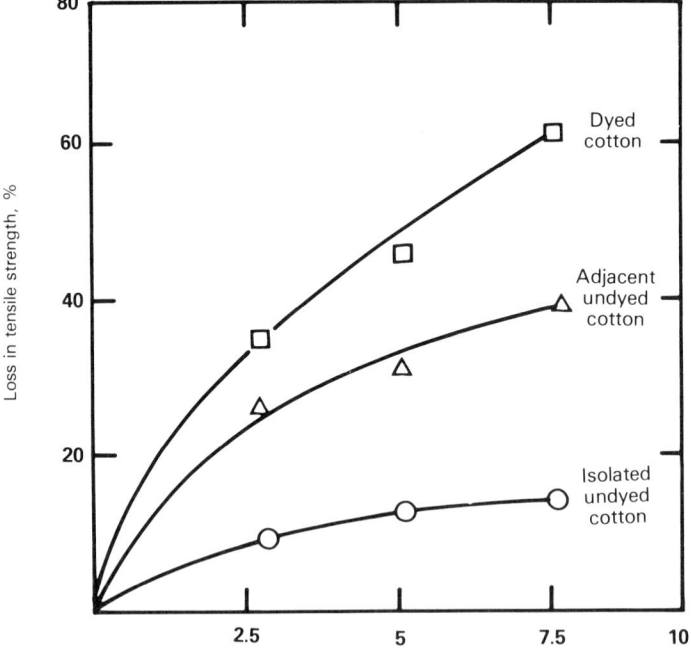

Figure 1.20 – Loss of strength of undyed cotton yarns and yarns dyed with Cibanone Orange R (SCI, C.I. Vat Orange 21) on exposure to sunlight in air at 100% r.h. (reproduced from ref. 1 by permission of Wiley Interscience, New York)

since such radiation is seldom encountered in the normal use of textiles, it is of less practical importance. A wavelength of 253.7 nm has frequently been used in studies of direct photolysis because it is readily obtainable with a quartz mercury-vapour lamp. In contrast to photosensitised degradation, direct photolysis is unaffected by the presence of oxygen and is inhibited by both vat dyes and water vapour. An interesting feature of this type of degradation is that it may continue in the dark for several weeks after irradiation has ceased. The rate of post-irradiation degradation increases with increasing temperature.

No account of the photolytic degradation of cellulose would be complete without some mention of the effect of what is often called 'high-energy radiation'; the term 'ionising radiation' is also sometimes used. Primarily these terms refer to X-rays and γ-rays, but traditionally they also include β-rays and other high-speed electrons, neutrons and streams of α-particles (high-energy helium nuclei). The subject has been discussed at some length by Arthur [90e]. Much of the work has been done with γ-radiation from cobalt-60. One effect of irradiation is the formation of free radicals that are remarkably stable in the presence of moisture. They have been detected in cotton cellulose by e.s.r. spectroscopy as long as seven years after it has been exposed to γ-rays. Since the spectrum consisted of a triplet with a signal strength ratio approximately 1:2:1, it has been suggested that radicals with structures XII, XIII or XIV (Figure 1.21) may be present, but confirmatory evidence is not available.

The e.s.r. spectrum of cellulose that has been irradiated *dry* consists of an intense but short-lived single line, which is most easily explained as arising from the species XV or XVI (Figure 1.21). These would be expected to lead to depolymerisation,

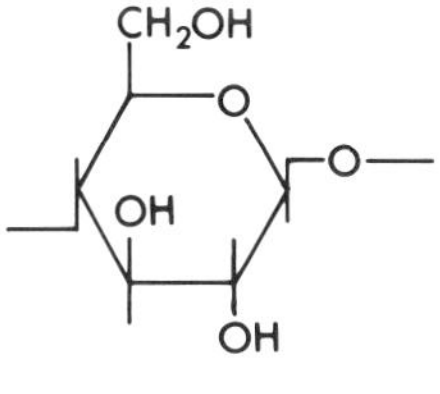

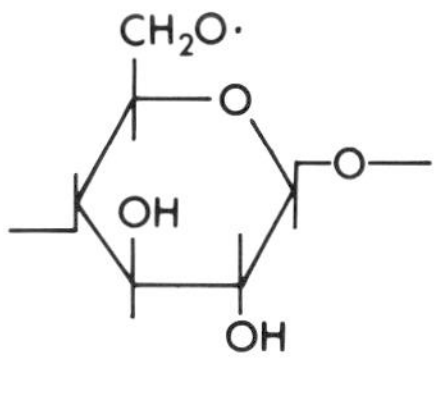

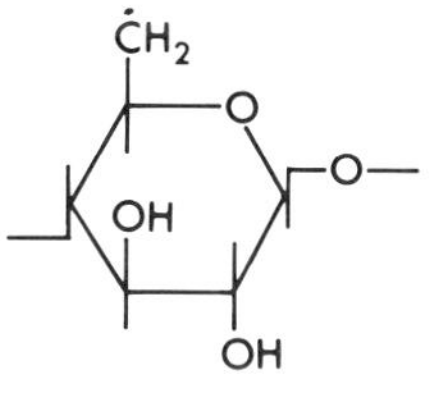

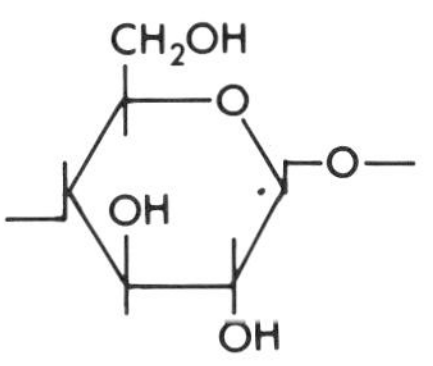

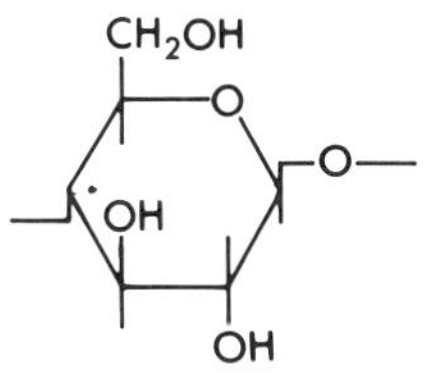

Figure 1.21 – Radicals thought to be responsible for the e.s.r. spectrum of irradiated cellulose

which has actually been observed, together with the formation of carbonyl and carboxyl, in γ-irradiated cellulose. Small quantities of carbon monoxide and carbon dioxide are also produced.

1.8.7 Enzymic Degradation

The enzymic degradation of cellulose forms an essential part of the carbon cycle by which life on earth is sustained. Cellulose is a potential raw material for the biotechnological production of aliphatic chemicals. Domestic waste represents a possible source, and vegetable cellulose may also be specially produced for this purpose in future [123].

In textiles biodeterioration is a serious problem and much effort has gone into finding methods of preventing it. If damp cotton is exposed to air, mildew may gradually develop on it, accompanied by the production of staining that is difficult, if not impossible, to remove. Prolonged exposure also causes a serious loss of tensile strength, but the fluidity of the material in cuprammonium is little changed. The degradation of cellulose by moulds and bacteria is thus easily distinguishable from degradation by acids [1], even though both involve the hydrolysis of glycosidic linkages. The distinction arises because the action of the micro-organism is localised in small areas, which become soluble in water, while the bulk of the cellulose remains undegraded.

Studies of degradation using cell-free enzyme preparations have proved difficult to interpret with certainty, although the mechanism of the process is now understood in broad outline [90f, 124]. Many cellulases extracted from fungi hydrolyse native cellulose only to a limited extent unless it has first been rendered more accessible by some form of swelling treatment (e.g. mercerisation). However, until recently certain extracts, notably those of *Trichoderma viride* and *Trichoderma koningii*, were thought to contain an 'activating' enzyme which had a similar effect to swelling in that it rendered the cellulose molecules more accessible to the hydrolysing enzymes. The activating enzyme in these preparations is often referred to as C_1 in the literature, and the hydrolysing enzyme as C_x, but the concept of a specific decrystallising enzyme has now been replaced by one of synergism between the component enzymes of the cellulose complex.

Unlike the undigested residue of fungal attack, cellulose that has been immersed in an active cellulase extract has a reduced degree of polymerisation. The fall in DP for a given loss of weight during enzymolysis is, however, less than that during acid hydrolysis [125], indicating that enzymolysis is not a random process. Although not confined exclusively to chain ends, it occurs more readily there, removing soluble oligosaccharide molecules from sites of sporadic attack.

1.9 DERIVATIVES OF CELLULOSE

1.9.1 General

The product of any reaction of cellulose with another substance may properly be described as a derivative. However, esters and ethers are the only compounds normally considered as cellulose derivatives, because of their industrial importance. A brief outline of the chemistry of these two classes now follows, together with sections on graft copolymers and cross-linked celluloses, which often fall into one of the two same classes. Derivatives with so-called unusual functional groups, such as chloro- or amino-deoxycellulose [90g], and cellulose dyed with reactive dyes will not be considered. For fuller information the reader is directed to Part 2 Chapter 9 and Part 5 Chapter 14 of *Cellulose and Cellulose Derivatives* [33, 90].

The intermediate chain unit of cellulose contains three hydroxyl groups capable of participating in derivative formation. The degree of substitution (DS) of a derivative is the fraction of hydroxyl groups that have reacted, and can therefore have any value between 0 and 3. It does not define a derivative uniquely, however, because substitution is seldom, if ever, uniform. Spurlin [33] has defined the highest possible degree of uniformity in a cellulose derivative as that which results if every chain unit is equally accessible to the reagents involved. This definition takes no account of the differing reactivities of the three hydroxyl groups. It is generally accepted that the primary alcohol group of C6 is considerably more reactive than the secondary groups at C2 and C3, but the relative rates differ from one reaction to another. Hence the reactivity ratio of primary and secondary alcohol groups is much higher for acylation with the bulky tosyl (*p*-toluenesulphonyl) group than with the small acetyl group. The overall relative reactivities of the three hydroxyl groups under heterogeneous conditions are determined by the combined effect of three factors: their inherent chemical reactivity, steric effects arising from the size of the entering group and steric effects arising from the supramolecular structure of the cellulose. In most reactions the reactivity decreases in the order $C6 >> C2 > C3$. As a consequence of these differences in reactivity and of the non-uniform accessibility of chain units towards chemical reagents, a large number of different derivatives having the same average degree of substitution may exist. The differences between them consist in different distributions of substituents along the chain molecules. The properties of derivatives, especially their solubilities and their mechanical properties in the solid state, depend strongly on the distribution of substituents. Properties also depend on the degree of polymerisation, and degradation nearly always accompanies derivative formation. A certain amount of depolymerisation is often desirable in commercial products, but care must be taken to control it.

Although interest in cellulose derivatives lies mainly in their industrial applications, it must not be forgotten that they have played an important role in the establishment of the chemical structure of cellulose [1, 11]. The acid hydrolysis of cellulose is too complex for satisfactory application to structural studies. Instead, cellulose derivatives (particularly methylcellulose) have been prepared under non-degradative conditions and subjected to either hydrolysis or methanolysis. The products of the complete hydrolysis of trimethylcellulose are 2,3,6-tri-*O*-methyl-D-glucose and one molecule of 2,3,4,6-tetra-*O*-methyl-D-glucose per non-reducing end group. Methanolysis gives the corresponding methylglucosides.

1.9.2 Esters

Cellulose can be esterified with most inorganic and organic acids by methods analogous to those used for simple alcohols. Many of the products have practical applications, but surpassing all others in industrial importance are the nitrates, acetates and xanthates.

Cellulose nitrate is manufactured at various values of DS between 2 and 3 (nitrogen content, by which it is frequently characterised, between 11.11 and 14.14%). The least-substituted materials can be used for plastics and the nearly tri-substituted for explosives; those in between are used for lacquers and similar products. Good solvents for di-nitrated esters (11.2–12% nitrogen) include methanol, various alkyl acetates, methyl ethyl ketone and acetone, but at higher degrees of substitution only acetone is suitable [33]. Although there are several ways of nitrating cellulose, industrial baths consist exclusively of mixtures of nitric and sulphuric acids and water. The composition of the mixture determines the degree of nitration. Unlike most esterifications of cellulose the reaction is rapid, even at low temperatures, and takes place without uniform dissolution throughout the fibres. It may be described as a homogeneous, or permutoid, reaction. The reactive species is the nitronium ion NO_2^+, formed in the presence of sulphuric acid in accordance with Scheme 1.16. Simultaneously the two acids ionise in the usual way (Schemes 1.17 and 1.18) and nitration can be represented by Scheme 1.19. The reaction is

$$HNO_3 + 2H_2SO_4 \rightleftharpoons NO_2^+ + H_3O^+ + 2HSO_4^-$$

$$HNO_3 + H_2O \rightleftharpoons H_3O^+ + NO_3^-$$

$$H_2SO_4 + 2H_2O \rightleftharpoons H_3O^+ + HSO_4^- + H_2O \rightleftharpoons 2H_3O^+ + SO_4^{2-}$$

$$R_{cell}OH + NO_2^+ + H_2O \rightleftharpoons R_{cell}O NO_2 + H_3O^+$$

Schemes 1.16–1.19

always allowed to proceed to equilibrium. A typical rate curve for the production of cellulose nitrate with a DS of 2.26 (12% nitrogen) is shown in Figure 1.22. Nitration is usually done at fairly low temperatures (20–40°C) to avoid excessive degradation. Cellulose nitrates produced in this way contain a few sulphate ester groups. If allowed to remain, these would slowly hydrolyse to sulphuric acid, which catalyses the decomposition of cellulose nitrate. Instead the nitrated product is immediately stabilised in boiling dilute acid, then neutralised with sodium carbonate solution and washed well with water. Sometimes, in addition, a stabiliser (e.g. a very weak base) is added to materials that are to be stored.

Cellulose acetates have already been mentioned as important textile materials; they are also used for transparent sheeting and moulded plastics. Acetylation is usually accomplished with acetic anhydride in the presence of an acid catalyst. The reaction is represented formally by Scheme 1.20, but its mechanism is more complex and involves intermediate combination of the catalyst with the cellulose [90h].

$$R_{cell}OH + (CH_3CO)_2O \longrightarrow R_{cell}OCOCH_3 + CH_3COOH$$

Scheme 1.20

Two separate processes are used: the fibrous process and the solution process. In the former, which is suitable only for the production of the triacetate, a mixture of acetic anhydride and acetic acid in a medium that does not dissolve cellulose acetate (such as an aromatic hydrocarbon or carbon tetrachloride) is employed; the catalyst is frequently perchloric acid. In laboratory investigations of properties of cellulose (e.g. reactivity) a mixture of acetic anhydride and pyridine has been used to effect partial fibrous acetylation [54].

In the solution process the cellulose is treated with a mixture of acetic anhydride, acetic acid and sulphuric acid. The reaction is slow and heterogeneous. The outermost layers are acetylated first and dissolve in the acetic acid, exposing unchanged cellulose to attack and dissolution in its turn. The process continues until a solution of cellulose triacetate (the 'primary' acetate) in acetic acid is obtained. Acetylation is an exothermic reaction; to prevent simultaneous degradation the reaction mixture is kept near room temperature by external cooling. The product, though substantially tri-acetylated cellulose, contains a significant proportion of sulphate ester groups. They are removed by hydrolysis, water being added under carefully controlled conditions. The primary acetate may be precipitated at this stage by the addition of more water. The secondary acetate (DS about 2.3) is also obtained by carefully controlled hydrolysis at about 40°C. Both the sulphate and the required proportion of acetate groups are removed, after which more water is added to precipitate the product. Secondary cellulose acetate prepared in this way is soluble in acetone, whereas materials with the same DS made by direct acetylation are not. This is a good example of the influence of uniformity of substitution on the solubility of a cellulose derivative.

Sodium cellulose xanthate is the sodium salt of the O-ester of unsymmetrical dithiocarbonic acid. It is made by the action of carbon disulphide on alkali cellulose (represented formally by Scheme 1.21). The ester itself is of little interest; its importance lies in its solubility in dilute sodium hydroxide. The viscose solution produced

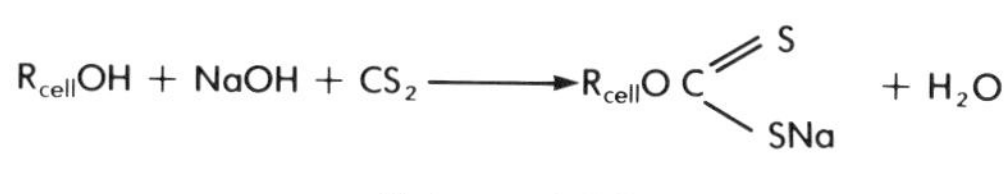

$$R_{cell}OH + NaOH + CS_2 \longrightarrow R_{cell}O\ C{\overset{\displaystyle S}{\underset{\displaystyle SNa}{}}} + H_2O$$

Scheme 1.21

is used for the manufacture of regenerated cellulose. The DS is usually 0.5 or a little more, but for the production of polynosic fibres it may be nearly 1.0. In the regenerated fibres industry the DS is often expressed as the γ-number, which is the number of xanthate groups per 100 anhydroglucose units ($γ = 100 × DS$). The technology of viscose production is too complicated to discuss here, but two important features of it may be mentioned. The first is that the alkali cellulose (i.e. cellulose impregnated with 18% sodium hydroxide) must be aged by keeping it for a day or more in the presence of air at 25 to 30°C. This is to reduce its degree of polymerisation to a suitable value. The second is that the viscose solution itself must be 'ripened' by storing it for one to three days at 15 to 25°C in order to bring it to the right condition for regeneration. The most important change occurring during ripening is gradual decomposition of the xanthate. The degree of ripening required depends on the particular final product.

1.9.3 Ethers

Cellulose ethers with high degrees of substitution can be prepared in the laboratory by any of the methods generally applicable to polysaccharides, provided that due account is taken of the difficulty of making the material completely accessible to the reagents [11]. The DS values of most commercial cellulose ethers lie between 0.5 and 2, and are commonly in the region of 1.5. These materials are usually made by reacting an alkyl halide or other suitable compound with alkali cellulose in an autoclave. The temperature must be prevented from rising too high; if it does, degradation may occur. The preparation of methylcellulose may be represented by Scheme 1.22. For carboxymethylcellulose ($R_{cell}OCH_2COOH$) sodium chloro-acetate would be used, and for hydroxyethylcellulose ($R_{cell}OCH_2CH_2OH$), ethylene

$$R_{cell}OH + NaOH + CH_3Cl \longrightarrow R_{cell}OCH_3 + NaCl + H_2O$$

Scheme 1.22

oxide. The addition of cellulose to activated olefinic compounds in the presence of alkali is also used to produce ethers. Cyanoethylcellulose is prepared in this way from acrylonitrile (Scheme 1.23). Vinylsulphones ($CH_2{=}CHSO_2R$) or compounds that generate vinylsulphones in the presence of alkali are also effective.

$$R_{cell}OH + CH_2{:}CHCN \xrightarrow{NaOH} R_{cell}OCH_2CH_2CN$$

Scheme 1.23

Most commercial cellulose ethers are soluble in water. Some, such as methyl-cellulose, are less soluble in hot water than in cold, but others, such as hydroxy-ethylcellulose, are soluble at all temperatures. They have a wide variety of practical applications, most of which stem from their capacity to act as protective colloids. Carboxymethylcellulose is usually incorporated in domestic washing powders to prevent soil redeposition in laundering. The only ethers manufactured with high enough DS values (about 2.5) to make them soluble in organic solvents are ethyl-cellulose and cyanoethylcellulose. The former finds limited use in lacquers and moulded plastics, whilst the latter, because of its high dielectric constant, is used in the manufacture of electroluminescent articles.

1.9.4 Graft Copolymers of Cellulose

The possibility of modifying the properties of cellulose by grafting other polymers onto it is obvious, but, although much work has been done in this field, it has proved less commercially important than might have been hoped. Methods of graft-ing have mostly been those used with synthetic polymers. Thus, if a suitable monomer is polymerised by a radical mechanism in the presence of cellulose, some of the product becomes attached to the cellulose by chain transfer. Initiation may be by means of a radical-producing catalyst (e.g. benzoyl peroxide) or an oxidation–

reduction system (e.g. a mixture of iron(II) sulphate and hydrogen peroxide) that forms hydroxyl radicals. The direct initiation of radicals in cellulose by ceric ion oxidation or by ozonation [90i] has also been proposed. The processes involved here are represented in Schemes 1.24–1.26.

$$R_{cell}OH + Ce^{4+} \longrightarrow R_{cell}O\cdot + Ce^{3+} + H^+$$

$$R_{cell}OH + O_3 \longrightarrow O_2 + R_{cell}OOH \longrightarrow R_{cell}O\cdot + HO\cdot$$

$$R_{cell}O\cdot + Monomer \longrightarrow Graft\ copolymer$$

Schemes 1.24–1.26

Initiation by γ-radiation has been studied extensively. The cellulose may be irradiated either together with the monomer to be grafted or prior to treatment with it. In either case a suitable swelling agent must also be used if a significant amount of grafting is to be achieved.

1.10 CROSS-LINKED CELLULOSE

Cellulose can be chemically cross-linked by any reagent containing at least two functional groups capable of reacting with alcohol groups. The process has been extensively studied for many years, largely with the object of imparting so-called easy-care properties to cotton and regenerated-cellulose textiles, and wet strength to paper. It is important to realise that chemical cross-linking may either increase or decrease the tensile strength of a cellulose *fibre* according to circumstances [126]. An imaginary fibre in which there were no lateral forces between chains would be weak, because the chains would be able to slide past one another and only those capable of spanning the gap between the jaws of a testing instrument could contribute to the fibre strength. The introduction of cross-links would increase the proportion of chains that would resist an applied stress. Tensile strength would therefore increase with increasing density of cross-linking. After a certain point, however, the introduction of further cross-links would begin to restrict the movement of adjacent chains to such an extent that the proportion of chains capable of resisting applied stress would begin to decrease and the tensile strength would fall. This is because a chain molecule resists stress only when it is fully extended. When the density of cross-links becomes high enough, the proportion of chains that can be fully extended is decreased. All cellulose fibres are cross-linked by a system of hydrogen bonds. In viscose the extent of this bonding is such that the introduction of covalent cross-links by chemical means at first causes a small rise in tensile strength. After passing through a maximum the strength falls. In cotton, however, the extent of inter-chain hydrogen bonding is so great that the introduction of further cross-links always causes a loss of strength. In industrial practice viscose, as well as cotton, usually suffers a loss of strength when cross-linked.

The strength of a cellulosic material depends not only on the intrinsic fibre strength, but also on the way in which the fibres are assembled. In textile yarns, and in woven and knitted fabrics, changes in fibre strength are reflected in similar changes in the strength of the material. In paper, however, where the fibres form a random web, the cross-links that most affect the strength are those between fibres rather than those between molecules within fibres. The effect on wet strength is profound, because the main source of strength in paper is inter-fibre hydrogen bonding, which is destroyed in the presence of liquid water. The extent of these changes in strength, in both textiles and paper, depends on the length of the cross-links as well as on their number and distribution.

The chemistry and technology of cross-linking has been fully documented [90j, 127]. In the textile field ether formation is the commonest type of cross-linking to be encountered. The earliest work was done with formaldehyde [128], which gives a methylene ether link, according to Scheme 1.27.

$$2R_{cell}OH + HCHO \longrightarrow R_{cell}OCH_2OR_{cell} + H_2O$$

Scheme 1.27

Not all the formaldehyde is used in linking adjacent chain molecules; some reacts with two hydroxyl groups in the same chain molecule. Of far greater practical importance are the N-hydroxymethyl (methylol) derivatives formed by the addition of formaldehyde and other aldehydes to acid amides and related compounds and to triazines, under mildly alkaline conditions. These precondensates react with cellulose on heating under slightly acid conditions. Dimethylolurea, formed by reacting a 2:1 mixture of formaldehyde and urea (Scheme 1.28), cross-links

$$2HCHO + NH_2CONH_2 \longrightarrow HOCH_2NHCONHCH_2OH$$

Scheme 1.28

cellulose, as shown in Scheme 1.29. Compounds XVII–XX (Figure 1.23) are examples of the large number of similar reagents that have been tried. Among

$$2R_{cell}OH + HOCH_2NHCONHCH_2OH \longrightarrow R_{cell}OCH_2NHCONHCH_2OR_{cell} + 2H_2O$$

Scheme 1.29

other ether-forming reagents that can be used to cross-link cellulose, activated vinyl compounds (such as divinylsulphone), epoxides (such as ethylene oxide) and dihalogenohydrins (such as 1,3-dichloropropan-2-ol) may be mentioned.

The cross-linking of cellulose by esterification with dibasic acids has not been used commercially but has proved valuable in fundamental research. So too has the use of reagents with two different functional groups of unequal chemical reactivity (e.g. N-methylolacrylamide ($HOH_2CNHCOCH=CH_2$)); with these stepwise cross-linking can be studied. Lastly the possibility of producing so-called reversible cross-links must be mentioned. These are cross-links that are capable of being broken and reformed under appropriate environmental conditions. In an attempt to simulate wool [129], 6,6′-deoxycellulose disulphide has been prepared by the series of reactions shown in Scheme 1.30, the last stage of which illustrates the reversible formation and destruction of cross-links by oxidation and reduction respectively.

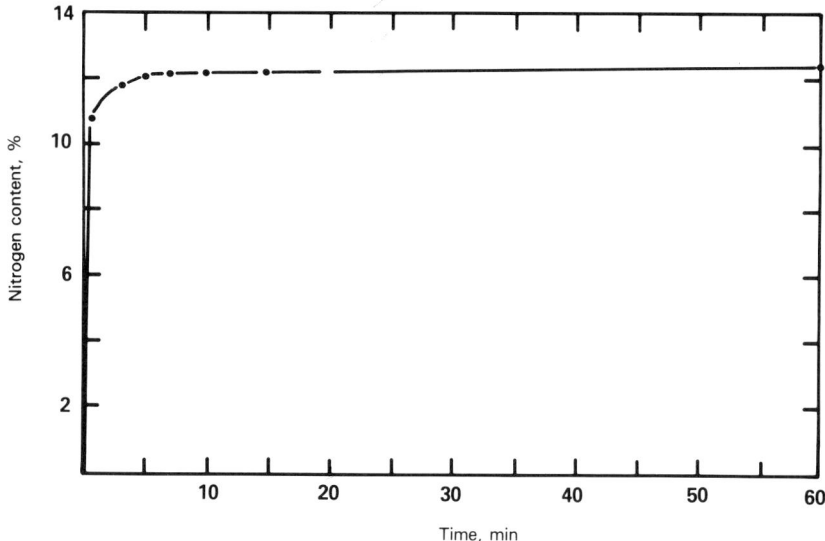

Figure 1.22 – Rate of nitration of cellulose in a mixture of nitric acid (21.0%), sulphuric acid (61.5%) and water (17.5%) (reproduced from ref. 33 by permission of Wiley Interscience, New York)

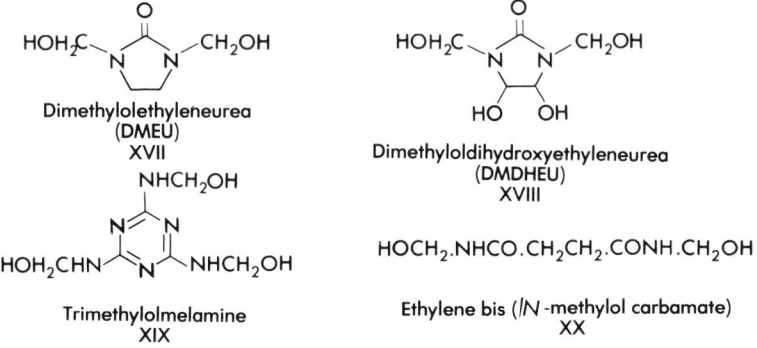

Figure 1.23 – Cross-linking compounds for cellulose

$$2R_{cell}\ OH\ +\ 2CH_3C_6H_4SO_2Cl\ \xrightarrow{C_5H_5N}\ 2R_{cell}OSO_2C_6H_4CH_3$$

$$\xrightarrow{CH_3COSK}\ 2R_{cell}\ SCOCH_3\ \xrightarrow{NaOH}\ 2R_{cell}\ SH$$

$$\underset{Reduction}{\overset{Oxidation}{\rightleftharpoons}}\ R_{cell}\ S.SR_{cell}$$

Scheme 1.30

REFERENCES

1. 'Cellulose and Cellulose Derivatives', 2nd Edn, Part 1, Ed. Ott, Spurlin and Grafflin (New York: Wiley Interscience, 1954).
2. Hoyle and Wickramasinghe, Nature, **268** (1977) 610.
3. Miller, Science News, **118** (1980) 377.
4. Haigler, Brown and Benziman, Science, **210** (1980) 903.
5. Payen, Compt. Rend., **7** (1838) 1052, 1125.
6. Nickerson, 'Matthews' Textile Fibres', Ed. Mauersberger (New York: John Wiley and Sons, 1954).
7. Jeffries et al., Cellulose Chem. and Technol., **3** (1969) 255.
8. Warwicker et al., Shirley Institute pamphlet No. 93 (1966).
9. Tripp, Moore and Rollins, Text. Research J., **21** (1951) 886.
10. Moncrieff, 'Man-made Fibres', 6th Edn (London: Newnes-Butterworth, 1975).
11. Aspinall, 'Polysaccharides' (Oxford: Pergamon Press, 1970).
12. Haworth, 'The Constitution of the Sugars' (London: Edward Arnold, 1929).
13. Marx-Figini and Schultz, Makromol. Chem., **62** (1963) 49.
14. 'Cellulose and Cellulose Derivatives', Part 4, Ed. Bikales and Segal (New York: Wiley Interscience, 1971).
15. Meyer and Misch, Helv. Chim. Acta, **20** (1937) 232.
16. Andress, Z. Phys. Chem., **B4** (1929) 190.
17. 'Cellulose Chemistry and Technology', Ed. Arthur (Washington, DC: American Chemical Society, 1977) 42.
18. Ellis and Bath, J. Amer. Chem. Soc., **62** (1940) 2859.
19. Liang and Marchessault, J. Polymer. Sci. **37** (1959) 385.
20. Hermans, 'Physics and Chemistry of Cellulose Fibres' (New York: Elsevier, 1949) 13.
21. Alexander, 'X-Ray Diffraction Methods in Polymer Science' (New York: Wiley Interscience, 1969) 54.
22. Manley, J. Polymer Sci. (A), **1** (1963) 1875, 1893.
23. Maeda, Kawada and Kawai, J. Polymer. Sci. (C), (30) (1970) 543.
24. Howlett and Urquhart, Chem. and Ind., (1951) 82.
25. Urquhart, 'Recent Advances in the Chemistry of Cellulose and Starch', Ed. Honeyman (London: Heywood, 1959).
26. Jeffries, J. Textile Inst., **51** (1960) T339, T441.
27. Urquhart and Williams, J. Textile Inst., **15** (1924) T433.
28. Hearle, 'Moisture in Textiles', Ed. Hearle and Peters, (Manchester: Textile Institute, 1960).
29. Staudinger and Döhle, J. Praktische Chemie, **161** (1942) 219.
30. Haller, Kolloid-Z, **20** (1917) 127.
31. Parnell, 'Life and Labours of John Mercer' (London: Longmans, Green & Co., 1886).
32. Mercer, B P 13296 (1850).
33. 'Cellulose and Cellulose Derivatives', 2nd Edn, Part 2, Ed. Ott, Spurlin and Grafflin (New York: Interscience, 1954).
34. Warwicker and Wright, J. Appl. Polymer Sci., **11** (1967) 659.

35. Sobue, Kiessig and Hess, Z. Physik. Chem., **B34** (1939) 309.
36. Vieweg, Ber., **40** (1907) 3876.
37. Coward and Spencer, J. Textile Inst., **14** (1923) T32.
38. Champetier and Ashar, Makromol. Chem., **6** (1951) 85.
39. Vignon, Comp. Rend., **110** (1890) 910.
40. Barratt and Lewis, J. Textile Inst., **13** (1922) T113.
41. Saito, Kolloidbeihefte, **49** (1939) 365.
42. Neale, J. Textile Inst., **20** (1929) T373.
43. Chédin and Marsaudon, Makromol. Chem., **15** (1955) 115; **20** (1956) 57.
44. Bartunek, Papier, **8** (1954) 78.
45. Barry, Peterson and King, J. Amer. Chem. Soc., **58** (1936) 333.
46. Hess and Gundermann, Ber., **70** (1937) 1788.
47. Clark and Parker, J. Phys. Chem., **41** (1937) 777.
48. Warwicker, Cellulose Chem. and Technol., **6** (1972) 85.
49. Davis et al., J. Amer. Chem. Soc., **65** (1943) 1294.
50. Segal, Nelson and Conrad, J. Phys. Colloid Chem., **55** (1951) 325; Text. Research J., **23** (1953) 428.
51. Creeley and Wade, Text. Research J., **45** (1975) 240; **48** (1978) 335.
52. Creeley, Wade and French, Text. Research J., **48** (1978) 37.
53. Loeb and Segal, Text. Research J., **25** (1955) 516.
54. Segal, 'Decrystallized Cotton' (Shildon, Durham: Merrow Publishing Co., 1971) 19, 31.
55. Marsh, 'An Introduction to Textile Finishing' (London: Chapman and Hall, 1957) 122.
56. Stamm and Tarkow, J. Phys. Colloid Chem., **54** (1950) 745.
57. Rebenfeld, USDA ARS Report 72–33 (1965).
58. Colombo and Immergut, J. Polymer Sci. (C), (31) (1970) 137.
59. Stamm, 'Wood and Cellulose Science' (New York: Ronald Press Co., 1964).
60. 'Solvent Spun Rayon, Modified Cellulose Fibers and Derivatives', Ed. Turbak, ACS Symposium Series No. 58 (Washington DC: American Chemical Society, 1977).
61. Schweizer, J. Prakt. Chem., **72** (1857) 109.
62. Clibbens and Little, J. Textile Inst., **27** (1936) T285.
63. BS Handbook 11: 1974, No. 5/61.
64. Clibbens and Ridge, J. Textile Inst., **19** (1928) T389.
65. Reeves, Advances in Carbohydrate Chem., **6** (1951) 107.
66. Nevell, Rev. Textile Prog., **3** (1951) 31.
67. Traube, Ber., **54B** (1921) 3220; **55B** (1922) 1899.
68. TAPPI Standard T 230 os-76.
69. ASTM Standard D1795–62 (reapproved 1979).
70. 'Polymer Handbook', 2nd Edn, Ed. Brandrup and Immergut (New York: Wiley Interscience, 1974).
71. Henley, Svensk Papperstidn, **63** (1960) 143; Arkiv Kemi, **18** (1961) 327.
72. Nevell and Shaw, Polymer, **15** (1974) 553.
73. Fowler et al., J. Amer. Chem. Soc., **69** (1947) 1636.
74. Schweiger, Chem. and Ind., (1969) 296.
75. Johnson, Nicholson and Haigh, J. Appl. Polymer Sci., Appl. Polymer Symposia, **28** (1976) 931.
76. Guthrie and Hardcastle, Polymer, **18** (1977) 203.
77. Girard, Compt. Rend., **81** (1875) 1105.
78. Witz, Bull. Soc. Ind. Rouen, **10** (1882) 416; **11** (1883) 169.
79. Cross and Bevan, J. Soc. Chem. Ind., **3** (1884) 206, 291.
80. Unruh and Kenyon, Text. Research J., **16** (1946) 1.
81. Clibbens, J. Textile Inst., **45** (1954) P173.
82. 'Methods in Carbohydrate Chemistry', Vol. 3, Ed. Whistler (New York: Academic Press, 1963).
83. Davidson and Nevell, J. Textile Inst., **46** (1955) T407.
84. Colbran and Davidson, J. Textile Inst., **52** (1961) T291.
85. Nabar and Padmanabhan, Proc. Indian Acad. Sci., **31A** (1950) 371.
86. BeMiller, Advances in Carbohydrate Chem., **22** (1967) 25.
87. Birtwell, Clibbens and Geake, J. Textile Inst., **17** (1926) T145.
88. Davidson, J. Textile Inst., **34** (1943) T87.
89. Sharples, Trans. Faraday Soc., **53** (1957) 1003.

90. 'Cellulose and Cellulose Derivatives', Part 5, Ed. Bikales and Segal (New York: Wiley Interscience, 1971) (a) 991, (b) 1007, (c) 893, (d) 1047, (e) 937, (f) 1079, (g) 987, (h) 760, (i) 909, (j) 835, 1095, 1205.
91. Pascu, J. Polymer Sci., 2 (1947) 565.
92. Schulz, J. Polymer Sci., 3 (1948) 365.
93. Fargher and Higginbotham, J. Textile Inst., 15 (1924) T419; 17 (1926) T233; 18 (1927) T283.
94. Davidson, J. Textile Inst., 25 (1934) T174.
95. Whistler and BeMiller, Advances in Carbohydrate Chem., 13 (1958) 289.
96. Meller, TAPPI, 34 (1951) 171; 36 (1953) 366.
97. Isbell, J. Res. Nat. Bureau Standards, 32 (1944) 45.
98. Lobry de Bruyn and Alberda van Ekenstein, Rec. Trav. Chim., 14 (1895) 203; 16 (1897) 262.
99. Speck, Advances in Carbohydrate Chem., 13 (1958) 63.
100. Samuelson et al., Svensk Papperstidn., 56 (1953) 779.
101. Corbett and Richards, Svensk Papperstidn., 60 (1957) 791.
102. Birtwell, Clibbens and Ridge, J. Textile Inst., 16 (1925) T13.
103. Clibbens and Ridge, J. Textile Inst., 18 (1927) T135.
104. Lewin and Epstein, J. Polymer Sci., 58 (1962) 991, 1023.
105. Nevell, J. Textile Inst., 52 (1961) T185.
106. Entwistle, Cole and Wooding, Text. Research J., 19 (1949) 527, 609.
107. Bone, J.S.D.C., 50 (1934) 307.
108. Bone and Turner, J.S.D.C., 66 (1950) 315.
109. Bogaty, Campbell and Appel, Text. Research J., 22 (1952) 75.
110. Madaras and Turner, J.S.D.C., 69 (1953) 371.
111. Jackson and Hudson, J. Amer. Chem. Soc., 59 (1937) 2049; 60 (1938) 989.
112. Davidson, J. Textile Inst., 31 (1940) T81; 32 (1941) T109.
113. Nevell, J. Textile Inst., 48 (1957) T484.
114. Rutherford et al., J. Res. Nat. Bureau Standards, 29 (1942) 131.
115. Head, J. Textile Inst., 46 (1955) T400.
116. Waller, Bass and Roseveare, Ind. Eng. Chem., 40 (1948) 138.
117. Major, TAPPI, 41 (1958) 530.
118. Peters and Still, 'Applied Fibre Science', Vol. 2, Ed. Happey (New York: Academic Press, 1979) 409.
119. Albeck, Ben-Bassat and Lewin, Text. Research J., 35 (1965) 836, 935.
120. Shafizadeh, Advances in Carbohydrate Chem., 23 (1968) 419.
121. Egerton, J. Textile Inst., 39 (1948) T305, Text. Research J., 18 (1948) 659; Nature, 204 (1964) 1153.
122. Phillips et al., Text. Research J., 36 (1966) 822.
123. Linko, 'Advances in Biochemical Engineering', Vol. 5, Ed. Ghose, Fiechter and Blakebrough (Berlin: Springer Verlag, 1977).
124. Finch and Roberts, 'Cellulose Chemistry and Its Applications', Ed. Nevell and Zeronian (Chichester, West Sussex: Ellis Horwood, 1985).
125. Selby, Biochem. J., 79 (1961) 562.
126. Gardon and Steele, Text. Research J., 31 (1961) 160.
127. 'Chemical Aftertreatment of Textiles', Ed. Mark, Wooding and Atlas (New York: Wiley Interscience, 1971).
128. Eschalier, J. Soc. Chem. Ind., 26 (1907) 821.
129. Schwenker, Lifland and Pacsu, Text. Research J., 32 (1962) 797.

CHAPTER 2

Preparation

KENNETH DICKINSON

2.1 INTRODUCTION

Cellulosic loose fibres, yarns and fabrics require treatment before dyeing or printing to remove natural and added impurities. This treatment is generally called preparation.

The need for good preparation has long been appreciated, but the developments which have taken place in dyeing processes, particularly continuous pad dyeing, have accentuated the importance of the correct preparation of cellulosic textiles. Over long continuous runs the fabric must be evenly treated to have excellent absorbency, low residual size and wax content, whiteness appropriate to the colour to be dyed and minimal fibre degradation. This technical standard has to be met against economic constraints relating to the cost of chemicals, labour, plant, power and water. In the last of these areas the direct cost of process water is only one aspect; environmental considerations relating to effluent disposal are of growing importance and add to costs.

Preparation processes for dyeing must also take into account subsequent finishing processes. Thus the presence of a residual substantive wetting agent is undesirable in fabrics to be given a waterproof finish, and the complete removal of waxes can lead to needle friction with consequent fabric damage in making-up operations.

2.1.1 Historical Background

The earliest methods of preparing cotton were based on boiling with potash lye, derived from ashes of plants, followed by exposure to sunlight, when bleaching was required. Some of the terms still in use in the industry can be traced back to such preparations. Thus a croft, which once was an open field where fabrics were exposed in light and air, is now the part of a works in which bleaching is carried out. Between alkaline boiling and crofting, fabric was rinsed and immersed in buttermilk, from which process is retained the term souring.

In the second half of the 18th century lime replaced potash, sulphuric acid replaced buttermilk and the methods of bleaching were revolutionised as the observations on the bleaching action of chlorine, discovered by Scheele in 1774, were developed. In the 19th century developments were related mainly to improvements in scouring techniques using lime or caustic soda. During the early 20th century considerable study was made of the control of hypochlorite bleaching. Knowledge then gained, and particularly that related to control tests for cotton quality, has been applicable to bleaching methods based on other chemicals that have since been introduced.

In the 1930s hydrogen peroxide and sodium chlorite bleaching processes were developed, though the former had then been in use for some 50 years for wool and silk bleaching. Most post-war developments have been associated with these two chemicals, hydrogen peroxide in particular being used in rapid continuous bleaching processes.

2.2 IMPURITIES IN CELLULOSICS

The impurities removed during preparation are those naturally associated with cellulose, those applied to assist spinning, knitting or weaving, and contaminants which may have been picked up during these operations.

The natural impurities vary with cotton quality and geographic source, and include waxes, proteins, mineral matter, colouring matter and residual seed. Though the presence of residual waxes can be advantageous for some fabric end uses, removal is generally required in order to develop good level absorbency for dyeing or printing. Other natural impurities interfere with dyeing to a lesser degree, but for practical purposes their removal is required.

Seed removal is essential for all white and coloured goods except those to be dyed to dark shades.

The extent to which bleaching is required depends on the shade of the dyeing which is to follow. However, with the increasing trend towards fully continuous preparation processes, it is not unusual to employ a preparation sequence providing a standard bleached base that can be used for dyeing a full shade range, including the darker colours.

The impurities applied during processing are essentially the constituents of sizes in woven fabrics and lubricants applied to assist spinning and knitting. Sizes for woven fabrics contain stiffening and lubricating components; the former are usually starches, cellulosic ethers, poly(vinyl alcohol) and polyacrylics used singly or in blends. Lubricants are of mineral or animal origin.

The undesirable contaminants of most concern are those associated with metallic impurities. These can cause local chemical damage during bleaching. Even when this is not severe enough to cause fabric damage, dye substantivity can be reduced with consequent resist marks. Metals can also be absorbed from the soil during the growth of the cotton plant, manganese being particularly troublesome as it can give bleached cotton a pink tone.

Problems can also arise from 'coloured fly', i.e. coloured fibres adventitiously introduced during cotton picking and subsequent carding or spinning. Although much has been done to eliminate this problem at source, some fabric preparation processes must be selected to ensure colour destruction.

2.3 CHEMICALS FOR PREPARATION PROCESSES

Many chemicals are used in preparation processes, including enzymatic desizing products, alkalis (caustic soda, soda ash, phosphates and silicates) and bleaching agents (hydrogen peroxide, sodium chlorite and hypochlorite). Apart from these, a wide range of commercial auxiliary products is also available. The detailed chemistry of these materials will not be discussed here, but some points on characteristics and guidance on selection is given below.

2.3.1. Wetting Agents

Good wetting of material is required to ensure penetration of preparation chemicals and evenness of treatment. Commercial wetting agents are usually anionic or non-ionic surfactants, or a blend of the two. The anionic products used by the textile industry are usually organic sulphates, sulphonates or phosphates. For most applications it is important that residues in effluents should be bio-degradable. Consequently products containing long straight carbon chains are preferred, these having largely replaced branched-chain alkyl or aryl bases.

In solution the compounds ionise, the surface-active component carrying the negative charge being thus the anion (Scheme 2.1, in which R is a long carbon chain).

$$R\ O\ SO_2\ ONa \ \rightleftharpoons \ R\ O\ SO_2\ O^- + Na^+$$

Scheme 2.1

By definition the non-ionic surfactants do not ionise in solution. Most commercial products used in the textile preparation processes are ethoxylated fatty alcohols with the general formula shown in Figure 2.1.

$$R\ O(CH_2CH_2O)_nH$$

Figure 2.1

The surfactant's properties are influenced by the relative lengths of the carbon (R) and ethoxylate (n) chains. Where n is low, products have lower water solubility and tend to have good emulsifying rather than wetting properties.

The following is a summary of the important factors affecting the use of wetting agents.

(a) Anionic products tend to have a greater adverse effect on enzymes than do their non-ionic equivalents. This is important where enzymatic desizing is performed.
(b) Stability to alkali is important in scouring and mercerising.
(c) When used in bleaching solutions the wetting agent must be compatible with the bleaching agent.
(d) For some end uses a surfactant with high affinity for the textile is not disadvantageous, but it is most undesirable if fabric is being prepared for waterproofing.
(e) The effectiveness of some wetting agents is influenced by temperature.

(f) The degree to which liquors foam is important with some processing machinery. Excessive foam in kiers, or other machines which circulate liquor, can cause cavitation in pumps with resultant poor circulation.

(g) In continuous bleaching using roller-bed steamers, including the Vaporloc pressure units, excessive foam can cause traction failure in the roller system that draws fabric into the steamer, and consequently poor piling on the roller bed.

(h) Foam can be an advantage in some chlorite systems, as chlorine dioxide liberation may be reduced.

2.3.2 Detergency Auxiliaries

A distinction should be drawn between surfactants that assist wetting-out and those that promote oil and fat emulsification. The latter are generally non-ionic with short ethylene oxide chains and may not contribute significantly to wetting-out. Hence when used in bleaching to promote fat and wax removal, e.g. in kier bleaching, a wetting agent is also required.

On the other hand it is possible to select wetting agents with little detergency value, an important factor in alkaline peroxide bleaching when retention of natural fats is required, e.g. when bleaching some knitted cotton fabrics.

2.3.3 Scouring Assistants

Some auxiliary products are designed to assist caustic scouring. These usually incorporate sequestrants that are effective complexing agents for calcium, magnesium and iron at high pH. Their inclusion is said to aid the removal of iron or other metal contamination (which can cause catalytic decomposition in subsequent bleaching) and to promote fabric absorbency by the extraction of the alkaline earth metals.

Reducing agents have also been included in commercial products. They assist the removal of iron contamination by reducing ferric to ferrous salts, which are more readily complexed by ethylenediamine tetra-acetic acid (EDTA). Furthermore they give some reductive bleaching so that scoured cotton is less brown in colour than is usual in caustic-scoured material.

2.3.4 Sequestrants

Apart from their application as noted above, sequestrants are used widely in peroxide bleaching systems. However, the stability of a given sequestrant can vary in different peroxide systems. Diethylenetriamine penta-acetic acid (DTPA) is preferred to EDTA in systems operating at temperatures above 60°C. Several organic phosphonate-based products also show good stability.

2.3.5 Organic Stabilisers for Peroxide Bleaching

Commercial products are based on various combinations of magnesium salts, organic sequestrants, protein degradation products and surfactants. Some products are designed to give stabilisation only, whereas others also combine detergent and softening actions. While many products give adequate stabilisation in long liquors, the range for pad–steam conditions is more restricted.

2.3.6 Chlorite Bleaching Auxiliary Products

Two types of product are commercially available. One type provides controlled activation of sodium chlorite through the gradual development of acidic conditions during processing. Products of the second type control chlorine dioxide evolution in processes through a predetermined level of acidity.

2.4 WATER QUALITY

Most bleachworks were situated initially where there was a readily available supply of good quality water, i.e. water with low suspended solid content and without metallic impurities, particularly iron salts.

The requirement for good quality water remains, though the original sources may now be inadequate. The two quality factors indicated are fairly self evident. Any suspended solids are likely to be filtered out onto yarn or fabric and iron salts may give rise to discoloration or catalytic damage during bleaching. Other metallic salts may also give rise to the latter problem, so that in hydrogen peroxide systems their presence must be avoided.

For peroxide bleaching some water hardness is advantageous. Ideally this should be about 60 mg/l (as $CaCO_3$). With water of lower hardness an addition of magnesium salts is usually made. Problems arising from using water of excessive hardness are usually encountered in alkaline scouring or bleaching liquors, when cloudiness of fabric appearance and unlevel absorbency can result. Such faults are usually corrected by scouring with hydrochloric acid.

The bleacher is concerned not only with process water quality, but also with its discharge. In many cases this may be to the local sewer system. For this or for discharge to natural waterways a consent limit for quality of effluent discharge must generally be met. The parameters of concern to the preparation department are primarily volume of effluent, biochemical oxygen demand (BOD) or other basis for assessing inorganic and organic chemical pollutant load, and suspended solids.

The efficiency of washing plant and process selection to minimise the number of washing stages can have a significant influence on effluent volume. To ensure minimum BOD care must be taken in the selection of chemicals and consideration given to the extent of breakdown of extracted material, particularly starches, during processing. Removal of high levels of suspended solids may involve filtration or at least settling-out in holding tanks before discharge. Such settlement may be aided by the use of flocculants, e.g. aluminium sulphate, which will also flocculate some colouring and other organic matter. The importance of cost in regard to both raw water purification and effluent disposal has already brought about changes and it is likely to become of ever-increasing concern to those responsible for cloth preparation.

2.5. METHODS OF PROCESSING CELLULOSIC TEXTILES

2.5.1 Loose Fibre

Most loose-fibre processing is based on circulation of liquor through a fibre pack in kiers or loose-stock machines. During the 1970s a continuous processing unit was developed in the USA by Cotton Inc. It provides mechanical cleaning prior to forming a loose-fibre mat which can be scoured and bleached continuously by pad–steam processes, similar to those used for woven fabrics.

2.5.2. Yarn

Yarn can be handled in hank form, the hanks being tied loosely into bundles for loading into kiers or hung in Hussong machines. Most yarn is handled now in package form, as cones or cheeses, these being processed in forced-circulation package machines.

2.5.3 Knitted Fabrics

Knitted fabrics require processing under low tension. Batch processing is done in winches. For continuous processing J-box or conveyor steamers are used widely, but an alternative approach, the PKS process (see p. 64) provides continuous treatment at a liquor ratio of up to 30:1 with bleaching taking place during a 10 min retention period.

2.5.4 Woven Fabrics

Fabric construction and fibre content determine whether woven fabrics are best processed in open-width or rope form. Machinery is available for continuous or batch operation for both forms. Winches, jigs, package and beam machines are used for both fabric preparation and dyeing. There are, however, some items of equipment used solely for preparation processes. These are described to facilitate the understanding of the processes covered later.

2.6 BATCH PREPARATION EQUIPMENT

2.6.1 Kier

The kier provides the means for treating a large batch, of up to 2 tonnes, of fabric in rope form, or yarn in hank form. The material remains stationary while liquor circulates through it. The effective liquor ratio is about 4:1. The desirable features of a kier for fabric are:

(a) Automatic piling to give even loading
(b) Chemical impregnation during loading
(c) Good circulation, obtained by collecting the liquor draining from the fabric in the false bottom of the kier, picking it up with a centrifugal pump and re-introducing it at the top of the kier through a circular spray pipe
(d) A multi-tubular heater between the centrifugal pump and the spray pipe; this is particularly desirable for hydrogen peroxide bleaching.

The automatic piler is a belt-driven device placed over the centre of the kier. It has a stainless steel or plastic trunk through which the fabric is allowed to pass. This is driven by a cam and rotates with an undulating motion. The length of the trunk can be varied in order, when necessary, to change the length of the fabric 'throw'. Clearly a longer throw is necessary in the early stages of piling than is required when the kier is nearly full. Apart from being a labour-saving device and ensuring uniform piling, there is the advantage of being able to introduce scouring or bleaching liquor into the trunk simultaneously with the fabric, thus giving a more even impregnation.

2.7 CONTINUOUS PREPARATION EQUIPMENT

2.7.1 Chemical Application

All continuous preparation processes require a consistent and continuous application of chemicals to the fabric, which is then usually passed through a steamer before washing-off.

It is not usually satisfactory to apply chemicals by means of a dyer's pad mangle as the fabric at this stage has poor absorbency. A saturator is required, and this should have an adequate volume to allow sufficient contact time between fabric and liquor.

Chemical application may be to dry or wet fabric and there is some difference in the controls required to give the required concentration on fabrics.

2.7.2 Wet-on-dry Application

This can only be used for the first preparation stage, e.g. where dry loom-state fabric is entering the saturator for impregnation, or after intermediate drying in multi-stage processing. It is possible to have a simple chemical feed system because the replacement feed liquor can be of the same composition as the liquor in the saturator.

2.7.3 Wet-on-wet Application

This is required in double- or multi-stage processing, where the fabric is entering one stage in a wet condition from a previous treatment. To assist interchange of saturator liquor with water held in the fabric it is advisable to ensure a minimum difference of 10% in the fabric's liquor content between entry and exit from the saturator. This small change means that concentrated chemical solutions must be metered to the saturator to maintain the correct liquor concentration. There are four basic types of chemical feed:

(a) Gravity feed from one or more header tanks, with flow control, preferably by rotameter gauges when multiple feeds are used

(b) Multiple proportioning pumps linked directly to fabric speed through the saturator and stopped automatically if the machine stops

(c) Proportioning system based on filling and emptying of predetermined volumes of chemical solutions to meet fabric requirements

(d) Fully automated system in which samples of saturator liquor are taken and titrated potentiometrically to determine rate of chemical addition (electronically controlled)

Many machines are available for fully continuous processing, offering choices of dwell time and operating temperature for rope or open-width processing. Brief descriptions follow.

2.8 CONTINUOUS ROPE PROCESSING

2.8.1 J-Box

The J-box was the first commercially accepted development for fully continuous preparation. Its basic design evolved from the Gantt piler, which had been used for a number of years for hypochlorite bleaching. This was a wooden structure shaped like the letter J with rolls at the bottom of the curve to facilitate movement of fabric. Two distinct types of J-box were developed which differ mainly in the method of fabric heating. In the Becco J-box heating is by direct application of steam to the pack of plaited fabric. With the DuPont J-box the fabric is heated by passing through a steam atmosphere in a 'heater tube' adjacent to the entrance of the J-box.

One fundamental problem associated with the J-box has been the difficulty in moving certain fabrics around the J-section. Modifications introduced to minimise this problem include an easy-slide liner, e.g. of PTFE, or a 'wet bottom', in which water can be introduced into the elbow to ease the passage of fabric and provide a degree of washing. Alternatively, in some cases bleach liquor is recirculated around the elbow

In addition to abrasion marks, rope creasing can sometimes occur. This latter point needs careful consideration when processing polyester blends, and only the lighter-weight blends of polyester/cotton can be processed by J-box. Partial heat setting of polyester/cotton prior to rope preparation will minimise the occurrence of permanent rope creases. However, the finisher must always bear in mind the possibiiity of permanent fixation of 'grey stains'.

2.8.2 Continuous Kier

The FMC continuous kier evolved from the principle of the 'wet bottom' J-box. Bleach liquor is continuously pumped from a circulation tank via a heat exchanger to the lower sections of the J-box, thus providing a liquor ratio of 6:1 to 8:1. The continuous kier has found acceptance particularly for single-stage bleaching of cotton knit goods.

2.9 CONTINUOUS OPEN-WIDTH PROCESSING

2.9.1 Pad Roll

Although the pad roll system is truly a batch operation, proper programming can allow an almost continuous flow of bleached fabric from the washers. The extension of the pad roll system by some machinery manufacturers to double-batch units does allow fully continuous operation, but with the addition of complex mechanical design features. These systems are limited to speeds of about 60 m/min. The pad roll unit was a popular choice for bleaching in Europe during the 1960s and 1970s, since it provides adequate open-width bleaching production capacity for the medium-sized textile mill.

The basic concept of chemical impregnation followed by storage of a batch of fabric in a steam-heated chamber does have inherent limitations. Careful control must be exercised to ensure a consistent standard of bleaching, since the inside of the batch will be in contact with the applied chemicals for about 1.5 h longer than the outside, and there is an inevitable risk of 'ending'. Furthermore if the temperature control is not precise 'listing' can be a problem. Listing can also be attributed to pressure effects in the batch which cause migration of chemicals from the centre to the selvedge areas of the fabric. Invariably these faults are more noticeable when the fabric is dyed by modern continuous rapid techniques. For these reasons and productivity factors the pad roll has given way to fully continuous systems.

2.9.2 Short J-Box
The open-width short J-box provides a dwell time of 8–12 min and is normally operated at 95°C for peroxide bleaching. It has, by necessity, a much smaller capacity than the rope J-box in order to minimise the frequency and intensity of fold marks caused by the weight of fabric moving through the J-box. It is important with this equipment to ensure that the metal of the box does not become overheated. If this does occur, the selvedge areas of the fabric that have touched the sides of the box can show different dyeing properties from the rest of the material.

2.9.3 U-Box and Roller-bed Steamer
It is convenient to group these two types of equipment together since the principle of operation is very similar, though the mechanical designs differ. In the U-box fabric is plaited down and eased round a roller bed in the configuration of the letter U. Dependent on fabric weight and depth of bed, dwell times of 5–15 min are obtainable with running speeds up to 100 m/min.

In the roller-bed steamer a flat bed of rollers is employed, normally with the end rollers slightly elevated. Fabric is plaited down on to the slowly moving roller bed, which transports the fabric in a relaxed state to the exit point. It is possible to maintain a required production speed while varying the retention time on a steamer by adjusting the depth of the fabric bed, and consequently the amount of fabric in the steamer.

Early machines provided dwell times of 3–5 min, but even with the roller-bed transport memory creases were found, especially on some polyester/cotton fabrics. Such creases are prevented by using a short tight-strand section prior to plaiting onto a roller bed. This combination is used in the second generation of roller-bed steamers. Dwell times have also been extended to 10–15 min, thus aiding seed removal in combined scour/bleach processing.

2.9.4 Conveyor Steamer
The conveyor steamer was introduced in the USA by the Mathieson Alkali Works in 1938–39 for chlorite bleaching. The impregnated fabric enters a steam-heated chamber and is plaited onto the first of three conveyor belts moving along the length of the machine. At the end of the first traverse the fabric is dropped onto a second conveyor and after another traverse onto a third conveyor. A temperature of 95°C and a dwell time of 45–60 min is typical. The system can be used also for peroxide bleaching. These machines have, however, largely been replaced by other systems because of their cost, and considerable maintenance and space requirements.

Single-bed conveyors, providing 30 min dwell, are being used for peroxide bleaching of knitted fabrics, as they give a very low-tension traction system.

2.9.5 Tight-strand Steamer
The atmospheric tight-strand roller steamer has been promoted, particularly in Europe, for bleaching and scouring under 'shock' conditions. Compared with the roller-bed steamer, it suffers from the disadvantage that the dwell period can only be changed by varying the production speed. Consequently steaming periods tend to be limited to 1–2 min.

2.9.6 Pressure Scouring and Bleaching
In the early 1960s James Hunter developed a commercial unit for scouring under pressure. Later Mather and Platt, and Kleinewefers, produced machines employing lip seals which overcame the inherent difficulties of roller seals in the Hunter machine. The lip seals use a pressure tube held against a metal plate, the pressure inside the tube being a little above that of the chamber. Although the fabric passes between the tube and the fixed bed, the chamber pressure can be held. In the Mather and Platt machine, with its Vaporloc unit, the fabric entry and exit are side-by-side, and the fabric is plaited into a roller-bed conveyor. The Kleinewefers machine has entry and exit points at opposite sides of the pressure unit, and the fabric passes through the machine under warp tension.

Since in the Mather machine fabric is transported in the relaxed state on a roller bed, the dwell time can be increased merely by increasing the plaiting density on the bed. The practical maximum storage time is short enough to ensure that the folds do not cause any problems. Normal dwell times vary in the range 1–3 min with production speeds of about 100 m/min. In the Kleinewefers machine, where fabric is transported by multiple rollers under slight warp tension, expanders are used to avoid creases going through at high temperatures. However, the only way to increase dwell time is by reducing running speed. Normally the capacity of the unit is 60 m, allowing a dwell time of 1 min when running at 60 m/min.

2.9.7 PKS Process
The PKS process, developed by Bayer, provides continuous bleaching under long liquor ratio conditions (between 25:1 and 30:1). Fabric is introduced into the reaction box under the liquor surface and transported through the liquor to give a dwell time in the order of 10 min at 90–95°C. Bleach liquor is constantly recirculated and provides a transport medium for the introduction of the fabric into the reaction chamber. The system has high energy and chemical costs compared with most continuous processes, and consequently it has only achieved limited acceptance.

2.10 PREPARATION PROCESSES
The chemical requirements for scouring and bleaching loose cotton, yarns and fabrics are very similar. Woven fabrics, however, have two particular requirements, singeing and desizing.

2.10.1 Singeing

Many woven fabrics require singeing to remove surface fibres. Various systems have been devised, the most usual having gas-fired burners through which the fabric passes at high speed. This treatment is usually the first one given to grey fabric, with a desizing liquor often used as the quench.

2.10.2 Desizing

Warp yarns for woven cotton fabrics are sized to enable the yarn to withstand the mechanical actions of the loom when weaving. Consequently the materials used and levels of application are determined by balancing costs against weaving production efficiency and quality. Most sizes are applied as a solution in water and dried onto the yarn to provide a protective film. The agents mainly used are:
(a) Native starches (potato, corn, rice, maize)
(b) Modified starches (starch ethers, esters, etc.)
(c) Non-starch polymers (e.g. acrylates, carboxymethylcellulose, methylcellulose and poly(vinyl alcohol))
(d) Gelatin, special starch derivatives, etc.
(e) Organic-solvent-soluble materials.

The starch-based sizes are widely used on 100% cotton as they are cheaper than other materials and good weaving efficiency can be obtained. The other products find applications, either alone or in combination with starches, where the higher cost is justified by improved efficiency. Thus poly(vinyl alcohol) is widely used when sizing cotton/polyester blends. The film-forming materials, which provide fibre cohesion, are combined with a fat or wax lubricant.

Though some sizes are completely water soluble and should dry to give a water-soluble film, in practice slight degradation of the size during application, singeing or heat setting can impair the water solubility.

The desizing operation, as part of the preparation sequence, is designed to remove the size film. Unfortunately all too frequently the finisher is not given details of the nature of the size on the fabric and must build a degree of flexibility into his process to deal with different sizing systems.

Size removal depends essentially on the following factors:
(a) Solution viscosity of the size
(b) Resolubility of the size
(c) Size loading
(d) Nature of lubricants
(e) Fabric construction
(f) Desizing route

Desizing processes use either water or organic solvents.

2.10.3 Aqueous Processes

Rot Steeping
In rot steeping fabrics are wet out with water only. It is little used in current practice because of the slow rate of desizing and non-uniformity of treatment.

Acid Steeping
Acid treatments degrade starch-based sizes and offer the further advantage of removing calcium and magnesium salts from cellulosic textiles. Hydrochloric acid is
preferred. The concentration of commercial acid (sp. gr. 1.14) used may be as high
as 2% when using short steeping times, and 0.2 to 0.3% for overnight steeping.
Care must be taken to avoid any drying out as this will damage the cellulose itself.

Enzyme Treatments
Enzyme treatments are used very widely on cotton fabrics sized with starch, with
bacterial α-amylase being the preferred product. Malt diastase, pancreatic amylase
and mixed α- and β-amylases are also employed. The process consists of three
stages:
(a) Application of the enzyme
(b) Digestion of the starch
(c) Removal of the digestion products by washing.

Control of pH, enzyme concentration, temperature and electrolyte are essential
for optimum desizing.

There must also be an adequate pick-up of liquor by the fabric in any process
based on a pad application of the desizing agent. With too low a liquor pick-up,
action on the size components and ease of washing-off can be impaired. Use of
good wetting agents is essential and these must be compatible with the enzyme. The
time required for the process is linked to the effective treatment temperature, and
in this connection enzymes with the higher temperature stability are now available
which permit process times to be reduced.

When used prior to hydrogen peroxide bleaching, washing-off after enzyme desizing must be very thorough as residual enzymes can have a deleterious effect on
the stability of the bleach liquor.

Oxidative Desizing
Oxidants have been used for many years as desizing agents. As a pretreatment
prior to hydrogen peroxide kier bleaching, desizing with sodium hypochlorite is
particularly useful. Though it is less effective than enzyme treatment in degrading
starches fully, the subsequent peroxide bleaching clears residual starch.

The use of sodium bromite for desizing was developed in France. It is claimed to
provide a degree of bleaching with starch degradation, but has not been adopted
commercially in the UK. One reason for this is the use of different starch and
lubricant size components in the two countries.

The term oxidative desizing is related more today to the use of persulphates and
hydrogen peroxide in alkaline pretreatments. Persulphates, and recently perphosphates, are recommended for use in caustic scouring processes to increase starch
degradation. The perphosphates are more difficult to manufacture and are not
available generally in commercial quantities. Whilst under laboratory conditions it
is not easy to identify differences in size removal in caustic scouring with and without the addition of oxidants, in practice their use gives improved uniformity of preparation in long continuous runs.

Hydrogen peroxide was developed initially for desizing fabrics sized with poly(vinyl alcohol). For fabrics sized only with poly(vinyl alcohol) desizing at about pH 9 is recommended. With mixed sizes a higher pH [1] can be used.

One reason for the increased interest in oxidative desizing is the mixed-size systems with which the finisher has to contend. Except in a few vertical companies, the finisher is not aware of size compositions on the fabric he has to process. Since the oxidative desizing processes are effective against a broad range of sizes, including starches, poly(vinyl alcohol) and carboxymethylcellulose, they assist the finisher to overcome this problem.

Oxidative desizing offers the possibility of reducing the number of processing stages required for fabric preparation, an important factor in minimising energy use. The oxidant can be added to caustic scour liquors to provide combined desizing and scouring. For this system little or no silicate or organic stabiliser is included. Alternatively some stabiliser may be added to give a degree of bleaching with desizing. This useful pretreatment extends the feasibility of combined scour/bleach processes, particularly when these would otherwise give inadequate bleaching and seed removal. In the general recommendations in Table 2.1 the lower levels of caustic soda provide desizing only. The higher levels provide oxidative scouring.

TABLE 2.1

Recommended Levels of Additions in Oxidative Desizing

Reagent	Amount of reagent applied (% o.w.f.) at:		
	100°C < 15 min	100°C 15–60 min	120–130°C 1–2 min
Magnesium sulphate (heptahydrate)	0.005	0.005	0.005
Caustic soda	2–6	2–4	8–12
Sodium silicate or organic stabiliser	0–1	0	0
DTPA (40% solution)	0.2	0.2	0.2
Hydrogen peroxide	0.2–0.35	0.2–0.35	0.1–0.2
or sodium persulphate	0.2–0.5	0.2–0.5	0.2–0.5

The following points are generally applicable:
(a) Rapid desizing treatments require more critical control of alkali and oxidant concentrations
(b) Increased alkali for a given oxidant concentration tends to increase chemical damage
(c) Increased oxidant over the minimum required for desizing increases chemical damage
(d) Persulphates promote desizing rather than bleaching, and require more critical control in concentration than does hydrogen peroxide
(e) Mixing persulphates and hydrogen peroxide is not recommended in pad–steam desizing.

Despite its many advantages, the use of oxidative desizing has been limited. This is due to the degree of control which is required and the unsuitable materials of construction of many quench boxes. However, in recent years ambient oxidative desizing processes have been found very useful as a pretreatment for one-pass pad–steam combined scouring and bleaching processes. Desizing liquors similar to those indicated for 15–60 min at 100°C are required, but fabric is retained for a minimum of 4 h ambient.

Hot Caustic Soda Treatments
Starch-based sizes can be removed by hot caustic soda treatments, and it is possible to combine size removal with grey mercerisation [2, 3].

This technique does, however, preclude recycling of mercerisation liquor. Care must be taken when using sizes containing poly(vinyl alcohol), as caustic soda treatments can fix the size. This difficulty is overcome by using the oxidative desizing technique. Caustic soda cannot be used to remove polyester sizes, e.g. Eastman WD, as hot alkaline treatments fix this size.

Hot Washing with Detergents
Simple aqueous washing removes some synthetic sizes. Developments in such products are directed towards low size solution viscosity and high solubility. Acrylate copolymers are amongst such products and the possibility exists with these and with some other water-soluble sizes, e.g. poly (vinyl alcohol), for size recovery and reuse. The washing procedures are quite simple; good control of pH, temperature and detergent concentration is required, and a plentiful supply of wash water with good mechanical agitation must be available A particularly attractive feature of recycling is the reduction in BOD from the desizing effluents.

2.10.4 Organic Solvent Processes

Solvent/Enzyme Emulsions
Apart from the removal of the film-forming component of size mixtures, it is necessary to clear added lubricants. Removal of these and natural fats by solvent extraction does not immediately provide good absorbency, hence an aqueous treatment is usually also necessary. However, there has been considerable interest in the use of solvents to clear the solvent-soluble materials.

Trichloroethylene was the first solvent used commercially, in a manner similar to that used for metal degreasing. Fabric is passed continuously through solvent vapour, which condenses on the fabric, dissolving out fats and waxes as it drains off. The system requires special equipment which includes solvent recovery. Even so, solvent losses contribute significantly to process costs. Though fats and waxes are removed, additional wet processing is required to remove other size components.

The Markal system, developed by ICI, whilst still requiring special plant, removed some of the disadvantages of solvent 'degreasing' and combined the removal of fat and wax with starch degradation.

In this process fabric is wet out in trichloroethylene containing a detergent. The fabric then passes into a steam box in which the trichloroethylene is removed by steam distillation. Condensation followed by water–solvent separation gives good, but not perfect, solvent recovery. The wetting-out in organic solvent gives complete penetration of the detergent, which remains in the fabric after steaming. Hot-water washing follows to remove fats and waxes, which had been made, in effect, self emulsifiable.

Introduction of an enzyme into the detergent solution gives starch degradation during steaming, allowing removal in the washing-off stage. The process provides fabric with excellent even absorbency.

The disadvantages are high capital cost, high solvent costs and effluent problems, all the residues being in the washing-off liquor. To overcome the problems of solvent cost, processes were introduced which used paraffin hydrocarbons, emulsified in aqueous enzyme solutions. These emulsions were padded directly onto grey fabric and, after appropriate storage for size degradation, washed-off. Good absorbency was obtained, but the effluent contained the hydrocarbons in addition to wax and size.

Development of the above-mentioned processes led to a fuller understanding of the chemical nature of those detergents most effective in promoting removal of fats and waxes, particularly in the pad application of desizing liquors. Whilst not strictly solvent emulsion processes, the use of these specialised auxiliary products has become common practice in many desizing and bleaching processes.

Solvent-soluble Sizes
A number of companies are active in the development of solvent-soluble sizes, which are applied and removed in non-aqueous media. Though they have the advantage of eliminating aqueous pollution, economic and technical factors have limited progress. The technology has been reviewed [4].

2.11 SCOURING
Natural and other fats and waxes may be removed prior to dyeing or printing, as indicated above, by the use of organic solvents, but most preparation routes use alkaline scouring. This may be a single process or be combined with the desizing and/or bleaching. Apart from fats and waxes, other non-cellulosic constituents can be removed, particularly nitrogenous matter and pectates. Most importantly cotton seed can be softened or burst for subsequent removal.

The natural oils and waxes associated with cotton fibres are mainly esters, most being triglycerides of unsaturated fatty acids, such as oleic acid, or of saturated higher molecular weight acids, with up to 30 carbon atoms per fatty acid chain. Their removal in caustic scouring is based on their saponification, or alkaline hydrolysis, to form the sodium salt of the fatty acid and a free alcohol.

Thus the water-insoluble esters are converted to water-soluble or dispersible materials. The water-soluble sodium salts or soaps are, of course, sensitive to precipitation by any calcium and magnesium salts. Hence, where lime was used in the initial boiling, acid scouring was required to release free fatty acid which could be solubilised in a subsequent soda ash or caustic soda boil.

In modern scouring practice it is more common to use scouring assistants based on sequestrants and synthetic surfactants. The choice of surfactants is important. They must be fully compatible with the caustic solution, assist in wetting out, and preferably also have good detergency properties in order to aid the removal of non-saponifiable oils and fats. The products most commonly used are anionic sulphates, sulphonates or phosphates [5].

The equipment normally used for batches of fabric in rope form is the kier. This type of plant was developed to provide the thorough scouring required prior to hypochlorite bleaching. Between 0.5 and 2 tonnes of fabric, according to kier capacity, is loaded into a kier and hot alkaline liquor is circulated for several hours. The process may be carried out at 100°C, but pressure boiling is also practised with temperatures up to 120°C. Methods of treatment are described in the literature [6].

Currently caustic soda is the most generally used reagent. The process is particularly effective for removing coloured fly. The materials extracted from cellulose contain reducing sugars, and the combined reductive and alkaline conditions clear the dye from the contaminated fibre.

In alkaline kier boiling care must be taken to ensure that air is not entrapped in the fabric, since its presence can lead to the formation of oxycellulose.

Kiers are also available for processing in open width, in which the fabric is batched onto perforated beams. These beams are run into horizontal autoclaves and, as in rope systems, the liquor circulates for several hours.

Scouring of small batches can be done in jigs or winches, the choice usually being dictated by the necessity or otherwise of open-width processing.

For fully continuous rope processing in a J-box system fabric is impregnated with a caustic soda solution, usually up to 80 g/l concentration, with a liquor retention of 80–100%, prior to steaming in the J-box at 90–100°C for 1–2 h. For open-width continuous processing similar concentrations are required for scouring, but it is not unusual to find much higher concentrations being used to provide a degree of causticisation, which improves dye yields.

In general, for non-oxidative scouring the alkali concentration is varied according to steaming time, very rapid processes requiring the highest caustic soda levels. This has been referred to as shock scouring. One disadvantage of using high concentrations of alkali is the difficulty of removing it when washing-off after scouring.

The times and temperatures used for treatment are those appropriate to particular machines and range from 1–2 min at 130°C in the Vaporloc and 3–12 min at 100°C in roller-bed steamers to 1–2 h at 90°C in pad roll systems.

Reference has been made previously both to the auxiliary products which may be used to improve caustic scouring processes and to combined desizing and scouring by the addition of oxidants. Though these appear contradictory to the need to avoid air entrapment during caustic scouring, provided that there is control of alkali and oxidant levels, good scouring, size removal and some fabric whitening can be obtained with little fibre damage.

2.12 MERCERISATION

Mercer's original invention was based on treatment of cotton fabrics with strong caustic soda solution, without tension, to improve strength and dye substantivity. Later it was found that the application of tension improved lustre.

Typically the caustic soda is a 25–26% wt/wt solution (56–60° Tw). At this concentration considerable swelling of the cellulosic fibre is obtained, accompanied by shrinkage if the fabric or yarn is not held under tension. Mercerising may be carried out at various stages of the processing route on one of two types of machine, classified as chain or chainless. The former applies tension directly to warp and weft whilst the latter only applies indirect tension across the weft. Consequently the fabric needs to be designed to allow for width loss, or must be stentered to a greater width prior to mercerising, which is difficult and sometimes impracticable. An important consideration in mercerisation is the speed of washing-out of the caustic soda.

The benefits sought in the process are improved lustre, tensile strength, dye uptake, coverage of dead cotton and dimensional stability. All these properties are influenced by alkali concentration, temperature and dwell time in alkali prior to washing-off [7].

The effects tend to be confined to the surface since full penetration into the fabrics by concentrated caustic soda at low temperature is not obtained, even with the aid of wetting agents. This is particularly the case when mercerising loom-state fabrics.

A further disadvantage of loom-state mercerisation is the fouling of the liquor by size, making caustic recovery and recycling difficult. However, there are a number of fabrics for which it is desirable to impregnate with caustic soda while they have their maximum strength, and hence there is still a considerable call for grey mercerisation.

In recent years a new development in mercerising has been proposed: so called hot mercerising. Some comment was made previously on this development (p. 68), and more detail is appropriate here. The basic principles are:

(a) Saturation with mercerising-strength caustic soda solution near to its boiling point
(b) Controlled hot stretching
(c) Controlled cooling
(d) Traditional tension-controlled washing followed by final washing

The advantages indicated for the process are:

(a) Shortening of the processing sequence providing cost savings
(b) Increased efficiency and uniformity
(c) Use of chain or chainless process with less problems related to fabric width
(d) Improved lustre, tensile strength and dimensional stability since greater fabric stretching is possible
(e) Increased dye substantivity, though this is dependent on the extent of stretch imparted; greater than normal stretch reduces dye substantivity with greater internal orientation of molecular structure
(f) Good response from fabrics containing lower-grade cotton
(g) Flash scouring effect obtained
(h) Good desizing

(i) Better fabric penetration by a hot caustic liquor than with normal mercerisation.

The main chemical and physical changes do not take place at the initial elevated temperature, but when the cooled fabrics go through the traditional section of the mercerising plant. The possibility of a combined scouring/mercerising process is of considerable potential interest, particularly as the degree of scouring, as a preliminary to peroxide bleaching, is said to equal that of a conventional caustic scour. However, since its introduction in 1977, this development has not achieved significant commercial success.

2.13 LIQUID AMMONIA TREATMENT
The use of ammonia has also been developed to treat cotton. The original Prograde process, as used on yarns, removes the ammonia in a hot water bath. This treatment brings about an increase in tensile strength, lustre and dye substantivity. However, the increase in the latter two properties is less than when mercerising with caustic soda, although the ammonia-treated cotton has greater resistance to thermal degradation.

For fabric processing the ammonia can be removed by dry heat. This gives very different properties to the Prograde system and should not be considered as a mercerisation process. As far as the influence on dye substantivity is concerned, this may vary from slight improvement to a reduction, depending on the dye. However, the dry-heat removal does give improved crease recovery to the fabric, and permanent easy-care finishes can be obtained with lower resin additions. Hence the benefits are associated primarily with improved properties in resin-finished cellulosic fabrics; the ammonia treatment may follow dyeing.

2.14 CHARACTERISTICS OF THE BLEACHING OPTIONS
The three chemicals used for bleaching are sodium hypochlorite, sodium chlorite and hydrogen peroxide. Whilst details of processing with each chemical will be given later, it is useful to note certain characteristics of these chemicals here.

2.14.1 Hypochlorite
Prior to bleaching with hypochlorite it is essential that the cellulose be cleared of natural impurities by thorough scouring. Although this may not seem to indicate complexity in processing, in practice one or two alkaline boils may be required with intermediate washing. These will be followed by souring and further washing prior to bleaching. Bleaching must be followed by washing and an antichlor treatment. The end result is, therefore, a process with relatively low chemical costs but high labour content, lengthy processing time and high water demand. Hypochlorite bleaching today is largely a batch process, and the better suitability of other chemicals to continuous production has considerably influenced its replacement by sodium chlorite or hydrogen peroxide.

2.14.2 Sodium Chlorite
Sodium chlorite bleaching, in contrast to hypochlorite or hydrogen peroxide bleaching, is carried out under acidic conditions. The scouring process, required for

hypochlorite, can be omitted and bleaching carried out on loom-state or desized materials.

When scouring is omitted, under the acid bleaching conditions, a relatively small amount of natural fats and waxes is removed, and this can be advantageous for knitting yarns and knitted frabrics. Chlorite bleaching is also relatively unaffected by low levels of iron or copper contamination. There are several disadvantages in chlorite bleaching. It is difficult to control chlorine dioxide release, a gas with a very low permitted threshold limit value (TLV). Hence considerable care must be taken in processing to protect operators by an adequate fume extraction system.

The acidic bleaching system is corrosive to stainless steel and special plant is often required. Chlorite bleaching has little or no effect on dirty oil stains. Several dyes are not resistant to chlorite bleaching, thus restricting the choice of fluorescent brighteners and colour woven effects. Also, in contrast to hydrogen peroxide, temperature, pH, etc. cannot be selected to provide very rapid bleaching.

2.14.3 Hydrogen Peroxide
Hydrogen peroxide bleaching for cellulosic textiles is carried out under alkaline conditions. Consequently scouring and bleaching can frequently be combined. Peroxide is adaptable to a very wide range of bleaching conditions, ranging in temperature from ambient to 130°C and in time from a few minutes to several hours. So the possibility exists for developing very rapid continuous bleaching processes. It may be used in many types of equipment and is now the major chemical in preparation processing in the USA, Europe and many other parts of the world.

2.14.4 Effect of Oxidants on Cellulose
It is interesting to note that oxidants have different actions on cellulose itself. Cotton oxidised with hydrogen peroxide is characterised by a high content of ketone groups, but very low aldehyde and carboxyl content. The ketones formed are 'inactive' carbonyls, i.e. they cause almost no yellowing on ageing or hot alkaline treatment. In contrast chlorine-oxidised cellulose has a high proportion of both aldehyde and acidic end groups [8].

2.15 HYPOCHLORITE BLEACHING
Although hypochlorite bleaching has been replaced very widely by processes based on hydrogen peroxide or sodium chlorite, a basic understanding is important. Hypochlorite is still used for bleaching, often in conjunction with other systems, as it is still a comparatively low-cost chemical. If only for historical reasons, the lessons learnt in establishing control of hypochlorite bleaching serve as a model of technological development. Moreover some of the test procedures for determining damage to cellulose, e.g. the cuprammonium fluidity test, have retained their value for control of more modern bleaching techniques.

It is essential that hypochlorite bleaching is preceded by thorough alkaline scouring. Bleaching is then carried out on 'clean' cellulose, the prime object being the destruction of residual natural colouring matter. This process is usually carried out by piling fabric into pits having a false bottom. Dilute hypochlorite liquor, typically with 2–3 g/l available chlorine, is then sprayed onto the goods, and drains through into a bleaching liquor tank prior to recirculation. Obviously uniform packing of the fabric into the pits is important, and this is best obtained using mechanical plaiting aids.

Sodium hypochlorite solutions as prepared, or available commercially, are alkaline, but some addition of alkali may be required to maintain alkalinity, particularly when regenerating the stock bleach liquor. Such regeneration is the general practice.

The bleaching is carried out at ambient temperature for several hours, frequently overnight, after which the liquor is allowed to drain and the fabric rinsed. This rinsing operation is usually carried out in the bleach pit.

While no insoluble residue should remain from sodium hypochlorite, calcium-containing residues are frequently produced in liquors prepared from bleaching powder. Such residues are readily removed by circulating dilute hydrochloric acid. This process is frequently included even when using sodium hypochlorite since it serves to decompose any residual hypochlorite, thus liberating free chlorine, and to clear other stains.

Despite thorough scouring, cotton may well retain some proteinaceous matter with which hypochlorite can react to form chloramines. When retained these can cause discoloration, though the major cause of colour deterioration in cotton may well be due to some residual waxes or the chemical action of chlorine on chlorine cellulose mentioned previously. An antichlor treatment with sodium sulphite or bisulphite or hydrogen peroxide is required to ensure removal of chloramines.

Partial bleaching with hypochlorite is used as a stage in some continuous bleaching processes. Cloth is saturated with a hypochlorite solution, typically to give a pick-up of 0.5% o.w.f. of available chlorine, and then held in a small J-box at ambient temperature for 15–30 min. Conditions should be such that all the hypochlorite is decomposed prior to subsequent impregnation with a hydrogen peroxide bleach liquor. The advantages of partial bleaching with a low-cost chemical have to be balanced against the cost of additional equipment and control.

The most important factors to be controlled in hypochlorite bleaching are pH, temperature and active chlorine concentration, the latter in relation to time of treatment.

2.15.1 Effect of pH
The active component in the bleaching system is governed by the equilibrium at different pH values, indicated in Scheme 2.2 for sodium hypochlorite.

$$\text{(a)} \quad NaOCl \rightleftharpoons Na^+ + OCl^-$$

$$\text{(b)} \quad HOCl \rightleftharpoons H^+ + OCl^-$$

$$\text{(c)} \quad HOCl + H^+ + Cl^- \rightleftharpoons Cl_2 + H_2O$$

Scheme 2.2

Above pH 10 reaction (a) predominates, while between pH 5 and 8.5 reaction (b) is most significant. Below pH 5 liberation of chlorine begins and below pH 3 the hypochlorous acid is converted to chlorine.

Though the equilibria were not studied in detail until the 1940s, over 50 years ago it was appreciated that there was a very great increase in degradation of cellulose by hypochlorite solutions in the pH range 4–10. Control in the range pH 10–11 can be obtained by adding lime to bleaching powder solutions or sodium carbonate to sodium hypochlorite solutions.

Attempts have been made to use activated hypochlorite solutions buffered to pH 7. Whilst much more rapid bleaching is possible, this is accompanied by the serious risk of fibre damage and the process has not been used to any significant extent.

The one area in which acid hypochlorite is used, with the intention of introducing free chlorine, is in flax and to a lesser degree jute preparation. This provides a chlorination rather than bleaching action to aid the removal of woody impurities frequently referred to as sprit. This has a high lignin content with which chlorine combines. A subsequent alkaline scour dissolves out the chlorinated lignin, so aiding sprit breakdown and removal. The removal of the sprit is important as a preparation for dyeing since sprit and clean fibre have different substantivities for many dyes.

2.15.2 Effect of Temperature
In the 1950s Derry established a quantitative relationship between oxidant use and fluidity increase, and also investigated the effect of bleaching temperature [9]. Increase in temperature gives a more rapid bleaching rate to the extent that the effect of 6 h bleaching at 20°C is matched by 6.8 min at 60°C. However, because of the risk of fibre damage through inadequate control, the influence of temperature has not been exploited.

2.15.3 Advantages and Disadvantages of Hypochlorite Bleaching
The main advantages of hypochlorite bleaching are low chemical costs and lower risk of catalytic fibre damage during correctly controlled bleaching. The disadvantages relate to the high labour and utility requirement, limited applicability of continuous processing and consequent long processing times for preparation. The importance of these factors led to the major move towards sodium chlorite and hydrogen peroxide in Europe in the 1950s. As costs of labour and utilities increase, these chemicals become increasingly attractive since overall savings in processing costs are possible. In addition they offer the possibility of greater uniformity in continuous processing.

Hypochlorite bleaching is likely to be retained in areas where pre-scouring is essential, e.g. when bleaching low-quality loose cotton, and where it is not possible to capitalise on the advantages of the more rapid processing potential of hydrogen peroxide. As will be detailed later, capital investment need not be a barrier to the use of the latter chemical since much traditional equipment, e.g. kiers, can be modified with very little capital outlay.

2.16 SODIUM CHLORITE BLEACHING

Acidification of sodium chlorite produces chlorine dioxide by two competing reactions, represented ionically in Schemes 2.3 and 2.4.

$$5ClO_2^- + 2H^+ \rightarrow 4ClO_2 + Cl^- + 2OH^-$$

$$4ClO_2^- + 4H^+ \rightarrow 3ClO_2 + \tfrac{1}{2}Cl_2 + 2H_2O$$

Schemes 2.3 and 2.4

Some decomposition to give chlorate and chloride also takes place (Scheme 2.5).

$$3ClO_2 \rightarrow 2ClO_3^- + Cl^-$$

Scheme 2.5

Having indicated that chlorine dioxide is formed, immediate attention must be drawn to the importance of controlling its rate of formation [10].

The rate of chlorite decomposition, and of bleaching, varies with pH and temperature. In neutral or alkaline conditions bleaching is virtually negligible and that which does occur is accompanied by fibre degradation.

In practice a balance must be struck between bleaching rate and chlorine dioxide evolution by accurate control of liquor pH. When bleaching cellulosic fabrics this is done most conveniently by using acetic or formic acids and buffering the system, preferably with acid phosphate salts. These not only control the bleaching pH but in high liquor ratio processes their addition results in improved whiteness.

For cotton the most suitable pH value for bleaching is 4 ± 0.2. The pH of the bleach liquor must not necessarily be adjusted to this value at the start of bleaching. Thus where the liquor ratio is very low, as in package machines and in impregnation bleaching, an initial pH of 4.5–5, or even higher, is often satisfactory when bleaching unscoured material. Impurities in the material liberate acid during bleaching, causing a fall in pH towards the optimum pH range.

Reduction of pH can be brought about also in short liquor conditions by incorporating chemicals that on heating liberate acid, e.g. sodium chloroacetate, chloroacetamide, triethanolamine, certain polyamines, ammonium persulphate. It is important to ensure that when such chemicals are used the final pH value attained in bleaching does not fall below 3.5. This can be done by incorporating a buffer such as sodium acetate or a phosphate in the bleach liquor.

Apart from pH effects, the amount of chlorine dioxide lost into the atmosphere, or available in the bleach liquor to cause plant corrosion, is influenced by the type of goods and the type of equipment. Where there is a large volume of liquor not directly in contact with the material being bleached, as in jigs and winches, chlorine dioxide is very likely to be released causing corrosion and presenting a health hazard. Less chlorine dioxide loss is generally experienced when bleaching in package machines or kiers and in continuous and semi-continuous pad–steam units, particularly when unscoured cotton is being bleached. In such cases the impurities in the cotton are in closer contact with the chlorine dioxide and can consume it more readily. This is particularly true in impregnation bleaching.

The odour from chlorine dioxide-containing chlorite solutions is most objectionable and is very apparent even at low concentrations. Moreover it is toxic. When buffer salt additions fail to give adequate control, the level of chlorine dioxide in solution can be reduced further, without impairing the whiteness, by the addition of various textile auxiliary products. These act by forming a loose combination with released chlorine dioxide or in some cases by producing a stable foam, which traps chlorine dioxide and so prevents its release to atmosphere.

Corrosion of stainless steel in direct contact with bleaching liquor can be reduced considerably by the inclusion of sodium nitrate in the bleach liquor. However, this contributes little to the prevention of vapour phase corrosion, and so it is necessary to use other materials of construction, e.g. titanium alloys, for certain parts.

2.16.1 Pretreatment

The type of treatment that cotton receives prior to chlorite bleaching varies, and is partly dependent on the amount of size which is present. Desizing is carried out as described previously.

The acidic conditions of chlorite bleaching provide minimal detergency action and with certain types of cotton it may be necessary to give a pre-scour followed by thorough washing. Any carry-over of alkali can lead to difficulty in pH control.

As an alternative to pre-scouring an aftertreatment with boiling soap and soda generally improves the permanence of the white and confers good wettability to the bleached material. Fats and waxes partially degraded by chlorite, but still in the form of an impermeable layer on the fibres, are removed rapidly by such an alkaline boil. Although the whiteness of well-bleached cloth may be slightly improved by this treatment, that of poorly bleached cloth may be impaired.

With the exception of pad–steam equipment, which gives short retention times, bleaching with sodium chlorite can be carried out in most systems. Typical application conditions are given below, these being subdivided according to the various types of equipment. In all formulae sodium chlorite expressed as 100% strength; though never supplied as such, recipes can be readily adjusted for commercial solid or liquid products.

2.16.2 Liquor Circulation Systems

Systems providing liquor circulation through static material are the kier, package and beam machines.

The most suitable kiers for sodium chlorite bleaching are those lined with ceramic tiles and fitted with a pump and piping made of similar material. It is also necessary to fabricate the base grids from ceramic material, and this has a limiting effect on the weight of cloth that may be loaded into the kier. The maximum weight is usually in the range of 1.5–2 tonnes. Direct steam may be used for heating. The full sequence of operations includes:
(a) Pretreatment
(b) Wash into kier
(c) Sodium chlorite bleach in kier
(d) Soap and soda ash scald
(e) Wash out of kier.

The chemicals normally used for kier bleaching are sodium chlorite (0.8–1.5% o.w.f.) and anhydrous sodium dihydrogen phosphate (NaH$_2$PO$_4$) (0.25–0.5% o.w.f.). A wetting agent is also usually required.

Chemicals should be dissolved in cold water in a separate stock tank with formic acid added immediately before use to enable the pH to be adjusted to between 3.8–4.2.

The fabric entering the automatic piler of the kier should not contain more than its own weight of moisture as this would interfere with the thorough saturation of the fabric by the bleaching liquor. Having loaded the kier, the liquor should be circulated for 15–20 min to obtain uniformity throughout the fabric.

The temperature of the bleach liquor should then be raised to 80–85°C in 1–1.5 h and maintained for a further 2–3 h. The pH of the bleaching liquor should be periodically checked and, when necessary, adjusted with suitably diluted formic acid.

On heavy fabrics that are difficult to bleach, it is better to give two treatments with, for example, 0.5–1.0% o.w.f. sodium chlorite, rather than one treatment with 1.5%. An intermediate wash is required between the first and second sodium chlorite treatments, entailing repacking the kier after the wash. Cotton as fabric, yarn or in loose form may be processed in package machines with similar regard given to pretreatments and aftertreatments, as in kier processing. Generally package and beam machines are constructed of stainless steel, so appropriate care must be taken to minimise corrosion. These machines operate with liquor ratios of between 5:1 and 8:1 and it is considered best to base chemical additions on liquor volume. Chemical requirements are:

(a) Sodium chlorite, 1.5–3 g/l
(b) Sodium dihydrogen phosphate (anhydrous), 0.5–1 g/l
(c) Sodium nitrate, 1–2 g/l.

As in kier bleaching a wetting agent is required and formic acid added to give pH 3.8–4.2.

When cotton is entered dry, the liquor should be circulated cold for 10 min and the pH then adjusted by addition of dilute acid. The temperature is then raised to 80–85°C and maintained for 1–2 h. Aftertreatments are quite widely used following kier and package machine bleaching. The fabric, still hot, may be taken out of the kier and passed through a washing machine containing 5 g/l soda ash and 1 g/l soap or detergent at a temperature of 80°C. Alternatively this treatment can be carried out in the kier or package machine. The fabric should then be thoroughly washed in fresh water.

While the above methods of bleaching with sodium chlorite may be used for fabrics containing dyed yarn effects, such as coloured stripes and borders, all colours should be tested for fastness before processing in bulk. Only certain dyes, e.g. selected members of the azoic and vat ranges, will be found compatible with the sodium chlorite bleaching process.

2.16.3 Winch Bleaching

Winches used for bleaching with chlorite should have a fume extractor fitted to remove chlorine dioxide fumes.

The liquor ratio may vary between 10:1 and 25:1, and at these ratios pre-scouring is seldom required. The usual sequence of operation is:

(a) Pretreatment (when required)
(b) Wash
(c) Bleach with sodium chlorite
(d) Wash
(e) Antichlor treatment (if necessary)
(f) Wash
(g) Soap and soda ash scald
(h) Wash.

Chemical requirements, influenced by fabric quality, are in the range:

(a) Sodium chlorite, 0.8–2.5 g/l
(b) Sodium dihydrogen phosphate (anhydrous), 1 g/l
(c) Sodium nitrate, 1–3 g/l.

The goods are run through liquor containing these chemicals for 5–10 min and formic acid is then added to give a pH of 3.8–4.2. The temperature should be raised gradually to 80–85°C and running continued for 1.5–2.5 h. The pH of the bleaching solution should be checked periodically and when necessary adjusted with suitably diluted formic acid.

After bleaching the fabric should be washed thoroughly prior to a treatment for 15–30 min at 80–85°C with

(a) Soda ash, 1–2 g/l
(b) Soap, 1 g/l.

This treatment hydrolyses degraded or partially degraded fats and waxes and improves absorbency; it should be followed by thorough rinsing. A softening agent may be used in the final rinse, if required.

When an antichlor treatment is required, e.g. prior to dyeing, sodium perborate (tetrahydrate) or sodium carbonate peroxyhydrate should be substituted for the soda ash. This process may be used for fabrics with certain dyed yarn effects, including those dyed with azoic and vat dyes. All colours should be tested before bleaching.

Winch bleaching with chlorite provides fabric of low fluidity with low weight loss.

2.16.4 Jig Bleaching

Enclosed jigs should be used, if possible, to minimise loss of chlorine dioxide to the surrounding atmosphere. Chemical requirements, based on fabric weight, are similar to those for kier bleaching.

2.16.5 Continuous Bleaching

As it is not possible to achieve very rapid bleaching with sodium chlorite, continuous bleaching can be performed only in equipment capable of providing a bleaching time at 85–90°C of at least 1 h, and preferably a few hours.

As in all continuous processes the fabric is impregnated first with sodium chlorite bleaching liquor. Chemical requirements are:
(a) Sodium chlorite, 0.8–2.5% o.w.f.
(b) Sodium dihydrogen phosphate (anhydrous), 0.3–0.5% o.w.f.
(c) Sodium nitrate, 0.2–0.3% o.w.f.
(d) Wetting agent, as required
(e) Formic acid to give pH 3.0–5.5.

The lower pH is needed when bleaching well prepared fabric.

In continuous production the impregnated cloth is heated and then held at 85–90°C for a period of 1–6 h.

The continuous bleaching systems can also use the activators referred to previously. With these the fabric is impregnated with a near neutral bleach liquor and acidity will develop during bleaching. After the fabric is bleached it is passed through an open soaper range for a soap or detergent and soda ash scour, followed by hot and cold water washing.

The general principles of this bleaching process are applicable also to linen, cotton, cotton/viscose blends, viscose and cellulose acetate.

2.16.6 Cold Pad–Batch Bleaching

Cold pad–batch bleaching can be carried out on loom-state or desized fabric. The basis of the process is simple impregnation of the fabric with sodium chlorite bleaching liquor. The temperature of cloth and bleaching liquor should be in the range 20–25°C. Bleaching takes place over a long period and activation is obtained by slow release of acidity. It is vital to obtain saturation and penetration, and to achieve uniform application of the bleaching liquor, this being assisted by the use of a good wetting agent. The concentration required depends upon the type of cloth and preparatory treatment. Best results are obtained by using a proportioning unit with two supply tanks, and a mixing vessel to facilitate the feeding of liquor to the mangle box.

A solution of sodium chlorite, soda ash and wetting agent is contained in one stock tank and a solution of activator in another. These are blended together in the mixing box so that the bleaching liquor is supplied, as required, to the mangle box. The concentrations of the two solutions are adjusted to suit the proportioning unit capacities. This arrangement gives superior conditions to those obtained from one stock tank, where activation begins at the moment of mixing. When the bleaching liquor is made up in one solution its stability is somewhat limited. A useful activator for this process is formaldehyde, with the saturator liquor providing the following chemicals.

For Loom-state Fabric
(a) Sodium chlorite, 1.5–2% o.w.f.
(b) Soda ash, 0.05–0.1% o.w.f.
(c) Wetting agent, as required
(d) Formaldehyde (40%), 0.3% o.w.f.

For Desized and Well-scoured Fabric
(a) Sodium chlorite, 0.6–0.8% o.w.f.
(b) Soda ash, 0.05–0.1% o.w.f.
(c) Wetting agent, as required
(d) Formaldehyde (40%), 0.2% o.w.f.

The amount of soda ash required is best determined by works trials. The quantity may require seasonal adjustment as at cooler ambient temperatures the saturator liquor is more stable. Generally the addition of 0.05–0.1% soda ash provides the required balance between stability of the saturator liquor and bleaching activity. Excess soda inhibits activation of the chlorite and consequently little bleaching occurs.

It is important that liquor pick-up by the fabric should be reasonably high, e.g. 85–100%, and that the fabric should be taken off the mangle in batch form. The batch should be covered with polyethylene film and tied onto the batch roller to form a complete enclosure before overnight storage. To prevent seepage of liquor from top to bottom of the batch slow rotation overnight is recommended; hot soaping off is then required. Desized and well-scoured fabric can be passed through an open soaper for hot and cold water washing. For large batch working, the first section of the soaper and the area over the batch should be hooded, and an extraction fan provided. Small batches can be put on an enclosed jig for hot and cold water washing. A short steaming for loom-state fabric is beneficial, e.g. on an enclosed jig with the fabric run for four passes through steam. The process then continues with a hot wash followed by four passes through a hot soda ash and soap liquor containing 5 g/l soda ash and 1 g/l soap or detergent. Finally there is hot and cold washing in fresh water.

Whilst application by a pad mangle is desirable, the process is capable of modification to suit individual requirements, e.g. for single batch working impregnation can take place on a suitable jig. Two or three passes ensure thorough penetration and, by experience of the quantity of solution required, the surplus liquor to be discarded need not be excessive.

2.17 HYDROGEN PEROXIDE BLEACHING

A prime advantage of hydrogen peroxide bleaching is the wide range of conditions over which it can be used for bleaching cellulosic textiles. However, as with hypochlorite and chlorite, correct process control is essential.

Although considerable progress has been made in the optimisation of bleaching conditions, the bleaching mechanism is not fully understood. The reason for this is the heterogeneous nature of the process and lack of absolute knowledge about the coloured matters that are destroyed. It is well known that hydrogen peroxide can break down into water and oxygen (Scheme 2.6). However, it is most unlikely that

$$2H_2O_2 \longrightarrow 2H_2O + O_2$$

Scheme 2.6

bleaching can be attributed to such a simple mechanism. Practical experience indicates that this direct decomposition is most undesirable, with liberated oxygen having little bleaching, rather a fibre damaging, effect.

On the basis that the rate of bleaching with hydrogen peroxide increases with rise in pH, it was proposed that the bleaching action is due to the perhydroxyl anion formed by ionisation (Scheme 2.7).

$$H_2O_2 \longrightarrow HO_2^- + H^+$$

Scheme 2.7

It is probable that the pigments responsible for the natural colour of cotton contain a chromophoric system of conjugated double bonds. These will be attacked by a free radical system and it has been proposed by Cates and Taher [11, 12] that

Scheme 2.8

peroxide bleaching takes place by such a mechanism (Scheme 2.8). Such free radicals might be produced by reaction of hydrogen peroxide with an electron donor, possibly derived from a metal cation or from a perhydroxyl anion. The reaction mechanism proposed is shown in Scheme 2.9.

(a) $H_2O_2 \longrightarrow H^+ + HO_2^-$

(b) $M^2 + H_2O_2 \longrightarrow M^{3+} + HO^- + HO\cdot$

Or   (c) $HO_2^- + H_2O_2 \longrightarrow HO_2^- + HO\cdot + HO^-$

(d) $HO\cdot + H_2O_2 \longrightarrow HO_2\cdot + H_2O$

(e) $HO_2 + M^{3+} \longrightarrow M^{2+} + O_2 + H^+$

Scheme 2.9

The free radicals are considered to induce decomposition through a chain mechanism. The decomposition within a given time interval is limited by the level of colour-bearing impurities or by inhibiting metal cations. The latter appear to protect the cellulose from chemical damage by minimising the production of molecular oxygen in the alkaline medium.

While absolute mechanisms are not fully understood, the bleacher still relies on control systems developed empirically. This control is often termed stabilisation. Reference to stabilisation in the context of alkaline peroxide bleaching should not be confused with the use of chemicals to give the commercial product stability during storage. These latter compounds are effective at about pH 4.5–5, the pH at which commercial hydrogen peroxide solutions are most stable. Correct process stabilisation conditions control the rate of bleaching and ensure a residual peroxide content prior to washing-off, while making the most economic use of the chemicals. In this way the required standards of whiteness with minimum chemical damage are obtained. In effect four parameters require to be balanced: time, temperature, alkalinity and stabiliser content. Each of these factors will now be considered.

2.17.1 Alkalinity

When peroxide bleaching cotton and its blends, the alkali added activates the peroxide bleaching and provides a scouring action. Bleaching processes are most effective when carried out within the pH range 10.5–11, since above this level peroxide bleach liquors are overactivated, giving excessive wasteful breakdown to water and oxygen. If a pH lower than 10.5 is used the bleaching activity is very slow. In practice the pH falls during a bleaching cycle as acidic by-products are formed and alkali is absorbed by the cellulose. A compromise is obtained between excess alkalinity at the start and an adequate final level. Below pH 9.5 bleaching is negligible. Alkalinity is usually provided by caustic soda, soda ash or phosphate. Sodium silicate, when used as a stabiliser, adds to the total alkali. The actual concentrations required are best determined by preliminary laboratory bleaching trials with the conditions optimised subsequently under plant conditions.

2.17.2. Stabilisers

The activity of the peroxide bleaching liquor brought about by addition of alkali is controlled by the action of stabiliser additives. The function of these chemicals is mainly two-fold. Firstly they act as buffers; secondly they serve to inactivate impurities, particularly metallic, which tend to cause catalytic decomposition of hydrogen peroxide. These impurities, the most common of which are copper and iron, can be introduced into the bleaching system from the fabric, water supply or chemicals used.

The stabilisers first used in bleaching cellulosic fibres with peroxide were the colloidal sodium silicates. These are highly effective and have an additional advantage of being comparatively low in cost. Metasilicate (Na_2SiO_3) may be used, and in some applications has been found to wash-out more readily than the colloidal sili-·cate. Recently the use of orthosilicates with a 2:1 $Na_2O:SiO_2$ ratio have been described [13]. In using either of these forms more caustic soda than provided by the colloidal silicate is in effect being added, and appropriate allowance must be made. Sodium silicates alone have little stabilising action and the presence of magnesium salts is generally necessary. These may be present to a sufficient extent in the cotton being processed, or may be present as salts in hard water supplies. When bleaching with soft water it may be necessary to add small amounts of magnesium in the form of sulphate or chloride.

Over the years there has been considerable discussion on the role of silicates in peroxide bleaching, particularly on their effectiveness to control iron and copper contamination. The following mechanism has been proposed:
(a) The silicates may form a silica gel with high specific surface area or colloidal magnesium silicate may be formed by reaction with magnesium salts, either of which product can absorb metallic impurities

(b) Silicate itself can complex with hydrogen peroxide to form unstable peroxides
(c) Silicate may bind free radicals formed in the presence of some metallic
    catalysts, and whether the addition of calcium or magnesium salts supports this
    action depends on the nature of the metallic catalyst
(d) Silicate may not only stabilise the peroxide but may also increase the efficiency
    of bleaching through the formation of peroxysilicate.

Most of the research work on the mechanism of stabilisation has been done
under long liquor conditions. Thus the proposed mechanisms may not be applicable
to the systems in which short liquors are employed. However, the simple explanation of magnesium silicate formation provides only a partial understanding of their
action.

When using silicates in peroxide bleaching it is important to establish correct
balance between the silica (SiO_2) content derived from the silicate and the sodium
oxide (Na_2O) content derived from the alkali and the silicate. The ratio in any formula can be calculated simply using the information given in Table 2.2. The proportions of Na_2O and SiO_2 shown may be used to calculate the total amounts in a
bleaching liquor. Thus in a typical long liquor bleaching formulation the
$Na_2O:SiO_2$ ratio is determined as follows:

– Sodium silicate (sp. gr. 1.4)   7 g/l provides 2.03 g/l SiO_2; 0.62 g/l Na_2O
– Caustic soda   0.5 g/l provides   0.39 g/l Na_2O
– Soda ash   1.8 g/l provides   1.04 g/l Na_2O

  Total SiO_2 and Na_2O is   2.03 g/l SiO_2; 2.05 g/l Na_2O

The above system therefore provides a 1:1 ratio of Na_2O to SiO_2.

TABLE 2.2

**Relative Na_2O and SiO_2 Concentrations in Peroxide
Bleaching Liquors**

Product	Na_2O (%)	SiO_2 (%)
Sodium orthosilicate (Na_4SiO_4)	67.4	32.6
Sodium metasilicate ($Na_2SiO_3 . 5H_2O$)	29.0	28.2
Colloidal sodium silicate (sp. gr. 1.4)	8.8	29.0
Caustic soda	77.5	
Soda ash	58.0	

The use of sodium silicate requires the provision of good washing-off facilities
after bleaching in order to prevent problems caused by residual silicates. Consequently, although sodium silicate is both effective and economic, there has been
considerable interest in the use of alternative materials for peroxide stabilisation.
There are now available several auxiliary products, generally known as organic or

non-silicate stabilisers. They are blends of organic materials with or without magnesium salts, and are mainly of three chemical types: organic sequestering agents, protein degradation products and certain surfactants. The commercial products are either designed to give stabilisation only or to combine stabilisation with other actions, such as detergency and softening. The use of these products was found particularly advantageous for long liquor processing in package machines, winches and jig machines. Washing-off processes were simplified with saving in processing time by the use of organic acids, e.g. acetic acid to neutralise residual alkali with no danger of precipitating silicates.

With the first generation of organic stabilisers the whiteness obtainable in the complete absence of silicate was a little inferior to that resulting from silicate stabilisation, though fully adequate for subsequent dyeing. Organic stabilisers were less suitable for pad–steam processes and it was usually necessary to include some silicate into the formulation, though less was needed than when using silicate alone. In recent years new products have been developed. These can be used without silicate in many continuous pad–steam processes, and allow bleaching to full whites without silicate addition on many fabrics.

The degree of preparation prior to peroxide bleaching influences the concentrations of alkali and stabiliser used.

Where pretreatment is limited to the removal of size by enzyme or aqueous extraction the presence in the cotton of natural impurities assists the stabilising of the bleaching liquor. However, acid pretreatment for removal of starches or other metallic impurities also removes natural calcium and magnesium complexes from the cotton. Under such conditions it may be necessary to increase the amount of magnesium sulphate added to the bleach liquor. Where alkaline boiling of the cotton precedes hydrogen peroxide bleaching, alkali addition to the bleach liquor other than silicate is normally low and in some cases may be omitted altogether.

The use of organic sequestering agents, e.g. DTPA, may be advantageous when small quantities of copper and iron are present in the bleaching system. Products of this type are less effective in the presence of high localised concentrations of metal impurity. It has recently been reported [14] that polyphosphates and EDTA eliminate or reduce the catalytic degradation resulting from metal ions, but only in baths stabilised with sodium silicate and magnesium ions. Experience indicates that this is not always the case, though it is acknowledged that silicates do play a major role in controlling catalytic metals during peroxide bleaching. Contamination, which under otherwise satisfactory bleaching conditions would give rise to catalytic damage, is best controlled by pretreatment and the use of less severe bleaching conditions, particularly in regard to alkalinity, temperature and time.

2.17.3 Temperature and Time

The general pattern for long processes is to keep alkali and temperature down. Continuous bleaching processing depends on a very rapid heating of fabrics. It is often necessary to adjust alkalinity in conjunction with time and temperature. At the other end of the scale, in high-temperature pressurised bleaching systems the time of bleaching is reduced to 1–2 min.

2.17.4 Kier Bleaching

The traditional kier used for alkaline scouring may be of vertical or horizontal design, although the hydrogen peroxide bleaching process is more easily adapted to the vertical kiers which have fabric capacities of 1–2 tonnes.

Where indirect kier heating is not available the puffer and steam injector type of heating system may cause excessive superheating at the point of steam entry, plus dilution and potential pollution from impurities in the steam. This necessitates restriction of bleaching temperatures to a maximum of 80°C, so limiting bleaching efficiency.

The kier pump and heaters are usually constructed of cast iron and mild steel. To permit use with hydrogen peroxide the kier itself requires a silicate/cement lining whilst the pump, heater and external pipes are passivated by circulating a boiling solution containing sodium silicate and magnesium sulphate.

The sequence of operations for kier bleaching is:
(a) Preliminary desizing or preparatory treatment
(b) Wash into kier
(c) Hydrogen peroxide bleach in kier
(d) Soda ash scald in kier
(e) Wash out of kier.

Prior to peroxide bleaching any of the desizing processes, referred to previously, can be used. A few relevant comments are made below.

Enzyme application must be followed by thorough hot and cold washing because carry-over of degraded starch or residual enzyme into the peroxide bleach liquor will reduce the bleach liquor stability.

Acid treatments are particularly advantageous for kier processing, since in addition to having a desizing action by hydrolysis of the starch the ash content of the fibre can be reduced considerably.

A pretreatment with a stabilised solution of sodium hypochlorite (2.7 g/l available chlorine with 5 g/l soda ash) is an effective means of degrading starch for subsequent removal in hydrogen peroxide bleaching.

When, because of particular mill conditions, the desired effect cannot be obtained by using the combined scour and bleach kier process, oxidative desizing may be a useful pretreatment to aid seed removal. Alternatively it may be necessary to pre-scour with caustic soda. In such cases, the caustic pretreatment may be less severe than that applied prior to hypochlorite bleaching. After such a caustic scour it is necessary to remove the fabric from the kier for washing and, if possible, souring. It is then piled back into the same or, more conveniently, a second kier for bleaching.

The necessity to consider the use of the caustic pretreatment to remove fats and waxes can in many cases be eliminated by the addition of a suitable detergent surfactant to the desizing process and/or to the hydrogen peroxide kier liquor. These auxiliary products must be selected to provide low-foaming conditions during the circulation of the kier liquor.

Chemical requirements for hydrogen peroxide bleaching in kiers are:
(a) Sodium silicate (79°Tw), 2–3% o.w.f.

(b) Caustic soda, 0.6–1.4% o.w.f.
      or caustic soda, 0.3–0.8% o.w.f. with soda ash, 0.6–1.0% o.w.f.
(c) Hydrogen peroxide (35%), 3–5% o.w.f.
      or hydrogen peroxide (50%), 2–3.5% o.w.f.
(d) Wetting agent, as required.

The caustic soda is omitted from the above formula when the cloth has been pre-scoured in caustic soda, silicate and soda ash only being required.

In operating the kier process the chemicals should be dissolved in a separate stock tank; magnesium salts should be added to soft water, or as required after acidic pretreatment, prior to other chemicals.

The alkalis should be added to about one-third of the total water required, with boiling to complete dissolution. The remainder of the water is then added cold to reduce the temperature to about 50°C, with the peroxide being added as the cold water runs in.

The fabric is preferably fed into the kier through an automatic piler with the bleach liquor circulating through the system. When the kier is about half full sufficient steam should be turned on to obtain a temperature of 40–45°C on completion of loading. The temperature should then be raised to 65–70°C in not less than 30 min; steam and circulation is then turned off to allow the load to 'rest' for 10 min, and to expel any air pockets.

The temperature is then raised to 80°C and the load rested again. (If a pressure kier is used it can then be clamped down and the temperature raised to the level required.) After reaching maximum temperature and pressure, the bleaching time normally lasts 2–3 h. With puffer or steam injection heating, where maximum temperatures will vary in the range 65–80°C, a longer time of from 5–8 h is necessary. The steady increase in activation by careful temperature control ensures even bleaching throughout the packed kier. At the end of the bleach cycle 10–20% of the initial peroxide should remain.

To improve whiteness, absorbency and quality of the finish, residual peroxide can be decomposed *in situ*, when most of the peroxide liquor has been drained from the kier, by running in a hot solution containing 2% o.w.f. soda ash and maintaining circulation at a temperature of 80–85°C for 0.5–1 h. Detergents and/or sequestering agents can be added to the soda ash solution to give improved results under certain conditions.

Where no soda ash aftertreatment is given the fabric can be withdrawn directly from the kier through standard washers. Any cooling prior to withdrawal should be gradual as the running of cold water onto the hot fabric is not advised. Rapid cooling tends to fix silicates in the fabric.

2.17.5 Colour Wovens

Hydrogen peroxide bleach can be used to advantage on goods containing dyed yarns. The omission of an efficient pre-boil leads to difficulties with traditional hypochlorite bleaching methods and many dyes are not fast to chlorite bleaching. The hydrogen peroxide process bleaches the white ground without any loss of

colour. In general milder conditions are used; caustic soda is omitted and temperatures are limited to a maximum of 80°C. Pretreatment with mild hypochlorite (e.g. 2.5 g/l available chlorine) is very useful for partially dyed fabrics.
Chemical requirements for bleaching are:
(a) Sodium silicate (79°Tw), 2–3% o.w.f.
(b) Soda ash, 1–1.5% o.w.f.
(c) Wetting agent, as required
(d) Hydrogen peroxide (35%), 2–4 o.w.f.
    or hydrogen peroxide (50%), 1.4–2.8% o.w.f.

The method of solution preparation and kier loading is as detailed for white goods, but with a lower operating temperature. Having loaded the kier the liquor is circulated and the temperature raised to 70°C in 2 h. This temperature is maintained for 1–2 h, after which bleaching is allowed to continue for several hours, usually overnight, without further heating.

2.17.6 Package Machine Bleaching
Similar processes are used for loose cotton or yarns, and for fabric processed on beam machines. When bleaching grey undyed cotton yarns that are wound to form cones, cops, cheeses or beams it is important that the yarn should not be wound too tightly (recommended density 0.5 g/cm³). Pretreatment of the yarn is generally necessary only for unusually dark brown cotton or heavily contaminated condenser yarn. For these dark yarns pretreatment may be with dilute hypochlorite.
    The use of organic stabilisers is particularly advantageous in the bleaching of cotton on a package machine, since it eliminates any possible problems arising from the deposition of insoluble silicates that may be filtered out by the yarn package.
    In the case of cotton yarns, where production of a soft handle is of importance, the circulation of a solution containing 2 g/l sodium tri-polyphosphate and a little wetting agent at 90°C for 5–10 min prior to bleaching is recommended. This pretreatment serves to remove any dirt or surface impurities and also to assist in the prevention of deposition of calcium and magnesium salts in the package.
    Typical chemical requirement for a package machine bleach are:
(a) Sodium silicate (79°Tw), 7 g/l
(b) Caustic soda, 0.5 g/l
(c) Soda ash, 1.8 g/l
(d) Wetting agent, as required
(e) Hydrogen peroxide (35%), 13ml/l
    or hydrogen peroxide (50%), 8 ml/l.

A bleach liquor of comparable strength utilising an organic stabiliser contains:
(a) Organic stabiliser (according to manufacturers' recommendations), 0.5–2 g/l
(b) Caustic soda, 0.5–1 g/l
(c) Wetting agent, as required
(d) Hydrogen peroxide (35%), 13 ml/l
    or hydrogen peroxide (50%), 8 ml/l.

For cotton knitting yarns it is often possible to reduce drastically the quantity of sodium silicate added, in some cases down to 2 g/l, though for these yarns an organic stabiliser is preferred.

For high-temperature bleaching, where advantage can be taken of shorter schedules, alkalinity can be increased and silicate concentrations lowered.

When bleaching in package machines the liquor should be introduced into the machine at a temperature not higher than 55°C. The temperature can then be raised to 90°C in 20–30 min and this temperature is maintained for a period of 1–2 h, by which time bleaching should be completed. After the liquor has been removed from the vessel the yarn is rinsed by circulation of first hot and then cold water.

Liquor is introduced into high-temperature machines at a maximum of 55°C. The temperature is first raised to 80°C in 20 min and the machine closed. The temperature is then elevated to 120°C (or to the machine limit, if lower) in 20 min and maintained at this level for a further 20 min. Prior to this stage it may be advantageous in some machines if compressed air is introduced at 1.5–2 atm (when the machine is closed) to prevent cavitation in the pump and consequent poor liquor circulation.

One way in which peroxide bleaching economies can be improved when using package machines is by the regeneration of bleach liquors. Instead of discharging to drain, at the end of a bleach cycle the liquor is pumped to a storage tank and, after cooling, brought to its initial strength by the addition of hydrogen peroxide and alkali.

2.17.7 Winch Bleaching

All the comments relating to non-pressurised package machine bleaching apply to winch bleaching. Although generally a longer liquor ratio is used in the winch, the formulae indicated for package machines are applicable. It is important that the fabric should be fully wet out before the bleach liquor temperature is raised above 50°C.

2.17.8 Jig Bleaching

Because of the low liquor ratio in normal jig processing it is usually necessary when bleaching in this type of equipment to give the fabric some type of pretreatment. Fouling of the liquor will rapidly occur if a considerable proportion of the size content of the cloth is not removed prior to bleaching, and bleaching will not be efficient. It has been found advantageous also to treat the cloth in a soda ash solution on completion of bleaching. The sequence of operations, therefore, comprises the first two or all of the following three stages:

(a) Preliminary desizing or preparatory treatment and wash-off
(b) Hydrogen peroxide bleaching in the jig
(c) Soda ash scalding.

The final washing-off and neutralisation stages are simplified by the use of organic stabilisers when bleaching cotton fabric in the jig, as it is possible to introduce a weak organic acid, e.g. acetic acid, immediately after the first end rinsing. This is not possible after sodium silicate stabilisation because of the danger of precipitating insoluble silicates.

Modern stainless steel jigs are best for peroxide bleaching. However, the older cast iron or mild steel varieties can be coated with silicate and cement. It is important that no copper, brass or iron components are present in any piece of the equipment that will come into contact with the hydrogen peroxide solution. Bushes and bearings of the guide roller under the surface of the liquor should be carefully examined to ensure that they are not constructed of these metals.

The degree and nature of the pretreatment given depends, to some extent, on the type of fabric and the type and quantity of the size resent on the fabric. Standard desizing treatments may be used. Frequently treatment with sodium hypochlorite will be adequate, the fabric being impregnated on the jig with a solution of sodium hypochlorite (equivalent to 2.7 g/l average chlorine) containing 5.0 g/l soda ash together with a suitable wetting agent. The fabric should be allowed to lie for a minimum of 30 min and then washed-off before bleaching with hydrogen peroxide. The composition of the bleaching solution depends on the degree of whiteness required and type of fabric.

Chemical requirements are usually within the following ranges, the higher quantities being for a full white.

Based on Silicate Stabiliser
(a) Sodium silicate (79°Tw), 3.0–5.0% o.w.f.
(b) Caustic soda, 0.25–0.8% o.w.f.
(c) Soda ash, up to 1.0% o.w.f.
(d) Hydrogen peroxide (35%), 2.0–5.0% o.w.f.
    or hydrogen peroxide (50%), 1.4–3.5% o.w.f.

Based on Organic Stabiliser
(a) Organic stabiliser (as recommended by supplier), 1.0–1.5% o.w.f.
(b) Caustic soda, 0.75–1.5% o.w.f.
(c) Hydrogen peroxide (35%), 2.0–5.0% o.w.f.
    or hydrogen peroxide (50%), 1.4–3.5% o.w.f.

To provide uniformity over the full length of the fabric it is recommended that all the alkali and half the hydrogen peroxide be added at the start of the bleaching cycle and the remainder of the peroxide added by a drip feed whilst the first end is being run. In the absence of a suitable drip feed arrangement the peroxide may be added half way through the first end or at the start of the second end. To prevent premature activation the bleach liquor temperature should not exceed 50°C during the first end. The temperature is raised to the boil by 20°C intervals over the first three ends and then maintained at the boil. After bleaching the fabric is thoroughly washed-off with or without an intermediate soda ash treatment.

The soda ash scald is of advantage when the fabric is to be given a high-quality finishing treatment. On completion of the hydrogen peroxide bleaching stage the liquor is dropped and, without intermediate rinsing, a hot solution containing 2% o.w.f. soda ash is run in. At least two ends should be given in the soda ash liquor at a temperature of 80°C, followed by washing-off.

2.17.9 Continuous Bleaching

Hydrogen peroxide bleaching processes for continuous operations were introduced in the late 1930s by American peroxide producers Becco and Du Pont. Many developments in machinery have taken place since that time, these taking advantage of the ability to use hydrogen peroxide under accelerated conditions at elevated temperature. Today a large proportion of fabric is bleached with hydrogen peroxide by continuous methods in rope or open-width form. Choice of process is dependent both upon fabric construction and production requirements, e.g. open-width treatment is preferred for poplins and sateens. Although a throughput of 100000 m weekly usually justifies pad–batch processing, for fully continuous rope or open-width bleaches not less than 500000 m a week is required.

The general principles of continuous processing fully apply when using hydrogen peroxide. This chemical can be used in a single preparation stage or it can be combined with one or more of the following processes:
(a) Desizing
(b) Alkaline scouring
(c) Sodium hypochlorite pretreatment
(d) Acid souring.

Much attention has been given to reducing the number of process stages in order to minimise plant investment and to provide savings in energy and water costs. The extent to which processing stages can be reduced depends on grey fabric quality and the preparation standards required, particularly whiteness, absorbency and seed removal. Much can be done by taking full regard of the relationships between stabilisation, alkalinity, time and temperature [15]. The most usual limitation is inadequate seed removal in the absence of an alkaline pretreatment. Oxidative desizing with hydrogen peroxide or a persulphate can minimise the need for separate hot alkaline scouring [16].

Some other differences between long liquor and short liquor bleaching warrant mention. In pad–steam processes sodium silicate provides the best stabilisation of the bleaching system and, until recently, was the only effective stabiliser. However, the organic stabilisers have been developed to an extent that silicate can be eliminated entirely from many bleaching processes and considerably reduced for others [17]. The alternative method for minimising silicate deposition is the use of the so-called silicate dispersants. These minimise, and in some cases completely eliminate, deposition of silicate onto machinery and fabric.

One technique popular in the USA is the use of two steamers alternated each week for caustic scouring and peroxide bleaching. Any silicate deposition onto machinery during the bleaching period is cleared by the caustic scour. Washing conditions play a major role in the adequacy or otherwise of silicate removal. Hot washing, preferably with added soda ash in the first wash boxes, is most desirable. Cooling of the fabric between bleaching and washing should be avoided.

Magnesium salts are beneficial in long liquor bleaching, but in short liquors with ratio 1:1 or less the presence of salts imparting hardness to water is of little or no advantage [18]. An exception to this may be found if goods are given acidic pretreatments that can remove natural bleach stabilising impurities. In long liquors caustic soda and soda ash mixture is often useful as the Na_2O content can be increased without raising the pH too far. Under pad–steam conditions no advantage is obtained by introducing soda ash. In fact it may well be deleterious because the stability of stock solutions can be impaired.

One further important factor is steam quality. When fabric is maintained at a high temperature for more than a few minutes the steam used for heating in the scouring and bleaching stages must not contain more than 3°C superheat. Failure to take this precaution can lead to degradation of the cellulose, particularly in the presence of metallic contaminations. Excessive superheat can be produced by rapid reduction of steam pressure and occurs when pressurised steam (over 3 atm) is fed directly to a steam spray pipe. It is recommended that high-pressure steam should be reduced to a pressure of 1 atm (15 p.s.i. gauge) some distance away from the bleaching machinery. An adequate length of unlagged piping should be used so that any superheat developed will be lost before the steam comes into contact with fabric containing bleaching liquor.

Chemical requirements depend on fabric quality and pretreatment. The formulations shown in Table 2.3 give a general indication of conditions for 100% cotton fabrics that have had a caustic scour or peroxide oxidative desize prior to bleaching. Where no such pretreatment has been given it is usually necessary to increase amounts of alkali and hydrogen peroxide by 50%. The silicate may be partially or wholly replaceable by an organic stabiliser.

TABLE 2.3

Chemical Requirements for Continuous Peroxide Bleaching

	J-box conveyor & pad roll	Short J-box & U-box	Roller bed	Pressure steamer
Sodium silicate (79°Tw) (% o.w.f.)	0.5–1.5	1.5–2.0	1.5–3.0	1.0–2.0
Sequestrant (% o.w.f.)	0.01–0.1	0.01–0.1	0.01–0.1	0.01–0.1
Wetting agent (% o.w.f.)	0.2–0.5	0.2–0.5	0.2–0.5	0.2–0.5
Caustic soda (% o.w.f.)	0.2–0.5	0.3–0.6	0.5–1.5	0.2–0.5
Hydrogen peroxide* (% o.w.f.)	0.4–0.8	0.5–1.0	1.0–1.75	1.0–1.5
Time (min)	60–120	10–20	3–10	1–3
Temp. (°C)	95–100	100	100–103	120–130

*Hydrogen peroxide requirements are expressed as 100%, though in practice the equivalent quantity of the 35% or 50% product is used.

2.17.10 Cold Pad–Batch Bleaching

This process consists of padding the grey fabric with a strong solution of alkali and hydrogen peroxide, and storing for several hours, usually overnight, at ambient temperature. An initial attraction of the process, where fabric was jig bleached and dyed, and where padding equipment was available, was the better utilisation of jigs for dyeing. In recent years interest in cold bleaching has increased as it provides a low-energy preparation route.

Fabric can be impregnated with the bleach solution on standard stainless steel pad mangles or open-width washers. Alternatively it can be saturated in two ends of a jig and then left batched up overnight on the jig or on stands.

Cold pad–batch bleaching requires:
1. Control of pad liquor concentration and temperature, preferably $25 \pm 5°C$
2. Minimum 80% liquor pick-up
3. Fabric storage without uneven drainage or surface drying
4. Washing-off at a minimum of 95°C.

A good wetting agent is essential to ensure good penetration of grey fabric by the bleaching liquor, with a detergent auxiliary to aid fat and wax removal and development of good absorbency. The use of vacuum impregnation or steam purging, recently developed by the Shirley Institute, can assist in the application of chemicals to grey non-absorbent fabrics.

The range of chemicals required for cold pad bleaching is:
(a) Sodium silicate (79°Tw), 0.8–1.2% o.w.f.
(b) Organic stabiliser, 0.6–1.0% o.w.f.
(c) Caustic soda flake, 0.8–1.5% o.w.f.
(d) Hydrogen peroxide (35%), 4.0–5.0% o.w.f.

Persulphates can also be added to the cold pad bleaching formula, up to 0.5% o.w.f. These aid the desizing action during bleaching.

Following impregnation the fabric should be batched up, covered with a plastic sheet to prevent drying and left for a period of 15–24 h. The fabric is then scalded-off at 95°C in a washing range or jig (two ends) through a solution of 1% soda ash, to which can be added soap, detergent, or sequestering agent. This alkaline treatment makes a significant improvement to fabric absorbency and increases brightness by 1–2%, compared with washing-off in water only.

2.18 REGENERATED CELLULOSIC FIBRES

One basic difference between cotton and the regenerated cellulosic fibres is the level of impurities. Consequently only a light preparation process is required for fabrics containing 100% regenerated cellulosic fibres; usually desizing with a mild scour or bleach is adequate. The second difference is the lower intrinsic molecular weight and hence greater care required to ensure minimum fibre degradation.

Two types of fibre will be considered, normal or high wet modulus viscose fibres and the acetylated celluloses.

2.18.1 Viscose Fibres

The impurities (apart from size and lubricant) most likely to concern the finisher are sulphur residues and catalytic metals, particularly iron absorbed during fibre manufacture. Sulphur residues are cleared to acceptable levels during a mild hydrogen peroxide bleaching process. The metallic impurities are present usually at a low level and distributed evenly through the fibre; their effect can be controlled by the use of sequestrants.

The form of the viscose will determine the type of equipment used. Yarn is processed in package equipment, while fabric may be processed on the various plants described. The effects of lower intrinsic strength compared with cotton are important, and tension and abrasion should be kept to a minimum. Milder conditions are used, in respect of alkalinity and bleaching agent, than those indicated for cotton. Generally concentrations should not be more than half those indicated for the various cotton bleaching processes.

The polynosic and other high wet modulus fibres have properties more similar to those of cotton than other types of viscose, and they may be subjected to somewhat more severe bleaching processes. Nevertheless certain precautions should be taken in their treatment. Alkali concentrations should not exceed 2% o.w.f., except in long liquors when up to 2 g/l may be used.

The use of the sequestrant DTPA is recommended for peroxide bleaching, the optimum quantity being determined for individual situations.

As an alternative to alkaline hydrogen peroxide or acid chlorite bleaching, peracetic acid can be used. When not available commercially this chemical can be prepared *in situ* using the following chemicals:
(a) Tetrasodium pyrophosphate ($Na_4P_2O_7$), 5.3 g/l
(b) Hydrogen peroxide (35%), 39 ml/l
(c) Caustic soda, 7.6 g/l
(d) Acetic anhydride, 45.6 g/l.

The chemicals, with the solids previously dissolved separately, are added to water in the order given, with continuous stirring. The final solution should be in the pH range 4.5–5.5 and will be about 25 g/l concentration ($CH_3CO.O.OH$). It may be diluted for use after about 30 min. The mixing vessel should be made of stainless steel. This method is only suitable for the preparation of small quantities of dilute peracetic acid. No attempt should be made to make a more concentrated product as there is a possibility of forming hazardous diacetyl peroxides. Only sufficient dilute peracetic acid should be prepared for immediate use because the product at this strength is not suitable for storage.

The 25 g/l stock solution so prepared is diluted to give 0.5–1 g/l peracetic acid (expressed as 100%) and bleaching carried out with the addition of 0.5 g/l sodium hexametaphosphate (($NaPO_3)_6$) and caustic soda to give a liquor pH of 6.5.

Apart from its use in bleaching sensitive regenerated cellulosic fibres, peracetic acid can be used for bleaching colour woven goods.

2.18.2 Cupro Fibres

The manufacturing process for cuprammomium rayon (cupro) gives rise to traces of residual copper salts in the yarn. Considerable care must be exercised in bleaching this fibre. In long liquors the use of disodium magnesium EDTA has been found beneficial in controlling catalytic degradation, which would otherwise occur with alkaline hydrogen peroxide bleaching.

2.18.3 Acetate Fibres

Acetate fibres are available as the diacetate or triacetate forms. The latter are relatively resistant to alkaline treatments. In contrast considerable care must be taken when processing the diacetate, and to avoid saponification a pH of 9.5 should not be exceeded. Saponification changes surface characteristics and, most importantly, the dyeing properties.

Tetrasodium pyrophosphate is preferred for alkaline peroxide processes. Even so, temperature must be limited to a 65°C maximum. Peracetic acid, as indicated for viscose, can be used but the safest chemical is sodium chlorite, since under acidic conditions there is no possibility of hydrolysis.

2.19 COTTON BLENDS

Preparation of cotton blended with other fibres requires removal of the natural and added impurities, including seed, as described for 100% cotton. This must be carried out with regard to the properties of the other fibre or fibres in the blend. The blends usually encountered are those with the regenerated cellulosics and the synthetic nylon and polyester fibres.

2.19.1 Cotton/Viscose Blends

In blends with regenerated cellulosic fibres the main consideration is the greater sensitivity of the regenerated fibre. Frequently the cotton fibre itself will have had good mechanical preparation prior to blending with the viscose. The other extreme may be met with relatively coarse cotton yarns used in conjunction with both acetate or viscose, particularly in furnishing fabrics. Here the differing dye substantivities are of importance in relation to design effects and great care must be taken to avoid hydrolysis of the acetate. Low-temperature combined scouring and bleaching by a cold pad hydrogen peroxide process or a chlorite bleaching process is preferred for such mixtures.

With well prepared cotton, such as is frequently used in knitted fabrics, good results can be obtained by the hydrogen peroxide or chlorite processes described for cotton, though some reduction should be made in chemical concentrations.

2.19.2 Nylon/Cotton Blends

These blends are met as mixed yarns and as fabrics, the latter containing independent cotton and nylon yarns.

Nylon is resistant to alkaline processes, but precautions are necessary when bleaching with either peroxide or chlorine-based bleaches. Some types of nylon are degraded by alkaline peroxide and, to the author's knowledge, no ready classification is possible; each quality must be assessed by preliminary testing. Protective auxiliary products are available commercially which, when added to alkaline hydrogen peroxide bleaching liquors, prevent degradation of the nylon.

The use of chlorine-based bleaches can also lead to fibre degradation because chlorine is retained from reaction with the nitrogenous nylon. Hot antichlor aftertreatments with bisulphite or hydrosulphite reducing agents are required to overcome this problem.

2.19.3 Polyester/Cotton Blends

Polyester/cotton fabrics are generally manufactured from 67/33 or 50/50 blended yarns. In dealing with the processing of these blended fabrics, compared with similar fabrics of 100% cotton, three factors have to be considered.

(a) Polyester fibres are thermoplastic and processing conditions must be selected to minimise the formation of crease marks. In general, therefore, it is preferable to process fabrics in open width, though for some lightweight fabrics rope processing can be considered. In such cases the prevention or removal of creases is assisted by heat-setting or mercerising treatments. The heat setting can be introduced at various stages in fabric processing, before or after bleaching. If it is used as an initial stage the fabric is less susceptible to crease marking during subsequent processing, but some stains present in the woven fabric may be less readily removed. At an intermediate or final stage the heat setting will help to remove any process creasing and may be combined with the heating of the fabric required for dye fixation or resin application.

(b) Polyester fibres can be degraded by caustic alkali, so the conditions of the preparation processes must be carefully controlled, with strict attention to alkali concentration, temperature and time. Manufacturers produce various grades of polyester fibre, which may show differences in resistance fo alkali; specific recommendations on the uses of particular grades of polyester are usually provided. It is common practice not to exceed a level of 1.5% o.w.f. caustic soda. Many polyester/cotton blends contain a high-quality cotton, which results in a fabric with a low seed content. Thus most polyester/cottons can be bleached with a single-stage hydrogen peroxide process without alkaline pretreatment.

(c) Polyester fibres are hydrophobic. This is an important factor to remember with regard to pad application of bleach liquor, as the liquor take-up by a polyester/cotton blend fabric will be different from similarly constructed fabrics of 100% cotton. In general the preparation of polyester/cotton blend fabrics on batch, or semi- or fully continuous plant is essentially the same as for 100% cotton fabrics, apart from restrictions on the use of rope processing as previously indicated. Pretreatments are typically as described for cotton. However, most polyester/cotton fabrics contain sizes other than 100% starch and oxidative desizing techniques may be advantageous. To obtain a well-prepared fabric, with the good absorbent properties required for subsequent pad dyeing or other finishing processes, it is necessary to ensure effective removal of oils and waxes. Ways of ensuring this have been discussed above. The addition of special detergent auxiliaries is very useful in processing polyester/cotton blends, usually eliminating the need for separate alkaline pretreatments. This is particularly so when using alkaline hydrogen peroxide bleaching processes. Since the polyester fibre itself will generally require no bleaching, adequate whiteness of the blended fabric is obtained by bleaching only the cellulosic fibre portion. In practice many polyester/cotton fabrics can be prepared by the rapid bleaching systems, which provide only a 2–3 min retention. This may not be acceptable for 100% cotton because of inadequate seed removal. For sodium chlorite bleaching conditions as given for 100% cotton are used. This system will provide some bleaching of the polyester, but as commented above this is seldom required prior to dyeing, or for a white finish, for which fluorescent whitening agents should be used.

2.20 LINEN

The final cellulosic fibre to be considered is linen, a bast fibre derived from flax. Unbleached flax shows a variation in colour to a greater extent than other natural fibres. This is due to climatic differences during growth and to variable retting conditions. Flax may be retted under water or on the ground, the latter tending to produce a darker heterogeneous fibre that is more difficult to bleach. Control of retting is important. An under-retted flax tends to have a reddish hue while an over-retted flax is almost grey in colour. It must be noted also that over-retting is accompanied by degradation of the cellulose.

The characteristics demanded after bleaching are no less varied than the unbleached material. Required whiteness may range from cream to full white. The presence of woody matter (sprit) that the mechanical operations (scutching and combing) have failed to remove may be desirable for certain uses or tolerated when weight loss must not exceed certain limits. If not removed prior to dyeing, uniformity of colour between sprit and linen can only be obtained by careful dye selection. When full sprit removal and full whiteness on material of high initial sprit content is required, the chemical treatments necessary result in some dissolution of the pectic cements bonding the elementary fibres together. Loss of this bonding results in 'cottonisation' of variable intensity.

Preparation processes are selected to avoid impairment of the special properties of linen and therefore have to strike an acceptable compromise between various criteria:
1. Whiteness
2. Chemical damage
3. Weight loss
4. Sprit removal.

Sprit is not the only impurity to be considered. Metallic impurities (mainly iron) are fairly often present in flax, originating from accidental contamination (rust and grease) or as microscopic iron or iron oxide particles left by earlier processes. The presence of these impurities necessitates the use of sequestering agents, sometimes in large quantities, particularly during processing by pad impregnation.

Linen may be bleached as tow, yarn or fabric. Its preparation is often multistage, using both chlorine- and peroxide-based bleaches. For maximum whiteness the alternative use of these two systems is preferred to repeated use of the same chemical.

Full details of the bleaching processes will not be given. The general considerations relating to control of hydrogen peroxide and chlorite bleaching, as indicated for 100% cotton, apply equally to linen. Chlorine may be used under alkaline conditions, as hypochlorite or as free chlorine, below pH 4.5 for sprit removal. In the latter process chlorination is followed by alkaline scouring, and the sequence is similar to that used for chemical wood pulp bleaching.

Chlorination is preferably carried out before alkaline scouring because certain technical advantages are gained. There is no need to cool the boiled fibre prior to chlorination. Also once the flax has been subjected to alkaline processing it has a fairly high buffering effect during subsequent acidifying processes. Consequently when chlorination follows alkaline boiling there can be a fairly long transition period in the dangerous pH zone (7–4) when hypochlorous acid, which degrades cellulose, is formed.

Gaseous chlorine is preferred for chlorination, although chlorine water may be prepared by acidification of a hypochlorite solution. In the latter case care must be taken to ensure that the pH never exceeds 4–4.5. When chlorination is conducted in a stainless steel apparatus the addition to the solution of 1.5–2 g/l of sodium nitrate as a corrosion inhibitor is recommended. In increasing order of severity, typical processing sequences for linen are as follows.

Two Stages: Scour–Peroxide
Alkaline scouring with up to 8% soda ash or 4% caustic soda (o.w.f.) is followed by a peroxide bleach. This process provides a cream shade with low weight loss (6–10%) and a fluidity of 2.5–3.0.

Two Stages: Hypochlorite–Peroxide
The hypochlorite stage must be maintained at pH 9 by the addition of alkali. It is carried out at ambient temperature (25°C) with 3–4% o.w.f. active chlorine. After rinsing a peroxide bleach follows. This process route will show weight losses of 8–12% and a fluidity of 4–5.

Three Stages: Hypochlorite–Chlorite–Peroxide
Precautions to maintain pH during the hypochlorite stage are required as in the previous process. It gives improved whiteness with little increase in fibre degradation.

Three Stages: Scouring–Chlorite–Peroxide
Good whiteness can be obtained by this sequence by optimising chemical concentrations. Very good washing after alkaline scouring must precede chlorite bleaching, particularly for pad bleaching of fabric.

Four Stages: Chlorination–Scouring–Chlorite–Peroxide
This full sequence is required when sprit is present in the unbleached linen to any significant extent. The acidic chlorination will use up to 9% active chlorine and is carried out at ambient temperature. Concentrations of chemicals in subsequent stages will depend on linen quality and allowed weight loss.

The traditional processes for linen fabrics involve multi-stage boiling with lime and soda ash with intermediate acid treatments and a final hypochlorite bleaching. However, more modern processes based on the guidelines given above, applicable to all linen processing, offer considerable savings in processing times. In fabric processing it is difficult to obtain acidic chlorination by the pad application of chemicals because the low solubility of chlorine does not allow preparation of concentrated chlorine liquors.

The general consideration in bleaching fibre mixtures containing linen is that process conditions must be dictated by the most sensitive fibre. Frequently the linen will be introduced as a partially prepared fibre. Cotton/linen fabrics are processed generally by the methods applicable to 100% cotton.

In blends with polyester or regenerated cellulosic, e.g. polynosic fibres, care must be taken to ensure that the caustic soda content of scouring or bleaching processes does not exceed the level approved by the fibre manufacturer.

2.21 CONTROL OF PREPARATION PROCESSES

Variations in the preparation processes influence subsequent dyeing and ultimate performance in wear. A useful review of the influence of bleaching on the dyeability of cotton fabrics indicates the nature of some of the variables [19]. Typical of the advantageous effects that can be obtained is the use of caustic soda, not necessarily of full mercerising strength, to improve dye yield. At the other end of the scale dye uptake is reduced when oxycellulose is produced. This can arise through the presence of occluded oxygen in alkaline scouring, or by metal-catalysed decomposition of hydrogen peroxide, or in incorrectly controlled hypochlorite bleaching.

There is therefore a need to understand the basic plant control systems that should be used and the tests that can be used for quality control.

2.21.1 Bleach Liquor Concentration

Measurement of bleach liquor concentration is advisable in all bleaching processes, from the simplest pit circulation hypochlorite system to the most sophisticated continuous bleaching range. Measurement may be by manual titration or incorporated into an automatic chemical feed system.

The iodometric method is applicable to hypochlorite, chlorite and peroxide bleaching liquors. When added to acidified potassium iodide solution, all these liquors liberate iodine, which can be titrated against a standard sodium thiosulphate solution. The following conversions may be used to determine the bleach liquor concentration based on the titration of a 10 ml bleach liquor sample with 0.05 mol/l thiosulphate. In each case a represents the volume (ml) of thiosulphate required.

(a) H_2O_2 (100%), g/l: $a \times 0.17$
(b) H_2O_2 (50%), g/l: $a \times 0.34$
                     ml/l: $a \times 0.285$
(c) H_2O_2 (35%), g/l: $a \times 0.486$
                     ml/l: $a \times 0.429$
(d) $NaClO_2$ (100%), g/l: $a \times 0.226$
(e) $NaClO_2$ (80%), g/l: $a \times 0.282$
(f) $NaClO_2$ (26%), g/l: $a \times 0.869$
                     ml/l: $a \times 0.71$
(g) NaOCl (available chlorine) g/l: $a \times 0.355$

For hydrogen peroxide a simple direct titration with potassium permanganate may be used. The sample of bleach liquor is added to dilute sulphuric acid, then standard potassium permanganate is titrated until a permanent pink colour is obtained. It is advisable to add a little permanganate to the acid before the bleach liquor sample to ensure that no residual reducing agents are present in the acid. Usually one or two drops suffice to give a pink colour.

When the permanganate titration is used to assess partially exhausted bleaching liquors a difficulty can arise from the presence of readily oxidisable impurities extracted during the bleaching. A tendency then exists for the coloration, which indicates full reaction with hydrogen peroxide, to fade as organic matter is oxidised. The iodometric method does not suffer from this difficulty.

Permanganate titration is still widely used for works control, and the conversion to peroxide concentration from a permanganate titration of a 2 ml sample of bleach liquor is given by the following, where a represents the volume (ml) of 0.1 mol/l permanganate:

(a) H_2O_2 (100%), g/l: $a \times 0.85$
(b) H_2O_2 (50%), g/l: $a \times 1.7$
(c) H_2O_2 (35%), g/l: $a \times 2.43$

2.21.2 pH Control

The simplest form of acidity or alkalinity measurement is that of pH. This measurement alone, however, provides only limited information and, particularly for hydrogen peroxide bleaching systems, determination of the alkali content by titration against acid is advised. Whilst this may not be essential as a routine control, when new processes are being established a much fuller understanding of the bleach liquor condition can be obtained.

During process optimisation compensation for over-rapid use of hydrogen peroxide can be achieved by reduction of alkali, increase of stabiliser or reduction of temperature. On the other hand, overstabilisation can be corrected by reducing stabiliser concentration or increasing alkalinity and temperature. Once optimum conditions have been established it is advisable to monitor subsequent operations, thus helping to maintain consistency of production and at the same time provide a record of process information should inconsistencies arise.

The level of alkalinity can be determined conveniently with bromothymol blue indicator. Taking a 25 ml bath sample, total alkalinity is given by the following conversion where α ml of 0.1 mol/l acid is required:

(a) Alkali as Na_2CO_3: $a \times 0.212$ g/l
(b) Alkali as NaOH: $a \times 0.16$ g/l
(c) Alkali as Na_2O: $a \times 0.124$ g/l

2.21.3 Control of Chemical Additions

The above tests may be applied by sampling liquors prepared for batch bleaching processes and for monitoring changes during the bleaching cycle. They are necessary also to check chemical dosing systems used in conjunction with continuous bleaching processes. In such processes it is necessary to maintain steady chemical concentrations in saturators. The setting up of chemical feed conditions, based initially on theoretical requirements, should be checked by titrations. This is done usually by manual titration, but automatic sampling and titration equipment is available commercially. Such equipment is usually linked electronically to activate chemical feeds as their requirement is indicated.

2.22 EVALUATION OF BLEACHED FABRIC
The need for a complete analysis of all prepared fabric will depend on the degree of quality control required for various end uses. A wide range of tests can be carried out, the most important of which are for whiteness, absorbency and chemical damage.

2.22.1 Whiteness
Whiteness of bleached fabric may be assessed visually or determined instrumentally by an electrophotometer. With the latter, comparison is made against a magnesium oxide standard. It is usual to filter the light source or reflected light to obtain a measurement at a wavelength of 464 nm since this shows the greatest reflectance differences for yellowness of fabrics. Fully bleached fabrics will normally have a reflectance of 83–85% without application of fluorescent whitening agent. Lower brightness, say 78–82%, is generally acceptable as a preparation for subsequent dyeing.

It is not a simple matter to judge visually the comparative whiteness of fabrics treated with fluorescent whitening agents. The efficiency of these agents is influenced by the quality of the base white. Perspex plates that will absorb u.v. radiation may be used, the fabrics being covered by the plate, in order to compare whiteness. Where possible the use of an electrophotometer with and without a u.v. illuminant is preferred.

2.22.2 Absorbency
Several methods of testing fabric or yarn absorbency are available. In practice simple tests based on the timing of a water drop to wet out the fabric, or for a sample of fabric to sink in water or dye liquor, are frequently used. Well-prepared fabrics should show a water absorbency of less than 1 s. However, it is not possible to differentiate critically between fabrics of good absorbency by the water drop test alone. The water may be replaced by a 50% sugar solution, which will give a much extended time scale with well-prepared fabrics.

The LINRA wipe test is more sophisticated but can be related to practical requirements in individual mills. In this test drops of dye solution are applied to the test paper, which is drawn under a piece of fabric. The fabric is held so that a constant load is applied. Highly absorbent fabrics rapidly absorb the dye and very short streaks are shown on the paper. Poor fabric absorbency is shown up by long dye streaks being spread onto the test paper. As with the drop absorbency test, the sensitivity of the test can be modified by using dye solutions of differing viscosity. As a control prior to the application of some finishes a simpler capillary absorption or wetting test may be used. A thin strip of material is suspended vertically above a solution, usually of a blue acid wool dye, with the lower edge just touching the liquor surface. The height to which the solution rises by capillary action is noted after a set time, e.g. 5 min.

2.22.3 Chemical Damage

Chemical damage tests were initially established to aid control of hypochlorite bleaching and the same tests are now applied for assessing fabric bleached with other agents. The fluidity method of test is sensitive to the onset of chemical damage before such damage would become apparent through a loss in tensile strength. Fluidity in cuprammonium solution is determined relatively simply, but does require standard viscometers.

In this test a weighed sample of the cellulose, finely chopped to give fibres of 1–2 mm length, is dissolved in standard cuprammonium hydroxide in a standard capillary viscometer. The quantity of cellulose to be weighed is that which will give a 0.5% solution for cotton or a 2% solution for regenerated cellulose. The viscometer must be filled completely to exclude air and covered to prevent exposure to light, whilst controlled agitation is given over 16 h. The viscometer and contents are then brought to 20°C in a thermostatically controlled bath and the rate of flow through the capillary measured. Standard viscometers are marked so that this flow measurement is simply a timing between two points. As each viscometer is pre-calibrated, from data provided, fluidity is then determined by dividing a viscometer constant by the time recorded. This gives a direct calculation of fluidity (in terms of $Pa^{-1} s^{-1}$ or reciprocal poises).

The principle of the test is that during dissolution no further breakdown of the cellulose molecular chain structure will occur. Long chain material, i.e. with low damage, will provide a high viscosity solution, hence low fluidity. Unbleached cotton shows a fluidity of about two. As a general guide bleached cotton with a fluidity of five or less is accepted commercially. Above a value of ten chemical damage shows up as a loss in tensile strength.

For regenerated cellulosic fibres, using the 2.0% solution, the high wet modulus products give similar fluidity levels to cotton, but the standard viscose has an unbleached fluidity of about ten.

In some countries, particularly in Western Europe, cupriethylenediamine (cuen) rather than cuprammonium hydroxide (cuam) is used. It is also more general to express the results as a degree of polymerisation (DP) value. In this case a high DP represents undamaged and a low DP damaged cellulose. The relationship between the two systems is given by Eqn 1 [20]:

$$DP = 2032 \log \frac{74.35 + F}{F} - 573 \tag{1}$$

A useful adaptation of the fluidity tests is the so-called rapid fluidity test devised by the Shirley Institute. For this test 0.125 g cotton is dissolved in 50 ml cuprammonium hydroxide in a wide-mouthed polypropylene bottle. Six drops of 50% pyrogallol solution are added and agitation aided by addition of twelve 6 mm stainless steel ball bearings. The bottle is mounted on a shaker and the cotton dissolves within 30 min. The solution is then transferred to a standard viscometer and the measured apparent fluidity converted to actual fluidity, using a conversion scale.

This method can be used for blends of cellulosic fibres with polyester or nylon, provided the composition of the blend is known. In such cases the weight of fabric taken is that which contains 0.125 g cotton. After agitation the cellulosic fibres can be separated by centrifuging. Whilst not giving absolute accuracy, the rapid technique is suitable for process control, and certainly indicates any serious over-bleaching situations. A modified method must be used for linen [21].

Other control tests can be used to give direct measurement of yarn or fabric tensile strength, bursting strength and abrasion resistance. These factors are influenced by both fabric structure and the degree of chemical damage. Tear strength may be influenced also by the degree to which natural lubricants have been removed. Details of such tests are not given here but can be found along with many others in the relevant British Standards handbook [22].

2.22.4 Spot Tests for Localised Chemical Damage

Highly localised chemical damage is not usually shown up in fluidity tests because the effect of a very small quantity of damaged cellulose can be masked by the surrounding good material. The fluidity tests given above assess the average for the whole sample dissolved. The presence of overbleached or tendered material shows up in yarn processing when an individual thread breaks during winding or knitting, or in fabrics when pin holes develop. This occurs particularly when the material is under tension as in stentering. Where the oxycellulose formation is less severe it may only show as a dye-resistant area.

Yarn or fabric breakdown may be caused by mechanical damage whilst dye resists may be due to residual size or silicates. It is therefore useful to be able to examine such faults and determine whether chemical damage has occurred.

A most useful and simple test is the Harrison test for oxycellulose. The test solution is prepared by adding dissolved silver nitrate to alkaline sodium thiosulphate solution. The quantities of chemical used are critical and the following procedure is suggested. For each 1 g fabric prepare 40 ml solution by adding 20 ml distilled water containing 0.08 g silver nitrate to 20 ml water containing 0.4 g sodium thiosulphate and 0.4 g sodium hydroxide. Addition of silver salt to thiosulphate should be made slowly with stirring. The prepared test solution is then brought to the boil and the test sample immersed. Boiling is continued, with stirring, for 5 min. Any oxycellulose will then show up as a dark brown or black coloration against the general background of slightly darkened fabric.

Apart from establishing that the cause of damage is chemical in nature, spot tests are also useful for identifying particular metallic contaminants. Iron can be detected with acidified potassium ferrocyanide solution, which will develop a blue coloration with ferric iron. Copper is shown up by sodium diethyl dithiocarbamate. When testing for copper it is advisable to spot the suspect area first with dilute nitric acid, then neutralise with dilute ammonia before spotting with the reagent. Details of these and other spot tests have been published [23].

2.22.5 Inorganic and Organic Residues

Inorganic and organic residues may be present on fabric after preparation as residual size components or from the actual scouring/bleaching preparation. Quantitatively they are usually determined by extraction or ashing procedures.

There are standard methods for such tests, comments here will be restricted to some observations relating to them.

Aqueous Extracts
Material extractable by demineralised water is usually assessed by measurement of fabric weight loss after washing for 20 min at 60°C at a liquor ratio of 40:1. Care must be taken to avoid losses other than the actual material extracted, e.g. fibre loss from frayed fabric. This test is usually coupled with pH measurement of the extract and serves basically to indicate the adequacy of washing-off processes. Some residual water-soluble sizes may be removed, but again this is indicative of poor rinsing.

Solvent Extracts
Chloroform is generally used in a Soxhlet extraction apparatus to determine solvent-extractable matter, i.e. residual material or size component fats and waxes. Where polyester is present in mixtures petroleum ether is used. For some specifications, notably loose cotton, dichloromethane is specified.

Apart from fats and waxes solvent extraction will also remove many residual surfactants.

Starch Content
One standard method is based on weight loss after extraction in an enzyme solution. A disadvantage of this method is that residual size which has resisted removal through preparation and hot washing may not respond to enzyme treatment. This method is most suitable for measuring the starch content of grey fabric.

Chemical oxidation methods to give a 'starch equivalent' are available but require the use of a correction factor to allow for oxidation of the cellulose itself. This factor changes with different pretreatments.

Simple staining with iodine, which can be semi-quantitative when used in conjunction with established colour scales, e.g. Tegawa, are very satisfactory for works quality control [24].

Ash Content
Inorganic residues can be assessed by ashing the fabric. The ash may be subjected to qualitative or quantitative analysis to determine the presence and levels of calcium, magnesium, iron, copper, silicate, etc.

2.23 FINAL COMMENTS
For many years the dyer and printer would be concerned to know that fabric was 'well bottomed' in the preparation sequences. The burden of this was carried by the alkaline scouring and acid scouring sequences. We have today an extensive range of machinery and auxiliary products which enable the preparation to be carried out in a matter of hours rather than days. Nevertheless the criteria demanded have not diminished. Rather they are, if anything, more severe so that fabrics suitable for the new dyeing and printing technologies can be produced.

The technology associated with preparation processes continues to develop and the reader should look upon this review as indicative of the 1985 situation, and in subsequent years note their developments.

REFERENCES

1. Rowe, AATCC National Technical Conference Book of Papers, (1977) 64.
2. Duckworth and Rusznak, Proceedings 10th Congress of IFATCC, Vol. 1 (1975) 343.
3. Duckworth and Wrennall, J.S.D.C., **93** (1977) 407.
4. Holmes, Dyer, (1977) 626.
5. Adams, Amer. Dyestuff Rep., (July 1978) 19.
6. Marsh, 'An Introduction to Textile Bleaching' (London: Chapman & Hall, 1946).
7. Sitver, AATCC National Technical Conference Book of Papers, (1977) 77.
8. Lewin and Ettinger, Cellulose Chem. Technology 3 (1969) 9.
9. Derry, J.S.D.C., **71** (1955) 886.
10. Chesner and Leigh, Textil Rundschau, **20** (1965) 217.
11. Taher and Cates, Text. Chem. Colorist, 7 (1975) 220.
12. Steinmiller and Cates, Text. Chem. Colorist, 8 (1976) 14.
13. Millsaps, AATCC National Technical Conference Book of Papers, (1977) 72
14. Soljacic et al., Tekske, **27** (1978) 27.
15. Dickinson and Heathcote, J.S.D.C., **88** (1972) 137.
16. Dickinson, Kindron and Curzons, Text. Chem. Colorist, **14** (1982) 126.
17. Hickman and Andrianjafy, J.S.D.C., **99** (1983) 86.
18. Kymel and Merk, Textil, **12** (6) (1975) 226.
19. Text. Chem. Colorist, **9** (1977) 281.
20. Deschler, Textil Praxis, **13** (1958) 927.
21. BS 3090 (1978).
22. 'Methods of Test for Textiles' (BS Handbook No. 11, 1974).
23. Garner, 'Textile Laboratory Manual', 3rd Edn, Vols 2 & 6 (London: Heywood Books, 1966 and 1967).
24. Deschler and Schmidt, Textil Praxis, **36** (1981) 1331.

FURTHER READING

Dyeing and Chemical Technology of Textile Fibres', 6th Edn, by E R Trotman (published by Charles Griffen, High Wycombe) is recommended, as are references 6, 21, 22 and 23.

CHAPTER 3

The Effects of Chemical and Physical Properties on Dyeing and Finishing

IAN HOLME

3.1 INTRODUCTION

One essential element leading to a greater understanding of the mechanisms of coloration and finishing processes is a sound knowledge of fibre structure. Indeed fibre physics and fibre chemistry play a fundamental role in all adsorption and diffusion processes, and are an integral component of dye–fibre interrelations in cellulosic fibres, whether of natural (native) or regenerated origin [1, 2].

In this chapter the structure and properties of fibres (as related to fibre morphology) and their modification by various treatments will be discussed in the context of their influence upon coloration and finishing processes.

The literature on the physical structure of native and of regenerated cellulose fibres is extensive, and often conflicting in terms of minor detail [1, 3–13]. Views of fibre structure have altered perceptibly in recent years as more powerful analytical techniques have been developed. Thus in the case of natural cellulose fibres, like cotton, there has been a distinct movement away from the older fringed-micelle and fringed-fibril theories [8], with the emergence of the crystalline-fibril theory [3, 6, 10, 12].

Nevertheless the assignation of a particular structure to a fibre is often still a matter of some debate; as Statton has pointed out, all theories of fibre structure are merely theories and all models are merely models [14]. The views expressed in this chapter are therefore intended to reflect those general proposals that have gained a wider acceptance and are based on a broad spectrum of evidence from many structural studies.

One final qualification must also be carefully considered, namely that it is normally presumed that diffusion and sorption of reagents take place within the disordered regions of the fibre that are accessible to the reagents [1, 15]. Comparatively little is known, and much has had to be inferred, about the structural arrangement within these disordered regions. The disordered regions are non-crystalline and are now considered to consist of parts that are either truly random (i.e.

amorphous) or of varying levels of higher structural order. Modern analytical techniques, while yielding much useful data on the crystalline or highly ordered regions, are often much less informative on the structural organisation within the regions of lower order or disorder [1]. This lack of precision concerning the detailed structure within the disordered regions, while a limitation at present, does not fundamentally detract from the utility of the general working hypothesis expressed in the order–disorder concept of fibre structure [1, 3, 5, 6, 12].

3.2 GENERAL THEORY OF FIBRE STRUCTURE

The structure of textile fibres has been considered [3] in terms of three essential parameters:
1. Degree of order
2. Degree of localisation of order and disorder
3. Length:width ratio of the localised units.

It has been pointed out, however, that two further parameters must also be considered for a rationalised theory of fibre structure, namely:
4. Size of the localised units
5. Degree of orientation.

All these factors will exert specific effects upon the fibre dyeability [3, 5].

However, a more rigorous definition of the fibre structure would require detailed consideration of a number of secondary factors. Thus the shapes of the localised units and the details of the chain packing are of importance, particularly for the crystalline regions. The nature of any crystal or lattice defects, the degree of order in the non-crystalline regions and the extent of chain folding or of intercrystalline links may also exert a subtle influence upon fibre dyeability [5].

It is generally considered that the relative proportion, size and shape of the crystalline regions, which give rise to the X-ray diffraction pattern, and those of the non-crystalline regions, in which there is a low degree of order, are of prime importance in determining the response of the fibre to coloration processes [2, 5, 15]. An essential feature is that diffusion and sorption of dyes are presumed to depend upon the extent to which the disordered regions in the fibre are accessible to the dye molecules. In some instances adsorption may occur on the accessible surfaces of the crystallites, but dye molecules are not absorbed *within* crystallites [5, 8, 16, 17].

The concept of the existence of a range of degrees of order or packing of chain molecules in textile fibres has been discussed by Howsman and Sisson [8] and is illustrated in Figure 3.1.

To summarise, probably the most useful general interpretation of fibre structure at the current time is to assume that in all fibres there exist regions of differing degrees of molecular order and disorder [1]. Within the crystalline regions and above a certain level of order, dependent upon the experimental conditions and the reagents used, the diffusion of dyes or other penetrant molecules is not possible, these regions being normally inaccessible to the penetration of reagents. The penetration of dyes and other reagents is thereby restricted to those disordered regions accessible to them. These regions range from low degrees of order to the

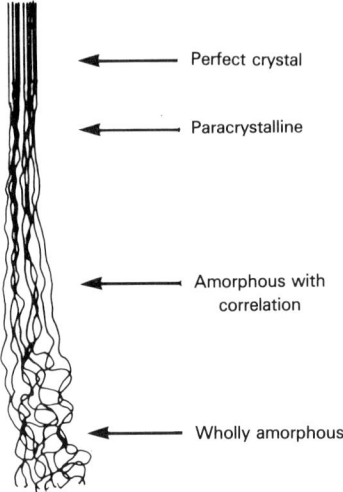

Figure 3.1 – Range in degrees of order in the packing of chain molecules

completely disordered (so-called amorphous) regions. In addition adsorption on the surfaces of crystalline regions may be possible depending upon the structural packing of the chain molecules [5, 12, 15, 17].

The fibre accessibility is therefore dependent upon the fine structure and this influences the rate, extent and uniformity of dyeing [1, 7, 13]. Transport of dyes or reagents inward to reaction sites and/or the movement of reaction products out from the reaction sites can thus occur within these less-ordered regions [18]. The microporosity and internal surface area of the fibre are therefore important factors. The degree of penetration and the fibre accessibility may, however, be altered by the ability of penetrant molecules, such as water and organic solvents, to swell and/or plasticise the fibre structure [1, 2, 6, 15, 18].

3.2.1 Structure of Cellulose Fibres

The properties of native or regenerated cellulose fibres are dependent upon the structure of the fibre at three levels [3, 19]:

1. Molecular level, i.e. the degree of order of the cellulose molecules
2. Fibrillar level, i.e. the orientation of the fibrils with respect to the fibre axis
3. Morphological level, i.e. the differences in structure between the surface and the interior, or other gross inhomogeneities.

In native cellulose fibres such as cotton, differences in degree of order, orientation and fibre morphology may occur as a result of modifications arising during growth. Likewise differences in regenerated cellulose fibres, e.g. viscose, may be caused by variations introduced either deliberately or unintentionally during production. Once formed, the fibre structure may be modified prior to coloration as a result of wetting, swelling, steaming or drying treatments, and indeed may also be modified during the coloration process itself [1–3, 5–8, 12, 15, 16, 18].

One very important feature common to the structure of both native and regenerated cellulose fibres is the fact that the fibre structure is usually heterogenous, particularly in the radial direction. This is seen clearly in the bilateral structure of native cotton [1, 20, 21] and in the skin–core structure of ordinary viscose fibres [1, 3, 5, 7, 8, 20]. The rates of diffusion of dyes and of other penetrants such as finishes may thus vary across the fibre radius, as the fibre structure varies in the degree of order.

In one study [22] of edgewise diffusion in swollen cellulose gel films, it was demonstrated that the diffusion of a direct dye was anisotropic, being more rapid along the axis of extrusion than perpendicular to it. However, it has been pointed out [23] that this is not so important for textile fibres in which radial diffusion is the predominant mode.

Both the fibre's morphology and its fine structure, and hence the dyeability, may be altered considerably by swelling treatments, e.g. mercerisation and causticisation [6, 24], or by anhydrous liquid ammonia treatments [25]. In these treatments factors such as the nature of the applied tension, temperature, time and reagent concentration all play an important role [24–26]. The structure of regenerated cellulose fibres, in particular the size of the crystallites and the orientation of the chain molecules, may be modified considerably as a result of the manufacturing process [1, 3, 7, 27–31].

Natural and regenerated cellulose fibres absorb dyes at different rates and to different saturation levels. Fibres from different sources will often differ in their dyeing behaviour, and for natural fibres the scouring and bleaching treatments used may also modify the dyeability. Cotton and linen are normally bleached to remove impurities to produce an absorbent fibre with stable whiteness [32, 33]. Jute is difficult to bleach and afterwards generally yellows on exposure to light. This has restricted the range of end uses for dyed jute [34].

Even in relatively simple aqueous dyeing processes, water as the distribution and circulation medium can also exert a positive or a negative influence on dye uptake. A coherent view of the nature of the aqueous dyeing process demands a detailed consideration of the relative importance of the various types of bonding interactions in the system [35].

In this chapter the theoretical aspects of dye–fibre, fibre–water and fibre–fibre interactions will be considered, but at the same time water–water, dye–dye and dye–water interactions must also be examined as possible competing or contributory factors. In solvent media similar considerations usually apply because the solvent merely replaces water as the circulation and distribution medium [5].

3.3 NATURAL CELLULOSE FIBRES

3.3.1 Structure of Cotton in Relation to Coloration and Finishing

The dyeing properties of cotton fibres depend on two general factors, namely fibre diameter and internal structure. Some typical mean values for the linear density (in μg per linear cm) of different species of cotton are given in Table 3.1. The range of fibre fineness can be as high as 5:1 for varieties grown in different parts of the world [6, 36]. Because fibre surface area per unit mass (a typical value is 200 m^2/kg) is of great importance in all wet-processing operations, fibre fineness is a particularly important feature. The finer the fibre, the faster is the rate of dyeing [27].

TABLE 3.1

Values of Average Fibre Weights per Centimetre of Typical Samples of Various Types of Cotton

Type	Fibre wt per cm (10^{-8} g)
St Vincent Sea Island	105
Montserrat Sea Island	140
Egyptian Giza 45	115
Egyptian Menoufi	143
Egyptian Ashmouni	184
Sudan Sakel L-type	160
United States 7/8 in. staple	225
United States 1 in. staple	205
United States 1 1/8 in. staple	180
Russian	185
Peruvian Tanguis	195
Indian Bengals	330

(Reproduced from ref. 36 by permission of the Textile Institute, Manchester)

Cotton may be regarded as being composed of structural units termed fibrils, which are essentially crystalline and built up from the close association of a number of identical unit cells of cellulose I (native cotton) [1, 3, 6, 10, 12]. The unit cell is the fundamental structural unit of crystalline materials and is the smallest highly ordered unit that by simple repetition forms the basis for the crystalline regions [3].

The crystalline regions form the bulk of the fibrils, the disordered regions being confined to the surface of the fibrils and to very short regions along their length. Accessibility and reactivity [37] are therefore explained by a system of voids bounded by fibrillar surfaces, rather than by 'amorphous' regions; penetration of dyes within the crystalline fibril is normally not possible [5, 6, 13, 16, 37].

Thus chemical reactions are regarded as taking place on the surfaces of fibrils of different sizes and also, in special circumstances, at imperfections within the crystalline lattice of the fibrils [5, 12, 37]. Swelling treatments may be considered as being a combination of interfibrillar and intrafibrillar processes [6]. In some cases interfibrillar swelling occurs first, but in some systems both processes take place simultaneously. This will be discussed in greater detail with reference to anhydrous liquid ammonia treatments on cotton.

An essential aspect of all chemical processes, including coloration and finishing treatments, involving cotton is the access to fibrillar surfaces. Thus the state of aggregation of the fibrillar units and the void spaces and their distribution are important factors in the chemical reactivity and morphology of cotton [1, 3, 12, 37, 38]. The way in which they are altered during swelling can exert a profound effect on the extent of subsequent reactions [6]. In addition, drying can modify both the fibrillar aggregation and the void distribution, so that the effects of such treatments must always be carefully considered [1].

In never-dried cotton (i.e. fibres removed from fresh closed bolls and maintained in the undried state) the formation of hydrogen bonds between cellulose fibrils is hindered by water molecules on the surfaces of the elementary fibrils. Cotton in this state has a large surface area available for adsorption, giving it a higher sorptive capacity both for water and for dyes than has dried cotton [39]. The plasticity of the fibrils in never-dried cotton also facilitates fibre extension during tensile stress, but this is irreversibly changed by the formation of hydrogen bonds during initial drying or by mechanical stressing of the never-dried fibre.

The uptake of C.I. Direct Green 26 (molecular weight 1350) has been used as a measure of the internal surface area of the cotton accessible to a large molecule [39]. It can be seen from Table 3.2 that the dye uptake is considerably higher for the never-dried fibres compared with normally dried fibres, but decreases with increase in growing time. Attempts at stabilisation of the never-dried structure by propylene

TABLE 3.2

Dye Uptake of Closed-boll Cotton Fibres

State	Boll age (days after flowering)	C.I. Direct Green 26 (mg dye/g cotton)
Closed bolls, never-dried fibres	35	37.3
	42	25.1
	49	25.0
Closed bolls, dried fibres	35	2.9
	42	2.4
	49	2.2
	Field opened	1.6
Never-dried fibres treated with PO	35	28.0
	42	13.5
	49	10.5
Rewet dried fibres treated with PO	35	13.0
	42	11.0
	49	12.7
	Field opened	16.3
Dried fibres, slack mercerised	Field opened	4.1

(Reproduced from ref. 39 by permission of the American Chemical Society, Washington DC)

oxide (PO) treatment of fibres pre-soaked in 6.5% sodium hydroxide can be seen to be partially successful, but this can give a greater dye uptake than conventionally picked, dried and slack-mercerised fibres. The initial drying out of the fibre thus reduces dye adsorption drastically, and while PO treatments are as yet only of academic interest, their potential for improving dye adsorption is clear.

Additional factors that may exert some influence on chemical reactions and on dyeing phenomena are weak zones and cracks, the nature of which are as yet little understood. Swelling can sometimes open up weak zones, e.g. transverse fissures, while the implications of such zones for fibre strength are obvious [6].

Recent research work, using scanning electron microscopy to detect surface cracks, suggests that the presence of surface damage in cotton fibres is an essential factor in promoting rapid wettability of the fibre in water [40]. Alkaline treatments such as scouring are important in facilitating the formation of sufficient surface damage to confer wettability and absorbency without tendering or degrading the main body of the fibre. Rapid wettability and absorbency are essential for all pad dyeing and finishing operations, but these factors are particularly critical for certain types of low wet pick-up systems, such as lick-roll systems [41]. Correct fabric preparation is thus essential for low wet pick-up coloration and finishing.

The disorder that is characteristic of the readily accessible surfaces of the elementary fibrils may be distributed uniformly along these surfaces or localised randomly. Sites of lattice disorder are considered to arise in two main regions: (a) on the surfaces of the elementary fibrils and (b) extending across the fibrils periodically along their length [37]. The latter regions of disorder are considered to be short in length, less than 5 nm or 10 D-glucopyranosyl units long, but reagents cannot readily enter because these regions do not behave in a non-crystalline fashion [12, 37].

An essential part of the fibre structure thus appears to be periodic regions of less than perfect order extending across the elementary fibrils. These allow the elementary fibril to undergo the curvature essential for spiral arrangement in a collapsed convoluted fibre, and in addition provide short regions that relieve strain beween the highly ordered rigid sections of the elementary fibril [12]. Discontinuities in the fibre crystallinity may thus be associated with twist and tilt boundaries up to 5 nm long scattered periodically to release strain between highly ordered segments of elementary fibrils that are typically around 60 nm long. This concept is illustrated in Figure 3.2.

It has been concluded by Rowland [12] that the elementary fibril is thus characterised by three types of regions:
1. Type A, having a high internal and surface order
2. Type B, having a high internal order with substantial disorder on the surface
3. Type C, having distorted and less-than-perfect order in the interior of the fibril, accompanied by complete disruption of the hydrogen bonding between the C6 hydroxyl of one chain to the C1 oxygen of another chain on the fibrillar surface.

Type A regions are relatively inaccessible in conventional textile finishing operations because of the strong hydrogen bonding or coalescing of the fibrillar surface to adjacent surfaces. The readily accessible surfaces in cotton fibres are thus repre-

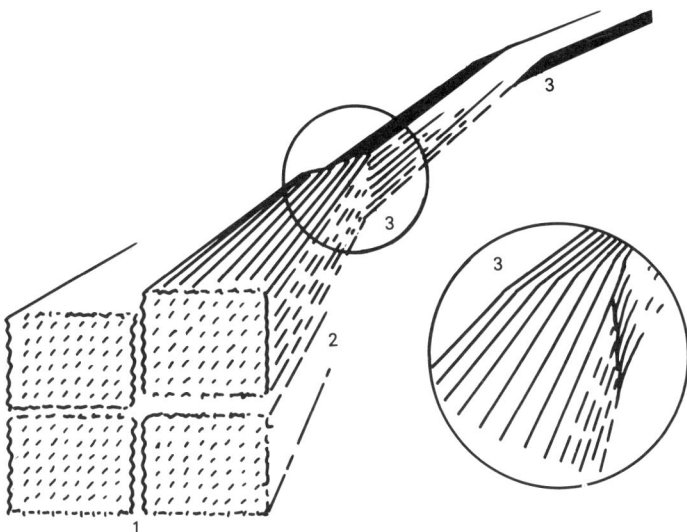

1 — Coalesced surfaces of high order
2 — Readily accessible disordered surfaces
3 — Readily accessible surfaces of strain- distorted tilt and
     twist regions

Figure 3.2 – Schematic representation of the elementary fibril (reproduced from ref. 12 by permission of the American Association of Textile Chemists and Colorists, North Carolina)

sented by types B and C, which together probably constitute less than 50% of the total surface area.

From the structural concepts outlined so far it has been shown that not all the hydroxyl groups in the cellulose chain molecule are equally accessible to chemical reagents [12]. In one study [42] of the reaction of N,N-diethylaziridinium chloride with highly crystalline hydrocellulose in aqueous media under mild conditions, the ratio of available hydroxyl groups at the C2, C3 and C6 atoms has been shown to be 1.0:0.28:0.54. In desized, scoured and bleached printcloth the relative availability of hydroxyl groups at C2, C3 and C6 was found to be 1.0:0.32:0.77 [43]. The higher availability of the hydroxyl groups at C6 in the cotton fibre, as compared with highly crystalline hydrocellulose, suggests that a fraction of the hydrogen bonding on the surfaces of the elementary fibrils from the C6 hydroxyl group to the C1 oxygen atom is disrupted. Nevertheless these results strongly suggest that reactions in fibrous cellulose occur, at least in part, on the surfaces of crystalline regions.

Evidence supporting the adsorption of direct dyes on lamellar surfaces has been reported by Johnson et al. [16], calculation of the accessible surface areas giving values consistent with other measures of accessibility. Steaming treatments following mercerisation under tension and drying were considered to lead primarily to an increase in the crystalline fusion of fibrils in those areas where the surfaces were already in alignment and in close proximity. Such a process was also envisaged to occur during first drying, to a smaller extent in subsequent drying operations, and also during mercerisation and acid hydrolysis; it led to a reduction in equilibrium sorption of dye [16].

3.3.2 Bilateral Structure of Cotton
The accessibility of the native cotton fibre to reagents is different in the convex (outermost) and in the concave (innermost) parts of the bean-shaped fibre cross-section, and the term bilateral has been applied to the fibre. The bilateral structure of mature cotton fibres has been revealed as a result of enzymatic degradation using a cellulase [21]. Figure 3.3 shows the three main zones A, B and C:
– Zone A represents the least accessible region of the fibre
– Zone B is more accessible to reagents
– Zone C is much more accessible and most reactive.

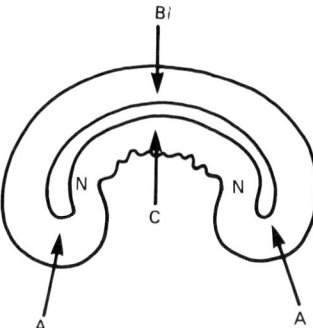

Figure 3.3 – Localisation of zones A, B, C and N in the cross-section of a mature cotton fibre (reproduced from ref. 21 by permission of the Textile Research Institute, Princeton, New Jersey)

Apart from the three main zones, limited areas located at the boundaries between zones A and C have been denoted as zones N. These are neutral zones and have been shown to the most accessible part of the secondary wall.

The differences in accessibility to enzymatic attack are believed to be reflected by the differences in the secondary wall. However, the differences observed in accessibility may also depend upon the size and shape of the penetrant molecules, so that the conclusions derived for high molecular weight cellulolytic enzymes may not necessarily apply to the comparatively smaller reagent molecules employed for the cross-linking of cotton, or even for some dyes.

3.3.3 Normal, Immature and Dead Cotton Fibres
'Normal' cotton fibres are those which, after swelling, appear rod-like with no continuous lumen and with no well-defined convolutions [36]. In 'dead' fibres the wall

thickness after swelling is one-fifth or less of the maximum ribbon width (i.e. the width of the widest portion of the fibre, usually midway between two convolutions). In addition there is a wide range of thin-walled fibres which do not fall into either the normal or the dead categories. These are 'immature' fibres and the fibre maturity is a measure of the thickening of the secondary wall of the fibre, established between the cessation of increase in fibre length and the bursting open of the fully developed boll [36, 44]. In any sample of cotton fibres there will be a mixture of fibres of different maturity, but under favourable growth conditions mature fibres with fairly thick walls result, although there will also be some poorly developed fibres.

3.3.4 Dyeing Behaviour of Immature Cotton Fibres

The wall thickness of the cotton hair may vary four- or five-fold in hairs from the same seed [45]. Of particular importance in coloration and finishing are the immature fibres in which there is little or no secondary wall thickening, for the primary cellulose reacts differently to dyes. These immature fibres during handling, ginning and carding roll up easily into knots and tangles normally called neps [45, 46]. A variety of methods are now available for determining the maturity of cotton fibres [44, 47].

Early work demonstrated that certain dyes will dye neps to almost the same colour as the rest of the fabric, while other dyes leave the neps a lighter colour [48]. In general only highly substantive dyes dye dead cotton fibres under normal conditions. Mercerisation prior to dyeing generally decreases the colour differences, while calendering treatments may often make the differences more marked. It has been demonstrated that differences between the fine structure of immature and mature cotton fibres lead to this differential response to dyeing processes, and this has formed the basis of a test for determining the maturity of a cotton [49, 50].

In most commercially dyed cotton fabrics the neps caused by immature fibres show as light specks, for in commercial dyeing systems equilibrium sorption is never reached and the effects of efficient washing and rinsing processes lead to a lower dye concentration in the immature fibre. However, the intensity of the colour depends not only upon the dye concentration, but also on the average path length of the light in the dyed fibre wall. The thin-walled immature fibres thus will appear paler even if the dye concentration is the same as in the mature fibres.

3.3.5 Factors Influencing the Dyeing of Cotton

The nature of the cotton fibre exerts a profound influence upon its dyeing behaviour. This has been recognised for a long time, and great care is thus taken in blending cotton fibre before spinning. It has been pointed out that, although colour variations arising from differences between the fibres within a fabric do not occur frequently, the likelihood of mixed batches of fabric containing different fibres is greater [51]. In either case redyeing is often the only remedy that can be attempted if variations in colour occur.

In a series of nine different types of cotton the colour obtained after dyeing separately with 1% Chlorantine Fast Green 5BLL (C.I. Direct Green 27) has been measured [51]. The fibres were subjected to a standard caustic soda scour and hydrogen peroxide bleach prior to dyeing. The resultant dyeings differed considerably in colour (see Table 3.3).

TABLE 3.3

Influence of Cotton Type on Colour After Dyeing with Chlorantine Fast Green 5BLL (1%)

Type	Staple length (mm)	$x^{(a)}$	$y^{(a)}$	Y	$\Delta E^{(b)}$
Pakistan Dessai	15.9	0.2369	0.2984	9.85	0
Middling American	27.0	0.2399	0.2971	9.60	1.47
Ashmouni	34.9	0.2382	0.2985	11.15	2.08
Bengal	12.7	0.2360	0.2971	10.70	1.46
Malaki	38.1	0.2359	0.2966	12.95	4.93
El-Paso	30.2	0.2377	0.2967	12.05	3.50
Karnak	33.3	0.2385	0.2967	11.20	2.24
Sudan Sakel	31.8	0.2381	0.2976	11.00	1.87
Tanguis	31.8	0.2353	0.2967	10.40	1.05

(a) $x = \dfrac{X}{X+Y+Z}$ $y = \dfrac{Y}{X+Y+Z}$

  where X, Y (lightness) and Z are tristimulus values

(b) ΔE is the total colour difference computed on the ANLAB 40 system

(Reproduced from ref. 51 by permission of the Textile Institute, Manchester)

In a series of yarns spun from different types of cotton dyed competitively with a grey mixture of three dyes the base colour of each cotton type varied considerably. The main factor giving rise to colour differences when yarns were dyed both competitively and separately was the inherent fibre dyeability. Thus Deltapine (the lightest base colour) and Short American (the darkest base colour) cotton fibres showed virtually no differences after dyeing competitively and only slightly greater differences when dyed non-competitively [51].

It has been demonstrated that the primary factor influencing the dyeing of cotton is the fibre structure, so that colour differences are more noticeable when yarns from different types of cotton are dyed together (i.e. competitively) rather than separately [52].

3.4 EFFECTS OF SWELLING TREATMENTS ON CELLULOSE FIBRES

3.4.1 Mercerisation

The mercerising of cotton and linen has been described in detail elsewhere [6, 7, 24, 53]. In this section the relevant effects of mercerisation upon the coloration of cotton fibres will be briefly reviewed.

Mercerised cotton is generally stronger and more lustrous, has a greater substantivity for dyes and is more chemically reactive as a result of fibre expansion and internal reorientation [6, 7, 53–55]. This creates more sites for chemical and physical bonding in mature cotton fibres. Immature fibres are also restructured, thereby improving their substantivity for dyes and reactivity in general.

A mercerised cotton fibre appears darker than an unmercerised fibre dyed with the same amount of dye, and the extent of this effect is dependent upon the dye used [6, 24–26, 56, 57]. Typical results using reactive dyes are illustrated in Figure 3.4, showing that a saving of 30% in dyes for pale depths (1–2% dye o.w.f.) and a

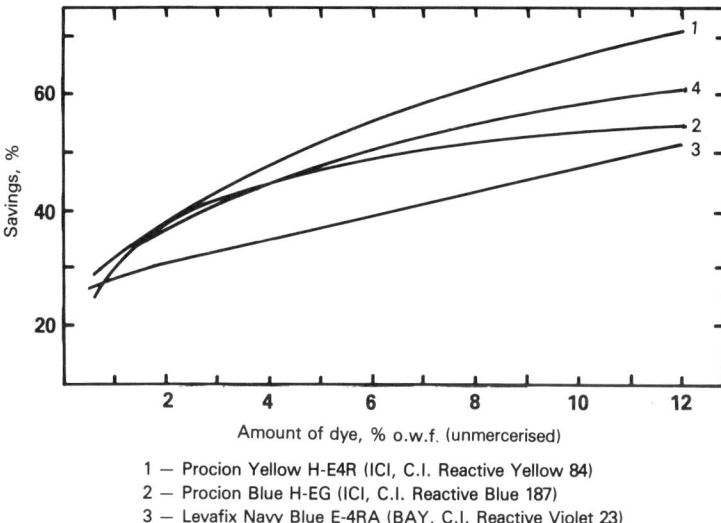

1 — Procion Yellow H-E4R (ICI, C.I. Reactive Yellow 84)
2 — Procion Blue H-EG (ICI, C.I. Reactive Blue 187)
3 — Levafix Navy Blue E-4RA (BAY, C.I. Reactive Violet 23)
4 — Levafix Black E-B (BAY, C.I. Reactive Black 5)

Figure 3.4 – Savings achievable in the dyeing of mercerised cotton fibres (reproduced by permission of the International Institute for Cotton, Manchester)

50–70% saving for deep colours can often be obtained if the fibre is mercerised [25, 56, 58]. For a range of light to medium depths of one particular dye, Goldthwait established that the darker dyeing or greater colour yield of mercerised cotton, as compared with the same cotton unmercerised, took place to different degrees at different depths of colour [57]; this is illustrated in Figure 3.5. Thus there was not a fixed ratio as might have been postulated if the effects were primarily associated with the changes of the original fibres to the more rounded form, with accompanying changes in the reflectance and scattering of incident light. Goldfinger has, however, asserted that the colour change resulting from mercerising cotton is chiefly due to a change in the efficiency of internal scattering. This seems to be the more likely explanation of this optical phenomenon, which is clearly of considerable economic benefit to the coloration industry [59].

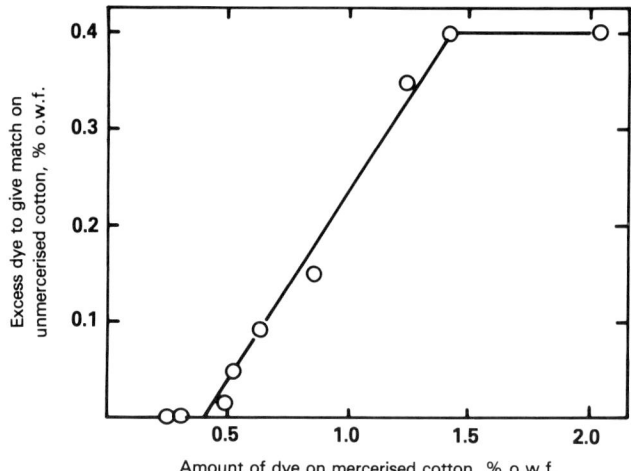

Figure 3.5 – Excess of dye necessary on unmercerised cotton to match the colour of a mercerised sample, plotted against dye concentration (reproduced from ref. 57 by permission of the Textile Research Institute, Princeton, New Jersey)

Apart from the effect of tension in the mercerisation process, the removal of the caustic soda and the drying temperature used also affect the accessibility of the resultant fibres (see Figure 3.6). Gailey has shown that the barium activity number (based upon the amount of barium hydroxide absorbed by the fibre) is greater for cotton mercerised without tension [26]. The barium activity number is progressively decreased as the drying temperature is increased, while a more noticeable reduction in accessibility occurs at temperatures in excess of 80°C. This has been attributed to different degrees of crystallisation of the disordered regions of the fibre, greater crystallisation taking place at higher drying temperatures. Thus, in practice, differences in the drying temperature, particularly above 80°C, may lead to greater variations of dye uptake. At short dyeing times these differences may be exaggerated, leading to skitteriness or unlevelness.

Early electro-osmosis measurements by Karrer and Schubert demonstrated that the electrokinetic potential of mercerised cotton is less negative than that of unmercerised cotton, which should favour an increased dye absorption [60]. There is certainly no doubt that increasing the concentration of aqueous caustic soda leads to a progressive increase in dye uptake for Benzopurpurine 4B (C.I. Direct Red 2) on cotton, the values appearing to approach a limiting value which is presumably controlled by the extent of the conversion of cellulose I to cellulose II in the fibre samples (see Table 3.4).

Treatment in caustic soda without tension generally is regarded as having the marked effect of increasing the amount of direct dye absorbed, although the effect is sometimes small and may even be in the reverse direction, depending upon the dye concerned (see Table 3.5) [61, 62]. It has been shown that the dye uptake is

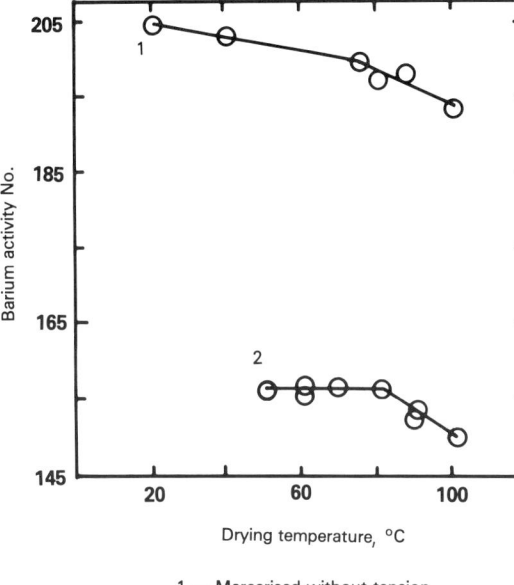

1 — Mercerised without tension
2 — Mercerised with tension

Figure 3.6 – Effect of drying temperature on sorptive capacity of mercerised cotton

TABLE 3.4

**Effect of Mercerising on the Absorption of
Benzopurpurine 4B by Cotton**

Caustic soda (%)	Benzopurpurine 4B (g/100 g fibre)
0.00	1.77
0.85	2.39
13.5	2.95
17.5	3.15
22.5	3.38
27.0	3.56
31.5	3.60

decreased when the mercerised fibre is subsequently dried (Table 3.6). This reduction is greater as the temperature of drying is increased, reflecting the change in fibre structure as a result of the rate of water removal employed during the drying process.

TABLE 3.5

Effect of Tension in Mercerisation on the Absorption of Benzopurpurine 4B and Chlorazol Sky Blue FF (ICI, C.I. Direct Blue 1)

Dye	Treatment	Dye absorbed (g/100g fibre)
Benzopurpurine 4B	Unmercerised	1.5
	Mercerised with tension	2.9
	Mercerised without tension	3.5
Chlorazol Sky Blue FF	Unmercerised	0.15
	Mercerised with tension	0.27
	Mercerised without tension	0.24

TABLE 3.6

Effect on Dye Absorption of Drying After Mercerising

Material	Absorption of Benzopurpurine 4B (g/100 g fibre)	Absorption of Chrysophenine G (C. I. Direct Yellow 12) (g/100 g fibre)
Unmercerised	0.8	0.3
Mercerised and dyed without drying	2.5	1.0
Mercerised and dyed after drying in air	1.6	0.8
Mercerised and dyed after drying at 110°C for 1 h	1.3	0.5

In summary, therefore, the mercerising process for cotton fabrics is currently employed to improve:
1. Colour yield and uniformity in dyeing
2. Dimensional stability
3. Lustre.

3.4.2 Anhydrous Liquid Ammonia Treatments

When native cotton (cellulose I) is treated with anhydrous liquid ammonia an un-stable adduct or ammonia cellulose compound is formed and extensive swelling occurs, resulting in disruption of the hydrogen bonding. Interfibrillar swelling is considered to occur with a limited amount of intrafibrillar swelling, the latter being less than that produced by the relatively larger dipole hydrate introduced as a result of mercerisation in caustic soda. If the adduct is then decomposed by evaporation of the ammonia with dry heat or through quenching treatments in organic solvents, cellulose III is formed [63]. Alternatively quenching in water or alcohols leads to the regeneration of cellulose I. Removal largely by dry heat, e.g. over hot cylinders, followed by steam to remove the last traces of ammonia, has been generally preferred in machinery for continuous fabric treatments because the fabric, when subsequently cross-linked (particularly by a low wet pick-up method), has an improved balance of physical properties compared with those fabrics from which ammonia is removed by water alone [25]. The latter process has, however, been used in the Prograde continuous yarn process for improving the strength, lustre and dye uptake of cotton sewing threads [64]. The flat-setting properties imparted by the ammonia–dry–steam process are superior to mercerisation (in which cellulose II is formed) in respect of the smooth-drying appearance and crease-shedding properties of such treated cotton fabrics. The changes in swelling occur more rapidly with the small ammonia molecule compared with the relatively large dipole hydrate in conventional mercerising, and the tensions developed are about three times greater, so that control of the fabric dimensions is important [28, 65].

It has been suggested that the ammonia–water process produces fabrics that are like mercerised cotton – only not quite, while the ammonia–dry–steam process produces fabrics like mercerised cotton – only better [25]. Thus the latter process gives consistently better crease recovery, tensile strength, tear strength and abrasion resistance for a given level of solids add-on in subsequent treatment with cross-linking agents, particularly if applied by the low wet pick-up method. The ammonia–dry–steam process gives effective fabric setting (reducing inter-yarn friction) and enables an improved distribution of the cross-linking agent to be attained through low wet pick-up finishing.

The differences in the response of bleached, mercerised and ammonia-treated fabrics are illustrated in Table 3.7. The influence of mercerising is generally to raise the critical application value (CAV), while ammonia treatment lowers the CAV when the time allowed for diffusion is short [66].

The CAV has been defined [66] as the lowest amount of finishing liquor that can be applied to a given cotton fabric without producing a non-uniform distribution of cross-linking after drying and curing. The CAV depends upon fibre type, fabric

TABLE 3.7

Print Cloth: Critical Application Values

	CAV (%)		
Treatment	Bleached	Mercerised	Ammonia treated
Immediate drying	36	41	31
Batch 1 h	22	20	25
Steam 5 s	18	18	18

(Reproduced from ref. 66 by permission of the Textile Research Institute, Princeton, New Jersey)

construction and also upon the level of fabric pretreatment. Type 1 non-uniformity (see Figure 3.7) occurs when the amount of applied liquor in padding is significantly higher than the CAV, so that migration of chemicals (e.g. resin finish) to the fabric surface takes place. Type 2 non-uniformity arises from an application level that is too low, causing a speckled or spotty appearance when the distribution of cross-linking is rendered visible by appropriate stains. Such white speckles or spots are areas of uncross-linked fibres where the liquor has never penetrated, while there is generally a difference between the face and back of the fabric. It has been concluded from radial wicking tests in which ammonia-treated fabrics perform better than bleached or mercerised fabrics (see Figure 3.8) that the lower rate and lower equilibrium level of swelling for ammonia-treated fabrics may allow a given volume of liquor more time for capillary transport outside the fibres [66]. Thus the rate of distribution and uniformity of spreading of the padding liquor is significantly improved with ammonia–dry–steam-treated fabrics which have been appropriately processed.

The ammonia/cellulose system is sensitive to the method of removal of the ammonia, to water and to temperature. Yarns and fabrics treated using the ammonia/water process give a remarkable improvement in colour yield, both in respect of a greater dye uptake (somewhat less than after mercerising, but often close) and the fact that the fabrics still appear to be more deeply dyed than un-

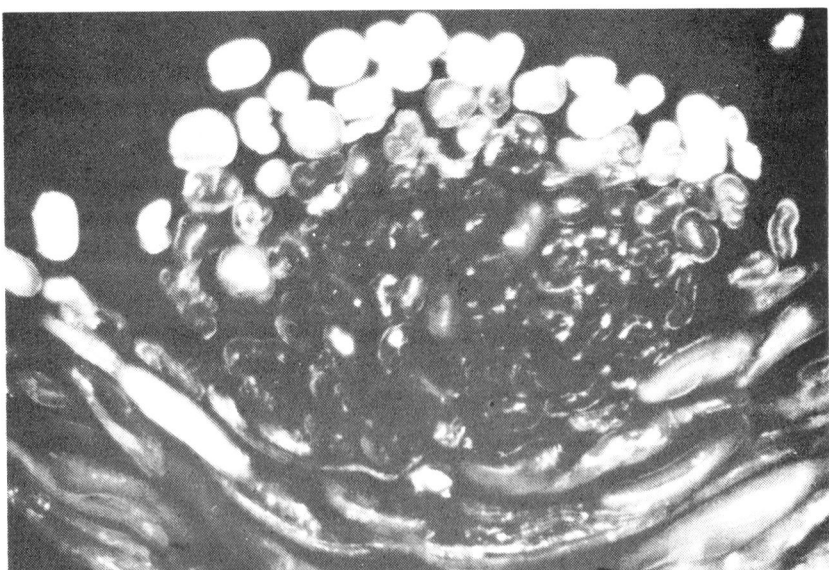

Figure 3.7 – Type 1 non-uniformity, caused by migration during drying, shown by staining the cross-linked areas with Rhodamine B, 70% pick-up (reproduced from ref. 66 by permission of the Textile Research Institute, Princeton, New Jersey)

treated fabrics, even when the same amount of dye is present in both fabrics [25, 64].

The improvements in colour yield from the ammonia–dry-steam process depend upon the specific changes in fibre morphology that occur, being particularly sensitive to the amount of ammonia remaining on the fabric at the time it enters the steamer [25]. The amount appears to be critical: over 35% ammonia yields a similar result to that of a water-based removal process, while less than 5% ammonia at the steamer yields the typical dry–steam process, i.e. the improvement over unmercerised cloth is small. If the ammonia content lies between 5 and 35% then intermediate properties result. Thus the changes in the dyeing and other properties are particularly sensitive and dependent upon this critical stage of the process.

The depth of shade obtained from the dyeing process may range from 'worse than untreated' to 'as good as mercerised', depending upon the particular dye and dyeing method. However, the small improvement usually obtained from the ammonia–dry–steam process results in a fibre that is more accessible to small molecules but less accessible to large molecules. The standard moisture regain is higher but the water retention value is lower. It has been concluded that more fibrillar surfaces may have been exposed but that some of the larger voids have

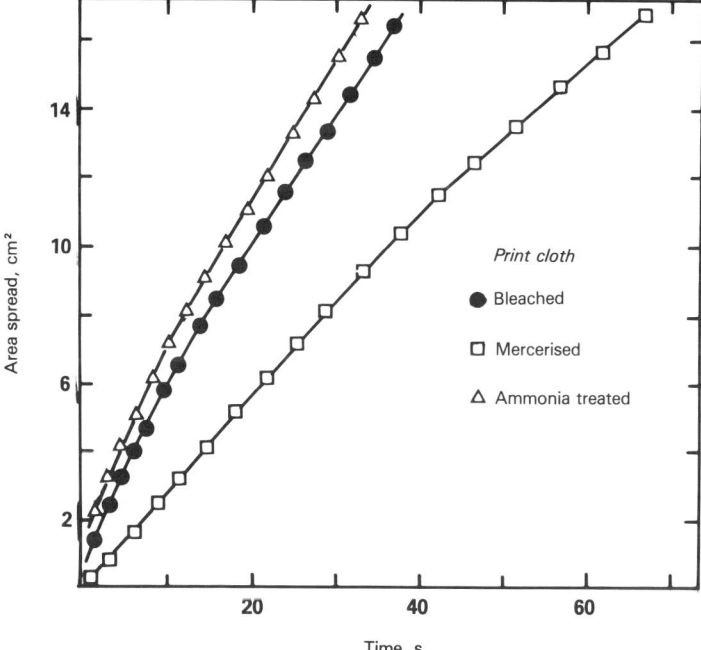

Figure 3.8 – Radial wicking in terms of area spread plotted against time (reproduced from ref. 66 by permission of the Textile Research Institute, Princeton, New Jersey)

been eliminated or at least reduced in size. An alternative view is that swelling in ammonia occurs principally in the ordered regions where dye molecules do not normally penetrate, whereas in conventional mercerisation extensive swelling of both the ordered and disordered regions occurs, thereby leading to a greater penetration of the disordered regions. As a consequence the rate of dyeing would be expected to be reduced by ammonia treatments, and this phenomenon has been observed. In addition there appears to be some difficulty in fixing large quantities of flame retardants [25].

3.5 REGENERATED CELLULOSE FIBRES

3.5.1 General Classification

The two main routes for the formation of regenerated cellulose fibres are those based on the viscose process and the cuprammonium process [1, 3, 5, 7, 67–72]. Viscose is by far the most important and is produced in a variety of fibre types with wide differences in structure, cross-section, physical properties and dyeability [1, 3–5, 69–72]. Cuprammonium rayon, or cupro, is spun by relatively few manufacturers, normally in the form of fine fibres simulating natural silk. With the advent of various silk-like thermoplastic man-made fibres with superior physical properties, its importance has further declined [68].

The relationship between fibre structure and dyeability is very complex, and many factors are important in determining not only the rate but also the extent of dye uptake [1, 5]. This is particularly the case with the various modifications of viscose fibres that have been produced, for apart from those designed to change the fibre lustre and opacity, great efforts have been made to improve the physical properties of standard viscose fibres. All this has led to fibres with different skin–core cross-sections, crimped fibres, and, through the incorporation of additives, the production of dye-variant and also flame-retardant fibres [1, 3, 5, 72].

The term viscose was formerly used to denote the solution obtained by dissolving cellulose xanthate in a dilute solution of caustic soda. The fibre formed by regeneration of the cellulose from 'viscose' by treatment with solutions of electrolytes (salts and acids) was then called viscose rayon. Current terminology now refers to viscose fibres rather than viscose rayon. Similarly cupro is the generic term for what used to be known as cuprammonium rayon fibres, which are the fibres regenerated from a solution of cellulose in cuprammonium hydroxide [73]. Both types of fibre are based on cellulose II, and their lustre may be varied by the incorporation within the fibre of suitable pigments in a finely divided state [67].

More recent modifications to the viscose process to produce regenerated cellulose fibres with improved physical properties in both the wet and the air-conditioned states have led to the introduction of other generic classes of fibres, namely high-tenacity polynosic, modal and also high wet modulus fibres [67, 71, 72].

Initially polynosic fibres with a wet modulus comparable with that of cotton were developed [71, 72, 74]. These were later termed standard polynosic fibres as two other variants emerged. The first of these was a high-strength polynosic in which the polynosic character was preserved to some extent while the wet-fibre tenacity was increased to match that of cotton. The second type was a high-elongation polynosic fibre, known as a modal fibre, in which the true polynosic character was sacrificed in order to obtain better dyeability, higher abrasion resistance, and also improved performance in processing and resin finishing. These developments have been described elsewhere [70–72, 74] and descriptions of the different fibre variants have appeared, although it must be pointed out that the distinction between polynosic and high wet modulus fibres in the earlier literature on such fibres is often not as clear as in later work, by which time the basic production methods were established.

3.5.2 Viscose Fibres

Regular Viscose
Regular (or standard) viscose is produced by the extrusion of cellulose xanthate into a dilute sulphuric acid bath containing sodium sulphate and zinc ions, usually in the form of zinc sulphate. Although cellulose xanthate cannot be oriented in solution, and only a very small degree of orientation (if any) can be introduced after regeneration [69], it can be oriented after coagulation. Therefore, by varying the relative rates of coagulation, neutralisation and regeneration, while applying stretch to the coagulated filaments, a wide variety of fibre structures and different fibre properties may be produced [1, 3, 5]. Major structural variations include differences in fibre cross-section, skin–core effect, crimp, orientation and crystallinity [67, 69–72]. In addition titanium dioxide pigments may be incorporated to vary the fibre lustre from bright (containing no delustrant) to fully matt (heavily delustred) [67].

Viscose fibres are characterised by an irregular serrated skin and core fibre cross-section. The existence of the skin–core structure has been described in many studies using staining techniques. The skin structure is believed to consist of many small-sized crystalline regions, whereas the core section of the fibre is indicative of a coarser crystalline structure [75]. The differences in the skin–core relationship thus reflect differences in the fine structure of the fibre, and the behaviour during dyeing and appearance after dyeing will differ according to the type of fibre under consideration.

The skin structure of viscose fibres normally begins to develop after only 0.1 s in the coagulation bath and is complete after 0.6 s. Changes in coagulation conditions lead to considerable changes in the surface structure of the fibre. Suitable modification of the spinning conditions can be employed to produce fibres that are highly oriented with a pronounced skin–core structure, in which the thickness of the skin is often arranged to be non-uniform [5, 76].

Chemically Crimped Viscose
These fibres are produced by altering the regeneration conditions so that the skin of the fibre bursts while in the spin bath [70]. The liquid viscose exposed is thus regenerated under slightly different conditions from the skin, and a bicomponent structure results. A permanent crimp develops as a result of the differential shrinkage in subsequent washing and drying. In the wet processing of such fibres high tensions

should be avoided because the force required to straighten a wet crimped viscose fibre is extremely small. Drying under strain or straining the fibres will remove some of the crimp, but this is normally recovered on rewetting [77]. Crimped fibre with its high degree of cover and attractive handle when made into fabrics is widely used in staple form, by itself and in blends with synthetic-polymer fibres.

The modification of the fibre structure does not lead, however, to marked differences in fibre dyeability, as compared with standard viscose fibres of comparable fineness, although the fibre crimp may lead to subtle changes in fabric appearance because of optical effects. Staple fibres of higher linear density for use in loop- and cut-pile carpets have been produced, while versions of carpet staple fibres with improved abrasion resistance have also been marketed, but the dyeing behaviour of the latter type is markedly different [78].

The effect of steaming on regular viscose and on cupro fibres is to reduce the uptake of direct dyes because of modifications in fibre structure [79]. Fibre density and crystallinity are increased, so that the dye absorption is markedly reduced as the temperature of steaming is raised (see Figure 3.9).

The structure of viscose fibres is manifestly different from that of cotton, and this is apparent not only during dyeing and finishing, but also in the properties of the resultant dyed fibre [80, 81]. Thus it has been demonstrated by Giles [82] that the light fastness grades of a number of direct dyes are higher on viscose than on cotton (see Figure 3.10).

Hollow Viscose Fibres
Hollow viscose fibres can be produced containing either discrete air bubbles or continuous hollow tubes [71, 72, 83]. One of the latter types of fibre is manufactured by spinning viscose dope containing sodium carbonate into an acid spinning bath. The carbon dioxide produced is enclosed within the fibre, creating a characteristic hollow fibre cross-section [71]. Such fibres are thus engineered to have a hollow centre similar to the lumen in cotton, only larger [72].

The lower fibre density of 1.15 g/ml (compared with 1.52 g/ml for regular viscose) is accompanied by a higher water imbibition (130% compared with 100%). In addition the greater surface area leads to a more rapid dyeing rate, although the equilibrium dye uptake and hue obtained are comparable to those achieved on regular viscose. The inner walls of the hollow fibre results in a lower colour yield for a given dye content than on regular viscose [83].

Therefore, while deep colours may require the use of more dye than on regular viscose, hollow viscose facilitates the production of solid colours in blends with cotton, in contrast to blends of regular viscose/cotton in which the cotton generally dyes lighter. Hollow viscose fibres also provide greater bulk and fabric cover for the same fabric weight per unit area and possess a soft handle of the type normally associated with combed cotton [71, 83].

3.5.3 Viscose Fibres with Improved Physical Properties
The physical properties of wet viscose fibres may be improved, and the fibre cross-section and dyeability dramatically modified, by reducing the rate of regeneration

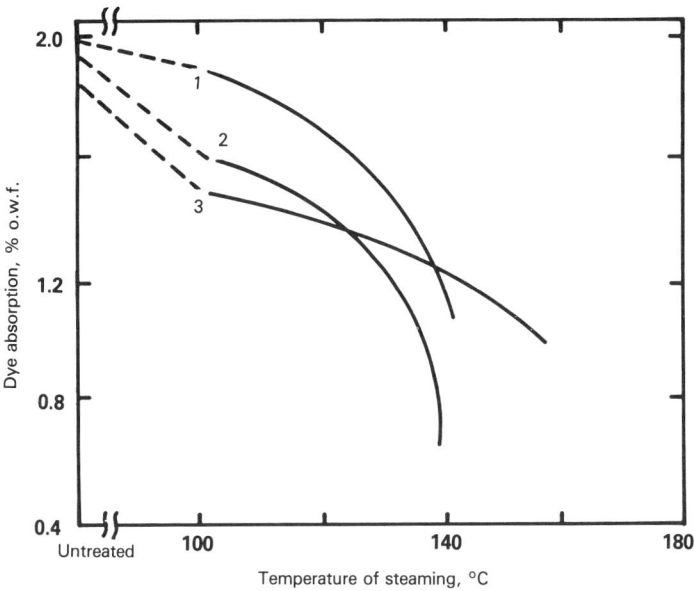

1 — Viscose, 0%, stretch, 20 – 25% water content
2 — Viscose, 30% stretch, 20 – 25% water content
3 — Cupro, 35% water content

Figure 3.9 – Dye absorption of cellulose fibres steamed for 1 h; dyeing conditions – Chlorazol Sky Blue FF (0.5 g/l), sodium chloride (5 g/l) for 2 h at 80°C

of the cellulose, so that stretching to produce a high degree of orientation may be employed [70–72, 74–76]. Such fibres have generally been termed high wet modulus (HWM) fibres. The regeneration rate may be reduced by a number of methods [75, 76]:

1. Use of a viscose dope with a high carbon disulphide content
2. Incorporation of additives or modifiers in viscose dope or in the coagulation bath
3. Lowering the coagulation bath temperature
4. Using low concentrations of sulphuric acid and high concentrations of zinc sulphate in the coagulation bath
5. Spinning at lower speeds.

Essentially two distinct sets of spinning methods have evolved:
(a) Zinc-based processes, as used to make regular viscose and high-tenacity viscose
(b) Spinning processes not based on zinc, which have led to the introduction of polynosic fibres.

The detailed development of both these spinning systems has been described elsewhere [70–72, 74, 75].

The prime factors of concern from the coloration point of view are the changes in the physico-chemical structures in the skin and core, the fibre surface, and the imbibition and tensile properties in the wet state.

The production and structure of high-tenacity viscose, polynosic and modified HWM fibres [67, 70–72, 74, 75] will now be briefly discussed.

High-tenacity Viscose Fibres
High-tenacity viscose fibres are usually produced by methods that confer a high degree of orientation, and the fibres are used largely in industrial applications requiring minimal coloration.

It is well established that the depth of dyeing on regular viscose is dependent upon the filament linear density, finer filaments requiring more dye for the same depth of coloration [80, 81, 84]. This optical effect can normally be allowed for by using the nomogram produced by Fothergill for calculating the ratio between the percentages of dye required to produce a given depth on filaments of different linear density [80, 85]. This is satisfactory on regular viscose fibres where the structure and the porosity of the fibres are relatively constant.

However, the high-tenacity viscose fibre Durafil is said [86] to require four times more direct dye to obtain the same depth as on regular viscose of the same filament linear density. The absorption of light by the direct dyes was considered to be greater in the length direction of the molecules. In highly oriented viscose fibres the resultant orientation of the direct dye molecules in the fibre length direction accordingly led to less absorption of light. Thus high-tenacity viscose fibres appeared to be less deeply dyed than regular viscose in which the lower fibre orientation led to a more random distribution of the dye molecules.

Polynosic Fibres
The term polynosic was first used in 1959 to designate a new class of regenerated cellulose fibres that differed fundamentally in properties from ordinary viscose staple fibre [74]. Polynosic fibres possess a homogeneous fibrillar structure and thus give a significant improvement in physical properties [67, 70, 74].

In the ordinary viscose process, the viscose, consisting largely of cellulose zanthate, is extruded into a spinning bath containing about 10% sulphuric acid together with other salts. Coagulation and regeneration take place almost immediately, and stretch is simultaneously imparted to the fibre [67, 70]. Polynosic fibres, however, are spun into a bath containing a dilute solution (3–7%) of sulphuric acid and less than 12% sodium sulphate. As a result the xanthate decomposes slowly and stretch is imparted to the filaments before regeneration is complete [70, 74, 75]. As the filaments are in a highly plastic state, a high degree of orientation exists during the formation of the crystalline structure. As stretching proceeds, the modulus increases, and because the degree of polymerisation of the cellulose is of the order of 500, which is about twice that in regular viscose, the retention of crystallinity is greatly facilitated.

Commercial production of Toramomen, the first polynosic fibre, followed some years after the process was invented by the Tachikawa Institute of Japan, in 1942.

Subsequently, however, apart from this process operated by a number of fibre producers under licence, several alternative processes have led to a wider range of polynosic fibres. While these various polynosic fibres differ in physical properties and dyeability, all have been classed [71, 74] into three main groups:
(a) Group 1, high-strength fibres with high air-dry and wet tensile strengths
(b) Group 2, standard group with properties intermediate between groups 1 and 3
(c) Group 3, high-elongation fibres.

The diversity in physical properties and dyeability does not detract from the common features of polynosic fibres [71, 74, 75]:
(a) High fibre modulus in the wet state, i.e. resistant to extension when wet
(b) Increased ratio of wet-to-dry breaking tenacity
(c) Increased resistance to swelling by caustic alkalis
(d) Fibres composed of cellulose chains with a high degree of polymerisation:

The similarity between cotton (imbibition 50%) and the polynosic fibres in terms of physical properties is demonstrated in Figure 3.11, in which the stress/strain properties are clearly seen to be superior to those of standard viscose staple (imbibition 100%). However, the physical properties, particularly the dyeability, depend upon the fine structure of the fibre, which has been shown [74, 75] to emanate from the:
1. High degree of crystallinity
2. High degree of orientation
3. High lateral order

which are all introduced as a result of the method of fibre manufacture.

X-ray diffraction and density studies suggest that polynosic fibres have a degree of crystallinity of the order of 55%, compared with 40–45% for viscose and 70–80% for cotton [74]. The size of the crystalline regions is considerably greater than for regular viscose fibres. Another factor of importance affecting dyeability is that the degree of orientation of the molecular chains in both the crystalline and the disordered (or amorphous) regions is greatly increased compared with regular viscose. The high lateral order is evidenced by the unique fibrillar structure in which fibrils are distributed uniformly through the cross-section, producing a fibre with a homogeneous structure and an almost circular cross-section. Thus the swelling and solubility properties of polynosic fibres differ markedly from those of regular viscose fibres.

HWM Fibres
The greater overall growth in use of HWM fibres relative to polynosics is primarily associated with the simpler and more economic manufacturing methods for the former [72, 75]. In addition HWM fibres are less stiff and do not tend to fibrillate as readily in the wet state, both important advantages [72].

HWM fibres are produced using the viscose spinning system and employing spinning bath modifiers or additives (or both) for the control of the regeneration process [67, 70–72, 74, 75]. The introduction of zinc into the spinning bath is believed to produce zinc xanthate complexes, which are more stable than cellulose xanthate

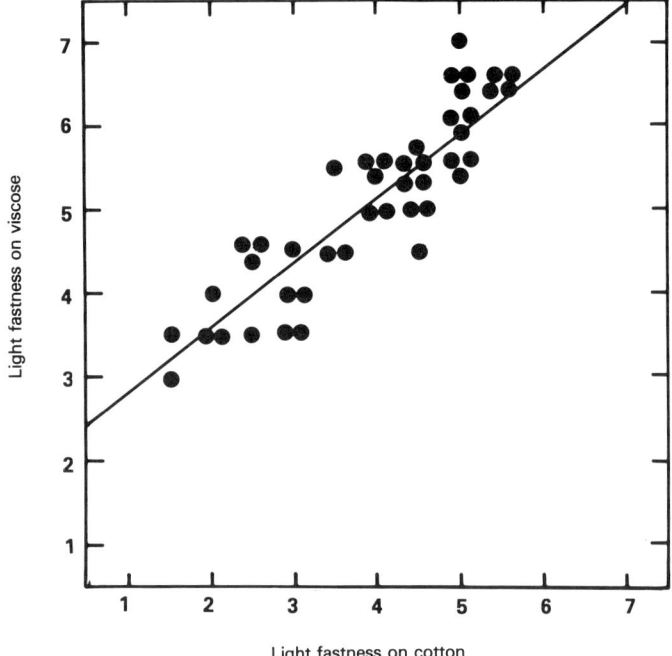

Figure 3.10 – Influence of the nature of the fibre on the light fastness of dyed textiles

and give greater control over the stretching process. Similarly formaldehyde added to the viscose dope or to the spinning bath stabilises the xanthate by forming an ester which is later decomposed [1, 74, 75]. Concern over the possible toxicity of formaldehyde has led to increasingly stringent regulations on the exposure of workers; recent advances in this field are summarised elsewhere [72].

HWM fibres differ in some physical, mechanical and fine-structural properties from the polynosic fibres, and this leads to differences in the kinetics of dyeing and the equilibrium dye uptake [75, 76].

3.5.4 Structure and Coloration of Regenerated Cellulose Fibres and Films
The characterisation of the structure of regenerated cellulose fibres may generally be described in terms of certain basic parameters [87, 88]:
1. Average degree of polymerisation (DP) (measured in terms of viscosity or osmosis)
2. Average crystallite length (measured using small-angle X-ray diffraction)
3. Perfection of lateral order (measured using wide-angle X-ray diffraction)
4. Degree of orientation (measured using infra-red dichroism or X-ray diffraction).

The DP of the regenerated cellulose chains and the molecular weight distribution within the fibre are of importance, not only because of their influence on the other three factors but also because of the general improvement in tensile properties in both the conditioned and wet states as the average DP is increased.

The dye and conditions used in the dyeing of regenerated (and also natural) cellulose fibres are certainly important, but the physico-chemical structure of the fibre is also crucial. This is particularly so with regenerated cellulose fibres, where the characteristics of the cellulose after dissolution (e.g. DP and chemical modification) and the structural changes induced in the fibre by the conditions employed during extrusion, coagulation and stretching and drying all modify the dyeing behaviour considerably [1, 5, 27–29].

Both the equilibrium absorption and the kinetics of dyeing are dependent upon a large number of factors [23]. Notable amongst these are:

1. Nature, concentration, distribution and degree of ionisation of the ionisable groups in the fibre and in the dye
2. Volume fraction, and detailed configuration, of the disordered regions accessible to the dye
3. Volume fraction, size, configuration and distribution of the 'crystalline' or ordered regions of the fibre
4. Molecular interactions occurring in the dyebath and in the fibre
5. Existence of elastic, or similar, stresses in the polymer structure.

The effects of processing conditions on dyeability are to be seen not only in regenerated cellulose fibres, but also in films [89, 90]. The diffusion of direct dyes in regenerated cellulose films occurs more rapidly in the highly swollen state of a never-dried film. After the drying process the rate of diffusion into the normal regenerated cellulose films, which are much less swollen and possess a more compact structure, is much lower than in the never-dried films, and moreover the equilibrium dye absorption is also lower.

Even in cellulose gel (i.e. never-dried) films studies of the edgewise diffusion of a direct dye demonstrated that the dye diffused anisotropically [89]. Thus the diffusion rate along the axis of extrusion was greater than in the direction normal to this axis. This has been interpreted in terms of the possible orientation of the cellulose chain molecules during extrusion [23].

The marked individuality of regenerated cellulose films and fibres is demonstrated in Table 3.8. Dyeing processes adopted during fibre manufacture that utilise the features of never-dried material have been described. These involve the padding of reactive dyes onto a never-dried viscose incorporating a cellulose aminoethyl ether after regeneration and washing, followed by steaming and washing [91]. Such processes may be employed as an alternative to mass pigmentation methods, described in detail elsewhere [86, 92].

3.5.5 Dyeability of Regular Viscose, Polynosic and HWM Fibres

Apart from fibres having a more or less circular cross-section, significant differences in fine structure are observed in fibres produced under different production conditions.

TABLE 3.8

Properties of a Variety of Commercially Available Viscose Fibres

Type	Dry tenacity (cN/tex)	Wet tenacity (cN/tex)	Dry extension (%)	Wet extension (%)	Water imbibition (%)
Standard viscose	17–22	8–11	18–30	20–40	90–100
Improved-strength viscose	22–26	11–14	17–25	20–30	85–95
Crimped viscose	15–21	7–12	18–40	25–54	90–100
Polynosic	25–45	18–35	6–12	9–15	55–75
Modal	30–40	19–28	12–15	17–21	70–80
High-tenacity viscose (tyre yarn)	35–65	25–50	4–17	6–33	65–75
Hollow viscose	19–24	9–13	13–15	16–19	120–140

(Reproduced from ref. 71 by permission of Shirley Institute, Manchester)

Vincel 64 (an HWM fibre), for example, has pores of smaller size and a lower degree of fibre swelling in water compared with cotton, so that the rate of dye diffusion is lower although the general dyeing behaviour is akin to that of regular viscose [76]. In such fibres dichroic effects, particularly with blue direct dyes, are common, this behaviour being associated with the close alignment of the dye molecules along the highly oriented fibre axis. In such cases the observed colour may well be flatter than that demonstrated on regular viscose. In general, studies indicate that the lower inter-pore volume of polynosic fibres leads to lower uptake of reactive dyes and lower water of imbibition compared with regular viscose.

Generally the degree of crystallinity, the length and thickness of the crystallites, the DP and the chain orientation all decrease in the order: polynosic > HWM > regular viscose fibres [75]. The accessibility of the hydroxyl groups to water is thus greatest with viscose and lowest for polynosic fibres. Thus there is a stronger internal structure in the HWM and polynosic fibres, which are characterised by less disorder and a greater number of intercrystalline links, than in regular viscose.

The orientation of the chain molecules is of great importance in determining the dye uptake; in general an increase in the degree of chain orientation leads to less dye being absorbed at equilibrium, while the rate of dyeing is dramatically decreased [23] (see Figure 3.12), although this relationship is not precise. While the methods employed to characterise the ordered crystalline regions lead to well-defined values, the disordered regions can only be imprecisely characterised. Any particular dye may or may not diffuse in the fibre, depending upon the number and size of the disordered regions and their individual level of orientation and lateral order. Nevertheless the net result is a decrease in the rate of dye uptake as the degree of orientation of the fibre is increased.

In one study the initial rate of dyeing was found to be closely related to the average void size derived from the degree of orientation and the average length of the

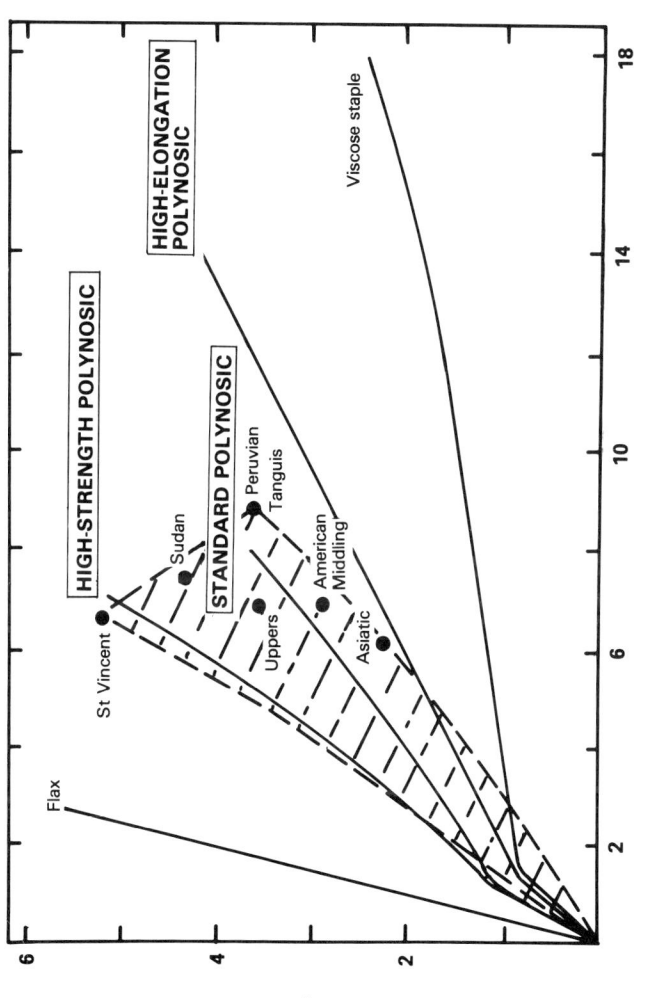

Figure 3.11 – Stress–strain curves, based on air-dry conditions, comparing three types of polynosic fibres with cotton, flax and viscose staple; the region including cotton is indicated by the cross-hatched area (reproduced from Text. Inst. Ind., 3 (1965) 55 by permission of the Textile Institute, Manchester)

crystallites in the fibre [88]. However, the number and accessibility of the reactive sites are also of importance for reactive dyes. A study concerned with the absorption of reactive dyes by cotton and eight different regenerated cellulose fibres demonstrated that cupro had the highest rate of dye uptake [93]. A continuous and homogeneous penetration throughout the whole fibre cross-section was obtained with polynosic fibres whereas more concentrated peripheral zones were detected in the other fibres. Dyeability variations were attributed to variable substantivity as well as to differences in the accessibility of the hydroxyl groups. These differences in dye uptake could be reduced markedly depending upon the concentration of sodium hydroxide used as a pretreatment.

In another study both HWM and regular viscose had an appreciable amount of skin as a uniform layer at the filament periphery [94]. Mercerisation destroyed the skin, and following treatment the fibre cross-sections showed equal staining.

Mechanical damage occurs during laundering and is severe in accelerated wear testing. Heat causes cleavage as well as cross-linking while u.v. radiation damage is confined solely to those portions of the fibre surface that are exposed, with evidence of some cross-linking. Clearly, therefore, the exposure of regenerated cellulose fibres to a wide variety of pretreatments has been shown to result in changes in physico-chemical structure, so that accompanying changes in the dyeing properties are to be expected [95].

In other studies the molecular weight distribution in various regenerated cellulose fibres has been shown to be markedly different, through using sophisticated polymer fractionation techniques [96]. More recent work also suggests that the uptake of vat dyes is affected by variations in molecular weight distribution and the degree of polydispersity [97]. The swelling, solubility and reactivity of regular viscose is particularly influenced by the proportion of low molecular weight fractions and their influence upon the fibre structure.

3.5.6 Effects of Changes in Specific Fibre Structure on the Dyeability of Viscose Fibres

Although many studies have been published on the dyeability of viscose fibres, there are relatively few in which a systematic study of the dyeability of model filaments has been reported and in which the changes in the fibre structure have been carefully controlled and characterised.

Filament Linear Density
Studies have demonstrated that, in general, the rate of dyeing is greater and the time to attain 90% exhaustion, $t(90\%)$, is lower the smaller the filament linear density [98]. However, the equilibrium exhaustion values show little variation between 1.12 and 5.4 dtex filaments. The dyeing rate is lower and the exhaustion value higher at 50°C than at 90°C, in agreement with general theories of dyeing [62, 99].

If d is the filament linear density and r is the radius of the filament cross-section, then $d \propto \pi r^2$. In a given weight of n filaments

$$n \propto 1/d$$

$$\propto 1/\pi r^2$$

The surface area of a filament (σ) is given by:

$$\sigma \propto 2\pi r . \frac{1}{\pi r^2}$$

$$\propto \frac{1}{r}$$

$$\therefore \ \sigma \propto \frac{1}{d^{1/2}}$$

However, because viscose fibres are often not circular and the cross-section is serrated, the serration coefficient (p/c), where p is the length of the periphery and c is the circumference of the surrounding circle of a viscose filament cross-section, may vary in value from 1 to about 2. In a series of specially spun viscose filaments, in which the linear density was varied but the serration coefficient kept constant, it was demonstrated that the rates of dyeing, expressed as the amounts of dye absorbed after 5 min, were directly proportional to the available surfaces of the filaments [98]. Thus the plot of relative dye absorption against $1/d^{1/2}$ was linear. This essentially means that the rate of dyeing on an equal area basis is independent of the filament linear density. The conflicting results from other studies are attributed to variations in filament orientation and structure in viscose filaments of different linear density [100].

Thus in a viscose fabric containing both coarse and fine fibres, the fine fibres will dye faster and absorb proportionally more dye from the solution, thereby prolonging the time required for levelling and equilibrium to be established. Differences in colour will still be apparent between fine and coarse fibres even though the equilibrium exhaustion values are the same. These differences are due to optical effects caused by the light being reflected from different surface areas, the finer fibres possessing a lower apparent depth than the coarse, even when the dye exhaustion values are the same [85].

Orientation
Orientation of the fibre structure in viscose is increased by increasing the stretch on the filament after coagulation [30, 98, 99]. The birefringence (a measure of fibre orientation) and fibre strength increase while fibre extensibility is reduced. Orientation exerts a marked influence on the rate of dyeing of viscose, a decrease in birefringence from 0.03 to 0.02 yielding an approximate two-fold increase in dyeing rate [98]. The dyeing rate (measured by the values of dye absorbed after 15 min) decreases linearly with increase in filament birefringence (and hence in filament orientation) when the results are plotted on an equal surface area basis. Thus the equilibrium dye uptake is approached more slowly the greater the fibre orientation [30, 98, 99].

At low birefringence values (0.15–0.25) and low orientation the equilibrium dye uptake decreases only slightly as the orientation is increased [30]. With increasing orientation the rate of decrease of the equilibrium dye uptake becomes greater and at a birefringence of 0.04 the equilibrium dye uptake is only 1 g per 100 g cellulose, compared with a value above 1.4 at a birefringence of about 0.15 [30].

Ripeness
Variation in the ripeness of viscose dope produces marked changes in the coagulation conditions and in the resulting fibres [98, 99]. The more unripe the viscose, the greater the number of xanthate groups combined with the cellulose. Ageing treatments for viscose dope prior to spinning ripen the viscose [99]. Increased ageing times lead to a slight decrease in initial dyeing rate and to an increase in the $t(90\%)$ values. This has been confirmed in another study in which as the ripeness decreased the orientation is increased, and the equilibrium dye absorption values thus showed a marked and progressive downward trend with increased ripeness [98].

Skin
The dyeing behaviour of no-skin and thick-skin viscose filaments differs, the thick-skin viscose dyeing at a slower rate, with the skin portion containing less dye than the core [99]. However, the equilibrium dye uptake values were the same for both types of fibre.

Degree of Polymerisation
The dyeing of 165 dtex/40 filament bright viscose yarns differing in average DP from 212 to 516 has demonstrated that, while the initial dyeing rate decreases with increase in DP, the $t(90\%)$ value and the equilibrium exhaustion progressively increase [99]. However, the changes in dye uptake, though real, are relatively small.

Period of Immersion in Coagulation Bath
Increasing the period of immersion of the viscose filament in the coagulation bath, at a constant spinning tension and speed, leads to higher wet and dry tensile strengths and lower filament extensibility. This indicates that the fibre orientation is increased the longer the immersion time, and hence slower rates of dyeing and lower dye absorption values are obtained [30, 98].

Latent Strain
When dry viscose yarns are extended beyond 2% or when they are dried without permitting free contraction, an appreciable amount of latent strain is retained; on subsequent wetting some, but not all, of this strain is released. The value of 2% extension is around the yield point for the fibre, which may reflect a closing or distortion of the accessible regions by which the dyes enter the fibre [98]. Where the recoverable latent strain exceeds 2% the dye absorption is reduced progressively as the strain is increased. The effect, however, is to reduce the rate of dyeing only, for the equilibrium dye uptake values are not affected. It would appear, therefore, that although the effective change in the accessible regions leads to a reduction in dyeing rate, there is no accompanying change in the internal surface available to dyes [98].

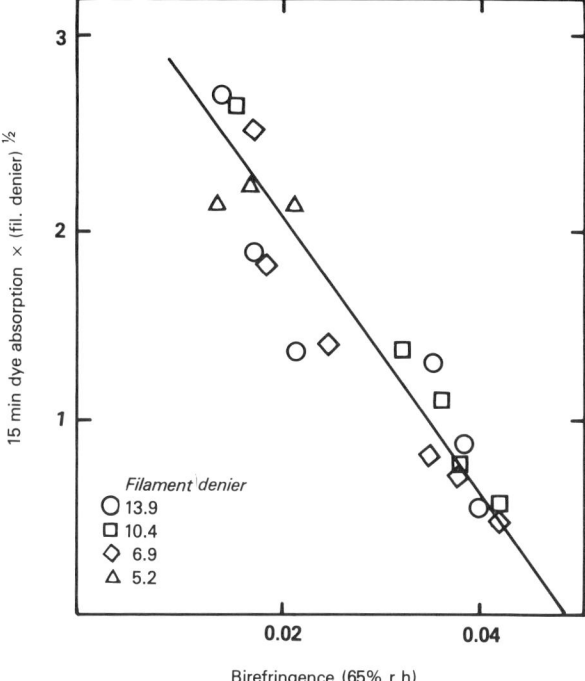

Figure 3.12 – Effect of orientation of viscose fibres on dye uptake

Volume Swelling
As the degree of fibre orientation decreases, as measured by a decrease in bi-refringence, there is an increase in dye absorption [30, 98]. It has been demonstrated that a decrease in both orientation and birefringence is associated with an increase in fibre volume swelling [101]. The volume swelling is a function of the amount of water or dyebath liquor imbibed by the fibres and an increase in the volume swelling is associated with an increase in the amount of dye absorbed at equilibrium. However, for fibres with very high volume swelling, the total internal volume is greater than the effective volume associated with the cellulose internal surface being dyed, so that the equilibrium dye uptake values approach a limiting value [101].

3.5.7 Viscose Fibres of Modified Dyeability
The attempts to produce viscose fibres with substantivity for acid dyes, to provide solid shades on wool/viscose blends, have a long history. Chemically basic additives were added to the viscose dope or amine–formaldehyde resins applied after fibre regeneration [1, 102, 103]. Various types were marketed but none had adequate fastness performance after dyeing and dyebath conditions were difficult to control.

A more successful approach was to link a cellulose derivative containing basic groups directly to the cellulose fibre. Such modified viscose fibres represent a near approach to a 'wool-dyeing' fibre but practical application difficulties persisted.

A more significant development has been the use of fibres containing a much lower degree of substitution, to yield deep-dyeing fibres [102], such as DD Sarille or Sarilluxe (Courtaulds). Using direct dyes, deep-dyeing viscose fibres dye much more rapidly and with greater exhaustion than normal viscose. Therefore dyeings on blends of deep-dyeing and normal viscose fibre produce tone-on-tone effects in which the degree of contrast between the two types of fibres may be varied according to the selected dyebath conditions.

However, in spite of many attractive properties, commercial production has virtually ceased because modified viscose fibres are expensive and of limited appeal.

3.5.8 Flame-retardant Viscose Fibres

The incorporation of water-insoluble phosphorus compounds into viscose prior to fibre extrusion by dispersing highly chlorinated or brominated alkyl phosphate esters such as tris(2,3-dibromopropyl)phosphate led to the production of durable flame-retardant viscose fibres like Darelle (Courtaulds) [5, 103, 104]. High additive levels (around 20%) led to slight dulling of the fibre lustre, reduced fibre tenacity and abrasion resistance, so that fibres of 5 dtex and above were required, although the handle was softer than regular viscose.

Practical precautions during wet processing to prevent progressive hydrolysis or loss of the additive included the avoidance of: high processing temperatures, alkaline conditions, extended processing times and the use of non-ionic detergents [104]. The colour yield from direct, reactive, vat or sulphur dyes was generally improved by up to 10% due to the lower percentage of cellulose in the fibre. However, because of potential toxicity hazards associated with tris(2,3-dibromo-propyl)phosphate, such fibres are no longer manufactured.

Viscose fibres modified by the incorporation of phosphorus-containing reagents to confer flame-retardant properties are currently produced, but the flame retardant causes a dulling effect [105].

Modern versions of flame-retardant viscose incorporate solid additives applied as aqueous dispersions mixed with the dope prior to fibre spinning. Solid flame-retardant additives such as those based on pyrophosphates are more durable to bleaching, washing, dry cleaning, dyeing and finishing procedures than are liquid additives [105].

3.5.9 Cupro Fibres

Cupro fibres are of minor commercial importance compared with viscose; they are coagulated initially in warm water, a slow process in which a comparatively large stretch is imparted, and are heterogeneous in the radial direction [106]. A distinct outermost layer of very low molecular weight (which has been termed the varnish layer) surrounds a layer in which lateral linkages are more or less intact but not well oriented. Deeper within the filament there is an oriented layer containing very few cross-linkages, and finally a core region containing a fair proportion of cross-links of low orientation.

The swelling capacity of the varnish layer (about 5% of the fibre) is about twice that of the intact fibre [106]. The varnish layer is considered to give rise to temporary filament adhesion after spinning, and to a greater abrasion resistance and more rapid penetration of dyes than regular viscose. Cupro filaments are very fine and this leads to a greater capillary attraction for dye liquor and a greater surface area available for dye uptake than with viscose [107, 108]. Cupro's higher substantivity for dyes thus renders the use of restraining agents advisable with certain direct dyes [109], while alkaline pre-scouring and rinsing to remove the varnish layer are generally recommended [107].

REFERENCES

1. Holme, Rev. Prog. Coloration, 1 (1969) 31.
2. Burdett, 'The Theory of Coloration of Textiles', Ed. Bird and Boston (Bradford: Dyers' Co. Publications Trust, 1975) 111.
3. Hearle and Greer, Text. Prog., 2 (4) (1970).
4. Meredith, Text. Prog., 7 (4) (1975).
5. Holme, Rev. Prog. Coloration, 7 (1976) 1.
6. Warwicker et al., 'A Review of the Literature on the Effect of Caustic Soda and Other Swelling Agents on the Fine Structure of Cotton', Shirley Institute Pamphlet No. 93 (Manchester: Shirley Institute, 1966) 10.
7. 'Cellulose and Cellulose Derivatives', Part 1, Ed. Ott, Spurlin and Grafflin (New York: Wiley Interscience, 1954).
8. Hearle and Peters, 'An Introduction to Fibre Structure' (Manchester and London: Textile Institute and Butterworths, 1963).
9. Hearle, 'Polymers and their Properties', Vol. 1 (Chichester, West Sussex: Ellis Horwood Ltd, 1982) 316.
10. Miles, 'The Setting of Fibres and Fabrics', Ed. Hearle and Miles (Watford: Merrow, 1971) 22.
11. Duckett, 'Surface Characteristics of Fibers and Textiles', Part 1, Ed. Schick (New York: Marcel Dekker, 1975) 67.
12. Rowland, Text. Chem. Colorist, 4 (1972) 204.
13. Johnson and Nevell, Rep. Prog. Appl. Chem., 56 (1971) 101.
14. Statton, 'The Meaning of Crystallinity in Polymers', Ed. Price, J. Polymer Sci., C18 (1967) 33.
15. Peters and Ingamells, J.S.D.C., 89 (1973) 397.
16. Johnson, Maheshwari and Miles, 1er Symposium International de la Recherche Textile Cotonniere, Paris (April 1969) 557.
17. Nelson and Oliver, 7th Cellulose Conference, Syracuse, J. Polymer Sci., C36 (1971) 305.
18. Ingamells, 'The Theory of Coloration of Textiles', Ed. Bird and Boston (Bradford: Dyers' Co. Publications Trust, 1975) 285.
19. Stone, Trieber and Abrahamson, TAPPI, 52 (1969) 108.
20. Morton and Hearle, 'Physical Properties of Textile Fibres' (London: Textile Institute and Heinemann, 1975).
21. Kassenbeck, Text. Research J., 40 (1970) 330.
22. Warwicker, J. Polymer Sci. (A1), 1 (1963) 3105.
23. McGregor and Peters, J.S.D.C., 84 (1968) 267.
24. Marsh, 'Mercerising' (London: Chapman and Hall, 1951).
25. Heap, Text. Inst. Ind., 16 (1978) 387.
26. Gailey, J.S.D.C., 67 (1951) 357.
27. Boulton and Morton, J.S.D.C., 56 (1940) 145.
28. Entwistle, J.S.D.C., 62 (1946) 261.

29. Tyler and Wooding, J.S.D.C., **74** (1958) 283.
30. Preston and Kapadia, J.S.D.C., **63** (1947) 434.
31. Joshi and Preston, Text. Research J., **24** (1954) 971.
32. Butcher, Rev. Prog. Coloration, **4** (1973) 90.
33. Sloan, Rev. Prog. Coloration, **5** (1974) 12.
34. 'Chemical Processing of Jute Fabrics for Decorative End Uses', Part I (Calcutta: Indian Jute Industries' Research Association, 1977).
35. Rattee, J.S.D.C., **90** (1974) 367.
36. Lord, 'Manual of Cotton Spinning', Vol. 2, Part 1 (Manchester and London: Textile Institute and Butterworths, 1961).
37. Jeffries et al., Cellulose Chem. and Technol., **3** (1969) 255.
38. Dolmetsch and Dolmetsch, Text. Research J., **39** (1969) 568.
39. Rousselle et al., Ind. Eng. Chem. Prod. Res. Dev., **19** (1980) 654.
40. Erol, PhD thesis, University of Leeds (1982).
41. Leah, Chem. and Ind., (14) (18 July 1981).
42. Rowland, Roberts and Bose, J. Polymer Sci. (A1), **9** (1971) 1431.
43. Rowland, Roberts and Wade, Text. Research J., **39** (1969) 530.
44. Lord, 'The Origin and Assessment of Cotton Fibre Maturity' (Manchester: International Institute for Cotton, 1981).
45. Balls, 'Studies of Quality in Cotton' (London: Macmillan, 1928) 18.
46. Clegg and Harland, J. Textile Inst., **14** (1923) T125.
47. Venkatesh and Dweltz, Text. Research J., **45** (1975) 230.
48. Lawrie, J.S.D.C., **43** (1927) 294.
49. Goldthwait, Smith and Barnett, Text. World, **97** (7) (1947) 105.
50. American Society for Testing Materials, ASTM Standards on Textile Materials (1956) Appendix X.
51. Roberts, Corless and Walton, 'Cotton in a Competitive World', Ed. Harrison (Manchester: Textile Institute, 1979) 264.
52. Cooper, Text. Month, (Feb 1980) 52.
53. International Textile Bulletin, Dyeing, Printing, Finishing, (2) (1970) 123.
54. Sitver, Amer. Dyestuff Rep., **69** (7) (1980) 24.
55. Bailey, Text. Industries, **143** (9) (1977) 82.
56. Greenwood, Text. Inst. Ind., **14** (1976) 373.
57. Goldthwait, Text. Research J., **47** (1977) 632.
58. Cotton Technol., **4** (Sept 1981).
59. Goldfinger, Text. Research J., **47** (1977) 633.
60. Karrer and Schubert, Helv. Chim. Acta, **11** (1928) 221.
61. Knecht, J.S.D.C., **24** (1908) 67, 107.
62. Vickerstaff, 'The Physical Chemistry of Dyeing', 2nd Edn (London: Oliver and Boyd, 1954).
63. Calamari et al., Text. Chem Colorist, **3** (1971) 234.
64. Gailey, 'The Liquid Ammonia Treatment of Cellulosic Textiles' (Manchester: Shirley Institute 1970) 9.
65. Heap, 'Textile and Paper Chemistry and Technology', Ed. Arthur, ACS Symposium No. 49 (Washington DC: American Chemical Society, 1977) 63.
66. Heap, Text. Research J., **49** (1979) 150.
67. Moncrieff, 'Man-Made Fibres', 6th Edn (London: Newnes-Butterworth, 1975).
68. Hathaway, 'Man-Made Fibers Science and Technology', Vol. 2, Ed. Mark, Atlas and Cernia (New York: Wiley Interscience, 1968) 1.
69. Von Bucher, 'Man-Made Fibers Science and Technology', Vol. 2. Ed. Mark, Atlas and Cernia (New York: Wiley Interscience, 1968) 7.
70. McGarry and Priest, 'Man-Made Fibers Science and Technology', Vol. 2, Ed. Mark, Atlas and Cernia (New York: Wiley Interscience, 1968) 43.
71. Welch and Woodings, 'Opportunities for Man-Made Fibres', 11th Shirley International Seminar, Shirley Institute Publication S36 (1979) 14.
72. Dyer and Daul, Ind. Eng. Chem. Prod. Res. Dev., **20** (1981) 222.
73. ISO 2076:1977(E) 'Man-Made Fibres – Generic Names'.

74. Griffiths, Text. Inst. Ind. **3** (1965) 54.
75. Schappel and Boekno, 'Cellulose and Cellulose Derivatives', Part 5, Ed. Bikales and Segal (New York: Wiley Interscience, 1971) 1115.
76. Madaras and Robinson, J.S.D.C., **89** (1973) 317.
77. Malabon, Text. Inst. Ind., **11** (1973) 240.
78. Cheetham, Bridges and Pratt, J.S.D.C., **81** (1965) 562.
79. Preston, Nimkar and Gundavda, J.S.D.C., **67** (1951) 169.
80. 'The Fibro Manual', Ed. Whittaker (London: Sylvan Press, 1949).
81. Boulton, J.S.D.C., **67** (1951) 522.
82. Giles, 'A Laboratory Course in Dyeing', 3rd Edn (Bradford: SDC, 1974) 39.
83. Priest, Text. Manuf., **77** (5) (Aug 1977) 22.
84. Boulton and Wardle, J.S.D.C., **63** (1947) 8.
85. Fothergill, J.S.D.C., **60** (1944) 93.
86. Butterworth and Cluley, J. Textile Inst., **45** (1954) P427.
87. Krässig, 'Man-Made Fibers Science and Technology', Vol. 2, Ed. Mark, Atlas and Cernia, (New York: Wiley Interscience, 1968) 121.
88. Krässig, TAPPI, **61** (3) (1978) 93.
89. McGregor and Peters, Trans. Faraday Soc., **60** (1964) 2062.
90. Warwicker, J. Polymer Sci. (A1), **1** (1963) 3105.
91. Courtaulds, BP 1271518 (1968).
92. Jordan, Bayer Farben Revue, (15) (1969) 1.
93. Valk, Kehren and Loers, Textilveredlung, **4** (1969) 46.
94. Morehead and Sisson, Text. Research J., **15** (1945) 443.
95. Dyer and Phifer, 7th Cellulose Conference, Syracuse, J. Polymer Sci., **C36** (1971) 103.
96. Cumberbirch, J. Textile Inst., **50** (1959) T528.
97. Lebedeva, Tekhnol. tekstil. Prom, No. 5 (96) (1973) 100.
98. Preston and Pal, J.S.D.C., **63** (1947) 430.
99. Royer, McCleary and de Bruyne, J.S.D.C., **63** (1947) 254.
100. Boulton and Wardle, J.S.D.C., **63** (1947) 8.
101. Preston, Mhatre and Narasimhan, J.S.D.C., **65** (1949) 17.
102. Ward and Hill, Text. Inst. Ind., **7** (1969) 274.
103. Best-Gordon, Text. Inst. Ind., **7** (1969) 162.
104. Dawson and Ward, J.S.D.C, **89** (1973) 493.
105. Wolf, Ind. Eng. Chem. Prod. Res. Dev., **20** (1981) 413.
106. Chamberlain and Khera, J. Textile Inst., **43** (1952) T123.
107. Higgs, J.S.D.C., **53** (1937) 305, 461.
108. Ashby, J.S.D.C., **61** (1945) 167.
109. Cheetham, 'Dyeing Fibre Blends' (London: Van Nostrand, 1966) 163.

CHAPTER 4

Dyeing with Reactive Dyes

(The late) MAURICE R FOX and HARRY H SUMNER

4.1 INTRODUCTION

Cross and Bevan, who added greatly to our knowledge of the structure and properties of cellulose [1], are credited with the first recognition of the advantages to be gained by creating a chemical bond between dye and fibre. In 1895 they treated cellulose with strong caustic soda solution and carried out the following sequence of reactions on the alkali cellulose formed: benzoylation, nitration, reduction and diazotisation. The product so formed could be finally coupled with amines or phenols to produce dyes which were linked to cellulose through an ester bond (Figure 4.1).

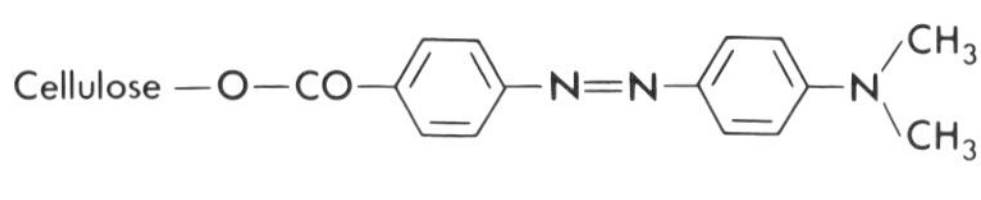

$$Cellulose\ -O-CO-\underset{}{\bigcirc}-N{=}N-\underset{}{\bigcirc}-N\underset{CH_3}{\overset{CH_3}{<}}$$

Figure 4.1 – Linkage of dyes to cellulose

Yellow and red colours with excellent fastness to washing were obtained, but the cellulose fibres suffered severe degradation during processing. Nevertheless other workers adopted this novel approach to coloration by exploring other means of forming ether or ester links between cellulose and dye [2–19]. These pioneering attempts proved to be of only academic interest, usually giving coloured cellulose which had been severely degraded. However, the studies of Haller et al. for Ciba [11] and Günther [4] came fairly close to the ultimate solution. Their approaches failed for different reasons. Thus Haller and Heckendorn, like Cross and Bevan, started with an alkali cellulose but reacted it with cyanuric chloride (the reagent responsible for later meeting the target successfully) and then substituted a second chlorine atom by reaction with aniline, the *para* coupling position of which was then available for coupling with a diazotised base (Scheme 4.1).

However, dyers were reluctant to use inflammable organic solvents. They also recognised the difficulty of producing a standard alkali cellulose and in any case this

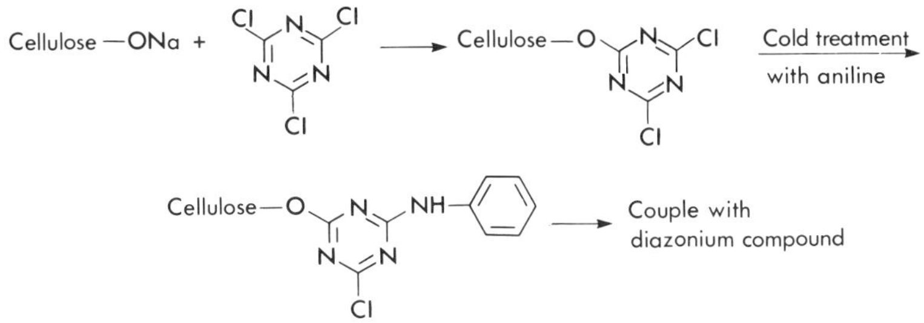

Scheme 4.1

process, like its predecessors, produced serious fibre degradation. Investigation of this patented route has since shown the process to be one of low efficiency combined with poor penetration when applied to cotton fabrics [20, 21].

Günther found that coloured azo derivatives of isatoic anhydride reacted with cellulose in the presence of sodium carbonate (Scheme 4.2). Beech [21] believed that this system, which avoided the need for the alkali cellulose step, was abandoned possibly because the dye–fibre bond was too readily hydrolysed.

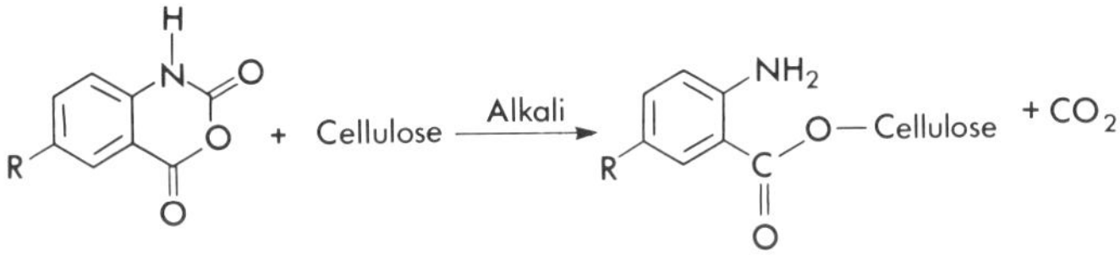

Scheme 4.2

4.2 FIRST COMMERCIAL REACTIVE DYES
During 1953 Stephen and Rattee of ICI were pursuing researches aimed at providing reactive dyes for wool to achieve exceptionally high wet fastness. In the course of his work Stephen submitted preparations of sulphonated azo dyes containing dichlorotriazinyl groups for Rattee to evaluate but the samples failed to meet the wool dyeing target.

Encouraged by the many earlier attempts to react dyes with cotton and inspired by a contemporary research project concerned with the reaction of alkali cellulose with cyanuric chloride [22, 23], it seemed possible to the ICI chemists that the chlorotriazinyl groups in these speculative dyes might be capable of reaction with alkali cellulose. Rattee found that, by first treating cotton in a 15% solution of caustic soda then immersing it in a cold solution of a dichlorotriazinyl dye and subsequently rinsing the impregnated material, he could produce a dyeing of remarkably high washing fastness with no staining of adjacent undyed material. That a dye–fibre reaction had occurred seemed almost certain, because an analogous levelling acid dye would have had no significant substantivity for cotton. The long-awaited breakthrough had taken place.

Rattee and his colleagues concerned themselves with demonstrating the existence of covalent dye–fibre bonds and developing technically sound application
techniques for evaluating further speculative reactive dyes. Stephen and his asso-
ciates attacked the fundamental difficulty preventing useful exploitation of the invention. This was the autocatalytic decomposition by hydrogen chloride of the
dichlorotriazinyl dyes, which could occur not only during preparation stages, including isolation and drying, but also during subsequent storage and use of the
commercial products [21, 24]. The work led to an ingenious and effective method of
mixing the dye with buffers; phosphates or disubstituted arylaminosulphonic acids
proved to be especially effective [25, 26].

Dyeing studies soon revealed that treatment of cotton with strong caustic soda
was not essential to ensure dye–fibre reaction. Dilute solutions of caustic soda were
effective in the presence of high concentrations of common salt. Whereas the first
dyes examined could be fixed by a cold treatment of this kind, later dyes required a
steaming step in order to bring about the optimum fixation. These investigations
led to the continuous dyeing sequence: pad (dye)–pad (caustic soda in brine)–
steam, which with some modification is still used for many classes of reactive dyes.
Further study showed that solutions of sodium carbonate, or even bicarbonate in
the presence of added salt, could be used for fixation. As a result, the first satisfactory fabric printing process and the following dyeing sequences were initiated and
proven [27, 28]:

(a) Pad (dye and sodium bicarbonate)–dry
(b) Pad (dye and bicarbonate)–dry–steam
(c) Pad (dye, urea and bicarbonate)–dry–thermofix (bake)

and eventually the cold exhaustion (batchwise) dyeing techniques were introduced.

The first three dichlorotriazinyl Procion (ICI) dyes were marketed in April
1956, a date almost coincidental with the centenary of Perkin's discovery of the
first synthetic dye. The names and structures of the three dyes are given in
Figures 4.2–4.4.

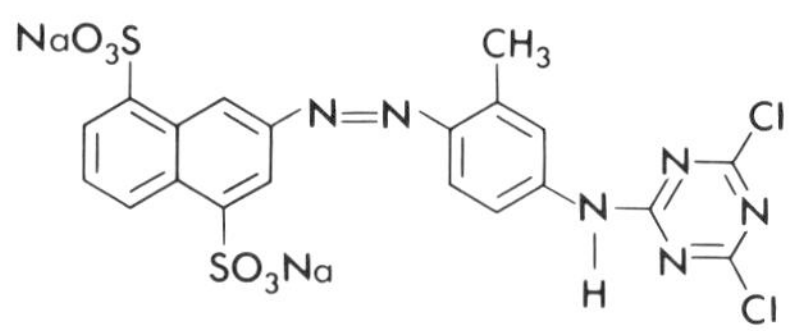

Figure 4.2 – Procion Yellow RS (ICI, C.I. Reactive Yellow 4)

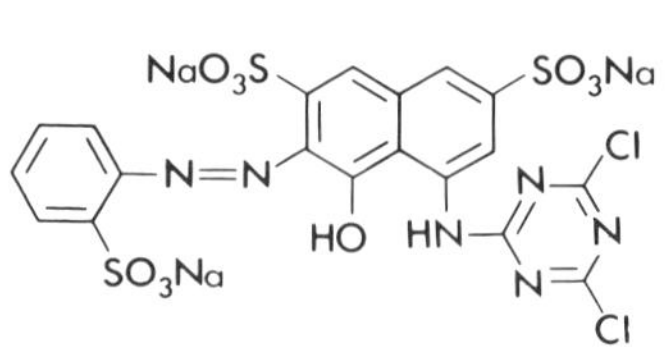

Figure 4.3 – Procion Brilliant Red 2BS (ICI, C.I. Reactive Red 1)

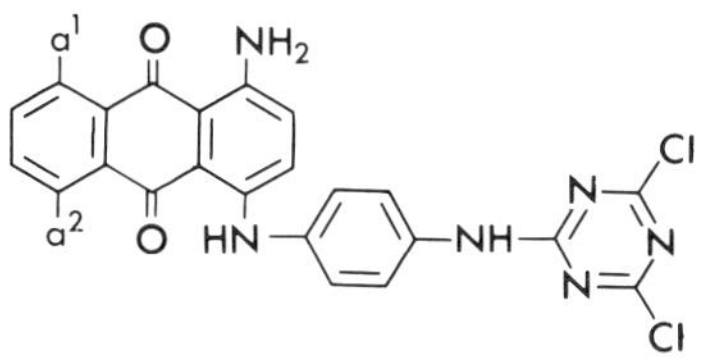

Figure 4.4 – Procion Blue 3GS (ICI, C.I. Reactive Blue 1), a mixture wherein the two components have NaO$_3$S either at a^1 or a^2

4.3 FURTHER DEVELOPMENT OF REACTIVE DYES

During 1957, mainly due to a recognition of the short storage life of textile printing pastes made from dichlorotriazinyl dyes, further research led to the introduction of the more stable monochlorotriazinyl derivatives in order to obviate this defect. The first member of this range is shown in Figure 4.5.

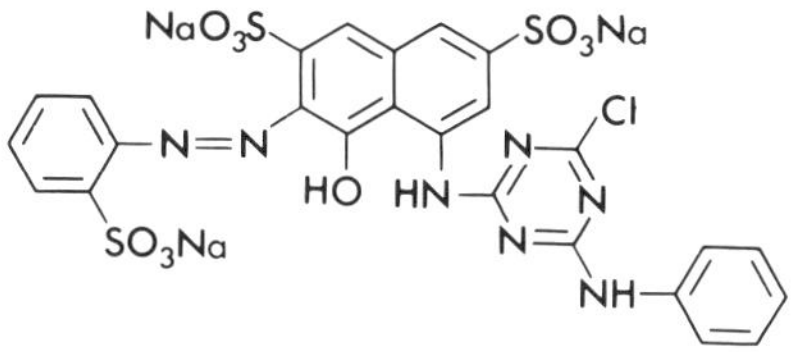

Figure 4.5 – Procion Brilliant Red H-3B (ICI, C.I. Reactive Red 3)

The introduction of reactive groups into the molecule of copper phthalocyanine yielded the first reactive turquoise dye (C.I. Reactive Blue 3) which showed relatively low reactivity. Nevertheless, because of its novel colour as a fashion shade, this dye found ready application in textile printing and was rapidly adopted by dyers for exhaust and continuous dyeing using hot conditions of application. These first steps led to rapid enlargement of the range for specific dyeing (and printing) uses. A later development was the production of dyes with more than one mono-chlorotriazinyl group per dye molecule in order to provide high exhaustion and fixation. Those designed for exhaust dyeing are called Procion H-E (ICI) dyes.

When ICI introduced chlorotriazinyl reactive dyes it was known that earlier Ciba patents had disclosed the use of monochlorotriazinyl groups in some of the latter's Chlorantine direct dyes. The fibre-reactive potential, however, had not been recognised. Ciba's work on monochlorotriazinyl dyes for wool before 1956 gave it a marked advantage in the new field of reactive dyes for cellulose so that, shortly after the first Procion H dyes had been released for sale, Ciba began to offer its similar Cibacron dyes. Since that time the chlorotriazinyl dyes have accounted for more than half of the world consumption of reactive dyes for cellulosic textiles and have been generally regarded as the most important group of cellulose-reactive dyes [29]. Expiry of the early patents has brought with it a further growth in the number of dye-making firms that have recognised the importance of this type. For example, BASF introduced the Primazin (sulphatopropionylamide) and Primazin P (dichloropyridazone) dyes in the early 1960s, but later entered the chlorotriazinyl field with Basilen dyes. The use of triazine chemistry has been extended in recent years with the introduction of the Cibacron F (CGY) monofluorotriazinyl dyes. Almost simultaneously with the successful launch of Procion dyes, all other leading dye makers began to search for patent-free reactive systems. Arising from the pioneering research of Heyna and Schumacher [30], Hoechst introduced its technically important Remazol reactive dyes for cellulose before the end of 1957. This range, commonly referred to as the vinylsulphone dyes, usually contains the precursor to this group (the sulphuric acid ester of β-hydroxyethylsulphone). These dyes, now greatly expanded in numbers, have retained their commercial importance and are widely used.

The Drimarene dyes of Sandoz, based on the dichloropyrimidinyl 'diazine' group, maintain their importance as Drimarene X dyes. Similar products were introduced by the former firm of Geigy as Reactone dyes in the same year. As a result of the Ciba–Geigy merger, the Reactone name has fallen into disuse but several of the dyes have been retained under the Cibacron T name.

The earliest Levafix (BAY) dyes (introduced in 1960) contained β-sulphatoethyl-sulphonamide groups, whilst the Levafix E dyes (1961) depend on dichloroquinoxalinecarbonamide groups for reactivity. Levafix P-A and E-A (BAY) dyes and the corresponding Drimarene R and K dyes (S) are monochloro-difluoropyrimidines; like Procion MX dyes these are often classified as 'cold-dyeing' products. Numerous fibre-reactive groups and systems of interest for dyeing and printing have been developed and protected by patents during the past 25 years [31–35].

When the first laboratory dyeing methods for applying reactive dyes were being developed, it was soon apparent that dyeing theory for dyes which entered into chemical union with cellulosic fibres required considerable investigation. However, it was not until a decade later that it was possible to develop the detailed theory to satisfactorily explain the rapidly gained but extensive practical experience. The interrelated factors and parameters governing the dyeing process were effectively brought to a state of order by the studies of Sumner and his collaborators [36–39]. Since then further refinement of theory has become possible and numerous investigations into the physical chemistry of reactive dyeing have continued.

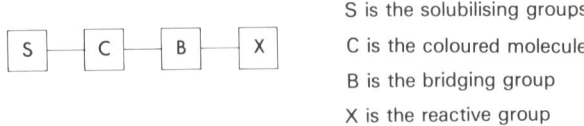

S is the solubilising groups
C is the coloured molecule
B is the bridging group
X is the reactive group

Figure 4.6 – Characteristic structural features of a reactive dye

4.4 ORGANIC CHEMISTRY OF REACTIVE DYES

In general reactive dyes for cellulosic materials have certain characteristic structural features, represented diagrammatically in Figure 4.6. When applied by the usual techniques in the presence of alkali the dyes fall essentially into two classes:

(a) Those that react by a nucleophilic substitution mechanism based on the presence of labile halogeno substituents in a heteroaromatic system, e.g. the chlorotriazinyl dyes (Scheme 4.3). Amongst the principal reactive systems of this type are the halogeno-substituted triazine, pyrimidine, pyrazine, quinoxaline, thiazole and pyridazone groups.

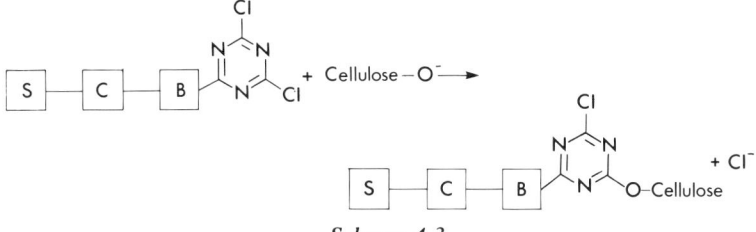

Scheme 4.3

(b) Those that react by the addition of a nucleophilic group to a carbon–carbon double bond of the reactive system (Scheme 4.4).

| S | C | B |—CH=CH$_2$ + Cellulose–O$^-$ →

| S | C | B |—CH$_2$CH$_2$O–Cellulose

Scheme 4.4

In most instances the unsaturated reactive group is not present in the dye as supplied but is formed from a precursor in the presence of alkali. The most important precursor for dyes of this type is the sulphuric acid ester of β-hydroxyethylsulphone, which forms a vinylsulphone in the dyebath by elimination of sulphuric acid (Scheme 4.5).

| S | C |—SO$_2$CH$_2$CH$_2$OSO$_3$H ⟶ | S | C |—SO$_2$CH=CH$_2$ + H$_2$SO$_4$

Scheme 4.5

4.5 PHYSICAL CHEMISTRY OF REACTIVE DYEING

The above-mentioned dye types, and indeed all reactive dyes for cellulose, rely on the reactivity of the cellulosate anion as the nucleophilic reagent. The need for ionisation demands the presence of a polarising medium (water in most dyeing systems). This in turn means that hydroxyl anions will always be present and thus hydrolysis will compete with the reaction desired.

4.5.1 Homogeneous Systems

The implications of this competing reaction in terms of reactive dyeing are best introduced by considering first a simple homogeneous system in which reactive dye is present in an alkaline aqueous solution of an alcohol. Here the two competing reactions are:

(a) Alcoholysis of the dye: $D + AO^- \rightarrow DOA$
(b) Hydrolysis of the dye: $D + OH^- \rightarrow DOH$

When two simultaneous reactions take place in a homogeneous system, the concentrations of the products formed after any given time, including when the reaction has proceeded to completion, are in the ratio of the two reaction rates (Eqn 4.1):

$$\frac{[DOA]_{t=t}}{[DOH]_{t=t}} = \frac{[DOA]_{t=\infty}}{[DOH]_{t=\infty}} = \frac{dA/dt}{dH/dt} = E \qquad (4.1)$$

where dA/dt = rate of alcoholysis
dH/dt = rate of hydrolysis
E = efficiency ratio of the alcoholysis reaction.

Since both reactions are bimolecular E can be expressed in terms of Eqn 4.2:

$$E = \frac{dA/dt}{dH/dt} = \frac{k_A[AO^-]_t[D]_t}{k_H[OH^-]_t[D]_t} = \frac{k_A[AO^-]_t}{k_H[OH^-]_t} \qquad (4.2)$$

where k_A and k_H are the bimolecular reaction constants of alcoholysis and hydrolysis respectively.

It has been shown [37, 39] that the ratio of bimolecular reaction constants (k_A/k_H) is a constant for a given alcohol and dye, independent of the pH of reaction. This expected result confirmed that the alcoholate and hydroxyl anions are the entities that react with the dye. Hence Eqn 4.3 can be written:

$$E = R_A \frac{[AO^-]}{[OH^-]} \qquad (4.3)$$

where $R_A = k_A/k_H$.

From the value of E obtained from Eqn 4.3 the percentage of dye that reacts with the alcohol can be calculated using Eqn 4.4:

$$\text{Percentage alcoholysis} = \frac{100E}{1+E} \qquad (4.4)$$

Consequently the efficiency of the alcoholysis reaction is determined not only by the value of R_A, which depends on the particular dye and alcohol used, but probably more on the value of $[AO^-]/[OH^-]$, which depends in turn on the dissociation constant (K_A) and concentration [A] of the alcohol and the pH of the reaction. In such homogeneous systems the rate of disappearance of active dye ($d[D]/dt$) is equal to the sum of the rates of the two competing reactions (Eqn 4.5):

$$\frac{d[D]}{dt} + \frac{dA}{dt} = \frac{dH}{dt} = k_A[AO^-]_t[D]_t + k_H[OH^-]_t[D]_t$$
$$= k_H[D]_t(R_A[AO^-]_t + [OH^-]_t) \qquad (4.5)$$

This equation is simplied if the dye is reacted with excess of alcohol at constant pH in buffer solutions. This means that the values of the terms in the bracket are virtually constant at any given pH and the equation becomes that of a pseudo-first-order reaction (Eqn 4.6):

$$\frac{d[D]}{dt} = k'_H[D]_t$$ (4.6)

where $k'_H = k_H(R_A[AO^-]_t + [OH^-]_t)$

4.5.2 Heterogeneous Systems – Cellulose and Water

The homogeneous system described above illustrates the basic ground rules of reactive dyeing. It is now necessary to adapt them to the far more complicated heterogeneous system of cellulose and water. In a two-phase system reaction between two entities can take place only if both are present in the same phase; therefore reaction between dye and cellulose can occur only when the dye has been absorbed into the cellulose phase. Thus any discussion of the kinetics must allow for the rate at which dye is absorbed.

The rate of diffusion of a sorbent into a solid medium with which it can react according to first-order kinetics has been considered by Danckwerts [40]. The solution for the dyeing of an infinitely thick plane slab of material in a dyebath of infinite volume can be written in the approximate form shown in Eqn 4.7:

$$\frac{dQ}{dt} = [D]_F \sqrt{Dk'_f}$$ (4.7)

where dQ/dt = rate of sorption of reactive dye per unit area of surface, which can be equated to the rate of fixation (since the material is considered infinitely thick and all the dye which enters will be fixed)

$[D]_F$ = equilibrium concentration of dye at the surface of the material

D = diffusion coefficient of the dye in the material

k'_F = first-order or pseudo-first-order reaction constant for the reaction between dye and substrate.

As in the homogeneous system described above, there are two competing reactions and the efficiency of fixation is given by Eqn 4.8:

$$E = \frac{\text{Rate of fixation}}{\text{Rate of hydrolysis}} = \frac{S[D]_F \sqrt{Dk'_F}}{L[D]_S k'_H}$$ (4.8)

where $[D]_S$ = concentration of dye in the aqueous phase

k'_H = first-order or psuedo-first-order reaction constant of hydrolysis.

The constant L, the liquor ratio, defines the difference in amount of the two phases (usually in terms of litres of dyebath per kilogram of substrate) and S, which defines the surface area of the substrate, is necessary because Danckwert's equation refers to diffusion per square centimetre of surface.

It has been demonstrated experimentally [35] that the ratio of the bimolecular constants (R_F) for the reaction of dye with the fibre (k_F) and with water (k_H) is a constant for a given dye over a wide range of alkaline pH values, thereby confirming that the kinetic relationships in the homogeneous system still apply in the heterogeneous cellulose–water system and that the reactive entity is ionised cellulose. Thus Eqn 4.9 applies:

$$k_F/k_H = R_F \tag{4.9}$$

and hence, since $k'_F = k_F[\text{Cell O}^-]$ and $k'_H = k_H[\text{OH}^-]$, Eqn 4.10 can be written:

$$k'_F = k'_H R_F \frac{[\text{CellO}^-]}{[\text{OH}^-]} \tag{4.10}$$

where $[\text{CellO}^-]$ = concentration of ionised cellulose.

Eqn 4.8 may therefore be rewritten in the form of Eqn 4.11:

$$E = \frac{S}{L} \frac{[D]_F}{[D]_S} \sqrt{\frac{D}{k'_H} \frac{R_F[\text{CellO}^-]}{[\text{OH}^-]}} \tag{4.11}$$

from which the percentage fixation may be calculated using Eqn 4.4.

Again, however, the efficiency of the process is only half of the story. Of equal importance to the practical dyer is the rate at which active dye is used up and hence the time required to complete the dyeing process. The total rate of disappearance of active dye is the sum of the rates of the two competing reactions (Eqn 4.12):

$$\frac{d[D]}{dt} = \frac{dF}{dt} + \frac{dH}{dt} = \frac{S}{L}[D]_F\sqrt{Dk'_F} + [D]_S k'_H$$

$$= \frac{S}{L}[D]_F\sqrt{Dk'_H R_F \frac{[\text{CellO}^-]}{[\text{OH}^-]}} + [D]_S k'_H \tag{4.12}$$

where dF/dt = rate of reaction of dye with the fibre.

Integration of Eqn 4.12 permits calculation of the amount of active dye that has been removed from the bath after a given time, following which Eqn 4.11 can be used to evaluate how much of this dye will have been fixed to the fibre.

It must be emphasised that these equations are in an abbreviated form which applies only under certain conditions. The full equation corresponding to the simple Eqn 4.7 has been given by Danckwerts [40]. Derivations of the equations for efficiency and rate have also been described [41, 42].

Although only strictly applicable to the ideal system of an infinitely thick plane slab of material, the validity of these equations in describing the behaviour of dyes in practical dyeing on cellulosic fibres and films has been demonstrated [43]. This required the accumulation of considerable data, too laborious a process for a study of all reactive dyes. However, the principles can be used generally to demonstrate the implications of the relevant variables for the practical application of these dyes.

4.6 PRACTICAL IMPLICATIONS OF THE PHYSICAL CHEMISTRY

4.6.1 Factors Outside the Dyer's Control

Fibre Shape Factor (S)
Although not merely a measure of surface area, the fibre shape factor is expressed in SI units as m^2/kg. It has been demonstrated that the lower the linear density of the fibre, i.e. the greater the surface area per unit weight, the more efficient is the dyeing. Clearly this would result in poor reproducibility if repeat dyeings were

carried out on materials of different linear density, and unlevelness would result in any one batch if fibres of different linear density were mixed.

Ratio of the Bimolecular Rate Constants (R_F)

Whilst R_F is a constant for any one dye over the range of pH values, it is different for different dyes as might be expected. There is insufficient experimental data to provide correlations between molecular structure and R_F value. From the equations, the greater the value of R_F the greater the efficiency and rate of reaction.

4.6.2 Factors Partly Within the Dyer's Control

Ratio of Concentrations of Ionised Groups $([CellO^-]/[OH^-])$

An increased concentration of electrolyte produces an increase in the value of this ratio, which in turn contributes to an increase in both efficiency and rate of reaction. Any attempt to increase the rate of reaction by raising the pH above 11 will not produce the expected effect in full. Above this pH value the ratio will fall, even in the presence of large concentrations of electrolyte.

Up to pH 11–12, in the absence of dye, the effect of increasing the electrolyte concentration above 0.1 mol/l is only minimal in terms of this ratio. In practical dyeing an electrolyte concentration of about 0.1 mol/l is typical, as a result of the alkali used to produce the desired pH (e.g. sodium carbonate, approx. 10 g/l). Why is extra electrolyte (sodium chloride) beneficial in terms of this ratio? As dyeing proceeds the concentration of dye in the fibre increases. But at an electrolyte concentration of 0.1 mol/l this results in a marked decrease in the ratio, which means that the efficiency becomes less and the rate of reaction diminishes as dyeing proceeds. Higher electrolyte concentrations overcome these effects; this is especially true at higher concentrations of dye in the fibre, when increasing the electrolyte concentration from 1 to 2 mol/l still produces a significant beneficial effect.

Pseudo-unimolecular Rate Constant for Hydrolysis (k'_H)

All known dyes react, in alkaline solution, with the hydroxyl ions present. Thus the observed value of k'_H will depend on pH. This dependence has been studied for dyes of the triazinyl and pyrimidinyl types [37, 43–55]. Nearly all reactive dyes of these types show a $\log_{10} k'_H$ vs pH relationship similar to one of the three general kinds shown qualitatively in Figure 4.7. One or two exceptions have been reported [37, 49], but such instances are rare. A full explanation of the shape of these curves is available [34, 35]. The majority of commercial dyes are of the type illustrated by curve C.

The effect of temperature on reactivity has been measured for a number of chlorotriazinyl dyes [43, 56]; on average an increase of 10°C in the temperature produces a 2.5-fold increase in the reactivity constant.

Substantivity Ratio of the Dye $([D]_F/[D]_S)$

This variable is the most influential of all since it is the only one, with the exception of S, that is not under the square root sign in Eqn 4.11. Numerous studies of this

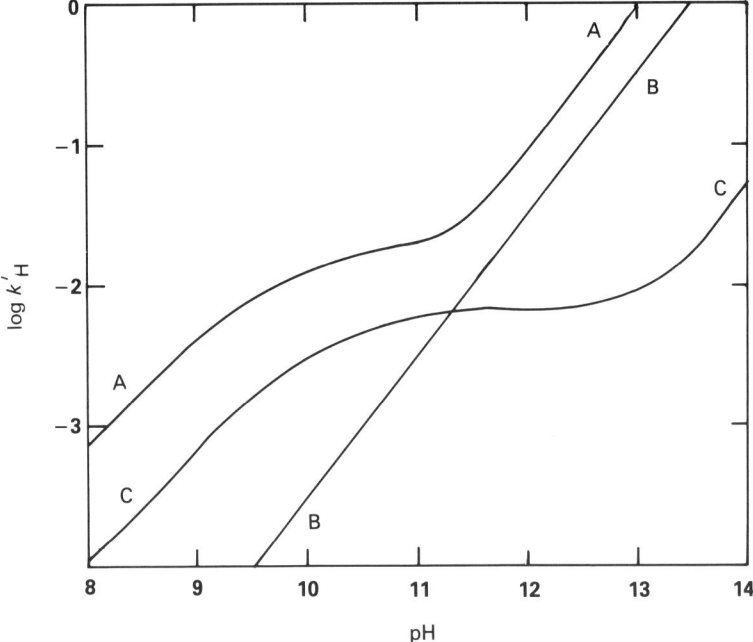

Figure 4.7 – Typical changes in the value of the pseudo-first-order reaction constant of hydrolysis with pH

variable have been reported for different dyes and dyebath conditions, but there remains the insuperable problem of directly measuring the substantivity ratio under fixation conditions. Obviously these are the essential values most required. Reasonable estimates have been achieved by extrapolation [38], but the necessary experimental work is extremely time-consuming. Nevertheless theoretical studies are capable of producing a reasonably accurate description of practical results [38, 57] and hence the trends to be expected as a result of changes in methods of application.

Effect of pH on Substantivity Ratio
Within the pH range 7–11 only minor changes in substantivity ratio occur in the presence of 1 mol/l total electrolyte concentration. Above pH 11 the effect is much more dramatic, particularly for dyes of higher basicity, and a very marked decrease in the substantivity ratio occurs. The magnitude of the effect is almost independent of dye affinity, but depends greatly on dye basicity. Thus an increase in pH above 11 reduces the fixation efficiency if other dyebath conditions remain unchanged, and the effect on rate of fixation is never as great as might be expected from the resultant change in reactivity. In fact, under certain conditions the rate may even be reduced.

If, for any reason, it is necessary to use a pH greater than 11, the adverse effect on substantivity ratio may be minimised by increasing the electrolyte concentration, although this will never eliminate the effect completely. The use of such large amounts of electrolyte may be undesirable from the point of view of cost and inconvenience, or impossible because of aggregation or precipitation of the dye. The effect of pH on substantivity ratio has implications for the application of dyes in admixture. If the component dyes have different affinities but the same basicity, there should be only small effects on the final hue due to accidental or deliberate changes in pH or electrolyte concentration. If, however, the dyes in the mixture are of different basicities then they will respond differently to such changes. This means that reproducibility of shade can *only* be assured if dyebath preparation is carried out precisely and that deliberate changes in dyebath conditions are not made without first investigating the possible consequences.

Effect of Dye Concentration on Substantivity Ratio
As the amount of dye applied is increased at constant electrolyte concentration, the substantivity ratio decreases and hence the efficiency of fixation and the rate of disappearance of reactive dye are reduced. For a given affinity the effect is more pronounced the greater the basicity of the dye. Thus heavier depths will require longer for the reaction to be completed and even then the result, in terms of percentage fixation, will be inferior.

The effect is reduced by increasing the electrolyte concentration but is never completely eliminated. Further electrolyte not only increases the fixation efficiency but reduces the time required to complete the reaction, particularly for deeper colours. Thus, in order to produce maximum efficiency and rate, an increase in depth applied should be accompanied by an increase in the electrolyte concentration. This, however, is not always possible since the dangers of aggregation or precipitation are greater at high dye and electrolyte concentrations.

Effect of Dye Fixation on Substantivity Ratio
The previous discussion of the effects of dyebath conditions on substantivity ratio has assumed that the fibre contained no fixed dye. This situation applies only at the beginning of the fixation step. As the fibre accumulates fixed dye during the course of the dyeing the position changes. The effect is not very significant for a dibasic dye, even at a full depth. For a tetrabasic dye, however, the effects are much more evident, so that for a 4% shade the substantivity ratio towards the end of dyeing is approximately half that at the start. Consequently the efficiency and the rate of fixation will be steadily reduced as the dyeing proceeds. Again the effect is minimised by increasing the electrolyte concentration but not completely eliminated, particularly with a dye of higher basicity.

Effect of Temperature on Substantivity Ratio
This effect depends essentially on the heat of dyeing of the individual dye. The limited information available indicates that there can be considerable variation from dye to dye. A reasonable estimate of the average change to be expected with

temperature, under normal conditions of application, would be a 1.5–2.5-fold decrease in substantivity ratio for a 20°C rise in temperature.

Integral Diffusion Coefficient of the Dye (D)
This, again, is a dye variable which cannot be measured under conditions where fixation occurs, but reasonable estimates can be made by extrapolation [38, 39]. The results reveal that the integral diffusion coefficients of reactive dyes, as a class, are much greater than those of direct dyes. Reactive dyes at 20°C possess diffusion coefficients in the range 10^{-10}–10^{-12} m²/min, whilst those for direct dyes at 90°C are 10^{-10}–10^{-13} m²/min. The near equivalence indicates that the rates of dyeing of the two ranges are similar at their respective temperatures of application. Assuming an average activation energy of dyeing for direct dyes of -60 kJ/mol (-14 kcal/mol), these figures mean that, on average, reactive dyes have diffusion coefficients approximately 100–200 times greater at the same temperature.

A detailed discussion of the effects of changing dyebath conditions on the value of the diffusion coefficient is not necessary because the integral diffusion coefficient does not appear to be a totally independent variable. Sufficient data are available [43] to demonstrate that changes in the value of the substantivity ratio are mirrored by changes in the diffusion coefficient, at least to a sufficient degree of precision to enable trends to be forecast.

Thus dyes of higher substantivity diffuse more slowly than dyes of lower substantivity. With any particular dye, changes in dyebath conditions which increase the substantivity will, at the same time, decrease the diffusion coefficient. The basis of these statements is illustrated in Figure 4.8 where the logarithm of the diffusion coefficient is plotted against that of the substantivity ratio. These results for C.I. Reactive Reds 1 and 6 illustrate the changes which take place in both variables as a result of concentration and pH effects [38]. The dashed lines indicate the region in which numerous results for various reactive dyes under different dyebath conditions are known to fall [43].

4.6.3 Liquor Ratio (*L*)
The remaining variable, the liquor ratio, is the only one largely within the dyer's control. Clearly, from its position in Eqns 4.11 and 4.12, any reduction in the magnitude of *L* must favour increases in efficiency and rate of dyeing. The full effects are never completely realised, however, even if all the other conditions of dyeing are kept constant; reducing the value of *L* means that for a given depth of shade the dye concentration must be increased. This, in turn, means that the substantivity ratio will decrease, offsetting some of the gain expected. Furthermore, in padding processes, the increased concentration of dye required means that the concentration of electrolyte must be reduced because of the hazards associated with precipitation of dye, so that the substantivity ratio is further reduced. Nevertheless decreasing the liquor ratio can produce a marked increase in efficiency [43].

4.7 TRANSIENT VALUES OF THE DYEING PARAMETERS
Throughout the discussion it has been repeatedly stressed that only trends in the values of the respective variables have been illustrated, because these are reactive

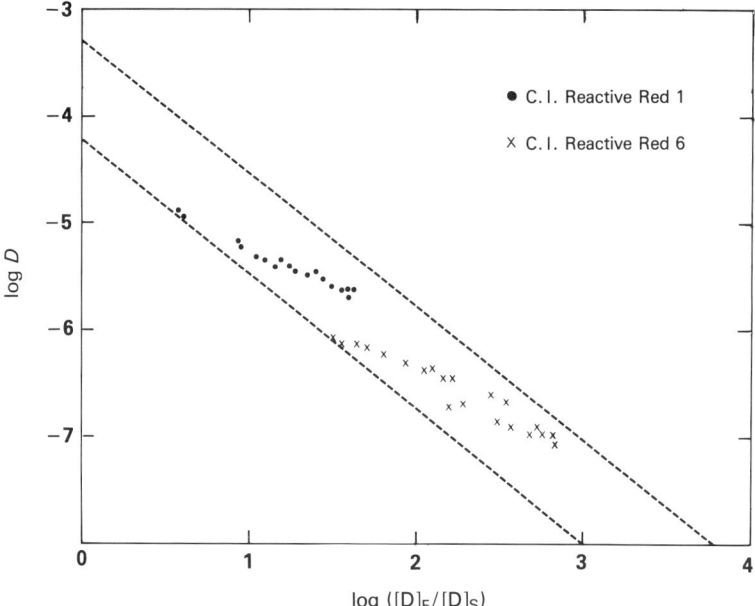

Figure 4.8 – Relationship between substantivity and diffusion coefficient

dyes and the ultimate efficiency of fixation depends on kinetic effects rather than on equilibrium.

In the theoretical treatment of non-reactive dyes, e.g. direct dyes on cotton, equilibrium sorption is dependent solely on the substantivity ratio at the end of dyeing. Provided the dyeing conditions have been kept constant, this is the result towards which the system has been aiming during the whole period of dyeing. Even if the dyeing conditions are deliberately or accidentally changed during dyeing, the result will be no different provided the final conditions are the same and sufficient time is allowed for the correct equilibrium situation to be achieved. This is because the dye is always free to migrate from dyebath to fibre and vice versa, thus always achieving the correct partition appropriate to any change in the dyeing conditions. Of course, for certain dye–fibre systems, migration may be so poor that the time required to achieve equilibrium may be unrealistically long in the practical sense. Nevertheless theoretically the opportunity always exists.

In reactive dyeing the situation is totally different. The end result, in terms of efficiency of fixation, is the *sum* of all the separate efficiencies obtaining at each instant of the dyeing time. Even if the dyeing conditions are kept constant after the addition of alkali, the efficiency will change as the dyeing proceeds, because the substantivity ratio progressively changes, penetration of the fibre increases, the dyebath becomes less concentrated in reactive dye and the fibre now contains fixed dye. All these changes affect the substantivity ratio and hence the efficiency of dyeing at each particular instant of dyeing time.

These gradual changes, which are dependent purely on the physical chemistry of the system, should in practice offer no problems in terms of reproducibility because, provided the dyeing sequence is carried out with precision, the changes will occur *reproducibly* and the end result will be the *same*. If, however, deliberate or accidental changes are made in the conditions during the fixation sequence which affect any of the important parameters, then the result will be different. This will not be corrected by a subsequent return to normal conditions because the dye is already fixed and is no longer free to migrate. Adequate precision in controlling the dyebath conditions must be exercised at all times if reproducibility is to be achieved, particularly in the application of mixtures of dyes when the component dyes are affected differently by changes in dyeing conditions.

4.8 COMPROMISES NECESSARY IN REACTIVE DYEING

All dyeing methods necessitate compromise, between the level of exhaustion and the time required to achieve it, between wet-fastness and level-dyeing properties, between technical performance and cost of different dyeing methods, and so on.

4.8.1 Essential Variants

One way to describe such compromises is to employ a method already published [43, 58]. Since Eqns 4.11 and 4.12 each contain seven variables, several assumptions must be made in applying them. The value of R_F has been found to vary in the range approximately 0.1–1.3 and so an average value of 0.7 has been used. An average value of 18 would reasonably represent the value of the ratio $[CellO^-]/[OH^-]$ for normal pH, electrolyte concentration and applied depth. The value of S was that used previously [43] for a sample of viscose fibre (i.e. 43) and the liquor ratio was taken at 20:1. This leaves the three dye variables: substantivity ratio, diffusion coefficient and reactivity to hydroxyl ions. Since substantivity ratio and diffusion coefficient are interdependent, the latter can be included as a function of the former. This leaves two variables, substantivity ratio and reactivity, and it is now possible using Eqn 4.11 and an integrated form of Eqn 4.12 to represent the interplay between them. In Figure 4.9 substantivity ratio ($[D]_F/[D]_S$) is plotted against reactivity (k'_H), both on a logarithmic scale, and curves A–E, calculated using Eqn 4.11, are drawn where constant levels of fixation are obtained when the reaction has been completed. It is clear that any increase in k'_H must be accompanied by an increase in $[D]_F/[D]_S$ if efficiency is to be maintained at any desired level, and that maximum efficiency will be achieved at high levels of $[D]_F/[D]_S$ and low levels of k'_H.

The curves F–L show the values of the two variables necessary to ensure 99% reaction with either the fibre or water in various lengths of time. It can be seen that a dye of low substantivity requires a greater reactivity than one of high substantivity to complete the reaction in a given time. In the practical situation, both efficiency of dyeing and the time required to reach completion are important. The properties of any dye that is required to give completion in less than 60 min and a fixation

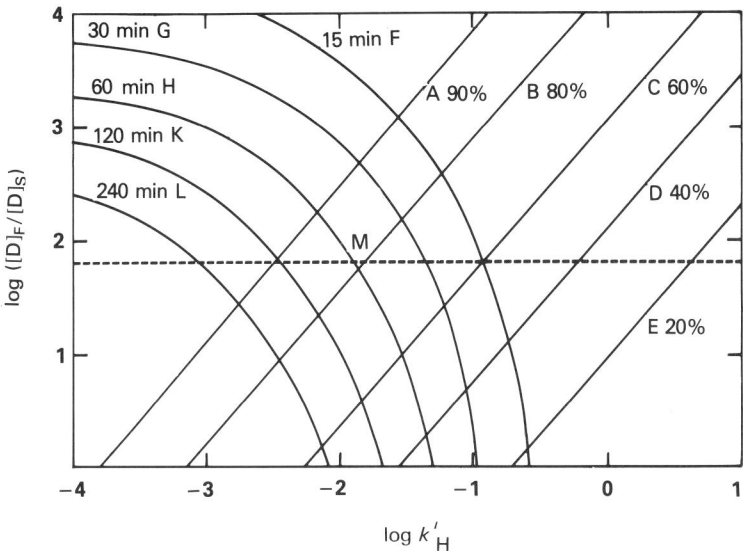

Figure 4.9 – Values of substantivity ratio and reactivity required (a) to produce various levels of fixation when all the dye has reacted (curves A–E), and (b) to complete reaction in a given time (curves F–L); calculated from Eqns 4.11 and 4.12 with $R_F = 0.7$, $S = 43$, $L = 20$ and $[CellO^-]/[OH^-] = 18$

better than 80% would have to fall in the area above the curves BM and HM. It is clear, therefore, that the more stringent the dyeing requirements the smaller the permissible variation in $[D]_F/[D]_S$ and k'_H. Equally, for the average dye, if maximum substantivity and length of time are specified then the fixation efficiency under any particular dyeing conditions is also defined within fairly narrow limits.

4.8.2 Factors Controllable by the Dyer
Although the values of the two variables under consideration are dependent on molecular structure, the dyer does have some control of them by adjusting pH, temperature and salt concentration.

pH
The effects of changing the pH of application may be illustrated by taking the substantivity vs pH profile of a typical dibasic dye in combination with the reactivity vs pH profile of dye A in Figure 4.7. Using Eqn 4.11 it is possible to predict what the percentage fixation would be if sufficient time was allowed for all the dye to react with either the fibre or water (Figure 4.10, curve A). The efficiency falls as the pH increases; this is due to the increase in reactivity. The rate of fall is accelerated beyond pH 11, since in this region the effect of increased reactivity is reinforced by a drop in substantivity ratio. Curve B shows the fraction of the total dye available that would have reacted in 60 min according to Eqn 4.12. A pH in excess of 10.5 is

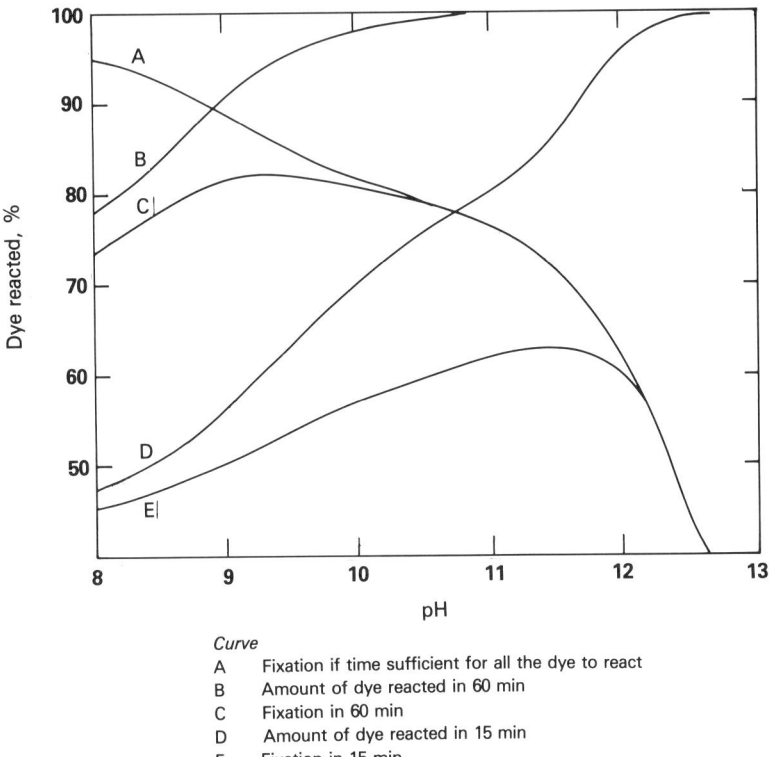

Curve
A   Fixation if time sufficient for all the dye to react
B   Amount of dye reacted in 60 min
C   Fixation in 60 min
D   Amount of dye reacted in 15 min
E   Fixation in 15 min

Figure 4.10 – Effect of time and pH on the amount of dye reacted and amount of dye fixed; calculated for a dibasic dye with a reactivity/pH profile shown in Figure 4.7, curve A, using other values as for Figure 4.9

necessary before all the dye can be considered, for all practical purposes, to have reacted. Combining curves A and B produces curve C, the fraction of dye that will have reacted with the fibre in 60 min. For this particular dye, under these dyeing conditions and for this time, there is a pH of maximum fixation at approximately pH 9.5 (which does not correspond to the pH of 100% reaction of the dye).

The effect of time of dyeing is also of interest. In Figure 4.9 curves D and E illustrate an available dyeing time of 15 min, and it can be seen that the pH of maximum fixation has moved from approximately 9.5 for 60 min to 11.5 for 15 min, with the maximum fixation changing from approximately 83 to 63%. Thus there is a further compromise – a saving of 45 min in time for a 25% loss in level of fixation. With this dye (Figure 4.7, dye A) the choice is available because the reaction can be accelerated by raising the pH, even though efficiency is lost, because little or no increase in rate of reaction results. In some cases the reaction may become slower, while still producing a decrease in efficiency.

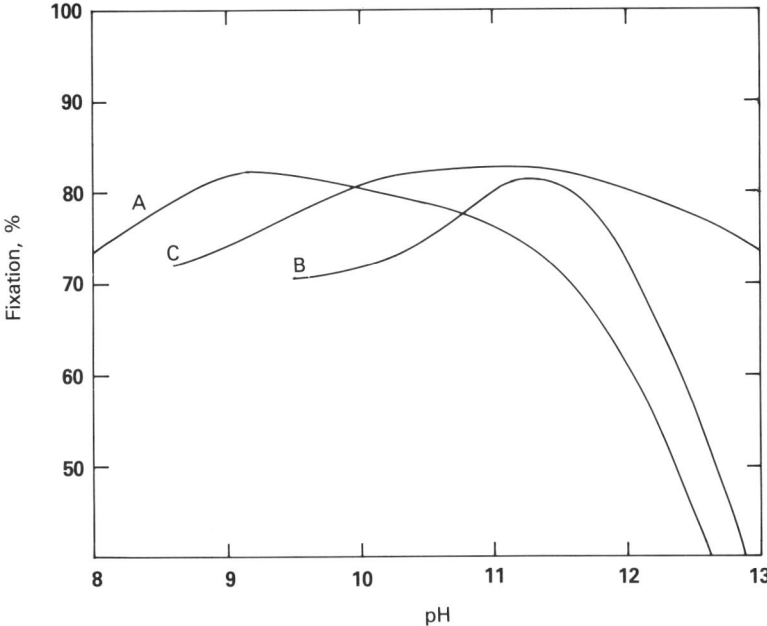

Figure 4.11 – Effect of pH on percentage fixation of dyes of different reactivity/pH profiles (dyeing time 60 min); calculated for dibasic dyes with reactivity/pH profiles as shown in Figure 4.7, curves A–C, using other values as for Figure 4.9

The pH of maximum fixation depends on the relative shapes of the substantivity and reactivity vs pH profiles. In Figure 4.11 three dibasic dyes are illustrated which all possess the same substantivity profile as the dye in Figure 4.9 but have reactivities according to curves A, B and C in Figure 4.7. The differences in pH of maximum fixation can be seen in Figure 4.11 (curves A and B), but of equal importance are the shapes of the curves produced. In curve A there is a region (pH 9.5–11) of relatively small change in fixation, since neither the substantivity nor the reactivity is changing drastically with pH. Above pH 11 the drop in substantivity is reinforced by a marked increase in reactivity. In curve B the sensitivity of reactivity to pH has produced a much sharper peak. For curve C the reverse is true, since over the pH range 10.5–13 the reactivity is relatively insensitive to pH. In this latter case the constancy of reactivity means that above pH 11 only the fall in substantivity is affecting the fixation.

If a mixture consisted of the three dyes illustrated in Figure 4.11, no single pH value would produce maximum efficiency in all three dyes and yet another compromise would have to be made. In addition the selection of a pH close to that of maximum fixation for one of the pH-sensitive dyes (A or B) would make the other sensitive to slight changes in the pH, with marked effects on reproducibility of shade. In this respect dyes of type C would be the most desirable because their level of fixation is relatively insensitive to small changes in pH; reactive dyes with this type of reactivity vs pH profile are quite common.

Temperature
The effect of changes in the temperature of application is to produce a further need for compromise between time and efficiency. Increasing the temperature reduces the value of the substantivity ratio and increases the reactivity; both effects reduce the efficiency. As far as reaction rate is concerned, the effect of temperature is not so clearly defined. In general, however, increasing the temperature by 20°C produces an increase in reactivity of some six to seven times. Since reactivity occurs as both k'_H and $(k'_H)^{1/2}$ in Eqn 4.12, the effect of a 20°C rise in decreasing substantivity by about 1.5–2.5 times is generally offset. The reaction therefore still proceeds at a faster rate, although not as fast as predicted from reactivity alone.

Electrolyte Concentration
Finally there is the question of electrolyte concentration. An increase always has a beneficial effect, in that it always produces greater efficiency and rate of reaction. These effects are most evident with dyes of greater basicity at higher pH and higher dye concentration. Apparently it has little effect on the reactivity of dyes except in so far as it can result in a reduction of pH due to activity effects. Thus the only limit on electrolyte concentration is determined by the hazards associated with dye precipitation or aggregation, and by the inconvenience and cost of excessive concentrations.

4.9 PRACTICAL APPLICATION OF REACTIVE DYES
Early practical dyeing procedures for reactive dyes were based on extensive empirical studies guided by the theories of dyeing extant prior to their discovery.

Dyeing processes have been refined in detail to accord with extensive experience on a large scale and with fundamental research. The practical maxims discussed above have helped to clarify the work of the dyer. Nevertheless many dyers have felt confused by the profusion of revisions to the basic recommendations published by dye makers.

In spite of the basic simplicity of reactive dyeing, the uniqueness of the various commercially available ranges of dyes can lead to some confusion, especially amongst colourists who wish to exploit some special feature in dyes selected from different ranges.

Few instances are met where dyes of one manufacturer are used in a common application recipe with dyes of another maker. Incompatibilities are feared and, indeed, often exist, because of the idiosyncracies shown by products from different ranges. In the foregoing respects reactive dyes differ from all other classes of dyes for cellulose. Even if competing dyes have identical chromophores, notable differences might be found in those fastness properties dependent on the nature of the dye–fibre bond. The first ranges of reactive dyes could be classified as cold dyeing (highly reactive) or hot dyeing (moderately reactive). More recently types have been introduced that are best suited to dyeing at intermediate temperatures. Certain ranges have been developed in order to satisfy particular requirements, including those designed specifically to meet the needs of long-liquor dyeing, textile printing or continuous dyeing. No other class of textile colorant has been so widely extended to meet the varying needs of the colourist.

4.9.1 Batchwise Dyeing
Reactive dyes can be applied by batchwise dyeing methods of all types to cellulosic materials. Most types of stock-dyeing equipment, paddle machines, package-dyeing vessels, jets, winches and jigs can be used. Stainless steel construction is preferred and copper fittings or vessels are to be avoided. The dyeing process consists of three stages:
1. Exhaustion from an aqueous bath containing common salt or Glauber's salt, normally under neutral conditions
2. Addition of an alkali to promote further uptake and chemical reaction of absorbed dye with the fibre
3. Dyed material is then rinsed and soaped to remove electrolyte, alkali and unfixed dye.

Processes whereby stages 1 and 2 are partly or fully combined have been developed to meet special requirements. The varying nature of dyes containing different reactive groups necessitates the use of dyeing temperatures that can range from ambient temperatures to the boil. Using specially selected dyes, temperatures above the atmospheric boil can be applied in pressurised package-dyeing equipment, but this is seldom necessary.

4.9.2 Preparation of Material to be Dyed
Except in special cases, batchwise preparation before dyeing is conducted either in the dyeing machine itself or in adjacent machines of similar design reserved for this purpose. Routines for the preparation of cotton, viscose and flax are well established. The essential requirements for batchwise dyeing with reactive dyes are that the goods must be made available to the dyer in a neutral, uniform and readily absorbent state.

In contrast to the dyeing of vat or sulphur dyes, typical reactive dyeing processes will not eliminate natural or added fats and waxes. When raw cotton is to be dyed, good results are readily obtained after a thorough batchwise pre-scour. However, acceptable results are often possible without lengthy pretreatment, e.g. batchwise dyeing of knitted fabrics with hot-dyeing reactive dyes in the presence of a powerful wetting agent, or the pad–batch dyeing of knitgoods with a similar auxiliary. Sizing materials must always be removed from woven goods because of their marked tendency to react with the dyes.

There is considerable variation in the ability of reactive dyes to cover dead or immature cotton. For this reason it may sometimes become necessary to causticise or semi-mercerise woven fabrics in order to produce a satisfactory appearance in certain colours. Such pretreatments (including full mercerisation) give the added effect of better colour value. Viscose fabrics are sometimes significantly improved by mild pre-causticisation. Because of the brilliance of many reactive dyes, sufficiently bright results are attainable on cotton without pre-bleaching of woven fabrics. Thoroughly desized and boiled-out goods can be used in many cases, thus presenting a financial saving. Where bleaching is necessary it is imperative to check that all traces of residual chlorine or peroxy compounds and alkali are removed prior to dyeing, otherwise loss of reactivity and even partial destruction of the dye can occur. Fabric for dyeing must be uniformly neutral; a pH no higher than 7 should be recorded when samples have been thoroughly extracted in boiling distilled water. Alkalinity can be corrected by careful addition of dilute acetic acid, but an excess should be avoided since carboxyl ions can catalyse the hydrolysis of many reactive dyes in solution.

4.9.3 Water for Dissolving and Dyeing
Apart from several well-publicised exceptions, reactive dyes have good solubility. Few show serious sensitivity to hard water, *but*, because the fixation stage demands alkali, precipitation of hardness constituents is inevitable. This is a serious hazard and soft water should be used for all dissolving and dyebath operations.

Where a water-softening plant is not available, *minimum* quantities of sodium hexametaphosphate (e.g. Calgon T (AW)) are permitted, but excess can lead to a notable reduction in colour yield. Uncontrolled use of organic sequestrants (e.g. ethylenediamine tetra-acetic acid) might lead to problems arising from colour change and loss in light fastness. All metal-complex dyes, with the exception of those derived from copper phthalocyanine, will give rise to this effect. However, where other methods have failed to reduce the adverse effect of free ions of copper or iron on metal-free dyes, careful application of minimal amounts of ethylenediamine tetra-acetic acid has been successful in eliminating the problem.

4.9.4 Common Salt and Glauber's Salt
The use of one of these salts, in large amounts, is essential to all batchwise dyeing processes. The relative price and availability of common salt and Glauber's salt varies considerably in different parts of the world and selection must take account of this. In the UK, for example, common salt is available in a very fine and pure vacuum-dried quality and is most widely used, except for most turquoise and green shades based on reactive dyes derived from copper and/or nickel phthalocyanine. Glauber's salt is preferred when there is a risk of dye aggregation in solution, e.g. it is considered essential for the brilliant blues of the vinylsulphone series of dyes.

Common salt is appreciably more soluble and easier to dissolve in water than Glauber's salt, so in most batchwise dyeing systems the necessary additions are made in the form of the dry product. Where salt consumption is high, however, a saturator to produce brine has positive advantages. Brine can be metered on demand, thus eliminating repeated weighing out and handling of salt, which is labour-intensive and costly. Marine salt, from evaporated sea water, contains a high proportion of magnesium and calcium salts, and should be avoided. On addition of alkali these impurities precipitate as hydroxides which cause considerable problems, especially in circulating-liquor dyeing machines. Not only do the precipitates interfere with flow and cause serious filtration problems, but they lead to reduced colour value, unlevelness and poor rubbing fastness. Precipitates of this kind are particularly difficult to remove.

Salt, from whatever source, must be free from alkali, since the latter causes premature fixation or hydrolysis of the dye. Calcined Glauber's salt is difficult to dissolve and does not readily lend itself to dry addition to the dyebath. Solutions are best made by first slurrying in very hot water and then completely dissolving by addition of cold water to the required volume; stirring whilst dissolving is essential. High-purity Glauber's salt, preferably in the calcined or dessicated form, should be used. Where only Glauber's salt crystals are available they should be used at twice the concentration recommended for the calcined salt.

4.9.5 Alkali

Whilst soda ash (98% anhydrous sodium carbonate) is probably the most widely used alkali in reactive dyeing, sodium bicarbonate and caustic soda are also important. These three agents, either separately or in binary mixtures, can span the range pH 8–12, of interest for all reactive dyeing methods. Soda ash of high purity is recommended. Additions are made to the dyebath from well-diluted solutions. Sodium bicarbonate is widely used in dyeing viscose and cotton, sometimes to provide a ready means of liberating sodium carbonate to increase pH during a rise in temperature. It may be used in conjunction with soda ash to provide conditions of intermediate pH. Sodium bicarbonate should not be stored in hot damp conditions and, as with soda ash, dry scoops should be used when weighing. Most importantly sodium bicarbonate should be dissolved at low temperatures, and direct heating by steam injection must be avoided.

Trisodium phosphate is seldom used nowadays; traces of calcium or magnesium ions can produce insoluble phosphates. These impart an undesirable hard handle to finished fabric and are a hindrance to winding and sewing because of friction effects.

Caustic soda, free from impurities, especially iron, is used in the form of solutions prepared from solid flake or, more frequently and for convenience, caustic liquors of known concentration.

4.9.6 Auxiliary Products

In normal circumstances, provided goods have been efficiently prepared for exhaust dyeing, it is unnecessary to add wetting or levelling agents to the dyebath. In conventional winch dyeing of tubular-knitted cotton, however, wetting agents provide a lubricating action for the avoidance of rope marks. If used, quantities should be minimal and consistent. Any excess of agent may exert a restraining action on one or more of the dyes in a mixture. After any pretreatment with wetting agent, thorough rinsing is advisable before a fresh bath is set for dyeing, in the interest of precise reproducibility. In many instances, however, dyeing can be carried out in the bath used for wetting out. Unwanted foam in dyeing machinery is eliminated by careful addition of selected antifoam agents. Defoaming agents are sometimes already incorporated in reactive dye formulations. Non-ionic wetting agents are frequently used when there is a risk of over-aggregation in electrolyte solutions, e.g. with certain turquoise and green dyes based on phthalocyanine, as well as other dyes of low solubility. Such agents, in the minimum quantity, should be introduced at the start of dyeing and never added to the hot dyebath. Cationic agents should never be used in the dyebath.

When dyeing in enclosed machines at temperatures higher than 70°C, some reactive dyes suffer reduction due to the combined effect of heat, alkali and the cellulose itself. If this problem is likely to occur it is advisable to add, at the start of dyeing, 1–2 g/l of an *m*-nitrobenzene sulphonate as a protecting agent.

4.9.7 Storage, Handling and Dissolving

All reactive dyes for cellulose are prone to hydrolysis in the presence of moisture, and unless carefully stored and handled they will deteriorate. Cool dry storage conditions are essential and the lids of packages must be firmly replaced after use; dry scoops, scales and containers must be used when weighing out. Bearing in mind that the dyes are *reactive chemicals*, there is always the remote possibility of respiratory allergies arising amongst workers who must handle them. For this reason it is sound practice to wear suitable dust-excluding respirators.

Dyes are usually dissolved by either of two techniques:

(a) By pasting with cold water followed by the steady addition, with stirring, of the required amount of water at the correct temperature (see below)

(b) By feeding a steady stream of the dye powder into the vortex produced by the high-speed stirring of water at the correct temperature.

Few types of reactive dye require boiling and most should not be so treated. However, Remazol dyes are dissolved in boiling water, followed at once by passing through a fine sieve into the required volume of cold water.

Highly reactive dyes (e.g. dichlorotriazinyl dyes) require water temperatures no higher than 50–60°C. Most dyes of lower reactivity (e.g. monochlorotriazinyl dyes) require a dissolving temperature of 80°C.

Chemicals used for dyeing should not be dissolved together with the dyes. The solubility limits of the individual dyes should never be exceeded. If these limits need to be approached, it is possible to improve the quality of solutions by the use of urea. This procedure is rarely necessary for batchwise dyeing, but urea is often used at 50–200 g/l in semi- and fully-continuous processes. When using Remazol dyes urea should not be dissolved together with the dyes. It should be separately sprinkled, in solid form, into the cooled dye solution before the start of dyeing. With the chlorotriazinyl dyes it is possible to dry-mix the urea with the dye powder, paste the mixture with water at 60°C and stir in the necessary volume of water. Urea absorbs heat on dissolving and the temperature of the final solution might need adjustment.

The inconsistencies and inefficiencies in dyeing that may arise from errors in weighing, and related dissolving procedures, have been discussed in detail [59].

4.9.8 Selection of Reactive Dyes for Batchwise Dyeing

It is inadvisable to mix dyes of different commercial ranges in a common recipe unless it is known with certainty that they are based on identical reactive systems. A comparison of a series of dyes based on a common chromophore but with different reactive groups is shown in Table 4.1.

TABLE 4.1

Examples of Competing Reactive Dyes with a Common Chromophore ©

Reactive group	Exhaust dyeing temperature (°C)	Common salt (g/l)	Soda ash (g/l)
	30	25–55	2–15
	80–85	30–90	10–20
	80–90	30–100	30–50
	40–50	20–80	5–35
	80–85	30–90	10–20

The brilliant red colours produced from these dyes not only show measurable differences in hue when dyed on a common substrate, but also differ markedly in requirements for optimum batchwise dyeing and in fastness properties [34]. Triazinyl and pyrimidinyl dyes give optimum wet fastness when the test is carried out at pH 6–7; vinylsulphones give best results at pH 4.5. At each side of these pH optima, hydrolysis of the dye–fibre bond can be either base- or acid-catalysed. The alkali sensitivity of Remazol dyeings is the reason for the warm acetic acid rinse recommended to remove alkali after dyeing.

A consequence arising from the large number of dyes based on different reactive systems is the multiplicity of recommendations in terms of electrolyte, alkali and temperature. Each separate range of dyes offered to the trade has demanded a specific set of compromises so that each dye will match a defined band of reactivity and efficiency conferred by the chemical and physical properties of the specific reactive system. It is clear that:

(a) Dyes containing different reactive systems have different detailed require-ments in a given dyeing method; additionally fastness properties may be influenced by the reactive system

(b) Dyes within a commercial range in which the individual products contain the same reactive group differ in the magnitude of the 'compromises' made to suit a given method of dyeing, but no more so than with other dye classes, such as direct or vat dyes.

The major practical criteria in the selection of dyes include the most *economical* means of obtaining the required *colour* and *fastness* with satisfactory *dyeing quality*.

4.10 BATCHWISE DYEING METHODS FOR REACTIVE DYES

The information given so far has been relevant, in a general sense, to all reactive dyes. In order to provide further practical details in a meaningful way, it is now necessary to refer to specific dyes. To simplify this presentation we have decided to select the chlorotriazinyl dyes as our point of reference, but to mention other reac-tive ranges where appropriate. This approach is less confusing than one referring to many individual types. The discussion will include those dyes which contain two chlorotriazinyl reactive centres per molecule.

4.10.1 Typical Dyeing Procedures for Chlorotriazinyl Dyes

These basic approaches to batchwise dyeing can be modified to fit local circum-stances and the requirements for producing satisfactory dyeing quality on the specific substrate. Typical modifications, including dye selection for jig, package and winch dyeing are discussed later.

For both dye ranges specified below, the procedure follows the sequence:

1. Load the machine with water and material as appropriate
2. Adjust bath temperature to that specified
3. Check pH (not to exceed 7) and correct with dilute acetic acid if necessary.

Dichlorotriazinyl Dyes
Start at 30°C and maintain the temperature throughout. Add dye solution over 5 min. During the next hour add the salt required in three portions of increasing size at intervals of 10–15 min. About 15 min after the final salt addition, add one-tenth of the soda ash required over 5 min. After a further 15 min add the remaining soda ash and continue dyeing for 30–45 min. Check a sample; if acceptable start rinse/soap stage.

Monochlorotriazinyl Dyes
Start at 50°C and add dye solution over 5 min. During the next 40 min add the salt required in three portions of increasing size at intervals of 10 min. Start to raise the temperature while adding the second portion. A rate of rise of not greater than 2°C/min should allow the required 80°C to be reached in approximately 20–30 min. Allow 15 min after the last salt addition before adding soda ash slowly over 15 min and continue dyeing at 80°C for 30–60 min. Check a sample; if acceptable start rinse/soap stage.

The above procedures are suitable for mercerised and unmercerised cotton. Similar processes are available for other reactive dye systems. Modification may be necessary, for reasons of dyeing quality or economic saving, to meet the needs of a specific machine design or substrate. Appreciable savings in times of treatment at certain stages are possible.

4.10.2 Jig Dyeing
In spite of inroads made by pad–batch dyeing, jig machines are still widely used for the dyeing of woven cotton. In dyeing with reactive dyes the jig presents a special problem in that marked variations in temperature can exist between the dyebath and various parts of the fabric roll. One set of observations [60] is shown in Table 4.2; the machine used was free from direct draughts.

TABLE 4.2

Fabric Temperatures in Open Jig Dyeing (Air in Dyehouse at 30°C, Dyebath at 85°C)

Temperature of cloth on draw roller (°C)	
(a) Centre of roll	67
(b) Extreme edge of cloth	57
(c) 1 cm inwards from (b)	61
(d) 2 cm inwards from (b)	63.5

Such differences between (a) and (b) result in 'listed' selvedges which are either pale or, in mixture shades, off-tone. 'Ending' can also be apparent because the draw roller (initially at 30°C) tends to abstract heat from the hotter fabric.

The jig dyer's normal practice of taking care to load the fabric 'lay-on-lay' to avoid overlapping selvedges does not provide sufficient safeguard against listing when dyeing with most of the hot-dyeing colours. The equilibrium uptake of dye is not greatly affected but the dye–fibre reaction rate is appreciably reduced at the lower temperatures. Increasing the recommended dye liquor temperature by 5–10°C does not eliminate the problem.

However, satisfactory dyeings can be achieved in enclosed jigs if care is taken to ensure that an elevated temperature is maintained in the liquor, so achieving a cloth temperature close to optimum (80°C), and if dyes of similar reactivity/temperature profiles are selected.

Use of highly reactive dyes of medium to high substantivity is the most effective solution to this problem. Dyebath temperatures of 30–40°C are conveniently closer to the air temperature, resulting in only moderate temperature differentials throughout the goods even under the most adverse conditions. Further advantage accrues from their good build-up at liquor ratios of 2:1 to 6:1 on the jig. Starting with goods prepared at about pH 6–7, adjusted using dilute acetic acid to prevent premature fixation and to aid levelling and penetration in dense, tight or irregular constructions, a normal procedure is as follows.

The dyebath is set at 40°C (30°C with some dyes), the dye added equally over the first two ends and then the salt likewise over two ends. When dyes of low to medium substantivity are used, dye and salt may be added together in the first two ends. The jig is run for a minimum of 30 min (at least two ends) and then alkali added over the next two ends; the jig is run for a further 30–60 min, depending on applied depth. After dropping the bath, the fabric is run for two ends of cold overflow washing and aftertreated if necessary. The bath temperature is raised to 50–60°C for a further two washes (repeated for full depths) and a squeeze or rider roller is applied if possible. Finally four to six ends in a detergent boil-off are carried out, depending on applied depth, followed by rinsing ends to clear.

Procedural details may vary, depending on dye choice, e.g. a few dyes showing solubility or aggregation problems require the use of Glauber's salt rather than common salt. Dyeing at 60°C might be necessary; in such cases enclosed jigs are preferred together with a 1:1 soda ash:sodium bicarbonate mixture. Pad–jig development gives improved surface appearance and penetration with difficult fabrics. The dry fabric is padded with dye solution and an anionic wetting agent. A high pick-up should be avoided to reduce the likelihood of seepage defects. The padded cloth may be passed directly to the jig, set with the full amount of salt, for immediate development. Alternatively quality can be improved by holding on the turning batching roll for about 30 min before passage to the prepared jig.

For reasons of fastness or colour it may be necessary to switch dye selection to hot-dyeing dyes. Caustic soda is best avoided as a further precaution against selvedge problems. Dyeing is started at 90°C with the dye solution divided over the first two ends, salt is divided over the next two ends and run for two ends before adding soda ash solution over two ends. The fabric is then run for sufficient ends at 85–90°C to give a fixation time of 45–60 min, depending on applied depth. The pad–jig process is also applicable to hot-dyeing dyes. Jig development should start at 90°C with all the salt present before the start of alkali addition. The jig dyeing of most turquoise dyes and recipes based on them normally demand Glauber's salt rather than common salt.

When minor shading adjustments on the jig are needed it is usual to drop half the volume of dye liquor from the trough and to adjust to the original volume with cold water. The necessary colour additions are dissolved and divided over two running ends. Sufficient amounts of salt and alkali are usually present to effect fixation when the bath has been raised to the appropriate dyeing temperature and two more passages of the fabric have been made.

Where large additions of colour are necessary the whole of the original bath should be discharged, followed by a thorough washing-off treatment to remove alkali and unfixed dye. A full redye process then becomes necessary.

4.10.3 Package Dyeing

Reactive dyes are well established for dyeing cotton yarns, including sewing threads. Hank dyeing has declined considerably in favour of circulating-liquor machines, in which hanks, warps, muffs, loose fibres, cones, cheeses or beams of material can be dyed. Modern units are controlled by fully- or semi-automatic systems, wholly or partially programmed to regulate temperature, process time, flow-direction cycles, dyebath additions, feed rates and sequence changes. Machine functions, together with the substrate (type of fibre and its form, uniformity and accessibility), determine not only the quality of dyeing but also the dyeing procedure.

Essentially the more thorough the access of dye liquor to the material the better the levelness and penetration. Relatively short dyeing cycles require rapid and uniform liquor circulation, which in turn depend on the efficiency of machine loading and the quality of package winding. The latter is determined by angle of wind, tension and overall density, and must allow uniform and consistent liquor flow.

In general liquor ratios in circulating-liquor machines fall within the range 8:1–12:1, but some units exceed this because piping and pumping demand a high volume of liquor. If circulation is poor or non-uniform, high-quality dyeings might still be possible but relatively long dyeing cycles are often necessary, particularly at the critical stages of salt levelling and alkali dosage. If feasible, chemical additions should be made when the liquor is circulating from outside to inside. Cold-dyeing dyes can be used with success at 40°C unless circulation conditions are poor. Where conditions are favourable it is possible to shorten the process by starting with all or part of the salt present before entering the goods, or even adding all the alkali at once after levelling has been achieved, although it is safer to add the alkali gradually. Special care is always necessary with yarns for plain weaving or knitting, as opposed to fine-effect threads in a coloured-woven design.

Where penetration problems are anticipated, as in certain mercerised, high-twist and/or multi-ply yarns, as well as most narrow fabrics, it is advisable to use hot-dyeing dyes. With these dyes, especially in enclosed machines, reductive degradation can be avoided by using a mild oxidising agent, which should be present from the start of dyeing. Care should be taken to optimise levelling prior to the addition of alkali.

With certain high-twist yarns on efficient machinery dyeing can proceed at 80°C throughout the process, provided the alkali addition is withheld until at least 30 min after the final salt addition. The opportunity arises when dyeing such materials as webbing, braid and zip-fastener tape to take advantage of the pre-alkali levelling function by raising the bath to the boil, or preferably 120°C; there is a good range of colours which suffer little or no change at 120°C for 45 min [61]. This technique is not always applicable and all copper-containing dyes, with the exception of copper phthalocyanine derivatives, are unsuitable. The dyebath must be set and maintained *below* pH 7 from the start and throughout the salt levelling period. Before the alkali is added it is imperative that the bath and the material be cooled to 80°C. A reduction inhibitor should be present from the start of dyeing.

A further modification when applying hot-dyeing dyes with good levelling properties in enclosed package-dyeing machines is to add all the salt at the start to avoid the physical inconvenience of adding large amounts of salt during dyeing. The so-called 'all-in' reactive dyeing procedures are frequently more attractive in title than in actual use [62] but they are often used for applying hot-dyeing dyes in conjunction with a wetting out of unscoured yarn before absorption and fixation of the dyes. In one workable process all the salt and alkali are added at ambient temperature and the liquor circulated for 10 min to ensure uniformity. The dye is added over the next 10 min and the liquor circulated again for 10 min, after which the temperature is raised to 80°C over 30 min and the dyeing continued for a further 60 min at this temperature.

Package dyeing procedures for Remazol dyes are available for dyeing temperatures of either 30–40°C or 30–60°C, depending on the difficulty of dyeing the substrate. Salt consumption averages 50 g/l; a mixed alkali system comprising caustic soda and soda ash (or trisodium phosphate alone) provides the pH for optimum dye–fibre reaction. Special recommendations, employing similar principles, exist for dyeing with selected Remazol dyes at 80°C using salt and soda ash.

4.10.4 Long-liquor Dyeing on the Winch

These procedures are of particular interest for knitted cotton, including blends with other fibres, as well as for those lightweight woven fabrics that will withstand processing in rope form without damage. Winch dyeing procedures are readily adapted to paddle dyeing machines. The typical salt/soda ash methods already outlined were based on practical winch dyeing procedures at liquor ratios of 15:1–30:1.

Special preparation techniques for tubular knitgoods are typically an alkaline detergent boil-off or a combined scour/peroxide bleach process, but some fabrics need only simple wetting out prior to dyeing. Particular care is necessary to avoid damage (e.g. abrasion, rope-marks, 'crow's feet' and running streaks) during preparation and dyeing. Whichever route is followed, all residual chemicals and impurities require thorough removal by hot rinsing, followed by pH adjustment with dilute acetic acid.

Satisfactory processing of tubular fabrics on the winch depends on efficient infla-
tion of the tube (ballooning) to avoid retention of permanent creases. The ballooning action is facilitated by careful sewing of the seams, by air injection from a series
of nozzles directed into the fabric tube and by certain anionic wetting agents which
exert a fibre-lubricating effect.

4.10.5 Dichlorotriazinyl Dyes on the Winch
The typical method already described is widely used. The 'low-alkali' variant is
basically identical to that described up to the stage of the first alkali addition. At
this point a considerably smaller quantity of soda ash is added over 5 min as a single
dose, giving a dyebath pH close to 9. After dyeing for 15 min, the pH is raised to
10.5–11.0 by addition of well-diluted caustic soda solution, in two portions, over a
10 min period; it is advisable to check the pH for each recipe. Dyeing is then continued at 30°C for 30–45 min before shading or proceeding to the washing-off stage.
Before making a shading addition, the bath is brought to pH 9 by the addition of
sodium bicarbonate (5 g/l); the dye is then introduced and after a further 10 min
sufficient caustic soda solution added to bring the pH back to the original level.
After 20 min the colour is checked again before starting the washing-off stage.
    The so-called 'bicarbonate-ash' dyeing process is designed for those 'difficult'
fabrics that do not respond satisfactorily to the standard approach. The fabric is run
in dye solution for 5 min at 50°C to obtain uniform initial uptake. The total salt
charge is then added and dyeing proceeds for 30 min. The dissolved (or slurried)
bicarbonate is added and, after a further 30–40 min still at 50°C, soda ash is added
to raise the pH. A final 30 min for fixation is followed by washing-off, unless
shading is necessary as already described.

4.10.6 Procion H-E Dyes on the Winch
In recent years, as the colour gamut obtainable from this range of dyes has been
extended, there has been a noteworthy growth in their use. These dyes provide
high standards of wet fastness and are especially valued because of high exhaustion
and fixation levels in long-liquor dyeing. Effective penetration and levelling at
80–85°C makes them useful for dyeing difficult constructions. The standard application process has been described. Normally the salt is added in portions, but there is
growing interest in adding all the salt at the start of the process, before adding the
dye and raising to the final dyeing temperature. Levelling is favoured by extension
of the migration period before alkali addition. Variants similar to those described
for package dyeing are applicable when necessary.

4.10.7 Short-liquor Atmospheric Jet and Overflow Machines
Several kinds of atmospheric jet and overflow machines have been introduced in
recent years. Advantages include shorter dyeing processes, savings in water consumption, lower volumes of effluent, and less salt and alkali consumption because
of the short (5:1–10:1) liquor ratios necessary. These machines are widely used for
the preparation and dyeing of knitted interlock and selected fine-ribbed cotton
fabrics. Abrasion problems may arise from the high speed of fabric running, often

about five times that in a conventional winch. Excessive foaming caused by vigorous turbulence at the jets can also cause problems. Even when antifoam agents are used, proper circulation might be hindered by slippage and level-dyeing quality might suffer. Reactive dyes of high exhaustion and fixation are particularly suited for dyeing knitted cotton fabrics in short-liquor atmospheric jets using methods described for conventional dyeing. It is generally accepted, however, that the jet machine (average liquor ratio 8:1) is inferior in respect of washing-off, when compared with a conventional winch (liquor ratio about 20:1). A jet machine is approximately two and half times less efficient than a winch machine in terms of electrolyte dilution and removal.

4.11 REGENERATED CELLULOSIC FIBRES, BAST FIBRES AND FIBRE BLENDS

4.11.1 Regenerated Cellulosic Fibres

Exhaustion and fixation on ordinary viscose are usually higher than on either cotton or linen; mercerised cotton falls between viscose and unmercerised cotton in these respects. These differences are also true for the various forms of high wet modulus (HWM or modal) fibres, but in the case of high-tenacity viscose and polynosic fibres no such generalisation can be made. The substantivity of dyes for these fibres varies over a considerable range. The fastness obtained from reactive dyes on ordinary viscose is especially noteworthy, since ratings for a given dye at a comparable depth on cotton can be as much as 1–1½ points lower.

In the earliest days of reactive dyeing the exhaust dyeing methods developed for cotton were used on viscose, but such methods were successful only with selected dyes on lightweight fibres of low linear density. The dyeing of heavyweight and high linear density viscose gave rise to poor penetration and severe surface frostiness.

The 'cold soda ash' process, i.e. dyeing at 20–30°C by the method described for dichlorotriazinyl dyes on cotton, is still used for selected colours produced with low- and medium-substantivity dyes. The 'warm bicarbonate' process for dyeing viscose with these dyes has long been preferred over other batchwise methods for viscose dyeing. It gives good colour yields with a level well-penetrated quality on materials of low and high linear density. Typical recommendations for dyeing loose fibre, yarn and fabric (particularly winch dyeing) are given below.

The bath is set with the appropriate dyes at 50°C. The goods are run for 10 min before starting the slow addition of salt. When this is completed dyeing is continued for 10 min at 50°C before adding the sodium bicarbonate. This provides an initial pH of 7.5 which rises steadily to pH 8.5. The time of dyeing after bicarbonate addition is dependent on filament linear density and applied depth. When more than 1% dye is applied dyeing is continued for a further 20 min after adding soda ash (equal to half the weight of bicarbonate used). This raises the pH to about 10.3 to allow full fixation. Shading is carried out by running half the dyebath to waste, refilling with cold water, adding the dissolved shading dye and running for 15 min. The bath temperature is increased to 50°C again and dyeing continued for 20–30 min, depending on the size of the shading addition. After checking the shade and adjusting if necessary, the final washing-off process is carried out.

Selected hot-dyeing dyes can often provide specific colours and fastness properties not obtainable with cold-dyeing dyes. Dyeing is at 70–85°C, according to dye selection, on materials normally difficult to dye level or insufficiently well-penetrated at lower temperatures. These dyes need less salt, especially if they belong to the high-substantivity group, often only half the quantity of salt used in cotton dyeing. Fixation normally requires 10–20 g/l soda ash but most turquoise dyes require special techniques.

The pad–jig procedure outlined for cotton gives satisfactory results with woven viscose fabrics and cotton/viscose blends. It is applicable to the pad–winch development sequence, following similar principles. Under alkaline conditions in enclosed machines viscose is especially prone to cause problems of dye reduction. It is essential that the viscose be thoroughly desulphurised, otherwise appreciable colour value will be lost. Addition of a reduction inhibitor from the start of dyeing is advised.

4.11.2 Bast Fibres

When adequately prepared, flax yarns and linen fabrics can be dyed by the usual routines for cotton. Residual 'sprit' and woody (ligneous) material usually takes up more dye than the normal fibre, resulting in a speckled effect and sometimes an off-tone colour, which is particularly unattractive. These deeply dyed specks are readily reduced in depth as colour losses occur during subsequent alkaline wet treatments. Every effort should be made to remove these impurities before dyeing.

Causticised linen dress fabrics generally behave well under normal cotton dyeing conditions. Here pad–jig development is considered to be the best approach for the coverage of slubs and other surface irregularities. Careful dye selection is necessary before applying resin finishes to linen.

Flax yarns package-dyed with reactive dyes show a level of penetration often better than that obtained with vat dyes. Dye–fibre reactivity and final fixation are closer to those of unmercerised rather than mercerised cotton and appreciably less than on ordinary viscose. Careful attention is needed at the critical levelling and diffusion stages of dyeing, particularly when making alkali additions. The pad–batch process is especially attractive for woven linen because of the excellent dye diffusion obtained. The quantities of linen fabric processed only rarely justify fully continuous dyeing, but many of these systems are technically suitable.

Limited quantities of ramie are still processed; reactive dyeing is carried out by the normal methods devised for cotton. Bleached jute is batchwise dyed with reactive dyes using salt and soda ash; stronger alkali tends to reduce the value and appeal of jute. Sisal is occasionally dyed with reactive dyes because of their bright colour, good light fastness and excellent water fastness; many constructions present problems of poor penetration, however. Low colour values are generally obtained on coir and those other bast fibres with a high non-cellulosic content and deep natural colour.

4.11.3 Blends of Cellulosic Fibres

Cotton/viscose blends are encountered in yarn, woven and knitted constructions. Tone-in-tone or solid colours call for considerable care in dye selection and dyeing procedures. Important factors include the quality and intimacy of the blend, weight/bulk ratios and distribution of the fibre components, and absorbency of the material. Compromise processes can be devised from those described for either fibre alone. For example, the cold soda ash exhaust process for dichlorotriazinyl dyes described for viscose is preferred to the warm bicarbonate route in which dye partition favours the viscose component.

With all dye types the chief criterion of choice centres on partition between the fibres. The ideal situation is reached only when either tone-in-tone or equal depth is achieved and a repeatable process has been developed. The precise nature and origin of the component fibres is rarely known by the dyer and hence there are always factors outside his control. Selection of dyes can be quite significantly influenced by uptake differences between carded and combed cottons in blends with viscose. This effect is more prevalent in long-liquor dyeing and is virtually eliminated where pad–development sequences are applicable. An excellent basis for the production of solid colours is the pad–develop procedure using soda ash at the final fixation stage. The pad–batch process is particularly attractive for wovens because there is no possibility of the gross migration that may occur in long-liquor development baths. However, the suitability of any process for a given blend should be established in trials.

4.12 SEMI- AND FULLY-CONTINUOUS DYEING WITH REACTIVE DYES

The effect of liquor ratio in reactive dyeing has been discussed earlier. Conventional batchwise methods take place at liquor ratios within the range 8:1–30:1. Pad dyeing, which is largely confined to woven goods, extends this range to 1:1 or even 0.5:1. Thus the advantages gained in exhaustion and fixation by dyeing in short liquor ratios can be significantly extended by the adoption of continuous processes. With reactive dyes it is possible to arrange for either long or short fixation times. Slow fixation is of special interest for achieving better diffusion, penetration and levelness on problematic materials, whilst rapid fixation is of greater interest for economy and productivity.

Fixation methods involving periods of 2–48 h are regarded as essentially semi-continuous, i.e. the cold pad–batch system. Fixation times of only 15–60 s are a feature of fully continuous processing, which can reach production rates of the order of 100 m/min. The capital outlay and running costs are considerably higher than for semi-continuous systems, in which processing costs are less than in batch-wise dyeing.

The most important continuous dyeing variants are described below. In each case the essential item of equipment is the padding mangle, of which many types exist [63, 64]. The most commonly used are those equipped with a low capacity trough and two (or three) large-diameter squeeze bowls. The trough has a V or U cross-section, often reduced in capacity by various displacement devices; full-width liquor feeds are normal and most are fitted with an accurate automatic level control.

From the earliest days of reactive dyes it was apparent that their generally low substantivity, good solubility and controllable reactivity held out great potential for their adaptation to continuous application. The following processes include several procedural variants designed to meet local needs.

Single Padding Methods (with simultaneous padding of dye and alkali)
(a) Semi-continuous sequences
   –Pad–batch cold, with 'short' or 'long' fixation times
(b) Continuous sequences
   –Pad–dry–wash
   –Pad–dry–bake(thermofix)–wash
   –Pad–dry–steam–wash

Double Padding Methods (with separate application of dye and alkali, with or without intermediate drying)
   –Pad–dry–pad alkali/salt–batch–wash
   –Pad–dry–pad alkali/salt–steam–wash
   –Pad–dry–impregnate alkali/salt–wash

In addition to their use on woven cotton, viscose or linen goods, these routines have been applied to cellulosic tapes and other narrow fabrics. Especially important is the dyeing of polyester/cellulosic blends by the application of disperse dyes and reactive dyes, either separately (in sequence) or simultaneously.

4.12.1 Pad–Batch Processes

Such processes follow the sequence:
1. Impregnation of the prepared dry fabric in a cold solution of dye and alkali
2. Expression of the surplus liquor uniformly as the goods emerge from the padding trough
3. Storage of the batched roll of wet fabric at ambient temperature for a predetermined fixation period (within the range 2–48 h)
4. Washing-off of unfixed dye
5. Drying.

When first introduced this method was of prime interest for the application of cold-dyeing dyes, but modifications to suit the less reactive types followed quickly. The success of the sequence pad(cold)–batch(cold)–wash is attributable to several factors, including the scope for selective control of the dye–cellulose and dye–water reaction rates. It is generally necessary to employ a liquor feed device, whereby dye and alkali are brought together immediately before the mixed padding solution comes into contact with the material being dyed. The equipment is simple and application costs are low. The technique, in terms of energy and water consumption, and labour cost, is the most economical approach to the production of high-quality dyeings of high wet fastness on cellulosic fabrics.

Batch lengths of 1000–10000 m to each colour, usually excessive for jig processing but too short to justify investment in fully continuous plant, can be processed conveniently. For many woven fabrics, especially dressgoods and furnishings, the pad–batch route has substantially displaced jig dyeing. Fundamental principles and practical details of the process for chlorotriazinyl dyes have been given by Marshall

[23]. Since the dyes react with water as well as with the fibre, attention must be given to maintaining a steady concentration of active dye in the alkaline padding bath.

An important development was that of devising an apparatus to mix and deliver aliquots of dye and alkali solution as demanded by the fabric during its passage through the impregnation trough. Several reliable feed systems have been devised for this purpose. A popular device is the stainless steel pneumatically operated ICI (Marshall-Jeffreys) tipping bucket in which solutions of dye and alkali are separately metered, in the volume ratio 4:1, and mixed *en route* to the padding trough, which has an integral automatic trough-level control to operate the feed system. Equally popular for this purpose is the electrically operated Klaus Fischer reciprocating pump, in which the feed solutions (4:1 dye:alkali) are metered, mixed and delivered to the trough at a predetermined flow rate.

Most pad–batch processes are designed for a dwell period of 2–8 h. For low-reactivity dyes batching may extend to 24 or even 48 h.

The recommended concentration of soda ash for applying dichlorotriazinyl dyes to cotton or linen using the short cold-batch procedure is equal to that of the applied concentration of dye (if within the range 5–30 g/l) for a liquor pick-up of 60–80%. The corresponding recommendations for viscose are a soda ash concentration half that of the dye (within 10–60 g/l dye) for a liquor pick-up of 90–110%. In both cases, at concentrations of dye below the lower limit 5 g/l soda ash is used, and at concentrations above the upper limit 30 g/l soda ash. The dye is dissolved and filtered into a storage tank. If urea is necessary (for deep shades or products of low solubility) it should be added at this stage. After adding well-diluted wetting agent and water to 80% of the total volume required for the run, the temperature is adjusted to the selected value between 20 and 30°C. This must be maintained throughout the run. Soda ash solution at five times the final concentration required is separately prepared in the alkali-storage vessel and adjusted to the same temperature.

Using the automatic feed and mixer unit, the trough of the padder is filled to the required level and padding is begun at constant speed. Woven fabrics are normally batched on the receiving roller or perforated beam, but certain loosely woven fabrics such as towelling or blanketing can be plaited down. When the run is complete the batch is first covered with a smooth end-fent sufficiently wide to overlap the selvedges of the dyed batch, and then an overall covering of polythene film is used to prevent evaporation and temperature change during storage. The roll is allowed to turn gently to minimise seepage effects. Peripheral drives to the batch should be avoided, and a centre drive selected wherever possible. The normal batching time for dichlorotriazinyl dyes for medium depths on cotton is 2 h; heavy depths and viscose dyeings might require up to 4 h. The temperature of the batch during storage should remain as close as possible to the padding temperature and should not be allowed to fall below 20°C. On completion of the batch-dwell period (during which time additional padding runs can be prepared) the goods may be washed-off on a jig or an open-width washing range, or sometimes in rope form in spiral becks. However, the most efficient washing-off process is that based on the principle of elution with hot water. The goods, as they leave the padding mangle, are batched onto specially designed perforated beams of suitable diameter. When fixation is completed the unit is transferred to a suitable washing station. This procedure provides highly efficient washing-off with a minimum of labour, water and capital cost. The concept of beam washing arose from the work of Marshall, who has detailed [65] the theory and practice of this widely adopted system. On viscose fibres with a filament linear density exceeding 1.5, viscose fabrics made from fibres of mixed linear density and certain mercerised cotton fabrics, dye penetration and surface appearance can be improved appreciably using a slower fixation treatment. The fixation time required for dichlorotriazinyl dyes at 20–30% can be conveniently extended from 2 to 24 h by simply replacing part (or all) of the soda ash by sodium bicarbonate. Thus a 4:1 bicarbonate:carbonate mixture is recommended for cotton or linen at a total concentration equal to that of the dye, while a concentration of bicarbonate equal to the dye concentration (within 5–30 g/l dye) is necessary for viscose. Shorter fixation times can be arranged by reducing the ratio of sodium bicarbonate to soda ash.

In order to meet demands of specific fastness, colour or dye costs, it might be necessary to apply dyes of lower reactivity by increasing the pH value of the padding liquor and the batching time. When applying monochlorotriazinyl dyes, for example, it is necessary to batch for 24–48 h and to use salt and caustic soda to attain optimum fixation. Typically the salt (up to 30 g/l) and alkali (10–15 g/l) are dissolved together in the alkali feed tank of the automatic feeding device. When caustic soda is used in pad–batch reactive dyeing there is some risk of poor fixation at the selvedges, due to neutralisation by carbon dioxide or other acidic vapour in the exposed regions of the fabric batch. As the dye applied there remains undisturbed, the fault is only revealed after washing-off. This problem of white selvedges cannot always be eliminated by improving the precision of edge-on-edge batching nor by minimising air movement in the batching zone. It is prevented by enclosing the batching area in a compartment (commonly a timber-framed housing covered in polyethylene film) containing a simple apparatus for carbon dioxide absorption consisting of a small electric extraction fan positioned to draw air through a bed of caustic soda pellets.

Fixation times for dyes containing other reactive groups vary within the range 3–48 h. Depending on their reactivity level, the pad bath pH is optimised using caustic soda alone or in admixture with either soda ash or sodium metasilicate (water-glass), with or without the addition of salt.

For a Remazol dyeing method, which includes silicate as the major component of the alkali feed, it is claimed that the white selvedge problem is virtually eliminated. Possible variants of the above processes to suit special requirements include the following sequences.

(a) Pad (dye only)–batch (1–2 h)–dry–pad(alkali)–batch–wash-off–dry. With certain qualities of viscose or cotton this route, which does not require a dye/alkali mixer, is capable or giving an excellent surface appearance. The batching stage before drying is essential with viscose to promote dye diffusion and reduce migration at the drying stage. Common salt and wetting agent may be added to further minimise migration.

(b) Routes for dyeing polyester/cellulosic blends:
   (i) Apply disperse dyes to the polyester portion, reduction clear, soap and dry, followed by pad (reactive dye and alkali)–batch–wash-off–dry
   (ii) Pad (suitable disperse and reactive dyes, neutral)–dry/thermofix–pad (caustic soda and common salt)–batch–wash-off–dry.

Manufacturers of reactive dyes have provided data on the 'affinity tailing' factors to be applied to individual dyes, so that drift of strength and hue does not occur before equilibrium is established during a run.

Now essentially of historical interest, the pad roll process [66] was carried out on a Svetema pad roll machine. The prepared fabric was padded with dye and alkali and then passed through an infra-red heating zone into a chamber of controlled humidity and temperature, in which it was batched onto a large-diameter roller. During fixation the batch was slowly rotated so as to avoid seepage of dye liquor to the lower regions of the roll. The yields obtained were generally lower than those obtained from the cold batching procedure described earlier.

4.12.2 Fully Continuous Dyeing

Installation of continuous dyeing equipment calls for considerable capital investment. Nevertheless, with skilled organisation and good management, this form of production offers advantages where large quantities of dyed and finished fabrics are required in a limited range of shades. Where pad–steam ranges have been originally laid down for vat or sulphur dyeing, for example, these can readily be adapted for reactive dyeing. Listing and ending can be avoided and excellent re-producibility is possible from run to run. There are notable savings to be gained in handling and labour costs, compared with batchwise processing of equal amounts of material. The minimum length to each colour on large multiple-unit ranges is usually estimated at about 10000 m, depending on local circumstances and avoidance of excessive downtime. The dye–fibre reaction takes place extremely rapidly in the presence of minimal amounts of alkali and water at elevated temperature. With highly reactive dyes of the dichlorotriazinyl type reaction times are sufficiently short to permit fixation simply by passing the padded goods through a conventional dryer. Fixation of low-reactivity dyes requires longer treatments under hot wet conditions, e.g. steaming.

Thorough and uniform preparation of the fabric and its presentation to the pad mangle in a crease-free state is crucially important. Processing before dyeing is determined by the state of the grey or loom-state cotton and might include: single–desize–scour–mercerise(optional)–bleach–dry–condition, followed by uniform cooling before dyeing.

Continuous routes for reactive dyes require either a single or a double padding operation. For single padding 'one dip–one nip' is preferable to a multi-dip and multi-squeeze system. The simpler system minimises tailing and permits the smallest possible pad trough volume consistent with thorough wetting and impregnation. Running conditions which allow a complete change of liquor in the trough every 2–3 min throughout the run are ideal for most purposes. Constant running speeds of 30–60 m/min are typical but some dyehouses achieve 100 m/min or more.

Mangle pressures are set to give a liquor pick-up of 60–80% at a constant padding temperature of 20–25°C. With few exceptions (e.g. those requiring urea addition), reactive dyes are notable for excellent solubility and rapid penetration of suitably prepared materials.

Tailing effects accompanying many padding processes arise from the selective affinities of the individual dyes for the substrate; a deeper colour at the beginning of a run progressively 'tails' (weakens) to a paler, sometimes off-tone, colour as the run continues. Tailing with reactive dyes is troublesome much less often than with direct dyes.

In pale depths under unfavourable conditions, however, preferential absorption can occur until a satisfactory equilibrium has been reached by feeding the trough with an adjusted dye solution. When dyes of different affinities are used together they can show selective absorption so that both hue and strength changes occur unless corrective steps are taken. Reproducibility of colour throughout the length of a run also depends on:
(a) Absorbency of the goods
(b) Temperature and time of immersion
(c) Volume of pad liquor and the efficiency with which this is controlled by the liquor-feed system
(d) Rate of uptake of liquor by the fabric passing through the pad bath at a given speed.

The theoretical and practical principles of affinity effects in padding have been described by Marshall and others [23, 67].

4.12.3 Continuous Sequences Based on a Single Padding Operation
These procedures comprise (a) padding the dye with a suitable alkali, followed by (b) fixation by drying alone, or drying and baking, or drying and steaming. All routes require a final washing-off stage to remove chemicals and unfixed dye.

Pad–Dry Processes
The first method of this type (the pad(bicarbonate)–dry process) makes use of a pad liquor containing dichlorotriazinyl dyes and sodium bicarbonate (10 g/l). Where doubt exists about the absorbency of the fabric to be dyed an addition of wetting agent may be necessary. The addition of other auxiliaries may be necessary, as detailed below.
(a) Urea to improve dye solubility. It also lowers the rate of removal of water by evaporation during drying. Even at high temperatures the solubilising and hygroscopic properties of urea are extremely beneficial in ensuring optimum fixation in medium to heavy depths, since dye–fibre reaction ceases when the fabric contains no residual moisture. Urea, however, frequently contributes to problems of migration during drying.
(b) Salt (5–10 g/l) or sodium alginate (up to 1 g/l) to minimise migration of colour at the drying stage (roller-type, hot flue or cylinder dryers are most commonly used).

Fortunately migration in pale depths (which are more prone to show tailing faults) is rarely severe and it is the medium and full depths which show most migration. Excess thickening agent such as sodium alginate can lead to inferior fabric penetration. In fact, before any pad bath additives are considered it is essential to determine the optimum pick-up (lowering this often brings improvement) and the optimum drying conditions. Migration shows itself as either 'mealiness' at the fabric surface or side-to-centre colour differences across the width of the fabric. Such effects could be attributed to faulty preparation, a pad bowl fault or excessive local heating in the dryer. Back-and-face difference effects, where one side of the cloth is lighter, may arise from the fabric construction or be caused by movement of the dye solution or dispersion toward the source of heat, owing to uneven distribution of heat between the two sides during drying. For optimum colour yield in the pad–dry process using a hot flue dryer, it is necessary to maintain a moisture content not less than 15–20%, i.e. a high wet-bulb temperature is required. Using dichlorotriazinyl dyes the minimum time of passage through a hot-flue dryer (depending on fabric type and applied depth) could be about 2–5 min at 103–105°C. By control of the air extraction system it is possible to ensure the presence of free moisture in the dryer. The time required to eliminate all moisture has to be longer than that to achieve complete dye–fibre reaction, since moisture is essential for the latter. Provided the dye–fibre reaction has reached completion, the treated fabric may be allowed to retain as much as 15% residual moisture content. Although considerable experience must be developed in order to obtain dyeings of satisfactory quality using a steam-heated cylinder dryer (drying cans), such equipment is widely used. A high rate of fixation is obtained with higher efficiency than with other forms of dryer. The main problems to be avoided are mottling due to 'sizzling' (or local boiling-off of water on the first few cans) and 'two-sidedness' (back and face migration). Both faults are controlled by reducing steam pressures on the entry-end cans and, in certain cases, by wrapping of the first two cans. Copper cylinders should be avoided because many reactive dyes combine with copper to give permanent colour changes; stainless steel cans are essential. Dyeing of fabrics with 'sculptured' surfaces presents exceptionally difficult migration problems and is best not attempted by this procedure. Cotton of simple construction, including raised fabrics (e.g. flannelette), and lightweight staple viscose behave well. The main function of heated cylinders is water evaporation. At a can surface temperature of 105°C, for example, an average fabric remains at about 70°C, so that it retains considerable moisture during most of the contact time. If dryness is reached the fabric temperature rises and dye–fibre reaction ceases. Conditions should be controlled so that complete dryness is not reached before the end of the run. Inadvertent stoppage of a hot-flue or cylinder dryer can be particularly harmful, since browning of the alkaline fabric occurs and this is extremely difficult to remove. Little detailed information exists on the principles of heating fabrics which contain reactive dye padding liquors [67].

Remazol dyes can be used in the pad–dry process, but it is necessary to replace the mildly alkaline bicarbonate bath by soda ash (10–30 g/l), and addition of urea (50–100 g/l) is advised.

Washing-off is carried out immediately on exit of the goods from the dryer, because in the presence of alkali any exposed areas are likely to show abnormally rapid fading even in diffuse light. Where typical open-width washing is available, the preferred sequence is: cold rinse, hot rinse, soap twice at the boil, two hot and two cold rinses. If necessary a dye-fixing agent can be added to the final cold rinse before mangling and drying.

The pad(bicarbonate)–dry process has been adapted to incorporate a crease-resist finish as part of the continuous sequence. Here it was found possible to replace the washing-off by a cooling air passage and immediate impregnation in the crease-resist formulation, followed by the necessary drying and curing stages. Any flushing of colour into the cold resin bath can be minimised using a cationic dye-fixing agent. Performance standards are acceptable for dress goods but this process is seldom used.

Pad–Dry–Bake (Thermofix) Processes
Shortly after the monochlorotriazinyl dyes were introduced, it was recognised that the pad(bicarbonate)–dry process, proving so successful with dichlorotriazinyl dyes, was valueless for these less reactive products.

Investigation led to the development of the pad–dry–bake process, still occasionally used when the expensive but versatile pad–steam ranges are not available. The thermofix route forms the basis of several dyeing processes for polyester/cellulosic blends.

On cotton fabrics the dye is padded together with 10–20 g/l soda ash and up to 200 g/l urea. During subsequent drying little fixation takes place; this stage is not particularly critical, except that precautions are essential to minimise migration. The dried fabric is led directly into the thermofixation unit (pin stenter or oil-heated cylinders), where baking takes place, e.g. for 1 min at 150°C. Open-width washing-off follows as described above.

Many viscose fabrics show excessive migration and poor diffusion of dye, which are manifested as inadequate colour penetration. This can be minimised by batching for 1–2 h before drying and baking, although such a step is neither convenient nor popular, since it lowers the daily output appreciably. Viscose is far more satisfactorily handled by pad–batch techniques, which have considerably lower energy costs, and by careful planning (e.g. using a multi-batch system) the daily output can approach that from fully continuous systems.

A further defect of the pad–dry–bake process is a lack of chlorine fastness from dyes that are normally satisfactory. They become less resistant to chlorine as the severity of thermofixation treatment increases. In association with water urea forms a mobile melt. Above 133°C molten urea decomposes rapidly, but when moisture remains the onset of urea decomposition is delayed. Apparently this is due to the formation of a stable eutectic mixture of urea and water [68]. The decomposition of urea in a dry atmosphere in the presence of certain dyes is accompanied by a deterioration in chlorine fastness of the dyeings and, in some cases, a reduction in light fastness. High-temperature (HT) steamers offer little advantage as alternatives to conventional thermofixation equipment when dyeing cotton; improved tinctorial yields can be obtained with certain dyes on viscose staple, however. With the padding recipe given above, typical HT steaming conditions are 1 min at 130°C or 30 s at 150°C.

When the pad–dry–thermofix route is adopted for polyester/cellulosic blends, i.e. with selected disperse and reactive dyes in a single padding operation, the urea concentration is reduced to 50 g/l or less in order to minimise staining of cellulose by the disperse dyes. In the so-called 'neutral thermofix' process it is now recommended that urea be replaced by dicyandiamide. Fixation is promoted by sodium bicarbonate and a migration inhibitor is added to control both classes of dye during drying. Thermofix treatment is given for 1 min at 200–220°C, depending on the properties of the disperse dyes selected. An alternative process is the two-stage sequence in which the disperse dyes are applied in a pad–thermofix stage and the reactive dyes by pad–steam. However, provided they can achieve similar depths, and there are characteristic limitations in certain regions of the shade gamut, dyers prefer the one-stage neutral thermofix process with dicyandiamide and bicarbonate (or bicarbonate/carbonate) at an initial pH of 7–8.

Pad–Dry–Steam Processes
Although mainly of interest to textile printers for grounds dyed with reactive dyes, this route is ocassionally preferred by dyers as an alternative to the pad(bicarbonate)–dry process when the available drying unit cannot be controlled satisfactorily for humidity, or when the maximum amount of urea has failed to give the optimum colour yield. Dichlorotriazinyl dyes are padded at 20–25°C with sodium bicarbonate (5–10 g/l), a reduction inhibitor and, if necessary, a wetting agent, dried and steamed for 30 s at about 102°C, and finally washed-off in a conventional open soaper. Where the process is incorporated in the production of overprint or discharge styles the sequence pad–dry–print–dry–steam–wash is followed.

Undue exposure of the padded and dried goods before printing should be avoided, since the unfixed alkaline dyeing is sensitive to daylight and acidic atmospheres. The ground colour and the print are fixed simultaneously during steaming. When dyes of lower reactivity are applied, soda ash (about 10 g/l) must replace bicarbonate and longer steaming times (3–10 min) are necessary.

4.12.4 Continuous Sequences Based on Two Padding Operations

Pad–Dry–Pad(Alkali/Salt)–Steam–Wash Processes
In the first practical dyeing method devised for reactive dyes the fabric was padded in a neutral solution of dye and then in a dilute solution of caustic soda in saturated sodium chloride before steaming to complete fixation. This 'wet-on-wet' system presented problems arising from 'bleed-off' of dye into the alkaline bath even at maximum salt concentration. This aggravated tailing effects, especially in the relatively large-volume padding troughs then in use. Partial hydrolysis of the dichlorotriazinyl dyes desorbed in this way resulted in reabsorption of inactive dye from the alkaline salt bath. Furthermore it was always difficult to ensure adequate pick-up of chemical solutions by the wet fabric, unless it was allowed to leave the second mangle in an unacceptably saturated state.

This process sequence was soon replaced by the 'wet-on-dry' technique, which was immediately adaptable to the du Pont pad–steam ranges already well established for vat dyeing. The wet-on-dry route follows the sequence: pad(neutral cold dye solution)–dry–pad(caustic soda in brine solution)–steam–wash. By hot-flue drying (then preferably cylinder cooling) the fabric after padding with neutral dye solution, highly efficient pick-up of the alkali/salt liquor is achieved. Where small-capacity troughs are fitted few colour-bleed problems are encountered. Dichloro-triazinyl dyes require only dilute (2 g/l) caustic soda and 15–30 s steaming at 100–105°C. Monochlorotriazinyl dyes, on the other hand, need at least 10 g/l caustic soda and steaming times of 30–75 s, depending on dye reactivity and applied depth. Slightly higher yields can be obtained from dichlorotriazinyl dyes by replacing caustic soda with soda ash (10 g/l) in the brine bath and extending the steaming time (30–60 s). Because of problems associated with the dissolution of soda ash in brine, however, the caustic/salt method is normally regarded as the standard route, although each commercial range of dyes requires slightly different steaming conditions. An addition of a reduction inhibitor is usually made to the dye solution.

Several designs of roller-type air-free 'wet' steamer with a cold water exit seal are suitable. The eight-box washing range is set for the preferred sequence already detailed for the pad–dry process. In full depths, however, extra detergent boil stages may be necessary. (With some fabrics, e.g. towelling, a continuous-spiral beck washing unit is recommended.) This process is the most widely employed of the fully continuous sequences. When dyeing polyester/cellulosic blends the basic pad–steam range is modified by the inclusion of a thermofixation unit between the flue dryer and the second padding mangle.

Pad–Dry–Impregnate(Alkali/Salt)–Wash Processes
This route is often referred to as the pad–wet-fixation process. Although rarely considered for chlorotriazinyl dyes, it has been of some interest for selected vinyl-sulphone dyes, especially if steaming equipment is not available.

The fabric is padded with neutral Remazol dye solution, dried and impregnated with caustic soda and common salt, or more often sodium silicate (water-glass), solution at 95–100°C for a contact time of 5–15 s. The specially designed Hoechst wet-fixation trough (with indirect heating to avoid dilution via condensation) is recommended for the boiling alkali step. Without due care this stage might prove hazardous for the operative.

4.13 WASHING-OFF AFTER DYEING
This is a process of *paramount* importance. At the end of dyeing the fibre contains unfixed hydrolysed dye and possibly some residual active dye. Before a reactive dyeing can show its true fastness such loose colour must be removed or rendered insignificant in amount.

It is remarkable how little unfixed colour causes an unacceptable stain on adjacent white material [69]. The average amount of unfixed colour necessary to produce a stain equivalent to a grey scale 4 rating is only about 0.003% o.w.f. dye, with a range of 0.002–0.007% depending on tinctorial strength. It must be stressed that these amounts do not represent how much loose dye can be left in the bulk of a dyed package, e.g. if there is a risk of migration during drying after washing-off. The amount must be sufficiently small to ensure that after migration the dyed yarn on the outside of the package still has adequate fastness. The need to limit the amount of unfixed dye to this extent means that washing-off can be laborious, time-consuming and wasteful of water. Much effort has been expended in defining ways by which this essential process can be carried out effectively. Batchwise and continuous methods will be considered separately.

4.13.1 Theory of the Batchwise Washing-off Process

All washing processes are essentially techniques for achieving progressive dilution. Indeed, the washing of dyed textiles would be entirely this if the dyebath contained only rapidly diffusing non-substantive molecules. A mathematical model of this system has been defined in which allowance is made for dye affinity [69]. A comparison with experimental data has demonstrated that this model does indeed represent the practical system, but the effort needed to accumulate such data precludes its adoption as a means of predicting the behaviour of individual dyes. Nevertheless the model is useful in predicting the essential features of the washing-off process.

Removal of Unfixed Dye

Calculations were carried out assuming that an 8% shade of dye of 50% purity was applied at 70°C, using a liquor ratio of 10:1, in the presence of 100 g/l sodium chloride and 20 g/l sodium carbonate to produce 50% fixation. This dyeing was washed-off, again at 10:1 liquor ratio, assuming a 300% o.w.f. carry-over between baths using the sequence: 2×10 min at 20°C, 1×30 min at 100°C and 2×10 min at 20°C.

The results for a dye of relatively high affinity demonstrate that the first cold rinse is relatively inefficient in removing loose dye still present on the fibre, because the substantivity of the dye increases as the temperature is reduced from 70°C in dyeing to 20°C in the first rinse. Moreover, although the total electrolyte concentration is reduced by dilution from 120 g/l it is still fairly high at about 36 g/l. The second rinse reduces this value further (to about 11 g/l) and desorbs almost half of the loose dye still retained. A further dilution, and an increase in temperature to the boil, means that this step is highly efficient in terms of dye desorption. Significant decreases in the total amount of loose dye in the system only occur after the fourth and fifth washes.

Reduction in Total Loose Colour on the Dried Fibre

The results discussed above suggest that the loose dye still retained by the fibre has been reduced to a sufficiently low level (i.e. 0.002% o.w.f.) by the end of the fourth wash. This, however, is not the complete picture. The dyed fibre is still wet with dye solution, the residual concentration of which depends on the degree of dilution that has already taken place. On drying, this dissolved colour will be redeposited on and possibly reabsorbed by the fibre. If the fibre is dried immediately after dyeing or after the first or second rinse, then practically all the loose dye present arises from retention by the fibre. After later stages, however, most of the colour on the dried fibre is attributable to redeposition of dye from carry-over liquor during drying. In fact, although the amount of dye retained by the fibre at the end of the fourth stage (less than 0.002% o.w.f.) suggests that the dyeing would have acceptable fastness, the total amount of colour present after drying (0.003% o.w.f.) is unacceptably high.

Clearly the washing sequence is initially a dilution of the electrolyte to a level which permits effective removal of the unfixed dye retained by the fibre. Once most of this has been desorbed the essential process is one of progressive dilution to ensure that a minimum of colour is present as entrained liquor at the drying stage.

Effect of Reducing the Carry-over Between Washing Stages
Although the effectiveness of washing increases with the degree of dilution, increasing the number of dilutions or increasing the liquor ratio may be uneconomical in terms of time taken and water consumption. Alternatively, if the amount of liquor carried over from one wash bath to the next is decreased from 300% to 50% o.w.f., the process becomes much more efficient. In particular the initial rinses become more effective in desorbing dye owing to the quicker dilution of the electrolyte, and that portion of the sequence in which virtually all of the dye on the dried fibre originates from carry-over of entrained liquor to the drying stage begins with the second rinse. Owing to the greater dilution at each step the process is much more effective and the previously quoted figure of 0.003% loose dye is achieved after three stages rather than after more than five of them. Under these conditions the third (boiling) stage may be regarded merely as a dilution step.

Reducing the carry-over is obviously a most effective means of increasing the washing efficiency. Although few dyeing machines have the facilities necessary for this, some improvement is possible by ensuring maximum drainage between successive stages.

Effect of Changing the Washing Sequence
The washing sequence discussed so far consisted of two cold rinses (each of 10 min), one boiling wash (30 min) and two further cold rinses. It is of interest to examine predictions from the model when this sequence is modified. The contribution of the boiling wash to efficiency increases as it is moved back from first place in the sequence, i.e. it becomes more effective as the electrolyte concentration is reduced. This effect, however, is offset by the extent to which the efficiency of the cold rinse which follows is impaired by the greater amount of loose colour in the carry-over from the hot wash. In terms of retention of loose dye after drying, a boiling wash in the fourth position has minimal advantage over a cold rinse since at this stage simple dilution of coloured liquor is the operative effect. A boiling wash in the second position is the most efficient and the more boiling washes in the sequence the better, although they must not be too near to the end of the sequence. It would be wrong to assume, from any of these figures, that treatment at the boil is unnecessary. Many dyes cannot be removed completely by cold rinsing; there is

always a small amount of dye retained by a different mechanism that cannot be incorporated in the mathematical treatment.

Batchwise Washing – Summary of Major Conclusions
1. The unfixed dye on the dried fibre consists of loose dye retained within the fibre after washing and dye redeposited on the fibre surface from the carry-over of the final rinsing bath into drying.
2. After most of the dye desorption has occurred in the early stages, reduction in the amount of loose dye on the dried fibre depends essentially on progressive dilution of the wash liquor.
3. Reducing the carry-over between washing stages ensures that this dilution begins earlier, making the sequence much more efficient.
4. Boiling washes are beneficial, the more the better as long as they are in the earlier desorption stages before the simple dilution effect starts.
5. A long liquor ratio favours desorption but increases the water consumption per stage.
6. Fewer stages means less time lost during filling and emptying.

4.13.2 Practical Aspects of Batchwise Washing
Staining onto adjacent materials is more prevalent with dyeings exposed to cold wet conditions (where contact transfer or capillary wicking can occur) than in warm or hot washing treatments. When stains dry out they are no longer removable by simple rinsing, but a thorough wash in hot detergent solution, thorough rinsing, hydroextraction and a quick drying normally give effective clearing.

Most machines encountered in practice are incapable of reaching 100°C even though the wash liquor may appear to be 'at the boil'. Enclosed atmospheric pressure dyeing machines are incapable of operating much above 90°C without cavitation developing at the pump, which interferes with effective circulation of the dyebath. The highest temperature attainable within the limitations of the machine should always be used so as to approach the boil as consistently as possible. In addition it is usual dyehouse practice to use a small amount of a suitable biodegradable anionic or non-ionic detergent in the boil-off. Such agents should be low foaming and insensitive to hard water. Washing-off efficiency is usually checked by the dyer on a sample of the dyed material taken before the load and the wash liquor have been removed from the machine. The wet dyeing is placed between two layers of size-free bleached cotton fabric. The assembly is then pressed with a hot iron or wrapped around an exposed section of a hot steam pipe until dry. The stain on the interior surfaces of the bleached fabrics is an indication of the degree of staining likely to arise from the finished product; the decision whether further washing is needed to meet target quality depends on this result. As already pointed out, this test will provide a better guide if the excess of entrained wash liquor is first removed by mangling or hydroextracting, so that it accurately represents the bulk dyeing just before the final drying treatment. It is recommended that reactive dyeings produced using vinylsulphone dyes should be given a preliminary cold rinse and a uniform neutralisation with dilute acetic acid at 40°C before proceeding to hot rinsing and soaping. It is obvious that an optimal technique for obtaining satisfactory wet fastness in all circumstances cannot be provided by a single set of instructions; at best only general guidelines can be given. Thus in jig dyeing only relatively small volumes of wash liquor can be used at each step and the only normal means of providing mechanical expression is the heavy ancillary rider roller running on the batch of cloth as it is received by the draw roller. After the exhausted dyebath has been drained as completely as possible at least two passages are given through cold water, preferably with a slow overflowing feed. This is followed by two ends in water at 50°C for cold dyeing dyes (but see later) or at 70°C for hot dyeing dyes. With deep colours the liquor is drained, replenished, and further hot passages given, followed by four or six ends in a 'boiling' bath containing minimal amounts of free-rinsing low-foaming detergent, and then successive pairs of ends in hot and then cold rinsing water.

When using circulating-liquor machines of the enclosed type the dyer has to operate blind, except for the sampling of liquor as it is being returned to the expansion tank. Considerable development work is necessary before a regular washing-off sequence can be programmed for repetitive manual or automatic control. Electrolyte removal is the controlling step before efficient removal of loose colour can take place. In-to-out flow cycles are most favoured, and when flow reversals are used the in-to-out direction is preferable for draining before bath changes. Sampling to check the efficiency is difficult, but where possible the 'bit' is taken from the centre of a package before the costly 'boiling soap' liquor is dropped. The bit is rinsed to remove detergent solution and hydroextracted before the wet-staining test described above.

The following guideline procedure is recommended:

1. At the end of the dyeing stage the assembly of packages is raised to allow drainage of residual liquor to be as complete as possible
2. Two or three fresh rinses are given, preferably at 50–60°C when washing-off highly substantive dyes of the hot dyeing type, allowing sufficient dwell time between liquor changes in permit maximum drainage
3. The material is soaped at the 'boil' for 15–30 min using free-rinsing detergent
4. A hot rinsing cycle follows, at 50°C for cold dyeing or 70°C for hot dyeing dyes
5. Finally the material is rinsed cold until clear.

Wherever feasible any of these separate rinsing operations may be replaced by a continuous overflowing 'through-rinse' to drain, in order to avoid redeposition problems. With highly substantive dyes it is advantageous, where machines can be pressurised, to soap at temperatures up to 110°C.

The above sequence is equally applicable to winch, jet or overflow dyeing. Sampling is considerably easier and there is the further advantage on the winch that longer liquor ratios are applicable. Liquor length should be at the maximum practicable. In short-liquor jet machines advantage accrues from forcing rinsing liquors into the fabric rope as it passes through the jet. Complete drainage of the dyebath after dyeing is normally followed by a continuously overflowing cold rinse lasting for about 10 min, or preferably two or three rinses at 50–60°C after dyeing with high-substantivity dyes of the hot dyeing type. This is followed by a short boil-off and final overflowing rinses to clear, before softeners or similar aftertreatments are applied.

4.13.3 Theory of the Continuous Washing Process

Continuous washing-off is usually carried out in an open-width washing range, i.e. a series of tanks filled initially with clean water. Each tank has a nip at the point of exit through which the material passes before entering the next tank. There are three possible modes of operation, as outlined below.

1. The range may be run with no further addition of clean water, i.e. a static tank system.
2. Clean water may be supplied to each tank separately and allowed to overflow to drain, i.e. an independent tank system.
3. Clean water may be supplied to the final tank which overflows into the preceding tank and so on, until the first overflows to drain, i.e. a counterflow system. For reasons of economy many systems which incorporate hot washing stages and/or addition of chemicals consist of a combination of static tanks and independent overflow tanks.

The performance of continuous washing ranges has been studied in detail [69–75]. It is proposed to give only a summary of these results. For simplicity the substantivity of the hydrolysed dye will be ignored and it will be assumed that each tank is a perfectly efficient washing unit [72]. A range of eight tanks used for continuous washing is taken as an example. The first three tanks might be used for initial rinsing, the next three for hot soaping and the last two to give a final rinse. With this division of the range it is possible to discuss the efficiency of the first three rinses in terms of degrees of dilution achieved.

Static, Independent Flow and Counterflow Systems

The first consideration is the difference in efficiency between these three commonly used systems. Static tanks have an obvious disadvantage; as there is no supply of fresh water to the system the concentrations of dye and electrolyte build up in each tank at a rate dependent on the tank volume and the liquor carry-over from the previous tank. After a certain running time these concentrations in the third rinsing tank rise to a point where the level of dilution achieved is inadequate for efficient desorption of dye in the soaping tanks; at this point the tanks have to be emptied and replenished if adequate dilution is to be restored. Irrespective of tank volume, the water consumption per metre is always the same when this maximum length is run because the process is merely one of dilution. Shorter runs use more water; but give a greater degree of dilution. If this is greater than that required then water can be saved on shorter runs by reducing the volume in the tanks. Comparative figures for three tanks with independent supplies of water and for a counterflow system indicate that the latter is much more efficient than independent supply in terms of water consumption. For short runs within the maximum permissible length, however, a static system is even more frugal with water.

Effect of Carry-over Volume
Calculations make it quite clear that the amount of liquor carried over from one bath to the next has a major effect on the efficiency of the range. Thus, in all three systems, reducing the carry-over from 200% to 100% o.w.f. reduces by half the quantity of water needed to achieve any given level of dilution. Whilst for mechanical reasons gross changes in carry-over may not be possible, it is clearly desirable to minimise this factor.

Degree of Dilution Required
The concentration of electrolyte that would permit the most efficient desorption of loose colour into the soaping bath is infinitely low, but this can be achieved only by rinsing in an infinitely large volume of water. The dyer must therefore ascertain the degree of dilution of electrolyte necessary before the fabric enters the hot detergent bath, in order to produce finished material of adequate fastness. If a 100-fold dilution is known to be adequate (it must be emphasised that this is an arbitrary figure) it can be shown that a 500-fold dilution uses 91% more water than that required for adequate dilution in independent tanks, or 78% more in counterflow tanks. The conclusion is clear: it is desirable to decide at the outset on the minimum degree of dilution required to ensure adequate final fastness. The volume of water supplied to the range should then be regulated in order to attain this level.

Dilution of Washed-off Dye
After the three hot soaping tanks a further dilution sequence is given to ensure that the residual concentration of colour in the liquor entrained in the fabric leaving the washing range does not exceed the minimum level, and hence produce unacceptable redeposition on the fabric during drying. In the last two tanks of the continuous range, therefore, the variables will be the same as for the first three and similar considerations apply.

Continuous Washing – Summary of Major Conclusions
1. The washing stages that come before or after the hot soaping are essentially dilution steps
2. Reducing the carry-over between baths makes such dilutions more effective
3. A counterflow wash system is more economical in water consumption for a given length of run than tanks with independent supply
4. In static tanks without a supply of fresh water the degree of dilution becomes inadequate for acceptable desorption of dye after a certain length of run, owing to the build-up of dye and electrolyte concentrations in the tanks
5. Overdilution should be avoided as this is wasteful of water. An adequate degree of dilution should be estimated and the flow of incoming water adjusted to achieve this.

4.13.4 Washing and Internal pH of Cellulose Dyed with Reactive Dyes
Reactive dyeings that contain dye fixed by nucleophilic substitution are prone to 'acid bleeding' of the dyed material. The severity of the effect depends on the structure of the dye in the vicinity of the reactive group. Dyes that react by a

nucleophilic addition mechanism, on the other hand, form a dye–fibre bond which is more resistant to acid attack but less stable under alkaline conditions. In either case there is always the possibility of hydrolytic degradation or tendering of the fibre. In extreme conditions most dyeings will apparently bleed to some extent because of hydrolysis of the cellulose chain, resulting in the release of dye–saccharide fragments in which the original dye–fibre bond is still intact.

It is obvious that such phenomena will depend on the conditions existing within the fibre phase and, in particular, on the pH in that phase. It has been shown [36, 58] that this internal pH is related not only to the dyebath pH but also to the electrolyte concentration and the fixed dye content of the fibre.

For a given amount of fixed dye, the external dyebath pH is reduced by dilution of the alkali, but the internal pH within the fibre is reduced even more by dilution of the electrolyte. The magnitude of the difference between internal and external pH increases with the concentration and basicity of fixed dye. Since this effect is associated with the dilution of alkali and salt, the internal pH reached in the later stages of washing will depend on the quality of water supplied. In a typical batchwise washing sequence using water at pH 7 which contains approximately 120 mg/l of neutral electrolyte (sodium chloride), the internal pH decreases progressively until values in the region of pH 4.5–5.5 are reached after six washes, the internal pH further decreasing as the concentration of fixed dye increases. Such prolonged treatment would be seldom necessary, even for deep colours at the lowest pH values observed. A few dyehouses, however, use exceptionally pure water, e.g. from melted snow or ion-exchange treatments; here a disastrous situation in terms of low internal pH (2–3) can be predicted if five or more washes are given. It should be noted that the internal pH values quoted refer to the fibre whilst still immersed in the washing bath. If hydroextracted to a moisture content less than 100% o.w.f. before drying, the internal pH will begin to rise gradually as drying proceeds, owing to the increasing concentration of electrolyte in the entrained water. It is reasonably certain, however, that a fibre interior which is already highly acidic will remain so throughout most of the drying process, and subsequent bleeding of dye will inevitably result from exposure to these hot acidic conditions. Similarly storage of such dyeings in the presence of normal moisture regain will cause serious hydrolysis of dye–fibre bonds and consequent loss of fastness.

The above discussion illustrates the danger, with certain dyes, of acidifying the washing bath to neutralise excess alkali. As the fibre enters the third boiling treatment the internal pH is already about 1.5–2 units lower than the external pH. If the previous cold rinse has been acidified to, say, pH 5, the internal pH during the boiling treatment would be only about pH 3–3.5, depending on dye content. Few dyeings could withstand such conditions and the possibility of cellulose degradation and dye bleeding would be most serious. By the same token, deep dyeings which required five or six washing stages would have a highly acidic internal pH, irrespective of the pH of the rinsing water, when they were taken for hydroextraction, drying and subsequent storage.

4.14 AFTERTREATMENTS

In the dyeing of certain deep shades, especially on closely constructed materials or on inefficient washing equipment, difficulties may arise in clearing unfixed colour. In these circumstances it is advisable to aftertreat with a cationic fixing agent of the type devised originally for direct dyeings. These products operate by electrostatic association with sulphonic acid groups in the dye molecule, forming an insoluble dye–agent complex. This is retained by the fibre during wet treatments at temperatures up to 60°C, so that staining is greatly reduced.

When the best possible washing-off treatment has been given, aftertreatment is carried out in a fresh bath of cold water and then the temperature is raised to the optimum level for the specific agent selected. A final rinse is not essential. If a cationic or non-ionic softening agent is applied to winch-dyed knitgoods the exhausted softening bath can be used to apply the dye-fixing agent. Treatment with a dye-fixing agent should *never* be regarded as a substitute for the most efficient washing-off process that circumstances allow. When an excess of loose dye remains in the washed-off goods there is always the risk that formation of the insoluble dye–agent complex will lead to unacceptable rubbing fastness, especially in subsequent wet-abrasive treatments. Certain reactive dyes also suffer a decrease in light fastness on aftertreatment with a cationic fixing agent, and changes in hue or brightness may occur.

Apart from inadequate washing-off, another possible cause of staining with dyeings of certain high-reactivity dyes is bleeding under mildly acidic conditions, either during storage in a humid acidic atmosphere or after exposure to a mildly acidic treatment. The latter may occur, for example, after an acidic softening treatment, especially if the wet fabric cannot be dried immediately. Certain types of rapid dryer for yarn packages may accentuate this problem.

It is not always easy to decide whether unwanted staining, marking-off or bleeding has arisen from inadequate washing-off or from acid hydrolysis. It may be necessary to counter both possibilities by first applying a specific type of amine before soaping and then finally aftertreating with a dye-fixing agent as described above.

The amine treatment was devised to minimise problems of acid hydrolysis on storage of certain sensitive brilliant red dichlorotriazinyl dyes applied in medium to full depths. Ethylenediamine was selected originally because it was capable of reacting with any reactive chloro substituent remaining in the fixed dye molecule at the end of the dyeing process. Although effective for this purpose, this diamine proved objectionable for practical use in the dyehouse and it has been replaced by more acceptable polyamines which function in the same way. Such agents are incapable of complex formation with loosely held hydrolysed dye; they are effective only by reacting with a residual active chloro substituent in the fixed dye molecule.

After initial rinsing before soaping, this polyamine (at least 0.5% o.w.f. but no more than half the amount of dye applied) is added to the soaping bath. For the agent to be effective the dyeing must be rinsed at a low temperature (preferably cold, but certainly never above 60°C); otherwise the residual active chlorine on the triazinyl group may be eliminated by hydrolysis and the agent would be no longer able to react in the intended manner. The agent should be added to the soaping bath (with the goods present) at a temperature below 60°C; the temperature is then raised to the 'boil' in the normal way for soaping. Where treatment with a cationic dye-fixing agent is necessary, it is carried out after rinsing away the residual amine and detergent. Only if high wet fastness cannot be achieved, even after thorough washing, should the aftertreatment approach be adopted. Resin-finished goods, especially viscose, rarely give rise to acid hydrolysis on storage.

4.15 STRIPPING OF GOODS DYED WITH REACTIVE DYES

Accidents and errors can never be eliminated completely. Sometimes it is necessary to strip reactive dyeings to permit redyeing of the desired colour. Destructive methods used for stripping other classes of dyes from cotton may be effective, but any reactive dyeings containing metal-complex dyes should be boiled first in a solution of a metal sequestrant (e.g. 2 g/l ethylenediamine tetra-acetic acid) and then thoroughly washed before either alkaline reduction or oxidative stripping treatment.

A full strip can usually be attained by boiling the material for 30 min in alkali (10 g/l soda ash or 5 g/l caustic soda flake) and sodium hydrosulphite (5 g/l), ensuring that a uniform treatment is given throughout. Soda ash is always preferable to caustic soda when processing viscose. After the reductive strip, a thorough washing-off is given, followed by a cold bleach in sodium hypochlorite solution (0.5–1°Tw). Before attempting the redyeing all bleaching and antichlor chemicals must be removed completely and a new dyeing recipe formulated and tested on a sample of the stripped material.

4.16 FASTNESS PROBLEMS

As with other classes of dyes, individual or related reactive dyes sometimes show specific fastness limitations. Although most reactive dyeings that have been applied and washed-off correctly show excellent fastness to washing, hardly any of them are fast to chlorine (hypochlorite or chlorite bleaching). Nevertheless many dyes will withstand treatment in chlorinated water (i.e. swimming pools) or washing with dilute hypochlorite present. Careful selection is necessary if dyeings are required to withstand peroxide bleaching, but many behave satisfactorily on washing in the presence of sodium perborate. Reactive dyes are not suitable for traditional bleaching processes involving a soda boil and hypochlorite bleach. Selection of reactive dyes for military fabrics is restricted by the usual requirements of infra-red reflectance and resistance to weathering.

Although few complaints arise from abnormal light fading, sporadic faults sometimes develop, as detailed below.

(a) Metal-complex reactive dyes normally exhibit high fastness to light but fade more quickly in the unmetallised form; the two forms usually differ significantly in hue. Demetallisation can occur if perspiration is dried into garments repeatedly during exposure, resulting in a marked change in colour and lower light fastness.

(b) Reactive turquoise blues derived from copper phthalocyanine, especially when aftertreated with a cationic dye-fixing agent or resin finish, tend to suffer a hypsochromic shift on exposure to daylight or u.v. radiation. This photoreduction is normally temporary; the turquoise hue usually returns after a few hours in a humid atmosphere. The rate of recovery is determined by rehydration of the cellulose, which is related to the amount and nature of the hydrophobic finishing agent present.

(c) When such turquoise blues are used in admixture with certain other reactive dyes, they may catalyse the fading of these shading colours when the goods are exposed to light in the wet state. This abnormal 'catalytic wet fading' occurs more often in pale to medium rather than full depths. The effect is more likely to arise when the substrate (e.g. towelling) dries slowly at ambient temperatures. Several reactive dyes exhibit abnormal wet fading when exposed to light under moist alkaline conditions. Resin finishes tend to minimise the incidence of this defect.

(d) The fault known as 'alkaline oxidative coppering' is responsible for substantial changes in hue, frequently contrasting strongly with the expected ground colour. This defect is not a function of the type of reactive group present; it is mainly confined to certain yellow, orange and red dyes which exhibit red to violet staining. Copper can always be detected in the stains, which do not respond to most attempts to remove them. Inorganic copper stains can be removed fairly readily by treatment with selected metal-sequestering agents. Subsequent oxidation by alkaline per salts (e.g. perborates in washing powders), however, produces a stain which no longer responds to sequestrant treatment.

4.17 TRENDS IN USAGE OF REACTIVE DYES

By 1970 consumption of reactive dyes for cellulosic dyeing (as distinct from textile printing) showed a ratio of 65:35 between batchwise and continuous dyeing methods [63]. Worldwide demand for this class of dye was already considerable [76] and since that time further progress has been made at the expense of azoic, direct, sulphur and vat dyes. The distribution of reactive dyes for exhaust dyeing in 1970 was estimated as 38% in yarn package and hank dyeing, 36% in winch and paddle machines, 15% in jig dyeing and 11% mainly for loose fibre.

Since 1970 the proportion dyed on the jig has greatly diminished in favour of pad–batch dyeing. There has been a significant growth in the use of reactive dyes for knitgoods, mainly on winches and jet machines, although in this area pad–batch dyeing has also made recent inroads. Steady growth has continued in reactive dyes for the cellulosic portion of blends of cotton with polyester, nylon or viscose. A recent account of dyeing in short-liquor machines [77] reported that 69% of the West German 1976 production of knitgoods was dyed with reactive dyes, compared with vat dyes (14%) and direct dyes (10%).

The growing preference for pad–batch dyeing is attributable to the relatively low consumption of energy in this process [78]. In the continuous dyeing sector, although investment in dyeing equipment has declined, reactive dyes have moved strongly into routine production on woven fabrics for workwear, service uniforms and sportswear, including the cellulosic portion of polyester/cellulosic blends, where they are sometimes displacing business traditionally held by vat and sulphur dyes. Their popularity for continuous dyeing has been further enhanced by the recent development of liquid brands of reactive dyes.

REFERENCES

1. Cross and Bevan, 'Researches on Cellulose 1895–1900' (London: Longmans, Green and Co.) 34.
2. Schröter, Ber. Deutsch Chem., **39** (1906) 1570.
3. Brigg, Z. Angew. Chem., **26** (1913) 256.
4. Günther and IG; USP 1567731 (1925).
5. Peacock, J.S.D.C., **42** (1926) 53.
6. Karrer and Wehrli, Z. Angew. Chem., **39** (1926) 1509.
7. Granacher; BP 346385 (1929), 347117 (1930), 347263 (1930).
8. Dreyfus, BP 344420 (1929).
9. Neithammer and König, Cellulose Chemie, **10** (1929) 203.
10. IG; German P 492062 (1930).
11. Haller and Heckendorn and Ciba; BP 342167 (1930), 363897 (1931).
12. Dinklage; BP 398279 (1932).
13. Riesz, Bull. Soc. Indust. Mulhouse, **99** (1933) 349.
14. Pancirolli, F. Boll. Rep. Fibretess. Vegitali, **32** (1937) 314.
15. Sieberlich, Rayon Text. Monthly, **18** (1937) 775.
16. Ciba; BP 533073 (1939).
17. Solodkov and Kursanov, Zh. Priklad. Khim, **16** (1943) 351.
18. Guthrie, Amer. Dyestuff Rep., **41** (1952) 13, 20.
19. Guthrie and US Dept of Agriculture; USP 2741532 (1952).
20. Rattee, Endeavour, **20** (1961) 156.
21. Beech, 'Fibre-reactive Dyes' (London: Logos, 1970).
22. Warren, Reid and Hamalainen, Text. Research J., **22** (1952) 584.
23. 'Procion Dyestuffs in Textile Dyeing' (Manchester: ICI, 1962).
24. Stephen, Chimica, **19** (1965) 261.
25. Heslop and Stephen and ICI; BP 839337 (1956).
26. Horrobin and ICI; BP 842933 (1957).
27. Alsberg et al. and ICI; BP 797946 (1954), 798121 (1954).
28. Vickerstaff, J.S.D.C., **73** (1937) 237.
29. Hildebrand, Schündehütte and Siegel, 'The Chemistry of Synthetic Dyes', Vol. 6, Ed. Venkataraman (New York: Academic Press, 1972) 124.
30. 'Remazol Dyestuffs – Ten Years of Success on the World Market' (Frankfurt: HOE, 1967).
31. Stead, Rev. Prog. Coloration, **1** (1970) 25.
32. Davies, Rev. Prog. Coloration, **3** (1972) 73.
33. Rosenthal, Rev. Prog. Coloration, **7** (1976) 23.
34. Rys and Zollinger, 'Theory of Coloration of Textiles', Ed. Bird and Boston (Bradford: Dyers' Co. Publications Trust, 1975).
35. Peters, 'Textile Chemistry', Vol. 3 (Amsterdam: Elsevier, 1975) 581.
36. Sumner, J.S.D.C., **76** (1960) 672.
37. Ingamells, Sumner and Williams, J.S.D.C., **78** (1962) 274.
38. Sumner and Taylor, J.S.D.C., **83** (1967) 445.
39. Preston and Fern, Chimia, **15** (1961) 177.
40. Danckwerts, Trans. Faraday Soc., **46** (1950) 300.
41. Rattee, J.S.D.C., **81** (1965) 145.
42. Rattee and Breuer, 'The Physical Chemistry of Dye Adsorption' (New York: Academic Press, 1974).

43. Sumner and Weston, Amer. Dyestuff Rep., 52 (1963) 442.
44. Aspland, Johnson and Peters, J.S.D.C., 78 (1962) 453.
45. Ingamells, Sumner and Williams, J.S.D.C., 78 (1962) 454.
46. Rattee, J.S.D.C., 85 (1969) 23.
47. Horrobin, J. Chem. Soc., (1963) 4130.
48. Rys and Zollinger, Helv. Chim. Acta, 49 (1966) 749.
49. Datyner, Rys and Zollinger, Helv. Chim. Acta, 49 (1966) 755.
50. Rys and Zollinger, Helv. Chim. Acta, 49 (1966) 761.
51. Rys, Schmitz and Zollinger, Helv. Chim. Acta, 54 (1971) 163.
52. Rys, Textilveredlung, 2 (1967) 95.
53. Ackermann and Dussy, Melliand Textilber., 42 (1961) 1167.
54. Ackermann and Dussy, Helv. Chim. Acta, 45 (1964) 1683.
55. Hildebrand and Beckmann, Melliand Textilber., 45 (1964) 1138.
56. Rattee and Murthy, J.S.D.C., 85 (1969) 368.
57. Liddell, McKay and Weedall, J.S.D.C., 90 (1974) 164.
58. Sumner. J.S.D.C., 81 (1965) 193.
59. Sumner, J.S.D.C., 92 (1976) 84.
60. Marshall, Amer. Dyestuff Rep., 58 (1969) 19.
61. ICI Technical Information Dyehouse 1210.
62. Fox, Text. Chem. Colorist, 5 (1973) 56, 197.
63. Fox, Marshall and Stewart, J.S.D.C., 83 (1967) 493.
64. Kretschmer, Textil Praxis, 25 (1970) 217.
65. Marshall, J.S.D.C., 82 (1966) 169.
66. Eriksson, Landqvist and Mellbin, J.S.D.C., 71 (1955) 894.
67. Marshall, J.S.D.C., 71 (1955) 13.
68. Lockett, J.S.D.C., 83 (1967) 213.
69. Sumner, Private communication.
70. Grew and Williamson, Chem and Ind., (1958) 78.
71. Coulson and Richardson, 'Chemical Engineering', Vol. 2 (Oxford: Pergamon Press, 1955).
72. Parish, J.S.D.C., 78 (1962) 109.
73. Bonkalo, Textil Praxis, 22 (1967) 510.
74. Schraud, Melliand Textilber., 52 (1971) 1426.
75. Gralen, J.S.D.C., 96 (1980) 52.
76. Booth, Rev. Prog. Coloration, 8 (1977) 2.
77. Von der Eltz and Wassner, Melliand Textilber., 60 (1979) 167.
78. Wyles, Rev. Prog. Coloration, 9 (1978) 37.

CHAPTER 5

Dyeing with Direct Dyes

BERNARD KRAMRISCH

5.1 INTRODUCTION

A review of the current position regarding the application of direct dyes shows that relatively little research has been undertaken in recent years, in marked contrast to the work in earlier years when the principal factors controlling the absorption of direct dyes by cellulose and methods of classifying them according to dyeing properties were determined. One exception is an examination of the possible application of direct dyes to cellulosic fibres by solvent dyeing processes but this has not yet been finalised to satisfaction.

The standard of wet fastness, particularly to washing, of dyeings of direct dyes, even when suitably aftertreated, no longer meets current consumer demands for the many end uses in the apparel and furnishing sectors of the textile trade and this accounts for their decreased use; in this regard they have been replaced to a great extent by reactive dyes which have improved wet-fastness properties coupled with good light fastness, cover a very wide range of hues and are also, mostly, suitable for dyeing dischargeable grounds.

Nevertheless there are still many applications in the textile industry for goods dyed with direct dyes, particularly where a high standard of wet fastness is not required. In many cases resin finishing after dyeing produces sufficient improvement in wet fastness, although careful dye selection is necessary on account of possible deleterious effects on hue and light fastness.

Examples of the current use of direct dyes include tufted carpets made from viscose, curtains and furnishings (not top quality) where good light fastness and moderate fastness to washing are usually adequate, cotton candlewick bedspreads which are washed only infrequently, lower-grade cotton dressing-gowns, viscose ribbons, cotton and viscose linings including glove linings, viscose shirts especially for cheaper sportswear in pale depths, flannelettes and winceyettes for baby-wear, and shoe and boot laces. Ground shades for subsequent discharge printing may be dyed with direct dyes, particularly if resin finishing is given as a final treatment. Direct dyes are also used for fabrics for casual wear and rainwear, provided that an appropriate durable-press or water-repellent finish is given. Additionally direct dyes are used in the non-textile field, in particular for dyeing paper and leather.

5.2 CHEMICAL CLASSIFICATION

5.2.1 Azo Dyes

The majority of direct dyes are in this group; the Third Edition of the *Colour Index* contains about 900 azo direct dyes. Approximately 45% are disazo and 25% trisazo dyes; the remainder are monoazo and polyazo compounds. A typical disazo dye (C.I. Direct Yellow 12) is shown in Figure 5.1.

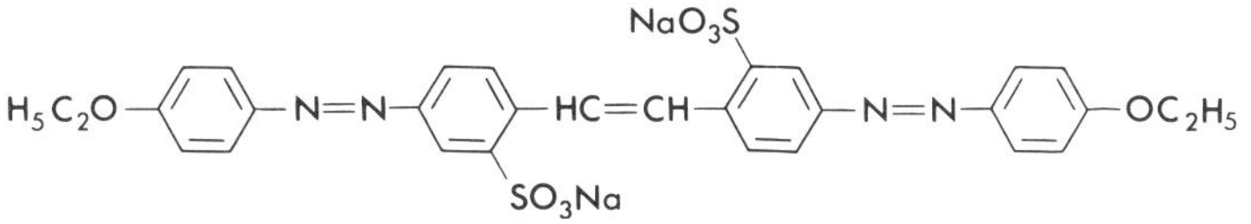

Figure 5.1

There are many premetallised direct dyes, water-soluble copper complexes of *o,o'*-dihydroxyazo dyes being first marketed about 1915. An example is shown in Figure 5.2. These copper complexes are of good light fastness, many attaining a figure of 6–7 on the BSI blue scale in standard depths (1/1) and 5 in pale depths (1/6).

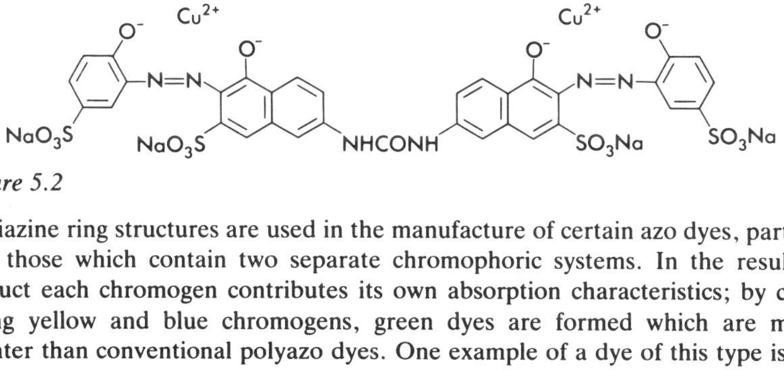

Figure 5.2

Triazine ring structures are used in the manufacture of certain azo dyes, particularly those which contain two separate chromophoric systems. In the resulting product each chromogen contributes its own absorption characteristics; by combining yellow and blue chromogens, green dyes are formed which are much brighter than conventional polyazo dyes. One example of a dye of this type is the bluish-green shown in Figure 5.3.

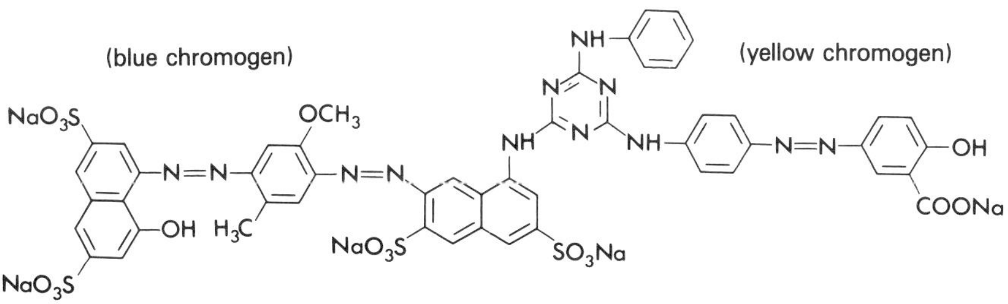

Figure 5.3

One of the amino-substituted intermediates may be replaced by an amino-substituted anthraquinone derivative, as in the bright yellowish-green dye shown in Figure 5.4. The use of aminotriazine linking groups in this way also results in the production of bright blue dyes [1, 2].

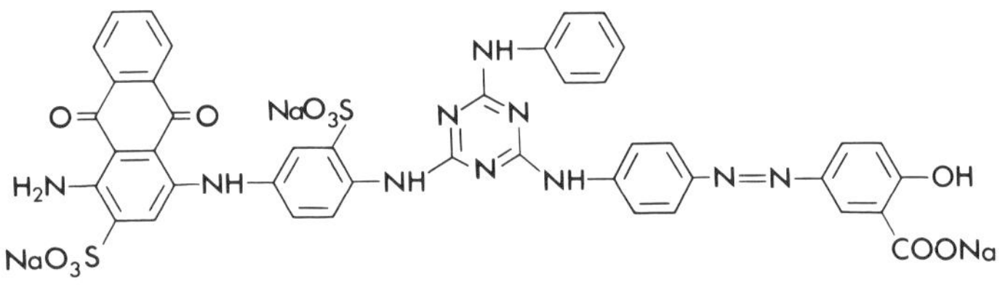

Figure 5.4

The first direct dye marketed was produced from benzidine and naphthionic acid (Figure 5.5). This dye, however, soon lost its importance for dyeing cotton because of its extreme sensitivity to acids, and was later used mainly as an indicator for mineral acids, changing from red at pH 5 to deep blue at pH 3.

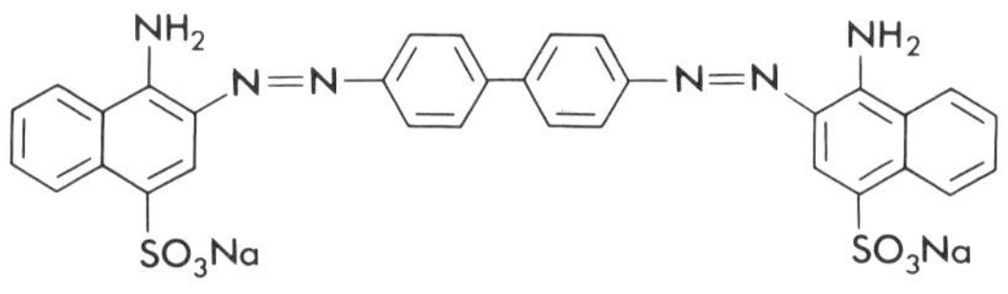

Figure 5.5

Many direct dyes of former importance made from benzidine have been withdrawn from manufacture in the UK and many other countries on account of the occurrence of carcinoma of the bladder in operatives, which is known to be caused by benzidine and certain derivatives [3]. This was first suspected and reported as far back as 1921 [4] and was proved in 1954 by Case and his co-workers, based on a survey carried out with the assistance of the Association of British Chemical Manufacturers [5]. Prior to the cessation of the manufacture of benzidine and benzidine-derived dyes in the UK in 1971, extra manufacturing precautions were taken by the use of special plant designed to prevent contact with benzidine by the operatives [6]. Safety and toxicological aspects in handling benzidine and other chemicals used in the colour-using industries has been discussed [7].

The prohibition of the manufacture of benzidine in the UK is the subject of government regulations [8–10]. As a consequence, the manufacture of many cheap and widely used direct dyes was discontinued, giving rise to problems both for the dye user and dye manufacturer. An intensive search was undertaken into alternatives produced from less hazardous intermediates [11], principally:

(a) The substitution of existing benzidine derivatives by analogous dyes in which benzidine is replaced by a structurally similar but less hazardous diamine such as *o*- or *m*-tolidine, or dianisidine; however, these diamines are also suspected of having carcinogenic activity and are controlled substances within the Carcinogenic Substances Regulations 1967

(b) The use of new diamines; the patent literature refers to a number of compounds including 4,4'-diaminodiphenylbenzaldehyde, 4,4'-diaminodiphenylether, 4,4'-diaminodiphenylsulphone and 1,5-diaminonaphthalenes.

Some examples of widely used benzidine-derived direct dyes and their current replacements may be of interest. For instance, Black BH (Figure 5.6) was manufactured at one time by many firms and used for dyeing cotton and viscose, frequently followed by diazotisation and development with several developers to give navy blue and black dyeings of good fastness to washing and dischargeability. Replacements for Black BH include C.I. Direct Blacks 265 and 266; it is possible, however, that the manufacture of these two dyes may have to be discontinued because of the intermediates used.

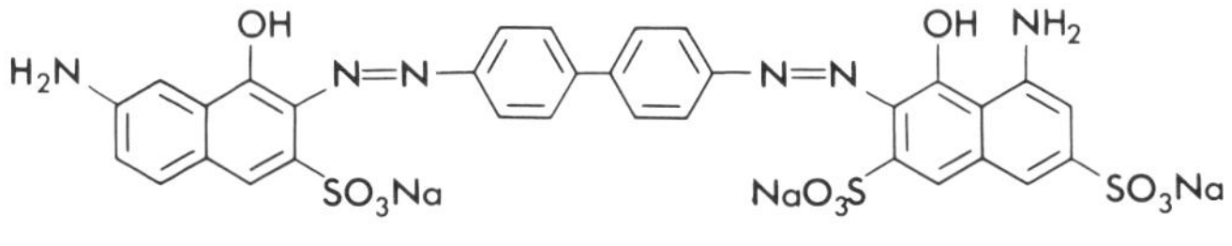

Figure 5.6

C.I. Direct Red 1, a cheap basis for the dyeing of deep red, maroon and wine colours on viscose carpets yarns, has been replaced by alternatives such as C.I. Direct Red 81.

Replacements for C.I. Direct Black 38, a cheap direct dye of high tinctorial strength on cellulosic fibres, leather and paper, include C.I. Direct Black 22.

Although the UK Carcinogenic Substances Regulations prohibit the manufacture of benzidine-based dyes, such dyes are still imported from countries where restrictions are less severe. In view of possible occupational hazards and the lack of available data on the free benzidine content of imported dyes of this type, a survey of current methods for the estimation of trace qualities of free benzidine in dyes was undertaken on behalf of the National Health and Safety Executive [12] and the free benzidine content of 44 imported direct and acid dyes was estimated. Current UK regulations do not permit the import and use of benzidine-based dyes containing more than 1% benzidine. All the dyes examined showed free benzidine contents well below the regulatory amount.

It has been suggested that any hazard in the use of these dyes can be effectively minimised by the enforcement of clean working practice in both manufacture and dyehouse conditions [12].

5.2.2 Stilbene Dyes

Dyes in this class are mainly yellow, orange or brown. They are mixtures of dyes of indeterminate constitution resulting from the alkaline condensation of 5-nitro-*o*-toluenesulphonic acid, either alone or with other aromatic amines. Azo and/or azoxy groups are probably the chromophores and these dyes are mostly non-dischargeable.

Stilbene-azo dyes of more precise constitution are prepared by tetrazotisation and coupling of 4,4'-diamino-2,2'-stilbene disulphonic acid (see C.I. Direct Yellow 12 in the above section on azo dyes).

5.2.3 Copper Phthalocyanine Dyes

These are water-soluble sodium salts of sulphonated copper phthalocyanine, e.g. the disulphonate with sulpho groups in the 3-positions (Figure 5.7). They have poor absorption properties so that deep dyeings are virtually unobtainable. Dyeing has to be done at about 95°C in order to facilitate absorption and this precludes their application in low-temperature dyeing processes such as pad dyeing; problems are also encountered as regards reproducibility in bulk dyeing processes and also in standardisation by the dye makers. They give very bright turquoise-blue colours of good light fastness but of poor wet fastness unless resin finished. They are applicable to paper where wet fastness is not as significant as on cotton and viscose. Dyeings similar in hue and light fastness but with appreciably better wet fastness properties are obtainable on cellulosic fibres with reactive dyes of the copper phthalocyanine type.

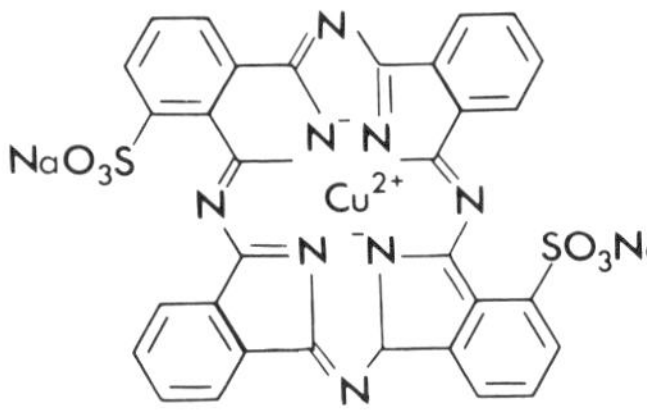

Figure 5.7

5.2.4 Other Types

There are a few direct dyes that are dioxazine, quinoline or thiazole derivatives. The patent literature refers to individual direct dyes that are anthraquinone derivatives produced by BASF and Hoechst [13].

5.3 BEHAVIOUR OF DYES IN AQUEOUS SOLUTIONS

In aqueous solutions most direct dyes exist as colloidal electrolytes and are present in the form of aggregates of several dye molecules. An increase in concentration of dye or electrolyte results in increased aggregation, but an increase in temperature decreases aggregation. A departure from linearity when absorbance is plotted against dye concentration is evidence of aggregation in aqueous solution. This departure from Beer's law is usually overcome by the addition of a polar solvent such as pyridine or dimethylformamide to the aqueous dye solution; this disaggregates the dye, facilitating reproducible colorimetric estimation of the dye concentration.

Dye aggregation in aqueous solution has been examined by making polarographic measurements, and the role of hydrophobic bonding has been emphasised.

Furthermore the addition of urea, a compound widely used in both dyeing and printing processes, was found to disaggregate direct dyes by reducing hydrophobic interaction [14]. The dyeing properties of direct dyes in electrolyte-free solutions have been examined and it was found that only those dyes that are able to form isoelectric micelles, because of their chemical constitution, show significant adsorption [15]. The relationship between structure, particle size in solution and rate of diffusion into cellulose of some direct dyes has been studied; additions of pyridine increased the rate of diffusion [16].

The behaviour of direct dyes in mixtures has been investigated by several workers and anomalous behaviour has been observed occasionally. In one such investigation it was found that the apparent adsorption capacities of direct dyes in binary mixtures are not always additive [17]. Another investigation into the behaviour of mixtures of C.I. Direct Blue 1 and C.I. Direct Yellow 12 led to the conclusion that interaction occurs even at 90°C, with the formation of a 1:1 complex [18]. In a study of the behaviour of certain direct dye mixtures the absorption spectra were measured and the equilibrium constants for the formation of 1:1 complexes were calculated [19].

5.3.1 Stability of Direct Dyes During Dyeing

Many direct dyes tend to decompose during dyeing at or above the boil. This is accentuated by prolonging the period of dyeing. Decomposition is due to reduction of the dye, occurring mainly with azo compounds, and is particularly noticeable with viscose fibres dyed under alkaline conditions, which have a reducing action [20]. This difficulty can be overcome by careful dye selection and control of the dyebath pH by the use of a buffer such as ammonium sulphate. Resistance of direct dyes to dyeing at 125°C is of importance when dyeing the polyester component of polyester/cellulosic blends at high temperature with disperse dyes when the cellulosic component has been dyed already with direct dyes. The importance of this subject is indicated by the number of investigations that have been published [21–26]. The position has been summarised by Fowler as follows [27]. Dye decomposition is caused by reducing conditions set up by the cellulose in the presence of alkali, and provided that such reducing conditions can be avoided the majority of direct dyes can be applied at 100–120°C. Butterworth examined a commercial range of 114 direct dyes applied to viscose at 120–130°C and showed that they could be classified into three groups [28]:

(a) Group I dyes are stable when dyed at high temperature under more or less neutral conditions and also show considerable resistance when dyed under alkaline conditions

(b) Group II dyes are not unduly affected by high temperatures in the absence of alkali but are completely destroyed under alkaline dyeing conditions

(c) Group III dyes decompose under either neutral or alkaline dyeing conditions.

Of the 114 dyes examined, only 13 fell into group III and the majority were placed in group II.

The relationship between the chemical constitution and the resistance of direct dyes to degradation during dyeing has been studied [29]. It was found that dyes containing exposed azo groups (Figure 5.8) are chiefly attacked, whereas those containing azo groups protected by *ortho*-substituted groups (Figure 5.9) are relatively stable.

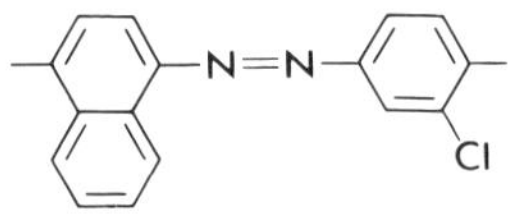

Figure 5.8

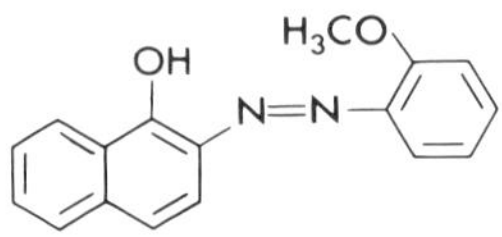

Figure 5.9

Apart from the use of alkalis such as soda ash and alkaline phosphates in dyeing with direct dyes, alkali can be introduced into the dyebath from diluents present in dyes that have been added during standardisation or manufacture, from auxiliaries and residual chemicals from preparatory processes such as scouring, and from softened water. The total exclusion of free alkali from the dyebath is not always possible and the use of a buffer such as ammonium sulphate is desirable to achieve a dyebath of pH 6. Where dye decomposition has been completely prevented the normal fastness properties associated with the individual dye are to be anticipated.

The effect of the addition of protecting agents has also been examined. *m*-Nitrobenzene sulphonic acid (Resist Salt) as a mild oxidising agent was found to be ineffective, but certain chromium salts gave the desired results, e.g. a mixture of potassium dichromate and ammonium acetate. These additives caused slight dulling with some direct dyes, probably due to chelation with chromium; this difficulty was overcome with a mixture of potassium chlorate and ammonium acetate, the former compound acting as the oxidising agent and the latter as a buffer to remove any alkali present. An alternative procedure is to use sodium perborate but it is necessary to exclude copper, which would cause catalytic degradation of cellulose, and the dyes used must be unaffected by sodium perborate.

The stability to visible light and ultra-violet radiation of a number of direct dyes in aqueous solutions has been examined; it was found that degradation in a natural aquatic environment would occur only after many weeks. This means that consideration has to be given to the presence and subsequent removal of direct dyes from textile effluents [30, 31].

5.4 GENERAL PRINCIPLES OF THE APPLICATION OF DIRECT DYES TO CELLULOSIC FIBRES

The Society of Dyers and Colourists defines a direct dye as being an 'anionic dye having substantivity for cellulosic fibres, normally applied from an aqueous dyebath containing an electrolyte' [32]. In practice direct dyes are usually applied with the addition of electrolyte at or near the boil. In some cases lower temperatures may be used, or dyeing may be done at temperatures above the boil, such as in high-temperature jigs or in package dyeing. An addition of alkali, usually sodium carbonate, may be made with acid-sensitive direct dyes and with hard water.

When cellulose is immersed in a solution of a direct dye it absorbs dye from the solution until equilibrium is attained, and at this stage most of the dye is taken up by the fibre. The rate of attainment of equilibrium or the rate of dyeing varies from dye to dye. The dyebath exhaustion at equilibrium is a measure of the proportion of the dye absorbed by the fibre compared with that remaining in the dyebath. Exhaustion is a measure of the substantivity of the individual direct dye.

The Society of Dyers and Colourists' definition of substantivity is the 'attraction between a substrate and a dye or other substance under the precise conditions of test whereby the latter is selectively extracted from the application medium by the substrate' [32]. For quantitative work the term affinity should be used as it is more rigorously defined and can be given a numerical value (usually in joules per mole). It is defined as the 'difference between the chemical potential of the dye in its standard state in the fibre and the corresponding chemical potential in the dyebath' [32].

5.5 ABSORPTION OF DYES BY CELLULOSE

Detailed treatment of this aspect of the subject is contained in several modern textbooks [33–36] and a study of the relevant chapters represents the most satisfactory way of gaining knowledge of this field.

Consideration has been given to the effect of dye structure in relation to absorption [37]. It has been established that dipole interactions are likely to be of importance in the bonding of direct dyes to cellulose; an examination of some of the important groups in direct dyes known to confer increased substantivity reveals the presence of certain dipolar groups, e.g. benzoylamino groups, ureide groups and imido systems, as well as the azo and other groups generally present as part of the chromogen.

The difference in equilibrium absorption of direct dyes by mercerised and unmercerised cotton has been examined [34]. The equilibrium absorption of C.I. Direct Yellow 12 and C.I. Direct Blue 1 on cotton oxidised with special oxidising agents and by the reduction of these oxycelluloses has been studied, and it has been shown that conversion of hydroxyl groups in cellulose to carbonyl groups does not influence dye absorption [38]. Heat of dyeing determinations carried out over a wide range of concentrations of several direct dyes on cotton, viscose and cupro fibres have led to the suggestion that direct dyes are adsorbed on specific sites [39]. This concept of a Langmuir-type of adsorption has led to an alternative way of calculating affinity that is considered [38] to be more realistic than the use of the conventional volume term [33]. Measurements of the absorption spectra of azo direct dyes on cellulose film have shown that dyes enter the cellulose as single molecules and then aggregate inside the cellulose [33]. The relationship between the structure of direct dyes and their substantivity for cellulose has been examined [40] and the relationship between adsorption and migration rate has been investigated [41]. A mathematical study of the absorption of C.I. Direct Blue 1 has been made [42] and the adsorption and diffusion of direct dyes in viscose film have been studied [43]. Equilibrium absorption isotherms and rates of dyeing at various temperatures for C.I. Direct Blue 1 on viscose applied in the presence of several electrolytes have been measured [44]. The presence of formyl groups in both unmercerised and mercerised cotton has been found to increase the absorption of direct dyes [45]. The effect of application temperature on the absorption of direct dyes has been compared at 70–90°C and at 130°C, and it was concluded that reduction in absorption at 130°C may be due to reduced substantivity or to decomposition. Copper phthalocyanine derivatives show an increase in absorption that is attributable to disaggregation in solution and an increase in diffusion rate [46]. It has been shown that one method of analysing the absorption of direct dyes by cellulose is to use the diffuse absorption model [47]. This method can account adequately for the absorption of mixtures of direct dyes by cellulose, provided that no interaction occurs between the dyes in either phase and that allowance is made for ionised carboxyl groups in the cellulose [48]. The last-mentioned investigation has called for comments from other workers [49].

In general it can be said that differences in dye absorption by different types of cellulose are due to variations in structural arrangement of the cellulose molecules. Such differences can be brought about by specific chemical treatments given to cellulosic fibres prior to dyeing, mainly those employing strong alkalis, resulting in the production of deeper dyeings. Mercerising is the principal commercial treatment of this nature and may be carried out under tension with caustic soda, without tension (slack mercerisation), or with a reduced concentration of caustic soda whereby extensive swelling of the fibre is avoided (causticising); all three treatments are normally performed cold, although recently attention has been given to hot mercerisation [50]. An alternative mercerising procedure is to use liquid ammonia instead of caustic soda, treatment taking place at −33°C (Prograde process of J & P Coats Ltd); in this process the resultant increase in dye absorption is approximately 80% of that brought about by conventional mercerising with caustic soda. An investigation into the comparative absorption of several types of dyes, including C.I. Direct Red 110 and C.I. Direct Green 26, by unmercerised and mercerised cotton fabrics, confirmed the marginally greater increase in dye absorption brought about by caustic soda in comparison with liquid ammonia [51].

Radical differences in the behaviour of cellulose towards direct dyes are obtained by chemical modification of the fibre during manufacture, e.g. by acetylation resulting in the production of cellulose esters. A similar effect is produced by crosslinking cellulose with a variety of resins applied in the crease-resisting of viscose. Other methods of esterification of cellulose alter its substantivity for dyes to:

(a) Confer substantivity for basic dyes and simultaneously reduce substantivity for direct dyes [52]

(b) Improve substantivity for direct as well as for acid and metal-complex acid dyes [53].

5.6 PARAMETERS AFFECTING DYE ABSORPTION AND LEVEL DYEING

The first stage in dyeing is adsorption of dye on the fibre surface and is termed the strike; ideally a uniform dyeing is obtained subsequently by diffusion of dye into the fibre to attain an equilibrium distribution between fibre and dyebath. The principal parameters effecting the absorption of direct dyes by cellulose from aqueous solutions are temperature and time of dyeing, liquor ratio, salt controllability, solubility of the individual dye, and to a lesser degree the influence of levelling agents.

5.6.1 Temperature

Strike and fibre penetration are in general governed by application temperature and are improved by an increase in temperature. Dyeing above the boil using totally enclosed pressure vessels has the advantage of shortening the dyeing period with resultant cost savings and the production of more level and better penetrated dyeings, an important factor when dyeing yarns on wound packages such as cops and cheeses. Dyeing above the boil facilitates level dyeing of direct dyes and this occurs to a greater degree in the absence of electrolytes [54]. Temperature and concentration of electrolyte affect the pore size of cellulosic fibres. The effect of an increase in the temperature of dyeing is to increase the so-called rate of dyeing, i.e. the rate of dye absorption by the cellulose, but at the same time it decreases the extent of equilibrium exhaustion. Consequently for a fixed dyeing time there is an optimum temperature at which absorption is at a maximum attainable level.

Examples of optimum dyeing temperatures for selected direct dyes applied to cotton for conventional periods of dyeing are:
(a) C.I. Direct Yellow 12   20°C
(b) C.I. Direct Red 81   60°C
(c) C.I. Direct Yellow 28   100°C.

In general the best levelling direct dyes show maximum absorption at 60°C or below.

5.6.2 Time of Dyeing

The production of level and well-penetrated dyeings is usually favoured by an increased time of dyeing, although prolonged dyeing at the boil when several successive additions of dye are made for matching purposes sometimes results in the decomposition of direct dyes. This difficulty can be overcome by the addition of ammonium sulphate to the dyebath [55].

5.6.3 Liquor Ratio

Dyebath exhaustion is governed by liquor ratio but other factors such as solubility of dyes in water, levelling properties and strike have to be taken into consideration. Appreciable variations in liquor ratio apply in dyeing cotton, viscose and other cellulosic fibres. Padding processes operate at very low liquor ratios (2:1 or less), jig dyeing machines operate at 3:1 to 5:1, and loose stock and yarn on wound packages are dyed at about 5:1; longer liquor ratios (20:1 to 25:1) are used when dyeing yarns in hank form in Hussong-type machines. Liquor ratios from 30:1 to 40:1 are necessary for dyeing loose stock in open vessels and for dyeing fabrics on the winch. In the case of fabric dyeing, however, jet and overflow machines have been constructed in which liquor ratios as low as 5:1 are possible.

5.6.4 Salt Controllability

The extent to which direct dyes are affected by the addition of electrolytes to the dyebath is known as salt sensitivity, and the ability of a specific direct dye to produce either a level or an unlevel dyeing is called its levelling power. Direct dyes vary appreciably as regards the effect of electrolytes, e.g. C.I. Direct Orange 20 is affected to only a slight extent whereas C.I. Direct Orange 34 is affected markedly.

The addition of electrolyte increases the rate of strike of the dye. The quantity of electrolyte required is governed by the concentration of dye in the dyebath; its effect depends on the individual dye and varies with the number of sulphonic groups present. In general the more sulphonate groups present, the less absorption can take place without electrolyte addition. The commonly used electrolytes are Glauber's salt (sodium sulphate) and common salt (sodium chloride), the latter being preferred with hard water. Glauber's salt may cause a precipitation of calcium sulphate on the dyed material, resulting in a somewhat harsh handle.

5.6.5 Dye Solubility

Dyes of good solubility are preferred particularly for package dyeing and for padding processes as low liquor ratios are employed, and also the padding temperature is often low. Salt-sensitive direct dyes should be marketed as concentrated brands containing a minimum amount of electrolyte as diluent. In addition the water used should have a low electrolyte content.

5.6.6 Levelling Agents

Several types of surface-active compounds are used with direct dyes to facilitate level dyeing. Many such compounds are non-ionic ethylene oxides derived from fatty alcohols, alkyl phenols or hydrophilic chemicals such as propylene oxide polymers. Other types marketed include alkylbenzimidazole sulphonates, phosphoric acid esters (either alone or combined with alkylarylsulphonates) and alkylarylpolyglycol ethers [56].

5.7 CLASSIFICATION ACCORDING TO DYEING BEHAVIOUR

It was appreciated by earlier workers that the behaviour of individual direct dyes varied considerably. This necessitated special care in selection, particularly in mixtures, in order to achieve optimum results and to prevent the occurrence of faults, such as uneven or insufficiently penetrated dyeings on all types of materials and listing or ending with jig-dyed fabrics. As a result attention was given to devising suitable laboratory test methods to characterise the dyeing behaviour of individual direct dyes and thereby enable the best selection to be made for a particular dyeing method, highlighting the parameters to be observed in controlling the dyeing cycle.

In the UK pioneer work in this area by C M Whittaker, John Boulton and their colleagues at Courtaulds in the 1940s was concerned with the dyeing of viscose. A characteristic of individual direct dyes, described as the time of half dyeing [57] (i.e. the time taken to reach 50% of the equilibrium absorption under specified conditions), is an indication of the rate at which a direct dye is absorbed by the fibre. In the direct dye range it varies from 0.72 to 280 min. Arising from this work, it was suggested that dyes exhibiting a similar time of half dyeing would be the preferred choice in mixtures. It was found later, however, that measurements of the so-called rate of dyeing, related to time of half dyeing, were inadequate to obtain a full understanding of the compatibility of direct dyes [58]. Subsequently it was confirmed that rate of dyeing alone is insufficient to predict compatibility and that rate of migration and salt controllability are of greater importance [59].

As a result of a detailed study of the subject by the Society of Dyers and Colourists' Committee on the Dyeing Properties of Direct Cotton Dyes [60] it was concluded that determination of four parameters was necessary, i.e. migration (or levelling power), salt controllability and the influence of temperature and of liquor ratio on exhaustion. Tests are prescribed for migration and salt controllability whilst the influence of temperature and liquor ratio are covered by a statement, no tests being prescribed.

The aforementioned SDC committee recommended that direct dyes be classified as follows.

Class A
Dyes which are self-levelling, i.e. dyes of good migration or levelling properties.

Class B
Dyes which are not self-levelling, but which can be controlled by addition of salt to give level results; they are described as salt controllable.

Class C
Dyes which are not self-levelling and which are highly sensitive to salt; the exhaustion of these dyes cannot adequately be controlled by addition of salt alone and they require additional control by temperature; they are described as temperature controllable.

Widespread use is made of the SDC ABC classification and it is included in many dye manufacturers' pattern cards and other technical literature. A typical dye maker's range of direct dyes would contain roughly 20% class A, 40% class B and 40% class C dyes.

The prescribed tests were based on the use of unmercerised cotton and were found subsequently to be equally applicable to mercerised cotton, viscose and linen [61].

Amplification and some modifications of the SDC ABC classification were undertaken by Beal [62] and the results were given in the form of graphs covering the following factors: rate of exhaustion and degree of migration (which are characteristic properties of individual dyes), time and temperature of dyeing, electrolyte concentration and liquor ratio (all the last four being external factors capable of control) [63]; these graphs are now seldom used. A study of the migration properties of direct dyes was made by Cegarra [64] to ascertain the effect of variations in temperature, electrolyte concentration, liquor ratio and agitation of the dye liquor. It was found that at low temperatures an increase in temperature improved migration more effectively with classes A and B dyes than with class C direct dyes. An optimum electrolyte concentration for maximum migration is shown by classes A and B dyes but with class C dyes the migration diminishes steadily as the electrolyte concentration is increased. Increase in liquor ratio increases migration of classes B and C but not that of class A dyes. Agitation increases migration of all three classes of dyes.

Temperature-range tests are useful for determining the behaviour of individual dyes at various temperatures of dyeing and are of particular value in the selection of compatible dyes for mixtures. The percentage absorption of dye under standard conditions of electrolyte concentration, liquor ratio and time of dyeing at a variety of temperatures is estimated visually or colorimetrically and the results are given in the form of graphs.

The selection of compatible dyes for padding and jig dyeing processes is not wholly covered by the SDC ABC classification and related tests. This can be done, however, by carrying out simple dip or strike tests in which fabric or yarn samples are dyed for short periods, e.g. for 1–2 min, removed from the dyebaths, replaced by fresh samples and the procedure repeated several times; the patterns are mounted in series and assessed visually for change of hue and depth. Marked changes of hue indicate incompatibility [65].

The various tests described are simple to perform, require the minimum of apparatus and skill, and the results obtained are easy to interpret. They provide valuable information on the performance of individual direct dyes, either alone or in mixtures.

5.8 COMBINED SCOURING AND DYEING

Many direct dyes are suitable for application by these techniques to either woven fabrics on jigs or knitted fabrics on winches. In the combined dyeing and scouring process the usual practice is to employ soda ash and a non-ionic detergent. Apart from alkali-sensitive dyes, most direct dyes can be used. In the combined scour–bleach and dyeing process either hydrogen peroxide or sodium perborate can be used.

Hydrogen peroxide is used together with sodium silicate, soda ash, caustic soda, an electrolyte and a non-ionic detergent. Alternatively sodium perborate is applied together with soda ash, a non-ionic detergent and an electrolyte. Direct dyes sensitive to alkaline oxidation should be avoided in both of these processes and copper-containing direct dyes must not be used with hydrogen peroxide [66]. These processes are of special interest for dyeing pastel pinks and blues on cotton flannelette, winceyette or candlewick fabrics, but deeper colours can also be produced.

5.9 COVERAGE OF DEAD OR IMMATURE COTTON

Direct dyes vary considerably in their ability to cover dead or immature cotton, which normally dyes lighter than mature cotton, but by careful selection a sufficient number can be found suitable for this purpose. In the case of dyes of poor to moderate wet fastness, specks of lightly coloured or undyed cotton may show after domestic washing. This defect can be minimised by treatment of the dyed fabric with a cationic fixing agent. If the final finish and handle of the fabric permit, mercerising or causticising before dyeing extends the range of suitable dyes appreciably. These treatments increase the absorption of both immature and mature cotton and thereby minimise the relative difference between them.

Fundamental studies [67, 68] of the behaviour of direct dyes on cotton fibres of different maturity using selected direct and after-coppered direct dyes have shown that maturity did not influence the amount of dye absorbed at equilibrium. The absorption and desorption rates, however, were more rapid for immature than for mature cotton fibres. Mercerisation prior to dyeing did not generally affect the differences. Apart from optical effects, differences in depth were thought to be caused by the more rapid desorption of dye from the immature fibres, and such differences are exaggerated by unsuitable processing. It was concluded that, in order to obtain optimum coverage of immature and mature fibres, dyeing should be carried out until equilibrium is attained. Washing-off and other aftertreatments should be given under conditions that limit dye desorption to a minimum [69].

A method proposed by Hoechst for the coverage of dead cotton is to pad the fabric with dyes together with a cellulose ether, followed by fixation in a solution of a salt of a polyvalent metal or a solution of a quaternary ammonium compound [70]. Coverage of neps or dead cotton is also possible by using a two-bath technique which includes the addition of a cationic fixing agent [71].

Unripe or dead cotton can be detected by dyeing with a mixture of C.I. Direct Red 82 and C.I. Direct Green 26; ripe cotton is dyed red, and unripe or dead cotton is dyed green [72].

5.10 DYEING OF VISCOSE

Certain types of cellulosic fabrics, e.g. viscose linings, may be dyed in the loom-state with selected dyes. The choice of size used for the yarn is important as it should be compatible with alkali and electrolyte. Acrylic sizes are recommended for this purpose [73].

A comparison of the dyeing characteristics of normal and desulphurised viscose with direct dyes included an evaluation of hue and fastness to light and washing [74].

The apparent depth of dyeings produced with the same percentage of dye on viscose varies with the filament's linear density. This is an optical effect, finer filaments appearing lighter in depth due to the greater degree of surface reflection. In order to achieve equal apparent depth on viscose filaments differing only in their linear density, the dye concentration must be inversely proportional to the square root of the linear density. A nomogram has been devised for this purpose [75].

5.10.1 Variable-substantivity Viscose

In the past problems were encountered in dyeing filament viscose fabrics. Satisfactory dyeings could be obtained by careful dye selection, in certain cases by making use of special dyes for the purpose. Streaky dyeings were often produced owing to physical differences arising during the drawing process in the manufacture of the fibre, which resulted in difference in dye absorption. Subsequent manufacturing improvements have virtually eliminated this difficulty. Variable-substantivity (at one time known as variable-affinity) viscose must not be confused with viscose having modified dyeability. Deep-dyeing viscose has been produced deliberately by chemical modification of the fibre during manufacture.

5.10.2 Deep-dyeing Viscose

At one time Courtaulds manufactured modified viscose that exhibited very different dyeing properties to the normal variety [76, 77]. Basic groups were introduced during manufacture, and these conferred enhanced substantivity for direct dyes. Normal viscose fibres carry a negative charge and therefore resist direct dyes unless an electrolyte is added to the dyebath. When acid is added to the dyebath, the positive charge on the deep-dyeing viscose increases and more dye is absorbed. For this reason, when blends of deep-dyeing and standard viscose are dyed with direct dyes, maximum contrast between the two variants is obtained under acid conditions. Direct dyes vary in the degree of contrast obtained between deep-dyeing and normal viscose, and acid-sensitive dyes have been found to be unsuitable. Furthermore the depth at which dyes are applied affects the contrast produced. In conventional dyeing methods, i.e. with electrolyte and without acid, the contrast between the two variants is lower and in some cases reasonable solidity can be obtained.

5.10.3 Viscose Carpets

Viscose is still used in the carpet industry, particularly for the production of tufted carpets, although it has been superseded to a great extent by synthetic-polymer fibres, particularly nylon. It has been used alone or in blends such as 40:40:20 wool/ Evlan/nylon and 85:15 or 80:20 Evlan/nylon, Evlan being Courtaulds' viscose carpet fibre. Dyeing can be done in the form of loose stock, yarn in hanks or on wound packages, or as tufted carpets winch-dyed using wide and low-set winches.

Although the general principles for dyeing cotton and the selection of direct dyes are applicable to the dyeing of viscose for the carpet trade, there are a number of special points to be observed with regard to colour fastness and dye selection.

Several direct dyes exhibit better light fastness on coarser viscose fibres than on cotton and this extends the range of suitable dyes. In general they have better wet fastness on coarse viscose for carpets than on the fine quality used for clothing.

A special problem arises with bright turquoise blues and greens which are important for floorcoverings. Direct dye derivatives of copper phthalocyanine give the desired hue, brightness and light fastness but have poor build-up and wet fastness. They also show poor reproducibility when applied with electrolyte; a similar situation applies with reactive dyes derived from copper phthalocyanine. A way out of this difficulty is to use Sirius Supra Blue 6G-LL (BAY, C.I. Direct Blue 264), also a copper phthalocyanine derivative. Whereas this dye exhibits the defects already mentioned when applied as a direct dye, satisfactory results are obtained when it is applied as a basic dye, the alternative designation being Astra Blue 6G-LL (BAY, C.I. Basic Blue 140). Dyeing is done without pre-mordanting using acetic acid and a non-ionic detergent at the boil. Bright greens can be obtained by subsequent topping with suitable direct yellows in a near-neutral second dyebath at 60°C containing the minimum quantity of electrolyte. The mechanism of absorption of this dye by cellulose when applied under acid conditions is similar to that of cationic fixing agents. As with these latter compounds, the absorption of dye can be prevented and dye already absorbed can be stripped off again by addition of electrolyte.

Direct dyes may show some differences in absorption rates, levelling and wet-fastness properties, but no difference in light fastness, on various viscose staple carpet yarns such as Evlan and Evlan M. As a result some class B dyes on Evlan may become class A dyes on Evlan M, so that more dyes are available for salting-on at the boil.

Space dyeing of viscose carpet yarns on such machines as the Crawford-Pickering unit can be done with selected direct dyes, frequently the fast-to-light products being preferred. The degree of fixation and fastness to both light and carpet shampooing are satisfactory [78].

5.11 APPLICATION AND SELECTION OF DYES FOR CONTINUOUS DYEING PROCESSES

Certain problems may be encountered with direct dyes applied by continuous dyeing techniques such as pad–dry and pad–steam processes. In the case of cotton it is often difficult to maintain uniformity of hue throughout the run with mixtures of dyes, owing to differences in substantivity. As far as possible close attention should be given to selecting dyes with similar absorption characteristics and to controlling the rate of supply of feed liquors. Direct dyes of good wet fastness diffuse slowly and prolonged steaming is necessary.

With certain amines, copper-complex polyazo dyes form loose complexes that diffuse rapidly into the fibre to give level dyeings [79]. The amines are released during subsequent steam fixation and are removed by washing-off, so that a normal dyeing is obtained. This method also permits simple and reliable application of highly sulphonated premetallised dyes. The application of direct dyes to viscose staple fabrics by continuous methods has been studied with the object of ensuring regularity of hue over a long run. This is of special importance in view of the selective absorption of substantive dyes during impregnation of the material. Methods for maintaining constant concentrations have been examined and include the use of spectrophotometric estimation at intervals. The wet fastness of direct dyes may be lower when they are applied by continuous processes than by conventional batch-wise methods, but this property can be maximised by adding electrolyte or by increasing the impregnation temperature [80].

A pad–dry continuous dyeing method, the Sandotherm (S) process, developed for the application of selected direct dyes to cellulosic fabrics, includes urea, a migration inhibitor (Sansopol M (S)) and a fixation accelerator (Sandotherm PD (S)). Fastness properties of the dyed fabrics are said to be equal to those produced by conventional batchwise dyeing techniques [81].

Many direct dyes are suitable for the continuous pad–steam dyeing of viscose carpets, but for dyeing fashion colours using a trichromatic combination the best results are obtained with class B dyes; class A dyes tend to migrate during steaming so that hue variations may arise if steaming is not uniform. Furthermore migration can occur during drying and the wet fastness of class A dyes is often inadequate unless aftertreatment with a cationic fixing agent is given. Class C dyes, on the other hand, tend to strike too rapidly resulting in a surface-dyed effect and inferior rubbing fastness [82]. In the pad–steam process for the dyeing of polyester/cellulosic blends with direct and disperse dyes, a method proposed is to pad the fabric with Sirius Supra (BAY) direct and Resolin (BAY) disperse dyes, dry, thermofix, pad in alkali and a cationic auxiliary Levogen RS (BAY), steam and wash-off. Levogen RS is stated to react with the hydroxyl groups in the cellulose and also to retain direct dyes on the cellulosic fibre by salt formation, with the result that dyeings will withstand several boiling washes [83].

5.12 DISCHARGEABILITY OF DYEINGS
Most direct dyes are azo compounds and without aftertreatment many show good dischargeability. They are suitable for dyeing fabrics that are to be printed with a white or coloured discharge; the lack of wet fastness is a disadvantage for many end uses but this can be overcome by subjecting the discharge print to a resin-finishing process.

Diazotised and developed direct dyes generally exhibit very good dischargeability, providing excess developer is removed. With fabrics intended for subsequent discharge printing it is essential to remove residual sodium nitrite and acid after diazotisation, otherwise during the subsequent coupling process undesirable by-products are liable to be produced. During subsequent discharge printing the reducing agent (stabilised hydrosulphite compound) reduces the azo groups in the normally diazotised and developed direct dyes but not in the by-products, and an unsatisfactory discharge may be produced [84]. Premetallised direct dyeings and those aftertreated with copper compounds are generally less readily dischargeable than those dyeings that do not contain copper. In the case of direct dyes that have no commercial value unless after-coppered, appreciable variation in dischargeability is shown. This is a limiting factor in their use for dyeing fabrics for subsequent discharge printing. The maximum discharge effect is obtained by dyeing, discharging and then after-coppering, but difficulties due to inadequate wet fastness arise when washing-off the uncoppered discharge print. Printers generally prefer to after-copper the dyeing before discharge printing. Stilbene derivatives are generally non-dischargeable.

5.13 AFTERTREATMENTS FOR DYEINGS
The wet-fastness properties (particularly washing, water and perspiration) of virtually all dyeings produced with direct dyes are inadequate for many end uses

but notable improvements can be brought about by aftertreatments. The wet fast-ness of direct dyes varies according to the depth at which they are dyed. Some after-treatments, e.g. with stilbene derivatives, confer reasonable wet fastness on pale dyeings. Similarly the light fastness of certain direct dyes can be improved by appropriate aftertreatments. All aftertreatments, however, incur increased proces-sing costs because of the extra time, energy, labour and chemicals involved. The more important aftertreatments are briefly described below.

5.13.1 Diazotisation and Development

Many direct dyes containing primary amino groups can be diazotised and coupled on the fibre with a variety of developers, including naphthols (e.g. β-naphthol), diamines (e.g. *m*-phenylene and *m*-toluylene diamine) and phenols, to give larger molecules with improved wet-fastness properties. A change in hue may occur, de-pending on the developer employed, and frequently the light fastness is downgraded.

There are three distinct stages in the process:

(a) Production of nitrous acid *in situ* by the action of cold mineral acid (hydro-chloric or sulphuric) on sodium nitrite (Scheme 5.1)

$$NaNO_2 + HCl \longrightarrow HNO_2 + NaCl$$

Scheme 5.1

(b) Formation of the diazonium chloride by the action of nitrous acid on the amino group of the dye, in the presence of a mineral acid (Scheme 5.2)

$$RNH_2 + HNO_2 + HCl \longrightarrow R\overset{+}{N}\equiv N \ Cl^- + 2H_2O$$

Scheme 5.2

(c) Coupling of the diazonium chloride with the developer, e.g. β-naphthol (Scheme 5.3).

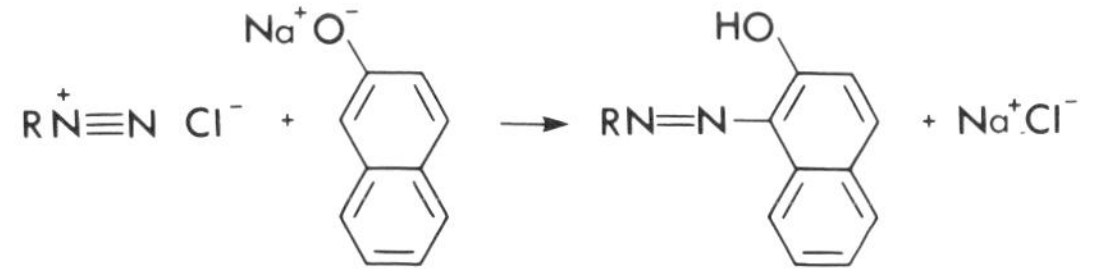

Scheme 5.3

In order to avoid decomposition of the diazonium compound, the temperature must be kept low, direct sunlight must be avoided and metals such as iron and copper must be absent. The vessel used for diazotisation should be constructed of earthenware, wood, GRP or stainless steel. Care must be taken in handling the diazotised dyeing to avoid the deleterious effect of perspiration, due to the pH sen-sitivity of the material, and splashing with water or other liquids prior to coupling must be avoided otherwise staining can occur. Developing baths must be kept alkaline or coupling will not take place.

A method suggested for overcoming the decrease in light fastness which frequently accompanies the diazotisation and development of direct dyes is to couple the diazonium compound with a copper complex of another azo dye, e.g. copper complexes of *o,o'*-dihydroxyazomethines of the benzene or naphthalene series, or *o,o'*-dihydroxyhydrazones or *o,o'*-dihydroxycarbazones of the benzene or naphthalene series [85].

Coupling with diazotised *p*-nitroaniline results in improved wet fastness in the case of some direct dyes. In order to avoid *in situ* diazotisation stabilised diazo compounds, e.g. C.I. Azoic Diazo Component 37, can be used. Diazotised and developed direct dyes were widely used at one time for the production of dischargeable ground colours on cotton and viscose. They have now been largely replaced by reactive dyes. Furthermore dyed viscose for these styles has been replaced by other fibres, e.g. polyester fibres for ties, and cellulose acetate for dressing gowns. In both cases the viscose was originally dyed with diazotised and developed dyes and then printed with a white or coloured discharge.

5.13.2 Metal Salts

Treatment with copper sulphate and acetic acid (usually with 0.25–2% copper sulphate and 1% acetic acid for 20–30 min at 60°C) results in a marked improvement in the light fastness of certain direct dyes, e.g. C.I. Direct Blue 1. Subsequent washing or alkaline treatment removes the copper, however, so that the light fastness reverts to the original rating. Ranges of direct dyes have been produced that are of no commercial value in the uncoppered state, but when aftertreated with copper salts produce dyeings of reasonable light and wet fastness. Many of the dyes of this type are pH sensitive before coppering and this necessitates care in handling. Control of application is essential, since once coppering has taken place unlevel results can only be rectified by stripping.

Apart from chelation taking place with certain direct dyes containing two hydroxyl groups in positions *ortho* to the azo group, it is also possible with dyes containing other groups such as *o*-hydroxy-*o'*-carboxy or salicylic acid groups (Figure 5.10), because sodium copper tartrate or Coprantex B (CGY) can be used in place of copper sulphate. Coprantex B is an amine–formaldehyde condensate containing a copper salt. This has the dual effect of after-coppering the dye and acting as a cationic fixing agent.

Certain dyes, including those containing salicylic acid groups, can be improved in fastness to washing, water and perspiration by aftertreatment with chromium salts

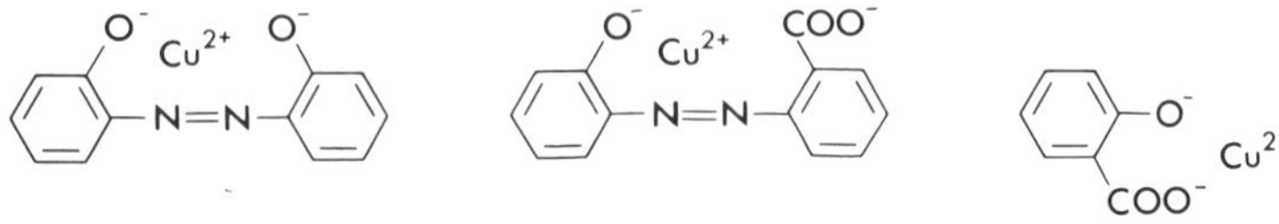

Figure 5.10

(e.g. chromium fluoride or acetate, or sodium or potassium dichromate) using 1–2% of the chromium salt and 1–2% acetic acid for 20–30 min at 60–80°C. An example of a dye suitable for a type of aftertreatment is C.I. Direct Red 23. Treatment with a mixture of copper sulphate and sodium or potassium dichromate will improve both light and wet fastness of certain direct dyes.

Dyeings containing copper complexes of azo dyes are unsuitable for use in the following circumstances.

(a) Copper compounds catalyse the degradation of cellulose during the rubber-proofing of fabrics by vulcanisation.

(b) Latex backing applied to tufted viscose carpeting extracts and sequesters copper, resulting in diminished colour fastness. Copper is also deleterious to the latex itself. The removal of copper has been reported with latex mixes containing dithiocarbonate accelerators [86].

(c) Copper catalyses the degradation of cellulose to oxycellulose during the combined dyeing and bleaching of cotton fabric using hydrogen peroxide.

(d) Selection of a suitable sequestering agent is necessary in hard water solutions of copper-containing direct dyes. EDTA (di- or tetra-sodium salt of ethylenediamine tetra-acetic acid) will sequester copper from dyes of this type with a resultant drop in light fastness and possible change in hue. This, however, does not take place with phosphates such as sodium hexametaphosphate.

5.13.3 Cationic Fixing Agents

These compounds interact with the sulphonic acid groups present in direct dyes [87] conferring increased wet fastness in all tests at temperatures below 60°C. They will also precipitate direct dyes from solution, and therefore the dyed material must be cleared of loosely held dye before treatment. Hue changes may occur and, in some cases, light fastness may be reduced. The dye–auxiliary complex usually dissociates in hot detergent solutions – partially in the ISO3 washing test at 60°C and almost completely in an ISO4 test at the boil. Many such agents are available, including quaternary ammonium compounds, complex fatty acid derivatives, aminotriazine condensates and pyridinium-derived bases. A typical example is Matexil FC-PN (ICI), a condensation product of dicyandiamide, formaldehyde and ammonium chloride. A theoretical study of the fixation process has been made and fixing agents have been classified according to their chemical constitution [88].

Two further applications of cationic fixing agents are to minimise staining of adjacent white materials during wet treatments and to reduce swealing of dyed materials (migration of dye before drying), e.g. with yarns in hank form suspended in a drying chamber.

5.13.4 Formaldehyde

Treatment of certain direct dyeings, mainly blacks, with 2–3% formaldehyde (30%) and 1% acetic acid (30%) for 30 min at 70–80°C improves the wet fastness (to both water and washing) of the dyeing. A drop in light fastness may occur, however. The improvement in wet fastness is most pronounced with dyes which have an end component with two hydroxyl or two amino groups *meta* to each other. There has been some controversy regarding the mechanism of the reaction that takes place between the dye and formaldehyde [89, 90]. The theory put forward by Fierz-David is that dye molecules are linked with the formation of methylene bridges to produce a compound of larger molecular size and diminished solubility in water with resultant improvement in wet fastness [91]. Scheme 5.4 (in which D is the dye molecule) is quoted in standard textbooks to represent the reaction taking place [92–94]. C.I. Direct Black 19 and C.I. Direct Black 22 are examples of dyes suitable for this type of aftertreatment.

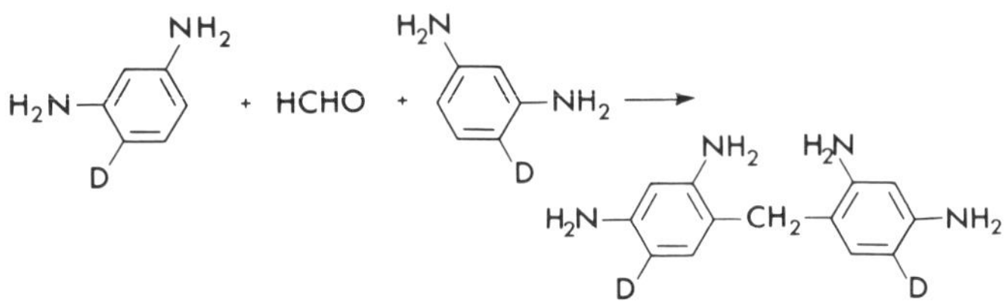

Scheme 5.4

5.13.5 Cross-linking Agents and Resin Treatments

Improvements in wet-fastness properties can be effected by treatment with amino–formaldehyde resins. Subsequent removal of the resin by acid treatment (e.g. formic acid at 90°C or hydrochloric acid at 60°C) leaves the untreated direct dye on the fibre and the dyed material regains its originally low level of wet fastness. Treatment with cross-linking agents in resin finishing improves the wet-fastness properties but hue and light fastness may be affected. The recently introduced Indosol (S) water-soluble reactant-fixable dyes are copper-complex direct dyes, which are fixed after dyeing using Indosol CR liquid or Indosol E-50 powder. Such dyeings show satisfactory light fastness and very good fastness to washing. They withstand the ISO3 wash test and are even of quite good fastness to the ISO4 test. Cross-linking of cellulose takes place with Indosol CR, giving dimensional stability and crease recovery. Application procedures and fastness comparisons with other classes of dyes for dyeing cellulosic materials have been summarised [95, 96].

5.14 EFFECTS OF FINISHING TREATMENTS ON HUE AND FASTNESS

5.14.1 Mechanical Finishes Without Added Moisture

A number of calender finishing treatments are given to cotton fabrics, e.g. chasing, friction and swizzing. Such treatments only involve heat together with pressure or friction. Additionally cotton fabrics may be given Schreiner or embossed finishes without the use of resins, where the same conditions apply. The only factor to be taken into consideration, as regards dye selection, with treatments of this type is in the case of heat-sensitive dyes, where change in hue and the time taken to revert to the original hue on cooling are significant.

5.14.2 Mechanical Finishes With Moisture Present

Apart from cylinder drying of damp or wet fabrics, certain finishing processes require the presence of moisture, e.g. the Sanforising (Cluett Peabody & Co.) and Rigmel (BDA) processes, which confer dimensional stability. In these cases both the resistance to heat and the fastness to water of direct dyes have to be taken into consideration.

5.14.3 Chemical Finishes

Any effect of durable finishes on hue and fastness properties depends on the chemicals and treatment conditions employed as well as on the individual dyes.

No significant effect on either hue or light fastness of direct dyes has been reported with either fluorocarbon compounds or acrylic and polystyrene resins used for the production of anti-soiling finishes on viscose carpets. The majority of softening agents applied to cotton and viscose, with the exception of those derived from N-methylol compounds, are unlikely to have any deleterious action on dyeings of direct dyes. Although some softeners are mildly cationic, no effect on the light fastness of direct dyes has been reported. Amongst compounds used for water-repellent finishing of cellulosic materials, only those containing melamine adversely affect either the hue or fastness of direct dyes.

Resin finishing and flame-retardant finishing warrant detailed consideration as both the hue and fastness of dyeings produced with many direct dyes may be affected.

5.14.4 Resin Finishing

The application of resin finishes is of great importance for conferring dimensional stability to fabrics made from viscose or cotton, either alone or in blends with synthetic-polymer fibres, especially polyester. Important treatments include crease-resist finishing of viscose fabrics, the production of smooth-drying, drip-dry and minimum-iron finishes on cotton shirting and bed linen, and durable-press finishes on polyester/cellulosic fabrics intended for trousers. Further applications of resins include calender finishing processes for cotton fabrics to produce durable chintz, emboss and Schreiner effects. An important purpose of resin finishing is to bring about a marked improvement in wet fastness of direct dyes. In the case of wash fastness, resin-finished dyeings will generally withstand the ISO2 wash test and in many cases even the ISO3 test, often in medium- to full-depth dyeings. This notable improvement in wet fastness on resin finishing means that direct dyes can be used for many end uses in which they would be quite unsuitable without this treatment. As a consequence of resin treatment, the dyed cellulosic material is coated with a layer of cross-linked resin, which acts as a hydrophobic barrier inhibiting the normal action of aqueous solutions of soaps and detergents [97, 98]. On the other hand, hue may be affected and light fastness may be increased or more frequently downgraded, the effect in both instances varying with the individual direct dye and the cross-linking system. For this reason it is advisable to consult the dye manufacturer's technical literature or to carry out preliminary trials under actual processing conditions.

There is a wide variety of processes used for cross-linking cellulose; these include the application of urea– or melamine–formaldehyde, *N*-methylol compounds such as dimethylolethyleneurea, dimethylolpropyleneurea and dimethyloldihydroxyethyleneurea, and acrylic and reactive resins. The mechanism of the application of such produu ts is the subject of several publications [99–102]. Certain inorganic salts are employed as catalysts in resin finishing, with curing conditions showing wide variations in respect of humidity and temperature.

Selection of both cross-linking agent and metal-salt catalyst are important, as many agents are in commercial use for resin finishing of cellulosic materials. Zinc chloride and zinc nitrate have a greater effect on both hue and light fastness than magnesium chloride [103]. Published data compare the effects of various cross-linking systems, including urea–formaldehyde, melamine–formaldehyde and dihydroxyethyleneurea, on a range of direct dyes [104].

As far back as 1954 a detailed study was made of the effect of urea–formaldehyde resin on the light fastness of direct dyes, using amine hydrochloride, diammonium phosphate, ammonium chloride and ammonium lactate as catalysts [105]. The relationship between dye structure and light fastness after resin treatment was examined and it was concluded that hydroxyl and amino groups are normally the most sensitive, and their number and position in the dye molecule play a significant role. It was found that formaldehyde, together with the catalyst, reduced the light fastness of naphthylazo dyes with an amino group located *ortho* to the azo group. Increase in the ratio of formaldehyde to urea increased the adverse effect on light fastness and metal-salt catalysts showed less effect on light fastness than ammonium salts. The possible action of formaldehyde on direct dyes during resin finishing with urea–formaldehyde is discussed in some detail in this paper and it is suggested that the formaldehyde may possibly react with the amino groups of the dye to produce a diphenylamine, since dyes of the diphenylamine class usually have poor light fastness.

Later investigations examined the effect of crease-resist finishing on the light fastness of direct, diazotised and developed [106] and reactive [107] dyes. The work on reactive dyes showed that accelerated fading is associated with auto-oxidation of the resin, this process leading to the formation of organic peroxides on the resin-treated fibre. It has been suggested that the peroxide and its decomposition products provide an environment of oxidising species that can react with the photochemically excited dyes to accelerate fading.

Another undesirable side effect which may arise during resin finishing of cellulosic materials dyed with direct dyes is photodegradation [108]. Photodegradation is independent of the structure of the individual direct dye but is related to the *N*-methylol cross-linking agent. Furthermore it was deduced that photodegradation is initiated by photo-oxidation of the dye induced by the *N*-methylol compound. The degree of photo-oxidation is related to the nature of the cross-linking agent and the oxygen consumption during exposure to light. Hence it is advisable to select *N*-methylol compounds that are either unoxidisable or are difficult to oxidise on exposure to light.

5.14.5 Flame-retardant Finishes

Flame-retardant finishes are applied to textiles for a variety of end uses, such as theatre curtains, aircraft furnishings, fabrics for tents and awnings, sewing threads and children's nightwear. Winceyettes and flannelettes are prohibited for sale following the issue of the Children's Nightdress Regulation 1964 unless they comply with BS 3121, 'Performance Requirements of Fabrics of Low Flammability'. Various chemicals are used for flame-retardant finishing of textiles, depending on the durability of the finish required. Organophosphorus compounds are used for the production of durable flame-retardant finishes and they vary in their effect on direct dyes, which are normally used on winceyettes and flannelettes. An organophosphorus compound is employed in the Proban finish. This improves the fastness to washing, water and perspiration but slightly lowers the light fastness of some direct dyes and may cause changes in hue [109]. If a melamine resin is also present both the hue and light fastness are liable to be adversely affected. In the case of C.I. Direct Red 76 treated with diammonium phosphate and dimethylolethyleneurea an irreversible change in hue occurs, attributed to the formation of a new complex [110].

It is interesting to note that the 'oxygen index' (the minimum oxygen concentration which will just support combustion of the cotton [111, 112]) is increased by the presence of certain direct dyes, lowering the flammability of the fabric [113].

5.15 CHEMICAL STRUCTURE AND PHYSICAL STATE OF DYES IN RELATION TO FASTNESS PROPERTIES

The physical state of direct dyes on viscose has been examined in relation to its effect on light fastness [114]. A correlation exists between chromatographic R_m values (Eqn 1) and the nature and position of substituent groups in the dye molecule; the fastness to wet treatments appears to be directly proportional to the R_m values [115].

$$R_m = \log \left(\frac{1}{R_f} - 1 \right) \tag{1}$$

Wet fading can occur with certain copper phthalocyanine derivatives, rapid fading taking place when the dyed material is exposed in the wet state to strong sunlight. This is particularly applicable in the case of materials that dry slowly, such as towelling.

5.16 PHOTOTROPISM OF DIRECT DYES

Certain direct dyes, principally copper phthalocyanine derivatives, exhibit a phototropic change on cellulose fibres, the hue changing from a bright turquoise to a violet or reddish-blue on prolonged exposure to sunlight or ultra-violet radiation. The hue reverts gradually to the original turquoise when the illuminant is withdrawn. This effect is accentuated by the presence of dye-fixing agents or crease-resist finishes, and is more pronounced if the dyed materials have not been washed-off after resin treatment and are left in an acid condition. The type of cross-linking agent used plays a significant part, the order of decreasing effect being: urea–formaldehyde > cyclic ethyleneurea > melamine–formaldehyde.

The degree of phototropic change is related to the intensity of the u.v. radiation and the ambient humidity. The drier the atmosphere, the slower becomes the reverse oxidation, which may be due to the connection between photogenerated hydrogen peroxide and the water present. Agents that lower the moisture regain, e.g. crease-resist finishes, greatly increase the tendency to show phototropic change.

The phototropic behaviour of copper phthalocyanine direct dyes appears to follow a redox mechanism. When dyeings of this type on cellulosic fibres are subjected to a vatting procedure with sodium hydroxide and sodium dithionite at 60°C, the hue changes rapidly from turquoise blue to violet. The dyeing reverts to its original hue on rinsing in water followed by air oxidation, thus producing similar changes to those taking place on illumination.

A similar reduction from turquoise blue to violet can take place in dyeing under bulk conditions, e.g. in jig dyeing of cellulosic fabrics at high temperature and in the continuous dyeing of viscose tow.

It is interesting to note that the unsulphonated water-insoluble copper phthalocyanine pigments do not exhibit the ready vattability of the sulphonated copper phthalocyanine direct dyes.

5.17 PHOTO-OXIDATION OF CELLULOSE PRODUCED BY DIRECT DYES

This phenomenon is well known with vat dyes, mainly certain yellow, orange and brown dyes. Degradation can occur on exposure of dyed or printed cellulosic materials to light, as with curtains, or during dyeing or hypochlorite bleaching under certain processing conditions. Dyes showing this behaviour are known as tenderers.

Instances of photo-oxidation of cellulose by direct dyes have been reported. In one investigation in this field dyed cotton was oxidised with buffered sodium hypochlorite solutions and an attempt was made to correlate the extent of fibre degradation and oxygen consumption during oxidation with the chemical constitution of the dye. The results of exposure to a fading lamp have also been examined [116].

REFERENCES

1. Allen 'Colour Chemistry' (London: Nelson and Sons, 1971) 66.
2. Bradley, 'Recent Progress in the Chemistry of Dyes and Pigments', Royal Institute of Chemistry Monograph No. 5 (1958) 52.
3. Scott, 'Carcinogenic and Chronic Toxic Hazards of Aromatic Amines' (Amsterdam: Elsevier Scientific Publications, 1962).
4. International Labour Office Studies Report, Series F, No. 1 (1921) 6.
5. Case et al., British J. Industrial Medicine, 11 (1954) 74.
6. Abrahart, 'Dyes and their Intermediates', 2nd Edn (London: Edward Arnold, 1977) 50.
7. Gadian, Rev. Prog. Coloration, 7 (1976) 85.
8. Carcinogenic Substances Regulations 1967.
9. Silk, J.S.D.C., 85 (1969) 458.

10. Health and Safety at Work Act 1974.
11. Stead, Rev. Prog. Coloration, **6** (1975) 1.
12. Jones, Patterson and Srinivasan, J.S.D.C., **96** (1980) 628.
13. BP 924258, 941009, 993594, 1241102.
14. Sivaraja Iyer and Singh, J.S.D.C., **89** (1973) 128.
15. Schaeffer, Melliand Textilber., **41** (1960) 980.
16. Melnikov, Teksstil. prom., **1** (1960) 111.
17. Neale and Stringfellow, J.S.D.C., **59** (1943) 241.
18. Derbyshire and Peters, J.S.D.C., **72** (1959) 268.
19. Morita and Sekido, Bull. Chem. Soc. Japan, **38** (1965) 2041.
20. Wilcock, J.S.D.C., **63** (1947) 136.
21. Armfield, J.S.D.C., **67** (1951) 297.
22. Ashpole, McFarlane and Wilcock, J.S.D.C., **66** (1950) 17.
23. Drijvers, Teintex, **17** (1952) 294.
24. Drijvers, Amer. Dyestuff Rep., **41** (1952) 533.
25. Herrmann, Melliand Textilber., **33** (1952) 1110.
26. Houser and White, AATCC Nat. Technical Conf. Papers (1976) 105.
27. Fowler, J.S.D.C., **71** (1955) 443.
28. Butterworth, J.S.D.C., **69** (1953) 362.
29. Schmitz, J.S.D.C., **71** (1955) 910.
30. Porter, Text. Research. J., **43** (1973) 735.
31. Khalil, Bendak and Agour, Amer. Dyestuff Rep., **70** (1981) 31.
32. J.S.D.C., **89** (1973) 4.
33. 'The Theory of Textile Coloration', Ed. Bird and Boston (Bradford: Dyers Co. Publication Trust, 1975).
34. Rattee and Brener, 'The Physical Chemistry of Dye Absorption' (New York: Academic Press, 1974).
35. McGregor, 'Diffusion and Adsorption in Fibres and Films' (New York: Academic Press, 1974).
36. Peters, 'Textile Chemistry', Vol. 3 (Amsterdam: Elsevier Scientific Publications, 1975).
37. Pal and Esteve, Text. Research J., **29**(1959) 84.
38. Daruwalla, Kangle and Nabar, Text. Research J., **31** (1961) 712.
39. Daruwalla and D'Silva, Text. Research J., **33** (1963) 40.
40. Bach et al. Angew. Chem., **75** (1963) 407.
41. Bubser and Eichmann, Textil Praxis, **19** (1964) 61.
42. Sivaraja et al., Text. Research J., **34** (1964) 807.
43. Ivanov and Schneider, Text. Research J., **26** (1956) 407 and **37** (1967) 11.
44. Iyer and Subramanian, J.S.D.C., **96** (1980) 185.
45. Goldthwait and Kirby, Text. Research J., **37** (1967) 136.
46. Gromova and Romanova, Tekstil. prom., **9** (1971) 58.
47. McGregor, Text. Research J., **42** (1972) 536.
48. Patel and Peters, J.S.D.C., **90** (1974) 50.
49. Liddell, Weedall and McKay, J.S.D.C., **90** (1974) 202.
50. Bechter, Textil Praxis, **33** (1978) 177.
51. Brederick and Weckmann, Melliand Textilber., **59** (1978) 137.
52. Lupton and Loughlin, Text. Research J., **45** (1975) 92.
53. Thomas, Chemiefasern, **20** (1970) 866.
54. Butterworth, J.S.D.C., **69** (1953) 362.
55. Millson, Amer. Dyestuff Rep., **47** (1958) 221.
56. Chwala, Anger and Chwala, 'Handbuch der Textilhilfsmittel' (New York: Verlag Chemie, 1977).
57. Boulton and Reading, J.S.D.C., **50** (1934) 381.
58. Boulton, J.S.D.C., **60** (1944) 5.
59. Lemin, Vickers and Vickerstaff, J.S.D.C., **62** (1946) 132.
60. First Report of the Committee on the Dyeing Properties of Direct Cotton Dyes, J.S.D.C., **62** (1946) 280.
61. Second Report of the Committee on the Dyeing Properties of Direct Cotton Dyes, J.S.D.C., **64** (1948) 145.

62. Beal, J.S.D.C., **72** (1966) 146.
63. Geigy Co. Pattern Card 500, 2nd Edn (1948).
64. Cegarra, J.S.D.C., **73** (1957) 375.
65. Whittaker, J.S.D.C., **54** (1938) 255.
66. ICI Technical Information Note 799.
67. Crespo, Invest. Inform. Text., **2** (1959) 189.
68. Rexroth, Melliand Textilber., **42** (1963) 602.
69. Furvik, J.S.D.C., **74** (1958) 290.
70. HOE, BP 1415542.
71. Roman et al., Industria Tech., **15** (1964) 673.
72. Goldthwait, Smith and Barnett, Textile World, (1947) 105, 201.
73. Rhodes, Dyer, **159** (20 Jan 1978) 64.
74. AATCC South Eastern Section, Amer. Dyestuff Rep., **50** (1961) 299.
75. Fothergill, J.S.D.C., **60** (1944) 93.
76. Ward and Hill, Text. Inst. and Ind., **7** (1969) 274.
77. 'Dyeing and Finishing Deep Dye Viscose Fibres' (Courtaulds Ltd, Droylesden Research Laboratory).
78. Beal and Warwick, J.S.D.C., **96** (1974) 425.
79. Wegmann, J.S.D.C., **71** (1955) 777.
80. Cheetham, J.S.D.C., **76** (1960) 95.
81. Oschatz, Textilveredlung, **9** (1974) 442.
82. ICI Technical Information Note D950.
83. Schiffer, Melliand Textilber., **59** (1978) 236.
84. Stott, Amer. Dyestuff Rep., **24** (1935) 217.
85. FP 852255.
86. Mohr, AATCC South Central Section, Amer. Dyestuff Rep., **45** (1956) 965.
87. Diserens, 'Die Neueste Fortschritte in der Anwendung der Farbstoffe', Vol. 2 (Basle: Verlag Birkhauser, 1949) 58.
88. Gill, J.S.D.C., **71** (1955) 380.
89. Fourness, J.S.D.C., **63** (1947) 178.
90. Whittaker, J.S.D.C., **63** (1947) 37, 179.
91. Fierz-David, 'Kunstliche Organische Farbstoffe' (Berlin: Springer Verlag, 1926) 195.
92. Bird, 'The Theory and Practice of Wool Dyeing', 4th Edn (Bradford: SDC, 1972) 154.
93. Trotman, 'Dyeing and Chemical Technology of Textile Fibres' 5th Edn (London: Charles Griffin & Co, 1975) 451.
94. Venkataraman, 'Chemistry of Synthetic Dyes', Vol. 1 (New York: Academic Press, 1952) 597.
95. Egger, Kissling and Robinson, Melliand Textilber., **62** (1981) 947.
96. Robinson and Egger, Textilveredlung, **18** (1983) 41.
97. Diserens, 'Die Neueste Fortschritte in der Anwendung der Farbstoffe', Vol. 2 (Basle: Verlag Birkhauser, 1949) 132.
98. Landolt, Text. Rundschau, **4** (1948) 108; **5** (1948) 152.
99. Bayer Farben Revue, No. 18, 193.
100. Marsh 'An Introduction to Textile Finishing' (London: Chapman & Hall, 1966) 360.
101. Skelly, Chem. and Ind, (9 Jan 1965) 50.
102. Smith, J.S.D.C., **70** (1954) 381; **77** (1961) 416.
103. ICI Technical Information Note 811.
104. Ciba-Geigy Pattern Card 3200.
105. Broden et al., Amer. Dyestuff Rep., **43** (1954) 6.
106. Goldstein and Koenig, Text. Research J., **29** (1959) 66.
107. Ingamells, J.S.D.C., **70** (1963) 651.
108. Fiebig and Howewel, Melliand Textilber., **57** (1976) 837.
109. Einsele et al., Melliand Textilber., **61** (1980) 180.
110. ICI Technical Information Note 849.
111. Feimore and Martin, Modern Plastics, **43** (1966) 141.
112. Reeves and Drake, 'Flame-resistant Cotton' (Shildon, Durham: Merrow Publishing Co., 1971) 19.
113. Segal, Timpa and Drake, Text. Research J., **44** (1974) 839.

114. Weissbein and Coven, Text. Research J., **30** (1960) 58.
115. Lörinc, Dobosy and Peter, J.S.D.C., **83** (1967) 184.
116. Datye, Nabar and Schroff, Text. Research J., **31** (1961) 813.

CHAPTER 6

Dyeing with Vat Dyes

ULRICH BAUMGARTE

6.1 INTRODUCTION

Dyeing with vat dyes is based on the principle of converting, by means of reduction, dye in a water-insoluble form into a water-soluble substantive compound (leuco dye), which penetrates into the fibre and is then reconverted, by oxidation, into the original insoluble form. These dyes contain carbonyl groups, separated by a conjugated system of double bonds. A distinction is made between the derivatives of indigo and of anthraquinone (indigoid and anthraquinoid dyes, Scheme 6.1), and also those of more highly condensed aromatic ring systems.

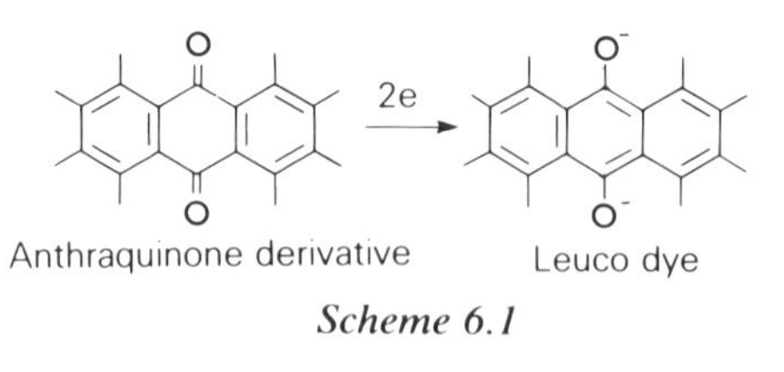

Indigo   Leuco indigo

Anthraquinone derivative   Leuco dye

Scheme 6.1

Vat dyes are used predominantly for dyeing cellulosic fibres. Although the leuco dyes also have substantivity for wool and nylon, technical reasons (e.g. fibre damage when dyeing wool, and the fastness properties on nylon) today restrict their commercial significance for these fibres to the dyeing of nylon/cotton blends.

The situation is quite different with the cellulosic fibres, i.e. cotton, regenerated cellulose and bast fibres. These constitute much more than half the quantity of all textile fibres produced, 15% of which are dyed with vat dyes (17% including indigo). Cellulosic fibres are likely to maintain this leading position, because their raw-material basis (water, carbon dioxide and solar energy) is not endangered.

The vat dyeing method has a long-standing tradition. Until the beginning of this century it was carried out on a cottage-industry scale using vegetable and animal dyes (e.g. indigo, Tyrian purple, etc.) with natural products as reducing agents (e.g. sugar and its decomposition products). However, the start of the 20th century was marked by the synthesis of dyes suitable for application to cellulose and the development of a sufficiently stable reducing agent with the necessary reactivity. Since then, it has been possible to operate the dyeing process on an industrial scale. Decisive steps in this direction included firstly the clarification of the structure of indigo, and its synthesis, followed by preparation of indanthrone from the alkali melt of β-aminoanthraquinone [1]. Of the dyes developed in Ludwigshafen up to 1909, 13 are still important members of the Indanthren (BASF) range. Equally important was the manufacture of a reducing agent with good storage stability, i.e. anhydrous sodium dithionite (hydrosulphite) [2].

6.2 FUNDAMENTAL PRINCIPLES

6.2.1 Dyes

Apart from indigo, the vat dyes used in dyeing applications are mainly derivatives of anthraquinone and of higher condensed aromatic ring systems with a closed system of conjugated double bonds. They may be homogeneous dyes or mixtures, and generally contain two, four or six reducible carbonyl groups.

The chemical constitution of the dye influences the properties of its leuco form in the dyeing process, e.g. its rate of adsorption, diffusion into the fibre, substantivity, thermal stability in the vat and levelling-out properties. It is also a key factor in the properties of the resultant dyeing, e.g. for the colour and fastness.

Figure 6.1 shows the structural elements of a number of important vat dyes.

The *indanthrones* are blue dyes (e.g. C.I. Vat Blues 4, 6 and 14). Since they are prone to over-reduction and over-oxidation, they can present problems in dyeing; however, because of their pleasing colours, very good fastness and reasonable price they still form one of the most important classes of vat dyes.

Flavanthrone (C.I. Vat Yellow 1) and its derivatives are, in common with the indanthrones, among the oldest synthetic vat dyes. In spite of certain shortcomings (e.g. slow oxidation, lower wash fastness and tendency to phototropism) this dye is still regarded as important because of its good light fastness.

The same applies to the *pyranthrone* types (e.g. C.I. Vat Oranges 2 and 9). Although these dyes also have certain shortcomings (inferior light fastness of the non-brominated product and fibre damage during dyeing) they continue to be widely used because of their good levelling properties, high colour strength and relatively favourable price.

The *isodibenzanthrone* dyes (isoviolanthrones) include some interesting deep violet colours (e.g. C.I. Vat Violets 1 and 9) that have a high colour strength and good fastness to bleaching, but lower fastness to rubbing, hot pressing and water spotting.

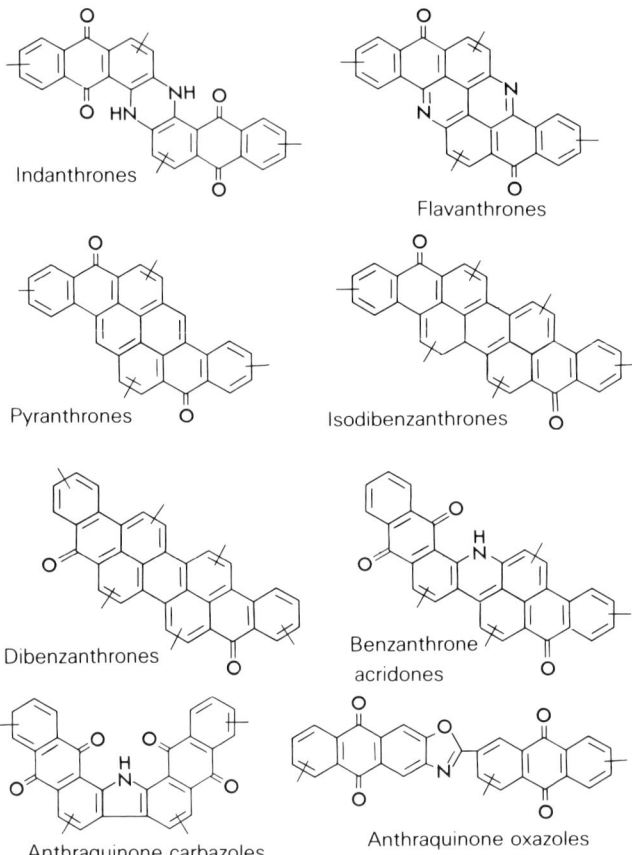

Figure 6.1 – Structural elements of some important vat dyes

The *dibenzanthrones* (violanthrones) form a particularly large group of dyes, with important examples in the dark blues, navy blues, greens and blacks (e.g. C.I. Vat Blues 16, 19, 20 and 22, C.I. Vat Greens 1, 2 and 9, and C.I. Vat Black 9). These dyes suffer from many of the same disadvantages as the isodibenzanthrones, but they have maintained their importance on account of their generally good levelling properties, very good fastness to light and to wet treatments, and because some colours cannot be produced by any other means.

The *anthraquinone carbazole* class of dyes is of similar importance for colours ranging from yellow and orange to brown, khaki and olive (e.g. C.I. Vat Oranges 11 and 15, C.I. Vat Browns 1, 3 and 44, C.I. Vat Green 8, and C.I. Vat Black 27).

In spite of their relatively flat colours, these dyes are extremely important because of their good levelling properties during dyeing and their excellent fastness to light, wet treatments and chlorine.

The *benzanthrone acridone* types represent another large class of dyes (e.g. C.I. Vat Greens 3 and 13 and C.I. Vat Black 25). These are relatively flat olive greens, olives, browns and greys. Although they are not easy to dye level, they have excellent fastness properties and also provide the fibre with a certain degree of protection against the action of light.

Figure 6.1 also illustrates the *anthraquinone oxazole* class of dyes. The main representative of this class is C.I. Vat Red 10, which is a strong brilliant red that levels well and has very good fastness properties.

Other types of vat dyes with important structural elements include:

(a) *Perylene tetracarboxylic diimide* derivatives, e.g. C.I. Vat Reds 23 and 32
(b) *Imidazole* derivatives, e.g. C.I. Vat Yellow 46, which is a very bright light-fast yellow
(c) *Triazinylaminoanthraquinone* derivatives, i.e. reaction products of amino-anthraquinone and cyanuric chloride. C.I. Vat Blue 66 is an important example, with very good levelling properties and good fastness, including fastness to chlorine. Furthermore, unlike the indanthrone blue dyes, it is not susceptible to over-reduction.

This summary does not claim to be complete. Further groups of vat dyes of similar structure are referred to in the literature [3–13] together with details of their preparation.

The leuco potential of all vat dyes, measured with a calomel electrode under standard conditions, lies between −650 and −1000 mV, i.e. satisfactory vatting can only be achieved with reducing agents that have a more negative reduction potential. The frequently postulated relationship between the leuco potential and the dyeing properties is still disputed.

After it has been synthesised a vat dye is still not in a suitable state for use, because reduction to the leuco form is normally an extremely slow process at this stage. All vat dyes must, therefore, first be converted into a suitable commercial form. This may involve a pretreatment, followed usually by a milling process with suitable dispersing agents. Over the years the demands placed on colorant formulations have increased considerably, particularly for batchwise pigmentation and semi-pigmentation processes in package equipment and for continuous piece dyeing, where a high standard of particle size distribution is necessary. The top-quality dyes available today generally have an average particle size of well below 1 μm.

Commercially, these products are available in the form of liquids, granules or dedusted powders. In the case of the powder and granular types it is essential that they should disperse readily in water. Apart from the particle size, other important properties of all commercial preparations include their storage stability, behaviour during preparation of the dye liquors and in the pigmentation process, and their vatting rate. The vatting rate is determined by the particle size distribution and the crystalline form of the dye.

6.2.2 Auxiliaries

Reducing Agents
The most important reducing agent in vat dyeing is sodium dithionite, generally referred to as hydrosulphite. Its reduction potential is adequate for all practical requirements. Other reducing agents can only be used for special purposes, or have not yet been accepted in practice. In this connection reference should be made to the hydroxyalkylsulphinates, which find application in vat printing and for dyeing at temperatures above 100°C. Examples of such products are Rongalit C (BASF), Rongalit 2PH (BASF) and Rongal HT (BASF). Although thiourea dioxide is a strong reducing agent, in alkaline solutions it is just as sensitive to atmospheric oxygen as hydrosulphite and thus offers no decisive advantages. Sodium borohydride reacts too slowly for vat dyeing. Further details of the latest investigations are to be found in the literature [14].

The properties of hydrosulphite are extremely important for the practical application of vat dyes. Its constitution as sodium dithionite ($Na_2S_2O_4$) has been known since the end of the last century [15], but the erroneous designation hydrosulphite continues to be used to describe its commercial forms. The structure of the compound, with an S–S bridging bond was also recognised [16] and later confirmed [17–19] (Scheme 6.2).

Sodium dithionite (hydrosulphite), $Na_2S_2O_4$
Structure of dithionite ion : $[O_2S\text{-}SO_2]^{2-}$

(a) Hydrolytic decomposition:
     Neutral medium:
     $2Na_2S_2O_4 + H_2O \rightarrow Na_2S_2O_3 + 2NaHSO_3$
     Alkaline medium
     $2Na_2S_2O_4 + 2NaOH \rightarrow Na_2S_2O_3 + 2Na_2SO_3 + H_2O$

(b) Reaction with atmospheric oxygen (alkaline medium):
     $Na_2S_2O_4 + 2NaOH + O_2 \rightarrow Na_2SO_3 + Na_2SO_4 + H_2O$

(c) Reaction with hydrogen peroxide (alkaline medium):
     $Na_2S_2O_4 + 3H_2O_2 + 2NaOH \rightarrow 2Na_2SO_4 + 4H_2O$

Scheme 6.2

In the anhydrous state the product is very stable, but in contact with water it forms sodium thiosulphate and sodium bisulphite [16]. The formation of acid products accelerates the decomposition, which proceeds exothermically and may result in spontaneous ignition. The same reactions occur in aqueous solution (without alkali) and both sulphur dioxide and sulphur have been identified as reaction products [16].

In the absence of air hydrosulphite is extremely stable in alkaline solutions. Under these conditions it is more stable than hydroxyalkylsulphinates and the formamidine sulphinate that is formed from thiourea dioxide under alkaline conditions. It is only under extreme conditions that sodium dithionite forms the thiosulphate and sulphite as reaction products [20]; at very high alkali concentrations and elevated temperatures some sulphide may also be produced [21].

In practice, the important factor is its behaviour in an alkaline solution in the presence of atmospheric oxygen. As shown in Scheme 6.2, sodium sulphite and sodium sulphate are formed.

Detailed investigations have shown that, depending on the conditions, more sulphite is formed than sulphate [22]. Apparently the free radical ion $\cdot SO_2^-$ is the initial transient formed from the dithionite anion ($^-O_2S-SO_2^-$), and the decomposition mechanisms still put forward for dithionite in aqueous media, which proceed via sulphoxylate ions (SO_2^{2-} or HSO_2^-), are certainly out of date. Oxidation with atmospheric oxygen is of the 0.5th order in relation to the dithionite concentration. For practical applications it is particularly important to note that sodium hydroxide is consumed in the oxidation. Therefore, it is necessary to ensure that there is sufficient excess present, otherwise the dye liquor will become neutral, or even acid, and enable the above-mentioned hydrolytic decomposition to take place.

In the oxidation of vat dyeings with oxidising agents other than atmospheric oxygen, only sulphate (e.g. with hydrogen peroxide) or only sulphite (e.g. with nitrobenzenesulphonate) are produced from the dithionite.

Since sodium dithionite is sensitive to atmospheric oxygen, an excess must always be present. The amount of this excess depends on the application conditions, particularly on the influence of certain factors on the rate of oxidation [23, 24].

1. Temperature: Given that the other conditions are constant, the rate of oxidation increases with the liquor temperature.
2. Dithionite concentration: Given that the other conditions are constant, a specific amount is oxidised in a given time, i.e. the more concentrated the initial dithionite solution, the longer it takes to become deactivated.
3. Movement of liquor and air: The greater the agitation of the liquor in the presence of atmospheric oxygen, the more rapidly decomposition proceeds. This is particularly relevant for hank-dyeing machines, winches and jigs.
4. Specific surface area: The greater the specific surface area of the liquor (i.e. the quotient of the surface area and volume), the more rapidly is the sodium dithionite oxidised. Since the time required for half oxidation is inversely proportional to the specific surface area, oxidation may take many hours in a large vessel with a relatively small surface area. On the other hand, because of the high specific surface area, a dithionite liquor padded onto a fabric is oxidised within 30–60 s, depending on its concentration and the prevailing conditions.
5. Presence of dyes: Assuming that the other conditions are constant, the reducing agent is oxidised more rapidly in the presence of leuco dyes than when these are absent.

On the other hand, under the conditions normally employed in practice (pH 12–14), oxidation of the sodium dithionite does not appear to depend to any significant extent on the alkali content of the liquor.

Other Auxiliaries

Apart from the reducing agent, other products are also necessary to ensure satisfactory dyeing or to improve the standard of the dyeing.

The most important of these is caustic soda, without which dyeing cannot proceed, because the leuco dyes can only be absorbed in the ionised form. To achieve this the liquor must have a pH of 12–13 to prevent formation of the practically insoluble vat acid, which has no substantivity for the fibre. Since caustic soda is consumed in the vatting process, and also by the action of atmospheric oxygen on the vat, a sufficient excess must always be present.

Neutral salts, e.g. sodium sulphate or common salt, can increase the substantivity of the leuco dyes for the fibre. Auxiliary products that form complexes with the leuco dyes are used to improve the levelness of the dyeings (e.g. Peregal P (BASF)) or to partially strip faulty dyeings (e.g. Albigen A (BASF)).

Wetting, complexing and dispersing agents help to overcome dyeing problems caused by inadequate pretreatment. For example, a wetting agent (e.g. Primasol FB (BASF)) is frequently necessary, especially when dyeing loom-state materials, to emulsify the waxes in the grey cotton and ensure satisfactory penetration of the dye liquor into the substrate. Complexing agents (e.g. Trilon TB (BASF)) bind the alkaline-earth ions contained in the grey cotton and the process water, and thus prevent the precipitation of pectins and of the almost insoluble alkaline-earth salts of leuco dyes [25].

The addition of supplementary dispersing agents (protective colloids) prevents the aggregation of undissolved particles and is particularly important in the oxidising and washing-off processes. These auxiliaries are of two types:

(a) Products that maintain the dye particles in a fine state of dispersion (e.g. Setamol WS (BASF))

(b) Products that prevent the flocculation of sparingly soluble leuco dyes (e.g. calcium salts) or of incompletely dissolved impurities from the grey cotton that are combined with leuco dye (e.g. Dekol S (BASF)).

For continuous dyeing with vat dyes by the pad–steam process with intermediate drying, padding auxiliaries (e.g. Primasol V (BASF)) [26] are necessary to prevent pigment migration in the drying operation. After dyeing, an oxidising agent (e.g. hydrogen peroxide, perborate or sodium *m*-nitrobenzenesulphonate, e.g. Ludigol (BASF)) is required, followed in the subsequent soaping process by the usual surfactants (e.g. Marseilles soap or Kieralon (BASF) types).

6.2.3 Vatting

Before the actual dyeing operation the water-insoluble dye must be converted into the water-soluble substantive form. This is achieved by 'vatting', i.e. reaction with a reducing agent – usually sodium dithionite – in the presence of sodium hydroxide to form the leuco dye. In this reaction the dithionite assumes the oxidation number of the sulphite (Scheme 6.3).

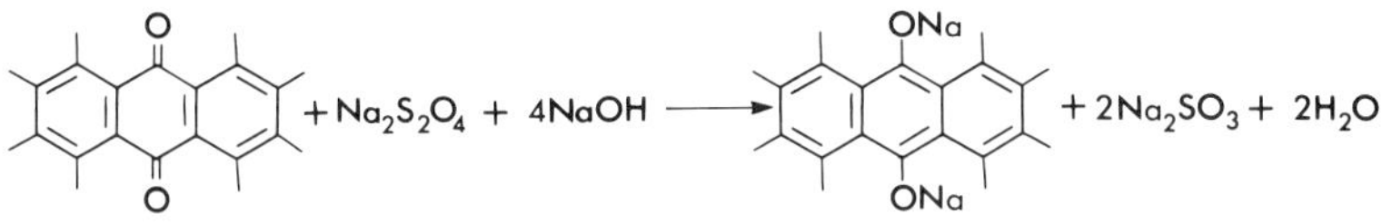

$$\text{(anthraquinone structure)} + Na_2S_2O_4 + 4NaOH \longrightarrow \text{(leuco structure with ONa)} + 2Na_2SO_3 + 2H_2O$$

Scheme 6.3

Experiments suggest that the actual chemical reaction proceeds as a two-electron transfer [27]. The rate of reaction is determined by association of the reducing agent with the oxygen atom in the keto group of the dye. This group is then rapidly split off by the action of the hydroxyl ions, leaving the two bonding electrons with the keto oxygen. Finally there is an electron shift to stabilise the dye in the leuco form. These reactions are of the first order with regard to both the dye and the reducing agent.

In practice a heterogeneous system is present, i.e. the dissolved reducing agent attacks the finely dispersed dye particles. In this case the vatting rate is not determined by the chemistry of the reaction but by the diffusion and transport stages [28]. Experiments have shown that:

(a) Vatting proceeds almost twice as rapidly with an increase in temperature of 10°C

(b) Above pH 12 the rate of vatting is not dependent on the hydroxyl ion concentration

(c) The higher the concentration of reducing agent and dye, the more rapidly reduction takes place

(d) The rate of vatting is dependent on the crystalline form and particle size of the dye.

The vatting rate is an important factor in practice, e.g. for the pigmentation, semi-pigmentation and continuous processes [29, 30].

To prepare a satisfactory vat it is necessary to have an adequate amount of reducing agent and caustic soda. The quantity of reducing agent is determined by that necessary for the particular dye [31] (number of reducible groups [32], molecular weight, content of pure dye) together with an excess, the quantity of which depends on the amount of air present in the dyeing process. In certain cases (grey cotton, or fibres damaged by oxidation) dithionite can also be consumed by the substrate. Since sodium hydroxide is consumed both in the vatting process and by the action of atmospheric oxygen, the alkali concentration has also to be so adjusted that the pH of the liquor remains sufficiently high during the dyeing process to prevent formation of the practically insoluble vat acids, or other complications (e.g. enol–keto changes [33]). Hence the amount of caustic soda required is determined by the number of carbonyl groups that have to be reduced and by the extent of oxidation due to atmospheric oxygen during dyeing. In the latter case approx. 1 ml caustic soda (38° Bé) is consumed in the oxidation of 1 g hydrosulphite.

6.2.4 Properties of Leuco Dyes

The leuco dyes are usually present in the dye liquor in a monomolecular form or as aggregates of a few dye molecules. From diffusion measurements, Valko [34] determined these to be aggregates of between two and four molecules. More recent investigations [35, 36] based on absorption spectra have shown that, depending on the concentration and temperature, planar molecules, such as the violanthrone derivatives C.I. Vat Blues 19, 20 and 22, and the perylene tetracarboxylic acid diimide derivatives C.I. Vat Reds 23 and 32, are dissolved in the vat in a monomolecular form or are present as dimers or (to a limited extent) also as higher aggregates. Violanthrone derivatives that do not have a coplanar structure, due to substitution by alkoxy groups in the 16 and 17 positions (C.I. Vat Greens 1, 2 and 4, and C.I. Vat Blue 16) are always present in solution as single molecules under dyeing conditions.

The substantivity of a dye for the fibre is determined by its constitution and is unaffected by the degree of aggregation. The aggregation can, however, influence the diffusion of the leuco dye within the fibre and thus affect the levelling behaviour.

Data concerning the solubility of the leuco dyes is provided in the dye manufacturers' pattern cards and manuals [31]. However, with certain dyes, e.g. C.I. Vat Blues 4, 6 and 14, vatting usually produces a supersaturated solution which, depending on the purity of the dye, tends to precipitate after a short time [5, 32].

In the presence of calcium, magnesium and iron ions some leuco compounds, e.g. C.I. Vat Yellow 1, Orange 2 and Blues 4, 6 and 14, form almost insoluble salts that have no substantivity for the fibre; precipitation can be prevented by using a complexing agent [31].

If there should be too little alkali in the vat an enol–keto change may occur or the vat acids precipitate [5, 32], resulting in paler dyeings with a lower rubbing fastness. With C.I. Vat Blues 4, 6 and 14 this conversion to the vat acid can even occur at pH 12, but not until much lower pH levels with the other dyes.

Certain leuco dyes, known as tenderers, can damage the substrate when there is a frequent alternation between oxidation and reduction in the dyeing process. This can be countered by the addition of pyrocatechol or tannin [31].

With some leuco dyes, chemical changes may take place in the alkaline medium at high temperatures [5, 32], e.g.

1. Hydrolysis of carbonamide groups
2. Dehalogenation (e.g. with C.I. Vat Blue 6)
3. Over-reduction (with the indanthrone types).

In the latter instance oxygen atoms are split off from the molecule at temperatures above 60°C, so that the original dye molecule cannot be re-formed on oxidation. The tendency to over-reduction increases with the concentration of caustic soda and hydrosulphite, and with the temperature and duration of the dyeing process. It results in flat colours, but can be prevented by appropriate additions of glucose or sodium nitrite [31].

6.2.5 Dyeing

Dyeing Stages
When a cellulosic textile is entered into the alkaline dyeing liquor that contains leuco vat dye, the dye exhausts out of the liquor into the fibre until, after a certain time, a state of equilibrium is attained. The higher the substantivity of a dye for the fibre, the higher its concentration in the fibre and the lower in the dye liquor.

It is a characteristic of vat dyes that they exhaust rapidly, even at relatively low temperatures [37–40]. A study of the dyeing kinetics shows that the dye exhausts in two phases (Figure 6.2). The major portion of the dye (generally 80–90%) exhausts within about 10 min (phase I), followed only slowly by the remainder (phase II). As a result there is the danger of the substrate being dyed very unevenly after the first phase, in which the dye is adsorbed initially on the outer, more accessible regions of the fibre, causing ring dyeing.

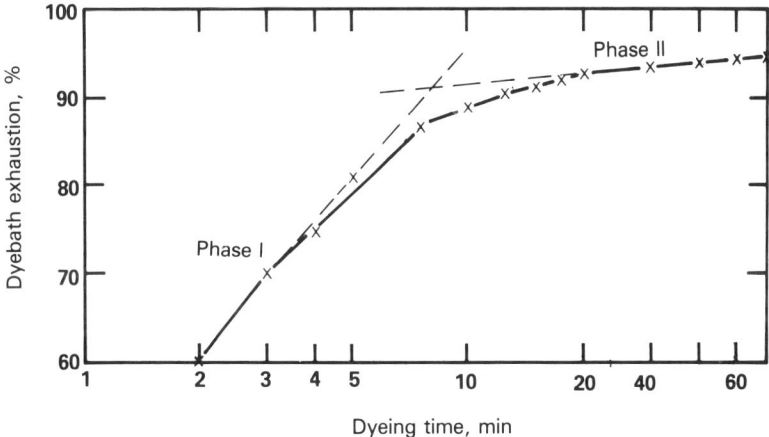

Figure 6.2 – Absorption behaviour of a leuco vat dye

If the change in dye concentration within an individual fibre is depicted in relation to the dyeing time, it is to be expected that the dye concentration will first increase rapidly in the outer part of the fibre (Figure 6.3, curves 1–3), and the bath will be largely exhausted. The second phase is determined by the diffusion of the dye into the inner part of the fibre (curves 4–6). In this phase the dye concentration in the outer part of the fibre falls again and only a small amount of dye can be taken up from the bath. This representation has been proved by trials with rolls of cellulosic film [41].

There are thus two phases in the kinetics of the dyeing process, one characterised by rapid exhaustion of the bath, due largely to the substantivity of the leuco dye for the fibre, and a second phase, dominated by diffusion of the dye into the inner part of the fibre.

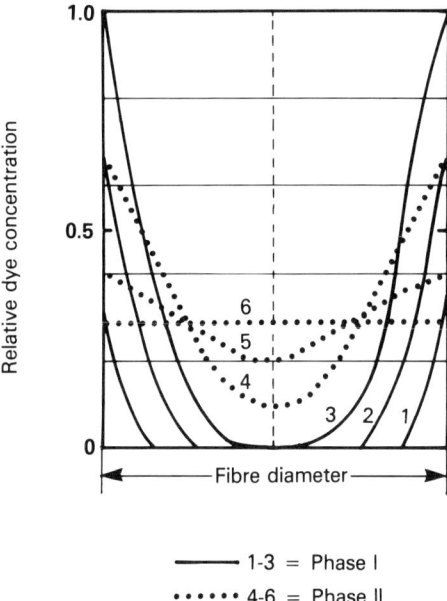

———— 1-3 = Phase I

•••••• 4-6 = Phase II

Figure 6.3 – Change in concentration in the fibre cross-section during the dyeing process

The rate at which the dye exhausts in the first phase is virtually independent of the rate of liquor circulation [40]. It is, on the other hand, influenced to a considerable extent by the textile material, e.g. the greater the surface area of the substrate in contact with the dye liquor, the more rapidly is the first dyeing phase completed. Furthermore, trials have shown that a rapid initial rate of dyeing is favoured by:
(a) Higher dyeing temperatures
(b) Shorter liquor ratios
(c) Less dye present [40, 41].

In practice the more rapidly the dye exhausts onto the fibre in this initial phase, the greater is the risk of obtaining unlevel dyeings.

Penetration of the individual fibres takes place in the second dyeing phase. The rate at which this proceeds is determined by the diffusion of the leuco dye molecules from the outer to the inner part of the fibres. The rate of diffusion depends on molecular structure, which can be characterised by a number [40]. Dyes with good levelling properties have values between six and eleven, whereas those with a limited levelling capacity have values of four or less. The rate of diffusion is influenced to a considerable degree by the dyeing temperature; it rises exponentially with increase in temperature, doubling with a temperature increase of around 14°C. Investigations have shown that dyes with a similar substantivity for cellulosic fibres and with a similar constitution diffuse more slowly if they tend to form dimers or higher aggregates (e.g. C.I. Vat Blue 20 in comparison with C.I. Vat Green 1) [36]. Such dyes also do not level out as readily, i.e. the levelling properties depend not only on the substantivity of the dye for the fibre – and thus on the concentration of the leuco dye remaining in the liquor after the exhaustion phase – but also on the rate at which the leuco dye molecules diffuse into or out of the fibre.

A dyeing equilibrium is attained after a certain time when a specific quantity of cellulosic fibre is added to a solution of leuco dye of known concentration and at a constant temperature, i.e. the dye becomes distributed between the solution and the fibre in specific proportions. Dyeing isotherms can be drawn by plotting the equilibrium concentrations in the fibre and solution for different dyes at different starting concentrations, as illustrated in Figure 6.4. It can be seen that the green dye exhausts much more completely than the two red dyes. The curves rise with increase in dye concentration in the bath, but the rise becomes ever more gradual and a saturation value is not attained.

Curves of this type are known as Freundlich adsorption isotherms and they can be expressed mathematically as in Eqn 6.1. Here the index n determines the form of the curve, and for the concentration range important in practice, with cotton as the substrate, n can be taken as closely approximating to 0.6. Even at different temperatures, and with dyes that vary considerably in their constitution, this index gives constant values (within the limits of experimental error), which serve as a measure for the substantivity of the leuco dye for the fibre. The higher these values,

$$\frac{[D]_F}{[D]_S^n} = \text{constant} \qquad (6.1)$$

where $[D]_F$ = equilibrium concentration of dye on the fibre
$[D]_S$ = equilibrium concentration of dye in solution
$n = 0.6$ for vat dyes on cotton.

the more dye is taken up by the fibre at equilibrium. At higher temperatures the values are smaller and the dyes have less substantivity for the fibre. Provided that allowance is made for factors such as dye concentration, liquor ratio, temperature and salt additions, these constants can be used to calculate the dye uptake at equilibrium [40]. These predicted values show good conformity to those obtained from production dyeings, which suggests that dyeings produced under plant conditions generally come very close to reaching equilibrium. In practice the dye uptake rises as the initial dye concentration in the bath, the liquor ratio and the dyeing temperature decrease and as the electrolyte (salt) content increases. It generally ranges from 85 to 95%.

The substantivity of the dye for the fibre depends on the former's molecular constitution and does not appear to be associated with the tendency to form leuco dye aggregates in the liquor, especially since it has been found that dyes which tend to form dimers in the liquor (e.g. C.I. Vat Blue 20) are mostly present in the monomolecular form once they have exhausted onto the fibre [35, 36, 41]. These conclusions have been drawn from a study of the absorption spectra of leuco dyes in a

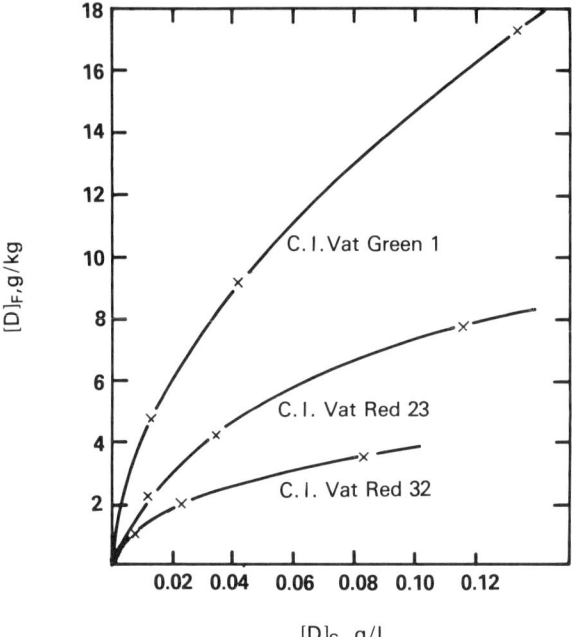

Figure 6.4 – Dyeing isotherms of vat dyes

cellulose film. As a general rule it is found that the absorption maxima show a bathochromic shift, indicative of interaction between the leuco dye and the cellulose molecules. This is attributed firstly to an ion–dipole attraction between the hydrated dye ions and the accessible hydrated polar groups of the cellulose molecules (polyether, polyalcohol or polyalcoholate), followed – as they approach closer – by interaction between the dipoles of the substrate with the π-electron system of the dye molecule.

The Freundlich equilibrium relationship is applicable up to very high dye concentrations. In experiments with regenerated cellulose films, dyeings have been produced which, after oxidation, contained up to 40% pure dye [34, 36]. After the same time the thickness of the film increased by 40%.

In the absence of complexing agents the behaviour of the leuco dyes under production conditions is determined by the initial extremely rapid bath exhaustion previously mentioned, with the attendant danger of unlevel dyeings. This danger is particularly great with pale colours, dyeings produced in short liquors or on mercerised cotton, and particularly with regenerated cellulosic fibres. If the bath exhausts too rapidly – even at room temperature – for level dyeings to be obtained, and the other parameters are fixed (i.e. substrate, dyeing equipment, recipe), all that can usually be done is to provide conditions that promote the levelling-out of unlevel dyeings. As already stated, the rate at which the dye diffuses into the fibre (and also, therefore, out of it) increases considerably with a rise in temperature. At the same time the dye's substantivity for the fibre diminishes, resulting in an increase in the dye concentration in the liquor. This facilitates the migration of leuco dye molecules, as shown in Figure 6.5 [40].

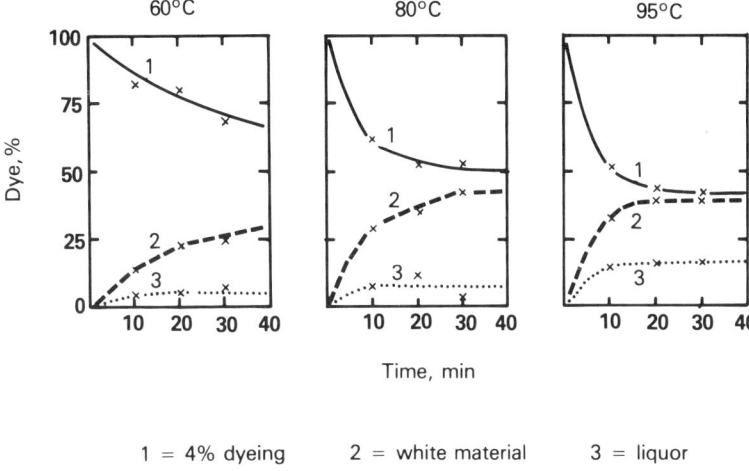

1 = 4% dyeing   2 = white material   3 = liquor

Figure 6.5 – Levelling of C.I. Vat Green 1 at various temperatures

In these experiments 4% dyeings were treated in a blank vat, together with the same amount of undyed material, and the dye content in the dyeing, the white material and the liquor was determined at regular intervals. It is quite clear that although the levelling process accelerates with rise in temperature, much more dye remains in the dye liquor at 95°C than at 60°C (curve 3). For this reason, after the levelling-out phase, the temperature should be reduced in order to allow the colour to reach its maximum depth.

However, the problem cannot always be solved in this manner, unless long dyeing times are acceptable; usually, therefore, there is no alternative to using levelling agents capable of complexing with the dyes used. The objective of adding such agents is to shift the absorption equilibrium in favour of the dyebath, in order to retard the rate of absorption of dye by the fibre or to promote the migration of dye that has already been taken up.

These complexing agents include polymers of ethylene oxide or ethylene imine of a specific chain length and polymeric hydroxyl compounds that are capable of associating with leuco dyes. This results in a bathochromic shift in the absorption spectrum [35, 36, 41]. The interaction normally takes place with the leuco dye in the monomolecular form, even with those dyes that dimerise in aqueous media. Formation of a dye–auxiliary complex is most likely to be initiated by an ion–dipole attraction between the hydrated dye anions and the polar auxiliaries that are also strongly hydrated (analogous to the interaction between a leuco dye and cellulose).

These relatively strong forces are responsible for bringing the dye and auxiliary molecules together so that the π-electron system of the dye can interact further with the dipoles of the auxiliary. These binding forces evidently depend on the size and planarity of the dye molecules.

The strength of the interaction between the dye and auxiliary determines whether the latter functions as a stripping agent (e.g. Albigen A) or as a levelling agent (Peregal P). For example, with C.I. Vat Blue 20, which is difficult to level out, a much better effect is obtained by adding 1 g/l Peregal P (calculated as 100% product) than by increasing the temperature by 15°C (Figure 6.6). On the other hand, under the same conditions, 1 g/l Albigen A (calculated as 100% product) has more of a stripping effect.

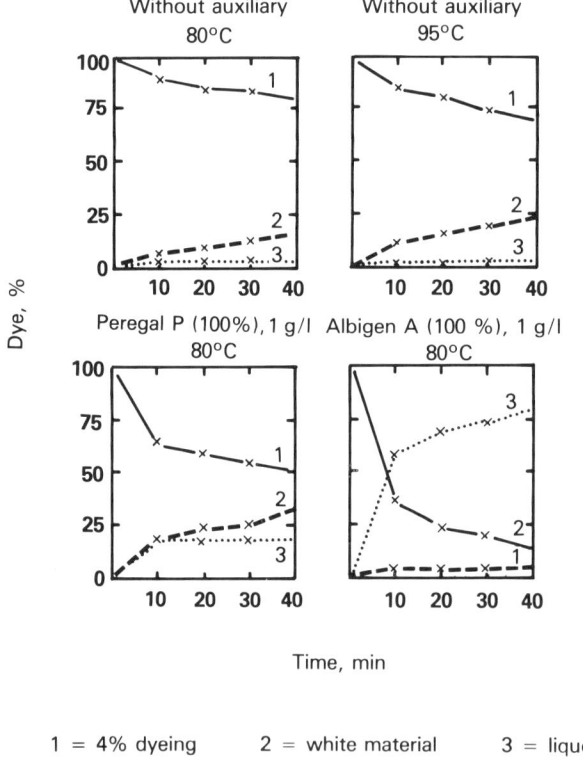

1 = 4% dyeing   2 = white material   3 = liquor

Figure 6.6 – Levelling of C.I. Vat Blue 20

Due to the similarity in the forces exerted on the dyes by the substrate and auxiliaries, the latter usually have a relatively pronounced effect on dyes that have particularly poor levelling properties and high substantivity. Conversely, however, this also means that such a product has only a low retarding action when it is used with less substantive dyes having good levelling properties. Consequently auxiliaries of this type can generally be used at higher concentrations when it is particularly necessary, e.g. for dyeing pale colours and at low liquor ratios [41]. If required, the retarding action of the auxiliaries can be diminished by raising the temperature. Their range of action extends from lowering the rate of exhaustion of the dyes (especially in the semi-pigmentation process) to levelling out unlevel dyeings at high temperatures.

Oxidation and Aftertreatment
When the exhaustion process is complete the dyeing is rinsed to remove loose dye and most of the residual reducing agent and alkali. The leuco dye is then reconverted into its original form by oxidation. Today this is generally carried out with hydrogen peroxide, perborate or, more recently, sodium *m*-nitrobenzenesulphonate. Other methods ('skying' or treatment with (a) hypochlorite or (b) acetic acid and potassium dichromate or (c) sodium chlorite) are not always possible and are now seldom used. In certain cases there can be problems with the indanthrone derivatives (C.I. Vat Blues 6 and 16, and especially with C.I. Vat Blue 4) due to overoxidation, caused particularly by atmospheric oxygen in the presence of high alkali concentrations. The yellow-green azine form of the dye is formed and the correct colour can then only be obtained by revatting.

After oxidation the dyeings are treated at the boil in an aqueous solution of a surfactant, an operation generally referred to as 'soaping'. This process is very important in vat dyeing; it removes loose dye and the properties of the dyeing are changed significantly, e.g. the fastness to washing may be improved and there may also be a change in colour (particularly with mercerised cotton and regenerated cellulose).

Current opinion concerning the aftertreatment operations is that the forces between the dye molecule and the cellulose chains are weaker after oxidation than before, and that the dye molecules are aligned mainly parallel to the fibre axis initially [34, 39, 42, 43]. In many cases the soaping process produces changes in the absorption spectra and in the dichroism of dyeings on film. From this behaviour it is concluded that the dye molecules associate to form submicroscopic crystals in the fissures of the substrate, and that in these crystals the dye molecules are predominantly oriented at right angles to the fibre axis [39, 42, 43]. Valko [34] has already succeeded in proving, by X-ray examination of extremely dark dyeings on cellulosic film, that in certain cases crystallisation takes place on soaping (e.g. with C.I. Vat Blue 6 and Orange 9). In other cases (e.g. C.I. Vat Blue 4) X-ray examination has shown the dye to be amorphous, both before and after soaping. Indigo dyeings were found to contain dye crystals even before they were soaped.

However, the phenomenon has not been fully clarified. For example, it has been observed that there are parallels between the crystallisation of dyes from polar and non-polar solvents and the behaviour of the dyeings before and after soaping. This has led to the conclusion that the metastable form of the dye crystal, formed during oxidation in the presence of the cellulose molecules, is converted into the stable form on soaping [35, 43, 44].

Two factors are important in practice, namely:
1. The efficiency of the soaping process is determined solely by the temperature and duration of the treatment and is not influenced by the pH
2. Dyes that show only a small change in colour are particularly useful for continuous processes, in which only a limited soaping time is available [31].

6.2.6 Properties of Dyeings

Dyeings produced with vat dyes on cellulosic fibres have an overall higher standard of fastness than is achieved with other classes of dyes. This applies not only to their fastness properties in use, e.g. fastness to light and washing, but also to those important during later processing, e.g. fastness to mercerising, soda boiling, chlorite and hypochlorite. Because of their excellent fastness to these processes vat dyes are ideal for yarn dyeing, particularly for coloured bleach goods such as handkerchiefs, shirting materials and terry towelling.

The following are brief references to certain special aspects, which are covered in detail in the manufacturers' technical literature (e.g. [31]).
1. If the dye is readily reducible, poor fastness ratings are obtained when the dyeing is washed at the boil in an alkaline medium. This applies to the flavanthrones (e.g. C.I. Vat Yellow 1) and the pyranthrones (e.g. C.I. Vat Orange 9). In these cases the fibre itself has a reducing action. The violanthrone derivatives (e.g. C.I. Vat Blue 20) are also sensitive in this respect. An increase in the molecular size and number of reducible carbonyl groups results in improved stability to this treatment [5]. The problem can be prevented by adding a mild oxidising agent (e.g. Ludigol).
2. The indanthrones are sensitive to hypochlorite. In this case 'over-oxidation' leads to the formation of azine groups and the dyeing becomes greener [5, 33]. C.I. Vat Blue 4 is more liable to this problem than C.I. Vat Blue 6.
3. The light fastness is particularly good with dyes that have a multi-nuclear ring system with integrated NH groups. With combinations of certain green and blue dyes with yellow types there can be a mutual adverse action on exposure to light or weathering, and this results in the blue or green component decomposing more rapidly than anticipated. This effect is commonly referred to as catalytic fading. The behaviour of such combination dyeings is influenced by (a) dye selection, (b) mixing proportions and depth of shade, (c) moisture content of the textile material, (d) u.v. content of the incident light and (e) the substrate itself. A particular yellow vat dye does not always show the same behaviour towards the different blue or green types with which it may be combined. There is, therefore, no general rule for determining whether a certain yellow dye is suitable for combining with green or blue dyes. Dyeings with a high yellow content are, however, more susceptible than those with a smaller proportion of yellow. The light fastness of such combinations diminishes with an increase in the atmospheric humidity. Hence these light fastness anomalies are hardly shown by textiles that have been given a water-repellent or resin-finishing treatment, because they take up less moisture. Dyeings on mercerised cotton or on non-delustred regenerated cellulosic fibres show the effect to a lesser extent than

those on unmercerised cotton [31]. However, certain dyes, e.g. C.I. Vat Green 3, may even have a positive effect on the light fastness of combination dyeings [5].

4. On exposure to light, degradation of the cellulosic fibre can occur more rapidly with a vat-dyed substrate than with undyed material, due to the formation of oxycellulose. The mechanism of this reaction can be explained as reduction of the dye in the fibre by the action of light, followed by its reoxidation by atmospheric oxygen during which peroxides are formed that degrade the cellulose [5]. This occurs mainly with those vat dyes that absorb radiation of short wavelength (e.g. C.I. Vat Oranges 2 and 9). Other vat dyes (e.g. C.I. Vat Green 3, and Blues 4, 6 and 14) have the opposite effect, inhibiting fibre degradation on exposure to light [5].

Further properties of vat dyeings, e.g. change in colour in artificial light, phototropism, infra-red reflectance, fastness to water spotting and pressing, behaviour on crease-resist finishing and coating, fastness to commercial laundering, dischargeability, etc. are described in the technical literature [31].

6.3 FUNDAMENTAL PROCESSES OF VAT DYEING

6.3.1 Pretreatment

Preparation of the material for dyeing is generally a very important processing stage. It should ensure that the substrate has a high and uniform dye uptake and absorbency, is virtually free of husks, has a sufficiently high standard of white (especially for pale dyeings), but must not cause any significant damage to the cellulose.

The requisite standard of absorption is achieved by removing the hydrophobic impurities from the cellulose. In the case of cotton the calcium and magnesium ions that are present in the pectin play an important part [25]. Pretreatment is carried out by boiling-off in the presence of alkali, dispersing agents and complexing agents. Further improvement in the absorbency can be achieved by a treatment with higher concentrations of alkali (causticising, mercerising). Prior to dyeing, size is removed from woven fabrics by the usual methods.

Since the vat dyeing of cellulosic fibres is carried out in relatively strong alkaline baths, it is also possible – in certain circumstances – to dye grey material. For example, with suitable auxiliaries grey yarn can be scoured and dyed simultaneously by the high-temperature process at temperatures above 100°C.

The substrate must be sufficiently lightened to obtain a dyeing of the requisite hue and brilliance. This is usually achieved by a preliminary oxidative bleaching treatment. As the leuco vat dyes are oxidised with peroxide or perborate after the dyeing process, this also has a certain bleaching action on the substrate, so that an oxidative pre-bleach may be unnecessary in certain circumstances, e.g. with dyeings in medium to dark colours.

6.3.2 Batchwise Dyeing Processes

Leuco Process

In the leuco process the material to be dyed is entered into a prepared dye liquor that contains the fully vatted dye, alkali (caustic soda) and reducing agent (hydrosulphite), together with various amounts of salt, dispersing agent, protective colloid, complexing agent and levelling agent, as required.

The amounts of caustic soda, hydrosulphite and salt – and the processing conditions – depend on the liquor ratio, dyeing properties and quantities of the dyes applied. Experience over many years has resulted in dyes with similar dyeing properties being classified in groups:

(a) IK dyes
(b) IW dyes
(c) IN dyes
(d) IN Special dyes
(e) Dyes that require a special procedure.

IK dyes have a relatively low substantivity for the cellulosic fibre and so are dyed at room temperature with a small amount of caustic soda and a high salt concentration. This group of dyes is diminishing in importance.

IW dyes have a much higher substantivity for the substrate and are dyed at 45–50°C with somewhat more caustic soda and less salt. Regenerated cellulosic fibres and mercerised cotton are dyed without salt.

IN dyes require still more caustic soda and are dyed at 60°C without salt. They have a high substantivity for the fibre, as have the IN Special dyes, but the latter differ from the normal IN dyes in requiring even more caustic soda.

The chemical additions required depend on the dye group, liquor ratio and amount of dye applied, as shown in Table 6.1. Certain dyes (e.g. C.I. Vat Red 23 and C.I. Vat Black 9) are dyed according to special procedures.

TABLE 6.1

Chemical Requirements for Dyeing by the Leuco Method at 20:1 and 10:1 Liquor Ratio

Dye group	Concn (% o.w.f.)	Caustic soda (38°Bé) (ml/l)		Hydrosulphite (g/l)		Sodium sulphate (g/l)	
		20:1	10:1	20:1	10:1	20:1	10:1
IK	0.1–1.0	4.0– 6.0	6.0– 7.0	2.0	2.0–2.5	7.5–15.0	7.5–10.0
	1.0–3.0	6.0– 7.0	7.0– 9.0	2.5–3.0	2.5–3.5	15.0–25.0	10.0–15.0
	3.0–5.0	7.0– 8.0	9.0–12.0	3.0–4.0	3.5–5.5	25.0–35.0	15.0–20.0
IW	0.1–1.0	6.0– 7.0	7.0– 9.0	2.0–3.0	2.0–3.0	5.0–10.0	5.0–10.0
	1.0–3.0	7.0– 9.0	9.0–12.0	3.0–4.0	3.0–5.0	10.0–15.0	10.0–15.0
	3.0–5.0	9.0–10.0	12.0–15.0	4.0–5.0	5.0–7.0	15.0–20.0	15.0–20.0
IN	0.1–1.0	10.0–12.0	15.0–17.0	3.0–4.0	3.0–4.0		
	1.0–3.0	12.0–14.0	17.0–22.0	4.0–5.0	4.0–6.0		
	3.0–5.0	14.0–16.0	22.0–26.0	5.0–6.0	6.0–8.0		

The classification of vat dyes into different groups according to their method of application is also described in the Third Edition of the *Colour Index*. This classification covers three dyeing procedures, methods I, II and III, referring to strong alkali and weak alkali at high temperature, and weak alkali at low temperature respectively. Individual dye manufacturers have adopted their own terminology.

Normally vatting is carried out in a long liquor for 5–10 min at dyeing temperature. Only concentrated dye preparations that contain little or no dispersing agent are pre-vatted in a highly concentrated stock vat, since vatting takes place more rapidly under these conditions.

With most dyes the dyeing temperature can be raised to 80°C during the dyeing process to achieve better levelling-out of any unevenness. It is also usual to raise the temperature to 80°C for shading purposes.

If the leuco process is employed at temperatures above 90°C (HT process) it is necessary to use IW and IN dyes that are sufficiently stable at these temperatures, together with a special reducing agent (Rongal HT). The chemical additions in this case are shown in Table 6.2. With vat dyes that are sensitive to over-reduction it is necessary to add suitable amounts of an inhibitor (e.g. glucose) when the dyeing temperature exceeds 60°C.

TABLE 6.2

Chemical Requirements for Dyeing at High Temperatures at 15:1 and 10:1 Liquor Ratio

Dyeing temp. (°C)	Concn (% o.w.f.)	Caustic soda (387°Bé) (ml/l)		Rongal HT (g/l)	
		15:1	10:1	15:1	10:1
95	1	10.8	12.8	5.0	5.0
95	3	12.4	14.4	5.0	6.0
95	5	14.0	16.0	5.0	7.0
115	1	12.3	14.3	5.0	6.7
115	3	14.0	16.0	5.7	7.6
115	5	15.6	17.7	6.5	8.5

The HT process is employed when it is necessary to brighten the substrate while dyeing pale to medium depths (at 115°C) or when there are levelling and penetration problems with certain substrates and dye combinations (at 90–100°C).

Pre-pigmentation Process
In this process the vat dye is distributed in the textile material as evenly as possible in the non-substantive insoluble form, i.e. prior to vatting. Only dyes with a fine particle size distribution are suitable for this method of application. Pigmentation is

begun at room temperature and the temperature is then raised slowly to 60–80°C, salt being added, if necessary, to promote exhaustion. This is followed by additions of alkali and hydrosulphite to vat the dye, which is then taken up by the fibre. Dyeing is continued to completion at the usual dyeing temperature, followed by after-treating in the usual manner.

Alternatively the HT dyeing process can be employed. If a brilliant colour should be required on a substrate that has not been pre-bleached, the pre-pigmentation can be combined with a peroxide bleach. The pre-pigmentation process can be carried out in all types of batchwise dyeing machine.

Semi-pigmentation Process
This process utilises the slower vatting rate of the dyes at low temperatures; the dyebath is set with dye and chemicals at 15–20°C and dyeing begun immediately. The temperature is then gradually raised, during which period dye that is not yet vatted becomes distributed in insoluble form in the substrate. Vatting begins at the same time, and the resultant leuco compound is taken up by the fibre. With this procedure a more uniform dyeing is obtained right from the outset than in the leuco process, where the leuco dye exhausts extremely rapidly. As in the pre-pigmentation process, the dyes must have a satisfactory particle size distribution.

6.3.3 Semi-continuous Dyeing Processes
The semi-continuous dyeing methods incorporate at least one continuous operation, i.e. impregnation of the material with the dye dispersion, usually coupled with an intermediate drying treatment. The dyeing is then developed in various types of batchwise dyeing equipment, usually on the jig (pad–jig process), with the dye being vatted and taken up by the fibre in the position where it has been applied. This process gives well-penetrated dyeings with good levelness. The chemical requirements are governed by the amount of dye applied, the liquor ratio and the method used (cf. Table 6.1). In principle the dyeing can also be developed by the cold pad–batch method, in which the fabric is padded with the dye dispersion, followed by intermediate drying if required; alkali and reducing agent are then applied in a second padding process and the fabric is batched up wet. The batch is wrapped with plastic film and allowed to rotate for 2–4 h at room temperature. As yet interest has only been shown in this process for certain special applications.

6.3.4 Continuous Dyeing Processes
A prerequisite for all continuous dyeing processes with vat dyes is that the fabric should have good absorbency so that it wets out rapidly and uniformly. The continuous dyeing of loom-state fabric or of material that has only been desized is restricted to special cases. Since the differences in substantivity of the leuco dyes for the fibre have less influence, the selection and combinability of the dyes is not as limited as in batchwise processes. Nevertheless dyes in the IN and IW groups have proved the most suitable.

The pad–steam process is the most reliable and popular continuous dyeing procedure for vat dyes. The fabric is padded with the dye dispersion and then dried immediately. In a second padding process alkali and reducing agent (usually hydrosulphite) are applied, after which the fabric is steamed in saturated steam for 60 s at a little above 100°C to reduce the dye and fix it on the substrate. This is followed by oxidation, rinsing and soaping on an open-width washer. The consumption of reducing agent depends on the quantity and type of the dye applied and on the processing conditions, because a certain proportion of the hydrosulphite is oxidised by the atmospheric oxygen during the development process. The quantities shown in Table 6.3 serve as a rough guide. It is also possible to ascertain the hydrosulphite requirement for a particular dye from the dye manufacturers' manuals [31] and to determine what excess is necessary by means of plant trials.

TABLE 6.3

Chemical Consumption in the Pad–Steam Process

Dye concn (% o.w.f.)	Liquor pick-up (%)	Caustic soda (38°Bé) (ml/l)	Hydrosulphite (g/l)
1	80	50	25
3	80	65	35
5	80	85	40
8	80	110	50
1	100	40	20
3	100	55	25
5	100	70	30
8	100	90	40

In the wet-steam process, after pad application of the dye dispersion, the dyed material is impregnated wet-on-wet with the requisite chemicals and developed immediately by steaming, thus eliminating the intermediate drying process. The padding trough that contains the chemical liquor can be situated either directly in front of the steamer, at its entrance, or inside the unit, immediately behind the entry slot. Lick-roll application of the chemical liquor has also proved very satisfactory.

6.4 DYEING METHODS

6.4.1 Dyeing of Loose Stock

Cotton is seldom dyed in the form of loose stock. However, if this procedure is used dyeing is always carried out by the pack system. The fibrous material is opened up, sprinkled with hot water and loaded into the dyeing vessel, in which it must be packed very tightly and uniformly to prevent channelling during dyeing. The loose stock is not usually pretreated prior to dyeing, which is mostly carried out by the leuco process at high temperatures.

6.4.2 Dyeing of Sliver

Cotton is dyed in the form of sliver when a large quantity of yarn is required with optimum levelness of colour and a high bulk, or when a fully penetrated dyeing is required on a high-quality yarn. Sliver can be dyed:
(a) Wound on beams
(b) Like loose stock, by the pack system
(c) Like wool tops, in the form of wound packages.

It is usually dyed by the leuco process or by the pre-pigmentation method with simultaneous bleaching.

6.4.3 Dyeing of Wound Yarn Packages

In package-dyeing machines the liquor circulates through the stationary material. Uniformity of liquor flow is particularly important, this being closely related to the resistance of the package, which in turn is determined by the type of fibre, the package density, the type of winding and package centre, the pH of the liquor and the dyeing temperature. Yarn that is liable to shrink during dyeing is wound on split or cardboard tubes combined with spring centres. Cotton yarn can be wound more tightly than viscose staple yarn, but uniformity of the winding is the most important factor. Air must be removed from the packages with steam or hot water, using a non-foaming wetting agent, before dyeing is begun.

Cheeses are generally dyed with an alternating liquor flow. In closed machines dyeing can be carried out at temperatures up to 115°C by the leuco, pre-pigmentation or semi-pigmentation processes already described. One rapid dyeing method [45] deserves a special mention. It consists of grey yarn being treated with saturated steam for 5–10 min at 110–120°C in a closed HT dyeing machine, and then cooled to 80°C before the addition of dye, caustic soda and hydrosulphite; dyeing is then continued for 20–25 min in the cooling liquor.

6.4.4 Dyeing of Yarn in Hank Form

The oldest procedure consists of dyeing the hanks of yarn in vats or becks by rotating them in the stationary liquor. In conventional hank-dyeing machines movement of the material is mechanised, whereas there are other machines in which the hanks remain stationary and the liquor is circulated. Both these principles are incorporated in the spray dyeing machine. The hanks are suspended on rods or perforated tubes, depending on the dyeing method employed. The pack system, as used for loose stock, is seldom employed today for hank yarn, although it has the advantage that even very fine yarns can subsequently be processed without difficulty when dyed in this manner.

Hanks dyed in becks are usually dyed by the leuco process. The vat is prepared and raised to the dyeing temperature before the hanks, suspended from rods, are entered and fully immersed. The hanks are then turned, frequently at first, then at longer intervals. On completion of dyeing the liquor is drained off and the dyeing oxidised and soaped in the usual manner.

Conventional hank-dyeing machines are employed for yarn qualities that are usually difficult to dye level, e.g. mercerised ply yarns, knitting yarns and sewing thread. Careful selection of the dye combinations is important, preferably from the IW group of dyes. The semi-pigmentation process with IN and IW dyes and direct black types is the most suitable method. Since one-third of the hank is permanently exposed to oxidation by atmospheric oxygen the hydrosulphite consumption is higher than when dyeing is carried out in becks, and so it must be checked constantly.

Enclosed hank-dyeing equipment is usually of the type employed for wool yarn (e.g. the cabinet system with alternating liquor circulation). The same yarn qualities are dyed in this type of equipment as in conventional hank-dyeing machines. The levelness of such dyeings is dependent on the uniformity of the liquor flow through the yarn. When the hanks are suspended on the rods care must be taken to ensure that they have sufficient play so that the suspension points are also completely penetrated by the dye. The dyeing methods employed are the same as for normal hank-dyeing machines, the best results being obtained with dyes that have good levelling properties. The use of levelling agents is also particularly important. The consumption of hydrosulphite is only 65–75% of that in conventional hank-dyeing machines.

6.4.5 Dyeing of Woven Fabrics
Woven fabrics composed of cellulosic fibres can be dyed by batchwise procedures in open-width or rope form, or semi-continuously or continuously in open width. The procedure employed depends on the type of fabric (fibre material, construction), size of the dye lot and dyeing equipment available.

Batchwise Methods
The most important types of dyeing equipment for the batchwise application of vat dyes are jigs, winches and beam dyeing machines.

The most suitable jigs are the covered type, fitted with an automatic reverse mechanism, with the fabric running at a low tension and a constant speed. The fabric must be desized before it is dyed. When the individual pieces and end cloths are sewn together there should be no longitudinal creases, seam marks or projecting selvedges. The more open the fabric construction, the smaller must be the size of the batch. The liquor ratio must not be less than 2:1. Since the fabric is liable to cool the dye liquor initially, it is important to check the liquor temperature carefully during the first pass and to keep it constant. Dyeing can be carried out by any of the batchwise processes already described. The dye liquor on the fabric must always contain sufficient hydrosulphite during the dyeing process to prevent a change in colour taking place at the selvedges due to oxidation by atmospheric oxygen. The concentration of reducing agent must be checked continuously and replenishing additions of reducing agent and caustic soda made as necessary.

Enclosed equipment is particularly necessary for winch dyeing to keep the consumption of hydrosulphite to the minimum. The process most frequently employed is the semi-pigmentation method, but the leuco and pre-pigmentation methods are also used.

In beam dyeing the levelness of the dyeing depends on the uniform flow of liquor through the textile material. The resistance to this flow depends, in turn, on the structure of the material and on the flow rate of the liquor. It is possible to estimate the influence of the fabric structure on liquor flow and utilise this information in the dyeing operation [31]. The most important dyeing methods for woven fabrics in beam dyeing machines are the semi-pigmentation process (for pale and medium depths) and the leuco process (for dark colours). On completion of dyeing the liquor is replaced by a cold rinsing liquor and the dyeing is then oxidised and after-treated in the usual manner.

Semi-continuous Methods [26]
The most important process in this area is the pad–jig process. The fabric, together with the end-cloth, is impregnated with the dye dispersion in the padder and wound into a batch. A good wetting agent is necessary, and also an anti-migration agent if the fabric is to be subjected to intermediate drying. If it is not to be dried before development the wet batch must be rotated slowly and continuously, possibly wrapped in plastic film.

In jig development insoluble dye is transferred mechanically to the liquor during the first pass.

It is therefore advisable to add some pad liquor to the development bath and allow this to vat before the first pass; a state of equilibrium is quickly reached in the liquor between the insoluble dye that is transferred and the leuco dye that is being absorbed, and this prevents end-to-end shade variations. The quantity of pad liquor that is necessary depends on the liquor pick-up of the fabric and on the liquor ratio in the jig development phase. The number of ends given is generally from four to six. The state of the vat is checked with vat yellow paper at the selvedge of the fabric before it re-enters the liquor.

Continuous Methods
The pad–steam process is the most important continuous dyeing method for vat dyes. The processing sequence and chemical requirements are described on p. 244.

The equipment necessary is indicated by the process sequence, namely:
1. Padding (dye dispersion)
2. Drying*
3. Padding (reducing agent)
4. Steaming
5. Aftertreatment.

In principle, any type of dye padder is suitable, provided it has a uniform squeezing effect. The coverings of both bowls must be of the same hardness (60–70°Shore). Several designs of padders are now available that compensate for roller deflection under load. A uniform liquor pick-up is the most important prerequisite for faultless

---

* The pad–thermofixation–pad–steam process for polyester/cotton fabrics is described in Chapter 9

dyeings. This can only be ensured if there is no variation in absorbency across the width and length of the fabric. For this reason the pretreatment processes should also be carried out continuously at open width. The dye dispersion should have a neutral reaction, and it is advisable to work with as low a liquor pick-up as possible in order to restrict migration of the dyes during drying. Liquor temperature is preferably below 25°C.

The fabric should be padded and dried in one continuous operation. Drying is usually carried out in two stages. The fabric is first pre-dried to a residual moisture content of 25–30% water in one or more infra-red units. Hot flues or cylinder dryers are usually employed for final drying operations. Stenters are not used for drying fabric that is still wet from the dye padder because the danger of insoluble dye migration is particularly great. Also cleaning of the chain would be very laborious.

The pre-drying and final drying of the fabric, padded with the dye dispersion, are operations that can have a decisive influence on the quality of the dyeing. Irregularities in drying can affect the migration of the insoluble dye particles and thus cause two-sided effects or listing, even when the fabric has been uniformly impregnated on the padder. It is advisable to allow the padded material an air passage of 15–20 s between the padder and the first drying unit. During this time some of the water at the surface of the cellulosic fibres diffuses into the fibre, thus reducing migration of the dye during drying. The temperature in the first section of a hot flue should be around 100°C with minimum air circulation. Drying can then be carried out in the other sections at higher temperatures (120–140°C) with a higher degree of air circulation. It is advisable that the first six to ten guide rollers be coated with polytetrafluoroethylene (PTFE)

If intermediate drying is carried out on cylinders, the infra-red pre-dryer stage is essential, otherwise a dye build-up would form on the first cylinders and dye migration would be severe. In order to reduce soiling the first six to eight drying, cylinders should be PTFE coated and temperature control carried out in groups of cylinders, the first of which should not exceed 100°C. The risk of two-sided effects is greater at higher temperatures, especially at low processing speeds. Nevertheless cylinder dryers have proved very suitable for smooth fabrics and are much more economical than hot flues.

For the full pad–steam process a conventional padder is usually employed to apply the alkali and reducing agent. The liquor trough must be of small capacity so that the contents are rapidly renewed by the feed liquor. The liquor should be kept cold, preferably below 20°C, and it is advisable to cool the fabric from the preceding dryer. The liquor pick-up should be as high as possible. This ensures that there is sufficient diffusion medium available for the dyes and chemicals and that exposed parts of the fabric (e.g. twill lines) are always saturated with sufficient reducing liquor. This gives an improved fabric appearance and prevents frosting.

In the wet-steam process chemical liquor impregnation is carried out so that there is the maximum difference in pick-up between wet fabric entering and leaving the liquor trough. This may be achieved by light squeezing by an unweighted top roller, or more recently by lick-roll application. After leaving the nip or the lick roller the fabric must pass directly to the steamer without passing over any guide rollers.

Steamers are usually of the tight-strand type with driven top rollers and compensator speed control to maintain correct fabric tension. The fabric capacity is between 15 and 60 m, so that according to speed the steaming time is in the range 30–60 s. For fabrics that are to be processed with minimum tension festoon steamers have proved suitable, provided that precautions are taken to ensure that chemical liquor does not accumulate at the bottom of the loops.

The atmosphere should be dry saturated steam, at normal pressure, with only slight superheating (dry-bulb temperature 103–105°C). It is imperative that the steam atmosphere should be as free from air as possible and that instruments are available for checking this state. The steamer exit must be constructed in the form of a water trap to prevent air from entering the steamer. The water feed should be 3–5 l/kg of material and the temperature in the water trap should not exceed 40°C, otherwise some of the vat dye may be removed. The water should be fed into the water trap across its full width but in such a way that none of it is sprayed onto the fabric. The water drains by overflow, again across the whole width. The design of the steamer must prevent condensation drops from the steamer roof and from the steamer throat entry.

The air passage between the padder and the steamer entry is critical and must be as short as possible in order to avoid decomposition of the sodium hydrosulphite (cf. p. 229). Likewise the air passage between the steamer water trap exit and the first wash box should be kept short; this applies especially to blue indanthrone derivatives which are susceptible to over-oxidation by atmospheric oxygen at high alkali concentrations. The dull yellow-green azine form of the dyes is then formed.

Aftertreatments consist of rinsing, oxidising, soaping and final rinsing, and are carried out continuously immediately after steaming. The most suitable equipment is an open-width washer, preferably with eight compartments. The fabric capacity of each compartment is approximately 15 m, although this depends on the speed of processing. Efficient oxidation and especially soaping depend on the processing time and concentration of chemicals, so the fabric capacity of these compartments should be proportional to the processing speed. Oxidation is by peroxide or perborate maintained at pH 8–9 and 50°C. The fastness of the dyeing and the final shade are affected by the soaping process. In the presence of water and at elevated temperatures a change takes place in the state of the reoxidised dye on the fibre that results in a more or less pronounced change in colour. It follows that dye selection for continuous processing should be from that group which shows only a small change in colour on soaping [31].

Two factors are decisive for the treatment: its duration and temperature. The time should not be less than 30 s and the temperature should be 95–100°C. To ensure good reproducibility of the dyeings, rinsing water and chemical additions should be controlled by flowmeters and specific temperatures maintained by automatic controllers.

Dyeing with vat dyes by continuous methods has become ever more reliable over the years and recent work [46] has concentrated on a number of critical stages, with special reference to pad liquor stability and the use of migration inhibitors.

6.4.6 Dyeing of Knitgoods [47]

Vat dyes are being used to an increasing extent in this sector, because dyeings on knitgoods are now expected to meet higher fastness requirements. This development has been facilitated by the use of jet and overflow dyeing machines, in which the dyeing conditions can be defined more precisely than in winches due to the rapid liquor circulation and uniform temperature.

Knitgoods have only a low dimensional stability to mechanical stress. Dyeing must therefore be carried out at the least possible tension to ensure that the finished fabric has a low shrinkage on subsequent washing. Cotton knitgoods were previously dyed mainly in rope form on winches, or on beams after slitting open. Today they are also dyed successfully in jet and overflow dyeing machines. Warp-knitted fabrics are dyed mainly in beam dyeing equipment.

The semi-pigmentation and pre-pigmentation processes are the main ones used for winch dyeing, the former having proved particularly suitable, e.g. for dyeing interlock qualities in pale to medium depths. The hydrosulphite content of the liquor must be carefully checked and replenished when necessary. It is advisable to increase the dyeing temperature to 70–75°C with IW or IN dyes to promote migration. In the pre-pigmentation process the hydrosulphite consumption can be reduced by extending the pigmentation phase and shortening the dyeing phase.

In jet and overflow dyeing machines the fabric is transported mainly by the liquor. Since products that tend to foam will cause problems in machines that are only partially flooded, care is necessary in the selection of the auxiliaries used. This restriction does not apply to fully flooded jet dyeing machines because no foam can develop. The following procedure has proved very satisfactory for dyeing grey fabric (pre-pigmentation process):

1. Set the liquor with a suitable auxiliary at 60–70°C
2. Enter the fabric, add 2 ml/l caustic soda (38°Bé) and heat to 105°C
3. After 10 min, cool to 85°C and add the dye
4. Add the remaining caustic soda as the temperature continues to fall
5. Add levelling agent and hydrosulphite at 80°C
6. Dye for 20–40 min at 80°C
7. Cool to 60°C and dye for a further 10 min at 60°C
8. Oxidise and soap in the usual manner.

Pretreated material can also be dyed by the semi-pigmentation method.

In the case of machines that are not fully flooded, the atmospheric oxygen in the air in the machine consumes a certain amount of hydrosulphite. Experience has shown that the oxygen in 1 m^3 air consumes 1.7 kg hydrosulphite and 1.7 l caustic soda (38°Bé), which must then be replaced. To improve the brilliance of pale colours the material can be bleached oxidatively during soaping without undue extension of the processing time.

6.4.7 Correction of Faulty Dyeings

Faulty dyeings can be corrected by levelling out, stripping or overdyeing. Levelling is carried out at 80–90°C, on the winch or jig, or even above the boil in package-dyeing machines. In addition to caustic soda, reducing agent and other auxiliaries, the liquor must contain a sufficient amount of a levelling agent (e.g. Peregal P). For stripping the dyeing is treated at 80–100°C in a liquor that contains caustic soda and hydrosulphite, together with a stripping agent (e.g. 2–3 g/l Albigen A). This complexes more readily with the leuco dye than does the levelling agent, and it rapidly forms very soluble leuco dye–polymer complexes in the liquor. The concentration of caustic soda should not exceed 20–30 ml/l (38°Bé).

6.4.8 Dyeing of Regenerated Cellulosic Fibres

Viscose fibres swell to a greater extent than cotton in the presence of alkali. This swelling action – and its effect on the strength and handle of the material – is less pronounced with yarns and fabrics in which the individual fibres are more densely compacted. An even better stabilising effect is obtained by blending with alkali-stable fibres. Viscose fibres can, for example, be dyed with vat dyes without difficulty when they are blended with polyester fibres or cotton.

Modal fibres (polynosic fibres or high wet modulus (HWM) fibres) are more stable to alkali than normal viscose fibres. In blends with cotton polynosic fibres form an alkali-stable substrate and can be mercerised. Although the HWM fibres are more sensitive to alkali, they are sufficiently stable to be dyed with vat dyes. The modal fibres are mostly used in blends with cotton or polyester fibres.

The strong swelling of the viscose fibre results in an increase in the diameter of the fibre, and particular attention must be paid to this fact in the dyeing of wound packages, since it increases the resistance to the liquor flow. For this reason packages of viscose staple yarn must be wound at a lower tension than cotton yarn. Since leuco dyes have a higher substantivity for regenerated cellulosic fibres than they do for cotton, there is a greater risk of obtaining unlevel dyeings; this can be counteracted by increasing the quantity of levelling agent used.

Regenerated cellulosic fibre yarns are dyed in wound-package or hank form by the leuco or pre-pigmentation process. Dyeing at as high a temperature as possible minimises swelling of the fibre and promotes levelling. On completion of dyeing the material must be thoroughly acidified because alkali is only removed very slowly from these fibres by rinsing.

Since woven viscose staple fabrics are readily deformed in the wet state care must be taken not to stretch the material during dyeing. They can be dyed (a) batchwise in low-tension jigs, beam dyeing machines and on the winch, (b) semi-continuously by the pad–jig process or (c) continuously, by the methods just described.

In blends of cotton and regenerated cellulosic fibres the latter fibres dye darker. There may also be differences in colour between the two components, although this can be prevented by suitable dye selection. A uniform depth of shade can also be obtained by varying the dyeing temperature. Woven and knitted fabric blends of this type can be dyed by the processes employed for pure cotton.

6.4.9 Dyeing of Linen

After retting, in addition to the bundles of cellulosic fibres, bast fibres still contain portions of the epidermis, the cortical cells and the woody zone, i.e. an amorphous

binding substance composed of lignin and hemicellulose [20]. This binding substance must not be removed during the dyeing process because it gives the linen its
distinctive handle.

The material is therefore only pretreated and bleached when it is to be dyed in
pale depths, since all alkaline treatments remove the non-cellulosic substances
present and thus result in an undesirable loss in weight. Dyeing at 60–80°C produces a loss in weight of 5–10%, but an alkali treatment under high-temperature
conditions followed by a reductive bleach can produce a weight loss of 20%. In
cheese dyeing it is difficult to achieve good penetration of the yarn and the yarn
cross-over points, particularly in the case of conical packages on rigid tubes. Hence
it is best to use combined cardboard and spring tubes, together with dyes giving
good levelling performance and a sufficient quantity of levelling agent. All the dyeing processes described for cotton yarn may be used for linen. The only problem in
dyeing linen fabrics is that of achieving satisfactory penetration. In this respect the
best results are obtained by beam dyeing at high temperatures. The pad–jig and
cold pad–batch processes are also suitable.

6.4.10 Dyeing with Indigo
Leuco indigo has only a low substantivity for cellulose, hence only pale depths are
obtainable by exhaust dyeing procedures. Indigo is therefore applied in a series of
'dips', with intermediate squeezing and atmospheric oxidation. By repeating the
process, dye is applied to the substrate 'layer on layer' to give deep dyeings with a
relatively low rubbing fastness. On cotton, indigo dyeings have a light fastness
rating of 3 at reference shade depth. Yellow decomposition products are formed on
exposure, which cause the blue dyeing to appear greener. Since these yellow products are water soluble the brilliant blue colour is obtained again on washing. When
assessed after washing a light fastness rating of 6 is obtained.

Indigo is usually dyed from a caustic soda/hydrosulphite vat. Cotton is dyed with
indigo in the form of ball warps, warp beams or in the piece, usually continuously
[48].

The batchwise dyeing of hank yarn is carried out in becks with repeated short
dips, followed by squeezing and atmospheric oxidation. Wound packages cannot be
dyed in full depths with indigo. Piece goods can be dyed on star frames or on the
jig. Generally speaking, however, the batchwise dyeing of indigo is now of little
importance.

In the continuous indigo dyeing of warp yarn, the yarn is in the form of a full-
width warp beam or a cable the thickness of a thumb (ball warp), containing
350–400 individual threads. It passes through several vats, each followed by an
air passage for oxidation. The processing speed is 20–30 m/min, with modern
machines providing an immersion time of 5–30 s in each vat. On leaving the vat
the material is squeezed to a liquor pick-up of approx. 100%, after which the
dyeing requires around 2 min for oxidation before it passes into the next vat.

A typical recipe for a dye liquor would be:
– Caustic soda (38°Bé), 5 ml/l

- Hydrosulphite, 1.5 g/l
- Stock vat, 62.5 ml/l

The stock vat is composed of:
- Indigo Pure (BASF, C.I. Vat Blue 1), 80 g/l
- Dispersing agent 4 g/l
- Wetting agent, 1 g/l
- Caustic soda (38°Bé), 130 ml/l
- Hydrosulphite, 60 g/l

Apart from the stock vat replenishing addition, it is also necessary during the dyeing process to add hydrosulphite and caustic soda in amounts that depend on the prevailing conditions. The content of reducing agent and caustic soda must be checked at regular intervals to determine what quantities are necessary. The continuous indigo dyeing of piece goods is carried out on the same types of dyeing machine, and in the same manner, as for warp beams.

REFERENCES

1. BASF, German P 129845 (1901).
2. BASF, German P 160529 (1904).
3. Venkataraman, 'The Chemistry of the Synthetic Dyes', Vol. 2 (New York: Academic Press, 1952) 861.
4. Venkataraman and Iyer, 'The Chemistry of the Synthetic Dyes', Vol. 5, Ed. Venkataraman (New York: Academic Press, 1971) 132.
5. Weiss, 'Die Küpenfarbstoffe' (Berlin: Springer Verlag, 1953).
6. 'Ullmanns Encyklopädie der technischen Chemie', 4th Edn, Vol. 7, 585.
7. 'Ullmanns Encyklopädie der technischen Chemie', 4th Edn, Vol. 13, 177.
8. 'Kirk-Othmer Encyclopedia of Chemical Technology', 3rd Edn, Vol. 8 (New York: John Wiley and Sons, 1978) 159.
9. 'Kirk-Othmer Encyclopedia of Chemical Technology', 2nd Edn, Vol. 11 (New York: John Wiley and Sons, 1966) 562.
10. 'Colour Index', 3rd Edn, Vol. 4 (Bradford: SDC and AATCC, 1971).
11. Fox, 'Vat Dyes and Vat Dyeing' (London: Chapman and Hall, 1948).
12. Kunz, Melliand Textilber., 33 (1952) 58.
13. Fox, J.S.D.C., 65 (1949) 508.
14. Baumgarte, Rev. Prog. Coloration, 5 (1974) 17.
15. Bernthsen, Ber., 14 (1881) 14.
16. Meyer, Z. Anorg. Chemie, 34 (1903) 43.
17. Simon and Küchler, Z. Anorg. Chemie, 260 (1949) 161.
18. Dunitz, J. Amer. Chem. Soc., 78 (1956) 878.
19. Dunitz, Acta Cryst., 9 (1956) 579.
20. Lister and Garvie, Canad. J. Chem., 37 (1959) 1567.
21. Baumgarte, Melliand Textilber., 53 (1972) 334.
22. Rinker et al., J. Phys. Chem., 64 (1960) 573.
23. Marshall, J.S.D.C., 72 (1956) 201.
24. Baumgarte, Textilveredlung, 2 (1967) 896.
25. Baumgarte, Melliand Textilber., 49 (1968) 1192, 1306.
26. Baumgarte and Schlüter, Melliand Textilber., 62 (1981) 555.
27. Baumgarte, Textilveredlung, 4 (1969) 821.
28. Porter, Text. Research J., 36 (1966) 289.
29. Marshall and Peters, J.S.D.C., 68 (1952) 289.
30. Baumgarte and Keuser, Melliand Textilber., 47 (1966) 286.
31. BASF Manual 'Cellulosic Fibres' B375e (1979).

32. Müller, Melliand Textilber., **13** (1932) 439, 488.
33. Müller, Textil-Rundschau, **5** (1950) 261, 303.
34. Valko, J. Amer. Chem. Soc., **63** (1941) 1433.
35. Wegmann, Amer. Dyestuff Rep., **51** (1962) 276.
36. Baumgarte, Textilveredlung, **15** (1980) 413.
37. Boulton and Morton, J.S.D.C., **55** (1939) 481.
38. Clark and McCleary, Amer. Dyestuff Rep., **38** (1949) 828.
39. Vickerstaff, 'The Physical Chemistry of Dyeing' (London: Oliver and Boyd, 1954) 299.
40. Baumgarte, Melliand Textilber., **55** (1974) 953.
41. Baumgarte, Melliand Textilber., **59** (1978) 311.
42. Sumner, Vickerstaff and Waters, J.S.D.C., **69** (1953) 181.
43. Peters, 'Textile Chemistry', Vol. 3 (Amsterdam: Elsevier Scientific Publications, 1975) 503.
44. Wegmann, J.S.D.C., **76** (1960) 282.
45. Fox, J.S.D.C., **78** (1962) 393.
46. Baumgarte and Schlüter, Text. Chem. Colorist, **17** (1985) 27.
47. Ruppert, Melliand Textilber., **60** (1979) 337.
48. Kramrisch, Amer. Dyestuff Rep., **69** (11) (1980) 34.

CHAPTER 7

Dyeing with Sulphur Dyes

COLIN SENIOR and DAVID A CLARKE

7.1 COMMERCIAL POSITION

The first sulphur dye is generally considered to be Cachou de Laval, a brownish-khaki colour discovered in 1873. Since that time there has been a steady improvement in dyeing and fastness properties, together with the development of different product types, in a range covering all colours except a true red.

Although sulphur dyes have been considered outdated by some writers, they still constitute the largest class in terms of quantity, with an estimated worldwide production of more than 80 000 tonnes in 1979, even though a different picture emerges if unit price is used as the basis of calculation.

Following the invention of reactive dyes, it was widely expected that this class would replace sulphur and direct dyes and take a large share of the vat market, but this has not occurred to date as Table 7.1 shows. Although it is impossible to relate exactly the different tinctorial strengths and production quantities of the various forms of sulphur dyes from the various producers, the figures do show very clearly that sulphur dyes are a major class of colorant in world terms.

Sulphur dyes are widely used for black, blue, brown, olive and green colours in medium to heavy depths, being relatively inexpensive. The liquid brands are ideally suited to long runs in continuous dyeing techniques. Their fastness properties vary markedly throughout the range, e.g. light fastness increases from yellow at about 3 to black at 7. Fastness to wet treatments in general is good, although fastness to bleaching is poor with certain notable exceptions, e.g. C.I. Sulphur Green 14, Black 11 and Red 10.

Sulphur dyes are widely used on cellulosic fibres and their blends, especially with polyester but also with nylon and acrylic fibres. Cotton and polyester/cotton drill and corduroy are dyed continuously or on the jig, whilst cotton/nylon and cotton/acrylic knitted and pile fabrics are winch or jet dyed. Yarn is dyed in package-, hank- or warp-dyeing machinery and loose stock in a variety of circulating-liquor machines. Sulphur dyes are also applied in limited quantities to paper and silk, and more widely to leather.

TABLE 7.1

**Percentage Share of the World Dye Market
Held by Different Types of Colorants [1]**

Consumption on cellulosic fibres		Consumption on all fibres	
Colorant class	(%)	Colorant class	(%)
Sulphur dyes	29.0	Sulphur dyes	18.0
Direct dyes	27.4	Direct dyes	17.0
Vat dyes	19.4	Disperse dyes	16.5
Reactive dyes	9.7	Acid dyes	16.5
Azoic dyes	8.1	Vat dyes	12.0
Pigments	6.4	Reactive dyes	6.0
		Azoic dyes	6.0
		Basic dyes	4.5
		Pigments	4.0

7.2 CLASSIFICATION AND COMMERCIAL FORMS

7.2.1 Colour Index Classification

The classification of sulphur dyes in the Third Edition of the *Colour Index* has become somewhat confusing owing to deletions from and additions to ranges and newly developed product types, although the main subdivisions are still clear. The four subdivisions are:

1. C.I. Sulphur dyes
2. C.I. Leuco Sulphur dyes
3. C.I. Solubilised Sulphur dyes
4. C.I. Condense Sulphur dyes.

The definition of a sulphur dye (group 1) is a water-insoluble dye, containing sulphur both as an integral part of the chromophore and in attached polysulphide chains, normally applied in the alkaline reduced (leuco) form from a sodium sulphide solution and subsequently oxidised to the insoluble form on the fibre.

As well as the traditional water-insoluble powder forms, this group includes the black grain types, which contain some sodium sulphide and possess limited substantivity but require additional reducing agent for dyeing, and the recently developed dispersed sulphur dyes which are available in powder and paste forms and are non-substantive in water. To complicate the issue, however, some dispersed products are of the so-called sulphur vat type, e.g. C.I. Vat Blue 43 and C.I. Vat Green 7, which require caustic soda/sodium dithionite reduction.

A leuco sulphur (group 2) dye has the same C.I. constitution number as the parent C.I. Sulphur dye but is a powder or liquid brand containing the soluble leuco form of the parent dye and reducing agent, usually sodium sulphide or hydrosulphide, in sufficient quantity to make the dye suitable for application either directly or with the addition of only a small amount of extra reducing agent.

A solubilised sulphur (group 3) dye has a different constitution number because chemically it is the thiosulphuric acid derivative of the parent dye, non-substantive to cellulose but converted to the substantive alkali-soluble thiol form during dyeing.

The condense sulphur dyes (group 4) are sodium *S*-alkyl or *S*-aryl thiosulphates. Although they contain sulphur, their constitution and method of manufacture bear little resemblance to those of traditional sulphur dyes. They do require sodium sulphide or polysulphide for dyeing, but conventional sulphur dyeing methods are unsuitable for the condense sulphur dyes.

The so-called sulphur vat dyes are not classified separately in the *Colour Index* but are a collection of dyes from both C.I. Sulphur and C.I. Vat classes which possess superior wet-fastness properties and better resistance to bleaching than traditional sulphur dyes; they are often applied by caustic soda/sodium dithionite reduction systems. The range includes C.I. Vat Blues 42 and 43, C.I. Vat Greens 7 and 20, and C.I. Sulphur Black 11 and Red 10.

7.2.2 Commercial Forms

Powders

Powders have, in the past, been the principal form in which sulphur dyes were sold. In general they are made from the dried presscake, finely ground and standardised with common salt, sodium sulphate or soda ash. They are prepared for dyeing by making a paste with water, which is dissolved by boiling with the necessary amount of reducing agent and further addition of water.

Pre-reduced Powders

These are usually made from presscake paste, to which a reducing agent such as sodium sulphide, sodium hydrosulphide or sodium dithionite has been added; these solubilise the dye in water. Before drying, the dye paste may be mixed with dispersing and stabilising agents to aid application.

Grains

Grains are usually pre-reduced powders. The quantities of sodium sulphide, hydrosulphide and mineral salts are adjusted to give a grainy product when the paste slurry is dried on a steam-heated drum dryer. Grains offer the advantage of having non-dusting properties.

Dispersed Powders

The principal use of dispersed powders is in pad–dry–chemical-pad–steam dyeing. They are normally made from presscake by ball or bead milling to microparticle size in the presence of dispersing agents. The drying is strictly controlled and is carried out in the presence of anticoagulants to prevent aggregation of the dispersed dye particles.

Dispersed Pastes

The milled pastes vary in strength, but for ease of handling the consistency of the dispersed pastes generally permits pouring from the container.

Liquids
During dye manufacture some liquid formulations are made directly from the thionation melt by additions of caustic soda and sodium hydrosulphide. Hydrotropic substances are sometimes added, either at the initial thionation stage or after the polysulphide melt is finished in order to keep the reduced dye in solution. Partially reduced liquids are also available. They are usually more concentrated than fully reduced liquids, thus saving packaging and transportation costs. However, they require a further addition of reducing agent to the dyebath in order to enable a full colour value to be obtained. On the other hand, fully reduced liquids are ready to use, since the amount of reducing agent for each dye has been carefully controlled to give maximum stability on storage and maximum colour yield in use. Unlike the dispersed pastes, they are not affected by low temperatures.

Water-soluble Brands
Solubilised sulphur dyes can be prepared in both powder and liquid forms. These dyes are the Bunte salts or thiosulphuric acid derivatives of the sulphur dyes. They are made by warming the polysulphide-free pastes with sodium sulphite or bisulphite until they dissolve. They are salted out from solution or isolated by drum drying of the liquor.
    Aqueous solutions of these dyes show little or no substantivity for cellulosic fibres until a reducing agent has been added. This assists the penetration of tightly woven materials.

7.3 AUXILIARIES

The two most important reducing agents for sulphur dyes are sodium sulphide (Na_2S) and sodium hydrosulphide (NaHS), and these products are commercially available in different forms at various concentrations. For simplicity and ease of comparison the recommended amounts applied are expressed here in terms of the full-strength product, i.e. 100% effective agent. Sodium sulphide is commonly available at 60% strength, i.e. one part full-strength product equivalent to 1.6 parts 60% product, while sodium hydrosulphide is widely used at 35% strength, i.e. one part full-strength product equivalent to 2.75 parts 35% product.

7.3.1 Reducing Agents
Sodium Sulphide
The traditional reducing agent for sulphur dyes is sodium sulphide, available as crystals (30–35%) or flakes (usually 60–62%, but may be as low as 50% in some parts of the world).
    The quantity of sodium sulphide required is dependent on the particular dyes being used and is usually directly proportional to dye weight, except in the case of pale colours when a minimum concentration in the region of 1.5–3 g/l full-strength (100%) sodium sulphide is used, the higher amount being recommended for yellow, orange, brown and khaki dyes.

Particularly when reducing the water-insoluble types, it is essential that at least 12 g/l full-strength sodium sulphide is present during dissolution and that sufficient of this solution is used to dissolve the dye fully. When dyeing very heavy depths at low liquor ratios it may be necessary to use the full dyebath volume to dissolve the dye. The amount of sodium sulphide required varies markedly for different dyes, and the recommendations of the manufacturer should be followed to obtain optimum results in most circumstances. However, it should be remembered that the recommendations are for normal conditions, such as jig or package dyeing, and abnormal conditions of use, e.g. excessive oxidation, may require some modification of the standard recommendations.

Sodium Hydrosulphide (Sodium Hydrogen Sulphide)
Sodium hydrosulphide is now widely used in place of sodium sulphide and is available at several different concentrations in liquid and powder form. Usage is as for sodium sulphide, but the amount of full-strength sodium hydrosulphide recommended is only 0.6 times that of the sulphide under similar circumstances, and an addition of alkali is necessary (10 g sodium carbonate or 5 g sodium hydroxide per 7 g sodium hydrosulphide).

This product is available from many sources, including the manufacturers of paper and viscose fibres. Although the quality varies, in some parts of the world it may be better than that of available sodium sulphide.

Caustic Soda/Sodium Dithionite
For many years this was the only sulphide-free dyeing system available for sulphur dyes, although it has never been universally popular; it is difficult to control and tends to give inconsistent results. The chief exception is the dyeing of certain sulphur vat dyes (C.I. Vat Blues 42 and 43, and C.I. Sulphur Black 11) which may be carried out in a caustic soda/dithionite bath only. A mixed system of sodium sulphide/caustic soda and sodium dithionite may be preferred in jig dyeing.

Typical recipes for package dyeing at 10:1 liquor ratio would range from 3.5 g/l caustic soda flake and 2.5 g/l sodium dithionite for a 1% dyeing to 7.5 g/l caustic soda flake and 7 g/l sodium dithionite for a 6% dyeing. These concentrations would be decreased (for example, by 30–40% at 20:1) or increased (correspondingly at 5:1) according to liquor ratio.

Traditional water-insoluble sulphur dyes reduced by this system have been used in warp dyeing of yarns for denims by the dye–dry–size system. Better colour yield is obtained than when using sulphide-reduced baths.

Sodium Carbonate/Sodium Dithionite
This is really only suitable for the water-soluble sulphur dyes as it is too weakly alkaline for the water-insoluble types and requires careful control if over-reduction and consequent low colour yield are to be avoided. Some dyes, for example C.I. Sulphur Red 6, Brown 15, Green 3 and Green 26 are not suitable for reduction with sodium dithionite, the colour being gradually destroyed.

Water-soluble black and blue sulphur dyes are well suited to this reduction system, and it is particularly useful for dyeing the flame-retardant viscose fibres that are sensitive to strong alkalis (e.g. Evlan FR). The flame-retardant properties are still satisfactory after this dyeing process (at 60–70°C), which is not the case with reduction systems employing caustic alkali.

The various dye manufacturers publish detailed information on the requirements of their different dyes. Typically 0.5–1.5 g sodium carbonate and 0.25–0.75 g sodium dithionite are recommended per gram of solubilised sulphur dye.

Glucose (Dextrose)
Together with sodium carbonate, caustic soda or a mixture of both, glucose is in increasing use where environmental considerations prevent the use of sulphide-based reduction systems, although it does present some problems of its own and not all dyes are satisfactorily reduced.

It may be used as additional reducing agent for the pre-reduced liquid brands, either in place of sodium sulphide or sodium hydrosulphide in order to lower the total sulphide content of the dyeing system, or together with sodium sulphide or sodium polysulphide when applying the water-insoluble types.

With the water-soluble dyes it may be used either as the total reducing system, i.e. a sulphide-free dye liquor, or together with sodium polysulphide to give improved dye yields, especially in continuous pad–steam systems (Figure 7.1) [2].

In package-dyeing systems the use of a caustic soda/sodium carbonate/glucose system has been found to give more consistent results than using either alkali alone. As glucose-based dyeing systems are both pH and temperature dependent, the combination of alkalis may well be buffering the system. At liquor ratios between

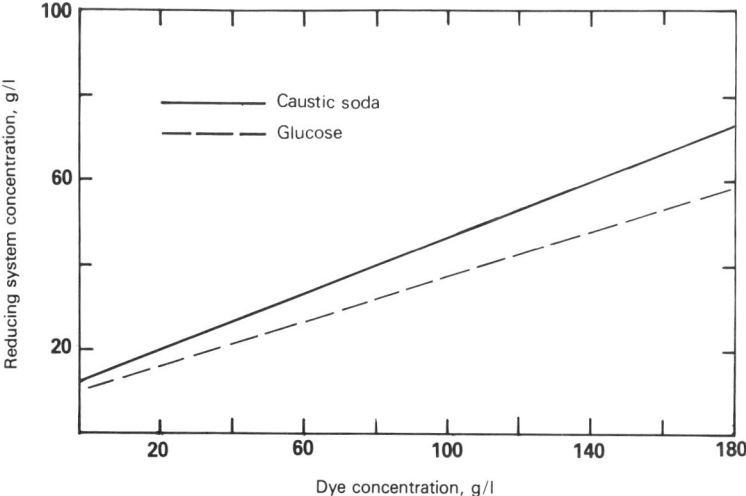

Figure 7.1 – Amounts of glucose and caustic soda required in the one-bath pad–steam process for applying solubilised sulphur dyes, in the presence of 7.5 ml/l sodium polysulphide

10:1 and 20:1 typical recommended concentrations are 3–8 g/l glucose, 4–10 g/l sodium carbonate and 2–6 g/l caustic soda flake, depending on applied depth. In all batchwise dyeing systems using glucose it is essential to maintain a temperature of 90–95°C for optimum results, regardless of the alkali selected. The system has a characteristic odour (of burning sugar) which may (or may not) be considered preferable to the familiar odour of a sulphide-reduced dyebath.

Mercaptoethanol
β-Mercaptoethanol (Molleskal SF, BASF) has been examined [2] for use with solubilised sulphur dyes, both by exhaust dyeing and by one-bath pad–steam processes. In combination with caustic soda, mercaptoethanol may be used in the application of most solubilised sulphur dyes although the colour yield is lower than from sulphide-reduced systems. Many of the water-insoluble dyes do not dissolve completely, and the sulphur vat types are not applicable from a mercaptoethanol-reduced dye liquor.

7.3.2 Dissolution Procedures
Dissolving sulphur dyes, especially the water-insoluble types, is generally considered to be the most important criterion in obtaining a satisfactory dyeing. The water-soluble and dispersed brands are much easier to prepare for dyeing, whilst the liquid brands are already in solution and should present no problem at all to the dyer.

Water-insoluble Dyes
These types are dissolved either by boiling for several minutes in a reducing solution (e.g. sodium sulphide) or by vatting with caustic soda and sodium dithionite in a similar manner to vat dyes.

In the first method the dyes are pasted with water and a suitable wetting agent, to which is added the required quantity of sodium sulphide (or sodium hydrosulphide/caustic soda) and sufficient water (approx. 30–50 ml per gram of dye to give a concentration of 20–30 g/l dye. This is the limiting concentration range below which most sulphur dyes readily dissolve. Notable dyes outside this range are C.I. Sulphur Black 1, which is normally soluble to 80–100 g/l and C.I. Sulphur Blue 13, which has a solubility of only 5–10 g/l.

The dye liquor should be thoroughly stirred, heated to the boil and allowed to simmer for 2–5 min with occasional agitation to ensure complete dissolution. When dissolving small quantities of dye it is essential to ensure that a minimum concentration of 12 g/l full-strength sodium sulphide is present. Conversely when dissolving large quantities of dyestuff it is necessary to ensure that the solubility limit of the dye is not exceeded.

Traditionally a small amount of sodium carbonate was added to the dyebath to neutralise acidity; nowadays this is more often to counteract water hardness. Alternatively a sequestering agent may be added. The dye liquor is then diluted to full dyebath volume at the required starting temperature.

In the alternative method the dyes are pasted with water and a suitable wetting agent, then 30–50 ml water per gram of dye are added, followed by the required amount of caustic soda. This liquor is heated to vatting temperature (60–70°C) and the sodium dithionite added. After stirring gently for 10–15 min to ensure complete dissolution, the leuco solution is added to the dyebath, which has been set with a small quantity of caustic soda and sodium dithionite.

Dispersed Powders or Pastes
These are simply sprinkled into warm water with vigorous stirring, preferably mechanical, to ensure uniform dispersion of the dye, which is then ready to use, either directly as a pad or pigmentation bath, or after reduction to a solution of the leuco form. Pale depths may require the addition of 1–2 g/l dispersing agent to maintain a satisfactory dyebath condition. When dyeing by a pad–dry–reduction method a migration inhibitor should be added to the pad liquor after the dye.

Liquid Dyes
These do not, of course, require boiling to dissolve as they are already in solution. However, some care is needed in the preparation of the dyebath and the following procedure is recommended:
1. Set the dyebath at 50–70% of its final volume
2. Add any required alkali (most yellow, orange and yellow-brown dyes require an addition of 1–3 g/l caustic soda flake for optimum shade and yield)
3. Add any required reducing agent (pale depths require an extra addition of reducing agent, 0.3–1.5 g/l full-strength sodium hydrosulphide, to maintain good dyebath reduction)
4. Add the dyes
5. Add the wetting agent and adjust to full volume.

The various dye manufacturers may recommend specific additions to individual dyes, and the appropriate pattern literature should always be consulted.

Water-soluble Dyes
These dyes should be dissolved by sprinkling into warm water (approx. 20–50 ml per gram of dye) containing the wetting agent and any sequestering agents. After stirring vigorously, the liquor is heated to the boil and allowed to simmer for 1–2 min to ensure complete dissolution, before dilution to full dyebath volume.

7.3.3 Oxidising Agents

Sodium Dichromate/Acetic Acid
Traditionally this is the preferred system for oxidising sulphur dyes. It is, however, increasingly under criticism on environmental grounds and for its adverse effects on handle and sewability.

For batchwise systems treatment in 1 g/l sodium dichromate and 0.8–1.2 g/l acetic acid for 15–20 min at 60°C is usually recommended. In continuous systems 5 g/l sodium dichromate and 6 g/l acetic acid is the usual starting bath at 60–70°C, with dwell times varying in the range 20–40 s.

Whilst the system is quite tolerant to variation in sodium dichromate concentration, better economy is obtained with close control and it is essential to maintain the pH at 4.5–5.5 for optimum oxidation. The addition of dispersing agents and sequestering agents to the oxidation bath has been recommended to improve rub fastness. Better wash fastness results are obtained if the goods are subsequently soaped-off.

Copper Sulphate/Sodium Dichromate/Acetic Acid
The addition of 1 g/l copper sulphate to batchwise oxidation baths of sodium dichromate and acetic acid improves the light fastness of material dyed with sulphur dyes by up to one point. The effect is most marked on yellow, orange, brown and khaki colours (traditionally the region of lowest light fastness). The treatment has a dulling effect, however, and gives a significantly harsher handle. It is not recommended for sulphur blacks, where the presence of copper promotes acid tendering. When carrying out this treatment it is essential that the copper sulphate is not added to the bath until all residual sodium sulphide has been destroyed and the pH is below 6. This avoids precipitation of copper as hydroxide or sulphide.

The copper is leached out by successive wet treatments and the effect is thereby diminished or lost altogether.

Potassium Iodate/Acetic Acid
This was possibly the first substitute for sodium dichromate but is now itself being replaced by a new generation of oxidants on environmental, economical and operational grounds.

Potassium iodate is normally used at either 0.2 g/l (batchwise) or 1 g/l (continuous) at 60°C together with acetic acid to maintain a pH of (ideally) 3.5–4.0. The oxidation rate slows markedly at pH levels above 4.5. Thermal decomposition at higher temperatures may partially reduce the iodate, and stronger acids, e.g. formic, may cause precipitation of the iodine formed, leading to corrosion and environmental problems.

Sodium Bromate
Although this product alone, or even with acetic acid, is ineffective as an oxidant for sulphur dyes, it has been found [3] that the addition of sodium metavanadate in catalytic quantities produces an oxidation system with properties approaching those of sodium dichromate and acetic acid. It is likely that this system will replace potassium iodate if the use of sodium dichromate becomes no longer permissible.

Dyetone (Olin), a proprietary solution of the catalyst-activated sodium bromate, is available and is used at either 1–2 g/l (batchwise) or 5–7 g/l (continuous) at 60–65°C. The pH should be maintained at 4–4.5 with acetic acid for optimum oxidation.

The fastness of dyeings oxidised with this system is similar to that from sodium dichromate or potassium iodate oxidation.

Hydrogen Peroxide/Sodium Perborate
The use of 1 ml/l hydrogen peroxide (130 vol.) or 1 g/l sodium perborate at 40°C for 10–20 min to give a brighter shade, especially with sulphur blues, is well known.

Unfortunately the wet fastness of the resultant dyeing may be lowered by one point or more (on grey scales) in respect of staining of adjacent fabrics, by comparison with sodium dichromate treatment. The treatment is also widely used in the oxidation of sulphur black, giving a bluer or lighter hue of marginally decreased wet fastness.

Under alkaline conditions the activity of peroxide is so great as to cause over-oxidation of the disulphide groups in the dye molecule, leading to the lower wet fastness referred to earlier. Hydrogen peroxide under mildly acid conditions gives a somewhat slower rate of oxidation, perhaps too slow for some red-browns, notably C.I. Sulphur Red 10, but a combination of 1 ml/l hydrogen peroxide (130 vol.) and 0.8 g/l acetic acid for 15–20 min at 50–60°C is widely used for the oxidation of package-dyed yarn.

Sodium Chlorite
This is the active constituent in a number of proprietary oxidising agents, e.g. Oxydurit SK (HOE), Protegal OD (Protex) and Sandopur DSC (S), the oxidation being carried out at alkaline pH (using sodium carbonate) at temperatures close to the boil. These proprietary products are understood to contain, in addition to sodium chlorite, stabilisers, EDTA-type sequestering agents and detergents. A French patent [4] claims that EDTA is essential to give the fully oxidised shade and optimum colour yield, whilst a Japanese patent [5] suggests that the absence of sequestering agent gives uneven dyeings.

Chlorite oxidation gives dyeings with good wet fastness and soft handle, but does not give complete oxidation with some sulphur red-browns, such as C.I. Sulphur Red 10. For batchwise systems a typical oxidation bath would be 2–3 g/l Protegal OD and 5 g/l sodium carbonate for 15–20 min at 90–95°C. Typical continuous conditions are 5–10 g/l Protegal OD and 5–10 g/l sodium carbonate for 1–2 min at 90–95°C.

Other Oxidants
The sodium salt of *m*-nitrobenzene sulphonate (Ludigol, BASF) is said to give uniformly complete oxidation on jet machines and winches. Typical concentrations are in the range 2–4 g/l in the presence of 2 g/l sodium carbonate for 20 min at 60°C.

It has been suggested [6] that the sodium salt of *N*-chloro-*p*-toluenesulphonamide (Chloramine T) can be used to achieve complete oxidation, at a concentration of 2 g/l for 10 min at 40°C.

In conjunction with sulphuric acid, sodium nitrite is an oxidant for sulphur dyes, but the risk of oxidative degradation of cellulosic fibres in such a system far outweighs any advantages.

7.3.4 Fixation Additives
Alkylating agents based on epichlorohydrin give dyeings of markedly improved fastness to severe washing treatments that use detergent/perborate formulations, such as are now standard practice in domestic washing. The alkylation treatment of the leuco dye also effectively oxidises the dyeing and so may replace a normal

oxidation treatment, except for those dyes which have a marked yellow leuco colour, e.g. C.I. Vat Blue 43 or C.I. Sulphur Blue 7, which should be given a mild oxidation treatment with hydrogen peroxide or sodium perborate before alkylation.

A typical product is Solidogen IH (CAS), which is applied at 2–3% o.w.f. with 1–2% sodium carbonate to give pH 10, beginning the treatment at 30–40°C (to ensure uniform uptake) then raising to 90–95°C for 10–15 min (to ensure full reaction).

The light fastness of the dyeing may be decreased by up to one point. In the event of the dyeing needing subsequent correction, alkylated sulphur dyes are difficult to strip and attempted removal will often entail destruction of the dye chromogen.

7.3.5 Crease-resist Finishing

Crease-resist finishing improves the fastness to wet treatments of sulphur dyeings by up to one point, whilst the light fastness is either unaffected or marginally improved. The effect on the colour of the dyeing is usually towards a redder/duller tone.

7.3.6 Antioxidants

Sodium polysulphide is widely used as an antioxidant in dyebaths reduced with sodium sulphide, sodium hydrosulphide or glucose. It is not compatible with sodium dithionite, however. It inhibits premature oxidation of the sulphide reducing agent, thereby promoting better dyebath stability, especially under adverse dyeing conditions, e.g. winch, jet or jig machines. This lessens the risks of bronzing, poor rubbing fastness and dark selvedges.

7.3.7 Wetting Agents

The number of wetting agents currently on the market and the rate of appearance of new products makes any specific recommendation impracticable. The majority of sulphur dyes are unaffected by most wetting agents, but several dyes, notably C.I. Sulphur Red 10 and Blue 13, are adversely affected by some products, which either inhibit the dye uptake in exhaust dyeing or precipitate the dye as a tarry leuco product. Surfactants of this kind usually contain non-ionic groupings and should be avoided, both in pre-scouring and in the dyebath itself.

7.3.8 Sequestering Agents

Sequestering agents based on sodium hexametaphosphate, ethylenediamine tetra-acetic acid or ethylenediamine tetracarbonic acid are widely used in dyeing with sulphur dyes where the water quality is low or variable. The presence of heavy-metal ions in the dye liquor or in the substrate will usually lead to poor rub fastness or uneven dyeings in some form; many dyers regard sequestering agents as essential insurance against these problems.

7.3.9 Rinsing and Soaping

Thorough rinsing *before* oxidation is essential with sulphur dyes if good rubbing fastness is to be obtained. It is most important that all loose colour should be removed before the acidic oxidation stage, which precipitates any unfixed dye on the surface of the fabric (or on the outside of a package), giving a 'bronzy' dyeing with low wet rub fastness.

Heavy-depth dyeings, but not usually pale to medium depths, are soaped-off after oxidation. This gives an increase in brightness, together with improved fastness to washing in respect of change in colour of the dyed pattern.

There is considerable difference of opinion on the relative merits of soap or synthetic detergent. The latter is undoubtedly preferable in hard water, but whichever is used an addition of soda ash is recommended. Thus 1–3 g/l soap or detergent and 2 g/l soda ash for 15–20 min at 90–95°C would be a typical recommendation for batchwise processing, whilst 5–10 g/l soap or detergent and 2–5 g/l soda ash for 30–60 s at the boil would be recommended for continuous processing.

7.4 APPLICATION METHODS

The dissolution of the various types of sulphur dye in preparation for dyeing has already been described in section 7.3.2. The substantivity of sulphur dyes for cellulosic fibres differs according to the particular substrate. Thus mercerised cotton and viscose fibres are dyed more heavily than unmercerised cotton. Substantivity varies from dye to dye and from one brand to another. Dye liquors prepared from the liquid brands containing the leuco liquid form, being virtually electrolyte free, are exhausted to a much lower extent than dye liquors prepared from the traditional powders, which invariably contain electrolyte added during dye standardisation. The quantity of diluent added in this way, however, is insufficient to give optimum exhaustion under batchwise dyeing conditions.

The rate of exhaustion of sulphur dyes is slow at low temperatures, but some dyeing can be expected to take place even at 45–50°C. In the case of liquid brands of leuco dyes this is very slight until electrolyte has been added. The rate of exhaustion may be controlled by temperature or by the gradual addition of electrolyte, and it is standard practice to add electrolytes to the dyebath, usually sodium chloride or anhydrous sodium sulphate, to promote exhaustion. It is essential to use good grades of these products, avoiding those containing calcium or magnesium salts. These tend to precipitate the dye and reducing agents as insoluble salts, and thus lower the rub fastness of the resultant dyeing, as do iron salts from rusty water pipes or machinery.

The addition of electrolyte to the dyebath in batchwise dyeing processes may be made either at the start or on reaching the top temperature; opinions vary as to which gives the best results. Where additions can be made with relative ease, e.g. on the jig, the addition of electrolyte at dyeing temperature is probably favoured as some dye has already exhausted onto the fibre. On machinery where addition is difficult, incorporating the salt at the start of the dyeing and gradually raising the temperature to control exhaustion is preferred.

For pale depths it may be preferable to forgo the electrolyte addition to reduce the possibility of an uneven dyeing. In pale to medium depths an addition of 5–10 g/l salt is normally adequate, adding 10–20 g/l salt in medium to heavy depths where there is less risk of unevenness.

In continuous dyeing, however, the presence of electrolyte may promote tailing, hence the preferred use of the pre-reduced liquid brands, which contain the leuco dye and minimal electrolyte, at padding temperatures as low as possible consistent with good absorption of pad liquor. This is often a compromise between what would be ideal and what is realistic, but for continuous dyeing fabric preparation should always produce a substrate with high and uniform absorbency.

Solubilised sulphur dyes may be used in pad–dry–chemical-pad–steam processes because they are not substantive to cellulose, hence tailing should not be a problem even at elevated padding temperatures.

7.4.1 Preparation

For special effects or fashion requirements minimal or even zero preparation may give the desired results, but to obtain high quality and reproducibility thorough preparation is essential. Yarn is often given a light scour only, but may be bleached for pale or brighter colours. Fabric should be desized and scoured to give good absorbency, especially for continuous dyeing, and may be bleached for brighter colours.

7.4.2 Yarn

In dyeing any form of wound package, be it cone, cheese or beam, thorough wetting out is essential. The most common method is a scour using sodium carbonate, a sequestering agent and a wetting agent or detergent, although some dyers prefer acetic acid instead of sodium carbonate when the yarn is known to contain calcium or magnesium salts. In either case treatment for 15–30 min at 80–90°C should be sufficient.

Whenever possible, soft water should be used in all package-dyeing operations.

Package Dyeing

The most suitable dyes are either the water-soluble sulphur dyes, which may be applied in a non-substantive form to obtain uniform penetration of the package, followed by reduction, or the pre-reduced liquid brands, which require no pre-boiling and may be more easily added to the machine, in portions if desired.

The preparation of packages suitable for dyeing is quite critical. For package dyeing the requirement is for consistent winding, as variation in tightness of packages within a dye lot will lead to channelling and uneven dyeing. Whilst soft packages are undoubtedly easier to dye, many dyehouses process hard packages quite satisfactorily using machinery capable of providing a good rate of flow of dye liquor.

For beam dyeing uniform density of winding is essential. If the beam is too soft or contains too few ends it will be more prone to 'bursting', i.e. dye liquor breaking through the mass of yarn and effectively ruining any chance of obtaining a level result.

A typical method for the pre-reduced brands, after wetting out or scouring, would be as follows:
1. Set the bath at 40°C with 0.6 g/l full-strength sodium sulphide, 1 g/l sequestering agent and 1 ml/l antioxidant and then circulate for 10 min
2. Add the dye in one to four portions over 10 min, then raise to 75–90°C and circulate for 10 min
3. Add 5–20 g/l salt slowly over 20 min and run for a further 10 min.

Throughout dyeing the flow direction should be changed every 5 min. Rinsing should be by overflow until clear, then rinse hot and oxidise. Heavy depths may be soaped-off.

Blacks should always be finished with an alkaline rinse containing 2–5 g/l sodium carbonate or 5–10 g/l sodium acetate to prevent possible tendering problems.

A typical method for the water-soluble brands would be:
1. Dissolve the dye by boiling for 30–60 s and circulate for 10–15 min at 35–40°C, then add the reducing agent and circulate for 10–15 min
2. Raise to 75–90°C and run for 10 min
3. Add 5–20 g/l salt over 20 min and run for a further 10 min.

The frequency of flow change, rinsing and oxidation stages are as for the liquid brands.

Sulphur dyes may be applied at 120°C with consequent savings in time and, it is claimed, some improvement in levelness. Dyebaths should be cooled to 70–80°C, however, before rinsing by overflow and oxidation as for normal-temperaure dyeings.

Beam Dyeing
Beam dyeing machines may be vertical or horizontal; in the latter design the beam is only partially immersed in the dye liquor and hence the flow is entirely in-to-out. Even on fully immersed beams the flow may be maintained in-to-out to avoid disturbance to the package and attendant risk of bursting of the beam. The following method would be suitable for dyeing with the pre-reduced liquid brands:
1. Set the bath at 20–30°C with 1–2 ml/l sodium hydrosulphide, 0.5 g/l caustic soda flake, 1–2 ml/l sequestering agent, 10–20 g/l salt and then circulate the liquor for 10 min
2. Add the dyes and circulate for a further 10 min
3. Raise the temperature to 80–90°C over 40–45 min and continue dyeing at 80–90°C for a further 30–45 min.

Rinsing is by overflow without dropping the bath until the rinse water is clear. The bath is then dropped and the material is given one cold rinse before oxidising as for package dyeing.

Continuous Warp Dyeing
The yarn in the form of a web or sheet, or sometimes in rope form, is passed successively through vessels containing wetting agent and soda ash, dyes, rinse

water and oxidation chemical, and then receives further rinsing (and possibly soaping). The process may be repeated when dyeing deep colours in order to build up the required depth. When the desired colour has been achieved the yarn is passed through a bath containing fibre lubricants, waxes, softener and (perhaps) size in order to facilitate the weaving operation, before finally drying. This dyeing method was widespread until the 1960s, but now is used in only a small number of dyehouses in its traditional form. However, the indigo dyeing range and the 'slasher dyer' or 'dyeing in the size box' are regarded as developments of warp dyeing, and sulphur dyes may be applied in both systems.

In the indigo dyeing machine cotton yarn is passed successively through tanks containing wetting agent and caustic alkali at the boil, four or five tanks containing indigo dye reduced with caustic soda and sodium dithionite (with airing passages between each tank), rinsing water and finally drying cans. In order to dye more economically some dyers add C.I. Leuco Sulphur Black 1 at relatively low concentration to the preparation tank before applying the much more expensive indigo. Other producers use a sulphur blue, e.g. C.I. Leuco Sulphur Blue 7 or 20.

Some dyers claim, however, that carry-over of sodium sulphide into the indigo tanks can adversely affect the chemical balance of the reducing system, lowering the colour yield. They suggest that applying the sulphur dye after the indigo in the last tank before rinsing is preferable. In this case a sulphur blue should be used, as black dulls the colour to an unacceptable degree.

Dyeing in the sizing machine or slasher is a very simple form of warp dyeing, widely used in dyeing warp yarns for the denim trade, where the processing is pad(dye)–dry–pad(size)–dry. Although not ideal for the process as usually practised, sulphur dyes are used in some parts of the world to produce 'coloured denim', i.e. colours other than blue. Pre-reduced liquid dyes (C.I. Leuco Sulphur liquids) may be applied by padding at 40°C, followed by a short air passage and drying. The yarn then enters the size box, which contains acetic acid to neutralise residual alkali and give some degree of oxidation in the drying stage.

Improved colour yields are obtained from the water-insoluble brands reduced with caustic soda and sodium dithionite, which are reoxidised much more readily than the sodium sulphide reduction system used in most leuco liquid sulphur dyes.

After a short air passage and drying, the acetic acid in the size box neutralises the residual alkali, and the full depth and yield of the dye is obtained.

7.4.3 Knitted Fabric

Knitted fabric in its many forms can be dyed in black, blue and brown colours on either winch or jet machines, usually after a light scour with detergent and sodium carbonate, although some fabrics may require more severe pretreatment incorporating a solvent in order to obtain a satisfactory dyeing.

Winch Dyeing

In general, the heavier the fabric, the better the result; lightweight fabrics are more difficult to process since they are more prone to float in the dyebath, leading to local oxidation and the possibility of bronzy patches. In addition such fabrics carry less dye liquor over the winch reel and hence tend to reoxidise more rapidly than heavier fabrics. The addition to the dye liquor of an antioxidant based on sodium polysulphide is essential in winch dyeing to prevent premature oxidation of the reducing agent.

The leuco or the solubilised sulphur dyes are preferred. A typical recipe for a black on 100% cotton knitted fabric at a liquor ratio of 20:1 would be:
- C.I. Leuco Sulphur Black 1, 15–20%
- Caustic soda flake, 0.5–1.0 g/l
- Sodium hydrosulphide (full strength), 0.6–1.2 g/l
- Antioxidant, 2–5 ml/l
- Salt, 10–20 g/l.

After scouring and rinsing, set the bath at 40–45°C with all the chemicals, including the salt, and run for 10 min before adding the dye. Run for a further 10 min before raising the temperature to 90–95°C over 30–45 min. Continue dyeing for 30 min before rinsing by overflow until clear. The temperature should then be adjusted as required for oxidation, e.g. to 40–45°C for oxidation with 1–2 ml/l hydrogen peroxide over 15–20 min. The goods are then rinsed and finished in a bath containing lubricant and softener, bearing in mind that all sulphur blacks should be finished on the alkaline side with 2–3 g/l sodium carbonate.

The following recipe has been suggested for solubilised sulphur dyes. After scouring and rinsing, set the dyebath at 40–45°C with a suitable wetting agent, add the dissolved dye and run the winch for 10 min. Add the required quantity of reducing agent, together with 2–5 ml/l antioxidant (sodium polysulphide) and raise the temperature to 80–90°C over 30–45 min. Then add 10–20 g/l salt over 15–20 min and continue dyeing for 20–30 min before rinsing and oxidising, using hydrogen peroxide and acetic acid, catalyst-activated sodium bromate and acetic acid, or sodium chlorite in alkaline solution (see section 7.3.3)

In some winch vessels it is impossible to maintain a temperature of 90–95°C throughout the machine. In these circumstances glucose-based reduction systems are likely to give unsatisfactory results since a minimum temperature of 90°C is essential to maintain full reduction.

Jet Dyeing
The first jet dyeing machines to be produced were largely unsuitable for dyeing sulphur colours because the turbulence created in the dye liquor effectively oxidised the reducing agents so rapidly that antioxidants were ineffective.

Modern machines, however, are generally quite suitable for sulphur dyes and give better results than winch dyeing equipment, especially when glucose-based reduction systems are involved, as the required temperature of 90–95°C may easily be maintained. In addition the enclosed conditions of the jet dyeing machine significantly minimise the problems of reoxidation which adversely affect winch dyeing with sulphur dyes.

The following recipe is typical of the application of a leuco sulphur black on a jet. Set the machine (after scouring and rinsing the fabric) at 40–45°C with:

- Caustic soda flake, 0.25–0.5 g/l
- Sodium hydrosulphide (full strength), 0.3–0.6 g/l
- Antioxidant (sodium polysulphide), 1–2 ml/l
- Defoamer (if required)
- Salt, 10–20 g/l.

and run for 15 min. Add the dye and run for a further 15 min before raising the temperature to 80–90°C over 30–45 min and run for 20–30 min. Rinse by pumping in clean water and running the dye liquor to drain, until the wash water is clear, then reoxidise as for winch dyeing.

The sulphide-free reducing system based on glucose is ideal for jet dyeing because many dyehouses operating jets are situated in areas in which sulphur dyes have tended not to be used. Hence permission to pass sulphides into the sewerage system is difficult, if not impossible, to obtain.

High-temperature dyeing machinery is more suited to sulphur dyes than atmospheric equipment, even when dyeing at temperatures of 90–95°C, as foaming tends to be a greater problem at atmospheric pressure. It can be controlled by defoaming agents, the long-chain fatty alcohol types (e.g. nonyl alcohol) having been found by experience to give the best results with sulphur dyes. As with all foaming problems, however, it is usually easier to prevent foam forming than to destroy it once it has formed.

The following procedure has been suggested for dyeing C.I. Solubilised Sulphur Black 1 on a jet machine, using caustic soda, sodium carbonate and glucose. In addition to being sulphide free, this reduction system also has the virtue of leaving dyeing machinery in a particularly clean condition, whereas sulphide-based systems and certain other classes of dyes usually require some cleaning down following the dyeing of full black shades:

- C.I. Solubilised Sulphur Black 1, 10–15%
- Caustic soda flake, 2–4 g/l
- Sodium carbonate, 4–8 g/l
- Glucose, 3–6 g/l
- Defoamer (if required)
- Salt 15–20 g/l.

After scouring and rinsing, set the bath at 40–45°C with the dissolved dye and run for 15 min. Add the pre-dissolved alkali and glucose (glucose dissolves readily in dilute alkaline solution) and run for a further 15 min before raising the temperature to 90–95°C. Run for 10 min before adding the salt over 15 min and continue for a further 20–30 min at 90–95°C. Rinse by flooding until clear, before oxidising with 1–2 ml/l hydrogen peroxide (130 vol.) for 15 min at 40–45°C. Rinse and finish with softener, lubricant, etc. (the final rinse should contain 2–5 g/l sodium carbonate to prevent any possibility of tendering).

This procedure could also be used in the dyeing of blues and browns using appropriate solubilised sulphur dyes.

Garment Dyeing
Some garments are dyed in Dytex machines, which are very similar to the drums used for dry cleaning. If possible, the dry goods are entered into the prepared dye liquor in order to achieve good penetration of the seams, which are invariably difficult to penetrate fully. Often, however, the goods must be pre-scoured with detergent and alkali to obtain a satisfactory ground for dyeing. Leuco liquid or solubilised sulphur dyes are recommended, the dyeing methods being suggested for liquor ratios of 10:1 or 15:1.

For leuco liquid dyes set the dyebath at 40°C with:
- Sodium hydrosulphide, 1–2 ml/l
- Antioxidant, 2–3 ml/l
- Caustic soda flake, 0.5–1 g/l
- Wetting agent, 1 g/l
- Dyes, x%.

Enter the goods and run for 15 min. Raise to 90°C over 20–30 min before adding 10–20 g/l salt over 10–15 min and running for a further 20–30 min. Rinse cold by overflow until clear, then oxidise and finally rinse.

For solubilised sulphur dyes set the dyebath at 40°C with the required pre-dissolved dyes and 1 ml/l wetting agent, enter the goods and run for 15 min. Add the required reducing agent and run for 15 min before raising the temperature to 90–95°C over 20–30 min. Add 10–20 g/l salt over 10–15 min and run for a further 20–30 min before rinsing by overflow until clear, oxidising and finally rinsing.

7.4.4 Batchwise Dyeing of Woven Fabrics
Sulphur dyes are widely applied on jigs, ranging in batch size from 200 to 1500 m and in width from 75 to 300 cm. Regardless of batch dimensions, complete removal of all contaminants such as size, fats and waxes is essential to obtain satisfactory results.

A thorough desize using an enzyme, followed by a caustic scour (and bleaching if necessary for brighter colours) or a combined caustic/peroxide scour/desize and bleach system may be employed. The fabric may be prepared on the jig immediately prior to dyeing, or alternatively on a pad–batch, pad–roll or continuous preparation range. Whichever system is employed, regular checks on starch and wax content should be made to ensure that a consistent quality of preparation is being achieved.

Full details of preparation techniques may be found in Chapter 2.

Jig Dyeing
The essential requirement in jig dyeing is a constant rate of uptake of dye, since there is little or no possibility for subsequent levelling. The dye liquor is normally divided into portions, two-thirds being added at the start and the remainder after the first end. All the chemicals, apart from any reducing agent necessary for the second portion, are added at the start. This is simple in theory, but much more difficult in practice, especially when dyeing medium to heavy depths with the insoluble powder brands, since the limited solubility may necessitate dissolving the

dyes in the jig trough. In these circumstances the jig roll should be 'swung' whilst the second portion is being prepared. The liquid brands may be simply divided into two portions and added over two ends with no need to stop the jig. Electrolyte is also added over two ends, and a typical dyeing procedure (20–32 ends) would be as follows:

1. Add dyes over two ends and run two ends
2. Add salt over two ends and run two to four ends
3. Rinse cold over four to six ends and hot over two ends
4. Oxidise over two to four ends and rinse over two to four ends
5. Soap over two ends and rinse over two to four ends.

With the steadily increasing size of jigs and batch sizes, the length of one end may be 20–30 min and the above sequence becomes impracticable and uneconomic. A shorter process is required and so modern jigs are equipped with spray bars for increased rinsing efficiency. The following modified process (14–18 ends) is increasingly in use:

1. Add dyes over two ends and salt over two ends
2. Run two ends and rinse cold over two to four ends
3. Oxidise over two ends and rinse hot over two ends
4. Soap (synthetic detergent) over two ends and rinse over two ends.

Proprietary oxidising formulations containing detergents are now available; these permit reoxidation and soaping in one step. Alternatively a detergent or dispersing agent may be added to the oxidation bath. The addition of a fatty alcohol polyoxyethylene adduct, e.g. Ekaline F (S), to dichromate/acetic acid oxidation baths has been recommended.

Bronzing of blacks and navies, due to premature oxidation of dye, or precipitation by metals such as calcium, magnesium or iron is a fairly common problem. It may be overcome or minimised by the addition of an antioxidant such as sodium polysulphide, or a sequestering agent. Lower dyeing temperatures (60–65°C) have been found to be beneficial in dyeing blue and navy colours.

Pad–Jig
The solubilised and dispersed sulphur dyes are the most suitable for application by this method owing to their lack of substantivity during impregnation. After padding the goods may be stored on a rotating batch or run directly into the jig already set with reducing agent and salt at 80–90°C, and then run for four to six ends before rinsing and oxidising.

Some dyers use the leuco liquid brands by this method, especially when heavyweight or tightly woven fabrics are being processed, in order to obtain better penetration. In this case the padded goods are run directly onto the jig set with a small quantity of reducing agent (1–2 ml/l) and 10–20 g/l salt at 80–90°C, and then run for four to six ends before rinsing and oxidising.

In all pad–jig processing an addition to the jig of 10–20 ml/l pad liquor is recommended in order to achieve equilibrium conditions more rapidly in the jig development stage.

The pad jig method is particularly useful in the dyeing of mercerised cotton or viscose fabrics, where the rapid strike onto the fibre makes subsequent uniform penetration of the fabric more difficult.

Pad–Batch and Pad–Roll
These processes were originally developed for the application of reactive dyes and have been used with limited success for sulphur dyes. The leuco liquid brands are preferred; extra reducing agent and antioxidant are added to the pad liquor to compensate for oxidation during the batching operation.

The additions required are 1.5–4 g/l full-strength sodium hydrosulphide and 2–6 ml/l antioxidant (sodium polysulphide), using the higher quantities for lower dye concentrations, together with a suitable wetting agent (5 ml/l). For heavier depths 10–15 g/l anhydrous sodium sulphate gives improved fixation.

For cold pad–batch dyeing a minimum of 3 h batching at room temperature is recommended. If large batches are being processed it may be convenient to store them overnight. In the pad–roll process, now virtually obsolete, shorter storage times of 15–60 min at 100–102°C in a saturated-steam chamber are sufficient.

A pad liquor temperature of 40°C with a pick-up of 80–100% is suitable for both processes, with rinsing and oxidation sequences as for pad–steam processing (see section 7.4.5).

7.4.5 Continuous Dyeing
Greater quantities of sulphur dyes are applied by continuous dyeing than by all other methods put together. Traditionally cotton pile fabrics have been a major market sector for sulphur dyeing and many millions of metres were dyed each week during the corduroy fashion boom of the late 1970s.

To produce good results in continuous dyeing it is essential to prepare to a consistently high level of absorbency, and this can only be achieved by close quality control of a continuous fabric preparation range. Any variation in residual starch or wax content will lead to variation in dye uptake and subsequent unlevelness, which is almost impossible to correct on a continuous basis.

Cotton fabrics are often mercerised before continuous dyeing for reasons of economy in dye consumption rather than any increase in lustre. Close control of the mercerising process is also essential if variations in dyeability along the warp yarns and from selvedge to selvedge are to be avoided.

Pad–Steam
The production of level dyeings is dependent on many factors, e.g. the pad mangle, air-free steam and efficient washing. Possibly the most important is fabric preparation. The fabric must be highly and uniformly absorbent so that padding may take place at as low a temperature as possible in order to minimise tailing effects. Increasingly dye manufacturers are supplying information relating to feed ratios, i.e. the dye concentrations in the feed liquor relative to those in the pad liquor at the start. But these data should be used as guides only, as the pretreatment of the fabric, running speeds and dwell time in the pad vary so widely as to make specific recommendations almost impossible.

Machinery requirements for pad–steam dyeing are simple to state but more difficult to achieve in practice and may be summarised briefly as follows. The pad trough should be as small as possible, equipped with an efficient constant-level device fed from one of two mixing tanks (the second being recharged to ensure a constant flow of dye liquor for continuous running). The mixing tanks should be equipped with good temperature control to maintain the required pad liquor temperature, stirrers and water supply to facilitate rapid rinsing down.

The pad mangle should be of high quality since uneven application of dye liquor will give uneven dyeings, there being no migration in a pad–steam dyeing system. For 100% cotton the pick-up will normally be 60–80%, whilst for polyester/cotton it might be 50–70%.

The steamer should be airtight and supplied with air-free saturated steam at 102–105°C, the design being such as to prevent condensation spots and provide a steaming time of 30–60 s at the desired running speeds. Typically these may be 30–100 m/min in Europe but up to 180 m/min in the USA. Air in the steamer may lead to premature oxidation of the dyeing, giving bronzing, poor rubbing fastness and possibly unlevelness, if air is drawn across the fabric causing local cooling and/or oxidation. It is usually quite easy to seal the exit via a water trough, but the entry seal is more difficult to achieve; machinery manufacturers adopt different approaches.

Thorough rinsing before chemical oxidation is vital to the attainment of satisfactory fastness. To this end the water seal at the steamer exit and the first wash box especially should have a very good water supply to give a high rate of liquor change. Subsequent wash boxes should, of course, also have good water supplies in which the countercurrent principle may be employed.

Oxidation may be performed in one or two boxes, depending on the particular system in use. Soaping off is preferable, especially with heavy depths, but regrettably some pad–steam systems have insufficient boxes to enable this operation to be carried out. The variation between washing ranges is wide, from as few as four to as many as 14 boxes, and running speeds also vary from 20 up to 150 m/min.

A typical pad–steam process, using an eight-box washing range is as follows:
1. Padding: Leuco sulphur liquid dye, x g/l
   Reducing agent, y g/l
   Wetting agent, 5 ml/l
   Temperature 40°C, pick-up 60–80%
2. Steam: 1 min at 102–105°C
3. Rinsing: Box 1 – Cold water
   Box 2 – Warm water 40–50°C
   Box 3 – Hot water 60°C
   Box 4 – Oxidation
   Box 5 – Hot water 60°C
   Box 6 – Soaping 90°C
   Box 7 – Hot water 60°C
   Box 8 – Cold water 20–30°C.

Up to 5 ml/l reducing agent would be added for pale depths, whilst many corduroy dyers add 3.5–7 ml/l full-strength sodium hydrosulphide to all pad liquors to counter-act the oxidation caused by air trapped within the pile.

Pad–Sky
The process sequence is identical to that for pad–steam, but the steaming stage is re-placed by a simple air passage of 30–60 s duration, followed by rinsing and oxidation as for pad–steam.

This system is really only suitable for relatively pale colours as heavier depths give poor colour yield and inferior fastness to washing and rubbing. The system has been used for speciality requirements, such as wash-down effects, where the desired result is obtained as a consequence of the decreased fastness properties.

Pad–Dry–Develop
In recent years a number of ways have been suggested for avoiding the steaming route, using dry heat fixation, with or without intermediate drying. For example, Hoechst has recommended the following process for solubilised sulphur dyes in pale to medium depths only; the rub fastness of heavy depths is unsatisfactory. Dissolve x g/l dyes and add 30–50 g/l urea, 25–50 g/l Hydrosol Fixer KT (HOE) (pre-dissolved), 5 g/l Cassapret P Conc (HOE) and 3–5 ml/l wetting agent. Pad at 20–30°C, dry at 120°C, fix for 1 min at 150–175°C. The dyeings are said to need only rinsing, no oxidation being necessary.

Pad–Dry–Chemical-pad–Steam
This system is claimed to give a much better surface appearance to the fabric, although it does have cost disadvantages for 100% cotton fabrics since it involves an intermediate drying stage. It is applicable to polyester/cotton blends by the inclu-sion of a thermofixation stage for the disperse dyes after drying.

Solubilised sulphur dyes may be used for 100% cotton fabric, with a chemical-pad reduction using any of the reducing agents mentioned in section 7.3.1. Alterna-tively the dispersed sulphur dyes now being introduced (such as Asathio Homodye (KKK), Sodyevat (RQ/SDC) or Sulphol Hi Fast (JR) types) may be used, probably with a caustic/dithionite reduction stage.

A third possibility is to use the pre-reduced liquid brands, and to reduce again with sodium sulphide or hydrosulphide at the chemical pad. This is claimed to give better surface appearance than the direct pad–steam system. The drying stage does give rise to more unpleasant fumes than from the other dye types. It is not suitable for sulphur blacks.

The subsequent rinsing and oxidation stages are similar to pad–steam processing.

Typical formulations for a black would be 100 g/l C.I. Solubilised Sulphur Black 1, 5 ml/l wetting agent and 10–20 ml/l migration inhibitor padded at 20–30°C, 60% pick-up and dried for 1 min at 120°C. This would be followed by 60 g/l full-strength sodium sulphide, 2 ml/l wetting agent, 2–5 ml/l sequestering agent and 10–20 ml/l dye-pad liquor padded at 30–40°C, 70–80% pick-up; steaming would be for 30–60 s at 102–105°C.

The addition of the dye-pad liquor to the chemical pad helps to establish a state of equilibrium in the chemical-pad liquor by preventing initial bleed-off of dye from the fabric into the chemical-pad liquor.

Electrolyte may also be added to the chemical pad to increase the fixation when dyeing medium to heavy depths; a concentration of 10–15 g/l anhydrous sodium sulphate is recommended.

The dispersed sulphur dyes are applied in a similar manner, although, as some of them are not dyeable from a sulphide reduction liquor, a combination of 20–30 g/l caustic soda flake and 40–60 g/l sodium dithionite would provide more suitable reducing conditions.

Leuco liquid dyes may be applied by the following method, bearing in mind that C.I. Sulphur Black 1 does not give satisfactory results. Pad x g/l dyes, 1–3 g/l sodium hexametaphosphate and 5 ml/l wetting agent at 40°C and dry for 1 min at 105–120°C. Then pad 5–17.5 g/l full-strength sodium sulphide or sodium hydrosulphide and 10–20 g/l sodium chloride or anhydrous sodium sulphate, steam for 1 min at 102–105°C. Rinsing and oxidation are as for pad–steam dyeing.

7.4.6 Dyeing of Blends

Polyester/Cellulosic Blends

Dyeing of polyester requires a high-temperature fixation stage. This is usually thermofixation, although it may be carried out on HT jet dyeing equipment. Carrier dyeing should be avoided since residual carrier has been shown to promote partial destruction of certain disperse dyes on the polyester during the subsequent sulphur dyeing stage.

In continuous dyeing disperse dyes for the polyester may be padded alone, followed by drying and thermofixation. The leuco sulphur dyes are applied in the second pad, followed by steaming. Alternatively the disperse dyes may be applied together with solubilised sulphur or dispersed sulphur dyes in the initial pad bath, followed by drying and thermofixation, the chemical pad being set with any of the reducing systems mentioned in section 7.3.1.

Advantages to be gained from the latter route are better fabric appearance, the possibility of using various reducing agents (including non-sulphide systems) and possibly some savings on initial capital cost, since it is possible to use a pad mangle of lower quality for the chemicals applied in the second padding stage. Disadvantages include lower colour yields and the need for more costly forms of sulphur dyes than the leuco pad system using the pre-reduced liquid brands.

There is normally no necessity for a reduction clear treatment after thermofixation when leuco padding with sulphur dyes on the cellulosic portion of a polyester/cellulosic blend. The reduction systems necessary for the fixation of the sulphur dyes also clears any unfixed disperse dyes, although it may be necessary to increase the quantity of reducing agent to allow for that used up by reaction with the disperse dyes.

Polyester/cotton drill and corduroy fabrics are important, although polyester is seldom used as a corduroy pile fibre. Coloration of the polyester, albeit only in the back of the fabric, still necessitates a full thermofixation process if good wash fast-ness of the disperse dyeing is to be obtained. The use of a lick roller to apply pad liquor to the back of the fabric only, instead of a normal pad application, helps to minimise the amount of disperse dyes applied to (and therefore to be subsequently removed from) the cotton, thereby increasing the efficiency and economy of the process.

The viscose component of polyester/viscose blends is often dyed with sulphur dyes, especially by continuous dyeing with leuco liquid brands in the USA. A typical recipe for the two-stage system (pad–thermofix application of disperse dyes followed by pad–steam dyeing with sulphur dyes) is as follows. Pad x g/l disperse dyes, 20 ml/l migration inhibitor and 0.8 g/l acetic acid at 20–30°C, 50–60% pick-up. Dry for 1 min at 120°C and thermofix for 1 min at 200–220°C. Then pad y g/l C.I. Leuco Sulphur liquid dyes, 2–3 g/l caustic soda flake, 3.5–7 ml/l full-strength sodium hydrosulphide, 2–3 ml/l wetting agent and 2–3 ml/l sequestering agent at 40°C, 60–70% pick-up, followed by steaming for 30–60 s at 102–105°C. Rinsing, oxidation and soaping are as for pad–steam processing.

With the 'all-in' system, using disperse dyes for the polyester and either solu-bilised sulphur or dispersed sulphur/sulphur vat dyes in the first stage, followed by a chemical pad and steaming, the following sequence of operations should be followed. Dissolve the solubilised sulphur dyes by boiling, dilute and cool to 20–30°C and adjust the pH to 4.5–5.5. Alternatively dilute the sulphur/sulphur vat dispersion to approximately two-thirds of the final volume and adjust the pH to 4.5–5.5. Add the disperse dyes and the pre-diluted solution of the migration inhibitor, recheck and adjust the pH to 4.5–5.5 if necessary, before making up to full volume. Pad at 20–30°C, 50–60% pick-up. Dry for 1 min at 120°C and ther-mofix for 1 min at 200–220°C. The chemical-pad liquor contains 25–35 g/l caustic soda flake, 40–60 g/l sodium dithionite, 3–5 ml/l wetting agent and 1–3 ml/l seques-tering agent. This is padded at 40°C, 60–70% pick-up followed by steaming for 1 min at 102–105°C. Rinsing and oxidation are as for the pad–steam process.

A single-bath method for polyester/cotton blends has been proposed by James Robinson & Co. Ltd [7] by a pad–dry–thermofixation route using thiourea as the fixing agent for solubilised sulphur dyes. Selection of the dyes is critical as some dis-perse dyes are unstable in the pad liquor. The process typically uses x g/l solubilised sulphur dyes, y g/l disperse dyes, x g/l thiourea (minimum 40 g/l), 10–20 ml/l migra-tion inhibitor, 3–5 ml/l wetting agent and acetic acid to adjust the pH to 5–6. Dis-solve the thiourea and solubilised sulphur dyes by boiling in water, cool to 30–40°C and adjust to pH 5–6 with acetic acid. Add the disperse dyes and migration in-hibitor and then dilute to the required volume. Pad at 60–70% expression, dry for 1 min at 120–130°C and then thermofix for 1 min at 200–220°C. Rinse cold, aftertreat with sodium dichromate and acetic acid at 70–80°C, rinse, soap off and finally rinse.

Nylon/Cellulosic Blends
Some of these blends may be dyed in selected solid colours, notably black or blue, using sulphur dyes only. Nylon is heavily dyed with certain products, especially C.I.

Leuco Sulphur Blues 7 and 13, Green 2, Brown 96, Red 10 and Black 11, as well as the sulphur vat types C.I. Vat Blues 42 and 43. The higher the dyeing temperature, the greater the uptake by nylon, to the virtual exclusion of the cotton in some cases. Solid colours may be obtained by simultaneously filling in the cotton with dyes that do not dye nylon. It must be emphasised that good laboratory dyeings are essential before attempting blend dyeing of this nature in bulk, as different nylon fibres vary in their uptake of sulphur dyes and the colours obtained on nylon may not be the same as on cotton. Blue and black in particular tend to give redder tones on nylon than on cellulosic fibres.

The possibility also exists to dye at lower temperatures (i.e. 50–70°C) using only those dyes capable of giving a similar depth on both cotton and nylon fibres under these conditions. The temperature control needs to be very precise to obtain reproducible results and is only practicable in isolated instances.

Of course, those sulphur dyes that reserve nylon may be used in a more conventional way to dye the cellulosic fibre before filling in the nylon with acid or premetallised dyes. Satisfactory solidity is easier to achieve at lower temperatures (45–55°C), where the partition of sulphur dyes strongly favours the cellulosic component.

The fastness to wet treatments of sulphur dyes on nylon is usually excellent, but the light fastness may be slightly lower than a similar depth on cellulosic fibres.

Cotton/nylon socks are often dyed in blue and black colours with leuco liquid dyes in Dytex rotary-drum machinery using recipes similar to those suggested in section 7.4.3.

Cotton/Viscose Blends
Blends of cotton and regenerated cellulosic fibres (including viscose and other variants such as high wet modulus fibres and polynosic fibres) are often dyed by processes similar to those used for 100% cotton, but the partition between cotton and regenerated cellulose varies widely between fibre variants and from dye to dye. Thus some dyes may give solid colours at all depths, e.g. C.I. Sulphur Black 1, whilst other dyes may be suitable only in pale depths, e.g. blue sulphur dyes. In general the cotton dyes to a lower depth than the viscose fibre.

Cotton/Acrylic Blends
Knitted pile fabrics with a cotton back and acrylic pile are popular in soft furnishings, upholstery and sweat shirts. The cotton portion is dyed with sulphur dyes and then the acrylic portion with cationic dyes in a separate bath.

Certain sulphur dyes colour acrylic fibre to a marked degree, which may be quite acceptable when dyeing solid colours but a considerable problem if a reserve is required on the acrylic fibre. In this case lowering the dyeing temperature to 45–55°C will greatly improve the degree of reservation.

7.5 EFFLUENT TREATMENT
Unless alternative reducing systems are used, the effluent arising from sulphur dye processes contains sulphides, the concentration of which depends on the dyeing

method, applied depth and the dye used. The discharge of sulphides to drain is not normally permissible because of the danger to life or damage to the fabric of the sewer from the bacterial oxidation of liberated hydrogen sulphide to sulphuric acid.

The leather industry has installed air-oxidation sulphide treatment plants at tanneries [8, 9] and similar methods are suitable and effective for the treatment of sulphur dye effluent, even when it contains relatively large amounts of sulphides.

Air oxidation can be accomplished by diffused aeration, surface aeration, ejectors or by coarse bubbles from sparge pipes.

Diffused aeration is achieved by generating fine bubbles from activated-sludge dome diffusers, which are set at one 20 cm diffuser per 1000 cm^2 cross-sectional area of treatment tank to achieve the best effect. Each diffuser requires 30–35 l/min of air and sulphide removal rates of up to 750 mg/l/h have been achieved. Diffusers suffer from suck-back and have to be removed regularly for cleaning.

Helixor modules [9] are considerably more expensive per unit than diffusers, but fewer are required and they are relatively maintenance free. Each helixor requires 1100–1250 l/min of air for maximum efficiency, and again rates of sulphide removal as high as 750 mg/l/h have been achieved. Operating units in the leather industry are utilising up to 65% of the available oxygen in treatment tanks of 6 m working depth. This rate falls to 15–30% utilisation in sulphur dye treatment tanks of 4 m working depth. A sulphide removal rate of 400 mg/l/h is regarded as a reasonable rate at such depths.

Typically 1 kg of sulphide requires about 1.1 kg of oxygen for complete removal, indicating that some sulphate arises by further oxidation of the thiosulphate formed initially (Scheme 7.1).

$$2Na_2S + 2O_2 + H_2O \longrightarrow Na_2S_2O_3 + 2NaOH$$

$$Na_2S_2O_3 + 2NaOH + 2O_2 \longrightarrow 2Na_2SO_4 + H_2O$$

Scheme 7.1

The observation that the oxidation of sulphide is difficult to drive to completion without a catalyst [10] is illustrated in Figure 7.2. The use of catalysts such as manganese sulphate, anthraquinone-1,2-disulphonic acid, hydroquinone, ferric chloride, copper sulphate or chrome either alone or in mixtures are useful in the oxidation of sulphides, but less so when sulphur dyes are present in the effluent. Presumably small amounts of sulphur dyes act as reaction promoters (Figure 7.2) through a redox mechanism. During oxidation the pH gradually falls from 12 to about 10, often marked by a slight increase just before the reaction is complete. It is absolutely essential that the pH is not allowed to fall below 9 during aeration, otherwise hydrogen sulphide is evolved. The oxidation of sulphide is exothermic; although the reaction proceeds more rapidly at elevated temperatures it is not necessary to raise the temperature by heating. The restrictions on the discharge of sulphate to sewer require that aeration should cease when all the sulphide has reacted, since excessive oxidation converts thiosulphate to sulphate.

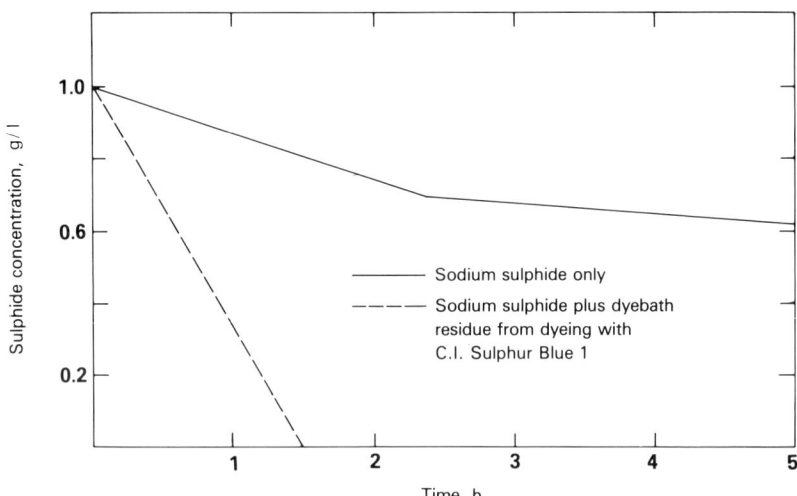

Figure 7.2 – Oxidation times of sulphide with no catalyst present

Whilst air oxidation is ideal for treating large amounts of sulphide, the technique has been applied in small dyehouses where batch liquors have been collected and treated either separately or after bulking together. For small quantities the use of either hydrogen peroxide or sodium hypochlorite is also very effective.

Below pH 8.5 the reaction shown in Scheme 7.2 predominates, and in more alkaline effluent the reaction gives sulphate (Scheme 7.3); hypochlorite also oxidises sulphide to sulphate.

$$H_2O_2 + H_2S \longrightarrow S\downarrow + 2H_2O$$

Scheme 7.2

$$4H_2O_2 + S^{2-} \longrightarrow 4H_2O + SO_4^{2-}$$

Scheme 7.3

Precipitation and settling using ferrous sulphate and alum is a technique that is also employed on the large scale.

Sulphide can be determined in two ways. The first method involves titration with ammoniacal copper sulphate solution using a platinum measuring electrode and calomel reference electrode. This method is easy to operate but gives unreliable results below about 150 mg/l sulphide. In the alternative method zinc acetate is added to the sample and the zinc sulphide separated by filtration; iodine and hydrochloric acid are then added and the excess iodine titrated with sodium thiosulphate.

Sulphide concentrations vary considerably depending on colour and application method. The following examples are typical of manufacturing experience.

(a) In pad–steam processing a full black was dyed with C.I. Leuco Sulphur Black 1.

The pad box contained 13 900 mg/l sulphide and the discharges were 380 mg/l sulphide from the first wash box and 28 mg/l from the second

(b) A full blue was dyed on the jig and had a final sulphide concentration of 1 300 mg/l while a similar pale depth had only 600 mg/l.

(c) The spent dyebath after dyeing a black on the beam contained 3 400 mg/l sulphide. This was air blown sulphide-free in 8 h at 5°C. The chemical oxidation demand fell from 4 550 to 2 600 mg/l. In general a reduction of up to one-third in the sulphide concentration can be expected after dyeing.

Typical treatment rates are shown in Figure 7.3.

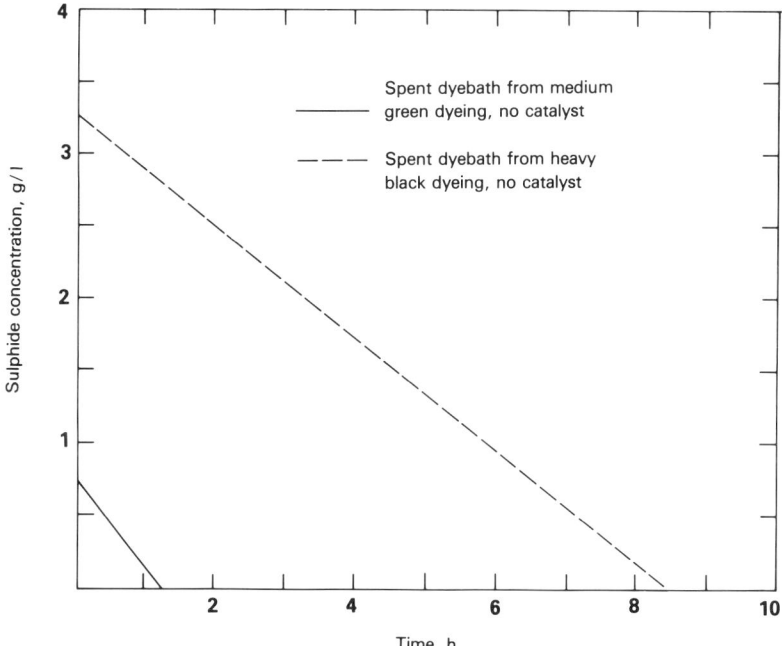

Figure 7.3 – Treatment times for the removal of sulphide; volume 1 700 l, depth 3.8 m, air flow 160 l/min through 5 × 20 cm Alunden fittings

7.6 PERFORMANCE

The fastness properties of sulphur dyes, as a class, fall between those of direct dyes and vat dyes. As with most dye ranges the fastness varies from dye to dye, but those of higher fastness, e.g. C.I. Sulphur Green 14 and Black 11 behave similarly to those vat dyes having the least impressive fastness properties.

Sulphur dyes, are, of course, considerably cheaper than most vat dyes and it is the area of medium to heavy depths, especially black, blue and brown, of reasonably good fastness at an economical price that demands their usage.

The fastness tests referred to are detailed in the 'Standard Methods for the Determination of the Colour Fastness of Textiles and Leather', Fourth Edition, published by the Society of Dyers and Colourists.

7.6.1 Fastness to Light
The fastness to light (test method BO2: 1978 xenon arc) essentially increases throughout the range from lowest in the yellows and oranges to highest in blacks and navy blues, although there are exceptions to this general rule, e.g. the yellow-browns: C.I. Sulphur Browns 51 and 60 are much faster than Brown 10.

Pale depths generally show quite poor light fastness, particularly yellow, orange and brown, although medium to heavy colours in most brown and khaki hues can be dyed to a light fastness of 5, whilst C.I. Sulphur Black 1 gives a rating of 5 even in relatively pale depths.

Blues and navies reach standard 5–6 or 6, as do most dark olive and green dyeings, and a full black dyed with C.I. Sulphur Black 1 will reach standard 7.

7.6.2 Fastness to Wet Treatments
Washing
Sulphur dyeings in general exhibit good fastness to washing tests based on soap (tests CO1–CO5), but are less resistant to laundering with detergents and perborates (CO6, A2–D2), although even here the fastness to washing is reasonable at temperatures not exceeding 50°C (i.e. tests CO6, A2 and B2). Some older green and red-brown dyes are not as fast to washing as newer types, e.g. C.I. Sulphur Red 10 and Green 14 are much superior to Red 6 and Green 3 respectively.

The use of alkylating agents based on epichlorohydrin condensation products is claimed to give improved fastness to severe washing treatments.

Perspiration
The fastness to perspiration (test EO4), especially at pH 5.5, is particularly good. Alkaline perspiration is generally good to very good, some exceptions being C.I. Sulphur Red 6, Green 3 and Blue 15 (a bluish-green).

Bleaching
Most sulphur colours are destroyed by sodium hypochlorite (test NO1), the exceptions being C.I. Sulphur Black 11, Green 14, Red 14 and the so-called sulphur vat dyes, C.I. Vat Blues 42 and 43, all of which have some resistance to bleaching with sodium hypochlorite. Some yellow, orange and brown dyes are only partially bleached, although the hue is usually considerably affected.

The effect of peroxide bleaching (test NO2) is not quite as severe as hypochlorite. Nevertheless most sulphur dyes lose considerable depth in peroxide bleaching, the exceptions being the same as for hypochlorite bleaching.

Mercerising
Although fabric to be dyed with sulphur dyes would normally be mercerised before dyeing, occasionally yarns dyed with sulphur dyes may be subjected to mercerising

after weaving into fabric. The fastness (test XO4) is good, with some apparent increase in depth, usually only marginal hue change and slight staining of adjacent undyed cotton.

Rubbing
The fastness to rubbing (test method X12) is so greatly dependent on the fabric itself, its preparation and the dyeing process, especially the efficiency of rinsing before oxidation, that absolute rubbing fastness ratings cannot be quoted. The fastness to dry rubbing is normally quite good. Even in heavy depths ratings of 4–5 for staining of adjacent fabrics are readily attainable. Fastness to wet rubbing in heavy depths is not usually as good and stain ratings of 2–3 are quite common on dark navy and black dyeings. In order to obtain the maximum rub fastness it is essential that the dyes should be completely in solution throughout, with sequestering agents and antioxidants present as necessary. The dyeing should also be thoroughly rinsed to remove as much unfixed dye as possible before the oxidation stage is reached.

Table 7.2 shows the fastness to light, washing and perspiration of a short range of dyes selected to illustrate some of the points made in sections 7.6.1 and 7.6.2.

7.6.3 Degradation
The phenomenon of tendering of black sulphur dyes has been examined many times, and it has been found that they all produce sulphuric acid under adverse storage conditions (high humidity and temperature). This problem may be reduced considerably or even eliminated by thorough washing before oxidation and alkaline rinsing as the final stage in processing.

It has been claimed [11] that resin finishing inhibits the tendering of sulphur blacks, whilst a proprietary cationic fibre-protective agent has been marketed by Hoechst as a more durable inhibitor than buffering with alkali.

No evidence has been reported of sulphuric acid damage by other sulphur dyes and the incidence of reports of tendering with sulphur blacks has been very much less frequent in recent years, even though the production of the dyes has increased. Apparently dyers are well aware of the problem and have adopted the necessary preventative measures.

7.7 COMMON FAULTS
When a dyeing is found to be faulty, the dyer is invariably held responsible, and he in turn blames the dyestuffs, although often the problem originated in preparation or by some operation being carried out incorrectly.

7.7.1 Yarn Dyeing
The problems here are usually unlevelness, either within the package or from package to package. The fault may be bronzing on the outside or a deposit on the inside of the package, as it is a very efficient filter. Light spots from cross-over marks or from entrapped bubbles of air may also be evident.

Variation in permeability from package to package is a winding problem caused by inconsistent tension during the winding of the packages onto dyeing centres,

TABLE 7.2

Comparative Fastness Ratings of Typical Dyes

C.I. Sulphur	Light fastness (2/1 depth)	Washing fastness (1/l depth)						Perspiration fastness (alkaline)		
		CO3			CO6 (C2)					
		Change in colour	Staining of		Change in colour	Staining of		Change in colour	Staining of	
			Cotton	Wool		Cotton	Viscose		Cotton	Wool
Black 1	7	4–5	4–5	5	4	4	4–5	4–5	5	5
Blue 5	6–7	4–5	4	4–5	3–4	3	3–4	4–5	4–5	5
Blue 13	5–6	4–5	4–5	4	4	4	4–5	5	4–5	5
Green 3	5–6	4	3–4	4	3–4	3–4	4–5	5	4	4–5
Green 14	6–7	4–5	5	5	3–4	4–5	4–5	5	5	5
Red 6	4–5	4	3	4–5	3–4	2	3	3–4	2–3	4
Red 10	6	4–5	4–5	4–5	4	4	4–5	4–5	4–5	5
Brown 10	4	4–5	4	4–5	4	4–5	4–5	4–5	5	5
Brown 51	6	4–5	4	4–5	4	4	4–5	4–5	5	5
Yellow 9	3–4	4–5	4–5	5	4	3–4	4	4–5	4–5	5

leading to different rates of flow through the packages. This can be corrected by rewinding the packages at constant tension and treating them in a blank bath of reducing agent (e.g. 6 g/l full-strength sodium sulphide) at as high a temperature as possible to partially strip the dyeing, before redyeing to shade. Variation within a package also requires a blank bath treatment at a high temperature; severe cases may need bleaching and redyeing.

A blank bath containing 4.5–9 g/l full-strength sodium sulphide together with 2–3 ml/l sequestering agent at 90–95°C will strip off 10–20% dye, whilst the addition of a stripping agent such as poly(vinyl pyrrolidone) will remove a further 10–20%. It is usually advisable to redye from a fresh bath. This becomes essential when using stripping agents as these will prevent exhaustion when further dye is applied.

Bronzing is usually attributable to premature reoxidation of the dyeing before the initial rinsing stage. This can be avoided by overflow rinsing until clear. A correction routine would be the same as for general unlevel dyeings.

Causes of unlevel dyeings include the following:
(a) Beginning dyeing at too high a temperature
(b) Raising the temperature too quickly at a slow flow rate
(c) Packages too tightly wound
(d) Addition of electrolyte too quickly or too early in the dye cycle
(e) Cavitation in the pump
(f) Inadequate rinsing before oxidation (this may also be a cause of poor fastness).

7.7.2 Jig Dyeing

The most common jig dyeing problems are ending (variation from one end of the jig roll to the other), listing (variation from selvedge to selvedge or centre to selvedge) and poor rubbing fastness.

Ending may be caused by adding all the dyes and auxiliaries in the first end, starting dyeing at too high a temperature or adding excessive quantities of electrolyte early in the dyeing cycle. Variations across the fabric width may arise from differences in temperature across the roll, possibly exacerbated by the selection of a combination of dyes that do not all have the same optimum dyeing temperature, e.g. yellow or orange with green. The use of an antioxidant is often helpful in such a case, as well as where light or dark selvedges result from poor batching of the jig roll. Poor rubbing fastness can be attributed to poor preparation, when residual size and/or wax may prevent full penetration and fixation of the dyes, or the presence of salts of metals such as calcium, magnesium or iron may interfere with dyeing behaviour.

Correction of all these faults involves treatment in a blank bath of reducing agent, e.g. 12–18 g/l full-strength sodium sulphide, for 30–60 min at 90–95°C with the addition of sequestering agents. Where a more severe treatment is required, the use of caustic soda and sodium dithionite will usually strip off 20–30% dye. However, because of the low liquor ratios involved, stripping is rather inefficient, and the treatment may need to be repeated to obtain satisfactory results before redyeing.

7.7.3 Knitted Fabric on Jet or Winch

The most common faults are streakiness, possibly with bronzing and rope or running marks. Streakiness and bronzing are often caused by premature oxidation, either in passing over a winch reel or floating in the winch beck. Streakiness is minimised by an addition of antioxidant, whereas bronzing due to floating may require the addition of a wetting agent to promote sinking of the fabric into the dye liquor.

7.7.4 Continuous Processing

Common problems in pad–steam dyeing are tailing, water or colour spotting, streakiness and skitteriness.

Traditionally tailing is taken into consideration by diluting the initial pad bath by 10–20%, thereby topping up the pad trough with a stronger feed liquor. This procedure is now considered to be somewhat inadequate under conditions of increasingly rigorous quality control, and manufacturers of leuco liquid dyes are supplying information on feed rates for dyes at different concentrations. Thus continuous pad–steam ranges may be adjusted with feed pad liquors that take account of the properties of the particular dye combinations being used. Tailing is further reduced by padding from a small-capacity trough at a low liquor temperature and a high running speed, all of which require high-quality preparation of the fabric.

Water spotting is a steamer problem, caused by condensed water droplets falling from the steamer roof onto the fabric. This fault may vary in severity from a virtually undyed spot to one only slightly weaker than the rest of the fabric. In the former case it may be necessary either to bleach and redye or to overdye to a much darker colour (usually black). Slight water spotting may be corrected simply by a batchwise treatment in a blank bath of reducing agent, or again it may be possible to overdye to a darker colour. However, prevention is better than cure, and heating the upper surfaces of the steamer, together with efficient lagging, should be sufficient to prevent the fault occurring.

Spots that are heavier in depth than the rest of the dyeing may be caused by foam picked up from the surface of the pad liquor or by insoluble dye particles in the solution. The latter cause is unlikely when pre-reduced liquid sulphur dyes are being used, unless an incompatible auxiliary is inducing dye precipitation. Low-foaming wetting agents and antifoams may reduce the incidence or prevent entirely the production of foam.

Streakiness may result from poor preparation, or a build-up of lint or other deposits on rollers in the pad mangle or steamer, whilst a skittery dyeing is invariably caused by poor preparation. If the cause is poor preparation this should be corrected at source if at all possible, although the use of a more efficient wetting agent may be tried if the problem is only a marginal one. However, any change of auxiliary should be thoroughly evaluated beforehand in the labratory to ensure that it does not create fresh problems.

It cannot be emphasised often enough that in all continuous processing thorough and uniform preparation, to give a highly absorbent fabric by consistent removal of size and wax, is essential. Only by this means can high-quality reproducible dyeings be obtained, with minimal problems or substandard material.

REFERENCES

1. Aeberhard, Textilveredlung, **16** (1981) 442.
2. Klein, J.S.D.C., **98** (1982) 110.
3. Olin, USP 3944782.
4. Protex, French P 2406691.
5. Protex, Japanese P (Appl.) 78/156936.
6. HOE, European P 121227.
7. Smithson, and JR, BP 1321453.
8. Bailey and Humphrey, J. Soc. Leather Technol. Chem., **51** (1967) 154.
9. BLMRA J., **19** (1976) 61.
10. Veno, Water Res., **10** (1976) 317.
11. Tigler, Amer. Dyestuff Rep., **57** (1968) 333.

FURTHER READING

Wood, Rev. Prog. Coloration, **7** (1976) 80.
Marshall, J.S.D.C., **71** (1955) 13.
Von der Eltz, J.S.D.C., **101** (1985) 168.
J. Water Pollution Control Federation, **46** (1974) 2778.
Wolf, Eckert and Theummler, Wasserwirt Wassertech., **19** (1969) 13.

CHAPTER 8

Dyeing with Azoic Dyes

HANS HERZOG (translated from the German by Bernard Kramrisch)

8.1 INTRODUCTION

Whereas the terms reactive, direct and vat dyes are clearly defined, as they represent classes of dyes categorised according to application method, the designations azoic dyes, developing dyes, insoluble azo dyes and naphthol dyes are not distinguishable with the same degree of accuracy. In the *Colour Index* [1] azoic colouring matters are defined as those which produce 'insoluble azo dyes *in situ*, usually on a textile substrate'. Azoic coupling components, according to the *Colour Index*, are often named naphthols, and azoic diazo components are primary amines or stabilised diazonium compounds, often called Bases or Salts respectively. So-called azoic compositions are described in the *Colour Index* as 'mechanical mixtures of an azoic coupling component and an azoic diazo component'.

The normal procedure for dyeing with azoic dyes includes application of the naphthol, removal of excess liquor, development in a solution of the diazonium compound and aftertreatment to achieve satisfactory fastness. In the first stage the material is impregnated with an alkaline solution of naphthol in a batchwise or continuous process.

The intermediate stage may consist merely of removal of water by suction, wringing, mangling or hydroextraction, or an intermediate rinsing with a solution of common salt; for fabrics a drying stage is introduced. Development is achieved by bringing the impregnated material, after intermediate treatment, into a solution of the diazonium compound, which has been prepared by diazotisation of a base or simply by dissolving a diazo salt. Aftertreatment is important and is carried out by soaping at the highest temperature attainable, followed by washing-off and drying. Except in continuous dyeing it is usual to soap twice, first at 60°C to remove loosely held dye and then at 80–90°C to achieve maximum fastness.

The first recommendation for the production of insoluble azo dyes on cotton was made in 1880 by Thomas and Robert Holliday of Read, Holliday & Co. Ltd, Huddersfield [2]. Their patent described a β-naphthol preparation followed by coupling with diazotised α- or β-naphthylamine to produce reds or bordeaux. In 1889 Gallois and Ullrich of Meister, Lucius and Bruning recommended the use of β-naphthol coupled with diazotised p-nitroaniline to produce Para Red (C.I. Pigment Red 1, first synthesised by Meldola in 1885), which was of importance over a long period for dyeing and printing [3]. In 1891 Fischesser and Pokorny recommended the replacement of β-naphthol by 2-hydroxy-3-naphthoic acid [4], which with tetrazotised dianisidine produced a blue with enhanced fastness to perspiration.

The use of β-naphthol and 2-hydroxy-3-naphthoic acid was followed by the introduction in 1911 of the anilide of 2-hydroxy-3-naphthoic acid, i.e. the first substantive azoic coupling component. The discovery of this product took place in an unusual manner as, according to the literature [5], a New York wine merchant used a red pigment to print tin foil wine bottle seals. This pigment, however, produced from 2-hydroxy-3-naphthoic acid, was insufficiently fast to light and attacked the tin foil. The problem was investigated at Griesheim Elektron by Winter, Laska and Zitscher, who recommended replacing 2-hydroxy-3-naphthoic acid by its anilide [6], which gave an improved pigment. The important factor was that this compound was found to have substantivity for cotton. It was marketed as Naphtol AS (HOE, C.I. Coupling Component 2). With diazotised 2-nitro-4-methylaniline (Fast Red GL Base (C.I. Azoic Diazo Component 8)) it gave the so-called Griesheim Red. Subsequently many other coupling components have been marketed (by several manufacturers), at least three-quarters of them being anilides of 2-hydroxy-3-naphthoic acid; many bases and salts have also been brought out. Theoretically about 1700 azoic combinations can be obtained with the available components, i.e. 34 naphthols and about 50 bases. Although not all these combinations are of commercial value, it does mean that azoic dyes offer greater versatility in selecting homogeneous hues than many other groups of dyes.

The main advantages of azoic dyes are:

(a) They are particularly strong in the orange, red and bordeaux regions, but the range also includes dark blue and black
(b) Dyeings can be produced in certain bright full depths not always attainable with other classes of dyes
(c) Materials can be dyed in virtually any form and on a wide range of machines
(d) Dyeings have excellent reproducibility
(e) In general, the standard of fastness is high
(f) Most combinations are dischargeable
(g) They are economically viable.

All the above advantages outweigh the disadvantages that are usually cited, i.e. complicated and time-consuming application procedures. The application of azoic dyes has been made easier by the availability of detailed literature issued by the dye manufacturers and new commercial forms of azoic dyes, such as liquids and more easily dissolvable powder forms. A further simplification in the dyeing of azoic dyes is the one-bath exhaust dyeing technique [7]; a highly substantive naphthol and a diazo–amine compound are applied simultaneously; coupling takes place by acidification of the dyebath.

The world production of azoic dyes in 1972 was estimated to be about 35000 tonnes [8], which represents 5% of the total world requirements for dyes for all fibres. Today azoic dyes still represent a significant class of dyes for cellulosic fibres. Apart from their use in dyeing, they have played an important role in printing of African prints and batiks.

8.2 CHEMICAL CONSTITUTION AND HUES OBTAINABLE [9]

Table 8.1 indicates the hue range obtainable with azoic dyes and the types of coupling component and base required. The hue range extends from yellow to black; most variation is obtainable in the red and bordeaux sectors, whilst there are gaps in greens and bright blues.

TABLE 8.1

Examples of Azoic Components

Colour	Coupling components (naphthols)	Diazo components (Fast Colour Bases or Salts)
Yellow	Amides of aceto acetic acid CH_3COCH_2CONHR (Yellow naphthols)	
Red	Arylamides of 2-hydroxy-3-naphthoic acid (Red naphthols)	Aniline derivatives
Bordeaux	Arylamides of 6-methoxy-2-hydroxy-3-naphthoic acid (Bordeaux naphthols)	(Fast Yellow, Orange, Scarlet and Red Bases or Salts)
	Arylamides of 2-hydroxy-3-naphthoic acid (Red naphthols)	Aminoazobenzene derivatives, e.g. (Fast Bordeaux, Garnet and Corinth Bases or Salts)
Violet and blue	Arylamides of 2-hydroxy-3-naphthoic acid (Red naphthols)	Substituted p-benzoylaminoanilines, diphenylamines and other compounds, e.g.

Table 8.1—*continued*

Green	2-Hydroxyanthracene-3-carboxylic acid *o*-toluidide	

(Green naphthol)   (Fast Violet and Blue Bases or Salts)

Brown	Arylamides of heterocyclic 2-hydroxyaryl-3-carboxylic acids	Various Fast Bases or Salts

(Brown naphthols)

Black	Arylamides of 2-hydroxy-3-naphthoic acid	Substituted aminoazobenzenes, polynuclear aromatic diamines and other compounds, e.g.

(Red naphthols)   (Fast Black Bases or Salts)

Arylamides of 7-hydroxy-benz[*a*]carbazole-6-carboxylic acid

Aniline derivatives

(Black naphthols)   (Fast Red Bases or Salts)

Yellow

Yellows are unobtainable with arylamides of 2-hydroxy-3-naphthoic acid and require the so-called yellow naphthols, which are amides of acetoacetic acid and are not derived from β-naphthol; various simple aromatic amines can be used as bases.

Red

Practically all red naphthols are arylamides of 2-hydroxy-3-naphthoic acid. As will be seen from Table 8.1, in principle the amines used as diazo components are the same as those for yellows. Naturally the constitution of the diazo components exerts a marked influence on hue; orange, scarlet and red bases on red naphthols give the corresponding colours, whereas the so-called yellow bases and naphthols give yellows only.

Bordeaux
Two different possibilities exist in the bordeaux sector. The older method, still widely used, is also based on the so-called red naphthols, together with bordeaux, garnet and corinth bases; the hue change to bordeaux derives from the batho-chromic effect of the diazo component. In many cases such diazo components con-tain an azo bridge, so that a disazo dye is obtained on coupling. The second way of producing bordeaux hues is to use the so-called bordeaux naphthols, in which a 6-methoxy group has been introduced into the arylamides of 2-hydroxy-3-naphthoic acid. As will be seen from Table 8.1, these compounds yield bordeaux hues with orange, scarlet and red bases.

Violet and Blue
Violet and blue bases are substituted *p*-benzoylaminoanilines, diphenylamines or other compounds. The so-called red naphthols are used as coupling components for violets and blues. Bright greenish-blues of the phthalocyanine type are unobtain-able and the hues produced are indigo and navy blue (Variamine Blues).

Green
The green naphthol in the anthracene range gives bottle greens when coupled with the blue bases. It is now possible to produce bright greens with azoic dyes of excel-lent light fastness. C.I. Azoic Coupling Component 108 is a condensation product of a copper phthalocyanine sulphochloride and an aminophenylpyrazolone, i.e. a combination of a blue copper phthalocyanine chromophore and the pyrazolone, which gives a yellow azo chromophore on coupling with a diazotised base. This green naphthol has, however, no substantivity for cellulosic fibres, its main applica-tion being in textile printing [10]. A further possibility is to use C.I. Azoic Diazo Component 118, another combination of blue and yellow components in one molecule; blue-green hues are obtainable on red naphthols and scarlet hues on yellow naphthols.

Brown
To obtain brown azoic colours it is necessary to use arylamides of heterocyclic 2-hydroxyaryl-3-carboxylic acids, derivatives of carbazole or dibenzofuran as coupling components. As the brown naphthols are highly substantive to cellulose, a batchwise dyeing process is preferred. Various bases or salts can be used as diazo components.

Black
As in the case of bordeaux, there are two main methods of producing blacks. Various red naphthols are suitable for continuous dyeing or printing with diazotised bases and salts, the naphthol-prepared fabric being dried before application of the diazo components. As will be seen from Table 8.1, blacks are produced by dyeing or printing with black diazotised bases and salts; selected derivatives of aminoazobenzene (similar to corinth bases) or multinuclear aromatic diamines con-taining azo groups are used. Blacks of high fastness are obtainable by batchwise

application of a black naphthol (arylamide of 7-hydroxybenz[*a*]carbazole-6-carboxylic acid) followed by development with a red diazotised base.

The chemical constitutions of both naphthol and diazotised base affect the hue obtained on coupling. An example is given in Scheme 8.1, showing the reactions of C.I. Azoic Coupling Component 11 (a red naphthol) and C.I. Azoic Coupling Component 113 (a bordeaux naphthol), which have closely similar structures, both being anilides of 2-hydroxy-3-naphthoic acid containing a methoxy substituent. The red naphthol is a *p*-methoxyanilide, whereas the bordeaux naphthol has a 6-methoxy group in the naphthalene residue. Virtually the same hue is produced when either the red naphthol (C.I. Azoic Coupling Component 11) is coupled with Fast Garnet GBC Base (C.I. Azoic Diazo Component 4) or the bordeaux naphthol (C.I. Azoic Coupling Component 113) is coupled with Fast Scarlet RC Base (C.I. Azoic Diazo Component 13). In the first case a disazo dye is formed and in the second a monoazo dye. The 6-methoxy group in the bordeaux naphthol, therefore, has the same bathochromic effect as a second azo group in the diazo component. Alkoxy groups in the 6-position of the naphthalene residue give a significant increase in substantivity. C.I. Azoic Coupling Component 11 exhibits poor substantivity as a coupling component, whereas C.I. Azoic Coupling Component 113 has moderate substantivity.

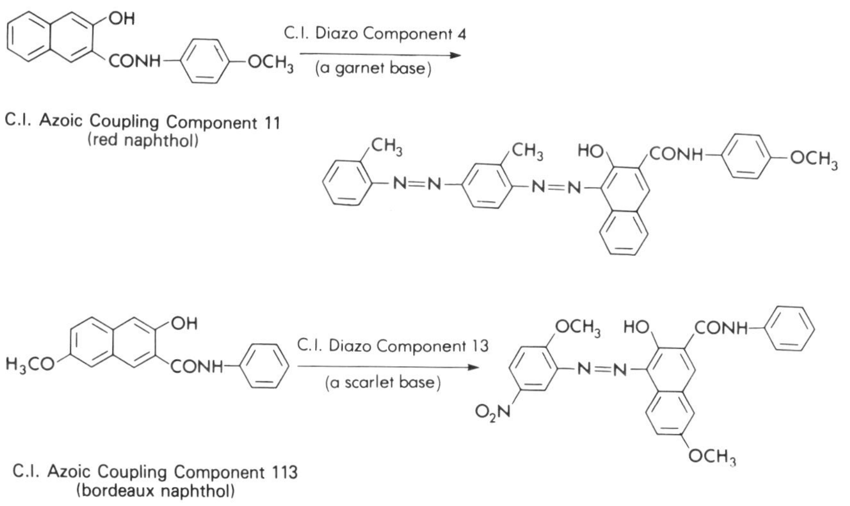

Scheme 8.1

8.3 TREATMENT WITH NAPHTHOLS

Unless specifically mentioned, the data in the following sections refer to the application of azoic dyes to cotton. Cotton is the most important substrate for the application of azoic dyes and special precautions are necessary when other natural or regenerated cellulosic fibres are dyed.

8.3.1 Preparation of Naphtholate Solutions

Naphthols are insoluble in water, but their sodium salts (naphtholates) are water soluble or can be dispersed in colloidal form; these colloidal dispersions are less stable than true solutions and require the addition of a protective colloid to render them stable. Both cold and hot methods of dissolving naphtholates can be used.

Cold-dissolving Method

The naphthol is converted to its naphtholate with alkali and dissolves in aqueous industrial alcohol. The naphthol can be pasted with industrial alcohol and warm water and then converted to the naphtholate by adding caustic soda; alternatively a mixture of water, caustic soda and methylated spirit can be poured over the naphthol, which is brought into solution by stirring. Dark brown to olive green solutions are produced that are highly concentrated and tend to show crystallisation unless they are diluted. Where necessary, formaldehyde is added to the concentrated solution, which is then diluted to form the application liquor containing a protective colloid and caustic soda. The diluted solution is ready for immediate use.

Hot-dissolving Method

A protective colloid and hot soft water are poured over the naphthol. After a short boil, the required quantity of hot caustic soda liquor is added, usually forming a clear solution which is ready for application. In the case of some naphtholates of low solubility the alkaline solution must be given a short boil before use.

Several naphthols of low or moderate substantivity, which are normally difficult to dissolve, are marketed in a special form in which they dissolve easily and quickly. In the hot-dissolving method these products can be strewn directly into the application bath already prepared with caustic soda and a protective colloid. After stirring briefly a clear liquor is obtained which is ready to use for padding.

The cold-dissolving process is used today when preparing naphtholate solutions for batchwise application. The hot-dissolving method is particularly important for padding processes, as padding is done near the boil, in contrast to batchwise processes which are carried out at room temperature. The simplest method of preparing naphtholate solutions is to use liquid brands of naphthols.

8.3.2 Selection and Application of Naphthols

When cotton is immersed in the naphtholate solution, exhaustion begins according to the substantivity of the naphtholate anion. Simultaneously non-substantive components of the absorbed solution are desorbed. Equilibrium absorption of the naphtholate is soon attained; treatment for 30 min is usually adequate for satisfactory levelling under bulk-scale conditions. Naphthols of low substantivity find their main application in continuous dyeing processes where high substantivity is not required. They can, however, be used with limitations in batchwise techniques by the addition of common salt.

Naphthols of moderate substantivity can be applied both by continuous processes in which the undesirable substantivity can be suppressed by increasing the padding temperature and running speed, and by batchwise techniques in which additions of electrolytes increase the absorption.

Naphthols of high substantivity are particularly suitable for batchwise techniques. With such products the concentration remaining in the exhausted bath is low, so that dyeings with good fastness to rubbing are obtained. If highly substantive naphthols are applied continuously the undesired substantivity must be controlled by setting the initial concentration in the padding trough lower than the concentration used for making additions. With such naphthols it is necessary to use high temperatures and running speeds in padding and to maintain a low liquor level in the padding trough, so that the absorbed solution is quickly replaced with fresh padding liquor.

8.3.3 Strengths of Azoic Dyeings

The depths of dyeings obtained with azoic dyes are controlled by the amount of applied naphthol; dyeings are defined by the quantity of naphthol fixed on the material (cotton) and designated as 'g/kg naphthol'. In batchwise techniques the depth of dyeing obtained with an individual naphthol and an individual diazotised base is dependent on the material used, concentration of the naphthol solution, liquor ratio and concentration of added salt, if any. For this reason the depth of a particular azoic dyeing cannot be specified by 'g/l naphthol' only and both liquor ratio and salt addition must be given. In continuous processes the depths of dyeings are dependent on the concentration of the naphthol added to the liquor and on the liquor retention of the fabric. Manufacturers of azoic dyes supply graphs and tables which indicate the concentration of naphthol for batchwise application at a specified liquor ratio to obtain the dyeing of the depth desired (expressed in terms of g naphthol per kg substrate). In padding processes, applied concentration (g/l) can be calculated from the desired depth (g/kg) by taking into account the liquor retention.

In section 8.5.6 an indication is given of the use of dye manufacturers' literature in calculating the quantities of diazotised bases required for development of fabric prepared with a given concentration of naphthol solution.

8.3.4 Additions to the Naphtholate Solution and Quality of Water Used

Water

Soft water should be used wherever possible for naphtholate application. If this is unavailable a sequestrant should be added; polyphosphates containing sodium hexametaphosphate (such as Calgon T (AW)) are suitable but complexing agents based on nitrilotriacetic acid or ethylenediamine tetra-acetic acid may also be used.

Protective Colloids and Wetting Agents

Addition of a protective colloid ensures that the naphtholate remains in solution and the addition of a wetting agent ensures rapid wetting-out of the material. Certain auxiliaries, such as Turkey red oil, combine the functions of a protective colloid and a wetting agent. However, in common with other sulphoricinoleates, Turkey red oil forms insoluble soaps with alkaline-earth metal ions present in hard water, so that it should be used only in soft or softened water.

The large number of protective colloids on the market can be classified into three groups:

(a) Purified sulphite cellulose waste liquors (salts of lignosulphonic acids)
(b) Protein–fatty acid condensates
(c) Sodium salts of naphthalenesulphonic acid–formaldehyde condensates.

Addition of a wetting agent may be needed should the protective colloid have insufficient wetting-out properties or if the fabric is difficult to wet out. Cold-wetting agents are necessary when using the batchwise technique; usually sodium salts of alkylnaphthalenesulphonates are suitable. When padding with naphtholate solution, the high temperature employed facilitates wetting-out of the fabric.

Caustic Soda
As already mentioned in section 8.3.1, it is necessary to convert the water-insoluble naphthols to the soluble form. Naphtholate solutions, whether prepared by the cold- or the hot-dissolving method, contain an appreciable excess of caustic soda. As a result there is a tendency for hydrolysis of the naphtholate to occur, both in the naphtholate solution and on the fibre. The formation of the free acid form of the naphthol must be prevented as it will not couple in this state.

The literature supplied by dye manufacturers indicates the amount of caustic soda absorbed by the material during naphthol application, and this is taken into consideration in calculating the required quantity of alkali binder.

Formaldehyde
Should hydrolysis of the naphtholate occur, resulting in liberation of the free acid form (as mentioned above), the treated material will react with atmospheric impurities and coupling in the subsequent development bath is prevented. Conversion of the dissolved naphtholate to the insoluble free naphthol form can occur on exposure to atmospheric carbon dioxide and to a marked degree in acid steam. The presence of formaldehyde together with excess of caustic soda provides good protection against formation of free naphthol while the treated fabrics are hydro-extracted or batched; methylol compounds of the naphtholate are produced.

Addition of formaldehyde is recommended when applying most naphthols by batchwise techniques, with the cold-dissolving method for preparation of the naphtholate solution being used. The protective action of the formaldehyde is brought about at 40–50°C by reversible formation of a methylol derivative from the naphtholate and formaldehyde, and the reaction is accelerated by adding the formaldehyde to a concentrated naphtholate solution. At temperatures above 50°C the methylol derivative combines with another molecule of naphtholate to give a methylene compound which will no longer couple (see Scheme 8.2). As a result of this reaction precipitation occurs with some naphthols, while with others the appearance of the liquor is unaltered. Furthermore formaldehyde must be omitted from the hot naphtholate solutions used in padding processes.

It is interesting to note that addition of formaldehyde produces a slight increase in the absorption of red naphthols, whereas in the case of bordeaux, brown, green and black naphthols the absorption is either unaffected or may even be decreased somewhat. The data issued by the dye manufacturers for the absorption of

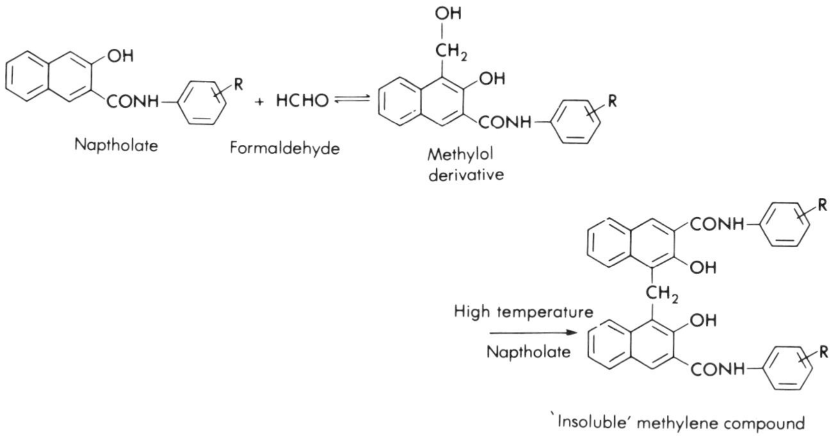

Scheme 8.2

naphthols relates to naphtholate solutions containing formaldehyde, if the addition of this chemical is recommended.

With black naphthols addition of formaldehyde improves the stability of the naphtholate solution. Formaldehyde must be omitted from solutions of yellow naphthols, however, otherwise less coupling takes place. Also the clarity of the naphtholate solution may be reduced and precipitation may occur.

Common Salt and Glauber's Salt
Additions of salt increase the exhaustion of naphthols, particularly those of low to moderate substantivity. For this reason addition of electrolyte is almost always recommended in the application of naphthols from long liquors but is not required in padding processes, where high substantivity is undesirable. Improved rubbing fastness can be obtained by adding common salt in package-dyeing machines or jigs, as the residual concentration of naphthol in the exhausted bath is thereby decreased. At short liquor ratios, with fabrics difficult to penetrate, naphthol application should be started without electrolyte, which can be added later. The amount of common salt required depends on the individual naphthol and ranges between 10 and 40 g/l. Common salt can be replaced by the same quantity of anhydrous sodium sulphate or by twice the amount of Glauber's salt ($Na_2SO_4 . 12H_2O$). The electrolytes must be free from impurities, so that salt obtained from sea water must not be used.

As already mentioned, naphthols differ in substantivity and the proportion absorbed depends on the depth applied, fibre quality, concentration and liquor ratio.

8.3.5 Temperature of Naphthol Treatment
The exhaustion of naphthols decreases with increase of temperature, so batchwise treatment is normally carried out at 20–30°C. Only when improved wetting or

penetration is necessary should the temperature be raised, and 50°C should not be exceeded if addition of formaldehyde is required. The temperature should be reduced to 30°C for the final 10–12 min in order to obtain adequate absorption.

Padding with naphthols should be carried out at higher temperatures (80–95°C) without formaldehyde.

8.3.6 Stability of Naphtholate Solutions
Naphtholate solutions are essentially dispersed colloids of limited stability, the degree of dispersion decreasing on standing, particularly when electrolytes are present. Furthermore the labile monomethylol reaction product of formaldehyde with the naphthol may be converted, on standing, to the stable methylene compound (see Scheme 8.2) which will no longer couple. The best procedure is to prepare the naphtholate solution immediately before use. At one time it was more common to use standing baths and, after treatment of the first batch of fabric, to add freshly dissolved naphtholate before treating the second batch. Coarsely dispersed naphthol is produced after a time and is absorbed by the substrate. After several additions of naphtholate the treatment bath becomes cloudy, partly because of impurities from the cotton. As soon as precipitation occurs the baths should be run off and fresh liquors prepared. Fresh baths are advisable when using naphthols that have high or moderate substantivity so that good reproducibility from batch to batch and good rubbing fastness can be obtained.

8.4 INTERMEDIATE TREATMENTS
In batchwise techniques an equilibrium between absorbed and residual naphthol is obtained usually after about 30 min. Material removed from the treatment bath includes absorbed naphtholate as well as some naphtholate solution absorbed within the fibre pores; the degree of absorption depends on the substantivity of the naphtholate, the amount applied and the liquor ratio.

The naphthol in the absorbed solution couples with the diazonium compound in a similar manner to the absorbed naphthol, but this loose azoic dye is produced only on the fibre surface and results in a decrease in fastness, particularly to rubbing and washing. Although most of the surface deposition is removed during subsequent aftertreatments, it should be kept to a minimum in order to achieve dyeings of maximum fastness. There are several methods of reducing the residual impurities which vary according to the material and equipment available. Complete removal can be effected by intermediate drying, but this is only applicable with fabric.

8.4.1 Removal of Water
Hydroextraction is the most efficient method of removing water and under optimum conditions can reduce the water content to 40% of the weight of cotton. Other methods comprise suction, squeezing or wringing, and their use depends on the type of material, i.e. loose stock, yarn in hanks, wound packages or fabric.

8.4.2 Rinsing
This is customary with fabrics prepared on jigs or yarn treated in package-dyeing machines, in order to reduce the final concentration of naphthol on the material. It

comprises treatment with 10–50 g/l common salt and 1–2 ml/l caustic soda (32.5%, 38°Bé) for 5–10 min; 10–30 g/l of common salt is used with highly substantive naphthols and 30–50 g/l with naphthols of low to moderate substantivity. If possible the rinsed material should be suction-extracted prior to development.

8.4.3 Drying

For fabrics intermediate drying is the most suitable form of treatment. In continuous dyeing processes it is advantageous to express the water on a pad mangle and then pass the fabric into a hot-flue dryer. Gradual evaporation of the residual liquor results in a steady increase in the concentration of naphthol present in the absorbed liquor, leading to a gradual and complete absorption of naphthol. Care must be taken to prevent sudden drying, as this can lead to oversaturation of the residual liquor and absorption of the naphthol can no longer be controlled, so that surface deposition of naphthol occurs.

The most appropriate drying temperature is between 90 and 110°C. It is important to ensure that the material is not overdried and with cotton a residual humidity of 9–12% is desirable. This is achieved by suitable regulation of the rate of passage of the fabric through the dryer. Careful drying after naphthol application, followed by development and aftertreatment according to the prescribed instructions, leads to dyeings of high fastness.

8.4.4 Sensitivity to Light

As already mentioned, the addition of formaldehyde overcomes the atmospheric sensitivity of naphthol-treated fabric since it prevents conversion of dissolved naphtholate to the insoluble free naphthol. Apart from atmospheric sensitivity, which occurs only under wet or damp conditions, the naphthol-treated material is affected by light, giving brownish areas on the yellowish background, the effect depending on the intensity of the incident light. On subsequent development dyeings are obtained that are unlevel or differ in hue from the standard. The most marked effects are caused by exposure to direct sunlight, although prolonged exposure to diffuse light can also cause changes. Damp naphthol-prepared material can be protected by covering with damp naphthol-treated fabric; naphthol-prepared and dried fabric can be rolled up, covered with other dry material or stored in wagons which are likewise covered. If suitably protected in this way dry naphthol-prepared fabrics can be stored for some weeks prior to further treatment, without damage occurring.

8.5 DEVELOPMENT

After naphthol application and subsequent treatments (such as removal of water, rinsing or drying), the material passes into the development bath which contains a dilute solution of a diazonium salt. This is produced either by diazotisation of an aromatic amine, a so-called Fast Colour Base, or by dissolving a Fast Colour Salt, which is a stabilised solid diazonium salt. Scheme 8.3 illustrates the diazotisation of a Fast Colour Base (a), the zinc double salt of a stabilised Fast Colour Salt (b) and the insoluble azoic dye (c). As soon as the naphthol-prepared material is introduced into the developing bath precipitation of the azoic dye begins, but more time is required before coupling is complete. The period of development depends in the first instance on the coupling energy and rate of coupling of the diazo component, and is less dependent on the chemical constitution of the naphthol.

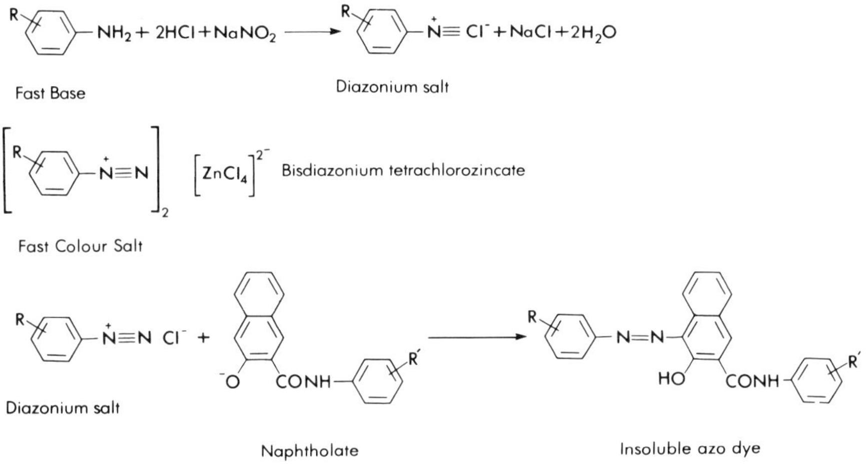

Scheme 8.3

Dye manufacturers today produce about 40 different Fast Colour Bases and Salts that can be classified into four groups according to their coupling energies. Table 8.2 illustrates typical examples from each of the four groups and also contains data on methods of stabilising the diazonium compounds in the form of Fast Colour Salts. The production of zinc chloride double salts has already been mentioned and represents the most widely used method of stabilisation; cobalt chloride and borofluoride complexes are also marketed. Another method of stabilisation entails precipitating the insoluble complex formed when a solution of a naphthalene sulphonic acid is added to a solution of a diazonium compound.

TABLE 8.2

Examples of Azoic Diazo Components

Fast Colour Base	Structure	Stabilisation of corresponding Fast Colour Salt	Coupling energy group[a]
C.I. Azoic Diazo Component 44	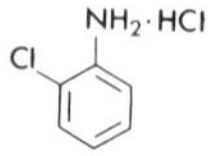	$ZnCl_2$ double salt	I
C.I. Azoic Diazo Component 2	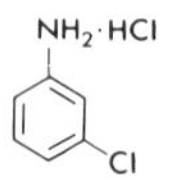	Borofluoride or naphthalene sulphonic acid	I

Table 8.2—*continued*

C.I. Azoic Diazo Component 6		ZnCl₂ double salt or borofluoride	I

C.I. Azoic Diazo Component 6		$ZnCl_2$ double salt or borofluoride	I
C.I. Azoic Diazo Component 3		$ZnCl_2$ double salt	I
C.I. Azoic Diazo Component 37		*p*-Chlorobenzene sulphonic acid or borofluoride	I
C.I. Azoic Diazo Component 32		Naphthalene sulphonic acid	II
C.I. Azoic Diazo Component 42		$ZnCl_2$ double salt	II
C.I. Azoic Diazo Component 36		$ZnCl_2$ double salt	I
C.I. Azoic Diazo Component 33		$CoCl_2$ double salt or oxalate	II
C.I. Azoic Diazo Component 5		Naphthalene sulphonic acid	I
C.I. Azoic Diazo Component 40		$ZnCl_2$ double salt	I
C.I. Azoic Diazo Component 39		$ZnCl_2$ double salt	II

Table 8.2—*continued*

C.I. Azoic Diazo Component 41	(structure: NH₂, H₃CO, CH₃, NHCO–phenyl)	ZnCl₂ double salt	III
C.I. Azoic Diazo Component 48	(structure: H₃CO, NH₂, H₃CO, NH₂ biphenyl)	ZnCl₂ double salt	IV
C.I. Azoic Diazo Component 20	(structure: NH₂, H₅C₂O, OC₂H₅, NHCO–phenyl)	ZnCl₂ double salt	III

(a) Optimum pH ranges for coupling: I – pH 4–5.5
                                        II – pH 5–6.5
                                        III – pH 6–7
                                        IV – continuous dyeing only
(b) Available as Fast Colour Salt only

8.5.1 Diazotisation of Fast Colour Bases

If the aromatic amine to be used is soluble in dilute hydrochloric acid, dissolved sodium nitrite is added slowly to this solution (direct diazotisation). If it is insoluble the amine is pasted with water and sodium nitrite, and the mixture added in portions to dilute hydrochloric acid. Difficulties can arise if the indirect diazotisation does not reach completion, so that a portion of the Fast Colour Base remains undiazotised. For this reason it is often advantageous to paste these aromatic amines with dilute hydrochloric acid and proceed in the normal manner. The dye manufacturers provide precise data for diazotisation, the concentration and amount of hydrochloric acid used in diazotisation, depending on the chemical constitution of the Fast Colour Base. Addition of ice is normally required to keep the diazotisation temperature sufficiently low.

It is important to add a suitable dispersing agent during diazotisation; non-ionic dispersing agents have proved ideal. An excess of free hydrochloric acid and sodium nitrite must also be maintained, which can be checked by the use of Congo Red (C.I. Direct Red 28) and starch potassium iodide papers. Completion of diazotisation of Fast Colour Bases that are insoluble in dilute hydrochloric acid is evident when the solution becomes completely clear. Observation of the end point with Fast Colour Bases that are soluble under these conditions is achieved indirectly as follows. Sodium acetate is added to a test solution until a neutral reaction to Congo Red is obtained. If the test solution remains clear after neutralisation then diazotisation is complete; if the solution becomes cloudy, however, the diazonium solution must be allowed to stand for a time until the reaction is complete.

With few exceptions diazotisation is normally carried out at 5–15°C. Heat is generated during diazotisation and this can have a deleterious effect on diazonium solutions, so that care must be taken to maintain the prescribed temperature. Diazotisation is simpler and quicker if liquid forms of Fast Colour Bases are used.

When diazotisation is complete the diazonium solution contains excess mineral acid and is stable if protected from the action of light and heat. Just before development the strongly acidic solution must be neutralised, otherwise coupling will not take place. Sodium acetate for neutralisation can be added directly to the concentrated diazonium solution. As a rule, however, the required amount is added to the developing bath prior to addition of the diazonium solution. Addition of sodium acetate results in the formation of free acetic acid through interaction with free hydrochloric acid and, depending on the coupling energy of the diazonium salt, buffering with further quantity of sodium acetate may be necessary.

8.5.2 Dissolving Fast Colour Salts

Fast Colour Salts consist of diazotised and stabilised primary aromatic amines and are readily soluble in water. As a rule, solutions are prepared by pouring over the Fast Colour Salt five times its weight of lukewarm water (25–30°C) containing a non-ionic dispersant and stirring until dissolved. Products having a solubility below 200 g/l must be diluted further with cold water to effect complete solution. Some Fast Colour Salts require an addition of acetic or formic acid. The clear concentrated diazo solutions should not be allowed to stand too long and should be diluted with water to the required concentration. The majority of Fast Colour Salts contain an alkali-binding agent (see below), so that in most cases no further addition is necessary and the prepared developing baths have the correct pH.

8.5.3 Stability of Development Baths

Hydrochloric acid solutions of diazotised Fast Colour Bases are more stable than neutralised acetic acid development baths, hence it is advisable to allow the prepared hydrochloric acid solutions to stand and to neutralise them only shortly before use. It is advantageous to dissolve Fast Colour Salts just prior to use. Addition of a non-ionic dispersant to the developing bath is essential. With few exceptions, developing liquors remain stable for half to a full day, but it is of advantage to prepare only as much developing liquor as is required the same day. Stored developing liquors should be kept cool and protected from direct exposure to light.

8.5.4 Water Quality and Additions to Dyebaths

In contrast to naptholate solutions, which must always be prepared with soft water, hard water can be used for the preparation of developing liquors. Non-ionic dispersants of the fatty alcohol–polyoxyethylene type are suitable auxiliaries to use in dissolving Fast Colour Salts and dispersing the insoluble azoic dye during development; there are many products of this type on the market. Addition of these dispersants ensures that the azoic dye precipitated in the development bath will be well dispersed, and as a result the deposition of azoic dye particles on the fibre surface will be obviated. Well-dispersed azoic dye is readily removed during washing-off. When the naphthol-prepared material is entered into the developing bath coupling takes place immediately, but some naphtholate is desorbed from the material. The degree of desorption depends on the substantivity of the naphthol and the coupling properties of the diazo component. Except in padding processes, desorption of the naphthol can be counteracted by addition of salt, but this should be omitted with Fast Colour Salts of poor solubility.

8.5.5 Alkali-binding Agents in Development Baths

Acetic acid is the most commonly used alkali-binding agent, and is produced after diazotisation by neutralising the excess of hydrochloric acid with sodium acetate. This amount of acetic acid, together with the quantity added on the normal diazotising instructions, is usually adequate to neutralise the alkali in the development bath. If necessary more acetic acid can be added to the developing bath. Most Fast Colour Salts contain solid alkali-binding agents in the form of aluminium, zinc or magnesium sulphate or, in a few cases, chromium acetate. An appropriate calculation specifies the additional quantity of acetic acid to be added to the development bath.

Acetic Acid
Dilute solutions containing 0.01 mol/l (1.2 ml/l of 50%) acetic acid have a pH of 3.35 and those containing 0.04 mol/l (5 ml/l of 50%) have a pH of 3.0. Addition of increasing amounts of sodium acetate (up to 20 g/l) raises the pH in the first case to 5.8 and in the second to 5.1. Thereby acetic acid–sodium acetate buffered systems can be produced over the pH range 3–6.

Aluminium Sulphate
This product has a strong alkali-binding action and Fast Colour Salts containing aluminium sulphate exhibit moderate to high coupling energy. As long as, during development, there is sufficient caustic soda, the aluminium sulphate will form soluble basic salts. If there is insufficient caustic soda insoluble basic salts are produced which cause clouding and finally flocculation of aluminium hydroxide.

Zinc Sulphate
This is less acidic than aluminium sulphate and is present in some Fast Colour Salts with low coupling energy. Zinc sulphate does not form basic salts with caustic soda but is precipitated immediately as zinc hydroxide, either partially or totally.

Chromium Acetate
This is present in a few of the blue Fast Colour Salts with a low coupling energy, which are speciality products used in continuous dyeing. Replacement of the

acetate ions in chromium acetate by hydroxyl ions takes place slowly in the cold and more rapidly when the solutions are warm. This dependence of the alkali-binding power of chromium acetate on temperature necessitates treating the fabric in an open-width washer with hot water after it leaves the developing unit, so that even and rapid development takes place.

8.5.6 Strength of Development Baths

Batchwise Dyeing
The applied concentration (expressed in terms of g/l) of Fast Colour Salt or Base is related to the applied depth (in terms of g/kg) of naphthol and the liquor ratio. In order to facilitate rapid and complete coupling with the absorbed naphthol, the development bath should be slightly acidic and contain excess diazo compound. Data on the appropriate concentrations are contained in the recipe discs and tabulated information provided by dye manufacturers.

Padding
The applied concentration (g/l) of Fast Colour Salt or Base is related to the applied depth (g/kg) of naphthol on the material, as in the case of batchwise dyeing. With the aid of the dye maker's recipe discs and tabulated data on applied depth of naphthol, it is possible to calculate the concentration of the developing solution required, depending on the diazo component used. As a rule, the quantities required are only slightly (about 10%) in excess of the theoretical. In padding processes liquor retention should be low to avoid a large excess of diazo solution. Development baths used in padding are highly concentrated, particularly if a high liquor retention is unavoidable, so that Fast Colour Salts of high solubility must be used.

8.5.7 Coupling Energy of Diazo Components
Diazo components are classified into four groups by dye manufacturers according to their fields of application and their energy of coupling. Table 8.2 contains examples from each group; groups I–III contain those Fast Colour Bases and Salts suitable for application by both batchwise and padding techniques, whereas the Fast Colour Salts in group IV are suitable only for padding.

Group I
These products have a high coupling energy and will couple fully even in the presence of a large excess of unbuffered acetic acid. The most suitable coupling range is pH 4–5.5.

Group II
These diazo components do not couple completely in the presence of excess acetic acid and an excess of sodium acetate is prescribed in the diazotising recipes for these Fast Bases. The coupling range for these products is pH 5–6.5.

Group III
Products in this group have a low coupling energy. They do not couple well even in the presence of small amounts of unbuffered acetic acid, so that in diazotisation there must be an excess of sodium acetate. The optimum coupling range is pH 6–7.

Group IV
This heterogeneous group contains Fast Colour Salts that couple with difficulty, complete coupling being possible only on a continuous range. Some Fast Colour Salts in group IV have a high coupling energy and are substantive aminoazo compounds (giving navy blues and blacks on coupling), but are unsuitable for batchwise dyeing except by special methods.

8.5.8 Mixtures of Fast Colour Bases and Salts
With few exceptions, mixtures of Fast Colour Bases and Salts are not recommended since their use can lead to unlevel dyeings and poor reproducibility. Should a mixture be essential, in order to produce a particular hue, it is advisable to use a mixture of naphthols.

8.5.9 Neutral Development
In exceptional cases, including the application of high-energy diazo components, it may be necessary to develop under near-neutral conditions. This is particularly advisable for the production of browns using C.I. Coupling Component 16 and a number of processes can be employed, outlined below.

Phosphate Buffer Method
Sodium dihydrogen phosphate is used to neutralise the caustic soda carried into the developing bath by the naphthol-prepared material, and the excess of hydrochloric acid used in diazotisation is neutralised with disodium hydrogen phosphate. The Fast Colour Base is diazotised according to the dye maker's instructions and filtered into the development bath without any addition of acetic acid or sodium acetate. The developing bath is prepared with the appropriate quantities of phosphates.

Sodium Bicarbonate Method
The Fast Colour Base, diazotised as prescribed and without any addition of acetic acid or sodium acetate, is filtered into the development bath which contains twice as much sodium bicarbonate as the amount of sodium nitrite that was used to diazotise the Fast Colour Base. Bases that are particularly sensitive to alkali cannot be applied by this method.

8.6 AFTERTREATMENT
This is an important part of the dyeing process and must be carried out just as carefully as naphthol application, intermediate treatment and developing. Aftertreatment includes rinsing, acidification after development, and alkaline soaping followed by rinsing, and only when these processes have been carried out thoroughly do the resultant dyeings exhibit the desired final hue and fastness standards.

8.6.1 Alkaline Soaping

Treatment in a boiling alkaline soaping liquor results in crystallisation of the major portion of the insoluble azoic dye within the fibre and only a small amount remains loosely adhering to the fibre surface. This process brings about some change in hue, and the loosely held surface dye dispersed by the soap solution is easier to remove on subsequent rinsing. Marseilles soap (olive oil soap) together with soda ash is suitable for alkaline soaping in soft or softened water. With hard water it is necessary to add a sequestrant, e.g. a polyphosphate of the Calgon T type, as such products not only soften the water but also have a dispersing action on the surface dye. If necessary synthetic detergents that are stable to hard water can be used, but soft or softened water is preferable.

8.6.2 Aftertreatment in the Batchwise Dyeing Process

It is customary to rinse cold with the addition of 2–3 ml/l concentrated hydrochloric acid to the first rinsing bath; this addition is essential in the development of Fast Colour Salts as it dissolves the basic metal hydroxides produced during development and facilitates their ready removal from the material. It also aids desorption of excess diazonium compounds and decomposition products from the protective colloids. For this reason the addition of acid is also recommended if the development using Fast Colour Bases or Salts did not include an alkali-binding agent.

After acidification the material is given another cold rinse and then an alkaline soaping for 10–20 min near the boil. A soaping liquor that has proved effective in bulk working comprises 1–2 g/l soda ash, about 3 g/l Marseilles soap or synthetic detergent, and 0.5–1.5 g/l polyphosphate of the Calgon T type. With yarns in hank form the soaping effect can be enhanced by efficient agitation. This is followed by treatment in a second bath containing a non-ionic dispersing agent for 10–15 min at 70–80°C. The overall procedure may be reversed, i.e. treatment first with a non-ionic dispersing agent followed by hot alkaline soaping. The soap solution containing the dispersed azoic dye must be removed as completely as possible from the dyed material by washing-off hot and cold. Particularly when using Marseilles soap, it is advisable to use soft or softened water for washing-off. When the washing-off liquor becomes highly coloured it should be replaced by a fresh bath.

8.6.3 Aftertreatment of Pad Dyeings

Development and aftertreatment are combined following padding and intermediate drying of the fabric, the first rinsing baths being part of the development process. At least three to four compartments of a continuous unit should be available containing 2–3 g/l soda ash, 3–5 g/l soap or synthetic detergent and 1–2 g/l Calgon T. This should be followed by treatment at 70–80°C with a non-ionic dispersing agent, and a final cold rinse.

If only a few washing compartments are available the fabric can be given a second run through an open-width washer to obtain the final hue. Usually the rubbing fastness of dyeings produced on a continuous unit is very good, as naphthol application is followed by intermediate drying prior to development.

8.7 DYEING OF MERCERISED COTTON AND OTHER CELLULOSIC FIBRES

Although untreated cotton represents the main substrate for the application of azoic dyes, consideration must also be given to causticised and mercerised cotton, bast fibres (particularly linen) and regenerated cellulosic fibres.

8.7.1 Causticised Cotton (Fabric)

Cotton fabrics can be causticised before dyeing to improve their dyeability and coverage of 'dead' cotton. The absorptive capacity of causticised cotton lies between those of untreated and mercerised cotton, but otherwise there is no difference in dyeing techniques when dyed with azoic dyes.

8.7.2 Mercerised Cotton (Yarn and Fabric)

Azoic dyes have a much greater substantivity for mercerised cotton than for untreated cotton and the following modifications in dyeing technique are necessary.

Naphthol Treatment

In view of the increased substantivity for mercerised cotton, the concentration of the naphtholate solution can be significantly reduced, particularly when naphthols of low substantivity are applied. The differences between untreated and mercerised cotton decrease as the substantivity of the naphthol increases. As mercerised cotton absorbs more alkali, a smaller excess of caustic soda is necessary for naphthol treatment.

Aftertreatment

Although the naphthol-prepared material is developed as for untreated cotton, it must then be treated immediately in a dilute hydrochloric acid bath (about 2–3 ml/l concentrated acid) to avoid delustring of the material. This procedure is necessary either with Fast Colour Salts or Bases. The amount of soda ash added to the boiling soap solution can be reduced (from about 2 g/l to 0.5–1 g/l); often 0.5–2 ml/l caustic soda (38° Bé) can be used in place of soda ash. Treatment with 0.1–0.5 ml/l acetic acid (50%) after soaping and rinsing will often increase the lustre.

8.7.3 Bast Fibres and Other Vegetable Fibres

Bast fibres, such as flax, hemp, jute and ramie, and other vegetable fibres, such as sisal and coir, contain impurities that interfere with the absorption of both naphthol and diazo component. As a result a significant proportion of insoluble azoic dye remains on the fibre surface and, unless the impurities are removed by appropriate pretreatment, dyeings of inadequate penetration and fastness are obtained. Flax (linen) represents the most important fibre in this category.

Pretreatment

Bleaching of linen results in the removal of some or all of the impurities, and the bleached linen behaves similarly to cotton. Unbleached linen must be boiled out with soda ash and a suitable wetting and dispersing agent, but a pre-bleach is advisable in order to obtain dyeings of maximum rubbing fastness.

Naphthol Application
In order to obtain satisfactory penetration, naphthol exhaustion should begin at
70°C or above, omitting the formaldehyde, and be completed in a cooling bath at
25–30°C. Addition of an alkali-resistant wetting agent to the naphtholate solution is
recommended.

Aftertreatment
Although azoic dyes are developed on linen in the same way as on cotton, a more
intensive aftertreatment is required to remove the greater proportion of loosely
held azoic dye from the fibre surface. In package dyeing it is necessary to prevent
filtration of the dispersed azoic dye particles by giving an initial treatment at
60–70°C, followed by soaping at the boil in a fresh liquor containing higher concentrations of soap and soda ash.

8.7.4 Regenerated Cellulosic Fibres
Viscose is the most important of the regenerated cellulosic fibres. It is available in
continuous-filament or staple variants, like the newer polynosic fibres. Absorption
of naphthol varies amongst these regenerated celluloses.

Pretreatment
Normally regenerated cellulosic fibres contain only small amounts of spinning
assistants and softeners. These are mainly water-soluble and can usually be removed by a weakly alkaline scour in soda ash with wetting and dispersing agents.

Naphthol Treatment
As naphthols have higher substantivity for regenerated cellulose than for cotton,
lower concentrations are required to attain the same depth. In batchwise processing
it is advisable to pre-wet the material thoroughly in a solution of wetting agent before addition of naphthol, to avoid uneven uptake owing to inadequate wetting-out
of the material. Regenerated cellulosic fibres swell to an appreciably greater extent
than cotton in alkaline liquors and have increased alkali absorbency, so that the
amount of alkali in the naphtholate solution can be reduced (usually to 4 ml/l
caustic soda 38° Bé)).

Intermediate Rinsing
The amount of caustic soda in the rinsing bath can be reduced (to 0.5–1 ml/l 38° Bé)
in view of the increased absorbency of the fibre.

Aftertreatment
Dyeings on regenerated cellulosic fibres are usually soaped at 80–90°C with 2 g/l
soap and 0.5 g/l soda ash. During soaping of certain azoic combinations 'blinding'
(delustring) of the fibre may occur, but this undesirable effect can be avoided by
soaping at 50–60°C. Preliminary trials are advisable to obtain optimum results.

8.8 EQUIPMENT FOR DYEING TEXTILES
Cellulosic textiles in the form of loose stock, sliver, tow, yarn, fabric, terry
towelling and knitted goods can be dyed with azoic dyes.

8.8.1 Dyeing of Stock, Sliver and Tow in Package Machines

Cotton is seldom dyed in the form of loose stock, but viscose staple is commonly dyed in these forms in package-dyeing machines. Cotton sliver can be naphthol-treated and developed in package machines or wound on perforated beams and dyed in beam machines. Two types of package-dyeing machine are available for loose stock: machines suitable only for this type of material and those that can be adapted for dyeing loose stock, cheese or beams by suitable choice of carrier. The loose stock must be tightly packed in a wet condition to prevent channelling and, as the tightly packed material has a strong resistance to flow, liquor circulation should be from inside to outside only. Depending on the type of material and machine used, it may be necessary to repack between naphthol application and development in order to obtain level dyeings.

Cotton can be yarn dyed in package-dyeing machines in the form of hanks or cheeses. Viscose can be dyed in cake form, particular care being taken that unsatisfactory packing does not cause unlevelness by channelling.

8.8.2 Hank Dyeing in Becks

Yarn in hank form was traditionally suspended on sticks and turned by hand while dyeing in large-volume becks (100–1000) made of wood or stainless steel. This method is seldom used today, although it gives azoic dyeings of particularly good rubbing fastness because the naphthol-treated hanks can be hydroextracted to about 50% before development and are then allowed to drain. Intensive aftertreatment follows in the boiling soap liquor in becks. In order to avoid undue cooling the hanks are seldom turned at the start, but turning is increased later. During turning the friction between adjacent hanks removes undesirable surface deposits. Dyeings of excellent rubbing fastness are produced after warm and cold rinsing, hydroextraction and drying.

8.8.3 Hank-dyeing Machines

Two types of machine are used, one in which the hanks are agitated and the liquor remains stationary and the other in which the liquor is circulated through the hanks. Spraying techniques are intermediate between these two methods.

In hank-dyeing machines of the first type the hanks are suspended in the liquor on rods which rotate and move up and down. This system can be used for naphthol exhaustion, development and aftertreatment, the dyeings produced being level and the yarns having a full handle. With the circulating-liquor type both open and closed vessels are available, consisting of rectangular tanks fitted with holders for the hanks at the top or side of the vessel. The yarn is completely immersed in the liquor, which is circulated by means of a pump. Most hank-dyeing machines have a stuffer box fitted outside the machine. This is used to fill the vessel with the dye liquor and to make additions of dyes and chemicals.

In the spray technique the yarn carriers are perforated and the dye liquor is pumped through onto the yarn hanks, which are suspended in the vessels without dipping into the dye liquor. The controlled addition of dye liquor is stopped at intervals during which the hanks are removed. This procedure can be used for both naphthol treatment and development and permits the use of short liquor ratios.

8.8.4 Cheese-dyeing Machines

Most yarns are dyed on conventional circulating-liquor machines, a method which is ideally suited for azoic dyes. Open machines are seldom used, in this case liquor circulation should be only from inside to outside due to the uneven pump action. Closed machines with two-way liquor circulation are preferred when applying azoic dyes. Machines with adequate suction are essential; suction treatment is desirable after each operation, particularly after naphthol application and intermediate rinsing. If soaping liquors become highly coloured by the azoic dye removed from the material it is advisable to run off the liquor and refill with a fresh soap solution. Furthermore during subsequent washing-off it is preferable to change the liquor frequently for the same reason rather than to continue with the same liquor for a longer period.

8.8.5 Beam-dyeing Machines

In this method cotton yarns are wound on perforated beams, uniform winding being essential to ensure the production of satisfactory dyeings. The beam or beams are fitted into the vessel either vertically or horizontally according to the type of machine used. Certain machines are suitable for dyeing either cheeses or beams and the basic principles or cheese dyeing apply to beams. In large beam machines there is considerable resistance to flow and the alternating cycle of flow direction should favour out-to-in rather than in-to-out.

8.8.6 Warp Yarns in Roller Vats

Warp yarns can be dyed in the form of wound packages in roller vats. The warps run continuously over guide rollers and pass through squeeze rollers, whereby the expressed dye liquor returns to the dye vat. After naphthol treatment the yarn is squeezed and placed in a truck and then passes into the developing liquor in a roller vat.

8.8.7 Naphthol Application During Warp Sizing (for Denim)

Most of the material not dyed with indigo or sulphur dyes in the production of blue dyeings on cotton denim fabric is dyed with azoic dyes during warp sizing. The warp yarns are simultaneously sized and treated with naphthol, mainly C.I. Azoic Coupling Component 2 or 20; carboxymethylcellulose, alone or in admixture with potato starch, is used as size. Increase in the proportion of carboxymethylcellulose gives a less viscous size liquor and consequently better penetration of naphthol into the yarn; however, this is not always desired. The warps can be dried in hot-air dryers or on heated cans, but rapid drying is not desirable if good penetration and rubbing fastness is required, since there is insufficient time for the naphthol to penetrate the yarn satisfactorily. The prepared warps are then woven with the weft yarn in the normal way. Care must be taken to ensure that the prepared warps and the woven fabric are not left exposed to direct sunlight and that no uneven friction occurs during weaving, as this can cause warp stripes. Both the beams and the undeveloped fabrics can be stored for a long period provided that they are protected from exposure to light, acid steam and high humidity.

Pad development of the woven fabric with Fast Colour Salts or diazotised Bases gives the best penetration. In principle jig development is also possible except for blues and blacks, although it is uneconomical. The concentration of the developing bath depends on the depth of naphthol applied. Since only the warp yarns contain naphthol the weight of weft yarn in the fabric must not be included when calculating the concentration of the bath. A normal aftertreatment is given, and in order to reserve the weft as much as possible, it may be necessary to include a boiling soap treatment, but this depends on the fabric construction. Bleached cotton must be used for the weft if the maximum white effect is desired, but undyed grey cotton is frequently employed. By the use of coloured weft yarns attractive two-coloured effects can be obtained that are of interest in clothing for casual wear [11, 12].

8.8.8 Winch Dyeing of Terry Towelling and Knitted Fabrics
Certain hues and depths difficult or impossible to obtain with reactive dyes can be produced with azoic dyes. Only highly substantive naphthols are applicable, and preferably diazo components with high or moderate coupling energy should be employed. Diazotised Fast Colour Bases and Salts with low coupling energy are less suitable.

Very good results are obtained if the prepared tubular-knitted fabric is removed from the winch and then hydroextracted and slit into open form for development on the winch. The time-consuming process of hydroextraction can be avoided by rinsing before development. Knitted fabrics treated with naphthol on the winch in tubular form may be developed continuously on special equipment in which air is injected to inflate the tubular fabric into balloon form. In this state it is immersed in the development liquor, and level dyeings should result.

8.8.9 Jig Dyeing of Fabrics
Piece goods are jig dyed only when small lengths of fabric are to be dyed or where continuous units are not available. In general rinsing is given between preparation and development. Where fastness requirements are particularly high, especially rubbing fastness, an intermediate drying stage is given. Intermediate drying of naphthol-treated fabric is also advisable before continuous development.

8.8.10 Pad–Jig Process
When a padder and drying unit are available, but a continuous range is not, an alternative process is the pad–jig technique. After padding with naphthol, with or without intermediate drying, the dyeing is developed and aftertreated on the jig.

8.8.11 Continuous Processing
This is the most important method for the azoic dyeing of fabrics. It has the advantage of low dye consumption and the possibility of dyeing long lengths of fabric. Standard colours can be dyed fully continuously; the naphthol-treated fabric is dried, developed and soaped on a continuous range. It is necessary, however, to cool the dried fabric before it passes into the development bath.

The most common method is padding with naphthol, drying and allowing to lie or batch. The best drying unit to use is a hot flue. The treated fabric is cooled and then developed, soaped and rinsed in a further padding and open-width washing range.

Naphthol Application

Two- or multi-roller padders with shallow troughs are used. Tightly woven cotton fabrics that are difficult to penetrate are preferably impregnated on a three- or multi-roller padder and given a double dip and nip treatment for the best possible penetration.

Preference should be given to naphthols with weak or moderate substantivity. As naphthol treatment takes place at 85–90°C it is advisable to dissolve the naphthols by the hot method or to use the readily soluble naphthols which only require sprinkling to form the hot naphtholate solution. Rapid and even wetting-out of the fabric is ensured by maintaining the naphtholate solution as hot as possible. The effect of weak or moderate substantivity of the naphthol is virtually eliminated and this has a positive influence on the levelness of the resultant dyeings.

Intermediate Drying

A hot flue is the best type of dryer and the most suitable temperature range is 90–100°C. A regular air stream is necessary to obtain level dyeings equal in depth on both sides of the fabric. If drying cylinders are used for intermediate drying, care must be taken to ensure that contact with the fabric changes from side-to-side as it passes through the dryer, and the first drying cylinder should be either kept at a lower temperature or lagged. Pin stenters are preferable to clip stenters for stenter drying, and the temperature in the first heating zone should be maintained at about 100°C to avoid premature drying of the fabric. The residual humidity should be within 8–12% in order to ensure rewettability and complete coupling; overdrying is to be avoided. The fabric should be covered with a wrapper to protect it from the action of moisture, water spotting, acid vapour and light.

Development

A continuous unit, i.e. a padder and open-width washer, is used. In many cases a two-roller padder is suitable for lightweight fabrics. For heavyweight fabrics, particularly when dyed with blue and black salts produced specially for continuous dyeing, a three- or multi-roller padder is recommended. The diazo compound is heat sensitive, so the development liquor should be as cool as possible in order to prevent decomposition. A small trough should be used which can be quickly refilled with liquor. The fabric is padded, skyed for a short time and then passed into an open-width washer. With most azoic combinations a skying period of 30–60 s is followed by a cold rinse and, if necessary, neutralisation with 2 ml/l concentrated hydrochloric acid, and in the next compartment the fabric is rinsed cold, sometimes using an overflow. The 'acid/soda' process is used with diazo components having a low coupling energy. The diazonium solution in the development padder is pre-pared with an excess of 10–20 ml/l acetic acid (50%) and, after skying for 30–40 s, the fabric passes into the first compartment of an open-width washer containing 10 g/l soda ash at 30–40°C. In the second compartment the fabric is rinsed again, possibly with overflow. In the case of weakly coupling diazo components, which decompose in the soda bath and lose their ability to couple, a third method is recommended. After padding and skying for 30–60 s the fabric is treated in water at 80–90°C in an open-width washer; if necessary, two treatments may be given. Finally in all three methods the fabric is soaped with a soda ash addition in several compartments of the washer, as near the boil as possible, and this is followed by warm and cold rinsing.

8.9 FASTNESS OF AZOIC DYEINGS

In common with vat dyeings, there are no water-solubilising groups present in azoic dyeings, which accounts for their exceptionally good wet fastness on cellulosic fibres, as illustrated in the manufacturers' pattern cards. Special mention should be made of the following fastness properties. All these naphthol combinations withstand washing at the boil and the light fastness properties are good to excellent. However, whereas dyeings of most dyes show a gradual lowering of light fastness with decrease in depth, the drop is more evident with many azoic dyes and this is one of the main reasons why azoic dyes are not normally applied in pale depths. The light fastness of some dyeings is affected by the moisture content of the atmosphere in which they are exposed; azoic dyes are prone to this effect. Most azoic combinations are fast to chlorine, so that they are suitable for materials to be bleached. With few exceptions, the fastness to mercerisation of azoic dyeings is excellent and the same is true of fastness to perspiration. Azoic dyes vary in fastness to hot pressing but there are many with excellent fastness. Inadequate fastness to hydrogen peroxide is frequently evident. Blue combinations are an exception, but they show lower fastness to chlorine. Most azoic dyeings are of good fastness to resin finishing [13–15]. Only slight changes in hue occur and light fastness is not adversely affected; in fact, in many cases it is even increased.

Similar comments apply to treatment with flame retardants [16]. The principal weakness of azoic dyeings is their moderate fastness to organic solvents used in dry cleaning and spotting [17]. There are, however, some exceptions to this statement and dye manufacturers' pattern cards should be consulted. Fastness to rubbing varies and is largely dependent on the dyeing process used.

Since azoic dyes are azo compounds they discharge readily and are ideal for dyeing fabrics intended for white and coloured discharge styles. Their commercial application, however, has declined somewhat in favour of reactive dyes in this area, because of the brilliant colour gamut and easier application procedures of reactive dyeing.

In general it can be said that the fastness standards of azoic dyeings are superior to those of reactive dyeings and only marginally below those obtained with vat dyes, although it must be borne in mind that many colours obtained with reactive or vat dyes cannot be produced with azoic dyes.

8.10 STRIPPING OF AZOIC DYEINGS

8.10.1 Stripping Naphthol-prepared Materials

Before development, naphthol-prepared materials, particularly where weakly substantive naphthols have been used, are relatively easy to strip using boiling alkaline liquors.

8.10.2 Stripping Dyeings

Azoic dyeings can be stripped with powerful reducing agents, although dyeings based on highly substantive naphthols are more difficult to deal with. Certain yellow azoic dyeings are resistant to reducing agents and can therefore be only partially stripped.

Stripping of azoic dyeings on cotton and other cellulosic fibres requires treatment with 5–10 ml/l caustic soda (38° Bé), 1–2 ml/l of a heat-stable dispersing agent and 3–5 g/l sodium hydrosulphite. An addition of 0.5–1 g/l anthraquinone powder results in an appreciable increase in the stripping effect. Care must be taken that sufficient sodium hydrosulphite and sodium hydroxide are present during the stripping process. Anthraquinone causes the stripping liquor to turn red. If it should turn yellow or brown a further addition of caustic soda or sodium hydrosulphite must be made. After running-off the stripping liquor, the prevention of stain formation is essential. Stains are caused by decomposition products and should be removed by giving the stripped material hot and cold rinses. An alternative process entails treating material with only caustic soda, dispersing agent and anthraquinone, cooling below the boil and then adding the sodium hydrosulphite.

8.11 USE OF DYE-MANUFACTURERS' LITERATURE

The most important factors to be considered in the preparation of recipes for dyeings are:
(a) Method of dissolving naphthols
(b) Absorption of naphthols (graphs or tables)
(c) Relationship between naphthols and Fast Colour Bases or Fast Colour Salts
(d) Quantities of Fast Colour Bases or Fast Colour Salts to be added for the production of pale, medium and full depths
(e) Diazotisation procedure for Fast Colour Bases
(f) Methods of dissolving Fast Colour Salts
(g) Alkali-binding capacity of diazotised Fast Colour Bases and Fast Colour Salts

Leading manufacturers of azoic dyes issue pattern cards for the dyeing of fabric and yarns, together with detailed technical literature of two types, i.e. handbooks containing a loose-leaf system of data relating to each naphthol, Base and Salt [18] and a double rotatable disc [19] giving the required data on the quantities of the various products necessary to prepare a dyeing.

8.11.1 Recipes for Batchwise Dyeing

Naphthol Application
As the concentration of naphthol determines the depth of the dyeing obtained, the

quantity of naphthol for a specific liquor ratio must be taken from the dye manufacturers' instructions. If the liquor ratio has to be changed, alterations in the amount
of naphthol can also be made.

Development
Data on dissolving Fast Colour Salts and on the diazotisation of Fast Colour Bases
are given by the dye manufacturers. Calculation of the concentration of diazo component can be done in two ways, in both cases based on the amount of naphthol absorbed. Tables or graphs provide data on the concentration of the naphtholate
solution applied and the amount of naphthol absorbed by the cotton can be read off
from the tables at various liquor ratios. The quantity of naphthol applied determines whether pale, medium or full depths will be obtained. Tables provide information, for each diazo component and for varying liquor ratios, on the amounts of
Fast Colour Bases or Salts required to produce various depths. This procedure
represents a simple and accurate method of setting up satisfactory development
liquors. Where standing baths are used this simplified method of calculating the
composition of developing baths is employed. If the development baths are used
only once, as is usual, there is a more precise method of calculation of the quantities of Fast Colour Bases and Salts, available from suppliers, resulting in a minimal
excess of diazo component (compared with the first method of calculation).

Calculation of Amount of Alkali-binding Agent
When development baths are set up according to the formula given previously, with
the prescribed quantities of Fast Colour Bases or Salts, it is important to add alkali-
binding agents to give the appropriate pH for development. The quantity of caustic
soda bound per kg Fast Colour Base or Salt prepared according to the prescribed
procedure can be obtained immediately by reference to the disc or handbooks. The
quantity of caustic soda taken by the material from the naphtholate solution is calculated first. The amount of caustic soda added to the naphtholate solution is
known and it is easy to calculate the uptake of caustic soda by reference to the
appropriate curves or tables for various liquor ratios. Thus the amount of caustic
soda remaining in the liquor is obtainable. If, after deducting the amount of caustic
soda brought over into the development bath from the total quantity that can be
bound to the diazo component, the result is negative, then the quantity of alkali-
binding agent present in the development bath is adequate. On the other hand if
the result is positive (i.e. not all the alkali is bound), then the difference must be
adjusted by increasing the amount of alkali-binding agent in the development bath.
Acetic acid is normally used and the necessary amount to be added can be seen by
reference to tables. With high-energy coupling components (group I) the excess
may be greater and the acetic acid does not need to be buffered, but with group III
coupling components (which couple most readily at pH 6–7) the excess acetic acid
is a minimum and may require buffering with sodium acetate.

8.11.2 Recipes for Continuous Dyeing
The preparation of padding recipes is simple. Where padding and development are
carried out at the same liquor absorption, reference to the disc or tables enables a

calculation to be made for the concentration of diazo component in relation to the concentration of naphthol.

Calculation of Amount of Alkali-binding Agent
This calculation is easy to carry out, as the amount of caustic soda in the naphtholate solution is known and the quantity absorbed by the cotton is related to the expression given. For example, with 100% expression using x g/l caustic soda in the naphtholate solution, there will be x g/kg on the prepared material. This figure has to be compared with the alkali-binding power of the diazo component used as detailed above for the batchwise dyeing technique and, if required, acetic acid must be added as alkali-binding agent.

REFERENCES

1. 'Colour Index', 3rd Edn, Vol. 1 (Bradford: SDC and AATCC, 1971).
2. Wallwork, J.S.D.C., **55** (1939) 477.
3. Staab, Melliand Textilber., **42** (1961) 1373.
4. Fischesser and Pokorny, French P, 212063 (1891).
5. Schneider and Schneider, Amer. Dyestuff Rep., **51** (1962) 1037.
6. Griesheim Elektron, German P, 256999.
7. Rys and Zollinger, 'Fundamentals of the Chemistry and Application of Dyes' (Chichester, West Sussex: John Wiley, 1972).
8. Hunger, Mischke and Rieper, 'Ullmann' 4th Edn, Vol 8.
9. Herzog, Chem. Rundsch., **26** (12) (1973) 7.
10. Gund, J.S.D.C., **76** (1960) 151.
11. Herzog, Melliand Textilber., **43** (1962) 848.
12. Herzog, Textilveredlung, **2** (1967) 205.
13. Herzog and Koszticsza, Textil Rundsch., **16** (1961) 782.
14. An Huef, Melliand Textilber., **50** (1969) 1349.
15. An Huef, Amer. Dyestuff Rep., **60** (1971) 56.
16. Einsele, Duran and Tarakcieoglu, Melliand Textilber., **61** (1980) 180.
17. Herzog, Textil Rundsch., **14** (1959) 494.
18. 'Naphtol AS – Directions for Use and Applications', Hoechst Publication 4026 (1971).
19. 'Naphthanilide Disc', Rohner Publication 148 (1980).

CHAPTER 9

Dyeing of Polyester/Cellulosic Blends

WILLIAM J MARSHALL

9.1 INTRODUCTION

Fabrics made from a blend of polyester and cotton fibres are used in half or more of all the shirts and raincoats in many advanced countries, in about one-third of all leisurewear trousers and in roughly a quarter of all workwear and sheets. Polyester/cotton thus occupies a very important position in the fabric markets and has displaced much 100% cotton, warp-knitted nylon, wool worsted and other materials.

In many countries polyester used in blend with cotton often comprises a third of all polyester consumed. In general throughout the world polyester/cotton is becoming the major application for polyester, and it is significant that no other man-made fibre has achieved such prominence in blends with cotton. Clearly polyester and cotton fibre properties must be specially compatible to have achieved this situation. The same cannot be said of their dyeing properties.

However, in the 1970s many complete fibre plants were designed and built specially for polyester staple fibre for polyester/cotton blends, and many fabric producers now have units or whole mills devoted entirely to polyester/cotton blends.

Polyester/cotton is increasing in use and is by now so important as to constitute a class of material on its own. The high price of cotton means that the blend is no longer a special product with new properties, the reverse becoming true as 100% cotton assumes a quality and comfort role while the blend is seen increasingly in lower priced articles where durability and good service are of paramount importance.

Although polyester/cotton is, by far, the most important and widely used of all the blends of polyester and cellulosic fibres, viscose and other regenerated cellulosic fibre blends are also very extensively used, for example in tropical lightweight suiting, in fashionwear, shirting, etc. Linen is also of considerable importance in blends with polyester, as a luxury fabric in household goods, such as tableware sheeting, etc., and in high-class fashion goods.

The general dyeing methods used apply to all of these materials, but there may be significant differences in the detailed requirements, with respect to both fastness and handling techniques. For example, viscose fibre blends will often be dyed in the winch or jet dyeing machine rather than in open width in order to preserve the handle; where thermofixation has been used for the disperse dyeing stage the subsequent treatment will often include rope soaping or relaxation in a winch. The choice of dyes will also be influenced by the fibre. Direct dyes are more likely to be used as their fastness is often higher on viscose fibre than on cotton.

Polynosic and other regenerated cellulosic fibres usually have their own special requirements, especially with respect to dye selection and the severity of certain treatments. These vary too much to specify, but the fibre manufacturers can supply the necessary details and the dye makers are usually able to make specific recommendations for dye selection.

Similarly blends containing linen have their own special needs which are familiar to those accustomed to dyeing 100% linen. The same precautions are required. Care must be taken not to spoil the characteristic nature of the linen texture. Vat or reactive dyes are normally chosen for linen and it is dyed in open width to avoid permanent creasing. There are other differences too. Disperse dyes often stain the lignin component in linen so that reduction clearing of the stain is more likely to be needed; this can be combined with the reduction stage of a vat dyeing.

These are not hard and fast rules. For example, there is a very large amount of polyester/viscose piece goods dyed continuously in open width. In some cases the material may be given a subsequent rope treatment to impart a softer handle. Sometimes the firmer handle associated with open-width treatment is preferred.

Throughout this chapter no clear cut distinctions will be drawn. The term polyester/cotton generally includes all classes of cellulosic blends. Where specific reference is made to another fibre the inference is that the method is especially appropriate to blends with that fibre.

9.2 PREPARATION OF MATERIAL FOR DYEING
Preparation of the material will not be discussed in detail in this chapter, but needless to say it is of great importance. Especially in continuous dyeing the material must be fully absorbent and easily wettable. Two particular aspects of polyester/cotton distinguishes it from 100% cotton, namely its behaviour on singeing and the requirements of heat setting. Incorrect procedures in either of these can give rise to faulty dyeings.

Polyester is a thermoplastic material and, when singed, small surface fibres may melt and form microscopic globules. These globules take up dye more readily than the bulk of the material and can give the finished dyeing a speckled appearance. Batchwise dyeing methods are more likely to suffer from this defect than are continuous methods. However, suitable singeing equipment is now available and much can be done to control this difficulty. In extreme cases singeing can be carried out after dyeing, but this usually involves additional processing and inconvenience. Cropping the material is an alternative that avoids the difficulty.

Secondly the polyester component must be heat set to stabilise the fabric structure and improve its crease-shedding properties. This is normally carried out, for piece goods, at or about 190°C for up to 30 s, usually on a stenter, either before or after dyeing; the temperature must remain uniform. Heat setting after dyeing removes minor creases introduced during dyeing, and allows the material to be pulled to its finished width and stabilised at that width. Especially if the dyed polyester fibres are not fully penetrated, subsequent setting may cause slight colour change (usually an increase in depth and brightness) as dye diffuses into the interior. More importantly with fully penetrated dyeings, particularly when softeners or other hydrophobic impurities are present, dye may diffuse to the surface of the polyester fibres and lower fastness may be observed in subsequent wet-fastness tests, a phenomenon known as thermal migration.

Heat setting before dyeing has the advantage that the material is less likely to crease during dyeing and dyeability variations arising from differences in thermal history of the polyester fibres may be less evident. Heat treatment of synthetic-polymer fibres influences the subsequent uptake of dyes. If batches of yarn or fabric have been subjected to different temperatures during manufacture, they may differ slightly in colour after dyeing.

Sensitivity to these differences is greater in batchwise dyeing than in continuous dyeing. If heat setting is carried out before preparation, care must be taken to ensure that there are no oil stains or other contaminants that might be set into the material and prove impossible to remove subsequently. On the other hand, heat setting after preparation tends to give a hydrophobic fibre with potential difficulties in subsequent continuous dyeing. Each dyehouse has its own special circumstances that will determine the best procedure for heat setting. This will depend on the variety and type of material processed, dyeing techniques, working methods and equipment available.

Finally, as with 100% cotton, polyester/cotton may be mercerised to enhance the appearance and increase the colour value of dye on cotton. Significant amounts of polyester/cotton blends are mercerised but the proportion varies according to the market.

9.3 DYES AND DYEING METHODS USED (GENERAL CONSIDERATIONS)

The polyester component of a polyester/cellulosic blend can be dyed by a continuous or by a batchwise method. Thermofixation is the basis of the very important continuous dyeing processes. The method that is adopted for dyeing the blend is dominated by the needs of the polyester, and there are three options available:

(a) Continuous dyeing (with the polyester dyed by a continuous method)
(b) Batchwise dyeing (with the polyester dyed by a batchwise (exhaust) method)
(c) Semi-continuous dyeing (with the polyester dyed either by a continuous or exhaust method).

The choice of dyes for dyeing polyester/cellulosic blends presents an intriguing combination of requirements to ensure that adequate fastness properties and dyeing quality are balanced against production volume, production costs, and dye and chemical costs, while making the most of the available equipment.

The dyeing properties of the two materials are so very different that a different class of dye is used to dye each of the two fibres. These dyes usually require different dyeing conditions even when superficially a single dyeing method is used. There are certain exceptions to this general statement which will be discussed later. In principle the two fibres can be dyed separately and in practice most dyeing methods used are essentially the telescoping of the two separate methods, although in some cases common application features, such as padding and drying, give a superficial appearance of a single dyeing method. To simplify the system the dyeing requirements of each fibre will be discussed separately, but in relation to dyeing in blends.

9.4 DYEING OF POLYESTER IN POLYESTER/CELLULOSIC BLENDS

9.4.1 Disperse Dyes in Dyeing Polyester

The requirements for dyeing polyester in polyester/cellulosic blends are often different from that of 100% polyester. The heat fastness of the dyeing is usually required to be higher, especially where permanent-press finishes are to be applied; thus C and D (medium to high energy) classes of disperse dyes are usually necessary, except in pale colours. These in turn require higher dyeing temperatures or more severe fixing conditions. Although dyeing under atmospheric conditions using carriers is possible, and was widely used before the availability of suitable pressure dyeing and thermofixing equipment, carrier dyeing is much less common nowadays except in special applications. Not only are the carriers and dyes expensive, but the cellulose is also heavily stained and it is not possible to obtain satisfactory deep colours with high fastness. The use of C and D classes of dye increases the problems of carrier dyeing.

The criteria for selection of disperse dyes on blends differ from those on 100% polyester, as the disperse dye stain on the cellulosic fibre may be difficult to remove and usually has low fastness to light and to wet treatments. Disperse dyes tend to stain adjacent nylon heavily in wet-fastness tests so it is essential that the staining of the cellulosic component during dyeing is minimal.

The dyeing conditions are important as will be explained later. Although the stain can usually be removed by reduction clearing, this is an extra process when direct or reactive dyes are being used. Where vat dyes are used reduction clearing can be combined with the reduction stage in vat dyeing. Even so the most effective reduction clearing requires the addition of an anionic or cationic clearing agent as well as reducing agents. As this restrains the vat dye, these agents must be applied as a separate process.

Clearly the choice of dyes is important. In spite of the low fastness of disperse dyes on cellulosic fibres, some disperse dyes have a significant substantivity for cotton and will stain it strongly, leading to difficulty in removal of unfixed dye and low fastness. A disperse dye with a low substantivity for cotton will show little staining.

Where material is dyed under pressure at 130°C with a dye of low substantivity for cotton, staining on the cotton is usually negligible. Residual dye in the dyebath is usually in solution, and if the dyebath is drained by blowing out under pressure without cooling, deposition of the dye is minimised. On the other hand, if the dyebath is cooled slowly the dissolved dye will reprecipitate and be redeposited on the fibre. Where the dye has substantivity for the cotton staining can be severe.

In continuous dyeing a low temperature of thermofixation or short treatment time prevents complete dye transfer from cotton to polyester, and hence staining of the cotton results.

Where the disperse dye is removed by reduction clearing, conditions are rather less stringent, although it is necessary to ensure that the dye can be satisfactorily cleared in this way. Taking all of these considerations into account it is clear that dyes should be chosen to give a minimum staining of the cellulosic component of the blend, even though this is less necessary when reduction clearing is carried out.

Apart from staining of the cellulosic component, choice of disperse dyes does not usually present many problems. Light fastness is usually adequate and after dyeing the dye is protected from many chemical effects by the hydrophobic nature and relative impermeability of the fibre. Nevertheless the dyer should be aware that a number of disperse dyes are sensitive to alkaline conditions in the dyebath and some dyes may be sensitive to metal contamination.

It is normally recommended that disperse dyes are applied under slightly acid conditions, e.g. at about pH 5, and, where a dye is sensitive to the presence of metal ions, addition of a small amount of sequestering agent should be standard practice. However, when dyeing in combination with alkali-fixing reactive dyes, some compromise in processing is required. Ideally alkali-sensitive disperse dyes should either be fully fixed before alkali is introduced to the dyebath or the disperse dye should not be introduced until the reactive dye is fully fixed and the dyebath neutralised, otherwise lower and perhaps erratic yields may be obtained. In practice a compromise is usually reached. This will be discussed more fully later. In the case of vat dyes reducing agent present with the alkali would in any case preclude using this type of single-stage condensed processing sequence.

This sensitivity to alkali can be put to advantage by using an alkaline scour to remove unfixed dye from the cellulosic portion of the fibre. One dye manufacturer has introduced a range of disperse dyes containing hydrolysable ester groups. Under hot alkaline conditions these dyes are converted to the water-soluble sodium carboxylate form, which has low substantivity for cotton and polyester. They were originally introduced for printing to avoid back-staining of whites in printing polyester and polyester/cotton blends. They are also promoted for the continuous dyeing of polyester/cellulosic blends in combination with reactive dyes. Tests show that this class of dye can be completely cleared in continuous processing and any problems of staining are due to the inadequate clearing of the reactive dye. This will be discussed more fully later (p. 328).

9.4.2 Continuous Dyeing with Disperse Dyes
The normal sequence of processes is pad–dry–thermofix–wash-off.

Padding
The pad liquor requires nothing other than disperse dye, but it is usual to add a migration inhibitor to ensure satisfactory dyeing quality, and often a wetting agent. An acid buffer, e.g. acetic acid, may sometimes be added to maintain the pH at around 5 with alkali-sensitive dyes. Dihydrogen sodium phosphate is also used as a

buffer but there is evidence that it can react with cellulose and inhibit dye absorption. Liquid forms of disperse dyes are preferred to powders as they are less prone to migrate during drying, they give less staining on the cellulose, give a higher colour yield and the pad liquors are easier to prepare in the large amounts usually required for continuous dyeing. On the other hand, liquid dyes can settle on long storage (they should always be thoroughly agitated before weighing); when stored in partly used containers they may dry out leaving a solid dye deposit on the side of the container at the air/liquid interface, giving rise to the possibility of specking. Carelessly stored material may also lose water and increase in strength. Manufacturers are aware of these problems and have done much to improve liquid disperse dyes in recent years. A compromise is to use liquid dyes where possible and to resort to solid powders or grains where dyes are used only in small amounts.

Padding temperatures for disperse dyes may be between 20 and 50°C according to circumstances.

Drying
The material must be thoroughly dry before thermofixation, otherwise the required conditions may not be achieved. Other special requirements to minimise migration are common to all dye classes and will be discussed below.

Thermofixation
Satisfactory thermofixation is essential for the production of level, uniform and reproducible dyeings with the desired fastness properties. Disperse dyes suitable for dyeing polyester/cellulosic fabrics usually require a fixation period of 30–60 s at 210–225°C. Certainly temperatures below 205°C are too low for the C and D classes of dyes normally used. Differences in fabric weight and equipment design affect the actual treatment time at thermofixation temperature and it is that which determines the efficiency of fixation. Bent, Flynn and Sumner in a classic study [1] clearly separated the complex factors involved in the continuous dyeing of polyester/cotton blends. They showed that disperse dye padded onto a 70:30 polyester/cotton blend after drying was partitioned with only 30% of the dye on the polyester but 70% on cotton, i.e. the opposite to the blend ratio; thus the concentration of disperse dye before thermofixation was more than five times greater on the cotton than on the polyester. During thermofixation dye was found to transfer from the cotton to the polyester, which could be fully explained by dye transfer through the vapour phase.

Some other important considerations are discussed below.
(a) At low temperatures or when the dyeing time is too short the dye is incompletely transferred from the cotton to the polyester. This leads to poor yields and excessive staining of the cotton, even with dyes that would normally be satisfactory in these respects when properly applied.
(b) Disperse dyes with a high substantivity for cotton do not completely transfer from the cotton to the polyester.
(c) At very high temperatures or if fixation is prolonged the dye volatilises and is

lost to the system. Apart from low yield this leads to contamination of the thermofixation unit and danger of spoiling subsequent dyeings by redeposition of the condensed dye on the new material.

(d) The optimum temperature for thermofixation is that at which the maximum amount of dye is transferred to the polyester without significant loss by volatilisation. This is also time dependent.

(e) The optimum temperature is closely related to the heat fastness of the dye. The class D dyes that are most fast to heat have an optimum fixation temperature of 225°C or even higher, while the class C dyes with the lowest heat fastness have optimum fixation temperatures in the region of 210°C. Class B dyes have even lower optimum fixation temperatures of about 200°C. If class B dyes are used at the higher temperatures serious contamination of machinery is likely. These are not hard and fast figures and are subject to depth of shade and variations in machine type and cloth being dyed. Treatment at the optimum dyeing temperature as well as giving the maximum dye yield and fastness gives the best conditions for good reproducibility, robustness to temperature variations, and colour stability after subsequent processing, e.g. permanent-press finishes.

(f) Disperse dye transfer is most efficient when there are as few auxiliaries present as possible, as these tend to retard volatilisation of the dye from the cotton component. Such auxiliaries can be dispersing agents (including those present in the original dye composition), migration inhibitors, electrolyte (neutral or otherwise), urea or any other non-volatile component that may have been added to control or improve the quality of the dyeing or as part of the dyeing system. At one time urea was thought to improve dye fixation. In fact this apparent improvement in fixation is due to increased staining of the cotton, giving rise to a visually deeper colour. Urea gives lower fixation of disperse dyes on the polyester, and the fastness properties are lower, unless the stain can be removed from the cotton. This limits the amount of urea that can be used as an aid to fixing reactive dyes in a one-bath process. Similarly liquid dyes give better yields than powders or grains because they contain less dispersing agent. Migration inhibitors of the hydrolysed polyacrylonitrile type do not interfere with dye transfer as much as alginates, when each is used at the normally recommended concentration. Transfer is improved at lower atmospheric pressures, and vacuum techniques have been applied successfully to transfer printing, particularly of carpet squares. However, vacuum transfer has not yet been extended to continuous dyeing.

At first sight there is what might appear to be an unexpected result of the dye transfer described above. If disperse dye only is applied the material will appear reasonably solidly dyed after padding and drying only. After thermofixation the material will now appear much weaker and skittery. The more effective the thermofixing the greater the effect, due of course to the melange effect of the blend of white cotton and heavily dyed polyester, compared with dye previously being distributed between both fibres. It follows that the more effective the dye transfer from the cotton, the whiter it will be and the paler the appearance of the dyeing.

Degradation of the cotton may also be caused by thermofixation at the temperature required to dye the polyester. This is affected by the following factors.

(a) Temperature and time of treatment, above 150°C degradation increases rapidly.
(b) pH, the optimum of the dye pad liquor is usually considered to be between 4.5 and 6. Alkaline conditions bring about degradation and severe browning of the cellulose as well as an increased possibility of disperse dye destruction. The pad bath pH is on the acid side of neutrality but the actual condition in the dry fibre at 200–220°C is unknown, although it will clearly depend on the buffer chemicals used. Acetic acid is a commonly used buffer but is a volatile acid and will be lost to the system. Buffers based on phosphoric acid are non-volatile but react with the cellulose. Experiments with the pad bath adjusted to pH 4.5 with phosphate buffer and added dicyandiamide gave material with a slightly alkaline reaction after thermofixation.
(c) The additives urea, dicyandiamide and similar reagents have a protective effect. Conventional additives, especially dispersing agents present in dye formulations, have a marked browning effect. It is a most revealing exercise to carry out a continuous 'dyeing' with all the additives except the dye but including the dispersing agent that would have been in the dye. Brown staining of the cotton is often severe, which is another good reason for using liquid forms of disperse and vat dyes, rather than grains or powders, in continuous dyeing as these help in keeping the need for dispersing agents to the minimum.

These comments on thermofixation would be incomplete without reference to high-temperature (HT) steaming, i.e. steaming at atmospheric pressure with superheated steam in the temperature range for polyester of 170–180°C for 6–8 min. This has become an established method for printing and has been of particular importance in the printing of texturised polyester. Lower temperatures of fixation can be used in HT steaming than in dry heat treatment. This is important in the printing of textured polyester, because conventional thermofixation causes unacceptable loss of crimp, even at the lowest fixation temperatures possible with class B disperse dyes. HT steamers are in widespread use in printworks. However, even at 180°C superheated steam is very dry and has a relative humidity (r.h.) of 10% in comparison with saturated steam at the same temperature. At 200°C the r.h. is 6.5%, and it appears that as the temperature is increased and the HT steam becomes drier the advantage of HT steaming over conventional thermofixation decreases. After initial interest, few dyers have adopted continuous HT steaming for polyester/cotton blends.

Washing-off Unfixed Dyes
As already mentioned, the main problem of removing unfixed disperse dye is clearing it from the cotton. Two methods are available, i.e. reduction clearing and alkaline washing. Until the recent development of a range of alkali-hydrolysable disperse dyes, reduction clearing was regarded as essential for the highest level of fastness in medium to heavy depths.

Reduction clearing cannot be used when the cotton has already been dyed, but when vat dyes are applied, either continuously or by a batchwise process, the reduction conditions used during vat dyeing are often sufficient to reduction clear the unfixed disperse dye effectively, so that separate clearing is unnecessary. This feature makes continuous dyeing with disperse and vat dyes a very attractive process. Under adverse conditions of material, colour or equipment, combined vat dyeing and reduction clearing may be inadequate for the standards required. Under these circumstances reduction clearing is carried out as a separate process after continuous dyeing with disperse dye but *before* dyeing the cotton. When reactive or direct dyes are used for the cotton component, any reduction clearing should always be carried out before dyeing the cotton.

Separate reduction clearing may be performed either in the normal continuous vat dyeing range, in which case the chemical pad liquor will consist typically of:
– Sodium hydrosulphite (hydros), 10 g/l
– Caustic soda (flake), 7 g/l
– Non-ionic detergent, e.g. Matexil DN-VL (ICI), 1–2 g/l.

This is followed by steaming for 30–60 s and washing-off in the continuous range. It is necessary to ensure that the reducing agent is fully destroyed and the caustic soda is 'neutralised' either with sodium bicarbonate or acetic acid. A high washing temperature should be maintained but if oxidation is necessary this should be at 50–60°C with a peroxy compound set at pH 8, if necessary with sodium bicarbonate. Higher temperatures will rapidly destroy the peroxide.

Alternatively, where no pad steam unit is available or it is preferable to use only an open soaping range, the first one or two boxes are set at 70°C with:
– Sodium hydrosulphite (hydros), 6 g/l
– Caustic soda (flake), 6 g/l
– Non-ionic detergent, e.g. Matexil DN-VL, 3 g/l

and washing carried out as above. In this case it is essential to make periodic additions of all components to maintain the reduction conditions.

Alkaline washing can take several alternative forms. It is clearly cheaper than reduction clearing, can be used after dyeing with reactive dyes and can be combined with washing-off unfixed reactive dye. It is therefore much more attractive than a separate reduction clearing provided that it is sufficiently effective in any given application.

The hitherto accepted method of continuous clearing unfixed disperse dye uses the following sequence: rinsing copiously with cold or warm water, thoroughly boiling-off with soda ash (2–3 g/l) and detergent (1–2 g/l), followed by rinsing and drying.

The initial rinsing is to remove mechanically, as far as possible, the unfixed dye and other soluble matter so that there is less contamination of the subsequent hot baths with dye that might have substantivity for either polyester or cotton. This method is still applicable, but work by ICI has shown that the initial cold rinse reduces penetration of alkali into the cotton, so that solubilisation of alkali-hydrolysable disperse dye is retarded. Since the hydrolysed dye has no substantivity for either cotton or polyester, contamination is less important. The method recommended for the alkali-hydrolysable dyes is either to pad with caustic soda (flake) (10 g/l) at 20–40°C or to set the first wash box with caustic soda (flake) (4 g/l) at 90–95°C. This is followed by boiling-off with caustic soda (1–2 g/l) and detergent

(1–2 g/l), rinsing, neutralising and drying. In both cases, after thermofixation the material should be entered dry into the alkali to ensure maximum alkali penetration.

The detailed sequence must be worked out according to the equipment used and material being processed.

9.4.3 Batchwise Dyeing Under Pressure Using Disperse Dyes

Continuous dyeing of disperse dyes has been dealt with extensively because it is a method used almost exclusively in dyeing polyester/cellulosic blends. On the other hand, batchwise dyeing of polyester/cellulosic blends has many features in common with the dyeing of 100% polyester, which has already been dealt with in a previous book of this series [2]. The main differences are in the choice of dyes, which has already been mentioned, and certain precautions required according to the nature of the material. The most noteworthy of these are the differences in handling texturised polyester and polyester/cotton blends. Dye choice again is important, with greater emphasis in the latter case being placed on heat fastness and freedom from staining the cellulose.

In the typical dyeing sequence dye is added below 70°C, and the temperature raised slowly to 125–130°C. This temperature is held for 30–60 min before blowing-out the bath under pressure (if possible), and rinsing clear or giving a light scour.

Brief comments only will be made on these operations. The disperse dye absorption rate is controlled by the rate of temperature rise through the critical temperature range, usually 15–20°C, which varies from dye to dye, tending to be higher with dyes of greater heat fastness. Staining of the cellulosic portion of the material is much less than in continuous dyeing, provided that a correct choice of dye has been made, and severe clearing treatments are seldom necessary, although reduction clearing can be used. It is highly advantageous if the exhausted dyebath can be blown-out immediately after dyeing under pressure and without cooling. This avoids redeposition and further staining of the cotton, since the dye remaining in the bath is usually soluble at the dyeing temperature. There is also a saving in dyeing time. However, the drains of the machine should be designed so that it is safe to blow-out the exhausted liquor under pressure, hence the practice is not suitable for jet dyeing machines or pressure winches (see p. 347). Blowing-out is particularly advantageous in yarn dyeing.

The additives to the dyebath are:
– Anionic dispersing agent, 1–2 g/l
– Acetic acid (30%) (to pH 5)
– Carrier (optional), 0.5–1 g/l
– Sequestering agent, e.g. EDTA, 0.5 g/l.

Again the preferred dyeing pH is 5–6.5. A carrier is not essential and many dyers prefer to avoid its use, but a small amount is sometimes advantageous in improving levelling and penetration. There is a wide choice available. Some dyes are very sensitive to small amounts of heavy metals, especially copper, and it is sensible to include a sequestering agent as a normal precaution unless it is known to be unnecessary.

Rinsing is necessary to remove dispersing agents and unfixed dye. Deeper colours may require a more thorough hot scour with detergent and alkali, followed by rinsing clear, and in extreme cases a reduction clear may be necessary. Much depends on the choice of dyes, depth of shade, construction of material, etc.

Reduction clearing is carried out with:
– Sodium hydrosulphite, 3 g/l
– Caustic soda (flake), 3 g/l
– Non-ionic detergent, e.g. Matexil DN-VL, 3 g/l

for 20 min at 80°C, rinsing clear and neutralising. The non-ionic detergent should always be thoroughly rinsed clear, otherwise thermal migration in subsequent heat treatment may lower the wet fastness.

9.4.4 Leuco Vat Ester Dyes in Dyeing Polyester

Polyester is almost exclusively dyed using disperse dyes. However, in blends with cellulosic fibres the use of leuco vat esters presents a very attractive method of dyeing pale to medium depths by a simple continuous process. In this process the leuco vat dyes the cellulose and initially stains the polyester; the dye diffuses into the polyester during thermofixation, which is an essential part of the process as it develops and stabilises the colour.

In applications requiring high fastness in pale depths this method of dyeing both components simultaneously is elegant and easy to use. The only drawbacks are that there is only a limited possibility of adjusting the proportions of the dye on the two fibres, and the dyes are expensive. In pale depths both of these disadvantages are of less importance, but they clearly limit the depth of shade applicable. Dye selection is important as, among other reasons, some vat dyes exhibit markedly different colours on the two fibres, but there is a useful short range of dyes covering the important colours.

9.5 DYEING OF CELLULOSE IN POLYESTER/CELLULOSIC BLENDS

Reactive, direct, vat and sulphur dyes are used for dyeing cellulosic materials in blends. The choice of dye class is complex, but all four classes mentioned are of major importance. The application of these dyes has been fully described in other chapters of this book so comments in this section are confined to additional factors introduced in dyeing the blend.

There are four additional features introduced by blend dyeing as opposed to dyeing a single fibre. They are:
(a) Cross-staining (staining of fibre by the dye intended for the other fibre)
(b) Interference between dyes or between dyes and processing chemicals
(c) Effect of the additional processing required to fix both dye for cellulose and the dye for polyester
(d) Effect of the second fibre component in increasing the effective liquor ratio significantly. For example, with a dyeing carried out at a 15:1 liquor ratio on a polyester/cotton blend where the blend ratio is 70:30 (i.e. containing 30% cotton) the liquor ratio with respect to the cotton is effectively 15:0.3, i.e. 50:1.

The importance of these effects differ according to dye class but can be crucial in the choice of processing sequence and its ultimate robustness.

An important and useful observation is that once disperse dye has been absorbed by and diffused into the polyester it is protected from most of the chemical or physical effects of subsequent processing. Thus disperse dyes are most susceptible to dyebath interactions *before* and *during* dyeing. This is not true of dye on the cotton component, e.g. reduction clearing will destroy direct and reactive dyes whether or not they have been absorbed by the cellulose, whereas it will only destroy disperse dye that has not been absorbed by the polyester. Likewise alkali will partially destroy some sensitive disperse dyes whilst in the dyebath but the dye is completely protected in the polyester fibre.

9.5.1 Dyeing with Vat Dyes

In continuous dyeing it is usual to use a disperse/vat dye combination. This system makes a convenient reference for comparing other systems. In general, other systems will only be preferred if they can provide a specific effect, an easier process, better equipment utilisation or lower costs with equally acceptable results. Vat dyes are almost invariably fixed on cotton after fixing the disperse dye, with the notable exception of the acid leuco esters (see p. 330). Vat dyes are stable to thermofixing conditions but some vat dyes will fix on polyester to a significant extent. In the oxidised form vat dyes are chemically stable to HT dyeing conditions but prolonged high temperatures (as in pressure dyeing) may cause dispersion instability if vat and disperse dye are applied simultaneously. It is preferable in batchwise dyeing processes to add the vat dye to the cooling dyebath after the HT fixation of disperse dye is complete.

In general, vat dyes are robust and suitable for one-bath, two-stage fixing processes, both in continuous and batchwise dyeing processes. There is pronounced cross-staining of the polyester, particularly in continuous dyeing.

9.5.2 Dyeing with Sulphur Dyes

Sulphur dyeing of polyester/cellulosic blends is widely used for continuous dyeing, where price is a major consideration. Similar comments apply as for vat dyeing. Sulphur dyes are cheap but their fastness is limited. Sodium sulphide is said to have an adverse effect on polyester and the preferred method uses sodium hydrosulphite to minimise this effect.

9.5.3 Dyeing with Reactive Dyes

Because of the very wide variety of dyeing methods and the different chemical types of reactive dyes, this dye class is technically the most interesting. It also offers the widest scope for compromise in processing conditions. A proper understanding is necessary to clarify the reasoning behind the choice of dyeing method and dye selection.

Cross-staining
Reactive dyes are almost completely free from cross-staining effects. The only

exceptions are a small amount of staining with the phthalocyanine-based dyes (turquoise blues and certain greens) and those dyes that may have traces of impurities introduced during manufacture. Cross-staining of polyester by reactive dyes can generally be ignored.

Liquor Ratio
In batchwise dyeing this can have an important bearing on dye choice for good reproducibility and economy. The effect on liquor ratio is illustrated in Table 9.1.

TABLE 9.1

Effective Liquor Ratios in Dyeing Polyester/Cellulosic Blends at Different Nominal Liquor Ratios

	Effective liquor ratio					
	50 PET/50 Cell		70 PET/30 Cell		80 PET/20 Cell	
Nominal liquor ratio	PET	Cell	PET	Cell	PET	Cell
5:1	10:1	10:1	7:1	17:1	6:1	25:1
10:1	20:1	20:1	14:1	33:1	12:1	50:1
15:1	30:1	30:1	20:1	50:1	20:1	75:1
20:1	40:1	40:1	30:1	67:1	25:1	100:1

PET – polyester
Cell – cellulose

This clearly shows that dyeing a 70:30 blend in the apparently very respectable liquor ratio of 10:1 or 15:1 effectively gives a liquor ratio of 33:1 or 50:1 with respect to the cellulose. This point is made in detail because it emphasises the advantage of using padding methods where possible and of choosing, for batchwise dyeing, reactive dyes giving high fixation at long liquor ratios. The use of low-substantivity dyes for batchwise dyeing is inefficient, expensive and leads to difficulties in dyeing reproducibility.

Interaction of Processes and Chemicals for the Two Dyeing Systems
The wide variety of processes available for dyeing reactive dyes described in Chapter 4 could lead to confusion in selecting the most appropriate method for blend dyeing. Owing to the special nature of reactive dyes, the possibilities of interaction between components of disperse and reactive dyeing systems must be taken into account and understood. These effects are not all clear cut, but over the years an understanding of the significant factors has been acquired, based on both practical experience and careful laboratory evaluation.

At the risk of over-simplification, the more important factors involved have been tabulated in Table 9.2 with a brief comment on the influence of each on the reactive dyeing of cellulose and on the disperse dyeing of polyester. From the practical point of view reactive dyes can be divided into three groups according to their reactivity. Although 'unofficial', it forms a useful basis of comparison. The groups are:

Group 1
Highly reactive dyes, e.g. dichlorotriazine (Procion MX (ICI)), dichloroquinoxaline (Levafix E (BAY)), fluorodichloropyrimidine (Drimarene R (S) and Levafix EA (BAY)), and fluorotriazine (Cibacron F (CGY)) types

Group 2
Moderately reactive dyes, e.g. vinylsulphone (Remazol (HOE)) types

Group 3
Dyes of lower reactivity, e.g. chlorotriazine (Procion H (ICI) and Cibacron E (CGY)), and trichloropyrimidine (Drimarene (S)) types.

This is not an exhaustive list but it indicates the types of dyes discussed.

Reactive dyes lend themselves to a wide variety of dyeing processes that are suitable for polyester/cellulosic blends. Although the wide variety of methods available may give an impression of complexity, they are quite straightforward. The range of colours available is excellent and the fastness is adequate for most uses. They are widely used for dresswear, children's wear, domestic goods, etc., especially in the brighter colours.

9.5.4 Dyeing with Direct Dyes
Direct dyes are widely used in the dyeing of polyester/cellulosic blends, especially blends containing viscose fibres. Their application is relatively straightforward. They are applied after the polyester has been dyed, either in the exhausted bath with the addition of salt, or in a fresh bath, which also serves as a soaping bath for clearing the disperse dye. Since the fastness of direct dyes is limited there is less need for a high standard of clearing of the disperse dye.

If the direct and disperse dyes are applied together, it is necessary to ensure that the direct dyes are sufficiently soluble and stable under slightly acidic conditions at the high temperature required to exhaust the disperse dyes.

By using special after-coppered direct dyes a high standard of light fastness can be obtained, combined with reasonably good wet-fastness properties. These 'high class' direct dyes are more expensive, require additional aftertreatments and are more difficult to apply than standard direct dyes, but they provide a useful range of drab colours and navies suitable for outerwear.

Direct dyes are normally dyed on polyester/cellulosic blends by batchwise dyeing processes only.

9.6 DYEING PROCESSES AND MACHINERY (GENERAL CONSIDERATIONS)
The dyeing process selected for use depends on the type of material to be dyed, the minimum fastness requirements, the size of the production run, the equipment available, its lay out and, of course, the overall economics. There is a complex

TABLE 9.2

Reactive and Disperse Dyeing Systems: Interactions of Dyes and Dyeing Assistants

Factor	Comment on reactive dyeing system	Comment on disperse dyeing system
pH	All reactive dyes require alkali for fixation. Severity of treatment required, i.e. pH and temperature increases in order group $1 < 2 < 3$. Group 1 dyes can react under neutral to slightly alkaline conditions when the temperature is sufficiently high.	Dyeing with disperse dyes is preferably carried out under neutral to slightly acid conditions. Alkaline dyeing conditions tend to give lower yield. Some disperse dyes are very sensitive to alkali.
Dye interaction	Reactive dyes can chemically react with dyes containing free amine or hydroxyl groups. Effects tend to be specific, but group 1 dyes are more reactive than group 3 dyes. In addition physical interaction can occur irrespective of dye reactivity.	Effect is highly specific to certain disperse dyes, and can be detected by effect of applying disperse dye in the presence of reactive dye. A reduced yield of the disperse dye is obtained on the polyester. Incipient interaction can also be detected chromatographically.
Salt	In batchwise dyeing salt is essential to promote dye exhaustion and satisfactory dye fixation. In continuous dyeing it is sometimes used to reduce migration of reactive dyes. It reduces the solubility of all reactive dyes. It is used in pad–develop sequences to promote fixation with alkali.	Salt decreases the stability of disperse dye dispersions and can lead to dye aggregation specking. It inhibits levelling and migration in dyeing. Powders and grains contain more dispersing agent and are therefore more stable than liquids.
Acid or alkaline hydrolysis	Reactive-dye–fibre bond is subject to hydrolysis to a greater or lesser extent. Under the HT, slightly acidic conditions used for batchwise dyeing with disperse dyes, some group 1 dyes and, to a lesser extent group 3 dyes lose some depth due to acid hydrolysis. Group 2 dyes are more stable under these conditions but are subject to significant hydrolysis during alkaline scouring, which is the best method of removing unfixed disperse dye.	Apart from reduction clearing, an alkaline scour is usually a good method of clearing unfixed disperse dye.
HT dyeing condition	Hydrolysis of the reactive group can occur, causing reduced reactivity. Chromophoric groups in certain reactive dyes are unstable during batchwise dyeing at high temperature. This results in reduction in final yield, whether or not the dye has been fixed.	It is possible either (a) to add disperse and reactive dye to the dyebath at the same time or (b) to apply the reactive dye before the disperse dye.

| Thermofixation and additives | Group 1 dyes are usually fixed by drying with alkali only. Deeper colours may require thermofixation at 120–130°C with urea (50 g/l) and alkali. Thermofixation at 210–220°C reduces the chlorine fastness in the presence of urea and alkali. Sodium bicarbonate is the alkali normally used. Pale depths of dichlorotriazine dyes can be fixed without alkali by thermofixation at 210–220°C.

Group 2 dyes are not recommended for fixation by dry heat, but thermofixation does not significantly affect the dyes adversely.

Group 3 dyes are usually fixed by thermofixing at 120–160°C with 200 g/l urea + soda ash. Thermofixation at higher temperature is more rapid but chlorine fastness is reduced.

Thermofixation of cellulose at 210–220°C, as required for applying disperse dye, degrades and browns the material to some extent. Degradation is greatest under alkaline conditions but urea tends to protect the cellulose. Under neutral to slightly acid conditions degradation is minimised. | Group C and D disperse dyes require minimum of 210–220°C for satisfactory thermofixation. The addition of alkali and urea inhibits disperse dye fixation, and urea increases staining on cotton. |

The resultant procedures for different conditions are as follows.

pH: In one-bath batchwise processes it is preferable to fix the disperse dye before alkali is added. If the reactive dye is fixed before the disperse dye the latter should not be added until the bath has been neutralised. If dyes from groups 1, 2 or 3 are used in a one-bath continuous process the disperse dye must be carefully chosen and the mildest possible alkali used. In double padding processes the disperse dye must be fully thermofixed before padding with alkali, or if the reactive dye is fixed first the alkali should be neutralised or washed-off before applying the disperse dye.

Salt: This is not generally a problem but care must always be exercised and the minimum amount of salt used where there may be a possibility of disperse dye aggregation. Glauber's salt is used in preference to common salt.

Acid or alkaline hydrolysis: If it is necessary to apply the reactive dye first an acid pH with group 1 and 3 dyes should be avoided. There should be no alkaline scouring after dyeing with group 2 dyes.

Thermofixation and additives: With group 1 and 3 dyes a compromise is necessary in one-bath processes. Both alkali and urea additions are reduced to minimise cross-staining, and this limits the fixation and build-up of reactive dyes. Group 1 dyes require least alkali and urea, and pale depths can usually be obtained without alkali or urea. Group 3 dyes require the most critical compromise.

interplay of factors. For example, if a full-scale continuous dyeing range is available the overall economics of dyeing a long production run may be better using disperse and vat dyes than dyeing in a batchwise system with disperse and direct dyes, although the latter are much cheaper than vat dyes. Furthermore the fastness of the dyeing would be higher. With this caveat in mind, the dyeing of polyester/cotton blends will be considered under three headings:
(a) Continuous dyeing
(b) Batchwise dyeing
(c) Semi-continuous and hybrid dyeing systems.

9.7 CONTINUOUS DYEING

Continuous dyeing of polyester/cellulosic blends is generally confined to woven piece goods. Typical materials processed in this way include shirting, trousering, rainwear, workwear and uniform material, the latter including both military and non-military items. The length of run in one colour is generally between 5000 and 10 000 m, at a running speed of 30–90 m/min. In certain circumstances the length of some runs may be only about 1000 m, but continuous equipment is not usually installed unless most production runs are at least 5000 m. The running speed depends to some extent on the weight of the material, but the design speed is calculated according to the production requirements of the plant. Speeds can go up to 120 or even 150 m/min. These higher production rates are better met by installing a second continuous dyeing unit, which has the advantage of increasing versatility, e.g. different widths of material can be processed, or one machine can be used for heavy depths and another for pale depths, thus cutting down cleaning time between runs.
Production runs will normally last 2–8 h, although they may be longer.

9.7.1 Continuous Dyeing Equipment
The full continuous dyeing range consists of the following equipment and is normally used in the sequence given.

Unit 1
– Two- or three-bowl padding mangle
– Infra-red pre-dryer
– Dryer (cylinder or hot-flue type)

Unit 2
– Thermofix range giving facilities for uniform heat treatment of 200–230°C for 30–60 s; hot flue and cylinder types are the most common; the Fleissner perforated-drum type is also used and suitable heat-setting stenters

Unit 3
– Two-bowl chemical padding mangle and steamer

Unit 4
– Continuous washing range optionally fitted with a 'skying' arrangement for oxidation of vat dyes or development of leuco vat esters

Unit 5
– Cloth drying unit (usually cylinders).

In the largest production plants these five units are placed in line and fabric is capable of running continuously from one unit to the next, in some cases without the possibility of breaking production at any point.

Bearing in mind the average time it takes to process any one part of the fabric, i.e.:

– Padding and drying	1–2 min
– Thermofixation	30–60 s
– Chemical padding and steaming	30–60 s
– Oxidation, reduction clearing, washing, etc.	3–8 min
– Drying	30–60 s
Total time in machine	5½–13 min

the amount of fabric in the machine will be 500 to 1000 m, and this length must be run before seeing the first piece of dyed material.

It is therefore common, and good practice, to allow the material to pile into a scray or miniature J-box capable of holding 50–100 m after thermofixation. This allows inspection or sampling of the material before further processing without having to interrupt production. When sampling or inspection is no longer required production can proceed fully continuously without having to stop the range.

Provision can also be made at this point for batching (on rolls or in trucks) for semi-continuous processes or for the production of cross-dyed or melange effects as described below. Although less common, it is useful to allow production to be interrupted between drying and thermofixing, especially if there are doubts about the dyeing quality or the colour. Since the disperse dye is not fixed at this stage there is no problem in removing the dye if quality or colour is unsatisfactory.

The success of continuous dyeing depends on the correct design of all its units, and especially the uniformity of treatment across the piece and absence of periodic changes in processing conditions (e.g. temperature). Correctly designed, properly installed and well-maintained machinery should take care of these items. However, certain aspects are of particular importance.

Unit Operation 1: Padding and Drying
In continuous dyeing of polyester/cotton blends the padding and drying stage is the most critical. The material before padding must have been well prepared so that it is uniformly absorbent, has not been overdried and has a uniform regain. Padding must be even across the material. Faults at this stage cannot be corrected later. The pick-up of dye liquor must not be too high as this increases the difficulties in drying, nor can it be too low as this accentuates weaving and surface faults. A typical pick-

up would be 55% for a 70:30 polyester/cotton poplin, but the most suitable level will vary from material to material.

After padding the material should pass directly upwards, preferably without coming into contact with guide rollers, into the infra-red (i.r.) pre-drying zones where the moisture content should be reduced sufficiently to prevent excessive migration at the next stage, which is hot-flue or cylinder drying. Where cylinders are used they should be graded in temperature to ensure that excessively rapid drying, and therefore migration, does not occur while the material still contains capillary water. Furthermore it is advantageous for the first six or eight cylinders to be coated with PTFE. The object of the i.r. pre-drying is to reduce the water content of the material sufficiently to prevent excessive migration of dye in subsequent drying, and also to prevent dye liquor from transferring (marking-off) from the wet fabric onto hot guide rollers or cylinders, where it can accumulate and possibly spoil later portions of the run by marking the fabric or depositing specks. For the same reason contact with rollers during i.r. drying should be kept to a minimum and the rollers should be placed in such a position that they are kept as cool as possible. Certain critical guide rollers should be shielded from i.r. radiation and (preferably) water cooled. However, if rollers are placed too far apart the fabric may tend to ripple lengthwise and this can introduce irregular results due to uneven dye migration. Correct tension control can reduce this tendency, but careful control is necessary to establish the best conditions for each material.

Migration control is important as excessive migration can bring about three different general types of fault, described below.

(a) Unsatisfactory appearance of the dyeing. This may emphasise weaving faults or irregularities, or be manifested as streaks, a 'salt and pepper' effect, or be just a general impression of poor dyeing quality. It can make a high-quality cloth have the appearance of a low-grade material.

(b) Unevenness from side to side or across the piece. The colour may have greater depth on one face due to more rapid drying on one side than the other. Similarly colour may not be uniform across the piece. This latter fault is often difficult to distinguish from uneven padding.

(c) Poor penetration. Even when material is evenly and fully penetrated during padding the final dyeing may exhibit poor penetration. During drying the water evaporates from the surface of the material to which heat is applied. This water is replaced by water from the interior of the fabric by capillary flow, carrying dye with it. Thus the dye that originally penetrated into the fabric is deposited on the surface of the material. I.r. heating gives better heat penetration of the material and hence less migration. The ultimate result of migration is that the material may be completely uncoloured under neps or loose threads. Similarly disturbance of the weave or the threads will reveal undyed material at the cross-overs and in the interior of the thread. This inevitably will occur in use and during washing, cleaning, etc., so that the material will appear to lose colour and have low fastness even with the fastest possible dyes. Wear points of garments will also quickly show as white patches. However popular this effect may be for certain types of leisurewear, it is not considered as satisfactory dyeing practice.

Because of these effects, migration enhances the colour value, with adverse results if the migration is unequal. If migration is kept under control and is completely uniform, the enhanced colour value is an asset, and few dyers would willingly sacrifice this by completely eliminating migration, even if it were possible to do so.

The measures a dyer can take to control migration are detailed in Table 9.3, which indicates the point of control, the reason and limitations. In practice it is usual to use a combination of the different approaches to achieve the best overall results. Some manufacturers supply migration inhibitors that are a mixture of products mentioned.

Migration as a problem in continuous dyeing is a subject that is well understood in general terms but few studies have been made in depth.

This discussion would be incomplete without reference to the Remaflam process developed by Hoechst in conjunction with Artos, the machinery manufacturer. In this system about one-third of the water in the padding liquor is replaced by methanol. During drying the methanol is ignited and contributes to very rapid drying and reduced migration. The advantages claimed include excellent wetting-out of the material during padding due to the high methanol content and reduced migration. Inherent difficulties of the process include the low flash point of methanol-containing pad liquor and control of the burning of the methanol during drying.

Although it is commonly considered that migration inhibitors are thickners and reduce migration by increasing viscosity, the true situation is much more complex and far from being clearly understood. The so-called 'thickners' used for vat and disperse dye combinations are ineffective for water-soluble dyes and almost certainly affect the behaviour of the dye dispersion. When selecting antimigration agents consideration must also be given to marking-off onto rollers during drying. For this reason, and to ensure optimum conditions for dye transfer from the cotton to the polyester during thermofixation, the total additions made should be kept to a mimimum.

It is again emphasised that the padding and drying stage is crucial in the production of high-quality and uniform dyeings.

Unit Operation 2: Thermofixation
The original Thermosol process was invented and developed by Du Pont for dyeing polyester with disperse dyes by applying dry heat. The term Thermosol is the property of the Du Pont company and refers specifically to dycing polyester. Reactive dyes may also be dyed on cellulosic material by the application of dry heat, and it is incorrect to use the Du Pont term Thermosol or worse Thermosoling in this connection. The more general term thermofixation should be used to describe fixation by dry heat, whatever the dye/fibre system concerned.

The process has been widely studied for fixing both disperse dyes on polyester and reactive dyes on cellulosic fibres, and important aspects have been discussed above.

The equipment used is important in determining the nominal time and temperature of treatment for a given dye and material. The *effective time* at a given tem-

TABLE 9.3

Conditions for Controlling Migration During Drying

Stage	Action	Principle involved
Cloth preparation	Ensure that the material is rapidly and uniformly wettable.	Irregular wicking of water through material during drying due to uneven wettability gives uneven redeposition of colour.
Padding	Adjust mangle pressure to give lowest pick-up consistent with quality.	Migration stops when water no longer forms a continuous film in the fibre capillary system, and is reduced as this condition is approached. There is no migration below this critical moisture content. In practice migration is unimportant at low pick-up levels significantly above this level.
Pad liquor composition	Add migration inhibitor(s) to pad liquor.	(a) For water-insoluble dyes, i.e. vat and disperse dyes, sodium alginate and poly(vinyl alcohol) derivatives are the most effective agents; their exact mode of operation is not fully understood. (b) For water-soluble dyes, i.e. reactive dyes, sodium chloride addition increases substantivity and reduces migration. (c) Certain non-ionic agents also improve the appearance of the dyeing although do not necessarily reduce migration; their mode of operation is not fully understood.

I.r. drying	(a) Run sufficient end fent through the machine with the i.r. dryers on to ensure they are fully operational before dyeing proper is started.	To be effective, i.r. pre-drying must remove 20–40% of the water content.
	(b) Ensure that guide rollers are in a position where they do not become overheated.	Dye migrates to hot surfaces.
	(c) Ensure that cloth tension and running speeds are adjusted to avoid rippling or fluting of the material.	Differential drying occurs at convex and concave surfaces.
Drying cylinders	Adjust temperature of the initial cylinders to be below 100°C, preferably about 80°C, with subsequent cylinders on a graded temperature range.	An excessive drying rate promotes migration. In general the higher the running speed over cylinders the better, as this gives more uniform treatment to both front and back of the fabric.
Hot-air driers	Ensure even air flow across the pieces and from side to side. Initial air temperature should be 100–110°C and not above 120°C. Ensure cloth is fully dry when leaving the drier.	Uneven air flow leads to uneven migration, which shows up as strength differences. Too rapid drying can lead to excessive migration. Incompletely dried material can give rise to difficulties at the thermofixation stage. With an efficient pre-dryer difficulties at this stage are not usually critical in a modern well-designed dryer.

perature (i.e. the time the fabric is at the temperature) is markedly different from the actual time of treatment. Air is a poor heat-transfer medium and it may take 45–60 s before the fabric temperature is within one or two degrees of the air temperature in a conventional hot-air thermofixation unit. The time taken also depends on the fabric weight and construction. A heavyweight fabric will take longer to reach equilibrium temperature than lightweight material. Shorter times can, to some extent, be made up by setting the equipment at a higher temperature, although this is a limited and dangerous expedient. If there is a large difference between the required temperature and the set temperature the actual temperature of the material will rapidly be increasing during the whole time it is in the machine, with the effective temperature being highly dependent on the running speed and small variations of air-flow rates, etc. Under these circumstances variations in colour readily occur. It follows that a recommendation for one machine may not be appropriate for another. Ideally the fabric temperature should be measured. Although this is possible in principle either from i.r. emission or by contact thermometry, there are practical difficulties and such measurements are rarely made. In practice this degree of sophistication is unnecessary. Provided the principles described above are taken into account, the thermofixation method provides a robust and reliable means of dyeing with disperse dyes.

As a guideline Table 9.4 lists, in order of relative efficiency of heat transfer, alternative methods of heating and gives a guide to treatment times for materials of average weight.

It is important that the material has been dried uniformly before entering the thermofix unit, otherwise the initial heating stage will be used to evaporate the water rather than raising the cloth temperature to its maximum. This will result in either uneven or inadequate dye fixation.

After thermofixation the material must be cooled if it is to be given a chemical pad–steam treatment. It is, in any case, advisable to cool before further processing, especially if the process is interrupted at this stage. Most thermofix units have provision for cooling, often a cylinder with water circulated in it.

The most widely used system in a custom-built continuous dyeing range is the hot-air unit with ducted air circulation, and the second commonest are cylinder systems of various design. The perforated-drum system of Fleissner is also popular. This consists of two rotating perforated drums of large diameter, over which the material passes and through which air is blown. Stenters are not normally incorporated into continuous dyeing equipment, although they are sometimes used for thermofixation in the absence of a custom-built range or to supplement production. The actual choice of equipment depends on the materials to be processed and the cost.

Unit Operation 3: Chemical Pad–Steam
The chemical pad–steam unit is essential for vat and sulphur dyeing, but is not necessary for dyeing with disperse/reactive dyes (except the vinylsulphone type). The Standfast molten metal machine is an alternative for the development of vat dyes, but this is not now a widespread method. The requirements for dyeing polyester/cotton blends are exactly as for 100% cotton (Chapter 6). Because of the

TABLE 9.4

Continuous Dyeing: Heating Rates for Different Systems

Heating system	Heating method and rate	Comment
Radio frequency and microwave	Radiation (very rapid)	Not used for thermofixation because of control difficulties[a]. Expensive.
Infra-red (i.r.)	Radiation (very rapid)	Not used for thermofixation because of difficulty in controlling fabric temperature.
Fluidised bed	Conduction (2–5 s)	Restricted use due to technical difficulties arising from high fabric tensions.
Cylinder	Conduction (10–30 s)	Highly efficient. Particularly useful for flat goods.
Perforated drum (Fleissner)	Conduction/ convection (15–40 s)	Highly efficient.
Stenter	Convection (15–40 s)[b]	Effective for most types of goods. Gives width control. Expensive.
Conventional hot air (with circulation)	Convection (30–90 s)[b]	Widely used. Often considered to give better (or different) handle to material being processed compared with cylinder and perforated-drum systems.
Laboratory oven	Convection (45–90 s)	Laboratory treatment times must be calibrated against bulk results to obtain reliable reproducibility.

(a) Information limited as loss factors which determine rate of heating are not known for either fibres or additives at thermofixation temperatures.
(b) At 200°C the walls of the equipment can produce significant i.r. radiation. The contribution from this source could be high if the emissivity of the internal surfaces is also high.

previous high temperature of the thermofixed material, special attention must be paid to ensure that the fabric is cool before padding and that the pad liquor temperature is kept below 30°C. The high temperature of thermofixation may also cause the material to be hydrophobic and steps should be taken to ensure that faults do not arise from this cause.

Unit Operation 4: Washing
The ultimate fastness of the dyeing depends on satisfactory washing-off and after-treatment conditions. The nature of continuous dyeing is such that processing times are reduced to the minimum, and it is therefore essential that these be carried out with the highest possible efficiency. In the past this has not been properly understood by machinery manufacturers and there have been a number of machines produced and sold that were unsuitable for the purpose. Fortunately the situation is

now very different and modern washing equipment is highly efficient. These newer developments have been led by the 'horizontal'-type washing machines, both pressurised and atmospheric, marketed by Kleinewefers and Artos respectively. In these machines the material is guided in a series of horizontal passes at successively higher levels and the wash liquor or treatment liquor is fed in at the top. The liquor flow is arranged to be truly counterflow, and that passing out of the unit at the bottom can be passed back into the previous unit. The horizontal machines are particularly compact owing to the high capacity achieved by vertical stacking of units, so that the overall length of the machine is minimised. Apart from technical efficiency in terms of dyeing quality, these machines are highly productive as a result of rapid heating and quick change-over between runs, and their consumption of energy and water is low.

However, claims are also made that the horizontal arrangement has certain deficiencies compared with the more traditional vertical disposition of the fabric, provided the same care in design has been taken. Indeed, most existing continuous ranges for polyester/cotton dyeing use the traditional eight (minimum) to ten box open soaping units with an optional 'skying' unit. The latter increases the versatility of the range by allowing air oxidation of vat and sulphur dyes, and dyeing with leuco vat ester dyes. If the latter are to be applied there should also be an impregnating box of suitable grade stainless steel for the sulphuric acid development stage.

The essentials of satisfactory treatment in the washing range are:

(a) Maintenance of correct reagent concentrations (this is a frequently neglected area of control)

(b) High wash water temperatures in the clearing and soaping baths (low bath temperatures are only too often a reason for unsatisfactory results)

(c) Correct control of feed water and overflows to avoid excess build-up of dirty water

(d) Sufficient processing time in the clearing and soaping baths to allow diffusion of unfixed reactive or disperse dye out of the fibre or to allow vat dyes to develop their correct shade

(e) Satisfactory interchange between fibre and treatment or wash water to allow rapid equilibrium.

If these various requirements are met the results should be satisfactory.

Unit Operation 5: Drying
The standard cylinder drying range is normally suitable for the vast majority of dyed polyester/cotton materials. It should be provided with a high standard of uniform lighting at the exit to ensure that any dyeing faults can be quickly identified and dealt with, so avoiding spoilt material.

9.8 BATCHWISE DYEING
As already mentioned, batchwise dyeing of polyester/cellulosic blends is always a two-stage process and the overall dyeing cycle is long. The methods used to shorten the process are compromises in which the processes are telescoped by carrying out

two successive processes in the same dyebath or without intermediate rinsing, etc. The exact method adopted and the detailed procedure depends greatly on the machinery used and this in turn depends on the type of material being processed. The individual dyeing methods have already been discussed, and this section will first describe the type of machinery used and then the way in which the different methods are fitted together.

9.8.1 Batchwise Dyeing Equipment

Polyester/cellulosic blends are almost entirely dyed either as yarn or in piece form. Yarn is mostly dyed in cones or cheeses or on beams, generally under pressure, i.e. under HT conditions. Certain blends may be dyed in hanks in impellor-type equipment. Piece goods were originally dyed in winches, pressurised winches or pressure jigs. Following the very great developments in jet dyeing, the pressurised winch has almost disappeared and the low liquor ratio of most modern jet machines is now comparable with that of the jig, and is often lower than that of the pressure beam dyeing machine. Most piece goods are now dyed on either the pressure jet machine or the beam, with smaller amounts still dyed on the pressure jig or on the atmospheric winch using carriers.

Thus the most important types of equipment for dyeing polyester/cellulosic blends are the jet machine and beam dyeing machine for piece goods, and the package and beam dyeing machines for yarn. These two classes of machines will now be discussed in more detail.

Package and Beam Dyeing Machines

Modern package (yarn) and beam (yarn or piece) dyeing machines for dyeing polyester/cellulosic blends are fully pressurised and designed to dye at temperatures of up to 150°C. The more usual maximum dyeing temperature used is 120–130°C. The principle of operation is to circulate the dye liquor evenly and rapidly through the material. This distinguishes these machines from those where the material passes through the dye liquor. Boulton and Crank [3] with their classic work in the early 1950s laid the theoretical foundation for package dyeing. Others have gone on to establish the practical requirements for level dyeing in such machines. It should be realised that initial dye absorption should be even throughout the material to ensure that the final dyeing is uniform. Some migration does occur but this cannot be relied on to produce level results.

In general, when there is significant depletion of the dye liquor as it passes through the closely packed material, the material that first comes into contact with the liquor will be more strongly dyed than that at the emergent side. The greater the depletion of dye during the passage of the dye liquor through the material, the greater the strength difference shown by the material. Thus a high dyeing rate or a slow circulation rate contributes to unlevel dyeing. To ensure level dyeing the increment of exhaustion for each circulation cycle should be not greater than a given amount, depending on the circumstances. Thus if the maximum permissible figure is 2% exhaustion per cycle then the maximum permissible rate of dyeing would be

2% per min for a circulation rate of one cycle per min, and 12% per min for a circulation rate of six cycles per min. (One cycle is the time taken to circulate through the system a volume of dye liquor equal to that of the dyebath.)

This is the theoretical basis of modern rapid dyeing systems in which high circulation rates are used to allow high exhaustion rates. The rate of exhaustion is controlled by the rate at which the temperature is raised. When disperse dyes are dyed by raising the temperature at a constant rate, say 2°C/min over the temperature range 60–125°C, the initial dyeing rate is slow. The rate increases as the temperature is raised, and at some temperature between 80 and 120°C the dyeing rate is at a maximum. The temperature range over which the dyeing rate is at its maximum is known as the 'critical dyeing temperature'. Slow-diffusing dyes (dyes of higher molecular weight) have a critical dyeing range of 105–130°C, while more rapidly diffusing dyes have a critical range between lower temperature limits. Manufacturers publish this information, but the figures they give are a guide only, as they are arbitrary and depend on the actual rate at which the temperature is raised, the dye concentration and other factors related to the flow rate, liquor ratio and material being dyed. Nevertheless the general principle remains as the basis for establishing the dyeing cycle. Thus the guiding rule is to add the disperse dye at a temperature below the lower limit of the critical dyeing range, raise the temperature rapidly to this value and then reduce the rate of heating over the critical range so that the maximum rate of exhaustion permissible for level dyeing is not exceeded. The temperature is then raised from the upper limit of the critical range to the top temperature at the maximum rate of heating.

Dyeing is continued for 30–90 min according to the dye used and depth of colour required. At the end of this period the colour is checked, and if it is necessary to make further dye additions the bath is cooled rapidly to 90°C, dye added, the temperature raised to 120–130°C and the process run for a further 30 min.

Following the dyeing cycle the unfixed disperse dye must be removed. Ideally this should be done by blowing the exhaust liquor to waste while the temperature is high, i.e. under pressure. This avoids the risk of reprecipitation and deposition of dye and oligomer on the fibre surface and minimises the stain of disperse dye on the cellulosic portion.

Where this is not possible the dye liquor should be run from the bath at the highest possible temperature. For the highest fastness the unfixed dye remaining on the material and the stain on the cellulose should be removed by a thorough soaping with detergent or by a suitable reduction clearing. In most cases the clearing treatment can be incorporated in the subsequent dyeing of the cellulose, e.g. soaping of reactive dye or reduction and oxidation of vat dye. Where reactive dyes are used and the highest standard is required it may be necessary to give a reduction clearing treatment separately before the reactive dye is applied.

Following the dyeing of the polyester with disperse dye the cellulosic portion is dyed with the appropriate dye in the usual way. In pale to medium depths the appropriate dyeing may follow on in the same dyebath without the clearing processes described above, provided that a suitable choice of disperse dye has been made to minimise staining of the cellulose and that the resultant fastness properties are acceptable.

In circulating-liquor dyeing machines it is clear that liquor flow through the package of fabric or yarn must be uniform and the material must not present too great a resistance to flow, or the flow rate will be too slow. Similarly the heat exchanger must not be allowed to build up a deposit of oligomer which would restrict heat transfer and circulation. In any of these circumstances unlevel dyeings will result. It is essential that the fabric or yarn is wound evenly with properly controlled tension. If the tension is too high flow will be restricted; if too low there is the danger of channelling and non-uniform flow will result. Similarly if packages of different winding density are dyed in the same machine the colour will vary from package to package. Winding density, i.e. the overall volume of the material divided by its weight, can easily be checked by ensuring that all packages are the same weight and diameter. With polyester/cellulosic blends there is the additional complication that shrinkage during dyeing may consolidate the material. If this is liable to occur the material must be relaxed or heat set prior to winding. Yarn can be wound onto collapsible tubes under low tension and steamed in a vacuum steamer 15 min at 5°C above the maximum dyeing temperature. The yarn is then rewound for dyeing. Piece goods should be given a comparable heat-setting treatment, e.g. 30 s at 180–200°C.

Jet Dyeing Machines
In jet dyeing machines the problems are different from those of circulation machines. A greater problem is that of creasing rather than unlevel dyeing. Although unlevel dyeing is possible, the slow rate of heating imposed by the need to avoid creasing is usually also sufficient to prevent uneven dye uptake. Furthermore the material is constantly moving through the jet and the body of the machine so that the same relations do not hold good as for package dyeing. Experimental evidence indicates that there is complete uniformity along the material, irrespective of the dyeing rate, although there may be local unlevelness under adverse circumstances.

After the dyeing has been completed it is not possible to blow out the exhausted dye liquor as previously described for circulating-liquor dyeing machines, and to avoid creasing the material must be cooled slowly at 1–2°C/min until the dyebath is below 80°C. Apart from this, similar considerations apply as already described for dyeing in circulation machines. Slow cooling of the dyebath need not be regarded as lost processing time if this period is used as part of the next stage of dyeing.

Choice between Jet and Beam Dyeing for Piece Goods
At one time beam dyeing would have been the natural choice for a number of materials (e.g. polyester/cotton sheeting) that are now commonly dyed on the jet machine. In fact there is a wide range of materials that can be dyed in either machine, but there are some restraints that apply to each system.

The beam machine is unsuitable for material that is of very low permeability, material with a sculptured surface structure and other materials with which it is difficult to control the evenness of tension and avoid possibilities of channelling. For example, knitwear is often difficult to wind evenly with suitable tension onto a beam.

On the other hand, the jet machine can produce crushing or creasing of material with sensitive surfaces, e.g. velvet. Very lightweight material may also give difficulties in the jet machine not related to intrinsic unsuitability but due to the very long length of an economical machine load. For example, a normal machine load per tube of 120 kg of material weighing 60 g per linear metre would be 2000 m in length. This is too long for satisfactory operation and the machine must be run underloaded. In such cases a beam machine may be more suitable.

In batchwise dyeing the liquor ratio is an important factor in determining the economics and reproducibility of dyeing, especially with reactive dyes. Modern jet machines often operate at a lower liquor ratio than beam machines, and this is an important factor to be taken into account.

However, the main consideration is the effect on the handle of certain types of material, e.g. polyester/viscose blends. The completely relaxed and tensionless dyeing conditions of the rope-dyeing system in jet machines allows relaxation, bulking and shrinkage that is physically prevented in the beam dyeing machine. This often results in a softer handle, which can be the main criterion for choosing the jet machine, although in other cases the firmer flatter results from the beam machine may be preferred.

9.8.2 Batchwise Dyeing Process Details

If a material contains at least 60% polyester, pale colours may be obtained by dyeing the polyester only. The reverse procedure is not recommended as the rubbing points of the garment would quickly show up as light patches due to the lower abrasion resistance of the cellulosic fibre. For tone-in-tone, cross-dyed and melange effects the polyester component should be the more heavily dyed for optimum fastness, but a better appearance is often obtained with the cellulose being the darker colour since the surface hairs and slubs are covered. For melange and cross-dyed effects where the maximum contrast is required it is necessary to ensure a thorough clearing of the disperse dye from the cellulose.

In most cases a solid colour (i.e where the material appears to consist of fibres that are all dyed to the same colour) is required. In batchwise dyeing the polyester and the cellulose are invariably dyed in separate stages, even though the dyes for both fibres may be added at the start of the dyeing. Even under atmospheric conditions, i.e. carrier dyeing, the addition of salt, alkali, reducing agent, etc. that are required for the dyeing of cellulose cannot be made until the disperse dyeing has been completed, without adversely affecting it.

There are a large number of possible sequences of processes, most of which have been tried at one time or another. Detailed considerations backed by practical experience have shown that the best and most reliable results are obtained by dyeing the polyester first, although shorter dyeing cycles can be devised.

The potential advantage of shorter dyeing times are usually more than offset by the disadvantages noted below.

(a) The dyed cellulose may suffer a change in colour during subsequent pressure dyeing with disperse dyes. This is unlikely to be easily reproduced, so that the time advantage will be lost by additional shading requirements.

(b) Shading the cellulosic component is much easier and quicker than the time-consuming shading of polyester.

(c) Although polyester is often the main fibre component, the cellulosic portion is found to migrate to the surface of a blend and has the dominant influence on final colour. Greater accuracy in colour is thus obtained by shading the cellulose.

(d) The auxiliary agents used for dyeing cellulosic fibres (alkali, reducing agent, salt, etc.) adversely affect the disperse dyes and call for appropriate treatment. The material must be freed from reducing agents, the pH must be adjusted to 4–5. If a salt is used in the prior dyeing stage Glauber's salt should be specified as it has a lesser aggregating effect on disperse dyes.

Disperse/Vat Dye Combinations
Combinations of disperse and vat dyes, when properly applied, give the highest all-round fastness. A wide range of colours is available but it is restricted in the bright orange, red and violet sectors.

The standard dyeing method follows the following sequence:
1. Dye with disperse dye (high temperature)
2. Add well-dispersed vat dye (unreduced) to cooling dyebath at 90–100°C
3. Ensure complete uniformity of dyebath
4. Add caustic soda and reducing agent after further cooling to a suitable temperature according to dye and conditions. The dyeing is then continued as for a normal vat dyeing.

There are several variants on the same theme.

The vat dye may be added to the dyebath at the same time as the disperse dye. This slightly simplifies the already complex dyeing sequence by eliminating one stage. It has the theoretical disadvantage that dye aggregation could occur at the high temperatures involved, but in practice this has not proved to be a problem. Some manufacturers offer disperse/vat dye mixtures and with these this sequence must be used. These mixtures have the advantage that the total number of dye weighings is halved and, if a polyester/cellulose blend only is dyed, the dye inventory may be reduced. There are disadvantages with these pre-mixed dyes. The choice of dye combinations is made by the supplier and the dyer is restricted in exercising his choice of the most suitable combination for his particular requirements. The balance of the combination is a compromise, so that poor solidity of dyeing may result with fabric blends that differ significantly from that tested by the supplier.

Where the fastness of the disperse dye component does not meet the fastness standard required, the clearing process may have been inadequate. This will normally occur with deep colours only. In this case a separate reduction clearing process should be used between the disperse and vat dyeing. Clearly pre-mixed disperse/vat dyes are unsuitable for such conditions.

In some cases it is attractive to use 'high-temperature' dyeing techniques for the vat dyeing stage, with the advantage of improved levelling of the vat dyes.

Disperse/Sulphur Dye Combinations
The low price of sulphur dyes makes disperse/sulphur dye combinations useful for heavy depths and when the fastness requirements are less stringent. The colour range is restricted to dull colours.
The standard dyeing process follows the sequence:
1. Dye with disperse dye
2. Cool bath to required dyeing temperature
3. Dye with sulphur dye in the same bath.

With sulphur dyes sodium hydrosulphide should be used as reducing agent in preference to sodium sulphide, as the former produces a 'cleaner' dyeing and there is less danger of degrading the polyester. With heavy depths it may be necessary to introduce an intermediate clearing as with vat dyes.

Disperse/Reactive Dye Combinations
Disperse/reactive dye combinations provide the widest range of fast colours normally available on polyester/cellulosic blends. Compared with direct dyes the wet fastness of reactive dyes is high; compared with sulphur dyes their light and wet fastnesses are high. Their wet fastness is similar to that of vat dyes and is adequate for most applications, except that they have general inferiority to chlorine bleaching. Their light fastness, although often below that of vat dyes, is adequate for a wide range of goods in which polyester/cellulosic blends are used. One might think that the minor fibre in a fibre blend would have a proportionally small influence on the light fastness of the dyed material. Unfortunately this is not so, for the reasons already given concerning the dominant effect of the cellulosic fibre on the resultant colour.
The standard method follows the sequence:
1. Dye with disperse dye
2. Drop the exhausted dyebath at the highest possible temperature
3. Refill and dye with reactive dye in the normal way.

In practice there are a large number of variants depending on fastness requirements, depth of colour and machinery used. The two most important variants are described below.
(a) The dyeing process is shortened by adding the reactive dye directly to the cooling bath followed by salt and alkali. When the dye is added at high temperature levelling is rapid. The alkaline fixation and thorough soaping required for high-substantivity reactive dyes will give satisfactory clearing of disperse dyes, even in heavy depths, if they have been chosen to have low substantivity for cellulose after alkaline treatment.
    This shortened process is particularly attractive in jet dyeing. Because of the slow cooling necessary in this type of machine to avoid creasing, the time saved can be considerable. In circulating-liquor machines, especially where the exhausted disperse dyebath can be blown to waste while still under pressure, the advantages are much less. In both types of machine there are savings in energy and water by using the one-bath process.

(b) Where the highest standard of wet fastness is required and is not being achieved because of inadequate clearing of the disperse dye, then it may be necessary to introduce a reduction clear between the two dyeing processes. After reduction clearing the dyeing must be thoroughly rinsed to ensure no reducing agent remains. Where capacity for pressure dyeing is limited, it may be convenient to transfer the material to unpressurised machinery for reduction clearing and reactive dyeing, but the double handling increases the labour required. Reduction clearing is most likely to be required if the disperse dye has been applied using a carrier at atmospheric pressure.

Various other sequences have been suggested from time to time with the objective of reducing the duration of the overall dyeing cycle. These include dyeing and fixing the reactive dye while raising the dyebath temperature; the bath is then neutralised, disperse dye added and the dyeing continued, a final soaping being given to clear both reactive and disperse dye. Another variant is adding the reactive dye at the same time as the disperse dye, to give maximum levelling of the high-substantivity reactives preferred for polyester/cellulose dyeing; salt is added at the end of the disperse dyeing, with alkali present in the cooling bath to complete the fixation. These methods both suffer from the danger of destroying the reactive dye during high-temperature treatment unless a very careful dye selection is made and salt is present during the disperse dyeing. Consequently achieving reproducibility in colour is made more difficult and any additional shading will more than offset advantages in a shorter dyeing cycle. With unpressurised carrier dyeing these objections largely disappear.

Disperse/Direct Dye Combinations
In general, disperse/direct dye combinations are most often used at the cheaper end of the market, so that the simplest possible dyeing process is required. Because of the limited fastness of direct dyes the freedom from staining of the disperse dyes is of less importance than with other combinations. Disperse/direct dye combinations are important for polyester/cellulosic blends, particularly polyester/viscose blends for suiting materials, and where the fast-to-light direct dyes can be used without the need for high wash fastness. Aftertreatment and resin finishing of dyeings can give materials of acceptable if limited wet fastness.

The standard procedure suitable for pale to medium depths is:
1. Add disperse and selected direct dye to the prepared dyebath and dye the disperse dye as normal (either pressurised or with carrier)
2. Cool to 90°C, add Glauber's salt and complete the dyeing of the direct dye
3. Rinse thoroughly with cold water
4. Aftertreat with dye-fixing agent if required.

In this process the direct dyes must be chosen to be soluble under the mildly acid conditions used, and to be stable to the high-temperature conditions if pressure dyed. Otherwise the direct dye must be added to the exhausted disperse dyebath after cooling to 90°C and adjusting the pH appropriately. This is followed by the addition of Glauber's salt, etc. as before.

For heavier depths, where the disperse dye is insufficiently cleared, a two-stage process must be used, as already described for reactive dyes.

9.9 SEMI-CONTINUOUS DYEING

Semi-continuous dyeing (i.e. a process in which one or both of the component fibres are dyed by a padding method delivering onto a batch) is usually confined to piece dyeing in polyester/cellulosic blends, although it would be perfectly feasible to develop methods for dyeing yarn (during sizing) or slubbing.

The advantages of semi-continuous dyeing are:

(a) Higher productivity than batchwise dyeing at the padding stage
(b) Continuity of colour compared with production of a number of discrete batch dyeings
(c) Suitable for batches that are insufficiently large to justify fully continuous processing
(d) Optimum use of available equipment.

Semi-continuous dyeing of polyester/cellulosic blends has a number of features that differentiate it from normally accepted semi-continuous piece dyeing processes. These are partly historical and partly due to the two-fold dyeing systems used.

Historically the continuous dyeing method for dyeing polyester blends was developed before fully satisfactory piece dyeing processes (pressure beam and pressure jet dyeing). Installation of semi-continuous machinery for short runs has therefore become established in dyehouses where production runs do not justify fully continuous dyeing methods. In such cases there may be no need to use expensive pressure dyeing methods, the cellulosic portion being dyed (if necessary) by conventional methods appropriate to the material.

The second distinguishing feature is the use of cross-dyed effects. In this case the base colour of, say, 5000 m of fabric might be dyed by pad–thermofix, this batch then being split into five batches of 1000 m each to be cross-dyed in batches to a different colour.

In addition to these comments, the previous remarks concerning the advantages of dyeing the cellulosic component last are also relevant, although they must be reviewed under the different circumstances of semi-continuous dyeing.

The machines used and the individual dyeing methods have all been described in this or earlier chapters so comments will be confined to the merits of the most attractive ways of putting these methods together. The semi-continuous operations in all cases are based on the following processes:

(a) Pad–batch (fixation of reactive dyes)
(b) Pad–thermofix (fixation of disperse dyes and possibly reactive dyes)
(c) Pad–batchwise develop (all dye classes).

9.9.1 Pad–Batch Methods

The cellulosic component is dyed by the normal pad–batch process and the polyester by normal batchwise dyeing processes. Section 9.9.2 also gives details of pad–thermofix methods that are applicable in pad–batch processing.

There are two variants, each with their merits, that are suitable for disperse/reactive dye systems.

Variant A
1. Pad–batch (normal method for reactive dyes) on prepared and dried material and store for required time
2. Split into batches of suitable sizes and load into machine for dyeing polyester
3. Rinse to remove alkali and adjust pH
4. Dye polyester with disperse dye
5. Rinse and soap thoroughly to remove unfixed reactive and disperse dye
6. Rinse and finish as usual.

Minor variations within this process are to batch into suitable machines loads immediately after padding, or on to perforated beams and rinse before loading for batchwise dyeing. The choice depends on the circumstances and the machinery available, the aim being to minimise the number of times the fabric is handled. With beam dyeing it is attractive to pad and then batch directly onto the beam, if sufficient beams are available.

Variant B
1. Batchwise dye polyester component with disperse dye
2. Reduction clear and rinse free of reducing agent (if necessary to achieve required level of fastness)
3. Remove material from machine, dry and assemble into padding lengths
4. Pad–batch as in variant A
5. Soap thoroughly to clear reactive dye (preferably using perforated beam).

Variant A is more productive because intermediate drying between the two dyeing stages is avoided (this only applies if the fabric is normally dried after preparation for dyeing). Variant B has the merit of dyeing the cellulose after the polyester, and it must be used if a reduction clearing is necessary to achieve the fastness required.

9.9.2 Pad–Thermofix Methods
All the comments made in section 9.7 on dye selection and dyeing techniques are applicable. After thermofixation dyeing is completed by a batchwise method as appropriate to the dye and material concerned.

Where dye fixation is still required this is carried out by the traditional method for cellulose, i.e. development on the jig or winch using salt/alkali or caustic soda/sodium hydrosulphite for reactive dyes and vat dyes respectively. If washing-off only is required then this is done by the usual methods, or alternatively on a perforated beam.

As well as catering for small batches semi-continuously, thermofixation followed by winch treatment can be used to achieve the required handle for some materials, especially certain styles of polyester/viscose fibre blend.

Where direct dyes are to be used they are applied in the winch or jig in the normal way.

Pad–thermofix processing combined with pad–batch dyeing offers a number of attractive features. Two especially useful sequences are given below.

Sequence A
1. Pad–thermofix (disperse dye only with usual additives)
2. Cool
3. Pad–batch with reactive dye and alkali
4. Soap, etc. as usual (perforated-beam method preferred)

Sequence B
1. Pad–thermofix (disperse and reactive dyes and usual additives)
2. Cool
3. Pad–batch with alkali only (and optional salt)
4. Soap, etc. as usual (perforated-beam method preferred)

Advantages of sequence A include the possibility of correcting the colour after thermofixation, no problems with reactive dye migration and elimination of potential loss of yield by interaction between disperse and reactive dyes. Undue emphasis should not be placed on the latter, but it is a point that must be taken into account when selecting the dyes for sequence B.

Sequence B has the production advantage that all colour padding is carried out in one stage.

9.9.3 Pad–Develop Methods

Pad–develop methods can be used for all dye combinations, e.g. disperse/vat, disperse/reactive and disperse/direct dye mixtures.

Their particular advantage is that, in making up one batch of dye liquor and padding onto the material, there is greater assurance that each batch is developed with the same percentage of each dye applied to the fabric. This eliminates weighing errors in dye and fabric which are a common reason for variation in colour. The pad liquor remaining after padding is equally divided into the number of batches for development and used for priming the development bath.

The development method chosen should be the same as that used for the normal batchwise dyeing method appropriate to the particular combination.

While applicable to most woven goods, pad–develop methods are of particular value in dyeing disperse/vat combinations where neither pressure dyeing machinery nor thermofixation equipment is available, and where development is in the jig (or in some cases in the winch) using a carrier for the disperse dye. Using the pad–develop method gives the best opportunity of a high standard of levelness combined with a minimum dyeing time.

9.10 OTHER CONSIDERATIONS

There are a number of miscellaneous items that are of importance in the dyeing of polyester/cellulosic blends. Throughout this chapter reference has been made to polyester blends with cellulose, both cotton and viscose fibres. This has been used as rather a loose nomenclature indicating the relative importance of the method for the particular blend. In continuous dyeing polyester/cotton is the more important material. Although viscose fibre blends may also be dyed continuously, they are in general less suitable, being both more difficult to dye (slower diffusion) and giving a less satisfactory handle. Thus reference to polyester/cotton in continuous dyeing does not exclude polyester/viscose, but is indicative of the lower importance of the latter, coupled with possible technical difficulties in some cases.

Various other miscellaneous matters are dealt with in this section.

9.10.1 Separation of Polyester and Cellulose in Blends

In establishing recipes, selecting dyes and fault identification it is often necessary to examine the colour of the two fibres separately. The simplest method during shade matching is to include a 'flyer' (small piece) of 100% polyester and 100% cellulosic fibre sewn to the main piece being dyed. The materials should be as similar as possible in characteristics to the individual fibres concerned and to the construction of the material. It is often difficult to find suitable materials and the results can usually only be taken as a guide to the colour of the material in the blend. However, it is a useful and simple technique, and if the appearance and colour of the blend is satisfactory using this method then nothing further need be done.

9.10.2 Removal of Cellulose Component from the Blend

Removal of the cellulose leaving the dyed polyester 'skeleton' is routine practice in many dyehouses when shade matching or checking the colour of polyester/cellulosic blends. As it is much more difficult to remove the polyester, the colour of the cotton is estimated by the difference in colour between the blend dyeing and the polyester 'skeleton'. The method is simple and can be easily fitted into a routine. A suitable method is:

1. Extract a suitable cutting (e.g. 5×5 cm) with 70% sulphuric acid (e.g. in 100 ml beaker) at room temperature (no higher) until the cellulose is completely dissolved (i.e. about 10 min)
2. Remove the polyester 'skeleton' and plunge into cold water
3. Neutralise in dilute ammonia
4. Rinse and dry.

The resultant skeleton is used in the assessment of colour, but it should be noted that some colours may be slightly affected by the strong sulphuric acid. This is uncommon but most likely in fawns and pale greys. Any doubts can be checked by treatment of a 100% polyester dyeing of similar colour using the same dyes and comparing it with the untreated control.

Although the method is simple the chemicals are hazardous and it should only be carried out in the laboratory under qualified supervision. Full safety precautions are essential. Goggles and rubber gloves should be worn. The spent sulphuric acid should be disposed of safely.

It is often convenient to purchase sulphuric acid as battery acid at sp. gr. 1.7, which is a suitable strength without dilution. The acid may be dispensed using a hand-operated peristaltic pump with an acid-resistant synthetic-rubber tubing, the acid being stored below bench level in a cupboard. These steps eliminate the main hazards in handling sulphuric acid.

9.10.3 Removal of Polyester Compound from the Blend

Solvents for polyester are generally unpleasant and often dangerous to handle. Being powerful solvents many affect the dyes remaining on the cotton skeleton. While methylsalicylate will dissolve polyester at 130°C leaving the cotton un-affected, it also dissolves vat dyes and will remove disperse dye stain from the cellulose.

The most useful solvent is hexafluoroisopropanol, which is used cold. Extraction takes about 15 min; the material should then be rinsed in fresh solvent and finally rinsed thoroughly in cold water and dried. It is very toxic and the dissolution must be carried out in a fume cupboard by experienced laboratory workers under proper supervision.

Although the solvent leaves the dye on the cotton unchanged, the method cannot be recommended as a routine procedure because of the hazards involved and the high cost of this solvent. Nevertheless it is a satisfactory procedure for special inves-tigations.

9.10.4 Physical Separation of the Two Components in a Blend

There is a method of separating the polyester and cellulosic components in a blend that is safe and effective. It depends on the physical separation of a finely chopped sample of material at the interface between water and a supernatent layer of white spirit.

Unfortunately, although simple and safe, it is relatively slow and requires some practice and manipulative skill. This makes it unsuitable for routine shade matching and assessment. However, because of the absence of powerful solvents it is particu-larly suitable for investigations of staining and partition of dye between the two fibres. Because the material is finely divided during processing, poorly penetrated dyeings will show up as weak compared with the original, and this can be used to give an assessment of migration during drying in thermofixation processes. Well-penetrated dyeings will, of course, be comparable with the original dyeing.

The procedure is as follows.

1. Prepare a finely divided sample of the material. This can be done by hand cutting into lengths of less than 2 mm so that they readily untwist into their com-ponent fibres. Alternatively use a micro-hammer mill, which prepares a suitable sample in 3–5 min.
2. Put the fibre sample (weighing approx. 0.1 g) into a 250 ml beaker and add 60–80 ml white spirit.
3. Add 100–120 ml water and stir well for 15–30 s.
4. Allow to stand until the two layers separate (1–2 min). The polyester and the cellulose will separate and collect at the two sides of the interface: the polyester above, in the white spirit phase, and the cotton in the aqueous phase.
5. Add 1–2 ml of a diluted wetting agent (5–10% solution) below the white spirit

surface, using a hypodermic syringe or pipette, and stir gently. The cellulose will fall to the bottom of the beaker.

6. Decant the upper layer containing the polyester, flushing out the final traces with water.

7. Each fraction is then filtered onto separate 25–50 mm diameter filter papers under vacuum, then rinsed with 20–30 ml water while adjusting the position of the fibres to give a uniformly distributed pad.

8. Finally a few drops of a diluted poly(vinyl acetate) dispersion are added to stick the fibres together for ease of handling, and the samples are then dried.

If direct dyes are involved 10 g/l salt should be added to the water.

As mentioned, the technique requires manipulative skills. These are best acquired by practice with cross-dyed material so that visual confirmation of successful separation is obtained.

With practice, the time taken to separate the two components is 7–8 min, sufficient to allow a preliminary assessment to be made. A complete separation including drying and sample preparation takes 20–25 min.

The method has been found reliable and useful, but if the material has been treated with finishing agents, such as waterproofing, soil-release and in some cases resin finishes, the separation is ineffective unless they are stripped from the fabric.

9.11 DYE SELECTION

No matter how meticulous the dyeing process is or how carefully it has been executed, an ultimate satisfactory result depends on the selection of suitable dyes and dye combinations. It is not possible to make general recommendations but with experience the user will establish a range of dyes that are suitable for his purpose. In most cases this should not exceed eight to ten different dyes for each fibre for any particular application. Familiarity with these dyes will soon indicate which dye, if any, is causing difficulties, and alternatives can be sought.

Dye manufacturers are aware of the problems involved, and are willing and able to make soundly based recommendations in particular cases. They also provide excellent technical literature on their products and give details of the dyeing methods they recommend.

Although no dye manufacturer has a monopoly of satisfactory dyes, it is sound practice to use, as a basis of dye selection, the recommendations made by a manufacturer whose technical excellence is acknowledged. Weaknesses in this selection can be filled in by using recommended products from other suppliers.

Apart from colour, fastness and dyeing properties of the dye for the individual fibres, the properties that are of particular importance in the dyeing of polyester/cellulosic blends are as follows.

1. Freedom from interaction, chemical or physical, with the dyes to be used for the other fibre. This is of particular importance with disperse/reactive dyes, where disperse dyes containing amino groups are capable of reacting with reactive dyes, but it also applies to other dyes where physical interaction can occur. This can be detected by a drop in yield when the sensitive dye is applied in the

presence of a dye of another class. Interaction can also be detected chromato-graphically, but such results can be misleading.
2. Freedom from cross-staining and low substantivity of the dye for the other fibre. This is of particular importance with disperse dyes where the stain on cellulose generally has poor wet fastness (staining of adjacent nylon is often a particular problem) and often poor light fastness. With vat dyes staining of polyester can sometimes cause problems due to the colour being significantly different from that on cotton. However, advantage is sometimes taken of a slight degree of staining in pale depths to give solid colours using a single dye class.

9.12 CONCLUSION
There are now many established procedures for dyeing polyester/cellulosic blends to give satisfactory end products, but only the continuous dyeing processes approach the high productivity achieved in dyeing 100% cellulose. All the batch-wise methods have a long and complex dyeing sequence. There is clearly room for improvement in these latter processes.

REFERENCES

1. Bent, Flynn and Sumner, J.S.D.C., **85** (1969) 606.
2. Broadhurst, 'The Dyeing of Synthetic-polymer and Acetate Fibres', Ed. Nunn (Bradford: Dyers' Company Publications Trust, 1979) 131.
3. Boulton and Crank, J.S.D.C., **68** (1952) 109.

CHAPTER 10

Selection of Dyes for Dyeing Cellulosic Fibres

JOHN SHORE

10.1 INTRODUCTION

Cellulosic textiles are found at all price levels, from the pinnacle of *haute couture* to the humblest cotton duster. Military fabrics, produced to rigid specifications of colour reproducibility, fastness and durability, depend heavily on cotton and its blends. Indigo-dyed cotton denim has the extraordinary requirement that the colour must readily bleed and fade to give the familiar washed-down worn-out look early in the life of the garment. All kinds of dyeing machine are suitable for processing cellulosic fibres in some form; numerous batchwise and continuous routes for preparation, dyeing and finishing of cotton fabrics have been discussed in earlier chapters.

In view of this remarkable versatility it is necessary to consider the selection of dyes for cellulose at several different levels. The titles of certain earlier chapters specify the important classes of dyes designed for application to this substrate. Within each class there are often significant sub-classes differentiated from one another by differences in application characteristics. Such distinctions may be decisive in selecting the most suitable dyes for a given set of dyeing conditions. In certain circumstances reference will be made in the following pages to the behaviour of individual dyes or groups of chemically related products, where these are sufficiently anomalous to be non-representative of the class or sub-class under discussion.

Most attention, however, will be focussed on the differences between the major classes of cellulosic dyes that determine whether a class is selected for a given substrate. The choice between sub-classes has been dealt with already in some detail under the appropriate chapters. Limitations of space prevent a detailed and comprehensive discussion of individual products and, in any case, selection between these can be fully meaningful only in the context of a specific set of economic and technological criteria. Before taking into account the numerous factors that have a bearing on dye selection at these various levels, it is first necessary to consider the following question.

10.2 WHY IS CELLULOSE DYED WITH SEVERAL MAJOR CLASSES OF DYES?

In the dyeing of non-cellulosic fibres [1, 2] one class of dyes invariably predominates on the substrate concerned, e.g. basic dyes on acrylic fibres, disperse dyes on polyester or cellulose acetate, anionic dyes on nylon or wool. Why then is this not the case on cellulose? The reasons are bound up with the way in which cellulose dyeing has evolved and with the somewhat complementary features of the various classes of dyes used on cellulose.

Direct dyes belong to the first of these classes to have become established, almost exactly a century ago. Before then, cotton almost always had to be mordanted before applying either natural mordant dyes or the newer synthetic products (basic dyes or anthraquinone mordant dyes). Most of the early fast colours were rather dull; there were no fast bright yellows, violets, blues or greens [3]. Mixtures were difficult to reproduce, especially if two or more mordants were present in the same recipe. Pale depths based on indigo were rather fugitive to light.

The breadth of colour gamut and ease of application of direct dyes, with their substantivity towards unmordanted cotton and good levelling properties, secured their ready acceptance in spite of the limited fastness to light and wet treatments of the early members of the range [4]. By the turn of the century, however, more expensive reds with high substantivity and good fastness properties were being developed. Nevertheless, the light fastness of many of the blue, green and grey direct dyes marketed then was so inferior to the major yellows and reds that they gave unbalanced fading in mixtures [5].

The first sulphur dye appeared before the direct dyes, but it was not until the development of the sulphur blacks in the closing years of the last century that this class of dyes made a major impact on cotton dyeing [6]. Sulphur Black T (C.I. Sulphur Black 1) quickly became the best-selling individual dye for textile coloration, a position it has retained ever since [7]. The gamut of sulphur dyes was soon extended to dull yellow, orange, brown, blue and green, satisfying the need for full-depth dyeings at moderate cost, with better fastness than direct dyes in general.

Indigo, the natural forerunner of the vat dyes, was by now available in synthetic form, but there remained a lack of brighter blues with good all-round fastness. This gap was filled by the indanthrone blues, which appeared at the beginning of the present century, closely followed in the next few years by other anthraquinonoid vat dyes in the orange, brown, red, violet, blue, olive, grey and black regions of colour space. Collectively this range offered, at a price, standards of fastness to light and washing that had not been approached hitherto by natural or synthetic dyes.

The early success of direct dyes had been tarnished by their limited wet fastness, particularly now that sulphur and vat dyes had shown what could be achieved, but the azo dye chemists were fighting back. Primuline Red, the first diazotisable direct dye, and Para Red (C.I. Pigment Red 1), the first successful azoic combination, had appeared in the same year (1887), but the orange, brown and blue dyes developed with β-naphthol were inferior to the reds from the viewpoint of cost, brightness and fastness. It was the discovery of the more substantive Naphtol AS (HOE, C.I. Azoic Coupling Component 2) in 1912 which provided the basis for a range of azoic dyes with improved colour gamut, brightness, build-up and fastness properties, although this development was not brought to fruition until after World War I [8, 9]. The enhanced wet fastness of diazotisable direct dyes after development inspired a search for other techniques to improve the performance of direct dyes. Structures were designed to achieve better wash fastness by aftertreatment with formaldehyde, but high light fastness was difficult to attain in this way. The discovery of the first metal-complex dyes for wool (1912) led to interest in copper-complex direct dyes, initially applied by an after-coppering technique but later synthesised as premetallised dyes for conventional application.

Thus the stage was set in the inter-war years for a struggle for supremacy between azoic, direct, sulphur and vat dyes, by now all well-established but still in a phase of active development. Demand for vat dyes began to grow, initially at the expense of azoic and direct dyes and later of sulphur dyes. This trend might well have been expected to continue, but several factors began to operate in the opposite direction in the later 1920s and the 1930s [10].

The surge of interest in vat dyes was stimulated in 1922 by the discovery of Caledon Jade Green (C.I. Vat Green 1), the first homogeneous fast green for cotton. Green had been an unsatisfied research target for many years. Basic greens were fugitive and direct greens dull, with unattractive dyeing properties; no green azoic or sulphur dyes had yet been found. Two years later the synthesis of the water-soluble leuco sulphuric ester Indigosol O, derived from indigo, initiated development of a new range of solubilised vat dyes.

An important factor that strongly influenced the demand for direct dyes was the introduction of viscose, the first regenerated cellulosic fibre. Direct dyeing represented a cheap and simple method of achieving acceptable fastness and brightness. The sensitivity of this fibre to caustic alkali (early forms of viscose were particularly low in wet strength) strongly favoured the use of direct dyes rather than Naphtol AS, vat or sulphur dyes. The synthesis of high-substantivity direct dyes by the judicious use of key intermediates such as J-acid and cyanuric chloride, and of fast-to-light copper-complex types, brought the direct dyes closer to their rivals in terms of fastness performance (and cost). As a result vat dyes in particular showed a decline in demand relative to direct dyes in the decade just before World War II [10].

In wartime conditions, however, the production of long runs in a limited range of colours was given priority. During World War II the United States, in particular, produced large quantities of military uniforms, tents and camouflage materials for the allied war effort. This urgent demand could be met only by the development and widespread adoption of continuous pad–steam dyeing of cotton fabrics with vat dyes. The increased use of durable resin finishes put more emphasis on fastness standards as an expression of quality. Labelling schemes were adopted and test methods for fastness against a wider range of agencies were developed.

As a result of these changes, by the early 1950s vat dyes had regained much of the predominance that they had attained 30 years earlier. On the verge of the discovery of reactive dyes, the main deficiencies of the anthraquinone vat range were identified as the absence of bright greenish-yellows, bright scarlets or reds, and bright turquoise or greenish-blues [11]. These outer zones of colour space represented notable targets for development in the first few years of the era of reactive dyeing. The growth in consumption of reactive dyes has been closely associated with the achievement of high wet fastness in bright highly saturated colours. The demand for cheap, dull, homogeneous members of the direct, sulphur and vat dye ranges has been least affected by competition from reactive dyes, which are usually applied as trichromatic mixtures when used for the dyeing of subdued tones [12].

A series of lectures with the following provocative titles was given at a VTCC symposium in Baden-Baden in 1970 and later published in *Melliand*; these papers still provide interesting reading:
1. Have vat dyes a future in the dyehouse? [13]
2. Can one with confidence forget about azoic dyes in the dyehouse? [14]
3. Has the age of vat leuco ester dyes passed by in the dyehouse? [15]
4. Have reactive dyes already reached their peak in the dyehouse? [16]
5. Have direct dyes still got a right to exist in the dyehouse? [17]
6. Are sulphur dyes out of date in the dyehouse? [18]

Since all the responses to these questions were presented by individuals from firms involved in dye supply, it is not entirely surprising that they all agreed on a vote of confidence in all classes of dyes for cellulose, in spite of the rapid growth in importance of synthetic-polymer fibres at that time. With the benefit of hindsight we can see that their optimism was not misplaced. A continuing decline in cellulosic fibres, especially viscose, had been foreseen [17], but successive oil crises in the 1970s helped to stabilise the relative demand for these fibres by increasing the relative cost of manufacturing synthetics.

The various classes of dyes for cellulose have continued to contend with one another. During the blue denim boom of the mid-1970s the price of indigo rose until it approached that of alternative blues (e.g. azoic or sulphur types) suitable for this outlet, and these latter products were able to take advantage of the world shortage of indigo [19, 20]. Efforts in recent years to minimise energy costs by operating at shorter liquor ratios have favoured the trends from winch to jet dyeing of knitgoods and from jet or jig to pad–batch processing; this has helped to further the continuing progress of reactive dyes. Azoic and vat dyes have been the main casualties of the growth in demand for reactive dyes over the last quarter-century. Direct and sulphur dyes continue to dominate the dyeing of cellulose in heavy dull colours, mainly on economic grounds. As will now be discussed in more detail, each dye class has several spheres of influence, e.g. direct dyes on viscose, reactive dyes on knitgoods, sulphur dyes on corduroy, vat dyes on military fabrics. No single class meets all requirements, each has its own strengths and weaknesses.

10.3 INFLUENCE OF COLOUR AND DYEING PROPERTIES ON SELECTION BETWEEN DYE CLASSES

As we have already seen, the advantages and limitations of colour gamut of the various classes have made a major contribution to trends in the development of new dyes, not least in securing a place in the sun for reactive dyes, latecomers to the cellulosic dyeing scene. By definition the azoic dyes are all unsulphonated monoazo or disazo pigments when fixed in the fibre. Almost all the direct dyes are disazo or polyazo compounds with two or more sulphonic acid groups. Sulphur and vat dyes, when oxidised to the pigment form in the fibre, are unsulphonated polycyclic compounds with characteristic disulphide (sulphur) or quinone (vat) groups present. These specific chemical categories impose restrictions on the colour gamut attainable within each dyeing class. Reactive dyes, however, are subject to no such limitation. The only common feature within this class is the presence of at least one fibre-reactive group. The chromophoric grouping may belong to one of several chemical classes (e.g. monoazo, disazo, metal-complex azo, anthraquinone, phthalocyanine. triphendioxazine). This versatility provides scope for attaining the widest possible range of hues.

10.3.1 Colour Gamut

Azoic dyes are severely limited in terms of their available range of hues, and sulphur dyes with regard to attainable level of brightness. Direct dyes and vat dyes offer advantages in both respects, but do not compete with reactive dyes in brightness attainable, except for direct dyes in the bright yellowish-red and bright turquoise sectors, where reactive dyes offer better wet fastness.

Azoic combinations cover only the range yellow–orange–red–violet–navy–black, and there are application limitations at both ends of these series. Only in the red sector is there real versatility, because practical problems arise with applying azoic components in mixtures. Bright blues and turquoises do not exist and the bright green naphthol is rather costly and lacks substantivity.

The direct range offers a complete circle of hues, but they are duller than reactive dyes in the yellow, bluish-red, violet, reddish-blue and green sectors. The direct dyes of higher fastness to light, particularly the premetallised and after-copperable sub-classes, tend to be somewhat dull. Reactive dyeings in dull colours are often based on trichromatic combinations of three relatively bright primaries, whereas with direct, vat or sulphur dyes there is a wider choice of dull homogeneous members of these ranges, from which a trio of much duller primaries closer to the target hue can be selected. The risk of unacceptable variations in hue arising from weighing errors is significantly lower in the latter situation, but corrective steps may be easier to carry out with bright primaries. Shading additions made with dull primaries often result in a match for hue that is stronger in depth than the target colour.

As already noted, sulphur dyes generally are restricted to drab colours and especially to cheap blacks. This limitation is attributable to their chemically complex and impure composition. Brighter red, violet and green members of the range are available but they are more costly than the duller more conventional products. Dichromate oxidation gives the best brightness from sulphur dyeings, but also poses the most serious effluent problems [21].

Although they contain impurities, vat dyes are more homogeneous than typical sulphur dyes and encompass a broader gamut of brighter shades. Nevertheless they lack the vivid brightness of azo chromophores in the greenish-yellow, scarlet, red and violet sectors and of phthalocyanine greenish-blues and turquoises. The vat dye range is well provided with duller homogeneous members in the central regions of colour space.

Yellow
In general reactive yellows are more economical than vat yellows. Special naphthols are required for azoic yellows; they are more costly and have lower substantivity than Naphtol AS, so they are only of interest for continuous application. Some sulphur yellows have poor light fastness and some vat yellows (e.g. C.I. Vat Yellow 2) are only moderate in this respect. Flavanthrone (C.I. Vat Yellow 1) is phototropic but otherwise exhibits good fastness to light. Certain vat yellows catalyse the phototendering of cellulose during dyeing or on storage of the dyed material. Some greenish-yellows (e.g. C.I. Vat Yellow 2 or 33) promote the catalytic fading of green vat dyes in mixtures. Catalytic wet fading imposes restrictions on the selection of direct and reactive dyes in greens; in pale to medium depths certain yellow members of these ranges fade more quickly in the presence of phthalocyanine or triphendioxazine blues.

Orange
Azoic and reactive dyes offer equal brightness in the orange sector; both are more economical and build up better than vat oranges. Certain sulphur and vat oranges exhibit inferior fastness to light. Pyranthrone oranges level well but C.I. Vat Orange 2 gives a different hue [22] by air oxidation than by chemical treatment (owing to over-oxidation); these dyes (C.I. Vat Oranges 1 and 2) catalyse the photodegradation of cellulose.

Red and Violet
Red is the strongest area for azo dyes. Azoic, direct and reactive dyes all achieve maximum brightness in the scarlet to mid-red sector, where azoics also offer maximum economy. The azoic range is, if anything, over-rich in cheap bright reds. Naphtol AS is the cheapest naphthol, but products are available at various levels of substantivity suitable for either batchwise or continuous application. The soaping-off of azoic reds on package-dyed cotton yarn can be difficult [23]. Azoic violets on Naphtol AS require special diazo components with low coupling energy.

Direct or reactive reds are more economical and build up better than vat reds; although not as cheap as azoic reds they are easier to apply. Cheap full reds dyed with diazotised and developed directs have good wet fastness but only limited light fastness; duller and bluer hues dyed with after-coppered directs show better fastness. Reactive reds offer better wet fastness and enhanced brightness in the bluish-red to violet sector. Certain types of dye–fibre bond are sensitive to acid, alkali or perborate-containing detergents (see below); these defects are often particularly troublesome with bluish-reds.

Full-depth reds and violets tend to be difficult and costly with vat dyes (e.g. C.I. Vat Red 23 requires a special method of application). The azole red C.I. Vat Red 10 has good levelling properties and very good fastness but it catalyses the photodegradation of cellulose. Dyeings of isodibenzanthrone violets can give problems of rubbing and water spotting.

Blue and Navy
In the blue sector vat dyes are able to compete with reactive dyes on cost grounds and provide better all-round fastness, although reactives have the edge with bright-

ness in greenish-blues and with ease of application. Dark blue azoic combinations are of interest only for continuous application, since the special low-energy diazo components required on Naphtol AS couple particularly slowly. They are fast to peroxide bleaching but have lower fastness to chlorine. The dull reddish-blue azo direct dyes build up well to navy depths and are of some interest on cheap outerwear fabrics, where the presence of a durable finish assists in providing adequate wet fastness. The unmetallised azo blue direct dyes have only borderline light fastness, especially if aftertreated with a cationic fixing agent or a crease-resist resin, but the after-coppered types are economical and show generally good fastness [24]. The navy blue and bluish-grey region is the most heavily represented amongst the recently introduced range of Indosol (S) dyes, which are selected premetallised copper complexes requiring aftertreatment with a special cationic auxiliary or a mixture of this with a cross-linking resin [25].

Good economy is offered by indanthrone blues (e.g. C.I. Vat Blue 4 or 6) in bright reddish-blues and by violanthrone blues (e.g. C.I. Vat Blue 20 or 26) in the navy region. They tend to exert a protective effect against photodegradation of cellulose when exposed to sunlight, but some blues show accelerated fading in the presence of the type of yellow (e.g. C.I. Vat Yellow 1) that promotes phototendering of the fibre. The indanthrone blues are sensitive to hard water, whilst indanthrones and violanthrones may give rub fastness problems in yarn dyeing. The violanthrone navies give only moderate coverage of dead cotton, and when exposed to soda boiling in the presence of cellulose they may suffer from over-reduction, leading to lower fastness ratings in subsequent tests. Nevertheless vat navy blues are important on sewing thread for both economic and technical reasons; thread intended for swimwear needs the chlorine fastness that these dyes provide. Certain reactive navy blues of the chloropyrimidine type may show difficulties of clearing after package dyeing in heavy depths [23].

Finally the importance of the sulphur blues and sulphurised vat blues at the cheaper end of the market should not be underestimated. Unlike the azoic dark blues they are highly substantive and build up well by exhaust methods [26]. The Hydron blues (sulphurised vats) are applicable with sodium dithionite as reducing agent, give good fastness to light and moderate bleach fastness, and are fast to washing at the boil if aftertreated with an S-alkylating agent (see Chapter 7, p. 284).

Turquoise

In many ways the turquoise sector is a special case in this context, because the ranges of azoic combinations and sulphur dyes are completely lacking in greenish-blues, whilst mixtures of even the brightest vat blues and greens are hopelessly dull in comparison with the direct and reactive turquoises based on the phthalocyanine chromophore. Even here it is really no contest. As a chemical class the sulphonated phthalocyanines tend to aggregate badly, especially in salt solutions, and are prone to solubility problems. With direct dyes the essential balance between adequate solubility, satisfactory substantivity and build-up, and acceptable wet fastness is particularly critical. Under unfavourable circumstances they show excessive swealing, bleeding and adverse staining in wet treatments [27]. The further degree of freedom attainable by relying on the covalent dye–fibre bond to ensure good wet fastness allows more scope in designing reactive phthalocyanine turquoises with better application characteristics.

Copper phthalocyanine has inherently very good fastness to light but, when aftertreated with a cationic fixing agent or a crease-resist resin, direct or reactive dyeings of this type become sensitive to photoreduction, i.e. they tend to show a shift towards violet when exposed to light rich in u.v. radiation. Clearly this problem will be more prevalent with the direct phthalocyanine blues, since their moderate wet fastness makes some form of aftertreatment unavoidable. Certain direct and reactive azo yellows are prone to catalytic wet fading in mixtures with phthalocyanine blues, but here again the practical situation favours reactive dyes because of the wider range of possible combinations from which satisfactory bright greens can be selected.

Green

As mentioned under the previous heading, really bright greens are possible only with direct or reactive dyes and, in practice, reactive dyes are mainly used because of their superior dyeing and fastness properties. A bright green naphthol is available but it is rather expensive and low in substantivity so it is of little interest except for printing. An olive green naphthol derived from anthracene can be used for exhaust dyeing but it is also somewhat costly. Cheap dull direct greens are important for olive dyeings on knitgoods, but unmetallised direct greens have only moderate fastness to light, especially if aftertreated. Certain olive green reactive chloropyrimidine dyes have given clearing problems in heavy depths on cotton yarn [23].

Most green sulphur dyes are dull, but they exhibit good light fastness; some of them break down in the presence of alkaline dithionite [28]. Bright green sulphur dyes derived from phthalocyanine do exist, but they are not widely used because they do not show the economic attractiveness of more typical sulphur dyes [7]. Where exceptional brightness is not demanded, vat greens and olives offer a desirable combination of good economy, level dyeing and excellent all-round fastness, e.g. for emerald and bottle greens on sewing thread [23]. Violanthrone greens (e.g. C.I. Vat Green 1) are necessary for the brighter hues and the acridone or carbazole types for olive greens. Light fastness in straight or lightly shaded recipes is generally extremely good, but combinations with phototendering yellows (e.g. C.I. Vat Yellow 1) should be avoided because of their catalytic effect on the fading rate of certain greens.

Brown

This colour is popular on corduroy, which is usually dyed with sulphur dyes by the one-bath pad–steam process [26]. Fastness to light and washing is satisfactory for civilian requirements, but one military workwear fabric dyed with sulphur brown gave acid tendering problems on storage owing to the prolonged storage times necessary before issue to servicemen. This was replaced by a more durable but more expensive azoic brown-dyed twill, but unfortunately this alternative caused allergy effects amongst sewing machinists [29]. Brown-shade naphthols have high substantivity towards cellulose and are thus restricted to batchwise application.

After-coppered direct dyes show economic build-up and good fastness in mode shades [24]. They are particularly useful in browns and greys since reactive dye recipes based on brighter primaries are often more sensitive to dyebath variables [27]. Solubility can be a problem with metal-complex reddish-brown reactive dyes, resulting in surface deposition in the package dyeing of cotton yarn [23]. Brown vat dyes of the carbazole type are reasonably economical and level well (although C.I. Vat Brown 3 is sensitive to immature or dead cotton). Their fastness ratings to light, chlorine bleaching and wet treatments are excellent.

Black
This is where sulphur dyes really come into their own. As noted earlier, Sulphur Black T has been manufactured in larger quantities than any other synthetic dye this century. Sulphur blacks are cheap and they have excellent fastness to light. Acid tendering of the dyed cotton on prolonged storage can be a problem, but aftertreatment with an *S*-alkylating agent converts the free thiol groups to the stable alkylthio derivative [26, 28]. Conventional application methods are preferred; sulphur blacks give lower yields and poor reproducibility using alkaline dithionite [28]. Most blacks on knitgoods are produced with sulphur dyes. They are also important for black sewing threads; here the yarn is usually protected from strength loss on storage by aftertreatment with a pH buffer and an *S*-alkylating agent [21].

Reactive dyes are second in importance for blacks on cotton knitwear [28]. The largest-selling reactive dye is C.I. Reactive Black 5, a dark navy rather than a true black. It is a versatile product used as the basis for dull hues generally by most methods of application of reactive dyes; fixation efficiency is good owing to the presence of two vinylsulphone reactive groups, although this type of dye–fibre bond is somewhat sensitive to strong alkali at elevated temperatures. The use of azoic blacks on knitgoods has declined in favour of reactive dyes, which are easier to apply and more versatile. Cheap blacks of moderate fastness on Naphtol AS are dyed continuously with special black diazo components of low coupling energy. Higher fastness is obtained from conventional red diazo components on more expensive black naphthols of high substantivity, which are suitable only for exhaust dyeing.

Grey and black polyazo direct dyes are cheap and easy to apply, but the unmetallised types have only moderate light fastness in general, especially if aftertreated with cationic agents or resins to achieve wet fastness levels acceptable for relatively undemanding end uses. After-coppered direct blacks provide better fastness to light and wet treatments, but the presence of excess copper in the effluent can cause problems [24]. Vat black dyeings based on violanthrone derivatives exhibit excellent fastness to light and wet treatments but may be only moderate in fastness to rubbing and hot pressing. Vat greys and blacks of the acridone type have poor levelling properties but excellent fastness, and they tend to exert a protective effect with regard to photodegradation of the dyed fibre.

10.3.2 Dyeing Properties
Simple exhaustion in the presence of salt using dyes of high substantivity is one of the least complicated of all dyeing processes. Typical batchwise processes for reactive dyes go much of the way towards this ideal, but they generally require more salt than direct dyes, as well as alkali to promote fixation with the fibre. Direct dyes, however, although offering a simpler procedure, do not attain adequate wet fastness in full depths without aftertreatment. Even in pale depths there may be limitations with low light fastness or catalytic fading of unmetallised azo dyes, or lack of brightness of copper-complex types, for example.

The need for a more prolonged and complicated washing-off for reactive dyeings is a criticism often levelled against them when compared with direct dyeings, but some form of aftertreatment is essential for the latter if they are even to approach the levels of wet fastness attainable with reactive dyes. Cationic aftertreating agents and resin finishes often cause colour changes sufficiently marked to result in difficulties of matching, and light fastness ratings may be lowered by the aftertreatment. Even the recently introduced Indosol copper-complex direct dyes require such aftertreatments to compete with reactive dyes in wet fastness performance.

The after-coppering stage is a critical process for those direct dyeings requiring this form of aftertreatment to achieve the desired hue, light fastness and wet fastness properties. Careful reoxidation and soaping aftertreatments are required to meet similar objectives for batchwise dyeings of vat or sulphur dyes, which also demand careful preliminary reducing processes to convert the insoluble pigment to the alkali-soluble leuco form in which it is applied to the fibre.

In padding processes low-substantivity reactive dyes selected for continuous dyeing normally give no solubility problems even in full depths, and they suffer much less from the tailing difficulties characteristic of direct dyes under these conditions. Solubilised derivatives of vat and sulphur dyes, i.e. the vat leuco esters and the S-aryl thiosulphates (Bunte salts), also have low substantivity towards cellulose and perform well in padding applications. Immediately after padding care must be taken to protect vat leuco ester dyeings from sunlight before they are given an oxidative development to regenerate the insoluble vat dye.

Probably the least attractive classes of dyes for cellulose from the viewpoint of ease of application are the azoic dyes, and the diazotised and developed direct dyes. Diazotisation and coupling are inconvenient processes to carry out under dyehouse conditions; they require careful control for reproducible results. The relatively complicated recipe calculations for azoic dyeings, although made as simple as possible in the technical literature of the manufacturers, are often cited as a drawback [14]. A dyeing of an already diazotised direct dye before development with the coupling component, or a cotton fabric that has been prepared with a naphthol but has not yet been coupled with the selected Fast Base or Salt, are both sensitive to sunlight and give unsatisfactory results if exposed to strong light before development takes place. Difficulty of application is probably the main reason for the marked loss of interest in diazotisable direct dyes nowadays.

Substantivity and Build-up
Probably the most decisive feature of a dye for cellulose is its substantivity towards

the fibre under the preferred conditions for dyeing. This property determines whether the dye will be successful mainly in batchwise or in continuous methods. As the major determinant of build-up properties, substantivity in relation to price thus has a dominant influence on cost-effectiveness, particularly in batchwise dyeing. Azo dye chemists have developed an impressive degree of control over those aspects of molecular design governing substantivity, more recently as a result of the efforts which have been devoted to the synthesis of more effective reactive dyes of this chemical class.

This approach really began many years ago, when azo chemists working on direct dyes found that by replacing, for example, γ-acid by J-acid, or phosgene by cyanuric chloride, analogous structures with intrinsically higher substantivity could be obtained. Many empirical rules of this kind were adopted before convincing explanations of the operation of substantivity forces were advanced. Almost by definition, direct dyes have to be high-substantivity products to achieve the desired economy and tolerable wet fastness in full depths, although some dyes added to meet special requirements, e.g. the bright turquoise blues of the sulphonated phthalocyanine type, have only moderate substantivity.

A wider range of substantivity levels is feasible for reactive dyes; these have been classified [30] as shown in Table 10.1.

TABLE 10.1

Classification of Reactive Dyes by Substantivity

Substantivity factor (%)	Category
>80	Very high substantivity
60–80	High substantivity
40–60	Medium substantivity
<40	Low substantivity

Many reactive dyes of commercial interest have substantivity factors within the range 40–80%. It could be argued that values above about 80% are too high, since such dyes tend to strike rapidly, migrate with difficulty and wash-off slowly. The most successful dyes for exhaust methods often belong to the 60–80% category. Dyes with substantivity values less than 40% are more suitable for padding methods; in exhaust dyeing, especially at long liquor ratios, they give poor yields and reproducibility problems.

Ideally the hydrolysed form of a reactive dye should have low substantivity and rapid diffusion properties to facilitate the washing-off process, but this is not always possible. There is greater scope for this with high-reactivity cold-dyeing dyes, since substantivity falls and diffusion coefficient rises as temperature increases. Such a dye may well be very much less substantive and more mobile during a soaping treatment at the boil than it was in a previous cold dyeing process in the presence of a high concentration of electrolyte. In long-liquor dyeing processes, however, the best results in terms of yield, build-up and reproducibility are given by high-efficiency dyes of the hot-dyeing type [31]. In jet dyeing the advantage of hot-dyeing reactive dyes is less clear-cut. Additions of large amounts of salt to jet dyebaths may be troublesome and more of this is necessary for reactive dyes, especially hot-dyeing types, than for direct dyes.

Direct dyes are inherently unsuitable for cold padding processes owing to their generally high level of substantivity. Reactive dyes are much more versatile in this respect, since products of relatively low substantivity can be selected to minimise tailing problems. Conventional sulphur dyes reduced to the water-soluble leuco form suffer much more than reactive dyes from substantive tailing, but solubilised sulphur dyes of the Bunte salt type are low in substantivity for cellulose and thus of particular interest for continuous dyeing [28].

Vat dyes perform well in continuous processes, either by pigment padding, since the insoluble vat dye has practically no substantivity until reduced at the later chemical padding stage, or in the form of the low-substantivity vat leuco esters, which are particularly suitable for pale depths. Substantivity is much more of a problem for vat dyes in exhaust dyeing. When reduced to the alkaline leuco form, vat dyes are highly substantive and generally give higher exhaustion values than typical direct or reactive dyes. Migration of these polycyclic compounds at normal dyeing temperatures is rather ineffective and non-ionic retarding agents are usually added to minimise the initial strike and to promote levelling. Better migration is possible by dyeing at higher temperatures (see Chapter 5, p. 243), but there is a risk of over-reduction.

When dyeing with azoic combinations the dyeing process selected often depends primarily on the substantivity of the coupling component, since this is applied first. Only in the red sector do the available naphthols cover the whole range from low to high substantivity. Those naphthols with relatively high substantivity are obviously more suitable for batchwise application, whereas a continuous method is preferable for those with relatively low substantivity (including Naphtol AS). Naphthols with an intermediate level of substantivity are less satisfactory for either approach. In batchwise application they require salt addition to promote exhaustion; this often results in inadequate penetration and poor fastness to rubbing. Conversely in continuous treatment they must be padded at a higher speed and temperature than usual to minimise tailing, but reproducible results are more difficult to attain under these conditions.

It is always difficult and often invidious to try to compare different classes of dyes in terms of value or cost-effectiveness, which is strongly influenced by build-up properties. As we have seen in the previous section, this relationship varies according to the sector of the colour gamut under consideration, owing to the chemical types represented in each class and other factors. Furthermore it is important to take into account differences between the dye classes in terms of process and chemical costs, as well as the cost of the dyes themselves [16]. Nevertheless it is possible to draw up an approximate order of decreasing cost:

vat leuco esters > vats > reactives > copper-complex directs > diazotisable and after-copperable directs > azoics and conventional directs > sulphurs

and to reiterate some of the differences between these classes that determine why there is a place for all of them. The more desirable characteristics, such as brightness, versatility and fastness, must normally be paid for and no single class has a monopoly of technical excellence.

For example, vat leuco esters offer water solubility, excellent reproducibility and superb fastness, but they do not build up economically. Conventional vat dyes are less costly for moderate to full depths, but only in the blue and green sectors do they compete with reactive dyes of the anthraquinone type. Azo reactive dyes in the yellow to violet sectors are cheaper than vat recipes generally; the chemical costs for reactive dyeing are also lower. Thus in turn the azo reactive dyes in general compete economically with the more sophisticated types of direct dyes, but the reactives usually have technical advantages in terms of brightness, wet fastness and versatility of application. Direct dyes requiring special aftertreatment processes are cheaper than these classes in terms of dye cost but they lack reproducibility and process simplicity. Conventional direct dyes are cheap to manufacture, easy to apply, but generally poor in fastness properties. Certain formerly important dyes of this kind derived from benzidine have been withdrawn for environmental reasons and replaced by more expensive alternatives. In their strongest suit of full bright reds, azoic dyes are cheaper than direct or reactive alternatives, but in other shade areas they are less competitive in terms of brightness, cost and ease of application. Sulphur dyes are the most economical of all within their restricted gamut of dull hues, notably for blacks. Dyed continuously they are cheap to apply, but batchwise methods are often troublesome and there are problems of reproducibility and light fastness in pale depths.

Diffusion, Levelling and Penetration
Since azoic dyes are applied by an ingrain method in which the diazo and coupling components react rapidly together within the fibre to form the azo pigment, problems of poor penetration attributable to slow diffusion are less likely than with other classes of dyes, which generally have molecular weights far in excess of those of most azoic components. Normally, of course, maximum penetration is highly desirable to achieve optimum fastness, but in one process for dark blue azoic dyes the opposite effect is preferred. Azoic compositions of the Rapidogen (BAY) type represent an alternative to indigo for the coloration of denim jeans. They can be applied to warp yarns on a simple two-dip sizing machine rather than a much more extensive indigo dyeing range. By avoiding the use of a wetting agent, thus ensuring poor penetration of the azoic components into the yarn, the hue and rub-down characteristics of indigo jeans can be imitated fairly closely [19].

Dyeing problems associated with slow diffusion and poor migration are often encountered with direct dyes because all chemical types represented (e.g. disazo, polyazo, stilbene, metal-complex azo, phthalocyanine) tend to have large molecules which readily aggregate together in salt solution. The levelling properties vary from one sub-class to another, those of lower solubility and higher wet fastness generally requiring careful control by salt addition and sometimes temperature regulation for level results. More rapid diffusion and better levelling are possible in the package dyeing of cotton yarn by raising the dyeing temperature to 100–120°C rather than the conventional 80–95°C, but the dyes must have adequate chemical stability under these conditions [32]. After-copperable direct dyes require careful control of pH, as well as temperature rise and salt additions, if unlevel results are to be avoided. When dyeing cotton the pH should be maintained on the mildly alkaline side with sodium carbonate during the dyeing stage, and the after-copper-ing bath adjusted to a mildly acidic pH with acetic acid; with viscose it is generally desirable to maintain a slightly acidic condition throughout.

Generally high substantivity and relatively slow diffusion behaviour are the two main reasons for the often unsatisfactory performance of direct dyes in continuous dyeing. The former causes tailing problems at the padding stage and relatively long times of fixation are required to attain acceptable penetration and wet fastness, especially on viscose. In the design of reactive dye structures, on the other hand, there is much more freedom to achieve a satisfactory balance between reactivity, substantivity and dyeing method, favouring both level dyeing and very good wet fastness. Selected high-reactivity dyes with relatively low substantivity are especially suitable for low-energy processes such as pad–batch and pad–dry, combining rapid fixation with process reliability.

In the conventional two-stage batchwise dyeing process those reactive dyes that combine low initial substantivity with high fixation efficiency are often prone to un-level dyeing, owing to the rapid and non-reversible strike taking place on addition of alkali. Certain sulphatoethylsulphone dyes suffer from this fault, since conversion to the active vinylsulphone form, on addition of alkali, lowers the solubility and en-hances the substantivity of the reactive dye. Similar difficulties of rapid strike are characteristic of high-substantivity high-reactivity dyes applied by the all-in method, where there is a little scope for migration to aid levelling before fixation takes place; slow-diffusing low-reactivity dyes applied at higher temperatures are more appropriate for this technique, so that dye uptake is slower and more uniform.

Nevertheless the degree of exhaustion of direct and reactive dyes is not too high to permit satisfactory migration and levelling when compared with the extremely substantive leuco forms of sulphur and vat dyes. These strike rapidly and migrate with difficulty at normal dyeing temperatures. A further risk of unlevelness with re-duced leuco compounds is the possibility of premature reoxidation at the liquor surface, a major problem frequently encountered with vat or sulphur dyes in winches or partly filled jet machines; these vessels are not well suited to the require-ments of this kind of process.

Solubility and Compatibility
Solubility in water is a feature that makes a major contribution to the ease of appli-cation of a dye to cellulose. As a rule an increase in molecular weight or a decrease in the degree of sulphonation of a direct dye tends to favour substantivity but may

well have an adverse effect on solubility, increasing the risk of aggregation and possible precipitation in salt solution. Hard water is undesirable, particularly for the copperable direct dyes. Reactive dye structures offer greater scope for modification to improve the balance between substantivity and solubility. Special care is needed to avoid precipitation, however, when applying low-solubility cold-dyeing dyes in full depths, especially by all-in or salt-at-start techniques.

Heavy depths of low-solubility direct or reactive dyes in padding processes present similar problems and solubilising agents may have to be used. Machine contamination is much more of a problem for vat or sulphur dyes, however, owing to the insoluble nature of the reoxidised dye that tends to be deposited on the vessel surface at the air–liquor interface. Thus it is difficult to follow dark colours dyed with these dyes on a pad–steam range by lighter or brighter colours, where the choice of direct or reactive dyes may be more appropriate [33]. Failure to keep the leuco solution of a vat or sulphur dye sufficiently alkaline, so that the relatively low-solubility acid leuco compound is formed, can be a further source of precipitation problems.

The satisfactory application of azoic dyes depends critically on the maintenance of adequate solubility before the coupling stage is reached. Naphthols require sufficient alkali to convert them completely to the naphtholate, and an alcoholic solvent is often required to ensure solubility at the padding stage. Insoluble Fast Bases must be completely transformed into the soluble diazonium compound by the diazotisation reaction, and anionic surfactants must be excluded to avoid coprecipitation with the diazonium ions.

When claims are made for the versatility of azoic dyeing, attention is often drawn to the theoretical possibility of obtaining about 1700 possible combinations from about 50 diazo components and 34 naphthols [14]. Only a relatively limited number of these are of interest with respect to hue and fastness properties. The potential scope for formulating mixtures of intermediate hue is even more restricted in practice. Naphthols vary in substantivity and diazo components differ widely in rate of coupling. It is possible with care to adjust a given Naphtol AS combination by adding another naphthol of good light fastness (e.g. C.I. Coupling Component 24 or 46), but if only traces are added the light fastness may drop severely [33].

The classifications of direct dyes and vat dyes into sub-classes according to the need to control dyeing behaviour by temperature control and chemical additions are well established. These differences complicate the selection of specific combinations on grounds of desirable hue or fastness properties, owing to the difficulty of arriving at a compromise method for mixtures of incompatible dyes drawn from different classes. In the field of reactive dyes there is generally no more variation in dyeing properties between members of a range sharing a common type of reactive group than there is between members of a sub-class of direct or vat dyes. Certain sub-classes of reactive dyes do, however, contain representatives of more than one type of reactive system.

The conventional leuco forms of vat and sulphur dyes vary in substantivity on a scale from moderate to very high; thus incompatible combinations show poor reproducibility in pad dyeing. Not only are all component dyes in a recipe progressively depleted from the bath, so that higher concentrations must be used to replenish them, but these tailing effects are selective and each component must be adjusted individually, or both hue and strength may vary.

Choice of Dyeing Method
As noted already, the choice between batchwise and continuous application of azoic components is usually determined by the substantivity characteristics of the naphthol, which is normally applied first. Considerations of compatibility seldom arise since these dyes are very often applied singly rather than in mixture recipes. A possible alternative to the conventional two-stage process is to pad with a mixture of the naphtholate and a suitable stabilised diazo component, batch cold for 1–2 h and finally develop with acetic acid to release the diazonium compound and form the azoic dye [26].

Batchwise dyeing methods are much more important than padding processes for direct dyes because of the limitations imposed by solubility, substantivity and diffusion, as discussed above. Careful selection of compatible recipes is important to minimise ending and listing on the jig, but the pad–jig develop method minimises such problems by ensuring a more uniform initial distribution. Compatible combinations with similar substantivity and diffusion properties at the fixation stage are particularly difficult to find for pad–dry and pad–steam processes, which are thus of relatively minor significance for direct dyes in practice.

Unlevel strike, excessive loss of reducing agent, premature reoxidation of the dye and contamination of the interior surfaces of the dyeing vessel are all reasons why winches and partly filled jet machines are far from ideal for the batchwise application of vat or sulphur dyes to knitgoods. With woven fabrics on open jigs listing is often a problem due to cooling and premature reoxidation at the selvedges. Fully enclosed jigs, beams or fully flooded jet machines provide more favourable conditions [32], but semi-continuous and continuous methods are more important for these classes of dyes. The one-bath pad–steam process is the main method of sulphur dyeing [28], e.g. in the dyeing of warp yarns for denim and the piece dyeing of corduroy fabrics.

Pad–steam application of vat dyes is the primary approach for high-quality woven goods, originally established for military fabrics during World War II. This process permits a wider selection of compatible dyes than do the batchwise methods. For lengths greater than 2000 m to a colour, the pad–dry–chemical-pad–steam sequence is cheaper than jig dyeing for vat dyes on cotton. When vat leuco esters are chosen the pad–batch–develop method is more economical than jig dyeing for runs of more than 1500 m, but equivalent cost is not attained by the quicker pad–develop process until batches of more than 5000 m are processed [34]. The two-bath two-stage sequence for continuous dyeing of polyester/cotton with disperse and vat dyes is high in process costs [24] but has remained a significant route for piece dyeing of this blend [35]. The one-bath pad–thermofix–chemical-pad–steam method is the most widely practised.

Reactive dyes are more versatile in application than any other class. All types of batchwise machines and many continuous sequences are available for accommodating numerous relatively simple dyeing methods [16]. Pad–batch processing is more attractive from the viewpoint of energy conservation, capital investment, productivity and simplicity than batchwise or fully continuous methods. Pad–batch application followed by a perforated-beam wash is an exceptionally economical process sequence; on average this approach uses only 9% of the water, 19% of the energy, 22% of the chemicals and 31% of the labour required for winch dyeing. The unit cost of dyeing by the pad–batch route is only about 20% of that for conventional winch dyeing, excluding the considerable contribution of dye cost [36]. A comparison that included the cost of the dyes demonstrated that the cost of pad–batch dyeing was 76% of the cost of jet dyeing for a batch of 1000 kg, dyed to a 3% depth with reactive dyes [37].

Pad–batch processing is of great interest for woven fabrics and has made considerable inroads into the knitgoods sector in recent years. Taking into account the cost of the dyeing stage only for reactive dyes on wovens, the pad–batch method was more economical than the jig for lengths greater than 1600 m to a colour. If the costs of washing-off were included, the semi-continuous method was favoured and the breakeven point was reached at about 1000 m [34]. The pad–dry process is another alternative for high-reactivity dyes of the cold-dyeing type, requiring only simple equipment with low energy requirements, but hot-dyeing dyes need a baking or steaming treatment for satisfactory fixation.

In the pad–dry–bake process dichlorotriazine dyes can be fixed with bicarbonate and 50 g/l urea at 120–130°C, but monochlorotriazine dyes require soda ash and 200 g/l urea at 150–160°C for optimum results. A useful possibility for the one-bath pad–dry–thermofix sequence on polyester/cotton blends is the neutral fixation of dichlorotriazine or difluorochloropyrimidine dyes in the presence of a fixation accelerator (dicyandiamide or ethylene carbonate). This permits a wider choice of suitable reactive and disperse dyes, since in the presence of bicarbonate such high-reactivity dyes tend to interact with certain disperse dyes and dispersing agents in the pad liquor.

Vinylsulphone dyes are not usually recommended for the pad–dry–bake process, owing to their tendency to become deactivated in the presence of urea. Rather than a direct reaction between the dye and urea, this is believed to depend on the thermal decomposition of urea to biuret and ammonia, followed by conversion of the vinylsulphone dye to the inactive aminoethylsulphone [38] (Scheme 10.1). The decomposition of urea during baking can be responsible for another problem; certain reactive dyes that normally show satisfactory fastness to light may be adversely affected under these conditions.

$$2H_2NCONH_2 \rightleftharpoons H_2NCONHCONH_2 + NH_3$$

$$DSO_2CH = CH_2 + NH_3 \longrightarrow DSO_2CH_2CH_2NH_2$$

Scheme 10.1

Environmental Problems

In recent years the choice of dyes and dyeing processes has been influenced increasingly by ecological and toxicological criteria [39]. Many cheap disazo direct dyes based on benzidine were withdrawn from manufacture and sale by the major manufacturers about ten years ago. Dyes introduced since then as replacements for the benzidine-derived products are generally more costly. Sporadic instances of skin allergy are occasionally reported with certain intermediates or dyes [29] and these may necessitate changes in product formulation or method of application to avoid the risk of exposure.

The handling problems associated with inorganic chemicals used in traditional dyeing processes and the impact of these products on effluent treatment costs have come under increasing scrutiny in recent years. In the field of cellulosic dyeing the simple and relatively innocuous chemicals required for conventional application of direct and reactive dyes are particularly attractive in this respect. Reactive dyes generally require more salt than direct dyes, as well as alkali to promote fixation, but some type of cationic aftertreatment or resin finish is almost obligatory for direct dyeings, to confer adequate wet fastness in moderate and full depths. In general, however, these classes of dyes present few problems with regard to effluent disposal.

After-copperable direct dyes are more troublesome, since the exhaust dyebath contains salt, alkali and relatively unstable unmetallised dyes, whereas the coppering bath contains acid and the excess copper salt, together with some desorbed dye in the form of its copper complex. Azoic dyes, and the diazotised and developed direct dyes, are unpleasant in use because of the unavoidable evolution of nitrous acid fumes during diazotisation and the strongly alkaline nature of naphtholate solutions. Heavy-metal salts are used to stabilise some of the Fast Colour Salts for azoic dyeing.

Probably the most difficult problems of effluent disposal from cellulosic dyeing processes are met in the batchwise dyeing of sulphur and vat dyes [40]. In the conventional pigment form both classes require reduction with sodium sulphide or sodium dithionite respectively in strongly alkaline solution, as well as further dosing during the dyeing process to make good any losses of these relatively unstable reducing systems. After dyeing both classes of leuco compound must be reoxidised back with peroxy compounds or dichromate solution, followed by prolonged soaping to complete the process. Staining of the internal surfaces of the dyeing vessel by prematurely oxidised insoluble dye necessitates regular cleaning with a further strongly alkaline reducing system. All the liquors needed for these various processes present some degree of environmental difficulty during preparation, application or effluent disposal.

10.4 SELECTION BETWEEN DYE CLASSES ACCORDING TO SUBSTRATE AND FASTNESS REQUIREMENTS

Enough mention has been made in Chapter 6 of the exceptionally good all-round fastness properties of vat dyeings to explain the consistent demand for these products on high-quality cotton and polyester/cotton materials, in spite of their relatively vulnerable position in terms of cost-effectiveness in a colouristic sense. The outstanding durability of vat-dyed cotton is well illustrated by reference to a showcase fabric of historical interest, which was dyed in 1910 using Indanthren Blue RS (BASF). This was reported to have been on exhibition and in storage for 60 years without perceptible fading [13] and no doubt it has withstood the further intervening years better than most of us. Even fabrics that have to be subjected to the rough-and-tumble of heavy-duty wear requirements, and frequent vigorous laundering cycles, such as vat-dyed workwear, towelling and military clothing, are able to take a great deal of punishment without significant colour loss. Textile damage, such as abrasion and fraying, is much more likely to be the first sign that the material is unable to endure these conditions indefinitely.

None of the other classes of dyes for cellulose can claim this stainless reputation; all show some weaknesses when exposed to certain agencies, although these sensitive areas vary from one class to another. Thus azoic dyes, particularly in their optimum sector of full bright reds, show up reasonably well for fastness to hypochlorite bleaching, although not to kier boiling, where they are liable to bleed. They are often criticised for borderline fastness to rubbing and dry cleaning, and for poor fastness to light at high humidity or in pale depths. Reactive dyes offer satisfactory all-round fastness for many applications on cotton and polyester/cotton blends, but their Achilles heel is their generally low level of fastness to chlorine bleaching treatments. Sulphur dyes generally rate badly towards this agency too; as a class they are not renowned for durability, particularly in view of the risk of fibre tendering under acidic conditions of storage, yet sulphur blacks and navy blues of the sulphurised vat type stand up well to light and wet treatments, especially if aftertreated.

Few direct dyes will meet all-round fastness requirements even for relatively modest quality standards without aftertreatment [24, 40, 41]. Even during the first decade after their discovery [6], when direct dyes displaced mordant dyes mainly on account of ease of application, dyers were finding that poor wet fastness was the penalty paid for this greater simplicity. Thus direct dyeings tended to gravitate towards the low-quality end of the market. Cheap cotton and later viscose fibres for a price-conscious mass market provided substantial demand, especially in the brighter hues not adequately satisfied by the dull sulphur colours. Viscose furnishing fabrics, curtaining and viscose-containing tufted or woven carpets, where wet fastness demands are less critical than most apparel outlets, have been dyed successfully for many years with fast-to-light direct dyes, although these materials have lost ground more recently with the growth in furnishings and carpets made from synthetics. Resin finishing of woven fabrics helped to overcome the major fastness limitations of direct dyeings, but on knitgoods, where considerations of softness of handle restrict the usefulness of this approach, reactive dyes have eventually replaced directs except in the least demanding applications.

10.4.1 Light Fastness
Outstanding fastness to light and weathering, even in pale depths, is one of the most characteristic features of the vat dye range. Yet this desirable state is not achieved effortlessly; thorough oxidation and soaping is necessary to promote the

morphological changes associated with development of the final hue and light fastness of the insoluble vat dye on the fibre. The leuco sulphuric esters are sensitive if exposed to direct illumination on the fibre before acid development to regenerate the parent vat dye. A small minority of vat dyes (e.g. C.I. Vat Yellow 2, Orange 9 and Blue 1) exhibit only moderate fastness to light, certain yellows (e.g. C.I. Vat Yellows 2 and 33) catalyse the fading of some blues and greens, and the photodegradation of cellulose is accelerated by certain dyes (e.g. C.I. Vat Yellow 2, Oranges 1 and 2, and Red 10).

Most of the azoic combinations of practical interest show good to very good fastness to light, if exposed in full depths under dry conditions. Unfortunately this stability declines more sharply with increasing humidity or decreasing depth than for dyeings of any other class of cellulosic dyes. Cotton fabric that has been prepared with a naphtholate solution but not yet developed in a solution of the diazo component is fugitive to light, even though the dye formed on coupling may be fully satisfactory in this respect.

The light fastness of reactive dyes ranges from moderate to very good, depending on hue and chemical class, but these dyeings are much less sensitive than azoic dyes to applied depth or humidity conditions during exposure. Not all members of this class are acceptable for all applications; the general standard is adequate for cotton dressgoods and polyester/cotton blends in most cases, but careful selection is needed to cover a reasonably wide gamut of hues on cotton furnishings [42]. Although reactive dyes of the anthraquinone, phthalocyanine and metal-complex azo subclasses are comparable with the premetallised direct dyes in this respect, some of the unmetallised azo directs and reactives show deficiencies, especially if aftertreated with certain cationic fixing agents.

Copper-complex directs and reactives usually hold their light fastness reasonably well in pale depths, but their duller hues tend to be less attractive for this purpose. After-coppered directs, and even more so the diazotisable and conventional unmetallised directs, afford only moderate light fastness in many cases. After diazotisation and development the resultant dyeing tends to fade more rapidly than the parent dye. Conventional direct dyes often require a cationic agent or resin treatment for adequate wet fastness, but these products usually have an adverse influence on light fastness.

Sulphur blacks have excellent light fastness and most blues and olive greens are reasonably good; only in the yellow to orange sector do some sulphur dyes have poor light fastness. Dichromate oxidation is preferred for optimum brightness and fastness. Light fastness in pale depths is frequently inadequate but this is not a serious drawback in practice, because dullness and poor reproducibility make these depths unattractive for sulphur dyeing [41].

Summarising these comments on light fastness, the following approximate order of decreasing stability is arrived at:

vats and vat leuco esters > reactives and premetallised directs > after-coppered directs, azoics and sulphurs > conventional and diazotisable directs

Azoics and sulphurs fare reasonably well in practice relative to their position in this series since their major consumption is in heavy reds and blacks respectively, with virtually no interest in them for pale depths. On the other hand directs, reactives and vats all have to meet the more demanding criteria of pastel dyeings as well as moderate to full depths.

10.4.2 Wet Fastness
This is the most difficult area in which to make generalisations about the relative performance of different classes of cellulosic dyes. Not only are there considerable differences between individual members of a range and for the same dye on different cellulosic substrates in a given test, but the results depend considerably on the methods selected for dyeing, washing-off and subsequent aftertreatments, including durable finishing. Numerous wet fastness tests of various degrees of severity are available. In the field of washing fastness in particular, major changes in test procedure have been adopted in recent years with a view to making the test conditions more representative of actual laundering practice [25]. Nevertheless it is possible to distinguish some qualitative trends and to arrive at an approximate ranking for the purposes of this discussion.

As with most fastness criteria, vat dyeings provide the quality standard against which other ranges are judged. They show very good to excellent fastness, even in severe washing tests at the boil; they are particularly resistant in fast blues, greens and heavy dull colours generally. Indigo has only moderate fastness to washing but it bleeds and fades on tone, a valuable characteristic for the special requirements of blue denim. Only in one respect can vat dyes be criticised relative to reactive dyes in severe wet tests: they do show a greater tendency to stain adjacent synthetic-polymer fibres. This feature can also be turned to advantage in another context, however. In the one-stage continuous dyeing of polyester/cotton blends with vat leuco esters the same dyes can be used to colour both fibre components in pale depths.

If properly soaped-off after dyeing to eliminate any loosely held pigment, azoic dyeings exhibit very good fastness to water, perspiration and washing at the boil. Like vat dyes, they are important for incorporation as coloured effect yarns in woven designs because they are fast to subsequent bleaching and mercerising of such fabrics, although they may bleed if kier boiled. As a class, reactive dyes cannot be considered for this purpose.

This limitation apart, reactive dyes achieve very high levels of wet fastness if given an effective washing-off process to eliminate the unfixed dye. They are almost completely free from cross-staining problems. The dye–fibre bond formed by dyes that react by a substitution mechanism (e.g. chloropyrimidines and chlorotriazines) is at its most stable in the pH range 6–7, so dyeings of the more reactive ranges in this category may show sensitivity to certain tests carried out under mildly acidic conditions, if not protected by a suitable aftertreatment (see below). Reactive dyes that react with cellulose by an addition mechanism (e.g. vinylsulphones) form cellulose ether-type bonds and these show maximum stability at about pH 4–5. Consequently the fastness of such dyes to severe alkaline washing treatments at elevated temperatures is moderate to poor, owing to alkaline hydrolysis of the dye–

fibre bond [38]. Most dyes of the monochloro heterocyclic category, on the other hand, rival vat dyes in their fastness to severe washing at the boil. Although reactive dyes are not fast to hypochlorite bleaching in general, products can be selected with satisfactory fastness to chlorinated water for swimwear, and many of the monochloro heterocyclic dyes are sufficiently stable on the fibre for post-bleaching with hydrogen peroxide [30]. The high level of fastness to perspiration of reactive dyes has favoured their selection for the growth area of knitted leisurewear and sportswear garments in recent years [43].

Sulphur dyeings are moderately fast to washing and perspiration, but they fail to withstand repeated severe laundering at temperatures much above 60°C [26]. The sulphurised vat dyes provide navy blues with generally better wet-fastness performance than the majority of conventional sulphur colours, especially after a stabilising aftertreatment

Inferior wet fastness is undoubtedly the chief cause of the 'substandard' reputation of direct dyes on cellulose. Their history has seen many attempts, none of them completely successful, to overcome this primary deficiency. Diazotisation and development was probably the most radical approach, but this brought other drawbacks in its wake. Dyes in this sub-class often have better fastness to scouring and acid cross-dyeing than many simple conventional disazo types. Most copper-complex and after-coppered dyeings are reasonably fast to washing, by direct dye standards, but there is a risk of demetallisation causing hue changes in acid perspiration tests. Cationic aftertreatment provides some improvement in wet fastness, but pad–bake application of a cross-linking resin must be added to the process costs if the dyeings are intended to meet severe washing criteria, even in the case of the recently developed Indosol range of copper-complex dyes [25].

The early conventional disazo direct dyes were a disastrous start in terms of sensitivity to wet treatments. Good levelling dyes of the class A type bleed and stain even in cold wet tests, and even after resin finishing they show only a modest degree of improvement. Such dyes will always have borderline acceptability in moderate to full depths and they can be considered only for the least demanding of applications.

In spite of the pitfalls implicit in drawing general conclusions regarding wet fastness performance of dye classes on cellulose, the following generalised order of decreasing fastness may be quoted:

vats and vat leuco esters > azoics > reactives and sulphurised vats > diazotisable directs > sulphurs and premetallised directs > after-coppered directs > conventional directs.

These rankings are based on overall response to a multitude of tests (washing with detergent (or detergent and alkali) at various temperatures, acid and alkaline perspiration, water, and so on), but the relative positions of some of the less fast subclasses vary somewhat in relation to specific tests. This is particularly evident for those washing tests carried out in the presence of a peroxy compound, e.g. sodium perborate.

Vat dyes do not exhibit any significant problems with regard to detergent–perborate tests. Most reactive dyes are satisfactory in general, but the chloro- and fluoro-triazine sub-classes are superior to the difluorochloropyrimidine types in many instances, and certain of the vinylsulphone dyes also show sensitivity. As a class, the azoic dyes are inadequate to most tests of this kind. Sulphur dyes likewise show low fastness, but thioalkyl stabilisation confers a marked improvement [26]. After-coppered direct dyeings are not fast to detergent–perborate washing and even premetallised copper complexes (direct and reactive) tend to be somewhat sensitive [39]. To temper the ratings of azoic and direct dyes in the above series, therefore, the revised list below may be taken as representative of approximate fastness to detergents containing peroxy compounds:

vats and vat leuco esters > reactives and sulphurised vats > azoics and sulphurs > diazotisable and premetallised directs > conventional and after-coppered directs.

10.4.3 Bleach Fastness
Response to this criterion is more specific: it is simply the relative resistance of typical members of the various ranges to conventional cotton bleaching routines, essentially based on powerful oxidising agents such as chlorite, hypochlorite or peroxide. Most azoic and vat dyes are highly rated. The azoic blues and the indanthrone vat blues (especially C.I. Vat Blues 4 and 14) will withstand peroxide but show inferior fastness to the chlorine bleaches. Indigo bleaches on tone with hypochlorite, another feature exploited by the wearers of blue denim to change the appearance of the garments. Direct, reactive and sulphur dyes generally put up only token resistance to bleaching agents, although sulphurised vat navies have moderate fastness and selected reactive dyeings will withstand chlorinated swimming pools or laundering baths containing modest hypochlorite additions. The differences noted above may be expressed in the following rankings:

vats and vat leuco esters > azoics > sulphurised vats > reactives > sulphurs > directs.

10.4.4 Fastness to Rubbing
This is another area in which hard and fast conclusions cannot be easily drawn. Fastness to wet and dry rubbing is tested by well-defined procedures and high ratings are not ambiguous. Unfortunately, unless the complete dyeing process including washing-off and drying stages is carried out most carefully, reproducible and meaningful performance will be difficult to maintain. With the more vulnerable dye classes under unfavourable circumstances (e.g. package dyeing of yarn) these problems can be just as troublesome as for disperse dyeings on polyester.

Vat leuco esters are seldom if ever concerned in problems associated with this agency. For economic reasons their usefulness is restricted essentially to pale depths, where adverse rub fastness results are rare. All fastness ratings vary with applied depth, but this dependence can be relatively acute for rubbing tests. It should also be borne in mind that chemically degraded cellulosic fibres may suffer abrasion and transfer of coloured fibrous debris. This can give the illusion of poor rubbing fastness even if the actual dye–substrate forces remain strong.

Class A (good levelling) direct dyes tend to have good solubility in salt solution and to show highly satisfactory fastness to rubbing even in full depths. The virtually complete freedom of reactive dyeings from the rub fastness problems characteristic of many azoic colours has been a major factor in the displacement of azoic by reactive recipes [27]. Typical class C direct dyes and certain reactive dyes with only moderate solubility in electrolyte solutions, such as the phthalocyanine turquoises, may exhibit borderline performance, especially in wet rubbing tests, if not properly washed-off and aftertreated where necessary in full depths. Copper-complex azo direct and reactive dyes are prone to rubbing [23], especially if hard water is present, and copperable direct dyeings suffer badly if not rinsed thoroughly before application of the copper salt.

The fastness to rubbing of typical sulphur dyeings leaves much to be desired [24]. They are often much inferior to reactive dyeings of comparable depth. A thorough wash of a sulphur dyeing before reoxidation may help (although more wasteful in terms of dye usage and processing time) but wet abrasion arising from dye-catalysed acid tendering of the cellulose may, in due course, aggravate a wet rub fastness problem. Except on blue jeans, where poor penetration of indigo is a virtue rather than a vice, vat dyes are always capable of giving unacceptably poor fastness to rubbing in full depths, especially with batchwise-dyed fabrics. Failure to reduce fully while vatting, excessive loss of reducing agent causing premature reoxidation, lowering of the pH with formation of the less soluble acid leuco compound, or insufficient attention to the effectiveness of reoxidation and soaping stages are all potential sources of surface deposition and inadequate rub fastness.

Azoic dyeings, almost entirely confined nowadays to heavy depths, are often problematical, usually in respect of wet rubbing and difficulties of mark-off onto adjacent materials. The level of fastness achieved depends on the process and substrate; careful control of the diazotisation, coupling and washing-off stages is essential. Naphthols of intermediate substantivity need special attention since they require more salt for exhaustion than do the high-substantivity products, whereas in continuous dyeing they must be padded under relatively adverse conditions to minimise tailing. It is difficult to remove deposits of unfixed azoic pigment from package-dyed yarn at the soaping stage [21, 23]. Slow and gentle drying is crucial or poor rub fastness may develop, even at this late stage, by thermal migration [33].

An approximate series in terms of fastness to rubbing may be represented as follows:

vat leuco esters > conventional directs and reactives > premetallised directs and reactives > sulphurs and vats > after-coppered and diazotisable directs > azoics.

This series should be interpreted, like the results of rub fastness tests themselves, with great care. It is intended to represent the increasing likelihood of encountering a rub fastness problem in the series from vat leuco esters to azoics. The fact should be borne in mind that azoic dyes are often criticised on these grounds, but they are almost always met with in heavy depths. Vat and sulphur dyeings at comparable depths tend to rub badly too. Conversely vat leuco esters are prohibitively expensive at depths where they might be expected to show this defect. Heavy depths of direct and reactive dyes, if processed and washed-off carelessly or inadequately, may well fail for poor wet rubbing [26].

10.4.5 Response to Dry Cleaning and Resin Finishing

Before leaving the topic of fastness performance, a few brief comments on the relative response of the major dye classes to these treatments may be in order. Direct dyes [17], reactive dyes and sulphur dyes [26] all exhibit very good fastness to dry cleaning, significantly better than some vat dyes. Azoic dyes in turn have only moderate fastness to this agency [27]; as in the case of rubbing tests, the level of performance achieved depends considerably on the conditions of application, rinsing, soaping and drying of the dyed material.

Sensitivity to resin finishing is much more a problem for direct and reactive dyeings than for azoics and vats, which are scarcely affected at all in hue or light fastness. The acidic conditions of resin fixation have a favourable influence on the subsequent wet fastness behaviour of sulphur dyeings; melamine–formaldehyde finishes in particular tend to enhance their fastness to bleaching. Most reactive dyes show detectable changes in hue and sometimes marginally lower light fastness after resin finishing. The effect on wet fastness is generally good, especially for dyeings on viscose. Few reactive dyeings bleed significantly in resin pad liquors, providing they have been washed-off effectively after dyeing.

Direct dyeings are more sensitive to resin finishing than any other class. Fluctuations in hue and decreases in light fastness are of a similar order to reactive dyeings. The beneficial influence on wet fastness performance is much more striking, however, because of the markedly lower level shown by untreated direct dyeings.

10.4.6 Response to Different Types of Cellulosic Substrate

The relative importance of the various classes of dyes for cellulose differs according to the type of fibre to be dyed. Special dyeing procedures are necessary for applying vat dyes to flax yarns and to tightly twisted mercerised cotton yarns in order to ensure satisfactory penetration. Caustic alkali is essential for dissolving naphthols and in the reduction of sulphur and vat dyes to their leuco compounds; viscose and linen fibres are more readily attacked by hot alkali than is cotton, so the use of direct and reactive dyes for these fibres is favoured. Nevertheless, to meet the highest standards of fastness, substantial quantities of vat dyes have been used successfully (particularly on viscose dyed in cake form).

Reactive dyes are sufficiently versatile to adapt to the special requirements of such substrates without difficulty. Improved penetration of high-twist yarns is achieved using hot-dyeing reactive dyes at 80°C or above. Certain mercerised fabrics benefit from the slower rate of fixation in the long-batch (bicarbonate) variant of the pad–batch process for cold-dyeing dyes, which is also a satisfactory technique for viscose. Reactive dyes diffuse readily in the pad–batch dyeing of woven linen, but the impurities present may cause off-tone or speckled effects in some instances. Transfer of recipes between these various substrates requires calibration; for a given visual depth, more dye is required on unmercerised than on mercerised cotton, whereas viscose usually needs less than unmercerised cotton.

Particularly good colour yield and purity of hue is shown by reactive dyes on cupro (cuprammonium rayon).

Viscose is the cellulosic fibre most suited to direct dyeing. Many textile fabrics made from short-staple cotton or viscose are cheap to manufacture and need to meet only moderate wet fastness criteria. Care in dye selection and choice of a suitable dyeing procedure is especially important for optimum results on viscose and its blends with cotton or polyester. It may be necessary to buffer the dyebath with ammonium sulphate to avoid alkaline reduction of certain simple disazo direct dyes during the dyeing of viscose. The premetallised copper-complex types are more stable in this respect and fast to light; they are of particular interest for polyester/viscose blends [17].

Polyester/cotton blends represent a special case in some respects, owing to the existence of a steady demand for certain good-quality fabrics produced in long runs by continuous pad–steam dyeing to relatively critical standards of fastness and reproducibility. The worldwide consumption of dyes in 1978 for the cotton component in continuously dyed polyester/cotton fabrics [35] was as follows: vats 40–50%, reactives 15–20%, azoics and directs 10–20%, sulphurs 10–15%, vat leuco esters 5–10%. For economic reasons the vat leuco esters can be considered only for pale depths, but they possess the ability to colour both fibres in the blend simultaneously, with any shortfall in yield being readily corrected with disperse dyes if necessary. Both dye and process costs must be taken into account in deciding the level below which leuco esters become economically attractive relative to conventional vat dyes [15]. There are marked restrictions of the usefulness of directs or azoics on polyester/cotton blends. The single-bath two-stage process for direct and disperse dyes is limited in permissible depths owing to problems of wet fastness and inadequate solubility of direct dyes under the mildly acidic conditions required for disperse dye application [32]. A two-bath process is unavoidable for azoic dyes and there are the usual limitations of hue and complicated procedure in this case [24]. Sulphur dyes are the preferred class for economy in black and dull hues generally; their market share has grown with the popularity of polyester/cotton leisurewear in recent years [26, 28].

Reactive dyes have gained more widely from the increase in demand for polyester/cellulose blends rather than all-cotton or all-polyester textiles [13], as well as for knitgoods at the expense of woven fabrics. The all-round fastness of reactive dyes is satisfactory for many polyester/cotton materials. High-efficiency dyes of the hot-dyeing type are particularly suitable for exhaust dyeing of this blend because the alkaline fixation bath for the reactive dyeing stage effectively clears the disperse dye stain from the cellulosic component [32]. Also the actual liquor ratio relative to the cellulosic fibre is three times the nominal value based on total fabric for a 67:33 polyester/cellulose blend, putting efficient exhaustion at a premium [13, 32].

Continuous dyeing with disperse and vat dyes is the accepted standard for many high-quality polyester/cotton materials. Although the process costs of the two-bath two-stage sequence are high, the second (vat dyeing) stage is a highly effective reduction clearing step for the residual unfixed disperse dye still present on the cotton, as is the chemical-pad–steam stage of the one-bath method. Until recently the armed forces have favoured polyester/cotton dyed in this way to replace former specifications based on all-cotton constructions because the strength loss on subsequent resin finishing is much lower and the blend fabrics need much less labour-intensive laundering and ironing procedures [29].

10.4.7 Dye Selection for Yarn Dyeing

Dye consumption in West Germany (1979–80) on cotton yarn and loose fibre [44] showed the following distribution: vats 42%, reactives 22%, directs 20%, sulphurs 11%, azoics 5%. Virtually all of this consumption was for batchwise dyeing. Colour fastness is particularly important for yarn as the ultimate requirements are more difficult to define than for piece-dyed goods [17]. The vat dyeing process is easier to control in yarn package dyeing than in many fabric-dyeing machines [44]. The cost-effectiveness of vat dyes is often favourable compared with reactive dyes in the dark blue and green sector, and the fastness of vat dyes to severe washing and bleaching is valuable for sewing thread dyeing [21, 23]. Reactive dyes are important for bright colours on yarn, including greenish-yellow, orange, turquoise and bright green. Azoic dyes are practically limited to bright reds based on high-substantivity naphthols and rapid-coupling diazo components [26] and sulphur dyes are mainly for aftertreated blacks [21]. Direct dye use is mostly confined to viscose and short-staple cotton yarns.

In sharp contrast to the conventional yarn dyeing sector, relatively low fastness to light, washing, rubbing and bleaching is regarded as acceptable in the dyeing of warp yarns for blue denim manufacture. This derives from the traditional selection for this purpose of indigo, which fades on tone to all these agencies. Since the application requires multiple dips and oxidation steps to attain the desired hue, indigo warp sizing ranges are costly to install and viable only for large-volume production [19]. The main alternative to this approach is the one-bath pad–steam process with sulphurised vat dyes [26, 28]. Most denim warps not dyed with indigo or sulphurised vats are dyed with azoics at the sizing stage. Stabilised azoic compositions are suitable for the one-bath combined dyeing and sizing process if an acid-stable size is used; they require only a simple two-trough sizing machine and are thus more appropriate for small-volume producers [19], since the capital expenditure required is low. An alternative approach is to apply a naphthol from an alkaline size bath, dry, weave and then develop in Fast Salt solution after weaving. Problems associated with this technique, however, are dusting of naphtholate during weaving, water-spotting of the naphthol-prepared warp yarns and cross-staining of the white weft during development.

10.4.8 Dye Selection for Knitted Fabrics

The West German data [44] for dye consumption (1979–80) was as follows for knitted fabrics: reactives 71%, vats 13%, directs 12%, sulphurs 3%, azoics 1%. Exhaust dyeing on winches and jets is the most important technique for knitgoods; these conditions are especially favourable for reactive dyeing. Reactive dyes offer a wide range of bright colours at fastness levels that are satisfactory for high-quality dressgoods and leisurewear. The dyeing temperature appropriate for hot-dyeing dyes ensures good running properties and level dyeing in jets and winches. The harshness of handle associated with after-coppered direct dyeings on knitwear is avoided. Reactive dyes in most cases have sufficient fastness to chlorinated water for use in swimwear [42] and sewing thread [23] for these garments. Careful selection for green mixtures on swimwear and towelling is essential owing to the risk of catalytic wet fading of certain yellows by phthalocyanine or triphendioxazine blues.

Before the advent of reactive dyes, direct dyes were well established on knit-goods and even in the early 1970s [17, 27] they were still widely used in winch dyeing. Premetallised copper-complex types provided satisfactory light fastness for pale-depth fashion colours and cheaper copperable or diazotisable direct dyes gave moderate wet fastness in fuller depths, but these recipes became increasingly vulnerable to competition from reactive dyes. Two recent trends to have favoured reactive dyes are the more varied wet fastness criteria adopted [25], and the replacement of some winch dyeing capacity by jet machines and pad–batch units in the interests of energy conservation [43]. Resin finishing is not usually favoured on knitgoods owing to the unattractive handle obtained; this limits the scope of after-treatments to enhance the wet fastness of direct dyes. Nevertheless there will always be a residual demand for cheap fabrics coloured with direct dyes, mainly for reasons of economy, e.g. viscose linings, cheap underwear and dressing gowns, toy covers and dusters [17, 27].

There was significantly more activity in winch dyeing of knitted fabrics with vat dyes at one time [27], but premature oxidation problems limited their usefulness under these conditions [26]. Sulphur dyes are of some interest, mainly for cheap blacks and other sombre hues. High-substantivity red naphthols retain a marginal share of the knitgoods market, notably on terry towelling, since they will withstand severe washing in the presence of hypochlorite.

10.4.9 Dye Selection for Woven Fabrics
The dyeing of woven cellulosic materials is dominated by the cheaper ranges of dyes, although certain high-quality articles demand the better fastness properties attainable with reactive and vat dyes. Thus the 1979–80 data for West German consumption on woven fabrics [44] showed the following breakdown: directs 30%, sulphurs 29%, reactives 21%, vats 17%, azoics 3%. Continuous dyeing methods (vat leuco esters in pale depths and conventional vat dyes in medium to full colours) are especially important for high-quality cotton poplin and polyester/cotton shirtings. The pad–steam route has remained the standard process for the almost exclusive selection of vat dyes for military uniforms, which require exceptional durability to light, weathering and severe laundering, as well as colour constancy over prolonged periods of storage and use. Equally demanding in terms of practical exposure to light and weathering are awnings and tents. Furnishing fabrics is another major area of interest for vat dyeing, although many curtain fabrics are dyed with selected reactive dyes or premetallised directs.

Workwear too demands good fastness to light and exceptional resistance to repeated severe laundering since the vigorous removal of obstinate stains and 'ground-in dirt' is an occupational hazard for these fabrics. Vat and sulphurised vat dyes are widely established in this field. Not quite so demanding are corduroys and velveteens, the traditional fabrics dominated by sulphur dyes (approximately 70% of the available market), applied by the one-bath pad–steam method [28, 33]. There were attempts in recent years to promote corduroy, dyed pad–batch with reactive dyes or continuously with vat leuco esters in pale depths, as a fashion fabric [33]. Cheaper qualities have been jig dyed with diazotisable direct dyes or azoic combinations but it is easy to run into problems of poor fastness to rubbing and wet treatments on pile fabrics of this kind.

Outerwear, rainwear and fabrics for subsequent coating or laminating present suitable opportunities for the selection of premetallised direct dyes and reactive dyes with above-average fastness to light. Direct dyes have been used widely in those domestic textiles where wash fastness is not critical, including candlewick bedspreads, curtains and tufted floor coverings, as well as sleepwear and low-cost leisure clothing. The application of a crease-resist resin or water-repellent finish after dyeing has a markedly favourable influence on the degree of wet fastness attainable with direct dyes in full depths. To some extent the bond between a reactive dye and the fibre is also protected from hydrolytic attack by the presence of a hydrophobic finish. Nevertheless producers of high-quality outerwear may choose the more expensive vats or vat leuco esters, so that they do not have to rely too much on the stability of the polymeric finish to provide durability of the coloured effect.

One field of application in which sulphur and vat dyes are definitely undesirable is the dyeing of woven fabrics for subsequent discharge printing. Until the discovery of reactive dyes, azoic dyes were popular with printers for their versatility in printing styles. As they are readily dischargeable they came to be widely used as dyed grounds for discharge styles as well. The economy and simplicity of the pad–batch process of reactive dyeing, however, as well as the sensitivity of vinylsulphone dyeings to the print(alkaline discharge)–steam treatment [38], has captured a great deal of this business. Reactive dyes have also replaced direct-dyed grounds for colours not previously obtainable with azoic dyes. Readily dischargeable diazotisable or conventional unmetallised directs tend to have low wet fastness, and reactive dyes are usually brighter and more readily dischargeable than the copper-complex types.

10.5 FACTORS GOVERNING CHOICE BETWEEN SUB-CLASSES WITHIN THE MAJOR DYE CLASSES

All classes of dyes for cellulosic dyeing may be further subdivided, the differentiation being based mainly on dyeing properties (Table 10.2).

An alternative approach would be to subdivide each dyeing class according to the chemical classification of dye structures, as used in the *Colour Index*. However, as mentioned already in relation to the limitations of colour gamut, each of these dyeing classes except reactive dyes is dominated by one main chemical class, so this approach would be much less useful.

TABLE 10.2

Basis of Subdivision of Dye Classes

Dye class	Basis of sub-classification
Reactive	Reactivity and dyeing temperature
Direct	Substantivity and dyeing rate
Vat	Substantivity and dyeing temperature
Sulphur	Substantivity and solubility
Azoic	Substantivity and coupling rate

10.5.1 Reactive Dyes

The obvious basis for sub-classification of reactive dyes is in terms of the relative reactivities of their characteristic reactive systems. Comments have already been made here and there in the above discussion on the behaviour of specific ranges, where this is markedly non-typical of reactive dyes in general. The relative reactivities of the major systems in descending order, together with typical values of fixation temperature under moderately alkaline conditions in batchwise dyeing are as follows:

dichlorotriazine (30°C) > difluorochloropyrimidine (40°C) > dichloroquinoxaline and monofluorotriazine (50°C) > vinylsulphone (60°C) > monochlorotriazine (80°C) > dichloro- and trichloropyrimidine (95°C).

This series corresponds reasonably well with the reactivity grid illustrated for the various ranges under their commercial names [30], but it should be noted that more than one type of reactive system is represented in some of these. It may be necessary to take account of differences in dyeing characteristics by even more subdivision. Thus the Remazol (HOE) vinylsulphone dyes may be placed in four categories based on differences in substantivity, and hence various conditions of fixation pH and temperature are possible to optimise yield and levelling properties. Moderately complex recommendations are necessary for the Levafix E, E-A and E-N (BAY) warm-dyeing range of dyes, in which four different reactive systems are represented. These dyes are classified into nine groups depending on their substantivity (low–medium–high) and reactivity (low–medium–high) ratings. An appropriate dyeing procedure is chosen, either a conventional two-stage sequence at 40, 50 or 60°C, or an addition of alkali (0.5–2 g/l sodium carbonate) to 'pre-sharpen' the dyebath before dyeing at 40 or 50°C. The pre-sharpening technique is adopted for dyes with low–medium substantivity and medium–high reactivity in order to minimise the risk of unlevel dyeing.

The fixation temperatures quoted in the above series for moderately alkaline conditions are thus only approximate and intended for purposes of overall comparison. It may be desirable to exhaust at a lower temperature to enhance substantivity before adding alkali at the optimum temperature of fixation. Applying a high-reactivity dye at a temperature above the optimum, however, results in loss of yield owing to premature hydrolysis of the dye before exhaustion is complete. For easy washing-off, low substantivity and rapid diffusion at the washing stage are desirable. Since substantivity falls as temperature increases, the high-reactivity dyes exhaust well at 30–40°C but are usually relatively low in substantivity during washing-off at the boil, especially when the electrolytes have been removed. Listing problems in jig dyeing are less prevalent for cold-dyeing dyes because cooling of the selvedges is less serious at 30–40°C than at 80–90°C. Short batching times in pad–batch dyeing are an attractive feature of high-reactivity dyes, but pad liquor stability is correspondingly more critical.

The low-reactivity dyes, on the other hand, benefit from the rapid diffusion and effective migration that are possible at relatively high dyeing temperatures; knitted fabrics dyed in this way show good running properties in winches and jets. A wide variety of fabrics can be dyed level with good penetration of high-twist yarns and densely woven fabric constructions. Hot-dyeing dyes tend to show outstanding reproducibility and to a considerable extent they are able to cover minor diffferences in pretreatment history [31]. Dyes of this type are sometimes criticised on grounds of higher energy consumption, but this is misleading. When dyeing knitted cotton at 40°C on a jet machine the cost of steam consumed in the dyeing stage is only about 4% of the total steam cost for the full process, and even at 80°C the steam cost is only 12%. If considered as a proportion of the total process costs, steam for dyeing amounts to only 0.3–4%, depending mainly on temperature, so that differences between the methods in this respect can be neglected for all practical purposes [36].

It is true that the difference in substantivity between that at the optimum dyeing temperature and that during soaping at the boil is less marked for hot-dyeing than for cold-dyeing dyes, but washing-off behaviour is not impaired if the liquor interchange is adequate for efficient dilution of the residual electrolyte in the system. Hot-dyeing dyes are more prone to listing on the jig as a result of inadequate fixation close to the cooler selvedges of the fabric. The need for longer batching times in the pad–batch process, however, is offset by the much superior stability of low-reactivity dyes in alkaline pad baths at ambient temperature.

Symmetrical reactive dye structures with two identical reactive groups, such as the Procion H-E (ICI) dyes containing two monochlorotriazine groups per molecule, provide scope for designing products with better compatibility, more reproducible exhaustion and higher fixation efficiency [30]. One of the earliest, but still probably the most important, of the vinylsulphone dyes, C.I. Reactive Black 5, contains two sulphatoethylsulphone precursor groups per molecule. There has been renewed interest recently in reactive dyes with two dissimilar reactive groups per molecule, including the Sumifix Supra (Sumitomo) range, in which each dye has both a monochlorotriazine group and a sulphatoethylsulphone group. Although it is claimed that the colour yield obtained with such dyes is less sensitive to dyeing temperatures [45], it is clearly impossible to select compromise dyebath conditions to provide optimum fixation efficiency for both of these disparate systems simultaneously.

The stability of the dye–fibre bond formed by the reaction of monohalogeno-triazine dyes with cellulose is exceptionally good. The level of fastness to alkaline washing at the boil achieved by these dyes is difficult to reach with other ranges of reactive dyes [30, 31]. Vinylsulphone dyes, on the other hand, exhibit poor fastness to severe alkaline washing [38] because the dye–fibre bond in this case is liable to alkaline hydrolysis at temperatures above about 70°C. A thorough rinsing in dilute acid is essential before soaping of dyeings of vinylsulphone dyes, but this is neither necessary nor desirable for dyes of the halogenoheterocyclic types.

In contrast to vinylsulphone dyes, cold-dyeing dyes of the dichlorotriazine or dichloroquinoxaline types form dye–fibre bonds that are somewhat sensitive to hydrolysis under mildly acidic conditions. If such dyeings are delayed for a prolonged period in the wet state before drying, or if damp fabric containing these dyes is exposed to an industrial atmosphere during storage, there is a risk that lower wet fastness will be observed. e.g. in subsequent perspiration tests [38]. This phenomenon is believed to arise by protonation of the oxygen atom linking the heterocyclic ring to cellulose, followed by hydrolysis [46]; the degree of sensitivity to acid hydrolysis varies from dye to dye, depending on the degree of activation of the oxygen atom by other substituents in the vicinity of the heterocyclic ring, which may favour or hinder protonation. Highly reactive red dyes derived from H-acid often tend to show this fault; the problem can be minimised by aftertreatment with a suitable primary amine, or preferably an oligomeric compound containing several amino groups. These agents are able to react with any residual activated chloro substituents on the heterocyclic ring of the fixed dye molecule, thereby decreasing the sensitivity of the dye–fibre bond to possible protonation and hydrolysis [27].

Unusual fastness problems were observed with dyes of the difluorochloropyrimidine type shortly after their introduction [47]. Dyeings that had been fast to washing deteriorated badly in performance if they were laundered with a detergent containing perborate (or given a cold steeping treatment in such a solution) and then exposed to sunlight. No immediate effect was observed at this stage, but if subsequently laundered again or simply rinsed in warm water the dye–fibre bonds in the areas exposed to light were found to be no longer effective, since considerable bleeding occurred immediately. Certain dyes of the dichloroquinoxaline and vinylsulphone types were also found to be somewhat sensitive, but dyes of the halogenotriazine sub-classes were generally satisfactory for resistance to these combined agencies [45]. The mechanism of this sensitivity of 2,4-difluoro-5-chloropyrimidine dyes has recently been elucidated [48]. The perborate anion acts as a donor of the hydroperoxy anion, which is capable of displacing the 5-chloro substituent, even if both fluorine atoms have been already lost by hydrolysis and reaction with cellulose. The heating effect associated with exposure to light is sufficient to catalyse the subsequent oxidative breakdown of the dye–fibre bond. This explanation also accounts for the fact that dyes of the s-triazine type do not suffer decomposition of the dye–fibre bond under these conditions, since all three positions ortho or para to the dye–fibre linkage are occupied by ring nitrogen atoms [48].

10.5.2 Direct Dyes

A classification of direct dyes on the basis of their dyeing properties was established many years ago [49] and this retains considerable practical significance. Self-levelling dyes of the class A type are generally monoazo or disazo dyes with at least two solubilising groups. They show relatively high solubility and thus a fairly low degree of aggregation in salt solution, which accounts for their good migration properties. In view of these characteristics they tend to build up well in padding methods and are suitable for the package dyeing of yarn in pale depths, owing to their good levelling and penetration. Class B dyes of the salt-controllable category are usually disazo or trisazo dyes with three or four sulphonate groups. They are relatively sensitive to salt concentration in terms of their exhaustion behaviour. Thus dyeing rate and levelling properties can be controlled by careful additions of salt during the dyeing process. The third category is represented by the temperature-controllable class C dyes; these are mostly disazo or trisazo dyes with only one or two sulphonate groups. They tend to be highly aggregated in salt solution. Owing to their relatively high substantivity they build up well by exhaust dyeing. Levelling tends to be more difficult, however, so careful control of both dyeing temperature and salt addition is necessary. Dyes of class C and especially class B generally show better wet fastness than those of class A.

Apart from this classification on the basis of dyeing properties, which is mainly of significance in selecting compatible combinations at the dyeing stage, direct dyeings may be categorised according to whether or not they have been given an aftertreatment (e.g. with a cationic agent, formaldehyde or a resin finish, or by diazotisation and coupling with a naphthol) and whether or not the dyeing is a copper complex (either dyed in the premetallised form or dyed as the unmetallised azo compound and aftertreated with a copper salt). These differences are important in terms of fastness performance as well as dyeing procedure, and this is why these categories have been mentioned more frequently already in this chapter than the class A–B–C subdivision.

If direct dyes with class B or C dyeing properties are selected for the package dyeing of yarn, they may be applicable at 120°C for optimum levelling and penetration [21]. Care in control of pH is necessary to ensure stability, particularly for unmetallised dyes under these conditions. Especially in the presence of viscose fibres there may be a risk of alkaline reduction; ammonium sulphate as an acid donor and a mild oxidant as reduction inhibitor are added to counteract this problem.

When dyeing with metal-complex dyes in the presence of hard water, hexametaphosphate rather than an organic sequestrant such as ethylenediamine tetra-acetic acid should be used, because the latter type of product can cause demetallisation of some copper-complex dyes. For optimum stability and reproducibility with copperable dyes on scoured cotton these should be dyed at a mildly alkaline pH but after-coppered in a weakly acidic bath. On viscose fibres or unscoured cotton, however, it is usually preferable to dye and aftertreat at a slightly acidic pH. Acid perspiration can cause demetallisation of some copper-complex dyes, and certain of these products are sensitive to alkaline washing in the presence of perborate.

10.5.3 Vat Dyes
Migration and strike levelling tests to characterise vat dyes were published a long time ago [50]. A classification of vat dyes based on substantivity data, with particu-

lar significance for rapid-dyeing techniques, was established more recently [51]. Cold-dyeing or IK types have relatively low substantivity. They are somewhat obsolescent and are mainly of interest in specific hues not readily attainable with dyes from other classes. The most important sub-class for batchwise dyeing contains the moderately substantive warm-dyeing IW brands applied with less salt at 45–50°C (compared with 20–30°C for IK dyes). Most IK and IW dyes can be applied without a retarder in full depths, but the best levelling and penetration is achieved in pale–medium depths if a non-ionic retarder is present. The high-substantivity IN dyes require an exhaust dyeing temperature of 55–60°C and a retarder but no salt; they are predominantly used in medium to heavy depths for reasons of economy and to avoid the levelling problems associated with pale dyeings. In continuous dyeing, however, the IN brands are generally preferred, both for performance and economy. Certain high-substantivity products require special dyeing methods, i.e. the IN Special A brands are vatted at 70–80°C and exhaust dyed at 50–60°C, whereas the converse is true for the IN Special B products [22].

10.5.4 Sulphur Dyes

The most important subdivision of the class of sulphur dyes is in terms of formulation or presentation of the commercial brand for dyeing. The traditional C.I. Sulphur dye is insoluble in its oxidised form as a dry powder or aqueous dispersion. Although the cheapest and most stable variant, this has become increasingly obsolescent for many purposes because of the necessity for boiling with sodium sulphide solution to form the soluble leuco form [7]. This is especially inconvenient for padding methods of application [28]. Sulphurised Vat dyes are also available as insoluble powders or finely dispersed in paste form.

Pre-reduced solutions of C.I. Leuco Sulphur dyes have been available in the USA since the 1930s and this is by far the most popular type of formulation there for continuous dyeing, since the reducing agent is already included [7]. European manufacturers of pre-reduced sulphur dyes have favoured solid mixtures of the leuco form with a stable reducing compound because they are more readily transported to export markets. For batchwise or continuous dyeing there is the further possibility of using the highly soluble but virtually non-substantive C.I. Solubilised Sulphur dyes. These are Bunte salts that are converted to the substantive leuco form during dyeing in the presence of an alkaline reducing agent.

10.5.5 Azoic Dyes

There is no formal classification of azoic coupling components but they vary in substantivity from low to high and this does impose some limitations of colour gamut attainable by batchwise and continuous methods. Thus the high-substantivity naphthols for exhaust application cover the rather dull series red–bordeaux–brown–olive–black, whereas the low-substantivity naphthols more suited to continuous padding provide the generally brighter but sometimes more costly range bright green–yellow–orange–red–violet–navy–black, although this does include the economical Naphtol AS colours. The diazo components with high coupling energy (class I, coupling at pH 4–5) provide the widest segment of the gamut: yellow–

orange–scarlet–red–bordeaux. The other classes of these components are much more restricted: red–bordeaux (II, pH 5–6), violet–navy (III, pH 6–7) and navy–black (IV, continuous application).

10.6 PRINCIPLES OF EVALUATION AND TESTING OF DYES

It is impossible to arrive at a rational selection of dyes without having first examined the available data on them, supplemented where necessary by further screening tests to confirm their suitability for the specific conditions of application under consideration. Brief comments on the general principles associated with gathering test data of this kind are relevant here; further details have been published elsewhere [52–54].

Most laboratories in the dyeing industry allocate substantial resources to dye evaluation, and this aspect of product assessment is most important for efficient purchasing of materials and cost-effective operation of the dyehouse. The methods employed in product development and standardising control by the dye manufacturer and in screening and quality checks carried out by the user have much in common. Research samples are screened until promising products emerge to justify commercial development. After exhaustive testing they are added to the manufacturing range and subsequent batches are tested for quality against an initial standard. In a broadly similar way the dye user carries out extensive screening tests on commercial dyes to select those suitable for his process, machinery and in-service requirements on the substrate to be dyed. Having selected a small range of dyes to achieve these targets, the user maintains routine checks on deliveries and compares similar products which may be available from several suppliers.

The manufacturer, however, is screening speculative dyes at an incomplete stage of development, whereas the user is testing finished products from a variety of sources. In establishing and maintaining a quality standard the manufacturer must attempt to meet the needs of users operating in widely different sectors of the textile industry, his product having to perform satisfactorily within a wide range of exposure conditions. An individual dye user may need to satisfy a much narrower range of machine–substrate–process criteria, enabling closer definition of the preferred selection of dyes for his requirements. A laboratory representing a group of dyeing factories, perhaps situated in different countries, may have to make compromises based on local circumstances in evaluating the dyes available and selecting those most suitable for recommended use within the group.

Numerous parameters have to be considered by both manufacturer and user of the product before it is eventually applied to an appropriate substrate for a specific end use. Properties of particular significance during safety testing, manufacture, standardising, transport and ultimate dissolving before use can be regarded broadly as the response of the dye itself, uncomplicated by the presence of the textile material, to its environmental conditions. Health and safety standards are increasingly significant and are particularly relevant to handling of the concentrated product during manufacture and application. Many more tests must be considered when the decision is taken to use the product in a dyeing process and these are all evaluations of the characteristics of the dye–fibre system, rather than of the dye alone. Cost-effectiveness is obviously essential for the user to retain any interest in the manufacturer's product, and the user's customer invariably lays down certain requirements to which the dyed textile must conform. There often has to be a trade-off in properties; a cheap dye may achieve only borderline fastness with difficulty, or it may only be possible to meet severe fastness requirements at the expense of level-dyeing properties.

Increasing economic pressures have compelled dye users to select dyes with greater care in order to use the minimum number of dyes to obtain the maximum colour gamut, to reduce stocks and to gain from bulk purchasing price concessions. More stringent technical requirements have meant that for certain end uses only a few dyes will meet the defined specification. The adoption of automation and the need for cost-effective processes both favour the use of rationalised small ranges of dyes. The choice of dyes, the determination of the recipe for a particular colour, and the definition of the application procedure and final treatment are the important steps in control of the dyeing process. Continuity of quality is essential and dyes are often chosen according to whether technical performance or price is paramount.

There are two commonly used empirical methods of selecting dyes to produce a given colour. One approach is to base most colours on a ternary combination of bright primary dyes and to supplement this by a small range of dyes compatible with the main combination, giving a wide gamut of attainable colours, particularly in depth and brightness. Approximately twelve dyes are required for this approach, which is adopted when cheaper and duller homogeneous dyes are not available for regions of the colour gamut fairly close to the lightness axis, e.g. with reactive dyes. In the second method a dye is chosen close to the colour required and small amounts of shading dyes are added to reach the desired target. This method gives a higher degree of reproducibility of colour from batch to batch, particularly if the concepts of internal primaries and colour mapping are employed. This approach is only possible for dye classes containing a sufficient number of well-spaced homogeneous dyes, such as direct and vat dyes. In an elegant application of the concept of internal primaries [52], reflectance data were used to construct colour maps, so that dyes in any given area of the gamut form a triangle of internal primaries. The technique is supported by a suite of computer programs to aid dye selection and recipe formulation. This work has been extended more recently and a summary of the steps in the selection process given [53].

Many aspects of testing for cost-effectiveness and dye application properties are linked indirectly with the end use of the material to be dyed. It is essential that quality standards for dyed textiles be considered, before any dye screening programme is undertaken, to provide guidelines for operating ranges and pass/fail limits in such tests. There are certain in-service requirements, however, of direct relevance to specific dye screening tests: fastness properties are an obvious example, because here the results of generally recognised tests play an important part in determining the commercial acceptability of the dyed textile. Many fastness tests are well defined in the appropriate published specifications and detailed reviews of developments in this field have appeared in recent years [55].

REFERENCES

1. 'Dyeing of Synthetic-polymer and Acetate Fibres', Ed. Nunn (Bradford: Dyers' Co. Publications Trust, 1979).
2. Bird, 'Theory and Practice of Wool Dyeing', 4th Edn (Bradford: SDC, 1972).
3. Shore, Dyer, 167 (Apr 1982) 21.
4. Pennington, J.S.D.C., 33 (1917) 142.
5. Whittaker, J.S.D.C., 61 (1945) 201.
6. Shore, Dyer, 167 (May 1982) 25.
7. Heid, Holoubek and Klein, Melliand Textilber., 54 (1973) 1314.
8. Rowe, J.S.D.C., 46 (1930) 121.
9. Peel, J.S.D.C., 68 (1952) 496.
10. Shore, Dyer, 167 (June 1982) 28.
11. Holbro, J.S.D.C., 69 (1953) 233.
12. Shore, Dyer, 167 (July 1982) 19.
13. Weigold, Melliand Textilber., 52 (1971) 90.
14. Heinisch, Melliand Textilber., 52 (1971) 99.
15. Goorhuis, Melliand Textilber, 52 (1971) 189.
16. Brunnschweiler, Melliand Textilber., 52 (1971) 192.
17. Renziehausen, Melliand Textilber., 52 (1971) 196.
18. Heid, Melliand Textilber., 52 (1971) 199.
19. Berenstecher, Textilveredlung, 13 (1978) 347.
20. Wood, Rev. Prog. Coloration, 7 (1976) 80.
21. Mackin, Rev. Prog. Coloration, 12 (1982) 13.
22. Wilcoxson, Amer. Dyestuff Rep., 71 (Sept 1982) 35.
23. Ferguson, J.S.D.C., 89 (1973) 281.
24. Balchin, Amer. Dyestuff Rep., 68 (Sept 1979) 35.
25. Robinson and Egger, Textilveredlung, 18 (1983) 14.
26. Klein, Dyer, 156 (1976) 282.
27. Fox, J.S.D.C., 84 (1968) 401.
28. Klein, J.S.D.C., 98 (1982) 106.
29. Morris, Rev. Prog. Coloration, 11 (1981) 9.
30. Bent, Davies and Phillips, J.S.D.C., 98 (1982) 326.
31. Kirner, Textilveredlung, 15 (1980) 13.
32. Norris and Ward, J.S.D.C., 89 (1973) 197.
33. Klein, Melliand Textilber., 60 (1979) 244.
34. Bartl et al., Textilveredlung, 9 (1974) 147.
35. Hildebrand and Marschner, Textile Asia, (Sept 1978) 80.
36. Shore, Rev. Prog. Coloration, 11 (1981) 58.
37. Rothweiler, Melliand Textilber., 60 (1979) 341.
38. Von der Eltz, Textilveredlung, 18 (1983) 99.
39. Anliker, Rev. Prog. Coloration, 8 (1977) 60; J.S.D.C., 95 (1979) 317.
40. Stetson and Petree, Asian Textile J., 2 (May 1974) 17.
41. Baumgarte and Schlüter, Melliand Textilber., 61 (1980) 258.
42. Ramsay, J.S.D.C., 97 (1981) 102.
43. Kreidler, Textilveredlung, 17 (1982) 295.
44. Schlüter, Dyer, 169 (Mar 1983) 20.
45. Fujioka and Abeta, Dyes and Pigments, 3 (1982) 281.
46. Rattee, J.S.D.C., 85 (1969) 23.
47. Rattee and So, Dyes and Pigments, 1 (1980) 121.
48. Rattee, Dyer, 171 (Mar 1984) 11.
49. SDC Direct Dyes Committee, J.S.D.C., 62 (1946) 280; 64 (1948) 145.
50. SDC Vat Dyes Committee, J.S.D.C., 66 (1950) 505.
51. Baumgarte, Melliand Textilber., 55 (1974) 953.
52. Mackin, J.S.D.C., 91 (1975) 75.

53. Mackin and Purves, J.S.D.C., **96** (1980) 177.
54. Park and Shore, Rev. Prog. Coloration, **12** (1982) 1.
55. Park, Rev. Prog. Coloration, **6** (1975) 71; **10** (1979) 20.

Index